Jean Epstein

Film Theory in Media History explores the epistemological and theoretical foundations of the study of film through texts by classical authors as well as anthologies
and monographs on key issues and developments in film theory. Adopting a historical perspective, but with a firm eye to the further development of the field, the
series provides a platform for ground-breaking new research into film theory and
media history and features high-profile editorial projects that offer resources for
teaching and scholarship. Combining the book form with open access online
publishing the series reaches the broadest possible audience of scholars, students, and other readers with a passion for film and theory.

Series editors: Prof. Dr. Vinzenz Hediger (Frankfurt), Dr. Trond Lundemo (Stockholm), Prof. Dr. Oliver Fahle (Bochum).

Film Theory in Media History is published in cooperation with the Permanent Semi-
nar for the History of Film Theories.

Jean Epstein

Critical Essays and New Translations

Edited by
Sarah Keller & Jason N. Paul

Amsterdam University Press

This book is published in print and online through the online OAPEN library (www.oapen.org)
OAPEN (Open Access Publishing in European Networks) is a collaborative initiative to develop and implement a sustainable Open Access publication model for academic books in the Humanities and Social Sciences. The OAPEN Library aims to improve the visibility and usability of high quality academic research by aggregating peer reviewed Open Access publications from across Europe.

Cover illustration: Jean Epstein during the shoot of Les Feux de la Mer, 1948. Courtesy Cinémathèque Française, Iconothèque.

Cover design: Suzan Beijer, Amersfoort
Lay-out: JAPES, Amsterdam

ISBN   978 90 8964 292 9
e-ISBN   978 90 4851 384 0
NUR   670

Table of Contents

Translations

Finis Terrae (Jean Epstein, 1929). © Musée Gaumont

Acknowledgments

This collection has developed over three years, originating in a two-day symposium on Jean Epstein's work that we organized in April 2008, while graduate students at the University of Chicago. That symposium far exceeded our already high expectations for it; and the extraordinary energy that surrounded the event inspired us to compile this volume, with increasing ambitions for its scope as it came together.

The symposium was made possible through the material and moral support of several individuals and groups at the University of Chicago, including the Franke Institute for the Humanities, the Department of Cinema and Media Studies, the France Chicago Center, the Film Studies Center, the Master of Arts Program in the Humanities, the Mass Culture Workshop, the New Media Workshop, and especially Julia Gibbs and Sabrina Craig for their support of the screenings and preparation of materials for the symposium.

We also wish to thank the editors at Amsterdam University Press, particularly Jeroen Sondervan and the editors of the series Film Theory in Media History, of which this volume is a part: Vinzenz Hediger, Oliver Fahle, and especially Trond Lundemo, who offered invaluable insights (and practical assistance) in selecting and securing support for the translations.

We greatly appreciate the generous support of the Dean of Faculty at Colby College (Ed Yeterian and, later, Lori Kletzer) for assistance with translations and other material concerns, as well as the Humanities Division for a 2010-11 Research Grant, which assisted in the costs associated with research for completing this volume. Thanks are due as well to the English Department for the support of a research assistant.

A number of remarkable archivists contributed to the progress of this book, including those at the Bibliothèque du film and the Cinémathèque Française in Paris and environs; the Cinémathèque québecoise in Montréal, especially Pierre Jutras and his colleagues, who helped arrange a special screening during a too-short visit to their amazing retrospective of Epstein's films in late January, 2011; Charles Silver at the Museum of Modern Art; and Robert Haller at Anthology Film Archives in New York.

We liked to say during the long process of putting together this volume that it was a labor of love among a true community of scholars. We shamelessly enlisted advice and every bit of help we could from some of the people whose work we most admire in this community, among them Richard Abel, Dudley Andrew, Robert Bird, Valérie Dionne, Leah Culligan Flack, Doron Galili, James Lastra, Christina Petersen, Ariel Rogers, Jennifer Wild, Tami Williams, and Josh Yumibe. We wish to thank them for their insights and support.

And there were those who allowed us to ask monumental favors (and even granted them!) with amazing good grace and generosity: Stuart Liebman, Christophe Wall-Romana, Arthur Greenspan, Franck Le Gac, and Audrey Brunetaux. We are deeply grateful for their expertise and their kind, even overgenerous natures, without which this work would be significantly diminished.

The boundless energy and gracious participation of Tom Gunning has been our guiding star throughout the process of compiling this collection, from his enthusiasm and advocacy for the Epstein symposium to his advice during the final stages of assembling the manuscript. Without his unstinting generosity, magnanimous presence, and wise counsel in this process, this volume would not exist.

Finally, we wish to dedicate this volume both to our extraordinary families – a pair of twins and a very positive and supportive partner for each of us – and to the memory of our teacher, Miriam Bratu Hansen, whose acute insights, formidable intellect, rigorous example, and love of cinema remain an inspiration to us despite her loss.

Abbreviations

Abel1   Richard Abel, *French Film Theory and Criticism: A History/Anthology*, *1907-1939. Vol. 1: 1907-1929* (Princeton: Princeton University Press, 1988).

Abel2   Richard Abel, *French Film Theory and Criticism: A History/Anthology*, *1907-1939. Vol. 2: 1929-1939* (Princeton: Princeton University Press, 1988).

ESC1   Jean Epstein, *Écrits sur le cinéma, 1921-1953: édition chronologique en deux volumes. Tome 1: 1921-1947*, ed. Pierre Lherminier (Paris: Cinéma Club/Seghers, 1975).

ESC2   Jean Epstein, *Écrits sur le cinéma, 1921-1953: édition chronologique en deux volumes. Tome 2: 1946-1953*, ed. Pierre Lherminier (Paris: Cinéma Club/Seghers, 1975)

A note on infra citations:
Throughout the endnotes in this collection, readers will find infra citations referring them to translations of Epstein's works included in this volume. Because some contributors have made their own translations of Epstein's texts, in many cases the two translations differ. We include the infra citation wherever possible so that when it is available, readers may have easy access to the larger excerpt of Epstein's writings from which these references are drawn.

Preface

Tom Gunning

> A senior film scholar once told me that when attending a conference on a famous American avant-garde filmmaker she asked one of the presenters why he hadn't mentioned the influence of Epstein.
> The presenter looked confused: "Did you say, 'Eisenstein'?" he asked.

The films and writings of Jean Epstein still remain one of the best-kept secrets of film studies, especially outside of France. Hopefully this rich and insightful new anthology may sound the trumpet blast that starts the walls of isolation tumbling. While I and a few other film scholars have enjoyed a certain sense of privileged pleasure in knowing the work of this extraordinary cineaste, I can only find this persistent neglect puzzling. To my mind Jean Epstein is not only the most original and the most poetic silent filmmaker in France, surpassing impressive figures like Abel Gance, Jacques Feyder, Marcel L'Herbier and even Louis Feuillade; I also consider him one of the finest film theorists of the silent era, worthy to be placed alongside the Soviet theorists (Eisenstein, Vertov and Kuleshov) and the equal of the extraordinary German-language cinema theorist, Béla Balázs. I recently amused another senior scholar when I claimed I thought an English translation of Epstein's writings on cinema could revolutionize American film studies. My interlocutor, who greatly admires Epstein, shook his head and replied, "I wish I had as high an opinion of American film studies as you do!"

I try not to assume that my own passions are universal, and it may still be some time before the name of Epstein sounds as familiar as Eisenstein. Nonetheless, I cannot help but welcome this new anthology of essays and translations as a possibly transformative contribution to media studies. And I say *media* studies rather than simply film studies or film history advisedly. Although Epstein's place in film history remains central and complex, I cannot regard him simply as a historical figure. Epstein entered cinema at its moment of greatest excitement and discovery – a period in which its possibilities seemed boundless and its implications yet to be theorized. We now are witnessing a moment in which the nature of moving images and sound, of media in general, is undergoing a similarly radical transformation – and Epstein's writings seem to me more relevant than ever. If Epstein is sometimes dismissed as a visionary (a poet, a mystic who naively sees cinema as offering an almost millennial promise), it may be that our times demand, once again, such a penetrating and untrammeled expectation of what our new media could achieve. It is not simply that Epstein's proclamations of the boundless novelty of cinema seem as inspired today as they did in the twenties; he saw cinema as more than a form of entertainment, a mass medium, or even a new art form. For Epstein, cinema offered a mechanical brain, a machine eye – a portal into a new world transformed by technology: a way for human perception to penetrate into the very life of matter. Epstein's conviction that cinema would open onto new domains of knowledge of the world by going beyond the limits of human consciousness represents more than just the quaint forgotten utopian prediction of a new medium from its first decades. Epstein reminds us of possibilities untapped and speculations unexplored, which emerge as a challenge today as media technology offers more than a means of subjugating the natural world. Can new technologies of vision and communication offer a way to rethink man's relation to his environment, rather than increased access to the ever-the-same? I believe Epstein provided a radically different way of looking at the cinema than that provided by the equally utopian but also instrumental and linguistic model of the Soviets. Unlike the Soviets or the semioticians of the seventies, Epstein's view of the possibilities of cinema surpassed their claims of a new visual language, by going beyond the linguistic model and seeking out instead a new way of seeing the world and interacting with it, based in the subconscious and the extension of our senses into new domains of sensitivity.

Thus I am calling for an approach to Epstein that a new anthology like this makes possible: a double vision of his work that makes use of materials newly available and perspectives newly opened. On the one hand, Epstein's place in film history remains unique and calls for reevaluation. This actually began a few decades ago and has been recognized in France, especially since the opening of new archives of material donated to the Cinémathèque française by Jean's sister, Marie Epstein, an important filmmaker in her own right, giving access to unpublished work by Epstein – of which several scholars in this anthology make intense use. Further, a new sense of the history of silent cinema, as well as new acknowledgement of Epstein's identity as both gay and Jewish, casts a different light on the man and the thinker. Epstein's work (the films and the writings, but the writing especially, some of it now made available in these new translations) may have undergone a certain eclipse, but their reemergence comes at a timely moment when their relevance appears clearer than ever.

First, let me sketch something of Epstein's unique historical position, but also indicate why he should not be grasped only as a historical figure. France could be considered the birthplace of cinema, in spite of subsequent claims made by Hollywood and the USA. France's role in the invention of cinema – first with the work of Etienne-Jules Marey on cinema's technical predecessor, chronophotography, and then the Lumière Brothers in devising an effective camera and projection system – was surpassed by the role of the Pathé Frères in industrializing the production and distribution of cinema internationally before WWI. However, with the near suspension of French film production during the war, and the consequent expansion of Hollywood internationally, the presence of French film suffered a drastic reduction on the world market and lost the international dominance Pathé had held before 1913. But in a sense the incredible bond France has always maintained with the cinema simply transmuted, shifting from industrial production to intellectual labor. The first widespread and coherent cinema movement, both in writing and filmmaking, the first attempt to articulate the nature of cinema and offer a theory of cinema's unique aesthetic, appeared in France shortly before and after World War I. While the market share of French films plummeted internationally, a serious intellectual discourse on the seventh art blossomed, sustained by the role of Paris as the international capital of modern art, willing to reach out towards this new art of the machine (unlike other artistic and intellectual centers which scorned film as vulgar). This burgeoning French film culture was nurtured by a new breed of intellectuals known as *cineastes* who founded film journals, created alternate forms for film exhibition in both cineclubs and specialized theaters, and fostered close contact among filmmakers, painters and poets (Apollinaire, Cendrars, Picasso, Léger, Man Ray, Colette, Cocteau, Artaud, Breton, were just a few of the Parisian intellectuals who flocked to the cinema in the teens and twenties and whose work was transformed by this encounter). The first "movement" in cinema, known (at least in retrospect) as the Impressionists (indicating only a vague relation to the movement in painting decades earlier, and possibly stronger relations to the music of Debussy and a definite debt to the subjective and ephemeral associations of the term) emerged from these intersecting forces. I have often thought it would be better to refer to this conjunction of theories and filmmaking as "Symbolist" because of its closer ties to the allegories and abstraction of the post-impressionist generation and its particularly strong ties to poetry, but the films did maintain a powerful link to the painter's obsession with vision under varying circumstances of light and atmosphere.

Epstein stands at the center of this first cinema movement, whose influence internationally on the avant-garde ideals of cinema has sometimes been obscured by the slightly later influence of Expressionism, Dada, Surrealism and Soviet montage. In many ways in spite of the extraordinary achievements of the French cinema after the war in the work of Marcel L'Herbier, Germaine Dulac, Abel Gance, Fernand Léger, Dimitri Kirsanov, Rene Clair, Henri Chomette, Louis Delluc, Jean Renoir and others (all touched to varying degrees and for varying lengths of time by the Impressionist influence), one could claim the true center of the movement lay in its theoretical discourse. Among the first self-conscious attempts to define the nature of cinema (and thus its difference from the other arts), the writings first of Louis Delluc, and then of Epstein and Germaine Dulac (and a host of other critics of writers, some of them filmmakers who wrote occasionally

– such as L'Herbier or Kirsanov) sparked an intense debate and polemic about the nature and possibilities of cinema. The initial term of these debates became *photogénie*, primarily introduced by Delluc, (although, as Katie Kirtland has shown, it had a long history, especially in art and literature, before the cinema). The term was debated, its relevance vaunted (and denied) by numerous voices, but its greatest exponent was Jean Epstein, at least in his early writings. Epstein's eloquent invocation of *photogénie* (and equally staunch refusal to offer a strict and easily paraphrased definition of the term) expressed his firm faith in cinema's unique quality, beyond logic and linguistic specification, his allegiance to the intuitive and subconscious sources of art and the enigmatic legacy of Symbolist poetry.

As I indicated, Epstein brings the Symbolist/Impressionist tradition in cinema to a climax in both his films and his writings. This in itself certainly makes him a crucial figure in film history and aesthetics. In spite of its eclipse by the more famous avant-garde movements, the influence of this current of cinema was international. One can trace its echoes not only in the later avant-garde movements of the 1920's – despite their polemics against it. The Surrealists denounced the Impressionists even as they appropriated aspects of Epstein's thought; the young Luis Buñuel apprenticed with the established filmmaker and apparently considered him an old-fashioned aesthete; yet the visual influence of *La Chute de la maison Usher*, on which he worked as an assistant, on *Un Chien Andalou* is evident, even if possibly carrying a mocking overtone. But Impressionist echoes also extended to the experimental cinemas of Latin America (Mario Peixoto's Brazilian masterpiece from 1930, *Limite*), Asia (Impressionist stylistics seem to me to dominate Teinosuke Kinugasa's 1926 *Page of Madness* in spite of more frequent comparisons to *The Cabinet of Dr. Caligari*) and the United States (especially evident in Webber and Watson's 1933 *Lot in Sodom*), not to mention the delayed surfacing of a Symbolist aesthetic in the films of Ingmar Bergman and Andrei Tarkovsky or, as Robert Bird has persuasively argued, Stan Brakhage. But as rich and in need of further study as this Impressionist legacy may be, as I indicated earlier, it should not circumscribe our understanding of Epstein by confining him to a brief period of film history rather than recognizing him as a still-vibrant force in thinking through the intersection of technology and perception in the modern era. Epstein's value lies in both embodying and surpassing cinematic Impressionism. Otherwise one might see Epstein as a slightly out-of-date turn-of-the-century decadent, whose thought and aesthetics seem caught in the wake of Baudelaire and Poe and whose sense of modernity lags behind the Surrealists and Constructivists, and whose theory remains poetic and impressionistic.

To launch a full claim for shaking Epstein out of this narrow frame, while acknowledging the importance of his Symbolist roots, lies beyond the scope of this modestly intended preface and my still-limited penetration into the full Epstein archive. I do not think it is wrong, though, to see it as one of the ambitions of this anthology as a whole, whose authors' knowledge surpasses my own.

While the approach and ideas of the authors assembled here differ, nonetheless they all reflect on Epstein as more than a circumscribed historical figure. The deep grappling with his work found here constantly affirms the excitement that his films and ideas still generate. The Epstein excavated in these pages is no mummy, but a vital gift to the future of media studies.

Noël Carroll has pointed out that the first generation of film theorists were primarily engaged in a polemic arguing for the value and uniqueness of cinema as an art form. This often led to a paradox of which these writers were aware to varying degrees. As a new art form, the cinema strove to define its difference from the other arts (especially from its closest cognate, theater). Thus, their arguments often assumed the form that became known as medium specificity. Cinema can do things other arts can't: it is luminous; it uses photography, but liberates it from stillness; it is produced by machines and can be distributed on a mass scale like an industrial product; it seems to attract even the uneducated; and it can communicate with limited (or even no) use of language. Conservative critics posed many of these qualities as limitations to cinema's ever attaining aesthetic parity with the traditional arts. Further, in the period before the First World War osocial critics denounced cinema as a vulgar fairground attraction, an example of mass-produced "trash," suitable only for the unwashed and uneducated. The response of those willing to defend the cinema primarily took the form of striving to infuse cinema with the values of traditional arts through adaptations of literary pieces, recreations of famous paintings, or obtaining the participation in film-making of well-known actors, writers and even composers. Gradually, however, a modernist backlash emerged, especially during and after the First World War, celebrating, rather than attempting to eliminate, film's fairground heritage and democratic audience, praising its mechanical rhythm, and embracing film's participation in the speedy tempos of modern urban life. The film theory of the late teens and twenties still wobbles a bit between these positions (an emulation of the established canons of art still competed with a view of cinema as a model for modern forms) and occasionally even attempted a synthesis.

The contested term photogénie, which will be discussed frequently in the pages of this anthology, can be seen as an attempt to define the uniqueness of the cinema, and, as I have indicated, to claim that cinema represented a new mode of perception and experience. As such, photogénie can be characterized as offering an argument of medium specificity. Yet at the risk of apparent contradiction, Epstein seems to locate the unique quality of cinema less in its difference from the other arts than in its achievement of a specifically modern synthesis and fulfillment of both the arts and the sciences, even providing new forms of knowledge that bridge the aesthetic and the epistemological (although perhaps the term "Gnostic" best indicates Epstein's view of cinema's new modes of knowing). Epstein's pre-cinematic career revolved around the dual centers of scientific research and modern poetry. His early writings seem inspired by Apollinaire's proclamation of a new poetry that could take its place alongside the new painting of the Cubist and post-impressionists. Cinema, Epstein might claim, fulfills the aspiration of new forms of poetry and painting, offering an entirely new way of making art, which grew out of a modern way of perceiving the world, and perhaps even provided a passage to this new world. Thus, film's synthesis of modern art resembled less a Wagnerian *gesamtkunstwerk* combining the arts of the past than a technical art aimed at the expansion and refinement of the senses. As a synthesis, cinema did not simply combine the various arts, but put them on a new footing, defining them not as a mode of representing the world, but as a way to penetrate it, even uncovering a world beyond human experience: exploring the realm of matter, of the *données* of consciousness, especially revealing the laws of time amid the deepest layers of motion and matter.

While I make no attempt here to give a synoptic account of Epstein theories, I do wish to point out how they evade a central dichotomy of traditional film theory. I have differentiated Epstein's concept of *photogénie* and theories of the photographic image from the syntactically based montage theories of Eisenstein, the only silent film theorist whose depth of thought could claim, in my opinion, to surpass Epstein's. Although postdating the period of Epstein's foundational writing, the essays of André Bazin, which date from the forties and fifties, offer a fascinating relation to Epstein (which merits a profound study). As recent revaluations and research make clear, Bazin stands as the most complex theorist of cinema after the silent era, and his discussion of the ontology of the photographic image at points recalls aspects of Epstein's description of *photogénie*, although Bazin seems almost to repress any reference to the earlier theorist. But if affinities exist between them, Bazin's approach to cinema certainly diverged from Epstein's. In a classic formulation, Bazin divided filmmakers into two broad camps: those who put their faith in the image and those who put their faith in reality. Epstein smashes through this division. For Bazin, those who put their faith in the image included those filmmakers who believed the essential art of cinema lay in developing the "expressive" devices of film, whether the montage of the Soviets, the plastic deformation of set design, composition and lighting practiced by the Expressionists, or the cinematic tricks beloved by the avant-garde, including the Impressionists (e.g. superimpositions, split-screens, manipulation of lenses). In his calls for a new avant-garde Epstein seems to belong firmly to the image camp. Especially in his early films, he employed most of these devices. However, he also expressed his suspicion of them and, especially in his Brittany films from the late twenties, sought to foreground cinema's interaction with real locations and the material surfaces of the world. But it would be too simple to see Epstein as gradually evolving into a Bazinian realist. Even in these later films, with their semi-documentary modes of location shooting and non-professional actors, we are hardly anticipating the styles of neo-realism, aspiring to capture reality yet avoid manipulating it. Epstein's cinema continues to intervene in the world, to present a world transformed rather than familiar. We could say Epstein felt that cinematic techniques failed if they obscured our contact with reality, but succeeded if they revealed new layers of the structures of the world, supplementing ordinary human perception.

I believe Epstein's third way, between the formalism of foregrounding artistic devices and the Bazinian faith in the sufficiency of photographic surface and the preservation of real time (as in the long-take aesthetic which has become nearly a fetish in current international film festival stylistics), represents not only a neglected and powerful tradition of filmmaking, but also a way of thinking about film that transcends medium specificity. Within the French film culture of the twenties the debates over *photogénie* eventually gave way to a discussion of *cinéma pur*, pure cinema, whose definition became as subject to disputes as the earlier term. Epstein seemed dubious about this even narrower focus on cinema maintaining a splendid isolation from other influences. Cinema existed within a network of modern arts and exemplified a modern poetry, and film's relation to the sciences supplied a vital realm of reference for Epstein. For Epstein, rather than simply contemplating its own nature, cinema opened onto the universe, both the human world of memory and emotion and the material world that films could open to human understanding. Thus, the devices of the cinema served less as artistic filters placed over the world than scientific lenses revealing new aspects, like the investigatory tools of laboratory or observatory. Epstein's fascination with the technique of slow motion clearly exemplifies this third way in which film explores previously undiscovered aspects of the world. Marey, the scientist who arguably made the greatest contribution to the technology of the motion pictures, had criticized the projected films of the Lumière brothers when they appeared at the turn-of-the-century, claiming such moving images simply reproduced common visual experience and did nothing to extend our powers of vision. Marey designed chronophotography to triumph over the human subjugation to temporal flow by stilling and capturing the otherwise invisible instant and subjecting it to observation and analysis. In the early twentieth century scientists recognized cinematic slow motion, along with its opposite, time-lapse photography, as providing major tools for observation and demonstration. Enabling through cinema the extension and compression of the flow of time respectively, these techniques revealed aspects of the world that human vision could not otherwise see, and yet they did not distort the world into an aesthetic image. Rather they opened up a new visual dimension. Epstein's manipulation of time in cinema revealed a different rhythm to the universe, a ballet of matter. Thus, the intuition of Roderick Usher, the protagonist of Poe's story, that matter itself may have a sentient and animate dimension was visualized in Epstein film's *La Chute de la maison Usher* through the use of slow motion. The constant vibration of the material world, whether the flowing of fabric caught in the breeze or the cascade of dust falling from a suddenly struck bell does not simply provide a visual metaphor for the haunted house of Usher. Rather, they capture a universal vibration shared by the soul of things and the structures of the psyche, invoking the senses of both vision and sound (and even touch) placed before us on the screen. In his penultimate masterpiece from 1947, *Le Tempestaire*, Epstein not only used slow motion to display the currents of ocean surf as he had in his earlier silent films made in Brittany, but innovatively introduced the timbre and resonance of slowed down recorded sound, enfolding us as auditors not simply in defamiliarized sonority, but allowing us to dwell within an extended soundscape filled with the uncanny echoes of nature.

I believe the future of media studies cannot simply ditch more than a century of moving images in order to vaunt the digital pleasures of video games. But I also find embalming the original potential of the moving image that emerged during the last century into a nostalgic longing for the vanished purity of cinema equally impoverished. I think Epstein's third way may serve as a clue to guide us through this new labyrinth of promises and false turns. Epstein saw cinema as a way of sharpening and intensifying not only our senses but our complex relation to the world – cinema serving as a device of exploration more than personal expression. For Epstein, time did not exist as a static given, but as a malleable dimension: inescapable perhaps, but also multifaceted when opened up by technology. *Le Tempestaire* provides a complex allegory of Epstein's visionary theory of film. The heroine, a young Breton girl anxious about the fate of her fisherman lover who may be lost in the tempest, finds little solace in the radio technology contained in a lighthouse and consults an old tempest master, a wizard who peers into a glass ball. This ancient tool of scrying resembles the cinema as vision machine, but Epstein's images of the tempest-tossed sea in slow and reverse motion and of clouds in fast motion scudding across the sky, reveals a powerful choreography of nature within a post-Einsteinian universe that exceeds the wizard's vision. The answer to the girl's fear does not come through the witch's ball, which falls to the floor and smashes. Occult vision does not resolve the narrative enigma, but rather cinema opens up another dimension of experience that actually cures the girl's fear of wind and sea. Epstein's unconventional rhetoric turns the viewer's attention away from the resolution of narrative expectations by overwhelming our concern for the outcome of the storm with an absorption into its awe-inspiring forms revealed through a new way of seeing and experiencing the world. As in the ending the Book of Job, in which Jehovah sidesteps Job's moral questions through an invocation of His sovereignty and the sublime structures of creation, here the structures of the world revealed through technology make a dangerous world inhabitable, if still uncanny. For Epstein cinema offered a means of revelation, but one essentially modern and technological.

The eclipse of Epstein's work has been pierced before, and this anthology should be seen as a culmination rather than an entirely new project. Although submerged, French scholarship has never entirely forgotten Epstein, and against

Bazin's silence Edgar Morin, in his crucial work of post-World War II film theory, *Le cinema ou l'homme imaginaire*, maintained Epstein's thought as an essential reference, while Henri Langlois of the Cinémathèque française undertook the effort to rediscover and preserve Epstein's films that will continue to fuel the revival I hope is now spreading beyond France. The opening of the new Epstein archives has been greeted by French scholars with new evaluations and publications, such as Jacques Aumont's invaluable anthology from 1998, *Jean Epstein: cinéaste, poète, philosophe*. And in spite of his relative neglect in English-language film studies, an Epstein revival did emerge in the 1970's with publications by the British journal *AfterImage* and a retrospective at New York City's Anthology Film Archive (which introduced me as young graduate student to his work, along with the insightful advocacy of Annette Michelson). Important subsequent scholarly work followed, ranging from David Bordwell's pioneering dissertation on French Impressionism (1974) to the penetrating dissertation by Stuart Liebman at NYU on Epstein's early work (1980). This culminated in Richard Abel's history of the French cinema of the Impressionist period, *French Cinema: The First Wave 1915-1929*, from 1987 (unfortunately long out of print) and the invaluable translations Abel made available in his anthology from 1988, *French Film Theory and Criticism: A History/Anthology 1907-1939*, a volume whose Epstein pages in my copy are dog-eared and heavily underscored. I am gratified that essays by some of these pioneering figures are included here. But it is primarily the work of a new generation of scholars that has produced this new anthology, and I am proud that I can claim some of them, including the dedicated and resourceful editors, as my students. The future of Epstein continues... and in new hands, who, with this volume, are now handing it on to all of us.

Introduction

Jean Epstein and the Revolt of Cinema

Sarah Keller

> As it sketched its very first aesthetic differentiations with the spectacles of nature, the cinematograph was choosing between God and Satan, and siding with the latter. Since whatever moves will transform and replace what has proven to be photogenic, photogénie, as a fundamental rule, clearly dedicated the new art to the service of the forces of transgression and revolt.[1]

As filmmaker and theorist, Jean Epstein has observed that the fundamental energies undergirding cinema are those that valorize both rapt attention (associated with stillness) and incessant flux (associated with movement), with a strong emphasis in his own work upon the latter. One of the cinema's most conspicuous tensions, for example, lies in the balance between its still frames and the way, when they are set into motion, that they revivify whatever these individual shots depict – a tension between stasis and change. Within his assertions about cinema as the ultimate negotiator of the *state of becoming* characterizing existence, we find a central connection among Epstein's theory, his films, and the world in which he conceived the theory and films. Epstein was a vigorous participant within the modern era of which he was a part and which witnessed the strengthening within intellectual circles of the idea of movement, change, and constant becoming as a means for understanding aspects of our experience. Simultaneously, that era itself witnessed immense social, technological, and aesthetic changes – changes that happened broadly and with harrowing rapidity. What better tool for comprehending such momentous transitions, Epstein argued, than cinema, born from a moment (and itself composed of the elements) of massive change?

Before attempting to answer such a question, we might do well to take a step back: first of all, who was Jean Epstein, this figure lingering on the outskirts of cinema studies' horizons, and why should the notion of change – and its attendant figure of transgression that the epigraph above points out – matter to cinema studies as much as it did to Epstein? In the history of cinema, and in the history of theories about cinema, where does his work fit in?

Jean Epstein was born in Warsaw, Poland in March 1897 – less than two years after the first public screening of cinema in Paris. By way of Switzerland for his boyhood education, Epstein came to France to continue his studies in medicine. His medical training at the Université de Lyon (from 1917-1920) does find later reflection in his film practice and theory, but within a short period of time, Epstein turned to the arts as his primary vocational interest, first as a literary critic and then (and finally) as a cineaste. While he was studying in Lyon, he made the acquaintance of Louis and Auguste Lumière, founding fathers of cinema who provided inspiration for him in establishing an arts journal, Le Promenoir. As this trajectory portends, Epstein's first foray into cinema came through writing, first in journals like his own, and then collected in a series of books. In fact, he wrote three books in quick succession from 1920 to 1922 and published them in short order through Parisian presses; he then moved to Paris partly through the encouragement he received for these works. In their approaches, these three foundational texts vary wildly, and in their content they range from discussions of literature to more general theories of aesthetics, social-psychology, and cinema. Epstein completed all three – Poésie d'aujourd'hui: un nouvel état d'intelligence (1921), Bonjour Cinema (1921), and La Lyrosophie (1922) – by the time he started work on his first film, a documentary on Louis Pasteur (Pasteur) later in 1922. From these auspicious, energetic beginnings until his death in 1953, Epstein was prolific in both filmmaking and writing about cinema: he completed over forty films and continually published articles, many of which he revised and collected in books published throughout his lifetime.

The writings and films range widely in their style and purpose. Epstein wrote articles about the parameters of cinema, philosophically inclined treatises, and books with a more creative bent. His films range from documentaries to feature films in a variety of styles. Among these are films that are broadly experimental or commercial, melodramatic or instrumentally subtle, with celebrated actors of the French cinema or non-actor inhabitants of the rugged islands off the coast of Brittany. In both the writings and films, he was restlessly engaged in developing ideas about the purview and potential of cinema, as well as about the character of the human, scientific, social, and natural worlds. His films are enthusiastically creative, capitalizing upon stylistic features available to the camera for dramatic and aesthetic purposes, such as a long, slow track out from a close-up of a woman's face, posing for a portrait, into an extreme long shot of the art deco apartment of her suitor, providing context for their romance (in Coeur des Gueux, 1936). And the films and the theory mutually inform each other, so that for instance Epstein's interest in the viability of creative uses of sound develops in tandem with film projects that explore what is possible to do with sound in practice. Thus Epstein was one of the rare figures of cinema history who conceived his creative practice parallel to an ambitious program of theorizing and writing.

As a young man seeking his vocation, he read widely in philosophy and psychology, the natural and physical sciences, poetry and literature, religion, and many diverse subjects, and eventually drew several of his ideas about the methods, aesthetics, and purposes of cinema from these sources. Although he did not initiate the potent idea for which he is most remembered – photogénie – he expanded and elaborated upon it productively, and in Anglophone cinema studies, he is the source on the matter to which most texts turn.[2] Photogénie, which for Epstein occurs in brief, electrifying flashes, signifies the quality which the filming of an object confers upon that object, a particularly photographic (with all of its effects) and cinematic (by dint of its mobile nature) quality that allows us to see the object in a new light. The concept has a number of implications – some of them unexpected – for the study of cinema, as we see in several of the essays in this collection.

However, Epstein's work goes well beyond his contributions to photogénie. Other issues that are raised in his work include his contributions to trends in French avant-garde filmmaking; his descriptions of the modernist condition which lead him to consider fatigue in relation to social conditions, binding him to the cultural critics of his time and beyond; and his innovative position on creative uses for sound after the cinema's transition from the silent era. One of the most provocative issues his work raises returns us to our initial question: we see that the notion of change, which draws its energy from the "forces of transgression and revolt," finds a particularly convincing and felicitous outlet in Epstein's critical and creative output. Cinema seen from Epstein's vantage point takes as its central motivation these transgressive yet ultimately life-affirming qualities of movement. Revolt may be diabolical, as Epstein's quotation suggests, but for him it is also a way of preserving vitality, of showing that cinema possesses a life of its own, its own intelligence.

Through the observations, obsessions, and arguments developed in his creative and critical work, Epstein became one of the very first to imagine and attempt to formulate a comprehensive notion of the cinema. As Richard Abel has noted, in France through the 1910s, a cohesive theory about the artistic mode of film failed to materialize.[3] However, by the 1920s, the far-reaching implications of the artistic potential inherent in cinema emerged from several corners. Jean Epstein belongs at the center of these efforts. In his earliest, most ebullient writings, he explores the potential of cinema to express constantly shifting modes of being – truly, modes of becoming. Epstein remains an optimist across his body of writing, even late in his career and even after being unable to make films for several years during the Second World War. The ways in which he understands the subversive nature of cinema and its capacity to harbor (positive) transgression develop over time in his critical and creative oeuvre. And from early on, always related to this foundational idea, Epstein navigates other concerns about the nature and purpose of the cinema, questions of great importance as several theories of cinema first develop.

In the present moment, anxieties have emerged about the nature of the cinematic medium and its future (or its imminent demise), as well as about the notion of being human both in a mechanized/digitized environment and across the realms of perception, intellect, reason, and sense. Accordingly, scholars have returned to earlier moments in cinema's history, when similar preoccupations reigned, for guidance on how to rethink cinema's foundations and its current status.[4] Indeed, the ways in which we have understood the founding questions of cinema studies appear not so much to be in a crisis moment at present as they are in crisis *again*: that crisis comes as part of the cyclical nature of cinema as it adjusts its parameters in the wake of irrevocable change, which Epstein identified as cinema's own central tendency. As a (relatively) new medium, cinema has always operated in an observable state of flux; its essential nature has proven elusive in part because of shifting contextual and technological terrain. As Epstein would warn us, setting one's sights on a moving object requires some flexibility of mind.

Within this medial environment, now is the perfect time to examine why Epstein's work is so important to the pre-digital age of cinema, as well as why it continues to carry great importance whenever we feel compelled to ask, as we often do: What is cinema? What can it do? And why does it matter? For Epstein, cinema is revolutionary. It provides an artistic mode for making sense of and, equally, for transforming the world it observes. Cinema triggers a revolt against the dullness of the senses and the habits of the mind; it recognizes and generates ecstatic attention; and it allows a representation of the world that is true to the nature of that world.

In his theory, more than any other theorist/filmmaker of the inter-war period – a period of decisive importance for the development of cinema as an art form – Epstein initiated debates about cinema's technological, perceptual, and cross-medial possibilities. He introduced formal innovations and new theoretical ideas, influencing film practice, criticism, and reception in the 1920s-1940s and well beyond. This anthology is the first comprehensive study in English of Epstein's far-reaching influence, and it arrives as several of the concerns most central to Epstein's work are undergoing productive reevaluations, including theories of reception, realism, the aesthetics and ontology of cinema, and the relationship between cinema and other arts. Epstein ought to be considered a requisite, cornerstone figure for scholars negotiating these enduring theoretical questions. He rails against taking the central aspects of cinema for granted – including its position as an industry, an art, and an apparatus – making him a necessary figure for any moment when we need to return to a consideration of the basics.

To demonstrate Epstein's importance, the present collection provides a panoply of different approaches to Epstein's work in a series of critical essays by scholars and filmmakers and also brings together a broad selection of Epstein's own written works, much of it translated for the first time into English. We hope that these efforts will lead in turn to the wider release of a greater portion of Epstein's complex, often stunning filmography, a necessary step for restoring his work to the stature it deserves.

For, up to the present moment, Epstein has been simultaneously an important and yet neglected figure for Anglophone cinema studies. Students of cinema know a few seminal translations of his written work very well, and a few films – including his adaptation of *The Fall of the House of Usher* (1928) – have found their way into the canon of film history. Recent work has rekindled Epstein studies in Europe, including Nicole Brenez and Ralph Eue's anthology of Epstein's work translated into German published as Jean Epstein: *Bonjour Cinéma und andere Schriften zum Kino* (2008), Prosper Hillairet's monograph on Epstein's *Coeur fidèle* (2008), Laura Vichi's *Jean Epstein* (2003), and the collection of essays published by the Cinémathèque française under the direction of Jacques Aumont, *Jean Epstein: Cinéaste, poète, philosophe* (1998).[5] However, aside from pioneering work by Richard Abel and Stuart Liebman in the 1980s and a few notable, recent exceptions, there has been a relative drought of sustained work on Epstein in the Anglophone world.[6]

This collection aims to correct that neglect and to inspire further work on Epstein both as a filmmaker and a theorist of cinema. Epstein is a distinctive presence in film history and accordingly the essays gathered here provide a provocative range of accounts for the intricacies of his thought and practice of cinema. Several issues of central importance to Epstein's oeuvre are discussed in detail within these critical essays, which fall into several primary categories of interest to cinema scholarship. First, Christophe Wall-Romana provides a foundation for understanding Epstein's thoughts on *photogénie* while arguing for an aesthetics of embodiment in Epstein's work. As such, he importantly resituates territory covered by earlier Epstein scholars, introducing Epstein's unpublished treatise on homosexuality to realign debates on the body as central to Epstein's idea of cinematic experience. Second, Stuart Liebman, Katie Kirtland, and Jennifer Wild – from strikingly different angles – address Epstein's complex notions of aesthetics, including the coincidence of ideas chez Epstein with the Russian formalists; the particular, kaleidoscopic subjectivity mobilized in Epstein's film work; and the idea of distance in Epstein's aesthetic filtered through Romanticism, notions of the sublime, and Epstein's own intervention in modernity wherein he navigates ancient, natural powers within contemporary experience.

Moving toward film form and style, essays by Laurent Guido and Ludovic Cortade address cinematic technique in Epstein's oeuvre, specifically in relation to his experiments with the temporal realm of cinema, including the implications of editing and rhythm for notions of cinematic time and modifications of time within a stretch of film (slow motion). Rachel Moore and the filmmaker James Schneider, from different perspectives, consider the important period of Epstein's career when he began making another kind of film altogether, using familiar stylistic strategies but for radically different ends, among the islands off the coast of Brittany. They examine the impact of that move on his concept of realism and on his filmmaking practice.

The significance of the cultural realm within Epstein's work finds expression in essays by Trond Lundemo, Nicole Brenez, and Érik Bullot, who in diverse ways consider the relevance of subjective and cultural experience within Epstein's theories and practice of cinema – through cinema's mechanistic, intelligent design; its relation to modernist concerns; and its plasticity (relating again to its dependence upon flux and instability). Finally, at the very end of this collection, Richard Abel contributes a reminder of several areas in need of attention related to the Epstein oeuvre, providing an afterword that ties together several of the issues raised in this volume. All of these strategies and topics suggest that the avenues of exploration for Epstein's written and film work readily open up to such wide-ranging, far-reaching considerations of his cinema within its psycho-social, cultural, technological, and aesthetic domains.

The nature and development of Epstein's oeuvre deserves the scrutiny and close readings these essays accomplish so well. To provide an introduction to the multiplicity of frameworks driving the writing collected in this volume, I will simply address one issue here that finds expression across Epstein's oeuvre and influences many of the concerns taken up in the critical essays, as a way of providing a thread to follow through them. In Epstein's earliest writings about cinema, the importance of a cross-medial aesthetic, especially one using a literary model as a point of reference, asserts itself. Looking at Epstein's interest in poetry in particular reveals both the coruscating quality of his theorizations and his strong connections with the artistic milieu of Paris, arguably the cultural capital of the 1920s. Such an aesthetic influences Epstein's subsequent theorizations about and practices of cinema in significant ways.

In addition to this contextualization of some of the broader concerns raised in the individual essays, this introduction will also familiarize the reader with Epstein's remarkable filmography, which because of its broader unavailability to the public requires some elaboration. It will therefore also provide a sense of how a handful of Epstein's preferred cinematic devices – especially the close-up and superimposition – manifest several of his theoretical concepts within the highly creative contexts of the films. Along these lines, Epstein's other enduring concerns, especially how to represent subjectivity or how to represent what he termed "the real world," are expressed through cinematic devices such as slow motion, editing, and sound.

Epstein's initiation: poetic cinema

It is essential that Epstein be situated in the context of modernist film and art movements and production in the 1920s and beyond. Like many of the artists who came to Paris at that time, Epstein envisioned the world transformed by the art of the modern age. Moreover, during this period in particular, international art movements were flourishing, dependent upon artists crossing both national and medial boundaries. Several movements developed in relation to artists migrating from country to country, picking up the nuances of differences across movements or theories and importing them wherever they alighted, and Epstein's theories accordingly developed in relation to or reaction against many of these movements – including Futurism, Dadaism, Surrealism, and what has become known as French Impressionism.[7] Epstein exemplifies a tendency that drew from many corners to create a centripetal energy whose center was Paris, buzzing with international ideas and figures.

At this early point in his vocational exploration, Epstein expressed the parameters of his views on cinema at first through his admiration for and understanding of literature and especially poetry. Notes taken even during his stint studying medicine in Lyon attest to his more artistic interests: circa 1919 his notebooks abound with reference to his literary reading and provide notes toward a comprehensive theory of modern letters.[8] Just after arriving in Paris in 1921, he published his first volume of writing – *Poésie d'aujourd'hui: un nouvel état d'intelligence* – which focuses first on literary concerns, but turns at the end to address cinema, in order to demonstrate affinities between poetic and cinematic strategies.

These affinities register in Epstein's methods for the writing in *Poésie d'aujourd'hui* as well. Even in the midst of making more theoretical points, the prose begins to take on poetic qualities: in sections, it resembles line breaks, and the statements are fragmentary, full of metaphors and imagery. In a section on "the aesthetics of proximity," for example, he describes the poverty of literary images in relation to the immersion of visual ones, and in so doing, employs poetic strategies:

> Between the spectacle and the spectator, no barrier.
> One doesn't look at life, one penetrates it.
> This penetration allows every intimacy. [...]
> This is the miracle of real presence,
>   life made manifest,
>   opened like a beautiful pomegranate
>   and stripped of its covering,
>   easily absorbed,
>   barbaric. [...]

Compared to the drama of muscles moving in close-up, how paltry a theatrical performance made of words![9]

To describe the phenomenon of the close-up, Epstein layers images and similes, using figures of speech to take the place of what usually looks like film criticism. Rather than simply using logical, deductive, argumentative, or strictly analytical structures (which he also does, often with equal *élan*), Epstein marshals poetic devices to make his point.

Later in the same chapter, Epstein describes cinematic devices and the contemporary cinematic climate according to principles he sees driving poetry. The collision of forms creates a network of poetic and cinematic languages in startling, fresh association:

The poem: a cavalcade of metaphors that rear up. [...]
The principle of the visual metaphor is adaptable in dreams and normal life; on the screen, it is a fixed given.
On screen, a crowd. A car pushes its way slowly through. Ovation. Hats off. White splashes of hands and handkerchiefs dance above heads. An indisputable analogy recalls these lines by Apollinaire:
"When human hands were all in leaf"[10]
and these others:
"The sky was filled with lakes of light.
And human hands flew up like milk-white birds."[11]

Epstein continues this elaborate citational-poetic theorization of imagery and its dependence on what seems to be a cinematic shorthand for visual imagery ("Ovation. Hats off...") by now adding language like that of a shooting script:

I immediately imagine a superimposition that emerges from
the fade-in, then jumps into focus and stops abruptly:
dead leaves falling down and swirling, then a flock of birds.
But:
QUICKLY (2 meters)
WITHOUT SYMBOLISM
(the birds should be neither doves nor crows, but simply birds)
Within five years we will write cinematographic poems:
150 meters of film with a string of 100 images that minds will follow.[12]

The text reads both like a poem (and *is* a poem at one point: it is, itself, both a simile and a metaphor for poetic language) and, simultaneously, like directions for filming such a scene. Of course, Epstein is writing neither a poem nor a shooting script here; instead, this is his first version of a sporadic film theory/

SARAH KELLER

literary criticism, and it makes use of the devices of both media – cinema and poetry – to promote an ambitious formal experiment in theorization. It then comments on its own strategies, remarking that more people will follow the model set by Epstein within the next five years.

What is it about the relationship between poetry and cinema that is so appealing and that assists Epstein in his theory? It appears that together, these artistic media provide paradigms that a more strictly analytical language cannot, just as Epstein's film practice looks to models outside of the hegemonic narrative norms rampant in the popular cinema of his day in order to effect experiments in perspective, subjectivity, and an often poetic relationship with mundane realities. He also seeks flexibility with time and space in the use of poetry, drawing on its unique tendencies, again in a way that will be pertinent to his film practice.[13] Poetic form offers access to the elusive qualities of the cinematic medium, a medium that is paradoxically adept at expressing both ephemerality and permanence, in a constant state of tension and fluctuation. This paradox is something Epstein explored throughout the full length of his writings on cinema. *Poésie d'aujourd'hui* initiates and mobilizes these poetic strategies at a very early stage in Epstein's career.

Bonjour Cinéma, published later the same year (1921), is best understood with reference to discourses more squarely belonging to the discipline of poetry, as well as to the popular domains of movie fandom – posters, fan magazines, etc. – all of which Epstein embraced as part of the intoxicatingly intermedial cinephilia that stimulated his generation.[14] *Bonjour Cinéma* is nearly equal parts prescient film theory, experimental poetry, illustrations, and textual experimentation (letters falling down the page, for example[15]), all bent toward paying homage to cinema.[16] Until the present volume, most representations of Epstein's work do not include this poetry or these illustrations; as such his investment in poetry and direct visual equivalents have been undervalued.[17] But *Bonjour Cinéma* – and indeed Epstein's film practice which was set to blossom at nearly the same moment (one year later, and clearly in nascent form here) – must be understood in relation to these ecstatic, cinephiliac, cross-medial impulses of which this text is a harbinger.

Epstein puts poetry, word play, and the visual (over the verbal) into action even before one opens the book: the cover depicts the word "Bonjour" with a "C" overlaid on top of it, out of which a triangular cut of white background (like a ray of light) emits a tumble of the rest of the letters in the word "cinema." Aside from its familiar and merry greeting to cinema (this is after all Epstein's debut in the cinema, his first full consideration of it as a central topic), the cover also effects simultaneity, superimposition, and visual design with simple tools: letters, layering, and a shifting field of background/foreground made by altering these two colors. Opening the cover, such play continues in a table of contents that puts each part of the book in the context of a theatre bill (in English: "This program is subject to alteration"), with parts for the orchestra and *mise-en-scène* credited to Claude Dalbanne, who designed many of the slim volume's images; even here, Epstein's mélange of random text, image, and poetry advances (through the use of different fonts, sizes of letters, and divisions of chapters strewn across the page and surrounded by advertisements for other books for cinephiles).

Epstein lays out the parts of the book by introducing multiple strands of ideas and strategies for expressing them, and then weaves them together into an almost giddy structure:

1. Textual play: Hayakawa and "Jazzimowa" (a play on Nazimova, one of Epstein's stars)
2. Poem: "Séances Continuelles"
3. Textual Play: Matinee Idol
4. (Prose) poem: "Le 14me episode," like script of a typical film scenario: (e.g., "Son voisin de cabine lui ressemble et se suicide. Echange de personnalités et de valises." ["The man in the ship's cabin next door, who resembles him, commits suicide. Exchange of personalities and luggage."])
5. Poem: "Aller et retour"
6. Textual play: Chas Ray, Chaplin
7. A short statement about *photogénie*
8. Prose criticism: "Le sens ibis"
9. Textual play: Douglas Fairbanks
10. Poem: "Écran"
11. Textual play: Los Angeles
12. Poem: not titled
13. 6 pages in fan magazine style (Hayakawa, Nazimova, Charlot, Charles Ray, Fairbanks)
14. Set of 5 poems: in praise of Hayakawa, Nazimova, Charlot, Charles Ray, Fairbanks. (N.B.: In the midst of these pages are some images and textual plays, relating to the subject at hand)
15. Prose criticism: "Grossissement"
16. Textual play: Amérique
17. Prose criticism: "Ciné Mystique"
18. Textual play: Bonsoir, Merci[18]

This truly eclectic collection of strategies and its arrangement of alternation are both complex and playful, especially for something that functions as a kind of film theory. The dizzying shifts of perspectives, the flouting of the conventions of rational order or thesis-driven exegesis, and the use of illustration alone demonstrate the creative, poetic inclination of Epstein's sense of theory and cinema, which continues in more subtle ways (for instance, through word play and superimposition, which allows the layering of ideas and images similar to *Bonjour Cinéma*'s textual strategies) in his later theory. In addition to this macro-level of complexity and structural innovation for the whole book's design, Epstein experiments with the individual components of the text: for instance, one of the poems comprising *Bonjour Cinéma*, "Aller et retour," is meant to be read both forwards and backwards.[19] However, within Epstein's penchant for play, serious consideration of the salient features of cinema's expressive capacities develops, and Epstein finds in this mélange of poetic, popular, cinematic experimentation a dynamic outlet for understanding what energies and methods undergird these media.

Take, for example, the first poem, in which Epstein includes a description of a scene in cinematic terms and with cinematic resonances:

In close up
pale sunshine
this face reigns
this enamel mouth stretches out
like a lazy awakening
then turns laughter upside down
up to the edge of the eyes[20]

The image, a face in close-up, has sunlight cast over it, and summons the concept of light essential to cinematic projection and/or recording (recalling the cover of the text as well as lighting effects more generally). Because Epstein has directed our attention to the minutiae of the movements across a face, the intensity of the face's features in motion may unfold. Close-ups are examined in a number of ways in *Bonjour Cinéma*: in this example, Epstein lays out the initial image and uses simile (like a lazy awakening) and synecdoche (enamel standing in for the teeth and lending the quality and feeling of hard whiteness to the image), as well as the image's mobility (the smile spreading from mouth to eyes), to focus upon the *effects* of that image. As such, he makes use of poetry's facility in invoking associations, even while appearing to treat an image directly.

Other parts of the book treat the same issue from another angle and by other means. Elsewhere in *Bonjour Cinéma* we find the more analytically inclined "Magnification" ("*Grossissement*") also treating the close-up. Epstein begins it by declaring: "I will never find the way to say how much I love American close-ups. Point blank. A head suddenly appears on screen and drama, now face to face, seems to address me personally and swells with an extraordinary intensity."[21] The close-up is a favored perspective for Epstein (as we've seen, the "aesthetics of proximity" are crucial for Epstein both in poetry and cinema) even before he starts making films, and it connects to issues having to do with his cinephilia, his cross-medial impulses, and his sense of cinematic subjectivity and perspective. For example, describing himself in terms of a spectator's interaction with a landscape of flowers, he insists on pointing to a specifically embodied sensorial perspective: "I look, I smell, I feel. Close up, close up, close up."[22]

The mixture of poetic figure and cinematic image continues throughout *Bonjour Cinéma*, serving as an intermedial connection between the two forms for an artist working (however briefly) in both. Excursions into poetry throughout *Bonjour Cinéma* allow for an interplay among Epstein's film theory, his film work, and the mandates of the traditions of poetry as refashioned by the modernist poets Epstein knew and/or admired. Epstein draws important conclusions about film art based on issues poets explore through poetry. For example, he arrives at the notion that one of cinema's central tenets depends on a poetics of visual images, with a much richer understanding of what a visual image is (and what it can accomplish, and how), by having compared it to a verbal image.

Even much later in his writings, Epstein is still reflecting on exactly this issue of the verbal versus the visual:

> Naturally, the style proper to the cinema defines itself in its use of close-ups and isolation of objects in drifting, incommensurable dimensions. [...] Thus the film is found to be particularly apt at both enriching and setting directly into motion the memory and visual imagination of spectators, without having to pass through the operations of crystallization and dissolution of a verbal intermediary.[23]

Epstein's interests in poetry and the visual/verbal image persist through many years in his writings and films. Certainly there are a number of arguments crucial to Epstein's work that draw upon their relationship to these concepts. The idea that poetry can allow critical exploration as well as access to creative reserves appealed very much to Epstein and enriched his film practice as well as the development of his film theory. Both an initiation to and perhaps a perfect crystallization of this interest, *Bonjour Cinéma* draws attention to the way in which Epstein literalizes and makes figurative the tropes of image making. The last two pages resemble a film strip in motion, in that you can see "Merci" at the bottom of the "Bonsoir" page and "Bonsoir" at the top of the page with "Merci" at the center, as if being pulled upward by the sprocket holes. Just as the image/words on the cover of the book – through a set of interrelated, simple graphic devices – invoke the projector, the final pages similarly cast our look into the spooling projector as a finale, effected through visual figuration.

Epstein's film practice

To understand the themes that Epstein developed in his critical work, it will be helpful to have a sense of the range of his creative work, from which his theories are drawn and through which they are developed. Although it is impossible in the context of an introduction to offer a comprehensive account of Epstein's complex filmography which so richly deserves plentiful detail, here it will suffice to present the major shifts in his efforts – to give a sense of the preoccupations of the films – and describe a few salient visual or auditory features of several works that are too seldom screened.

Epstein's career as a filmmaker spans almost thirty years and comprises over three dozen finished films. While he worked in diverse cinematic modes, as we have seen, several features cohere across his oeuvre. More commercially inclined feature films like Le Lion des Mogols (1924), which was unfortunately a commercial disappointment, stand comfortably in the company of more experimental fare like La Glace à trois faces (1927). Indeed, several enduring concerns for Epstein inform both kinds of projects: for instance, both of these films embrace the contradiction of an interest in narrative conventions coupled with visual experimentation through editing (e.g., Le Lion des Mogols's opening sequence and La Glace à trois faces's closing sequences each utilize fast cuts, but for very different narrative and thematic purposes).

Epstein's career offers incisive insights about cinema and the experience of modernity and demonstrates his efforts to realize in practice concepts that originate in his theory. Therefore, in his films, the exceedingly abstract concept of photogénie, as well as several of his other interests including the relationship of the "real" to the cinematic, finds more concrete articulation in the use of devices specific to cinema (the close-up, slow motion, superimposition, editing, focus, lighting, etc.). Epstein ambitiously employs and tests the limits of these devices that flaunt cinema's natural flexibility in presenting time and space. For instance, the consistent confrontation of the character with the camera – breaking the fourth wall, as it were – in several of Epstein's films (unlike the classical mode, in which characters deny the presence of the camera) points to the eruptive power of cinema which Epstein often sought to bring to the fore.

Epstein often allows cinema's seams to show, or takes a sequence to a point of cinematic excess, as we shall see, and thereby calls attention to the process of picturing the world, emotional states, and intimate environments. Certain sequences remove the viewer even further from the anchor of contextualizing space and put her directly into the realm of the image as synecdoche, as for instance in the sequence in Coeur Fidèle where Jean is confronted by Marie's fiancé (Petit Paul) and several of his roughs. The images betray the shifting emotional terrain: suspicion, readiness, confrontation, aggression, disdain. Here we have the components – at first seen in successive isolation, primarily through the most expressive parts of the body (faces and hands) – of a bar fight. The sequence ends with a long shot returning us to the context for these several close views, but because the close-ups occur quickly and in a fluid montage, without any reference to their larger environment, they place us in the center of the fight on the level of its emotional impact – angry faces, menacing looks, fists, bottles about to be broken, one individual against a mini-mob. As René Clair commented in relation to the film, Coeur Fidèle might be faulted for going "into technical experiments which the action does not demand"[24]: that is, which the narrative does not demand. But, as Clair also realizes, Epstein's excess in terms of the function of his camerawork creates the peculiar drama in this and others of his films. Rather than causal, the drama is emotional, photographic, and visual.

Visuality is indeed the foundation upon which Epstein's concept and practice of cinema rests: *photogénie* lays bare the nature of the object as photographed; it helps us to see in a way we haven't seen before. Famously, in "Le Regard du verre" (1925),[25] Epstein envisions cinema as a spiral staircase lined with mirrors which, by dint of their sheer objectivity but complicated by their multiplicity, help one to see what can no longer be seen when simply presented before the naked eye:

> The camera lens…is an eye endowed with nonhuman analytical properties. It is an eye without prejudices, without morality, free of influences; and it sees in the face and in human movement traits which we, weighted down by likings and dislikings, by habits and considerations, can no longer perceive.[26]

Because it is objective (the lens in French is *l'objectif*, a fact in which Epstein delights), the camera helps us to lay aside our preconceived notions and to see anew. Mirrors, cameras, reflections on water and in glass, and similar patterns are accorded a special place in the Epsteinian *mise-en-scène*, as a closer look at the more general course of Epstein's work on film reveals.

Several critics have distinguished distinct periods in Epstein's development, often coinciding with his choices of material, writers, or production companies. The way this story goes, his oeuvre may be characterized first by a concern with "the visual and dramatic effects…of movement on the screen"[27] (roughly 1922-1925), then with experimentation in cinema's spatial and temporal dimensions (1925-1928). Later, his work turns to the natural world as a backdrop and/or subject of his films (1928-1936) before, finally, turning to groundbreaking experiments with sound (the 1940s). While this too-tidy and often repeated formulation falters in that all of these impulses drive most of Epstein's work across his career, and in that this division of his concerns places much too much emphasis on certain better-known films than others,[28] it does help us to get a handle on some of the major movements in his career. Keeping this map in mind may help us to understand some of the evolution of Epstein's concerns over the course of a life in film.

An overview of Epstein's first films 1922-1928

Epstein's debut as a filmmaker came after his first written volumes that deal with cinema, including *Bonjour Cinéma*. In 1922, Jean Benoît-Levy hired him to make a documentary for the occasion of the centennial of Louis Pasteur's birth. After completing the film, Epstein was awarded a contract with Pathé Films, where he made his first fiction films, *L'Auberge Rouge* and *Coeur Fidèle*, in 1923.[29] Also in 1923, Epstein made a short documentary film on the eruption of Mount Etna (*La Montagne infidèle*, now lost), an experience that eventually fueled his reflections on cinema in essays collected in *Le cinématographe vu de l'Etna* (Paris: Les Écrivains Réunis, 1926). This extraordinarily productive year closed with Epstein's production of *La Belle Nivernaise* (1923), whose long tracking shots on the Seine proved influential to Jean Vigo's 1934 film *L'Atalante*. The production packet distributed by Pathé describes the ending of the film as "a fairy tale," and indeed the broad strokes of the film's story situate it in the narrative simplicity of that mode while allowing Epstein to innovate his film style. The same give-and-take of narrative and style occurs across all of these films: *L'Auberge Rouge*'s scenes of fortune reading, diamonds gone missing, and mistaken identities match (in a different register) *La Belle Nivernaise*'s long, spectacular scenes of the river boat, for instance drifting down the river with no one at the helm toward certain mayhem. For this last film of 1923, as Epstein put it, "the greatest actor, the most powerful personality that I know most intimately [in that film] is the Seine from Paris to Rouen."[30] The plasticity of the objects and people Epstein filmed take a central role in his first efforts at making films.

In 1924, Epstein served briefly as director of *La Goutte de Sang*, but abandoned it, reportedly because of difficulty with the Societé des Cinéromans.[31] Soon after, Epstein began his association with Les Films Albatros, a production company founded by Russian émigrés. His first feature for Albatros was *Le Lion des Mogols*, a vehicle for Ivan Mosjoukine, who starred in it and wrote the script.[32] Other films from this remunerative producer-director relationship include *L'Affiche* (1924) and *Le Double Amour* (1925), neither of which should be dismissed out of hand, but which often are, since they subscribe to more narrative-driven, sentimental scenarios (notably they were both written by Epstein's sister, Marie). *Le Double Amour*, for instance, concerns a woman whose lover has a gambling problem, to which she subjugates her income (and scandalizes the charity whose money she uses to rescue him), only to be left by him (at the urging of his father). Unbeknownst to him, however, she bears a son who, twenty years later, becomes an inveterate gambler as well. Like the films from 1923-1924, the story and the style are conflictingly compelling at several points: *Double Amour*'s long tracking shot down a row of admirers listening to the heroine sing does add the arguably narrative-driven character information of her capableness and lovability. However, the bravado of the camera movement, which is in excess of that narrative information, shows again Epstein's commitment to subverting the hold of narrative by letting its margins decenter it.

Bookending Epstein's (reportedly) only film entirely experimental in design, *Photogénies* (1925, lost), are two adaptations of classical texts from theater and literature, *Les Aventures de Robert Macaire* and *Mauprat*.[33] The first represents the final film Epstein made for Albatros. A serial adventure, it is the longest of Epstein's films and follows the episodic adventures of the title character. Of Epstein's films, it seems to be one of the few (the much later *Marius et Olive à Paris* [1935] is another[34]) that takes comedy as one of its primary goals. On the opposite end of the comedy spectrum, but similarly episodic, *Mauprat*, a costume drama, lacks almost entirely the vigor described by Epstein about the effects of cinema on an audience in an interview he gave during the filming (while simultaneously driving a Chrysler-Six automobile, on loan to him at that time). The interviewer recounts Epstein's recollection of a formative experience even prior to Epstein's own moviegoing:

> As a child, I was afraid to go to the cinema. I had heard perfectly reasonable adults speak strongly about horrific details of the conflagration at the charity bazaar where, it seemed, a bishop was burned alive. In my premature logic, I told myself that if a bishop can die at the cinema, all the more reasonable that I would, since I was surely not so well protected by the will of God; I would cry and stamp my feet and enter into mad crises of despair when I would see my parents prepare to go to the cinema: I was never sure they'd return alive.[35]

This risky cinema-going, coupled with the wild ride in the automobile with Epstein, whom his interviewer described as dangerously distracted, portended a new wave of filmmaking for Epstein's career (and simultaneously presaged the death-wish drive of his protagonist in *La Glace à trois faces* [1927] made at the crest of that wave). Despite *Mauprat*'s conventional and somewhat clunky plotting, it is the first film of Epstein's own production company, Les Films Jean Epstein, and marks the beginning of an important new period for his work.

The creative freedom that resulted from working through his own production company drew Epstein toward a series of films that proved highly productive for his sense of the possibilities of cinema: *Six et demi, onze* (1927), *La Glace à trois faces* (1927), and *La Chute de la Maison Usher* (1928). While Marie Epstein assures his audience that Epstein's *La Chute de la maison Usher* "dominates the whole of the second period" – a period characterized as revealing the animism of things and beginning to be more emphatically concerned with the treatment of time (several slow-motion sequences serve as the centerpiece of that film) – all three are masterpieces of specifically cinematic brio in at least one way, if not several. Since *Usher* and *La Glace à trois fois* have received some important critical attention in Anglophone cinema studies, while *Six et demi, onze* remains almost completely neglected, some exploration of this latter film's conspicuous charms in thematic content and stylistic panache is warranted here.

Written by Marie Epstein and produced by Films Jean Epstein, the production of *Six et demi, onze* allowed Epstein to explore several pet themes. The title refers to a standard format of Kodak camera, making the film immediately self-referential in its photographic processes. The primary dramatic movement of the film depends as well on photography, inasmuch as the dual heroes of the film – two brothers quite unalike in all ways except their care for each other and their unfortunate liaisons with Mary Winter (an undeserving, selfish, greedy young beauty) – discover the duplicitous nature of the (deeply flawed) heroine by the passage of a photograph from one brother (Jean) to another (Jerôme) after the first brother's death. Literalizing the claim that he made about La Belle Nivernaise that, in his mind, the trees and the river played starring roles, in the credits for Six et demi, onze Epstein includes the roles of "the sun" and "the lens" in addition to each of the human actors.

The first half of the film depicts Jean's love affair with Mary. While Jean's brother Jerôme, a doctor, is seen among the glass bottles of his profession, Jean is seen with Mary in his "palace of love," a hotel out in the country where they run off together before she throws him over for a flashy young dancer, Harry Gold (in keeping with the English, symbol-laden character names of the film). The film explores the beautiful grounds of their love palace and all the stunning imagery of their romance: one sequence shows them on the water in a boat, with sharp, sparkling cinematography fixated on the water and the moonlight; another shows them driving alongside the seashore in a car and superimposes water, their car driving, and a medium close-up of them kissing. It appears that they are driving through the water, and the image serves as a mobile, dynamic update on the pining lovers Jean and Marie in Coeur Fidèle, here with a disastrous conclusion based on the heroine's coeur completely infidèle.

The second half of the film begins anew, with the aftermath of Jean's suicide and Marie's seduction of Jerôme. Again, while the film appears to transpire in melodramatic territory, the complexity of the themes and the filming, in excess of the needs of the narrative, tell another story altogether. Between the first and second half, the pivotal scene wherein the camera plays the central part most readily illustrates that story.

Jean buys a camera and brings it back to the love palace, where he takes Mary's picture. She demures, saying she doesn't like photography. Her image is reflected in a shot of the camera lens. A close-up of the sun follows – a cameo of the light necessary to take her photograph – then the lens again. Jean takes several photos, and then Mary walks away (in long shot), covering her face. Without really any definitive sign of a break in time, Epstein then gives us a close-up of Jean's face. Several images – the waves of the sea, pigeons flying, the grounds at the hotel – are intercut with beautifully lit close-ups of his face before shifting to long shots of him searching for Mary: we are in another, later moment in the diegesis. Shortly thereafter, there is a shot of Jean looking seriously into the mirror in his room. Epstein superimposes this long shot with an extreme close-up of his eyes and a close-up of his face. Thus, including the mediating frame of the mirror into which he looks, Epstein gives us four images in combination here. Jean then shoots his four-fold image in the mirror with a little gun (taken from Mary). Finally, he turns this gun to his heart and shoots. Shots of the camera and its lens follow before the image fades, signaling Jean's demise.

Here, the camera becomes a crucial character in the drama, as well as a means, a variation of a *deus ex machina*, for the complicating action and climax. Epstein calls to mind both the mechanical quality of the camera (the idea that Jean need only push a button and his unfaithful lover will be revealed, even in a later time and context) and the agency of the cameraman in exacting his revenge (à la *The Cameraman's Revenge*, a trope frequently cited in early accounts of itinerant cinemas). Photography is rampant as a device and theme in the film: Jean's picture at Jerôme's home alerts Mary to the connection between the brothers; Jean's picture falls from Jerôme's wall when he dies; and the revelation that saves Jerôme from Mary's machinations arrives via the development of film left in Jean's camera. The photographic theme is mobilized, as well as served, by Epstein's use of superimposition, the close-up, lighting, and temporal ellipses, such as that effected in Jean's search for the missing Mary, often in a very literal way (lens = the revealer of the truth about Mary).

After *Six et demi, onze*, the "more dominant" final film of this period, *La Chute de la maison Usher* – with some of its footage shot in Brittany – led to another, very different series of films, including *Finis Terrae* (1929), *Mor'Vran* (1930), *L'Or des mers* (1932), and *Chanson d'Ar-Mor* (1934). Thus commenced another phase in Epstein's development, toward a more explicit exploration of the relationship between reality and the filmic image.

World and film: 1928-1948

Even before his transformative encounter with cinematic reality marked by his Brittany films, in *La Chute de la maison Usher*, with its excessive digressions, Epstein scrutinized the relationship between pro-filmic and post-filmic reality. While Roderick Usher is solicitous toward his wife Madeline, and tends to her in her apparent illness, the fascination of her representation in Roderick's portrait of her overcomes him in the end – to the point of not noticing that she has died. In the sequence depicting her death, images of the painting, the person, and the object are swapped within a frame insert. The painting, a still image, is represented by a mobile (filmic, photographic) inset of Madeline: one can see her mildly blinking at the camera although she is supposed to be a painting, which points to the life-likeness of Roderick's representation of her. Meanwhile, when Epstein means to depict the "real" woman outside of her portrait, he gives the viewer a still, negative image, superimposed over several shots of a mobile Madeline. Much is made over the "truth" of the image, so much so that Epstein equates it with life: "*C'est la vie même!*" In fact, for Epstein and for Roderick Usher, what is filmed is *greater* than life: the realm of the photographic exposes something more fascinating about the thing (or person) photographed than that thing (or person) holds on its own.

In the series of films he made on several of the islands off the coast of Brittany over the course of two decades, Epstein demonstrates his investment in the relationship between reality and representation, between documenting and narrating. Although Finis Terrae on the one hand tells a story about a small group of kelp fishermen on a remote island, on the other hand it focuses more on the experience of the island life itself than on the characters populating that island. Indeed, Epstein noted that among its other directives, Finis Terrae covered documentary ground:

> Finis Terrae endeavors to be psychological 'documentary,' the reproduction of a brief drama comprising events which really happened, of authentic men and things. Leaving the Ouessant archipelago, I felt I was taking with me not a film but a fact.[36]

Moreover, the film examines the subjective distortions of reality through the perspective of a hallucinating character, further demonstrating Epstein's interest in the often blurry line between reality and the perception of it in images. Accessing the inaccessible 'reality' of subjective experience proved to be something of an anthropological project for Epstein's film work in this region.

Like Finis Terrae, Epstein's 1930 film Mor'Vran opens with a series of images and text meant to situate the striking imagery and fictionalized account that will follow in documentary realms. After the opening credits, Epstein's camera observes the open ocean in an establishing shot. This seascape will serve as the backdrop for the simple story of the islanders whose rough lives both depend upon and are deeply threatened by their environment. The next shot cuts to a drawn map, over which Epstein's camera pans, in pursuit over the expansive sea for the string of islands about which he wishes to demonstrate something. An initial shot of the map is followed by a closer view of the same, drawing us closer to the island in question.

A title interrupts to tell the audience about where we are: Ouessant, "queen of the archipelago." A series of shots that adumbrate life on the island ensue:
- a long shot of a church (center of social contracts and life more generally for the islanders), followed by
- a close-up of a crucifix,
- a long shot of boats resting on land at low tide,
- a close view of a windmill,
- two shots of sheep (first in the medium distance, then from a further distance)

The regular variation of camera distance alone (long view, close view) creates a feeling of rhythm underlining the harmony of the simple life Epstein sees being led by the island inhabitants. The lives of the islanders are sketched out by these visual references to the church, the boats, the sheep: the bucolic and the aquatic life. Moreover, several levels of signification are introduced from the beginning, allowing multiple ways to access the image, the nature, and the mediated state of these islands. For instance, the titles offer one sort of "documentary information," while maps are icons of another sort, and the photographic images that then accumulate are of yet another sort. Additionally, the photographic images also register multiple valences: one leans toward documentary, the other toward fiction, and they assist each other in the making of meaning. So an islander ("played" by an actual islander) acts out a common occurrence in the lives of his fellow islanders: a death at sea, lent pathos by a trip to the fair to buy souvenirs before the fateful trip. In telling this story, Epstein focuses on the natural landscapes and the people who occupy them. He emphasizes the "documents" of the islanders' lives, which pervade the film: more maps, a registry of funeral costs, an icon on the necklace (which serves as both a souvenir and the sign that marks the death of the sailor at sea: it is a tangible reminder of something passing). As such, we might say that during this period, Epstein was especially interested in navigating, through filmmaking, the impulse to document the world and to make meaning from its sea of details.

One of the most interesting of the films Epstein made in this vein, L'Or des mers, derives from a novel Epstein himself wrote, partly in response to his experiences in the region over several years. Conceived of first as a written text (one of two novels Epstein wrote, both of which deal with experiences on the islands off Brittany), and filmed with astonishingly disorienting continuity effects, it also features equally disorienting uses of sound (added after the fact, which may contribute to the disembodied feeling it creates). Together, all of these aspects of the film generate a highly moving yet somehow disturbing portrait of the inhabitants of a remote, wind-swept island. It addresses the character of the wind as readily as it does its apparent protagonist, an unlikeable fellow who in his impoverished state imposes himself upon his neighbors until one day he finds a treasure from a shipwreck washed up on shore. Although the treasure turns out to be a box of junk, his neighbors, none the wiser, ply him with wine and food. Before his untimely death, he tells his abused daughter where he has stashed the box, which leads her, under threat by her fiancé's father, to a dangerous area of quicksand, where she nearly perishes. In this climactic scene, the images – alternating between close-ups of the girl's face on the vertical axis, long shots of her body stuck in sand on the horizontal axis, and extreme long shots of her fiancé crossing the treacherous beach toward her rescue – in addition to the very close-up recordings of her voice calling weakly out for help even when she is in long shot – provide a jarring set of collisions in our expectations for the rules of continuity, heightening our sense of distress and confusion about the innocent girl's plight.

L'Or des mers, just like Finis Terrae, Mor'Vran, and the other Brittany films, thus mixes Epstein's interest in the rough natural features of this landscape with narrative and experimental concerns. A stunning sequence of superimpositions, lasting impossibly long near the end of L'Or des mers, both provides narrative context – the villagers exiting the church will not be there to rescue the girl, and their circle of dancing shows the march of their lives despite the dangers of the sea – and cinematic excess. The ability of the camera to show several places/images from several different angles and distances – a layering effect similar to the strategies of Bonjour Cinéma – serves Epstein's purpose in multiple ways.

Moreover, we should note that within this period of greater documentary emphasis, Epstein did not entirely abandon more strictly fictional filmmaking either, as most accounts of his artistic trajectory suggest. During this same period, he also made Sa Tête (1929), a short film about a young man tried and eventually released for a murder he did not commit, with a remarkable sequence involving the intercutting of images of cigar smoke, a miniature guillotine, tarot cards, and the unwitting guilty consciences of the protagonists. The swift, deft filming and editing of this thirty-six minute long film – including another fairground attractions sequence used to an entirely different purpose than the fête foraine sequence in Coeur Fidèle – demonstrate Epstein at the height of his powers even when treating a slight subject. L'homme à l'Hispano (1933), La Chatelaine de Liban (1933), and the aforementioned Marius et Olive à Paris (1935) and Coeur de Gueux (1936) also come out of this period, as well as La Femme au bout du monde (1937), which could reasonably be considered a hybrid of the two instincts driving Epstein's creative output during this time. In this last film, a woman running an inn on a remote island must navigate the rabid attraction every man to come through the village discovers he possesses for her; however, while the film employs a greater proportion of film actors than the more documentary Brittany films, and spends more time developing its narrative, the sound of the wind and the rough geography of the island as well as the sea that borders it on every side are of strong interest to Epstein's project in addition to the woman's plight.

This series of later films – both those more inclined to documentary and those more inclined to narrative conventions – also developed alongside several shorter projects filmed by Epstein for a variety of commercial or cultural interests, which fall into two main categories. First, Epstein made several filmed songs. For example, Les Berceaux (1932), a popular song with lyrics based on a poem by Sully Prudhomme and with music composed by Gabriel Fauré, features a great deal of abstract images meant to (elliptically) illustrate a song about babies rocking in their cradles and the men who feel drawn back from their sea ventures by their loved ones. Second, Epstein accomplished a series of short documentary features made for a variety of purposes. These included La Bretagne and La Bourgogne (both 1936), made with a certain degree of exasperation on Epstein's part for the Exposition of Arts and Technology in the troubled years just before Epstein unwillingly left filmmaking and Paris in the late 1930s, just prior to the war. After this period of multivalent activity, it was not until after the war that Epstein's film practice resumed with *Le Tempestaire* (1947), which is treated within the essays of this collection, and *Les Feux de la Mer* (1948), Epstein's final cinematic work. The fact that this last film is a documentary, as was his first film, rounds out the trajectory of the oeuvre of this filmmaker so much more interested in multiple, radiating and circuitous paths than in one linear one.

★ ★ ★

In the next section the reader will find a dozen essays by an international collection of scholars at several stages in their careers. Together, these essays offer a range of ways to think through Epstein's complex oeuvre. While this introduction, then, has offered broad context for the work of Epstein over the course of his career, it falls upon the critical essays as well as Epstein's own writings to lay some groundwork toward the recovery of Epstein's significance in Anglophone cinema studies.

The twelve critical essays that follow grapple with the complexities of Epstein's thought and point to the crucial and comprehensive terms of his film theory and practice. Arranged according to both the historical trajectory of Epstein's work and the major themes that preoccupy each stage of his career (which have been outlined above), the organization of the essays allows the reader to begin with Epstein's earliest work and observe its development over time, with several recursions, ellipses, and moments of significant overlap that should begin to feel quite natural to anyone becoming familiar with Epstein's work.

Notes

1. Jean Epstein, *Le cinéma du Diable* (Paris: Éditions Jacques Melot, 1947), p. 45.
2. Louis Delluc is generally credited with originating the concept. As Stuart Liebman notes in his dissertation on Epstein, "though a theory of film...can be discerned in his work, no single essay by Delluc elaborates his position fully. It is also significant that Delluc rejected the role of theorist, preferring to think of himself merely as an interested observer" (Stuart Liebman, *Jean Epstein's Early Film Theory, 1920-1922* [PhD Dissertation: New York University, 1980], pp. 44-45). For further reading, also see Richard Abel's "*Photogénie* and Company," Abel1, pp. 95-124.
3. Richard Abel, "Before the Canon," Abel1, p. 23.
4. See for instance Paolo Cherchi Usai's *The Death of Cinema: History, Cultural Memory, and the Digital Dark Age* (London: BFI, 2008). Also note editor Sumiko Higashi's collection of position papers in *Cinema Journal* 44.1 (Fall 2004) on the "historical turn" in cinema studies, which examines such approaches from several angles.

5. Jean Epstein: Bonjour Cinéma und andere Schriften zum Kino, eds. Nichole Brenez and Ralph Eue (Wien: Österreichisches Filmmuseum, 2008); Prosper Hillairet, Coeur Fidèle de Jean Epstein. (Crisnée: Éditions Yellow Now, 2008); Laura Vichi, Jean Epstein (Milano: Il Castoro, 2003); Jean Epstein: Cinéaste, Poète, Philosophe, ed. Jacques Aumont (Paris: Cinémathèque française, 1998).

6. Those important works include Liebman's dissertation, Jean Epstein's Early Film Theory, 1920-1922, which lays the groundwork for further investigation of Epstein admirably and comprehensively; and Richard Abel's edited collection, French Film Theory and Criticism, 2 vols. (Princeton: Princeton University Press, 1988), which brings Epstein's work into greater relief, both through comparison with a large volume of contemporaneous essays and through Abel's perceptive analysis of Epstein within that context.

    More recently, Malcolm Turvey's Doubting Vision: Film and the Revelationist Tradition (New York: Oxford University Press, 2008) places Epstein in a central position for a particular strain of film theory and history, one in which he claims human vision is trumped by cinematic vision; for Epstein, he argues, the importance of cinematic vision arrives as part of a faith in the cinema's mechanical superiority to the body. Turvey critiques Epstein's position, but through consideration of a small set of examples of Epstein's texts. As the texts included here from L'Intelligence d'une machine, Cinéma du diable, and Esprit du cinéma demonstrate, the idea of cinema's relation to the "real" world and human perception for Epstein actually depends less on "doubts about human vision" or "the human [eye's failure] to see the true nature of reality due to innate handicaps," and much more upon his notion of the way that the world, like the cinema, operates in a constant state of change, demanding a similarly fluid relationship with the visible. Also, while Epstein receives significant attention in Turvey's formulation, he must share the spotlight with three other theorists of cinema (Siegfried Kracauer, Béla Balasz, and Dziga Vertov).

    Several shorter works in English have also recently contributed in important ways to Epstein scholarship, though we note that many of them come from non-Anglophone scholars. These include Chiara Tognolotti, "Jean Epstein's 'Intellectual Factory': An Analysis of the Fonds Epstein, 1946-1953," in Dall'inizio, alla fine. Teorie del cinema in prospettiva/In the Very Beginning, at the Very End: Film Theories in Perspective, eds. F. Casetti, J. Gaines, and V. Re (Udine: Forum, 2009), pp. 515-524; Viva Paci, "The Attraction of the Intelligent Eye: Obsessions with the Vision Machine in Early Film Theories," in The Cinema of Attractions Reloaded, ed. Wanda Strauven (Amsterdam: Amsterdam University Press, 2006), pp. 121-137; and Ludovic Cortade, "Le Cinéma du diable: Jean Epstein and the Ambiguities of Subversion," SubStance 34, no. 3 (2005): 3-16.

    And indeed, the present collection, we are told, has inspired one of its contributors to write the first monograph on Epstein in English, which is just the sort of effect we seek: Christophe Wall-Romana, Jean Epstein (Manchester: Manchester University Press, forthcoming 2012).

7. See Marjorie Perloff, The Futurist Moment: Avant-Garde, Avant-Guerre, and the Language of Rupture (Chicago: University of Chicago Press, 2003).

8. Jean Epstein, [Manuscript notes, 1918-1920], Fonds Jean et Marie Epstein, Bibliothèque du film, Paris, EPSTEIN289-B88.

9. Jean Epstein, *Poésie d'aujourd'hui: un nouvel état d'intelligence* (Paris: Éditions de la Sirène, 1921), pp. 171-172; infra, 272-73.

10. Guillaume Apollinaire, "L'émigrant de Landor Road/The Emigrant of Landor Road," in *Alcools*, trans. Donald Revell (Hanover, CT: Wesleyan University Press, 1995), p. 103.

11. Apollinaire, "L'émigrant de Landor Road/The Emigrant of Landor Road," p. 101. Epstein cites these passages in *Poésie d'aujourd'hui*, p. 176; infra, 274.

12. Epstein, *Poésie d'aujourd'hui*, pp. 176-177; infra, 275.

13. Likewise, Maya Deren, who herself may have been drawing upon Epstein's example (she cites him briefly in her *Anagram of Ideas on Art, Form, and Film*), elaborates the "poetic" tendency of cinema as a temporal tendency, where cinema should be made to explore time "vertically," like a poem does, versus horizontally, according to the causal logic one finds in narrative forms.

14. "*Photogénie* and Company," *Abel1*, pp. 95-124. See also Christophe Wall-Romana, *French Cinepoetry: Unmaking and Remaking the Poem in the Age of Cinema* (PhD Dissertaion: University of California at Berkeley, 2005), pp. 176-215.

15. This textual word play may also be occasionally inflected with Epstein's Polish background. One example, "Jazzi-mowa," emphasizes the letters "mowa" (Polish for "language") by depicting them a bit separately and vertically (while "Jazz i" is horizontal). Thus, possibly Epstein has arranged the letters to allow for the reading "Jazzi-language" simultaneous to them being a play on the name of one of his most beloved actresses (Nazimova). Epstein's connection to contemporary and avant-garde music is briefly pointed out in Liebman's dissertation as well. I am grateful to Robert Bird for pointing out this possible connection to Epstein's heritage evident in *Bonjour Cinéma*.

16. Compare Epstein's experiments with text on the page to other poetic experimenters in France, including (much earlier) Mallarmé's seminal *Un coup de dès* (1897) and, not so much earlier, Guillaume Apollinaire's *Calligrammes* (1913-16), both of which feature poetry that dismantles the lexical signs of the words that comprise their poems.

17. See, for example, the representation of *Bonjour Cinema* in *ESC1*, pp. 71-104; all of the poetry is absent.

18. The table of contents does not divide the parts into these sections: its layout is shorter and simpler. This is meant to describe how the book itself unfolds.

19. Epstein carefully crafted this poem, apparently arriving at the idea of forward and backward reading after he inserted a marginal note about reading a train schedule upside down; in *Bonjour Cinéma*, an arrow, pointing back up the page appears alongside the last lines of the poem. Early drafts of this poem may be seen in Epstein's papers, Fonds Jean et Marie Epstein, Bibliothèque du film, Paris, EPSTEIN176-B82.

20. Jean Epstein, *Bonjour Cinéma* (Paris: Éditions de la Sirène, 1921), p. 13; infra, 277-78.

21. Epstein, "Magnification," *Abel1*, p. 235.

22. "Je regarde, je flaire, je palpe. Gros plan, gros plan, gros plan" (*Bonjour Cinéma*, p. 100).

23. Jean Epstein, "Cine-analyse, ou poésie en quantité industrielle," *ESC2*, p. 54.

24. René Clair, "*Coeur Fidèle*," *Abel1*, pp. 303-305.

25. Included in this volume as a footnote to *Cinema Seen from Etna*, from which "Le Regard du verre" was drawn. See infra, 309.

26. Jean Epstein quoted in P. Adams Sitney, "Image and Title in Avant-Garde Cinema," *October* 11 (Winter 1979), p. 112.

27. Gideon Bachmann in his formulation of the development of Epstein's career, which may be seen in the program notes accompanying a retrospective of Epstein's works in the United States. See *Anthology Film Archives Presents the Films of Jean Epstein in Cooperation with La Cinémathèque française and the Film Society of Lincoln Center* (New York: Anthology Film Archives, 1971).

28. For example, this trajectory depends on *Coeur Fidèle* for the first movement, *La Chute de la maison Usher* for the second, the Brittany films for the third, and *Le Tempestaire* for the fourth, all but the third of which have been released in video formats.

29. The trajectory of Epstein's early film career and affiliation with various production companies is recounted in Liebman, *Jean Epstein's Early Film Theory*, pp. 7-14.

30. Cited in program notes for an Epstein retrospective housed at Anthology Film Archives (my translation).

31. The film was finished by Maurice Mariaud, who received credit for it.

32. See François Albéra's *Albatros: des russes à Paris, 1919-1929* (Paris: Cinémathèque Française, 1995) for an account of the history and provenance of Albatros in Paris.

33. *Les aventures de Robert Macaire* is based on the 1832 play *L'Auberge des Adrets* by Benjamin Antier; *Mauprat* is a novel of the same name first published serially in 1837 by George Sand.

34. This film was left off the Epstein filmography as late as the Séghers edition of Epstein's *Écrits* in the mid-1970s.

35. Cited in *Cinémagazine* (12 November 1926).

36. Epstein, "Approaches to Truth," *Abel1*, p. 424.

Essays

Epstein's *Photogénie* as Corporeal Vision: Inner Sensation, Queer Embodiment, and Ethics

Christophe Wall-Romana

Let us begin with a puzzle. In the following passage, Jean Epstein is referring to *something*...

> ...all the planes and volumes of which have been rounded and polished by patient forces into a symphony of forms that unfold out of each other [*se déroulent les unes des autres*], that conjoin each other [*s'entr'épousent*] into a complex yet unbreakable unity, like that of revolving solids – these spatial matrices defined by the movement of a mathematical function.

This language of serial and kinetic fusion will be familiar to readers of silent cinema theoreticians who found ever more ingenious ways of describing how the fluid motion from frame to frame and shot to shot produces the effect of filmic animation. But in point of fact, Epstein is not talking about cinema here – at least, not explicitly. He is describing teeth, the human dentition whose beauty is for him "a living crystal," and "an ivory landscape erecting its scintillating peaks, inclining its soft slopes hollowed with glens."[1] According to an annotation by his sister Marie, this unpublished text, titled "The Echo of Pythagoras," dates from the years 1918-1920 and thus predates Jean's first writings on cinema as well as his involvement in the film industry. Although Epstein was then a medical student in Lyon, not only is this lyrical focus on teeth clearly not a medical gaze on the human body, but it strikingly encapsulates what would become over the 1920s part of the stylistic signature of the *photogénie* movement: the extreme close-up. I take this cryptically cinematic close-up on teeth as my point of entry into Epstein's corporeal vision of *photogénie*.

The word *photogénie* has itself been grinded down like a bad tooth. From astronomer Arago's original coinage in 1839, to denote a model, object, or scene having a signal aptitude for photographic capture, *photogénie* was redirected in 1919 by Louis Delluc into a broad didactic slogan calling attention to the filmic image as such.[2] By the mid-1920s, after Delluc's early death, Epstein became its erstwhile proponent, notwithstanding the fact that his mentor, the poet Blaise Cendrars (also production assistant to Abel Gance, the 'master' of early *photogénie*), assured him the word was, "*cucul-praline-rhododendron*."[3] This slang expression means at once 'cheesy' and 'airy-fairy' – we shall return to the effeminate and homosexual connotations later.[4] Although his work with documentary and sound in the 1930s to the late 1940s foregrounded other aspects of his filmmaking panoply, Epstein never wavered from his commitment to *photogénie*, which he reasserts in his last (posthumously published) text, *Alcohol and Cinema*, written in the 1950s. For contemporary film studies, *photogénie* conveniently labels the group of filmmakers also known as the first French film avant-garde and the French Impressionist School of the 1920s. In spite of the painstaking recovery and careful analysis of its theoretical writings by the likes of Nourredine Ghali[5] and especially Richard Abel, the term *photogénie* has now been reduced to denote an exalted but now obsolete technical aestheticism, a naïve fetishism for the filmic shot, even a mistaken theory of cinematic vision.[6]

I take the "Echo of Pythagoras" as an intimation to rethink Epstein's theory and practice of *photogénie* in terms of corporeal vision. I will argue that Epstein's cinematic vision is corporeal in two ways: first, because for him cinema is an apparatus of vision of and into the body, especially the male body, and second, because cinema's mode of vision and spectatorship is tightly intertwined for Epstein with bodily affects and non-visual sensations, especially what he calls "coenaesthesis," the inner sensations that the body has of itself:

> The inconstancy and fuzziness of lived time are due to the fact that the ego's duration is perceived by a complex, obtuse, imprecise inner sense: coenaesthesis. It constitutes the general feeling of living, in which a host of indistinct sensations coalesce and fuse, collected by the very imperfectly conscious sensibility of our viscera. A primitive, fetal, and very much animal sensibility...[7]

Reframing Epstein's *photogénie* as corporeal vision opens a number of perspectives on his writings and film work, three of which we will examine here. First, it makes for a productive confrontation with the influential ideas of a critic of cinematic spectatorship who came after Epstein, Walter Benjamin. Second, together with Epstein's unpublished book on male homosexuality, it points to a different gendered and ethical mode of spectatorial experiencing. Finally, its immersive haptic quality relates to models of vision developed in the post-digital era by perception researchers, new media theoreticians, and video artists such as Bill Viola.

1

Let us begin by looking at the span of Epstein's use of the term *photogénie*. Its canonical definition comes from "On Some Conditions of *Photogénie*" (1923), collected in *The Cinema Seen from Etna* (1926): "I will term photogenic any aspect of things, beings and souls that enhances its moral quality through cinematographic reproduction."[8] *Photogénie* is thus the filmic as such, yet not devalued as a copy or simulacrum less essential than its model, but on the contrary as the enhancement of the model's "moral quality." The latter is a fuzzy expression in French, since 'moral' ranges from the spiritual to the ethical and social, and 'quality' has the Bergsonian ring of duration. Fortunately, Epstein twice alters his definition, to add that only "mobile aspects" are photogenic, and further on that "only mobile and personal aspects of things, beings and souls can be photogenic."[9] Here the moral would seem to have merged into the 'personal,' which connotes a Bergsonian vitalist singularity. Epstein recognizes elsewhere that "you fall flat on your face trying to define [*photogénie*]," yet from the examples he gives we can infer the following.[10] First, *photogénie* is a hyper-aesthetic phenomenon – that is, a heightened mode under which things and beings animated by film appear to perceivers; and second, *photogénie* involves an emotional response by the perceiver to this very mode of appearance (besides the contents themselves). There is also a curious temporality and interpersonality to *photogénie*, since Epstein writes that "*Photogénie* is to be conjugated in the future and imperative. It is never a state." This echoes Bergsonian duration and its sense of becoming, yet with an interpellative and intersubjective dimension – a calling, as it were.[11] The mobile-temporal aspect is associated with the notion of cinema as non-human sight, but also with music and poetry as arts of time functioning always through a certain form of virtuality. The personal-interpersonal aspect is linked to the beauty of film stars (the trivial sense of *photogénie* in movie culture), to a physical sense of promise, pleasure, and the extraordinary, and also to temporal retention and protention.[12] At the intersection of both series, Epstein formulates *photogénie* as "sensorial logarithms," an apt expression conveying the poly-sensorial compression of the photogenic sequence.[13] Let us sum up provisionally. Epsteinian *photogénie* is at minimum a triadic relation between the perceiver as embodied, the profilmic as hyper-aestheticized, and the filmic as a kinesthetic condition of and ethical potential for the relation of perceiver to profilmic.

This view of *photogénie* may be productively compared to Walter Benjamin's aura through their remarkable operative similarity: minimally, both *photogénie* and aura stage a scene of beholding between a subject and an object-field in which a qualitative change results from cinematic mediation itself. The canonical formulation of aura, from Benjamin's "The Work of Art" essay is, "A strange weave of space and time: the unique appearance of a distance, however near it may be."[14] Both *photogénie* and aura are then products of middle terms in so far as they alter time and space, since Epstein writes, "The photogenic aspect of an object results from its variations in space-time."[15] This deserves emphasis in terms of aesthetic philosophy. No longer is immediacy between subject and object privileged or even posited – the common premise of both Romanticism and realism – but on the contrary, a new form of semi-agency arises between them and mediates them. Benjamin's auratic 'distance' proceeds also from cinema, as is made plain from another passage in the essay: "[F]or the first time – and this is the effect of film – the human being is placed in a position where he must operate with his whole living person, while forgoing its aura."[16] In other words, cinema's pressure destroys auratic distance while generating a new mode of embodiment. Thus, while Benjamin's aura as a qualitative loss is the exact opposite of *photogénie* as a qualitative enhancement, both describe the very same phenomenon at the level of the body: a qualitative shift in the mode of embodiment due to cinema and cinema alone.

We can push the similarity further. If the close-up in Epstein's hyperbole is "cinema's soul," he adds immediately: "it may be brief, for *photogénie* is a value of the order of the second."[17] We might recall Abel Gance's rapid edits of medium close-ups and iris shots during Sisif's flashback as he is about to fall from the mountain in *La Roue* (1922) or Epstein's own *Coeur fidèle* (1923) with the famous merry-go-round sequence. Rather than the isolated or still close-up, Epstein favors in fact a sequence of shots of alternating scales. Hence he states that "the dance of the landscape is photogenic," not any one shot of the landscape itself.[18] Epstein propounds shot variation around close-ups, for example describing an actual dance filmed with a mobile camera taking very close shots of dancers, then pulling back to their periphery.[19] I belabor the importance of scale shift here because of Benjamin's enigmatic illustration: "To follow with the eye... a mountain range on the horizon, or a branch that casts its shadow on the beholder is to breathe the aura of those mountains, of that branch."[20] In her essay on the *aura hysterica*, Ulla Link-Heer points out an instance of a hill returning Marcel's gaze in Proust's *La Recherche* as a possible source for Benjamin's image.[21] Yet a more complete similarity is found in the first section of *The Cinema Seen from Etna*, where Epstein writes, "One of cinema's greatest powers is its animism. On the screen there is no still life. Objects have attitudes. Trees gesture. Mountains, like this Etna, signify. Each element of staging becomes a character."[22] Of course, this is just the kind of magical animism Benjamin warns against: cinema's reproductive "mass existence" replacing the "unique existence" of things to satisfy "the desire of the present-day masses to 'get closer' to things."[23] Yet Epstein's animism is not "a passionate concern for overcoming each thing's uniqueness" as Benjamin adds, but exactly the contrary: a vision of the singularity of filmic objects, preserving their "character" and "gesture." This is what Epstein calls "the persona of the gaze [*le personnage du regard*]," that is, the filmed object's gaze-like emanation.[24] That is why the third definition of *photogénie* is crucial – "mobile and personal aspects of things" – because, like philosopher Emmanuel Levinas, who holds that the face/gaze is irreducibly human, this "persona of the gaze" contained in the filmic image is foremost ethical. This explains Epstein's paradigmatically photogenic objects – a telephone, a gun, a door handle – in that they convey inter-human involvement: they crystallize intersubjectivity into a material form disclosed through the film's singularized motion. Hence, while Benjamin's profound skepticism about cinema (at least at one pole of his thought[25]) raises the traditional objection of the simulacrum, within the very same operative model Epstein theorizes photogénie from the ethical standpoint as the filmic's capacity to disclose the human gaze and implicate inter-human relations. While this return of the gaze is fundamental to Benjamin's aura as well, the latter structurally excludes the mediation of technology.[26]

In view of this closeness between them, we might ask whether Benjamin was aware of Epstein's theoretical work from the 1920s. I believe that he must have known of it and very probably also read it. The direct link between them is Léon Pierre-Quint, the French critic who wrote the first book on Proust in 1925. Two words of general context are needed first. As Michael Jennings has shown, when Benjamin turned his attention toward popular culture and cinema around 1924, after his failed Habilitation, he became close to the Gestaltung group of Berlin for whom photomontage and film constituted an intermedia franca where all arts could meet.[27] Hans Richter was its main figure and a journal was launched in 1922 around Moholy-Nagy, El Lissitsky, and Mies van der Rohe. Yet the prototype of such postwar interart journals was L'Esprit Nouveau, edited by Ozenfant and Jeanneret (later to be known as Le Corbusier), starting in 1920. It is in that journal in 1921 that Epstein contributed an early version of his first book under the title "The Literary Phenomenon," which ran through six issues.[28] Perusing the list of L'Esprit nouveau subscribers for the years 1920-21, we can find the names of Moholy-Nagy, Lissitsky, and Tzara – among hundreds of well-known artists (Brancusi, Duchamp, Pound, Stevens, Gide, Faure, etc.).[29] If Benjamin did not directly discover Epstein in L'Esprit nouveau, certainly the latter's theories were disseminated within the group. The only direct link I have been able to find so far comes from footnotes to the "Work of Art" essay that mention L'Art cinématographique, second volume.[30] It is a 1927 collection of essays on cinema (one of eight volumes) by Germaine Dulac, Abel Gance, Lionel Landry, and Léon Pierre-Quint. Taken together, these essays may be seen to push Impressionist theory in a direction very close to what Benjamin would theorize after Freud as innervation (Bahnung) – the counter-impulse capable of undoing the anesthetic effects of shock or trauma by reviving the path of the original impulse. In her essay, Dulac writes for instance: "It was cinema which revealed progressively to us the presence within our unconscious [inconscient] of a new emotional sense allowing for our sensorial comprehension of visual rhythms."[31] Minus the idea of rhythm, this progressive new sense of "sensorial comprehension" is closely related to Benjamin's innervation via the optical unconscious.[32] Now, it is the essay by Léon Pierre-Quint in this collection – from which Benjamin cites a passage from Pirandello – that establishes a link between Benjamin and Epstein. In his essay, Pierre-Quint tells of his recent conversion to cinema in the following terms: "The ray of light from the 'surreal eye' as Mr. Jean Epstein puts it, has lit my darkness."[33] Benjamin's "Paris Diary" of 1930 indicates that Léon Pierre-Quint was Benjamin's closest friend in Paris, both men sharing a daily breakfast.[34] Pierre-Quint adds in his essay, "A wholly new image [...] prolonging the reach of our senses, creates in ourselves a stimulation until now unknown in our consciousness."[35] This "prolonging" into a "new stimulation" is again a close approximation of innervation via the optical unconscious. A third passage by Lionel Landry, who refers to films of Epstein including *Le Lion des Mogols* (1924), reads: "Should we hope that, through a fusion, a progressive simplification, through some unconscious 'facilitation' of associations ['*frayage' inconscient d'associations*], a pure cinematic sensibility might be created?"[36] The word "*frayage*" is the sanctioned translation of Freud's "*Bahnung*" into French from *Beyond the Pleasure Principle*.

From this quite sophisticated volume, Benjamin excises for the "Work of Art" essay three flat-footed passages in the most exulted of the four essays, that by Abel Gance. Benjamin willfully leaves the link between *photogénie* and the optical unconscious by the wayside.[37] His citational strategy aims only at illustrating "the obtuse and hyperbolic character of early film theory," insofar as "these theoreticians [...] attribute elements of cult to film – with a striking lack of discretion."[38] Epstein's comment about the "surreal eye" concludes the 1923 essay, "On Some Conditions of *Photogénie*," collected in *The Cinema Seen from Etna* (1926), and Pierre-Quint obviously read it carefully. In view of his conversion, it is quite probable that he either gave it to Benjamin to read, or at minimum talked to him about Epstein's *photogénie*. Thus very likely aware of the theoretical and psycho-physiological savvy of French photogenists, Benjamin refuses any acknowledgment.

As Miriam Hansen's recent exhumation of Benjamin's formulation of aura previous to "The Work of Art" essay attests, the tactical dissolution of aura occluded "broader anthropological, perceptual-mnemonic, and visionary dimensions" in Benjamin's earlier work not inimical in my view to Epstein's *photogénie*.[39] Both share as profound inspirations the sensory nature of remembrance and childhood mediated by Proust, the paradoxical temporality of the past informed by Bergson, and the Kabbalah as a messianic mode of making present rather than representation.[40] Among more minute similarities, we could mention Epstein's "The Literary Phenomenon," which opens with a long section on modernity's technological erasure of distance, "*le loin*," in terms that are very close to those of Valéry's 1933 "The Conquest of Ubiquity," an excerpt of which opens the last version of "The Work of Art" essay.

It isn't very difficult to see why Benjamin would repudiate *photogénie*. Epstein embraces neither the Hegelian dialectic (rejected in *La Lyrosophie*) nor Freud's ra-

CHRISTOPHE WALL-ROMANA

tionalization of the unconscious which he denounces as a detective scenario of bourgeois sexuality (in "Freud or the Nick-Carterianism in Psychology"[41]). Epstein's financial backers were Russian émigrés around the production company Albatros – the landless white bird of long migrations – and Marxism plays no explicit part in Epstein's thought. Moreover, Benjamin attempted to get close to André Breton from the late 1920s onward. Epstein's use of the word "surréel" – similar to Ivan Goll and Paul Dermée titling their new journal Surréalisme in 1924 – would have triggered a violent anathema from the surrealist's group proprietary control of Apollinaire's word.[42] By comparison to Benjamin's silence, we may cite his friend and editor Siegfried Kracauer who freely refers to Epstein in his Theory of Film, in fact more than to Béla Balázs, Fritz Lang, and Hans Richter combined. Kracauer would most certainly have brought Epstein to Benjamin's attention as well, and perhaps further comments are yet to be found in Benjamin's correspondence and archive.

2

Although Epstein's thought about cinema begins, as will Benjamin's, with its place in mass modernity and its homeopathic potential to alleviate modernity's anaesthetizing effects, it points to a very different set of implications. Epstein's view of mass culture, for instance, lacks the intellectual condescension and fear for cultural capital deflation that are all too palpable in André Breton's and Theodor Adorno's allergies to commercial cinema and jazz respectively. He even grants a putative confidence to popular film spectators that they have the ability to derive from the culture industry an "autopsychology" of their own state of psychosomatic exhaustion. Popular culture comes first phenomenologically for Epstein, who defines modernism as the avant-garde's belated realization of the new psychosomatic economy it deploys. In a way, then, surprisingly close to Marx's attention to the history of the senses, in The Poetry of Today, A New State of Mind (1921), Epstein bases his theory of modernist poetry entirely on the sensorial conditions dictating pulp literature and cinema.

Rather than the psychic unconscious (l'inconscient), what he places at the core of the new homeopathic art he tries defining is a somatic subconscious (le subconscient) that functions on an energetic model of counter-anaesthetizing or restoring the individual's sensorium. Melodramatic cinema for Epstein exemplifies this restorative psycho-corporeality with its strict finalism of feel-good logic, artificial justice, Manichean characters, and happy ending. Epstein neither condones nor condemns pulp culture: his analyses are meant only to understand why and how it has become dominant, and in the second part of The Poetry of Today he shows that modern literature from Proust to Aragon has implicitly extrapolated its counter-anaesthetic traits into a new organization of the literary text. At the very center of the subconscious sensorium, Epstein locates "vegetative life": "This life has been called vegetative, sympathetic life. It is a diffuse, deep, active, silent and animal life."[43] This vegetative life – which recalls Freud's vesicular body in *Beyond the Pleasure Principle* – regulates fatigue and sensorial erosion, nervous discharge and sexual over-excitation, psychosomatic ailments and revivification, involuntary memory, and even intellectual stimulation. For Epstein, "[the modern mind] reaches to it, leans over its rumor, examines it by auscultation, scrutinizes it, interrogates it and expects marvels from it."[44]

The sensory disposition that corresponds to this attention to one's vegetative life Epstein calls "coenaesthesis," the inner sense of one's own senses, that which "summarizes the sensory state of an individual at any given time.... the physiological face of the subconscious."[45] Epstein's *photogénie* – to which we can now return – is intimately tied to coenaesthesis: in fact, his general philosophy of aesthetics amounts to finding the best possible means of disclosing how human and inter-human experience springs from coenaesthesis.[46] Cinema would seem better suited to give it expression than medicine, poetry, or philosophy: "Beyond the scenario's drama, the screen violently resonates with an immense trove of wild desires and continual worries, the spirit, *photogénie*'s sweet smell like that of sainthood, poetic persona."[47] Cinematic techniques such as the close-up, rapid editing, slow motion, and slow-moving staging, among others, aim to make perceptible the inner sensory state of the actor – especially in the case of the non-professional actors in Epstein's Brittany films between 1928 and 1947 – as well as re-amplify the inner sensory state of the spectator. But the style of writing that Epstein adopts – empirical, clipped, steeped in the logic of affect – also foregrounds the coenaesthetic rhythms of embodied subject-position over the trappings of anonymous rationality.[48]

This centrality of embodiment in *photogénie* might be related to the fact that Epstein was a homosexual. I should preface this statement with my sense of surprise when, consulting the Epstein archives at the Bibliothèque du film in Paris, I stumbled upon a 300-page manuscript entitled: *Ganymède: Essay on Masculine Homosexual Ethics*, dated circa 1930-1940, and written under the pseudonym of Alfred Kléber. In the perhaps unique French mélange of respect of privacy and hypocrisy, nowhere had I read that Epstein was a homosexual, and no reference had ever been made to this work. The manuscript itself makes it clear that it is for social and not for personal reasons that Epstein dissimulated his homosexuality, since he presents it as a civil right: "[S]uicide, contraception, and homosexuality are discoveries of the same, and I will say, highest order... [in terms of] the acceptance of the priority of essential individual rights upon certain collective imperatives."[49] *Ganymède* seems to me an important document for the history and self-theorization of homosexuality. Epstein asserts for instance that, "the least prejudiced minds are rallying around the conception that homosexuality is an innate disposition" (G, 44), and he questions both the model of inversion and the notion of heterosexual norm (G, 53). After systematically debunking arguments against homosexuality (from the purviews of nature, reproduction, heterosexual masquerade, and society), Epstein presents various configurations of male homosexual couples, including those with a large age differential, and looks towards the future of homosexuality. Rejecting "anatomical and physiological determinations of the homosexual," Epstein steers clear of essentializing or even characterizing a homosexual sensibility, and in this sense it may be more precise to speak of a queer aesthetics (G, 41).

While nothing indicates therefore that male homosexuality informs *photogénie* in any direct way, we may note nonetheless that Epstein's films focus equally on male and female bodies, that the male body is explicitly a site of *photogénie* in his writings, especially in *Bonjour cinéma* (1921), and that Epstein's coenaesthesis emphasizes a non-phobic relation with inner bodily sensations, whether one's own as spectator or that of a male body on cinematic display.[50] His films such as *La Glace à trois faces* (1927) and *Finis Terrae* (1929) feature male heroes wrestling with coenaesthesis, whether it be a fatal restlessness and unexplained dissatisfaction towards three different women in the former (none of whom seem capable of reflecting back his desire), or a fever due to an infection of the main character's (phallic) thumb following a dispute with his best friend in the latter. Epstein's most famous film, *The Fall of the House of Usher* (1928), stages two older males competitively hovering over Roderick, himself splenetically involved in painting his wife Madeline and progressively robbing her of life. Certainly, this film circumvents heterosexual desire with a morbid narcissism involving fetishized female likeness.[51] Even *Coeur fidèle* (1923), a film featuring a reciprocated and seemingly victorious heterosexual love, ends with a scene of deflation or distraction, which more than suggests that the male rivalry that propelled the plot acted as its affective center as well. Yet any such 'readings' of queer elements in silent film should take care to gauge contextually cinematic norms of gender coding. Thus the elegant and thin male character of *La Glace à trois faces* appears to wear more, or more conspicuous, make-up than may be the norm for contemporary male leads – but is it really so? The repugnantly abusive and caricaturally straight husband in Germaine Dulac's *The Smiling Madame Beudet* (1927) seems to wear about the same amount of make-up. The love triangle in *Coeur fidèle* resembles the one in Abel Gance's *J'accuse* (1919) in that male rivalry leads to a form of accommodation: is the former more 'queer' than the latter? One single scene in Epstein's oeuvre stands out as staging a homosexual pickup. In *Le Double amour* – another of Epstein's ambiguous titles – a rich son finds himself in a large jail cell where he encounters an *apache*, a working class hoodlum in French slang, whose demeanor, dress, and high-top hairdo with thin sideburns, as well as his odd pet mouse, display clashing masculine and feminine attributes. In *Ganymède*, Epstein makes a special case for what he calls "homosexuality by confinement," as opposed to "essential homosexuality," and it is unclear which kind is displayed in that scene (G, 126). With super-impressions of an ostrich feather fan and a viola, the two men are shown circling each other in a diegetic ellipsis that may or may not be taking place, or may be the phantasm of either or both of them.

There is very little critical work available on homosexuality and silent cinema, especially in France.[52] Germaine Dulac, another central figure in the *photogénie* movement, was a lesbian who co-founded a film production with her scriptwriter and lover Irène Hiller-Erlanger in 1915, and Marcel L'Herbier was also a "known" homosexual, although this is again undocumented. Several critics such as Ruby Rich have noted the crisis of masculinity and male embodiment following World War I: the fascination of Delluc and Epstein for the bodies of actor Sessue Hayakawa and Chaplin, for instance, in their exotic extremes of hypo- and hyper-activity, might be understood in such a context of traumatology.[53] This does not preclude, however, a homoerotic component whether related to it or not: in *Bonjour cinéma*, two of the titles for Epstein's poetic sequences are "Amour de Charlot" and "Amour de Sessue" – which read ambiguously in French as either "Lovely Chaplin" or "Love for Sessue." I believe that the experimental motivation to find cinematic techniques for objectifying subjective states from a 'queer' perspective represents a promising area for future research on the *photogénie* movement. There might be similarities to pursue as well between Jean Epstein, Jean Cocteau, and Derek Jarman, all three queer filmmakers influenced by and having written poetry, belonging to the avant-garde yet at an idiosyncratic remove from it, and all three exploring the thematic tension between "the mirror and the sea"[54] – that is, between on the one hand narcissism and self-exploration, and on the other hand the dissolution or sublimation of the ego within a broader engagement with reality.[55] Perhaps, then, Epstein's formulation of the self belongs to this queer dialectic in its essential fluidity:

> Individuality is a mobile complex, that each of us, more or less consciously, must choose and construct for himself, then rearrange ceaselessly, through a diversity of aspects which, themselves, are far from being simple or permanent, and within the mass of which, when too numerous, the individual succeeds with great difficulty in keeping a clear form. Then, so-called personality becomes a diffuse self, whose polymorphism tends towards the amorphous and dissolves itself in the watery current of motherly depths [*le courant de ses eaux-mères*].[56]

The sea, moving water, and fluidity are indeed central to Epstein's *photogénie* in bringing into sensorial intimacy visual mobility and non-visual coenaesthesis: "The world of the screen...constitutes the privileged domain of the malleable, the viscous, and the liquid."[57] From a non-human living environment in his Brittany films, the sea becomes in his last major feature, *Le Tempestaire* (1947), a kind of quasi-human figure of *photogénie*'s ethical relation. The famous shots of the sea in slow motion and in reverse motion embody and index – underneath the diegetic conceit of a magical taming of the ocean – the magmatic affects stirring between the two distant and off-screen lovers. It is a Baudelairean "correspondence" running along sensorial experiences of vision, kinesthesia, fear, nausea, and longing. In *Esprit de cinéma*, (1955), Epstein reformulates this slowed-down *photogénie* as,

> What the mind does not have time to retain, what the eye has neither the time nor the field to see in one expression: the premonitory symptoms, the evolution, the strife among emotional inter-currents [*sentiments intercurrents*] that compose their synthesis – all this is what slow-motion displays at will.[58]

Photogénie as mobility of vision correlates both with the liquid element and the churning of affects; what Epstein qualifies as, "the perpetual flux and reflux agitating the affective domain," which finds in cinema a privileged mode of objectification, the "revelation on the screen of a deeper inner life, with its perpetual palpitation, its crisscrossing meanders, its mysterious spontaneity...."[59] This coenaesthetic life constitutes the fluid bedrock of meaning:

> ... In the reality of the psyche, verbal thought... only smothers under it and rejects in the shadow, in most cases, other modes of visual, auditory, olfactory, tactile, gustative, and coenaesthetic representations. And this thinking via the evocation of sensorial impressions can organize itself in concepts no less precise than those used in verbal thinking...
>
> Repressed in the subconscious, the memories of sensorial impressions constitute nonetheless the feeding roots on which words graft themselves and upon which they continue drawing their greatest resource of meaning.[60]

Epstein's coenaesthetic *photogénie* suggests a broad affect-based theory of experience compared, for instance, to Freud's arch-determinism of the sex drive. Given the centrality of (heteronormative) psychoanalysis in film studies' classical construal of spectatorship, whether in Jean-Louis Baudry's apparatus theory or in Laura Mulvey's pioneering essay, Epstein's *photogénie* offers an alternative historical model. I would propose that *photogénie* implies a particular mode of scopophilia whereby the apparatus concentrates and reflects back optical desire in a way that discloses the spectator's body as sensorially self-relating – sensing itself viewing – through the 'enactive' aspect of filmic images (see section 3 below). We could contrast this mode precisely with Benjamin's reticence at the apparatus' reflex reach within the spectator's body. In "The Work of Art" essay, Benjamin's references to cinema as "the most intensive interpenetration of equipment and reality" and "the desire of the present-day masses to get closer to things," betray a worried if not phobic relation to haptic-optical closeness.[61] Whereas the magician and the painter "maintain the natural distance between [themselves] and the person treated," the surgeon and the filmmaker, "greatly diminish...the distance from the patient by penetrating the patient's body."[62] I wonder whether auratic distance, for Benjamin, safeguards the (male) body from contact and disclosure via the reflex reach of *photogénie* into the spectator's coenaesthetic affects. In a 1926 piece on Klages, Benjamin writes: "The erotic life is ignited by distance. On the other hand, there is an affinity between nearness and sexuality."[63] Benjamin, it seems, remains here within an early Romantic sensibility, found in Rousseau's *Letter to Monsieur D'Alembert on Theater* and Diderot's *Paradox of the Comedian*, for instance, whereby the danger inherent to theatrical spectatorship is that it might feminize the male viewer's body by disclosing its sensorial insides, by moving and emoting his affects through interoceptive sensations – precisely what Epstein means by coenaesthesis. What makes such a model of non-Freudian and hetero-abnormative spectatorship ethical, again recalling Levinas, is its vulnerability – its "cucul-praline-rhododendron" corporeal openness towards the other.[64]

3

I have suggested that Epstein's *photogénie* results equally from the technological mediation of the apparatus and the embodied experience of the viewer. Truncating either condition leads to mischaracterizations of Epstein's theory. This is just what Malcolm Turvey does in a recent book on what he calls the "revelationist tradition" that, besides Jean Epstein, includes Béla Bálazs, Dziga Vertov, and Siegfried Kracauer.[65] Turvey's central argument is that Epstein and other revelationists exaggerate the failings of unaided human vision in order to inflate cinema's capability as a technological medium. Bracketing the psycho-sensorial and ethical aspects of *photogénie*, Turvey aims to discipline cinema theoreticians by way of gauging the truth-value of their propositions regarding sight. This approach is all the more perplexing given that a previous essay of his had keenly brought to light the centrality of immanence and corporeality in Epstein's thought.[66] Turvey's objections are nonetheless useful to further define *photogénie* and introduce links between Epstein's corporeal vision and contemporary research on perception, the immersive sensorium, and digital media.

Turvey sets out to demystify a number of claims that revelationists like Epstein make regarding cinema's "ability to uncover features of reality invisible to human vision" (DV, 3). He claims that for Epstein these features are: the mobile aspect of reality (DV, 28), the fourth dimension which is time, in particular the future (DV, 12, 52), the inner emotional life of human beings (DV, 59), the personality or interior life of an object (DV, 60), and family resemblance (DV, 61). In addition, Turvey asserts that for Epstein, "the naked human eye is unable to see the true nature of reality" (DV, 23) and moreover that "skepticism about everyday sight is a very general feature of modernism" (DV, 108). In prosecuting his case, Turvey is careful to adopt a narrowly optical model of cinematic vision, so that he grants cinema's capacity as art for "revealing truths that we are capable of seeing unaided but that were previously concealed or that we did not pay attention to" (DV, 128). Hence, he condemns revelationists for their claims about cinema's novelty as an optical prosthesis, and not for their claims about cinema's novelty as a new form of expression (even though his critique of modernism ultimately links both). This is important, in Turvey's view, because "film theorists are woefully confused about what it is we actually see when we watch films" (DV, 130), and they tend to echo and amplify a general skepticism about human vision that is nothing but a "category mistake" inherited from the modernist creed.

There are a number of problems with Turvey's general thesis, the first of which is that nowhere does he describe what he thinks human vision does, nor does he acknowledge the unsettled debates taking place in human vision science today. Instead, Turvey takes it for granted that we know what we see unaided and what we see in films. This is a crucial point because experiments in perception studies are increasingly confirming the general conclusion that we idealize our own perceptual processes, and in fact build for ourselves a deeply skewed sense of what our vision does.[67] The work of visual perception theoretician Alva Noë shows that perception makes little sense if we abstract our bodily involvement in what we see.[68] Noë propounds an "enactive" theory of visual perception based on our sensorimotor knowledge of our environment – that is, on the fact that we only see insofar as we (potentially) interact with what we see. Vision for Noë cannot be explained as the result of optical stimuli deciphered by the brain, because it is our sensorimotor involvement that allows us to decipher what we see. This means that vision, besides being optical in a trivial sense, is more interestingly haptic, proprioceptive, kinesthetic, and projective: we see not 'in' our heads but 'in' what we see, 'in' the world. Failing to present a reliable scientific theory of human vision against which to gauge that presented by revelationists invalidates Turvey's logical critique. For example, Noë demonstrates on an experimental basis that at any one time we construct only a very small part of our visual field, the rest (most) of which remains cognitively virtual – at the ready, as it were, but not in any tangibly sensorial way present. Hence Turvey's indictment of Epstein for proposing that "the naked human eye is unable to see the true nature of reality" (DV, 23) takes for granted that reality is fully given to human vision, like a photograph. Noë shows that such a "snapshot" hypothesis misrepresents our limited focus and its inferential reconstruction of the perceptual field. Epstein's point that without cinema we cannot access the mobile aspects of reality would also seem to be confirmed, in that our vision is hyper-mobile both muscularly (saccadic) and cognitively (focal invariance), so that we have a remarkable ability to 'lock on' moving objects within our visual field, and thus do not ordinarily experience visual mobility *as such*, that is, as other than non-focal blur. When Epstein writes that, "an aspect is photogenic if it moves and varies simultaneously in space and time," we must understand underneath the oxymoron (nothing can move in space but not in time!) that cinema presents us with the composed spectacle of space-time variation in an enframing way that the human eye – because of its locking mechanism – ordinarily cannot.[69] The difference between natural and cinematic vision is aptly couched in terms of "secondary intentionality" by Vivian Sobchack.[70] Phenomenologist Edmund Husserl renamed consciousness 'intentionality' to indicate that its perceptual-cognitive beholding of something is its basic character. Because cinema's beholding, for Sobchack, resembles and precedes our own, it can be termed a secondary intentionality, and for Epstein this secondary intentionality – which he calls "the gaze of the lens" – lets us attend to composed motion in a way qualitatively beyond what our eyes can do.[71]

By positing that Epstein's invocation of the fourth dimension shows his modernist bias, Turvey diminishes Epstein's quasi-phenomenological approach to temporality. Turvey cites Epstein's comments from "The Photogénie of the Imponderable" that "Man...seems constitutionally unsuited to capture a continuous event in four dimensions all by himself."[72] If this was really the case, we would not be able to drive a car or catch a ball! But Epstein is talking only about "capture" – that is, cinema as a "recording" device (mentioned in the previous sentence in both versions) – and Epstein's point here is simply that human vision is incapable of such recording because our perceptual apparatus locates us overwhelmingly in the present. Two pages later, Turvey misrepresents this simple observation:

But does this mean that humans are confined to the present due to the weakness of our perceptual and mental faculties? Is time really something that we could see or experience more of if our eyes were only stronger, as Epstein claims? This claim suggests that time is like a spatial whole that we can see more or less of. (DV, 52)

Turvey is disingenuous on three counts. First, Epstein does not make the claim Turvey says he does, but asserts only that cinema records time better than man. Second, the spatialization (quantification) of time is precisely what Bergson's qualitative duration opposes most strenuously: Turvey can hardly argue both that Epstein is thoroughly Bergsonian (DV, 49-51) and that he misses Bergson's basic thesis. Finally, (and this is precisely why Bergson distrusted cinema) a film is indeed a "spatial whole that we can see more or less of," whether it be on a celluloid strip or in a series of bits. Adducing comments by Augustine and Wittgenstein, Turvey concludes: "It is therefore nonsensical to accuse the human eye of failing to see the fourth dimension of time, as Epstein does, and equally nonsensical to argue that the cinema is capable of revealing it" (DV, 54). While the first part of this conclusion plainly misrepresents Epstein's comment, the second part is more intriguing. Turvey explains that "making the fourth dimension of time visible" does not merely consist in altering the diegesis of the film with flashbacks or flash-forwards, but in allowing "the viewer to see the flashback when it was shown at the previous night's screening" (DV, 54). This reference to Wells' time machine misses the mark (although Laura Marcus has recently shown that cinema was precisely what allowed Wells to dream up time travel![73]). Epstein's thought about the fourth dimension is not primarily based on reordering the diegesis, but on technical manipulations associated with the cinema of attractions which Turvey entirely fails to mention: slow motion and acceleration, and to a lesser extent, reverse motion. Epstein calls cinema "the time thinking machine" in that it assists us in a meditation on time "by experimentally effecting very broad variations, unknown until then, of temporal perspective."[74] Epstein adds:

> A short documentary describing in a few minutes twelve months of the life of a plant, from its germination to maturity and decay, up to the formation of the seeds of a new generation, is enough to take us on the most extraordinary trip, the most difficult escape, that man has ever attempted.[75]

Turvey eschews such capabilities of cinema probably because they are clearly beyond what the human eye can do. Unfortunately, slow motion in particular is essential to Epstein's claim that cinema allows us to see the inner emotional life of humans in a way the human eye cannot. In Finis Terrae and The Fall of the House of Usher, it is slow motion – various speeds of slow motion in fact – that loosens the dramatic diegesis to create small eddies of four-dimensional affect exemplifying the coenaesthetic or interoceptive reception of the photogenic image. This is how Epstein describes his use of slow motion in The Fall of the House of Usher:

> I know of nothing more absolutely moving than a face in slow motion freeing itself from an emotion. First a long preparation, a slow fever, which might be compared either to a morbid incubation, or a progressive ripening or, more crudely, a pregnancy. Finally, this whole effort bursts out, breaks away from muscular rigidity. A contagion of movements animates the face... Such a power of discrimination of the mechanical and optical super-eye [sur-oeil] clearly reveals time's relativity.[76]

Although Epstein's views on cinema include a reverence that occasionally verges on mysticism, his photogénie remains solidly anchored in a phenomenological description of the corporeal basis of visual perception and of its 'enactive' involvement in the filmic image to which Turvey's critique of logical inconsistencies simply does no justice.

4

To conclude, let us briefly point to recent developments in digital art and new media theory that unknowingly recoup or revive Epstein's photogénie. Filming staged emotions of human subjects with high-speed equipment and projecting these images at normal speed (thus appearing to us in slow motion), video artist Bill Viola has focused on the ethical aesthetics of bodily and facial expressiveness in his *Passions* series, in a way that is so closely reminiscent of Epstein's films and theories that his work should be plainly termed photogenic.[77] Viola's *Passions* series has, in turn, been taken up by Mark Hansen as the cornerstone for a theory of new media that seeks to elude "the 'cinematocentrism' plaguing most accounts of new media."[78] Hansen cites Viola's characterization of his work as creating a "subjective image... an image that can only be experienced internally" (NP, 268) to argue that Viola's images uniquely link "the domain of properly imperceptible microphysical stimuli and the phenomenological dimension of affectivity" (NP, 267). Yet this, again, was exactly Epstein's *photogénie* program of using various speeds to show how "the theater of the skin" is rooted in coenaesthesis.

Setting aside Hansen's declaration of independence from cinema, we might see his theory of digital media as a way to understand *photogénie* as enactive in Noë's sense – that is, in Hansen's words, "demonstrat[ing] the plasticity of the nervous system and the operative role of bodily motility in the production of sensation" (NP, 39). Moreover, by characterizing the originality of new media through the formula "affect as interface" (NP, 127), via facialization and the close-up (NP, 130), but also beyond them, Hansen substantially enlarges the conceptual reach of *photogénie*. It is, nonetheless, a mark of Epstein's originality that it has taken so long for artists and theorists like Viola and Hansen to reconstruct a conceptual-affective context akin to *photogénie*, and to which a fuller recovery of Epstein's writings on *photogénie* and of his still-misunderstood films such as *The Fall of the House of Usher* have much to contribute. Hansen's reliance on the thought of Gilles Deleuze – whose profound absorption of Epstein's *photogénie* in his two *Cinema* books also deserves close scrutiny – represents a direct, if occluded, channel of influence.

While Cendrars thought little of *photogénie* as a word and as a practice, it seems that we are now past the intimation that focusing on pre-subjective affective and ethical experience in both perception and film studies is an 'airy-fairy' project. It nonetheless took three-quarters of a century to catch up with the 'queer eye' of Epstein's corporeal *photogénie* of cinema's 'hyper-eye.' Perhaps it is due in part to the difficult recognition of the close ties between the virtual, ethical, and corporeal aspects of vision. For while Levinas considers that the gaze alone holds the ethical calling of the face, we might wonder, to return in closing to "The Echo of Pythagoras," whether teeth for Epstein – as the very trivial emblem of glamorous *photogénie* – do not disclose another ethical injunction through the non-visual aperture of the human face, accessible to the other not only visually but physically. Thus superimposing the mouth as metaphoric 'eye of the body' on the traditional image of the eye as the 'window of the soul' would be in keeping with Epstein's cinematic revaluation of the base, the popular, and the bodily.

Notes

1. Jean Epstein, "L'Écho de Pythagore" [Manuscrits divers 1918-1920]. Fonds Jean et Marie Epstein, Bibliothèque du film, Paris, EPSTEIN282-B88.
2. Colette's and Henri Diamant-Berger's references to "photogenic arc" lamps are two possible sources for Delluc's updating of the term. See Gilles Delluc, *Louis Delluc, 1890-1924: l'éveilleur du cinéma français au temps des années folles* (Périgueux: Pilote 24 éditions, 2002), p. 227n230. The most thorough discussion of *photogénie* is Richard Abel, "*Photogénie* and Company," in Abel1, pp. 95-124.
3. Jean Epstein, "*Mémoires inachevées*," ESC1, p. 32.
4. The term "cucul" by itself – a reduplication of "cul" [ass] – means shallow and ridiculous, while "praline" in slang can refer to the clitoris; "rhododendron" is unclear but "rose" and "rosette" can refer to homosexuals. See Jean-Pierre Colin, *Dictionnaire de l'argot* (Paris: Larousse, 1992), entries for "cucul," "praline," "rose," "rosette."
5. Nourredine Ghali, *L'Avant-garde cinématographique en France dans les années vingt: idées, conceptions, theories* (Paris: Paris expérimental, 1995), pp. 123-36.
6. See below for a critique of Malcolm Turvey's view of *photogénie* as "category mistake" in his *Doubting Vision: Film and the Revelationist Tradition* (New York: Oxford University Press, 2008).
7. Jean Epstein, *Le Cinéma du diable* [1947], ESC1, p. 367.
8. Jean Epstein, *Le Cinématographe vu de l'Etna* [1926], ESC1, p. 137; "On Certain Characteristics of *Photogénie*" [1924], trans. Tom Milne, Abel1, pp. 314-18; infra, 293. Throughout this article, I will amend the excellent translations made or provided by Richard Abel and the translators in the present volume only in order to provide a more literal rendition of the language.
9. Epstein, *Le Cinématographe vu de l'Etna*, ESC1, pp. 138, 140; infra, 294, 295.
10. Jean Epstein, *Bonjour cinéma* [1921], ESC1, 91; "The Senses 1 (b)" [1921], trans. Tom Milne, Abel1, p. 243.
11. Epstein, *Bonjour cinéma*, ESC1, 94; "Magnification" [1921], trans. Stuart Liebman, Abel1, p. 236.
12. These are Edmund Husserl's terms for our sense that time gathers what has just happened (retention) and projects towards what is going to happen (protention). See Malin Wahlberg, *Documentary Time: Film and Phenomenology* (Minneapolis: University of Minnesota Press, 2008), p. 24.
13. Epstein, *Bonjour cinéma*, ESC1, 94; "Magnification," Abel1, p. 236.
14. Walter Benjamin, "The Work of Art in the Age of its Technological Reproducibility" [Second Version, 1936], trans. Edmund Jephcott and Harry Zohn, in Benjamin, *Selected Writings, Volume 3: 1935-1938*, eds. Howard Eiland and Michael W. Jennings (Cambridge, MA: Belknap Press of Harvard University Press, 2002), pp. 104-05.
15. Epstein, *Le Cinématographe vu de l'Etna* [1926], ESC1, p. 139; "On Certain Characteristics of *Photogénie*," Abel1, p. 316; infra, 294.
16. Benjamin, "The Work of Art in the Age of its Technological Reproducibility," p. 112.
17. Epstein, *Bonjour cinéma*, ESC1, 94; "Magnification," Abel1, p. 236.
18. Epstein, *Bonjour cinéma*, ESC1, 97; "Magnification," Abel1, p. 237.

19. Epstein, *Bonjour cinéma*, ESC1, 98; "Magnification," *Abel1*, p. 237.
20. Benjamin, "The Work of Art in the Age of its Technological Reproducibility," p. 105.
21. Ulla Link-Heer, "Aura Hysterica or the Lifted Gaze of the Object," in *Mapping Benjamin: The Work of Art in the Digital Age*, eds. Michael Merrinan and Hans Ulrich Gumbrecht (Stanford, CA: Stanford University Press, 2003), pp. 122-23.
22. Epstein, *Le Cinématographe vu de l'Etna*, ESC1, p. 134; infra, 289.
23. Benjamin, "The Work of Art in the Age of its Technological Reproducibility," pp. 104, 105.
24. Epstein, *Le Cinématographe vu de l'Etna*, ESC1, p. 140; "On Certain Characteristics of Photogénie," *Abel1*, p. 317; infra, 295.
25. For Benjamin's fundamental ambivalence, cf. Miriam Hansen, "Benjamin and Cinema: Not a One-Way Street," in *Benjamin's Ghosts: Interventions in Contemporary Literary and Cultural Theory*, ed. Gerhard Richter (Stanford, CA: Stanford University Press, 2002), pp. 41-73.
26. It is in the context of Baudelaire's condemnation of the daguerreotype that Benjamin formulates the auratic gaze: "Experience of the aura thus arises from the fact that a response characteristic of human relationships is transposed to the relationship between humans and inanimate or natural objects. [...] To experience the aura of an object we look at means to invest it with the ability to look back at us" (Walter Benjamin, "On Some Motifs in Baudelaire" [1940], trans. Harry Zohn, in *Selected Writings, Volume 4: 1938-1940*, eds. Howard Eiland and Michael W. Jennings [Cambridge, MA: Belknap Press of Harvard University Press, 2003], p. 338).
27. Michael Jennings, "Walter Benjamin and the European Avant-Garde," in *The Cambridge Companion to Walter Benjamin*, ed. David S. Ferris (Cambridge: Cambridge University Press, 2004), pp. 18-34.
28. Jean Epstein, "Le Phénomène littéraire" [1922], in *Jean Epstein: cinéaste, poète, philosophe*, ed. Jacques Aumont (Paris: Cinémathèque française, 1998), pp. 39-83. The first section of this essay appears as "The New Conditions of Literary Phenomena," *Broom* 2, no. 1 (April 1922): 3-10.
29. For the archival records of *L'Esprit nouveau* held by the Fondation Le corbusier, see http://www.fondationlecorbusier.fr/corbuweb/zcomp/pages/EditR3%281%29.htm. Accessed 2 December 2011.
30. Benjamin, "The Work of Art in the Age of its Technological Reproducibility," pp. 122n3, 125n14-15, and 126n20.
31. Germaine Dulac, "Les esthétiques, les entraves, la cinégraphie intégrale," in *L'Art cinématographique*, vol. 2 (Paris: Félix Alcan, 1927), p. 32; "Aesthetics, Obstacles, Integral Cinégraphie," trans. Stuart Liebman, *Abel1*, p. 390.
32. For Benjamin's homeopathic view of cinema as "second technology," see Hansen, "Benjamin and Cinema," pp. 52-55.
33. Léon Pierre-Quint, "Signification du cinéma," *L'Art cinématographique*, vol. 2, (Paris: Félix Alcan, 1927), p. 2.
34. Walter Benjamin, "Paris Diary" [1930], trans. Rodney Livingstone, in Benjamin, *Selected Writings, Volume 2: 1938-1940*, eds. Howard Eiland, Michael W. Jennings, and Gary Smith (Cambridge, MA: Belknap Press of Harvard University Press, 1999), pp. 340, 350.

35. Pierre-Quint, "Signification du cinéma," p. 20.

36. Lionel Landry, "Formation de la sensibilité," *L'Art cinématographique*, vol. 2, (Paris: Félix Alcan, 1927), pp. 80-81.

37. We may wonder how come Benjamin chanced upon only volume two of *L'Art cinémato-graphique*. In volume one, René Allendy's "The Psychological Value of the Image" defines an optical unconscious, concluding that, "a deep knowledge of the affective value of images and unconscious processes would be the indispensable know-how of the filmmaker." See René Allendy, "La Valeur psychologique de l'image," *L'Art cinématographique*, vol. 1 (Paris: Félix Alcan, 1926), p. 103.

38. Benjamin, "The Work of Art in the Age of its Technological Reproducibility," p. 110.

39. Miriam Bratu Hansen, "Benjamin's Aura," *Critical Inquiry* 34, no. 2 (Winter 2008), p. 338.

40. See Jean Epstein, "Nous kabbalistes," *L'Esprit nouveau*, no. 15 (February 1922): 1709-1713. Reprinted in Jean Epstein, *La Lyrosophie* (Paris: Éditions de la Sirène, 1922), pp. 83-95; and more recently in *Jean Epstein*, ed. Aumont, pp. 119-24.

41. Jean Epstein, "Freud ou le nick-cartérianisme en psychologie," *L'Esprit nouveau*, no. 16 (May 1922): 1857-1864. Reprinted in *Jean Epstein*, ed. Aumont, pp. 139-46.

42. For the connections between Epstein and another reject of surrealism, Georges Bataille, see Ludovic Cortade, "*Le Cinéma du diable*: Jean Epstein and the Ambiguities of Subversion," *SubStance* 34, no. 3 (2005): 3-16.

43. Jean Epstein, *La Poésie d'aujourd'hui, un nouvel état d'intelligence* (Paris: La Sirène, 1921), p. 153.

44. Epstein, *La Poésie d'aujourd'hui*, p. 156.

45. Epstein, *La Poésie d'aujourd'hui*, pp. 82-83.

46. For a fascinating history of philosophical reflections on this inner sense, see Daniel Heller-Roazen, *The Inner Touch: Archaeology of a Sensation* (Brooklyn: Zone Books, 2007), esp. chapter 22, "Coenaesthesis," pp. 237-51.

47. Jean Epstein, *Le Cinématographe vu de l'Etna*, p. 74; infra, 308. I cite the original text because the last two pages, "Amour de Sessue," on Sessue Hayakawa, were inexplicably withheld from the collected writings.

48. The main thesis of *La Lyrosophie* is that affects represent a more comprehensive logic than rationality since mathematical evidence is itself a kind of affect.

49. Jean Epstein, *Ganymède, essai sur l'éthique homosexuelle masculine*, p. 28. Fonds Jean et Marie Epstein, Bibliothèque du film, Paris, EPSTEIN227-B59. Hereafter cited in the text as "G."

50. See the following homoerotic passages on male beauty from Epstein's *Bonjour cinéma*: "sensual like the hip of a woman or a young man" (43); "Glass gloved faces / Living luxury in which I gaze / At my desire" (53); "The mechanics' tanned faces / Under the wind of their engines / And that of merchant marine boys / Who were tender towards their elders" (54).

51. For a misreading of this film based on "the impulse of the heterosexual romantic in Epstein," see Darragh O'Donoghue, "On Some Motifs in Poe: Jean Epstein's *La Chute de la maison Usher*," *Senses of Cinema*, no. 30 (2004). Available online at http://archive. sensesofcinema.com/contents/04/30/la_chute_de_la_maison_usher.html. Accessed on 2 December 2011.

52. For general evidentiary problems, see Anthony Slide, "The Silent Closet," *Film Quarterly* 52, no. 4 (Summer 1999): 24-32. See also Darwin Porter, *Hollywood's Silent Closet* (New York: Blue Moon Press, 2001); and Vito Russo's classic, *The Celluloid Closet* (New York: Harper & Row, 1981).

53. Ruby Rich made her comment at the opening of the retrospective *Duty, Deviance, Desire: The Films of Germaine Dulac*, 14 September 2003, University of California at Berkeley.

54. I cite the subtitle of Steven Dillon's *Derek Jarman and Lyric Film: The Mirror and the Sea* (Austin: University of Texas Press, 2004). Dillon connects Jarman to Cocteau.

55. See Stuart Liebman, "Sublime et désublimation dans la théorie cinématographique de Jean Epstein: *Le Cinématographe vu de l'Etna*," in *Jean Epstein*, ed. Aumont, pp. 125-137.

56. Epstein, *Le Cinéma du diable*, ESC1, p. 394.

57. Epstein, *Le Cinéma du diable*, ESC1, p. 347.

58. Jean Epstein, "Photogénie de l'impondérable" [1955], *Esprit de cinéma*, ESC2, p. 15.

59. Epstein, *Le Cinéma du diable*, ESC1, pp. 353, 357.

60. Jean Epstein, "Finalité du cinéma" [1949], in *Esprit de cinéma*, ESC2, p. 34.

61. Benjamin, "The Work of Art in the Age of its Technological Reproducibility," p. 116.

62. Benjamin, "The Work of Art in the Age of its Technological Reproducibility," p. 115.

63. Walter Benjamin, "Outline of the Psychophysical Problem" [1923], trans. Rodney Livingstone, in *Selected Writings, Volume 1: 1913-1926*, eds. Marcus Bullock and Michael W. Jennings (Cambridge, MA: Belknap Press of Harvard University Press, 1996), p. 397.

64. Although Jewish mysticism is an influence on Epstein, Greek thought from the pre-Socratics to Plato, including its integration of homosexuality in pedagogy, is probably more important; further study of this topic is warranted.

65. Turvey, *Doubting Vision*. Hereafter cited in the text as DV.

66. Malcolm Turvey, "Jean Epstein's Cinema of Immanence: The Rehabilitation of the Corporeal Eye." *October*, no. 83. (Winter 1998): 25-50.

67. Perception is attention-dependent, limited, focal, and consequently inferential. For instance, see Jeremy M. Wolfe et al., *Sensation and Perception* (Sunderland: Sinauer Associates, 2006), p. 202.

68. Alva Noë, *Action in Perception* (Cambridge, MA: MIT Press, 2004).

69. Jean Epstein, "L'Essentiel du cinéma" [1923], ESC1, p. 120.

70. Vivian Sobchack, *The Address of the Eye: A Phenomenology of Film Experience* (Princeton: Princeton University Press, 1992), esp. chapter 2, "The Act of Being With One's Own Eyes," pp. 51-162.

71. Turvey's emphasis on cinema's quantitative visual difference, modeled on the microscope, fails to convince in the case of Epstein, all the more so because he insists that Epstein follows Bergson, who always favors the qualitative over the quantitative.

72. Turvey, *Doubting Vision*, p. 50. The translation is from "Photogénie of the Imponderable" [1935], trans. Richard Abel, Abel2, p. 189. The original is Jean Epstein, "Photogénie de l'impondérable" [1935], ESC1, p. 250. Epstein later revised the passage, however, in a way that softens his observation: "In this, [cinema] proves superior to the human mind, which does seem constituted so as to capture easily the totality of a four-dimensional continuity" (Epstein, *Esprit de cinéma* [1955], ESC2, p. 12).

73. Laura Marcus, *The Tenth Muse: Writing About Cinema in the Modernist Period* (New York: Oxford University Press, 2007), pp. 44-67.

74. Jean Epstein, *L'Intelligence d'une machine*, ESC1, pp. 282, 284.
75. Ibid., p. 285.
76. Jean Epstein, "L'Âme au ralenti" [1928], ESC1, p. 191.
77. Compare Viola's focus on "the *phenomena* of sense perception as a language of the body" and his belated premonition that "the late twentieth century will prove to be an important turning point in visual art when images moved into another dimension, the fourth dimension of time." Bill Viola, *Reasons for Knocking at an Empty House: Writings, 1971-1993* (Cambridge, MA: MIT Press, 2002), pp. 275, 278.
78. Mark B. N. Hansen, *New Philosophy for New Media* (Cambridge, MA: MIT Press, 2004), p. 267. Hereafter cited in the text as NP.

Novelty and Poiesis in the Early Writings of Jean Epstein[1]

Stuart Liebman

More than half a century after his death in 1953, Jean Epstein remains too much of a prophet without honor in American annals of European film theory and film-making. Despite some impressive archival work and several pioneering studies over the last couple of decades, as well as a number of recent reassessments, it is nevertheless correct to say that Epstein's films and film theory figure largely as *terrae incognitae* on current maps of cinematic achievement, at least in the English-speaking world.[2] Many topics must still be pursued in greater depth. A fuller understanding of how Epstein's theories informed his cinematic practice over the course of his three-decade-long career awaits more intensive analyses of many of his films and the circumstances in which they were made. The complex, quite often dissonant relationships his theoretical writings and films sustained with the various European avant-garde filmmaking ventures of his time certainly deserve more concerted attention. A searching exploration of the sinuous course of his later quasi-philosophical reflections on cinema has never really been attempted, while the reason for his marginal position in the shifting intellectual milieus of French film culture since the 1940s remains an important topic for further scholarly investigation. Happily, Epstein's catalogued archive was opened to the public several years ago and, as the present essay collection demonstrates, scholars are now beginning to unpack it for new insights into the work and thought of a man who is as fascinating – though also as elusive – as he is mis-understood and undervalued.

One area in particular that has been too little studied is the relationship between Epstein's earliest intellectual venture, his construction of the poetics subtending the French modernist verse produced by his contemporaries, and his assessment of the capabilities of that newer medium with which he had grown up and to which he would contribute so much: the cinema. In my dissertation, completed thirty years ago, I argued that Epstein's first book on poetry, *La Poésie d'aujourd'hui, un nouvel état d'intelligence* (1921), the series of critical essays on literature entitled *Le Phénomène Littéraire* (1921-22), as well as his quasi-philosophical speculations in *La Lyrosophie* (1922) and other essays of the early 1920s ought to be closely examined because they constituted the basis for his earliest theoretical speculations about film.[3] In this respect, to be sure, Epstein was not entirely alone; a number of European writers of his day – Reverdy, Soupault, Canudo, and Cendrars, just to name a few of his peers in France – also used their reflections on poetry as jumping-off points for fledgling theories of cinema.[4] Compared to their rather circumscribed remarks in brief, occasional essays, however, Epstein's analytic framework was incomparably more ambitious, detailed, and far-reaching. It warrants further investigation.

Indeed, as of 1922, when the publication of *La Lyrosophie* capped off a remarkable two years of achievement for the young critic, one may fairly say that Epstein's theorization of modernist verse in his earliest books aided him in developing – in his famous *plaquette Bonjour Cinéma* and related writings – a theory of film that was unmatched in scope or daring anywhere in Europe. By that year, for example, Kuleshov had written but a few of the short essays on montage that would soon make his reputation, while his erstwhile pupils Vertov and Eisenstein had barely published a word. As Sabine Hake has noted, the "cinema's third machine" had only just started to function in Germany: "Most contributions [to film criticism and theory up to that time] remained essayistic: short, fragmentary, spontaneous..."[5] And, to conclude this brief summary of the state of film theory in 1922, the exiled Hungarian poet and librettist Béla Balázs only took up writing film criticism in Austrian newspapers toward the end of the year. His famous theoretical tract, *Der Sichtbare Mensch* – claimed by some to be the first major European text on film theory – would not appear until two years later.[6]

Indeed, the sophistication of Epstein's ideas about poetry was arguably only comparable to the formulations proposed by another group who would also soon turn their attention to the theorization of cinema: his near contemporaries collectively known as the "Russian Formalist" critics, preeminently Viktor Shklovsky, Roman Jakobson, Yuri Tynianov, and Boris Eikhenbaum.[7] In my dissertation I had, in fact, noted in passing that Epstein's and the Formalists' reflections on the poetry of their times often converged to a surprising degree, though the context of my argument did not require me to pursue the comparison further at the time. I also did not explore how markedly *different* their explanations for the psychological and cultural dynamics motivating modern poetry were, nor how these differences would eventually bear significant consequences for their visions of what cinematic art could/should be. The aim of the present essay is, then, precisely to revisit some of the intellectual territory I passed through too quickly years ago. By exploring both the convergences and divergences between Epstein and the Formalist critics, I want to highlight the range and singularity of Epstein's theoretical voice on several issues – the nature of cinematic representation, the relation of the new medium to modernity, and the dependence of film structure on narrative logic, among others – that were crucial to the film-theoretical debates of the 1920s.

The Russian Formalists, of course, had begun their meetings to discuss poetics before Epstein had finished his secondary education. As is now well-known, the Russian Formalists formed two somewhat informal groups in St. Petersburg and Moscow in 1915-1916, following on the publication of a few groundbreaking critical and theoretical essays about poetics by Viktor Shklovsky and others.[8] One of Shklovsky's signature early essays, "Art as Technique," published in 1917, laid a famous foundation stone for the group's perspective on literary art. In a well-known passage, he lamented the extent to which social and linguistic routines had taken hold of experience, dulling perception of the world. "Habitualization," he wrote with comic hyperbole, "devours works, clothes, furniture, one's wife, and the fear of war. If the whole complex lives of many people go on unconsciously, then such lives are as if they had never been."[9] He later echoed this concern in a strikingly graphic image: "We live as if covered with rubber...," and in the early essays of this most colorful of Formalist critics one can find many similar passages decrying the linguistic ciphers through whose agency people filtered – and also occluded – the world of things and experience.[10]

Happily, Shklovsky added, art – and he, more than most of his peers, included visual as well as language arts in his thinking – rescued individuals from this malaise.[11] Art's innovative linguistic or imagistic techniques fulfilled a key existential function: they removed screens of habit – including veils of routinized language – that beclouded perception, and by doing so reconnected individuals to the world. Art made objects and experiences palpable once again, releasing them from the deadening grip of the already "known."

> Art exists that one may recover the sensation of life; it exists to make one feel things, to make the stone stony. The purpose of art is to impart the sensation of things as they are perceived and not as they are known. The technique of art is to make objects unfamiliar. [...] Art removes objects from the automatism of perception....[12]

His hyperbole later went so far as to attribute "all the horror...of our present day – the Entente, Russia" to "the absence in us of a sensation of the world, by the absence of art....To this end, in order to make an object into a fact of broad art, it has to be extracted from the quantity of facts of life."[13] This "extraction," yielding a work of art he deemed ontologically distinct from ordinary things, was achieved through innovating artistic forms, as poets and visual artists deployed new techniques to challenge and thus to refresh perception.

Unfortunately, even older art of the highest quality was subject to a tendency to become conventionalized over time. Repetitions of earlier modes of poetry or painting styles degraded the effectiveness of existing artistic structures in accomplishing their assigned task. Roman Jakobson forcefully insisted upon this point. "There comes a time," he wrote in 1921, when the traditional poetic language hardens into stereotype and is no longer capable of being felt but is experienced rather as a ritual, as a holy text in which even the errors are considered sacred. The language of poetry is as it were covered by a veneer and neither its tropes nor its poetic licenses any longer speak to consciousness. [...] Form becomes stereotype and it is no longer alive.[14]

For both these Russian critics, the power of art declined whenever its audience became habituated to the conventions it used. Experience of the world then grew stale; what had formerly been vibrant and alive became bland, or even sterile. The antidote Shklovsky and Jakobson proposed involved a breaking of the vessels, a renovation of form by constituting new prisms of language or original visual vocabularies through which the world could be made to feel new once more, in which stones, in Shklovsky's phrasing, could again be perceived as *stony*. In this stirring credo, the stakes both for art and human existence were high indeed.

In the very same year in which Jakobson warned against the threat of stereotypical language in art, hundreds of miles away to the West another young literary critic of East European Jewish background was writing texts that would soon make him famous in his adopted country of France. Jean Epstein, then at the ripe age of 24, had already published the first of his two monographs on contemporary poetry, and the second was then appearing in the pages of Le Corbusier and Ozenfant's prestigious review, L'*Esprit nouveau*. Over the next eighteen months, he would add his now famous film-theoretical tract *Bonjour Cinéma*, the speculative philosophical book, *La Lyrosophie*, as well as essays on diverse intellectual topics: the alleged follies of Freud's psychoanalytic theory, Rimbaud, contemporary scientific thought, the Kabbalah, and love.

Using a vocabulary strikingly reminiscent of his Russian Formalist contemporaries in his analysis of modern poetry, he decried the torpor of the age – symptomatized by what he called modern "fatigue" – and stressed the need for new forms of verbal art to respond to it.[15] Indeed, in the following quotation that referenced Pavlov more than once, Epstein seems to have echoed Formalist views; he sounded almost like a proto-Eisenstein in his insistence on "conditioned reflexes" as the foundation for a reader's or spectator's reactions to artistic techniques.

Habit, which deadens, renders blasé, fatigues and extinguishes aesthetic emotion, steadily demands that new details, novel processes, and original ideas be added to the more durable characteristics of works of art – a change corresponding to a change in the conditions of life. This is necessary if one wishes to awaken beauty from its torpor, to astonish, to strike the intelligence and stir the sensibility. The impression of the beautiful is a sort of *conditioned reflex* and undergoes the physiological law of all reflexes, which eventuates at length in extinction. It becomes necessary to introduce new conditions into the production of phenomena of beauty in order to revive this *conditioned reflex*.[16]

Epstein's warning was, in any case, as clear as the Russians' had been: formal innovation was crucial because "The extinction of the aesthetic emotion specific to each literary school marks the end of these schools. There is no eternal beauty."[17]

Clearly, these young literary critics all perceived the verbal art of their day to be in crisis, and they understood the symptoms of that crisis in strikingly similar terms. Their analyses converged in the observation that modern societies had increasingly oriented themselves to a certain mental economy based on practical transactions employing utilitarian ciphers with which to communicate. The result was a kind of "algebraization" of thought – effective, perhaps, in encouraging daily social intercourse and pragmatic action, but with dire consequences for the human sensorium and intellect. As Shklovsky suggested, for most modern individuals it was as if the world *were* covered with rubber. Moreover, the linguistic art that had formerly broken through the veneer dulling the vividness of the world had itself been neutralized by burdensome, outmoded tropic and formal conventions. It was therefore no longer capable of fulfilling art's special social role, namely, to reestablish a vital connection to the world through a renovation of perception. What was needed, all agreed, was nothing less than a far-reaching renewal of poetry's words and phrasings; novel concatenations of imagery and rhythms had to be developed to allow the world to blossom forth once more. An analysis of these new techniques embodied in the works of poets they admired became the key gateways to the perspectives they offered.

The basic orientation and the prescriptions offered by Epstein and the Formalists were, in fact, so close in both letter and spirit as to raise the question of influence. I have found no evidence that Epstein, who did not know Russian, was aware of any of the essays by Shklovsky or Jakobson I have cited; these were, as far as I know, not translated into any West European languages until many years later.[18] It is true that by the first years of the 1920s, both Shklovsky and Jakobson were in exile in Berlin and Prague respectively. In these cultural capitals they might very well have gained access to Epstein's books in French, a language they surely knew well, and almost certainly could have perused some of his many texts in the internationally distributed *L'Esprit nouveau*. Two of Epstein's early short texts on cinema, moreover, were even translated into Russian and published in the Moscow journal *Zénith*.[19] Epstein's writings on poetry, however, post-date most of the Shklovsky and Jakobson essays already cited by several months, and in some cases, by years; the Russian critics would, at best, probably have found confirmation of some of their own insights in Epstein's independent writings. The apparent absence of contact or any genetic influence in either direction therefore likely points to a shared source or sources, which might be profitably explored by future researchers. The celebrated French philosopher Henri Bergson's writings are most certainly one possible discourse they might all have read, as some scholars are beginning to suggest.[20] For now, it is enough to note how much the prescriptions for formal innovations recommended by these critics in both Eastern and Western Europe overlap.

In general terms, Shklovsky and Jakobson argued that the language of poetry had to be "roughened," made difficult so as to retard or even "impede" the reader's ease in consuming the poem. The Formalists' jargon for this process was "defamiliarization" (ostranenie). In their view, poets used language to make objects "strange." By this procedure, automatized responses were derailed, allowing "things" to be perceptually redeemed. Epstein did not use the word "defamiliarize," but he did employ one quite closely related to it: déformation. He opined that artists – and at this early stage of his career he was thinking primarily of poets, but soon the work of visual artists was encompassed as well – had to "deform" the world, rendering it more complex and new by multiplying not entirely compatible perspectives on it.[21] He likened the procedures as akin to those of scientists who used diverse instruments and not always congruent standards of measurement in their research to bring new phenomena into sharper relief.[22]

What is more, their general orientations and vocabularies were echoed to an astonishing degree in their descriptions of the linguistic devices characterizing poems capable of defamiliarizing or deforming the world. Jakobson catalogued many of them in his famous text on Xlebnikov from which I have already quoted. First and foremost, Jakobson praised Xlebnikov's verse for what he termed the "self-developing, self-valuing word" as the ground of a poetry importantly divorced from its communicative function. Indeed, Xlebnikov's strikingly original works often reached the state of zaoum, that is, "trans-sense," chiefly by rejecting any logical motivation or connecting threads among the words through such strategies as temporal displacement, anachronism, arbitrary arrangements of story elements, linkages by formal likeness or contrast, and a tendency toward "verblessness," among others. Such techniques complicated language; denotations were suspended and the range of connotative meanings expanded. This "roughening" also conferred greater emphasis on the phonic dimension of verbal representations in and for themselves. "Cumulatively," Jakobson observed, "these devices became exemplary indices of the differentia of poetry as language in its aesthetic function.[23] In Shklovsky's words, these strategies restored "density (faktura) [to objects]... the principal characteristic of this peculiar world of deliberately constructed objects, the totality of which we call art."[24]

Epstein was no less alert to similar techniques in the works of the contemporary French poets he admired. Approximation, slant rhyme schemes, exaggerated metaphors, and the abandonment of rhythmic regularity were only some of the strategies he isolated in verses by Cendrars, Cocteau, and Aragon, French counterparts to the Formalists' list of exemplary contemporary poets topped by Maya-

kovsky, Kručenyx, and Xlebnikov.[25] In one of the installments in L'Esprit nouveau of
"Le Phénomène Littéraire," the monograph-length article series on poetry Epstein
published over several months in 1921 and 1922, he wrote:

> ...writers are obliged to make their grammar more supple, to make it more
> flexible – and this is not always so easy – even to the point of completely re-
> nouncing grammar and phrasing, and contenting themselves with words, el-
> lipses, fragmented phrases, even syllables. Likewise, the punctuation that cer-
> tainly exists in literature, rather less in speech, and much less so – indeed is
> almost non-existent in our thoughts – has been attenuated or even suppressed
> by certain authors.[26]

Rejecting syntax led to a new "flexibility" of grammar, sometimes even reaching a
point where it seemed to be suspended entirely. The French poems he prized
indulged in such linguistic escapades to open conundrums, producing a kind of
verbal hash that at times seemed to elude meaning of any kind, almost in the
manner of *zaoum* poetry. And this evasion or displacement of logical sense was,
Epstein noted, often augmented by the way a text was laid out on a page.

> Thus the reader sometimes finds in modern works a word in capital letters
> larger than those related to it, sometimes a space between two words, some-
> times a space in the middle of a word cut into two or three parts, sometimes a
> single word in the middle of a line, sometimes an entire phrase in letters smal-
> ler than those surrounding them, sometimes a group of words and letters dis-
> posed in such a way as to form a design corresponding to the idea of the text,
> etc., etc. At first glance, people are surprised, and criticize it [the layout] as
> willfully bizarre. Not at all. It is but a way of translating and measuring...the
> architecture and three-dimensionality of thoughts. It is also a way of arousing
> the reader's fatigued attention.[27]

So typography, too, could be enlisted to disable ordinary reading procedures,
thereby conjuring different, more engaging, and potentially signifying visualizations that complemented the poets' experiments with tropes, syntax, and
rhythms. With such observations, Epstein highlighted what were some of the
most advanced poems in the Western poetic canon of his time: Un coup de dés by
Mallarmé and the "calligrammes" of Apollinaire, in addition to diverse works by
Max Jacob, Cocteau, Aragon, and Epstein's own mentor, Blaise Cendrars.

The search for *new* linguistic forms was for both Epstein and the Russians the
lynchpin of any solution to the perceived crisis in art in their time. As Epstein
stated pointedly in La Poésie d'aujourd'hui, "a search for the new is the springboard
of the aesthetic."[28] But what was to count as new? And how was formal innovation to register with the reader or viewer? Jakobson's answer was straightforward.

"Only against the background of the familiar does the unfamiliar reach and impress us," a statement which Epstein would have been quick to second. "The new conditions of life," he wrote,

> have determined a literature, a necessary and sufficient literature, a new literature. However, it is not necessary to believe that this modern literature has completely rejected all traditions, that it has broken completely with the past, that it has entirely created itself as a thing in no respect comparable with what has been. Even had it wished to do this, it would not have been able...In the most 'advanced modernism' there survives an abundant heredity.[29]

Even Shklovsky, the most strident exponent of introducing striking new strategies almost for their own sake, argued that the linguistic and formal novelties he championed only assumed meaning as they altered older artistic conventions which remained at least liminally present.[30] For all three, artistic innovation derived from a necessarily dialectical process engaging past and present, the old and the new.

If, however, there was a surprising degree of agreement in their characterization of modern poetry and of the crucial role it potentially played in the mental well-being of the societies in which they lived, Epstein and the Formalists parted company in major ways. This is most apparent, perhaps, in the scope of their explanations of the circumstances in which modern art was generated and the nature of the processes motivating art. Joined by Boris Eikhenbaum, for example, Shklovsky and Jakobson were convinced that linguistic and formal changes in and of themselves were all that was needed to effect the desired renovation of perception through verse. This renewal took place entirely at the level of the signs of literary discourse by poets consciously acting on their own artistic initiatives. Social conditions had little or no effect on such changes. In fact, in these early Formalist writings, one can at times detect an almost belligerent resistance to the idea that any broader social process might lie behind the impetus to transform artistic practices. "Historical materialism is fine for sociology, but it's impossible to use it as a substitute for a knowledge of mathematics and astronomy. [...] It's equally impossible to proceed from historical materialism to explain and reject, or accept, a work of art or a whole school of art," Shklovsky truculently observed in an essay on the Suprematist painters.[31] This and other rather cavalier pronouncements were obviously at odds with the Marxist authorities and increasingly risky in a Soviet Union moving toward exclusive government control of the arts.[32] Such anti-Marxist pronouncements even drew the critical attention of no less a figure than Trotsky himself.[33] But for Shklovsky and his colleagues, the realm of art simply lay beyond the grasp of sociological or political categories – it was a world apart. In Erlich's paraphrase of Eikhenbaum's argument: "No cultural phenomenon [could] be reduced to, or derived from, social facts of a different order. To

STUART LIEBMAN

account for literature in terms of sociology or economics [was] to deny the autonomy and inner dynamism of literature...."[34]

Epstein would not have agreed with such a statement, and in comparison to the early Formalists the larger scope of his analysis is striking. He sought to ground the modes of modern poetry in a theory of the changing conditions of work in modern capitalist economies. There had been, he noted, a marked transition from manual to intellectual labor in recent times. New technological developments raised the speed and intensity of mental operations as work demands and advanced communication and transportation networks projected increasingly "cosmopolitan" individuals ever more rapidly through physical, as well as mental, time and space.[35] Escalating numbers of burdensome mental operations were now of necessity demanded in the emerging modern society, and these resulted in what Epstein, following many psychologists of his day, called "fatigue" as a major psychological effect. Developing a schematic sociology and from it a theory of social, psychological, and aesthetic effects suggests how much less cloistered and more ambitious Epstein's explanatory scheme was than that of his Russian counterparts.[36] Reminiscent at times of themes from Mosso, Durkheim, Simmel, and Weber, among others, Epstein's theorization of the dynamics of the modern social order almost certainly would not have passed muster with Marxist orthodoxy. Nevertheless, as noted briefly above, Epstein's attempt to ground his more rarified psychological speculations in large social trends is certainly worth greater scholarly exploration than is possible in this essay.

Conservative thinkers regarded fatigue as a malady and as a reason to contest the rationalizing forces of modernity. Epstein, however, did not equate this new condition simply with exhaustion, loss of focus, and mental depletion. Rather, he considered it simply an inevitable, irreversible, and ultimately positive consequence of modernity. According to him, fatigue favored a descent into subconscious modes of cognition that were rich in soothing emotion beyond the reach of the "logic" he identified with the strenuous pragmatic calculations and algebraic communicative speech increasingly demanded of the growing class of white-collar workers. The poets' delving into these layers of imagery and experience yielded works that helped to relax and soothe jangled brains, affording compensation to them for their extraordinary exertions. The poems thereby acted as a kind of therapy. Modern poetic works were in this respect both signs of the times as well as a kind of haven for many workers in an increasingly abstract, distracted world.

The Formalists could not have disagreed more fundamentally. As the historian of Russian Formalism, Victor Ehrlich, reminds us, the Russians were inclined to regard the process of literary change as supra-personal, and highly conscious. Innovations were a "deliberate application of techniques to materials rather than as self-expression, as a [change of] convention rather than as a confession."[37] So deep-seated was their distrust of psychology that they saw no need to invoke any faculty of mind allegedly conducive to poetic creation or apprehension. Boris Ei-khenbaum, a leader of the Formalists, perhaps formulated it most succinctly: "Not a single phrase of a literary work can at any time be the direct expression of the author's personal sentiments; it is, rather, always a construction and playful."[38]

Epstein, however, insisted on pursuing precisely this line of inquiry by attempting to map the "subconscious" – the site, he claimed, of all aesthetic experience.

> Attention brought to bear on one's inner life discovers rather quickly that if inner life that is fully conscious is very rich, there exist zones within it which are infinitely more bountiful and strange because they have not been explored. These zones are the liminal states of the subconscious. Authors have turned toward this subconscious in order to look closely at it and examine it more closely. [...] Sometimes, the subconscious has risen spontaneously into the poet's consciousness...[39]

And, in a later installment of the same essay series, he forcefully asserted:

> ...Poetry in general seems to me impossible without the intense, distinctive engagement of the *subconscient*. The enormous speed of thought, the rapid comprehension of metaphorical analogies, the singular perspective of its mental framework, the succession of imagistic details, create poetry because they engage the life of the *subconscient*, setting this hundred-faceted, mirrored top spinning.[40]

By monitoring the aesthetic transactions he believed took place in this "neuropathic" realm, by burrowing down to explore the poet's intense engagement with what he called "*coenesthésie*," Epstein hoped to anchor an explanation of how the specific characteristics of the formal innovations he advocated, especially the abandonment of grammar and the increased density of tropes, came into being.[41]

Epstein, then, regarded the poet's efforts to introduce formal changes as an ultimately *personal*, though not fully conscious experience. *Pace* the Formalists, poetic renewal was not the result of playing with or consciously reconstructing poetic language. Rather, it involved a physiologically motivated plunge into subconscious depths where words, if not entirely dispensed with, existed unconstrained by rigidly grammatical aspects of ordinary communicative speech and logic. The poet's task consisted of faithfully noting down the very pattern of the thought process as it was expressed in the strange, irrational linguistic forms native to that realm. In the subconscious, he observed,

> Writers have perceived that if thoughts are – at least for the most part, made of words – [...] they are hardly composed of phrases; and if thoughts admit a

logic, that is, an order determined by how its elements are linked, then this logic is infinitely mobile, changing, complicated; in short, it is illogical, and has nothing to do with the simple, stiff logic of expression, a part of which forms grammar.[42]

In Epstein's conception, innovative poetry had, in fact, become – and should become – a kind of exquisite reportage of the twisting, meandering course of thought necessarily transacted at the deepest cognitive levels of the poet's "subconscious." Modern poets had grasped that their reports of fatigue-induced experience could only be authentic if rendered in phrases that at times made no sense, but whose elliptical, eccentrically metaphorical figures were highly expressive and restored density to words that, in turn, lent a new weight to the world they somehow so tellingly disclosed.

> Literature has progressively discovered the vast domain of thinking. [Literature] is therefore no longer a function of the contingent truth of facts that for so long were understood as the sole truth, at a time when the mind was not yet perceived as capable of being its own mirror and its own nourishment. From now on, one will seek to represent the thought process. The truth would be the precise representation of the course of thought. Next to the truth of action, an external truth, the truth of thinking, an internal truth, has been born.[43]

Without mentioning his name, Epstein was engaged in theorizing what would soon come to be known, preeminently through the work of James Joyce, as the "stream of consciousness." Such ideas would continue to inspire other filmmakers, preeminently Eisenstein during the late 1920s and, decades later, Stan Brakhage.[44]

The details of Epstein's theories of the subconscious and his intricate mapping of the "irrational, ... irresistible" transactions that purportedly shaped aesthetic response in it would require at least another essay to sort through.[45] However precocious and resourceful the young critic was even to broach an explanation of poetic innovation in such terms, there are certainly more than a lot of arcane, questionable, and just plain confusing dimensions of his theorization of this allegedly more profound cognitive apparatus. Suffice it to say that in attempting to theorize this realm as the ground for his poetics, Epstein embraced the possible opportunities for artistic innovation it opened, but by doing so he was very far removed from the orientations of the Russian Formalists.[46]

One might confirm this comment by jumping ahead in time a bit in order to compare Eikhenbaum's remarks on what he called "internal speech," the putative process through which, he believed, spectators negotiated the sequences of silent film images. Interpreting such image structures, Eikhenbaum noted, required a "new type of mental labor which does not normally develop in everyday life"; the film viewer had to connect the frames (i.e., shots) in order to "continually form a chain of cine-phrases, or else he will not understand anything."[47] This general description of the process of experiencing a film, however, was conditioned by a key specification: the editing of the shots must operate so that contiguous shots were perceived as *preceding* and *following* each other in time. "This is the general law of cinema. The director, submitting to this law, makes use of it for the construction of time; i.e., he creates the illusion of continuity."[48] Similar strictures also held for the construction of space. Cinema's inherent dynamism, its ability to join together pictures of different places, needed to be reined in so that spectators could negotiate the gaps between shots and create at least the illusion of continuity so that "time-space relationships...play the role of a basic semantic link, outside of which the viewer cannot orient himself..."[49] Only when the film's narrative and montage complied to motivate such transitions between segments could internal speech "give the viewer of a film the impression of completeness and logic."[50] At this point, it seems clear that the Formalists had retreated from their bolder claims about poetry and now advocated, as it were, a kind of cinematic prose.[51]

Epstein's conclusions about how film images should engage with narrative demands directly opposed such prescriptions, a point I will return to in a moment. The divergence of their views about the function of editing and narrative structure is all the more striking because both Epstein and the Formalists shared the same fundamental conviction that the building blocks of film art – the punctuated flow of moving images – were not simple reflections of the world, but the stuff of poetry constituted by the devices of the medium. Shklovsky had referred to verse writing as a "dance of the articulatory organs."[52] For Epstein, the literary critic turned cineaste, the Bell & Howell, "a brain in metal," was the vital articulatory organ that enabled cinema to "dance" as modern poetry did.[53] As recorded by the camera, the things appearing on screen were endowed with a new vivacity and immediacy. These film images, all agreed, were essentially "photogenic."

Epstein, of course, was intimately familiar with the elusive concept of "*photogénie*" which was first deployed in the influential film criticism of Louis Delluc for whom he had served as an assistant on the production of *Le Tonnerre* (1921). By the beginning of the 1920s, *photogénie* had already become part of the common currency of film discussions, not only in France, but even as far away as the Soviet Union, where it was embraced by Formalists as a basic principle of their theory of film. Eikhenbaum, for example, cited Delluc and identified *photogénie* as "the 'trans-sense' essence of film" that could be observed "on the screen – in faces, in objects, in scenery – apart from any connection with plot." However, while Delluc had thought many modern objects – locomotives, ocean liners, etc. – were inherently photogenic, Eikhenbaum disagreed. The cameraman, who knew how to position objects in the frame, who arranged the lighting, distance, and angle from which they would be seen on screen, was the individual most responsible for

STUART LIEBMAN

creating *photogénie*.[54] As I have already suggested, this insistence on the act of fashioning through the conscious deployment of the devices of a medium was entirely consistent with the emphases of Formalist poetics.

I have repeatedly stressed that Epstein's poetics were rooted in a similar assertion of the need for new artistic techniques. It is not surprising, therefore, that the essays in *Bonjour Cinéma*, dependent as they were on his poetics, were replete with paeans of praise for cinematic structuring devices, especially novel ones, and the way in which these techniques radically transformed the world depicted on screen. Close-ups and camera movements (especially rapid, whirling ones), among other filmic procedures, extracted things from their ordinary contexts; their removal often suspended denotations, refashioned referents, and thereby broadened the scope of connotations.[55]

Interestingly, Epstein signaled the affiliation of his poetic and emerging film theory by conveying his observations about cinema in a complex metaphorical language that itself recalled some of the poetic strategies he championed in the verse of his times. Consider his laudatory description of a face seen in close-up in his remarkable essay "Magnification." It opens with a gust of emotion and never lets up.

I will never find the way to say how much I love American close-ups! Point blank. A head suddenly appears on screen and drama, now face to face, seems to address me personally and swells with an extraordinary intensity. I am hypnotized. Now the tragedy is anatomical. The decor of the fifth act is this corner of a cheek torn by a smile. Waiting for the moment when 1,000 meters of intrigue converge in a muscular denouement satisfies me more than the rest of the film. Muscular preambles ripple beneath the skin. Shadows shift, tremble, hesitate. Something is being decided. A breeze of emotion underlines the mouth with clouds. The orography of the face vacillates. Seismic shocks begin. Capillary wrinkles try to split the fault. A wave carries them away. Crescendo. A muscle bridles. The lip is laced with tics like a theater curtain. Everything is movement, imbalance, crisis. Crack. The mouth gives way, like a ripe fruit splitting open. As if slit by a scalpel, a keyboard-like smile cuts laterally into the corner of the lips. The close-up is the soul of the cinema.[56]

In this high-spirited description of what Epstein would certainly have identified as a quintessentially photogenic moment, he conspicuously jettisoned simple description. Instead, in a manner akin to the poetic work he prized, he yoked together disparate notions to pulverize the language through which he evoked this spectacular close-up. He translated the face – seen in unnatural proximity and enlarged to fantastic scale on the screen – as a string of incompatible, stunningly mixed, metaphors: the facial expanse was a theater set, a cloudy sky, a mountain range, a theater curtain; the mouth was a ripe fruit and the teeth a piano keyboard.

Metaphor assumed a central role in articulating this oblique, "roughened" discourse that suggested that viewers had to "read" images as differently as they read poems; it was a process Epstein believed to be more rewarding and emotionally engaging. Indeed, one may think of the description – it is really more properly regarded as an evocation – of the face in this passage as a kind of prose poem of the sort Epstein lauded in his critical writings on literature. Through its reconstitution as metaphor, those who read it were thereby enabled to "see" a face appearing like no other seen before. Torn from its habitual context, several semantic frameworks evolve around it as one reads, loosening the bond between sign and object.[57] As the metaphors shift, the identity of the object oscillates, its sensory texture and polysemic density heightened by the eccentrically patterned language representing it. Through such evocations of things, spectators became deeply imbricated in the almost magical kind of cinematic representation Epstein called the "photogenic." This is by no means a unique example; there are many others in Epstein's early writings.[58] All point toward a theory of cinematic representation very far removed from any notion of "realism," and it deserves a much more detailed and extensive account than is possible here.[59]

Throughout *Bonjour Cinéma*, Epstein repeatedly extolled such effects and tended to neglect larger concepts of structure beyond the idea of sequences representing subjective experience or unprecedentedly dynamic physical action. Unlike the Formalists, however, he rejected any need for temporal or spatial continuity as a precondition for spectator comprehension and pleasure. On the contrary, he regarded the imposition of such constraints as attempts to reintroduce a narrative "logic" reflecting dryly rational or conventional predispositions of the intellect that he quite conspicuously scorned. Cinema was "true," while the conventions of an imposed story were a "lie." Cinema did not render anecdotes very well and "dramatic action was an error." "The cinema assimilated the rational armature of the feuilleton badly," he noted. "...so why tell stories, narratives that always presuppose an ordered series of events, a chronology. [...] There are no stories. There have never been any stories. There are only situations without heads or tails; with no beginning, no middle and no end..."[60]

The gap separating Formalists and Epstein on this point is as obvious as it would be difficult to bridge. His stunning refusal of plots with a beginning, middle, and end, at least in his film theory, should not surprise readers of his poetic texts.[61] Such radical claims clearly reflected the fundamental illogic he defined as the essential dynamic of the subconscious that was, in turn, the source of all aesthetic emotion. This was as true for the new medium of photogenic film as it was for the more traditional arts. To impose story logic would be to betray the needs of a modern mass audience in search of a spectacularly photogenic world of cinematic poetry. It would limit – perhaps even banish – wonderment and reinstall the stultifying expectations and all too familiar reading procedures of what Epstein referred to – scornfully – as "literature." For Epstein, one might say, the new world of cinema would be poetic, or would not be.

Notes

1. This article is a revised, expanded version of a talk given at the conference "Jean Epstein's Interdisciplinary Cinema and the French Avant-Garde," held at the University of Chicago in April, 2008. I thank the organizers, Sarah Keller and Jason Paul, both for their invitation to speak, as well as their suggestions for revision, and their patience while awaiting the final version of this text. Unless otherwise indicated, all translations from Epstein's writings are my own.

2. See David Bordwell, *French Impressionist Cinema: Film Culture, Film Theory and Film Style* [1974] (New York: Arno Press, 1980); Stuart Liebman, *Jean Epstein's Early Film Theory, 1920-1922* [1980] (Ann Arbor, MI: University Microfilms International, 1981); Richard Abel, *French Cinema: The First Wave, 1915-1929* (Princeton: Princeton University Press, 1984); *Jean Epstein: cinéaste, poète, philosophe*, ed. Jacques Aumont (Paris: Cinémathèque française, 1998); Vincent Guigueno, *Jean Epstein, Cinéaste des îles* (Paris: Jean Michel Place, 2003); Laura Vichi, *Jean Epstein* (Milan: Il Castoro Cinema, 2003); and Malcolm Turvey, *Doubting Vision. Film and the Revelationist Tradition* (New York: Oxford University Press, 2008). One should also mention the very first extensive assessment of Epstein's work by Pierre Leprohon, *Jean Epstein* (Paris: Éditions Seghers, 1964).

3. See Liebman, *Jean Epstein's Early Film Theory*.

4. Cendrars served as Epstein's mentor and introduced him to the Parisian avant-garde scene, including Paul Lafitte, publisher of *Éditions de la Sirène*.

5. Sabine Hake, *The Cinema's Third Machine: Writing on Film in Germany, 1907-1933* (Lincoln, NE: University of Nebraska Press, 1993), p. 62.

6. See Joseph Zsuffa, *Béla Balázs, The Man and the Artist* (Berkeley: University of California Press, 1987), dust jacket.

7. Interestingly, all four would, like Epstein in France, later go on to work in the Soviet film industry, though primarily as scriptwriters. Epstein, however, began his filmmaking career at least three years earlier.

8. The best history of their work remains Victor Erlich, *Russian Formalism: History, Doctrine*, 3rd ed. (The Hague: Mouton, 1969). The inspiration of early Russian Futurist verse by Mayakovsky, among others, to their theoretical initiatives should be underscored.

9. Viktor Shklovsky, "Art as Technique" [1917], in *Russian Formalist Criticism: Four Essays*, eds. and trans. Lee T. Lemon and Marion J. Reis (Lincoln, NE: Bison Books, 1965), p. 12.

10. Viktor Shklovsky, *Literature and Cinematography* [1923], trans. Irina Masinovsky (Champaign, IL: Dalkey Archive Press, 2006), p. 13.

11. See, for example, Shklovsky's comments in his seminal essay, "The Resurrection of the Word" [1914], trans. Richard Sherwood in *Russian Formalism*, eds. Steven Bann and John Bowlt (New York: Barnes and Noble Books, 1973), pp. 41-47. The visual arts also play a major role in Shklovsky's *Knight's Move* [1923], trans. Richard Sheldon (Normal,

IL: Dalkey Archive Press, 2005), pp. 54-72. Note that all the articles in this book had been published in Russia between 1919 and 1921. See also Shklovsky, *Literature and Cinematography, passim*.

12. Shklovsky, "Art as Technique," p. 12. In his later *Theory of Prose*, Shklovsky referred to this kind of automatism as "generalizing perception" (Viktor Shklovsky, *Theory of Prose* [1923; 2nd enlarged ed., 1929], trans. Benjamin Sher [Elmwood Park, IL: Dalkey Archive Press, 1991], p. 5).

13. Shklovsky, *Literature and Cinematography*, p. 13.

14. Roman Jakobson, "The Newest Russian Poetry: Velimir Xlebnikov," [1921], trans. Stephen Rudy, in Jakobson, *My Futurist Years* (New York: Marsilio Books, 1997), p. 189.

15. For his notions of fatigue, Epstein drew on a number of thinkers that were well known at the time, including Charles Féré and Angelo Mosso. For a survey of ideas about social energy and exhaustion in the twentieth century, see Anson Rabinbach, *The Human Motor. Energy, Fatigue, and the Origins of Modernity* (New York: Basic Books, 1990).

16. Jean Epstein, "A Necessary and Sufficient Literature," trans. Gorham Munson, *Broom* 2, no. 4 (July 1922), p. 309. Originally published as part of "Le Phénomène Littéraire" in *L'Esprit nouveau*, no. 9 (1921), p. 967. See also Epstein's more extensive elaboration of the idea of aesthetic reflexes in *La Poèsie d'aujourd'hui*, pp. 32-37.

17. Epstein, "A Necessary and Sufficient Literature," p. 309.

18. One tantalizing point of convergence is the appearance in the little journal Epstein edited in Lyons of an undated "Poème" by "Chlebnikoff," translated from the Russian by H. Izdebska. See *Promenoir*, no. 6 (1921), p. 74.

19. See "Cinéma," [identical to "Le Sens 1 bis," a section of *Bonjour Cinéma*] in *Zénith* (October 1921); and "Le Bel Agonisant" [that had appeared in Epstein's Lyon-based journal *Promenoir* in June 1922] in *Zénith* (May 1922).

20. One possible common influence might be the writings of Henri Bergson, which were influential in Russia as well as France. Curiously, Victor Erlich, the leading historian of the Formalist movement, mentions Bergson only once in *Russian Formalism* as part of a general description of the intellectual interests of the era; he does not mention any significant influence by Bergson on the Formalists' emerging notions of literature and fails even to list his name in the index. More recent commentators, however, have begun to highlight the possible connections between Bergson and readers in Russia. See James M. Curtis, "Bergson and Russian Formalism," *Comparative Literature* 28, no. 2 (1976): 109-121. For a more general view, see Hilary Fink, *Bergson and Russian Modernism, 1910-1930* (Evanston, IL: Northwestern University Press, 1999). There are also obvious similarities between the Formalists' views and those of Jean Cocteau, one of Epstein's favored poets during the late 1910s and early 1920s, who clearly was influenced by Bergson. In "Le Secret Professional," Cocteau wrote: "Suddenly, as if in a flash, we *see* the dog, the coach, the house for the first time. Shortly afterwards, habit again erases this potent image. We pet the dog, we call the coach, we live in a house; we do not see them anymore...Such is the role of poetry. It takes off the veil...It reveals...the amazing things which surround us and which our senses usually register mechanically. Get hold of a commonplace, clean it, rub it, illuminate it in such a fashion that it will astound us all with its freshness, with its primordial vigor, and you shall have done the job of the poet. *Tout le rest est littérature*." By the way, Erlich attri-

butes the dating of Cocteau's text only to its late publication in book form. "Le Secret Professional" was delivered as lectures in 1921, published in 1922, and finally reprinted in Cocteau's *Le Rappel à l'Ordre* (Paris: Editions Stock, 1926), pp. 215-216. Erlich only cites the last date. See Erlich, *Russian Formalism*, pp. 179-180.

21. See, for example, Jean Epstein, "Fernand Léger," *Les Feuilles Libres* (March-April 1923): 26-31.

22. Epstein, "Le Phénomène Littéraire," *L'Esprit nouveau*, no. 8 (1921), p. 858.

23. Jakobson, "The Newest Russian Poetry," *passim*.

24. Shklovsky, *Knight's Move*, cited by Victor Erlich, *Russian Formalism*, p. 177.

25. Jean Epstein, *La Poèsie d'aujourd'hui* (Paris: Éditions de la Sirène, 1921), pp. 47-55.

26. Epstein, "Le Phénomène Littéraire," *L'Esprit nouveau*, nos. 11-12 (1922), p. 1221. See also Epstein, *La Poèsie d'aujourd'hui*, pp. 95-98.

27. Epstein, "Le Phénomène Littéraire," *L'Esprit nouveau*, nos. 11-12 (1922), p. 1222. Mallarmé's famous poem "Un Coup de dès" and Apollinaire's *Calligrammes* were surely the models for this practice. There are clear parallels in the layouts of poems by Futurist artists and poets in Russian books of the period. See Susan R. Compton, *World Backwards: Russian Futurist Books, 1912-1916* (London: British Library, 1978); and Margit Rowell and Deborah Wye, *The Russian Avant-Garde Book, 1910-1934* (New York: Museum of Modern Art, 2002).

28. Epstein, *La Poésie d'aujourd'hui*, p. 12. Epstein was certainly not alone among West European poets in calling for "the new." Pound and Apollinaire, among many others, made similar appeals. See also the writings on art by T. E. Hulme, which were mightily influenced by Bergson. See his *Speculations* (New York: Harcourt Brace, 1967 [1924]). In his article "Bergson and Russian Futurism," James Curtis calls attention to the procedural similarities between Bergson and Shklovsky's writings, which tend to stress the de-automatizing devices in a work at the expense of more general structural considerations of the work of art. I would argue the same holds true of Epstein, and will briefly revisit the issue later in this essay.

29. Epstein, "A Necessary and Sufficient Literature," p. 309.

30. Jakobson, "The Newest Russian Poetry," p. 189; Epstein, *La Poésie*, p. 40. See also Shklovsky, *Theory of Prose*, p. 20: "I would like to add the following as a general rule: a work of art is perceived against a background of and by association with other works of art. The form of a work of art is determined by its relationship with other pre-existing forms." See also Yury Tynianov's phrasing of this relationship in his "Problems of Poetic Language" [1924], trans. Tzvetan Todorov, in *Théorie de la littérature*, ed. Tzvetan Todorov (Paris: Éditions du Seuil, 1965), p. 118.

31. Viktor Shklovsky, "Space in Painting and the Suprematists," in *Knight's Move*, p. 58.

32. Viktor Shklovsky, "Ullya, Ullya, Martians," in *Knight's Move*, pp. 21-24.

33. Leon Trotsky, *Literature and Revolution*, trans. Rose Strunsky (Ann Arbor, MI: University of Michigan Press, 1971), pp. 162-183.

34. Erlich, *Russian Formalism*, p. 109.

35. Epstein's stress on speed and individual mobility in modern vehicles reflects the broad social effects of Italian Futurist manifestos as well as that of related avant-garde artistic groups.

36. Gerard Conio's edition of *Le Formalisme et le Futurisme Russes devant le Marxisme* (Lausanne: Éditions L'Age d'Homme, 1975), makes clear the extent to which by 1924, if not sooner, the absence of a theory of society and social change led to political problems for the Formalists in the Soviet Union.

37. Victor Ehrlich, *Russian Formalism*, p. 190.

38. Cited in Conio, *Le Formalisme et le Futurisme Russes devant le Marxisme*, p. 11.

39. Epstein, "Le Phénomène Littéraire," *L'Esprit nouveau*, nos. 11-12 (1922), p. 1220.

40. Epstein, "Le Phénomène Littéraire," *L'Esprit nouveau*, no. 13 (1922), p. 1433.

41. For Epstein, "coenaesthesia" was the "physiological aspect of the subconscious," a variant of what other artists of an earlier period referred to as synesthesia. See Epstein, *La Poèsie d'aujourd'hui*, pp. 82ff.

42. Epstein, "Le Phénomène Littéraire," *L'Esprit nouveau*, nos. 11-12 (1922), p. 1222. Again, see also Epstein, *La Poèsie d'aujourd'hui*, pp. 95-98.

43. Epstein, *La Poèsie d'aujourd'hui*, p. 100.

44. Eisenstein specifically took up Joyce's example in his "A Course in Treatment," trans. Jay Leyda, in *Film Form* (New York: Meridian Books, 1957), pp. 84-107. For a fine reading of the Russian director's reading of Joyce, see Annette Michelson, "Reading Eisenstein Reading *Ulysses*: Montage and the Claims of Subjectivity," *Art & Text* [Australia] no. 34 (Spring 1989): 64-78.

45. Epstein, *La Poèsie*, p. 33.

46. Epstein, *La Poèsie*, p. 181ff.

47. Boris Eikhenbaum, "Problems of Film Stylistics" [1927], trans. Thomas Aman, *Screen* 15, no. 3 (Autumn 1974), pp. 14-15.

48. Eikenbaum, "Problems of Film Stylistics," p. 21.

49. Eikenbaum, "Problems of Film Stylistics," p. 25.

50. Eikenbaum, "Problems of Film Stylistics," p. 27. In many of his texts on film from the mid to late 1920s, Shklovsky, too, stressed plot as providing the logic binding images. See, for example, his remarks in various texts collected in *The Film Factory*, eds. Richard Taylor and Ian Christie (Cambridge, MA: Harvard University Press, 1988), pp. 133, 153, 178, and 182.

51. Rising political pressures may well have played a role here, but it is also true that the Formalists' familiarity both with the demands of the film market and the attendant political pressures while actively working within the Soviet industry may have influenced their theoretical notions.

52. Cited in Ehrlich, *Russian Formalism*, p. 178.

53. Jean Epstein, "Le Sens 1 bis," *Bonjour Cinéma* (Paris: Éditions de la Sirène, 1921), pp. 38-39. The camera "brain" was only a synecdoche for all the estranging powers that cinema had at its disposal. Editing, rapid and slow motion, stop motion, as well as close-ups and camera movements constituted images that were, for Epstein, the equivalents of poetic tropes whose appeal and process addressed the fatigue of modern individuals in a manner similar to poems. See also the list of cinematic procedures akin to poetic devices in chapter 18, "Le Cinema," in *La Poésie d'aujourd'hui*, pp. 169-180; infra, 271-76.

54. Eikenbaum, "Problems of Film Stylistics," p. 9.

55. See, for example, the many suggestions for the use of close-ups and moving cameras mounted on cars and airplanes in "Grossissement," in *Bonjour Cinéma*, pp. 93-108.

56. Jean Epstein, "Magnification," trans. Stuart Liebman, *Abel1*, pp. 235-236.

57. I am here paraphrasing Ehrlich in *Russian Formalism*, p. 177. "By tearing the object out of its habitual context by bringing together disparate notions, the poet gives a coupe de grace to the verbal cliché and to the stock responses attendant upon it and forces us into heightened awareness of things and their sensory texture. The act of creative deformation restores sharpness to our perception, giving *density* to the world around us."

58. "...the photogenic and a whole new rhetoric are similarly concealed in the close-up. I haven't the right to think of anything but this telephone. It is a monster, a tower, and a character. The power and scope of its whisperings. Destinies wheel about, enter, and leave from this pylon as if from an acoustical pigeon house. [...] It is a sensory limit, a solid nucleus, a relay, a mysterious transformer from which everything good or bad may issue. It has the air of an idea." See Epstein, "Magnification," *Abel1*, p. 239.

59. A valuable study might be made of the way in which André Bazin read – and creatively misread – Epstein. Bazin's emergence as the most important critic of the generation following Epstein may explain in part Epstein's marginalization in French film circles in his last years and over the decades since he died.

60. These quotations are all taken from "Le Sens 1 bis," *passim*.

61. Clearly, Epstein's filmmaking was constrained by the realities of the marketplace. As Katie Kirtland points out in her essay in this volume, his celebrated *Coeur fidèle* is based on a crude melodramatic scenario, and it was not alone in this regard. Perhaps the films that best represented his vision of story-less cinema were the documentary *La Montagne infidèle* (1923) and the compilation film, significantly named *Photogénies* (1925). Both are unfortunately lost.

The Cinema of the Kaleidoscope

Katie Kirtland

Silent or sound, pure cinema is a cinema that would like to dispense with words: the cinema, as the etymology already indicates, is essentially the painter, the narrator of mobility, of all mobility, of mobility alone, because it alone is photogenic…. But the word constitutes a fixed form, a stable state, a stop, a crystallization of thought, an element of immobility.
Jean Epstein[1]

In 1926, film theorist Pierre Porte invokes Jean Epstein's Bonjour Cinéma (1921) in support of his argument for a 'pure cinema' whose fundamental principle is "to express itself through the harmony and melody of plastic movement," regardless of whether such visual abstraction is embedded in a narrative structure.[2] Epstein's response in the same journal two weeks later, an essay called "L'Objectif lui-même," protests this use of his work. While he acknowledges that, at the time, the purely plastic qualities of passages of Abel Gance's La Roue (1922), Dudley Murphy and Fernand Léger's Ballet Mécanique (1923-24), and the absolute films of Viking Eggeling were products of genuine inspiration, they no longer represented the path of artistic advance for the cinema. The central objective of Epstein's essay is instead to celebrate the possibilities of the camera lens as an "inhuman eye, without memory, without thought," capable of "escaping the tyrannical egocentrism of our personal vision," thus also relegating the subjective cinema, until then predominant among the avant-garde, to obsolescence.[3]

That Porte associates Epstein with a cinema of plastic deformation is largely a function of the renown of Epstein's 1923 film, Cœur fidèle.[4] Upon its release, the film created a sensation in the press. Some writers criticized its scenario as *merely* a melodrama. Likewise, L'Auxiliaire Financier finds it bizarre to have a film with no action, "that is to say, without interest, with a deplorable predilection to adapt cubism to the cinema."[5] According to Epstein's account, the mobility of the film wreaked havoc when it opened at the Omnia, a theater catering to a bourgeois audience accustomed to films more conventional in execution, prompting its removal from the program within two days.[6] But by 1926, Cœur fidèle was regarded as a classic achievement of the nascent art cinema; the film enjoyed pride of place in the repertoire of the Parisian ciné-clubs until the occupation. The prominent critic of painting, Waldemar George, for instance, describes Cœur fidèle as a melodrama reduced "to the state of an optical poem" by a masterful artist, "the sole poet of the screen of today."[7]

Most notable was its *fête foraine* sequence, in which a rhythmic accumulation of rhyming rotational motion culminates in the dizzying spectacle of the vantage point of a passenger on a carnival ride. In addition to its musical or poetic visual abstraction, the sequence is also among the most subtle and effective instances of the subjective cinema of the period. By placing the camera in the cart with the characters, this vertiginous phantom ride performs a powerful transposition of stasis and motion. The viewer's access to the male character, Petit-Paul, is neutralized by his paroxysms of glee and abandon. Edmond Van Daële's almost clownish physical performance in the role reflects Epstein's conception of the character as a distillation of "the rough force of man: brutal desire; human and animal, drunk and passionate like Dionysus."[8] But the close-up of the heroine, Marie, remains a stable and compelling anchor in shots that internally maintain a fixed relationship between her and the viewer. As the ride accelerates and the background becomes an amorphous rotational force, the viewer is equally subject to Marie's impotence and immobility in the face of utterly disorienting circumstances. The powerful construction of identification with Marie is underscored when, just after the sequence ends and her fate as Petit-Paul's possession is sealed, she engages the viewer by looking directly and plaintively into the camera (Fig. 1).

Fig. 1: Marie's direct look in Cœur Fidèle

As Epstein continues extricating himself from a subjective cinema of pure visual abstraction in "L'Objectif lui-même," he addresses the unavoidable issue of the *fête foraine* sequence:

> In *Cœur fidèle* the turns of sleight-of-hand of the *fête foraine* have very much un-balanced the way I would wish that the film be understood. [...] If this abstract cinema enchants some, let them buy a kaleidoscope, a toy for a second child-hood, in which a very simple device can give a speed of rotation, regular and variable at will. As for me, I believe that the age of the cinema-kaleidoscope has passed.[9]

Epstein here seems to equate the idea of the kaleidoscope with mere visual ab-straction in order to dismiss such formal exploration as antiquated child's play, a trick akin to sleight-of-hand. In doing so, however, he elides the importance of the kaleidoscope in his thinking of the early 1920s. The operation of the device is analogous to the model of subjectivity and its relation to language that shapes his work at this time. Indeed, in his 1921 book, *La Poésie d'aujourd'hui: Un nouvel état d'intelligence*, Epstein claims that modern poetry and cinema display an "aesthetic of the kaleidoscope."[10] *Cœur fidèle* may be read as illustrative of this aesthetic, but less for its groundbreaking visual abstraction than for its subversion of conven-tional forms.

Both Epstein and his sister Marie recount that the scenario for *Cœur fidèle*, a formulaic melodrama whose execution rubs against the grain of the formula, was written in the course of a single, feverish night, but that the photogenic possibi-lities of a drama set in a *fête foraine* had preoccupied Epstein for quite some time. In his 1921 essay, "Magnification," for instance, he writes:

> I yearn for a drama aboard a merry-go-round, or more modern still, on air-planes. The fair below and its surroundings would be progressively con-founded. Centrifuged in this way, and adding vertigo and rotation to it, the tragedy would increase its photogenic quality ten-fold.[11]

Marie Epstein writes that in 1920 he submitted a scenario for a project called *Week-End*, which was set in a fair, to a competition, and that when finally given the opportunity to direct a film on his own, *Pasteur* (1922), he was disappointed that there was not a feasible means by which to depict Louis Pasteur on a carnival ride.[12] *Pasteur*, however, finds other means of exploring the capacity of the me-dium to transform the viewer's perspective, both through what Epstein later deemed an excessive reliance upon the bird's-eye-view,[13] and through a pervasive investigation of the evocative hybrid worlds created by reflections in the curved glass – an on-screen analogue of the camera's lens – of Pasteur's scientific appa-ratus.[14]

It is likely that the idea for the *fête foraine* sequence was developed in conversations with the painters Pierre Deval and Fernand Léger. In early 1921, while still in Lyon pursuing a medical degree, Epstein founded a short-lived cultural review called *Promenoir*, whose first two issues featured his meditation on the close-up, "Magnification." Deval also contributed an essay on the close-up to *Promenoir*, "Agrandissement," which demonstrates the depth of the integration of both the fairground and the close-up into the larger avant-garde conversation. Parroting Epstein, Deval claims that cinema, by virtue of its close-ups in space and in time – slow-motion photography – is "more amorous sentiment than art." He quotes André Breton who, in the context of a preface to a Max Ernst exhibition, emphasizes the capacity of slow- and accelerated-motion photography to render the ordinary marvelous and to transform visual perception. Finally, Deval draws a parallel between the close-up and the riot of color in the posters, paintings, and painted sculptures of fairground attractions, citing the enthusiasm of Pablo Picasso, André Derain, and Léger for this kind of popular imagery. He concludes: "Fairs and the cinema, and the magnification that is in them both – there is the modern, fecund and full."[15]

Léger's contribution to *Promenoir*, "La Couleur dans la vie (Fragment d'une étude sur les valeurs plastiques nouvelles)," is distinctive among his other writings in that it bears in tone some resemblance to the staccato rhythm of the simultaneist prose poems of Blaise Cendrars celebrated by Epstein. It begins: "Action and influence of new visual phenomena – conscious and unconscious." Its third paragraph proposes a consideration of a *fête foraine*.

> To conceive the popular fête in all its brilliance, to save it from current decadence. To conceive it on the scale of surprise, by the magnification of employed values. To admit the floats, follies or grotesques, to 'enormify' the volume and the color to 100%, higher than the houses. To outshine the gray and lifeless houses. To erupt like the unexpected thing. To invent an enormous and new object, expressing the opposite of all the average and habitual measures in which one lives. Violent and aggressive object, tragic in the grossest popular taste, contrary to gray and nuanced, dreary and faded bourgeois taste.[16]

This directive is fully in keeping with Léger's notion of a "realism of conception," developed in his critical writings of the 1910s. According to Léger, the art relevant to a modern environment marked by visual rupture, fragmentation and hyperstimulation demands a pictorial practice that orders line, volume, and color according to a structural principle of maximum contrast, with the aim of offending the bourgeois taste for a tasteful tone-on-tone decorative concept and a sentimental narrative. Ten years before *Ballet Mécanique*, Léger writes that "the screen of any cinema" intensely captures this mode of realism.[17]

The eruption of mobility, magnification, and plastic deformation in the *fête foraine* sequence of *Coeur fidèle*, housed within the framing device of the melodramatic formula, which Epstein describes as "sub-literature" pandering to the taste of "a people of vulgar organisms," fulfills Léger's prescription.[18] Indeed, of this sequence, among others, Léger writes, "It is plasticity, it is the image alone that acts on the spectator, and he submits to it, is moved, and conquered. It is a beautiful victory...."[19] But although the rapid editing, tight framing, and pervasive rotational motion serve to fragment and abstract images as the mirrors in a kaleidoscope do, it is the ironically-employed word *amour* iced onto a chocolate pig in a graceful looping gesture as the sequence winds down that is more relevant to the aspects of the aesthetic of the kaleidoscope that are at issue in this discussion.

The image in a kaleidoscope is largely a function of the relationships between the objects of vision, as created by the device which itself remains invisible, rather than a function of properties inherent in the objects themselves. It is only with the operation of the device, and the unsettling of fixed relationships, that the principle governing the image becomes discernable. For Epstein, the underlying principle that governs both love and aesthetic effect is the operation of the subconscious, which can only be perceived askance. Thus, an aesthetic of the kaleidoscope requires constant mobility. This is not a question of the literal mobility of the *fête foraine* sequence, however, but rather one of establishing friction between a rationally governed representation – the lifeless house of a word, or the melodramatic form – and its meaning.

As Epstein describes it in *La Poésie d'aujourd'hui* (1921), the melodramatic formula is comprised of a logical progression toward a just dénouement for characters clearly delineated by their moral stature. In privileging logic, morality, justice, the institution of marriage, and the sentimental, the melodrama reiterates each of the hackneyed, artificial forms in which subconscious sentiment generally is contained. The function of all literature for Epstein is to serve as a cathartic device when the flood of sentiment emerging from subconscious memory – as physiological a phenomenon as a glandular secretion – exceeds the capacity of one's available object of desire to embody it. The melodrama provides a tidy and hygienic effigy. In short, it is the perfect foil to more elevated modes of literature, in that it privileges many of the rational structures that, to Epstein, modern poetry disrupts.

The scenario for *Cœur fidèle* is a rather spare document of less than three pages. What little specification it provides conforms rather closely to the melodramatic formula.[20] Marie, an orphaned young woman, suffers the desire of the thug Petit-Paul to whom she has been promised by her indifferent adoptive parents. When Petit-Paul learns that he is under surveillance by the police – a motivation that is only scantily suggested in the actual film – he seizes the opportunity to spirit her away to the *fête foraine*, which to him is tantamount to a wedding and its subsequent consummation of his desire. Marie's true love, the honest dockworker Jean, is thwarted in his attempt at rescue and serves a year in prison for brawling with Petit-Paul, where he pines for her. Upon his release, he immediately seeks and finds her. Marie's oppressor is then vanquished by her neighbor, the little crippled girl who serves as the free-floating force of justice and good in the world by shooting Petit-Paul in both the head and the heart. Finally, Jean and Marie have unfettered access to the fair.

The epilogue of the film is a comment on this conventional structure, and the layers of cliché that factor into a formulaic marriage plot. It opens with a shot of exploding fireworks intercut with Jean and Marie on the carnival ride and an image of the crippled girl caring for Marie and Petit-Paul's infant child. After a final burst of fireworks, there is an intertitle that wryly alludes to the relationship of love to subconscious memory: "Love makes it possible to forget everything." Epstein had a collection of postcards marketed to sailors, and conceived of the passage that follows the intertitle as an allusion to this genre of popular imagery.[21] First, there is a superimposition of a pan over a bed of roses and a formal floral arrangement. The bed of roses fades out as another layer of the image irises in on a close-up of the two lovers. Then, the floral arrangement fades to the image in a rotating kaleidoscope, which fades to hand-written words. The image of the couple irises out, and the last image of the film is a single exposure of the words "for ever."

Note the role-reversal in the film's two episodes on the carnival ride. In the dénouement of *Cœur fidèle*, justice and the freedom to love without obstacle have done nothing to dispel the mood of deflated and impotent dissatisfaction that has pervaded Jean's mien throughout the film. His emotional base remains constant, but with the turn of events, relationships have shifted, dislodging the one-dimensional roles from their inhabitants, and now it is Jean who appears to be in need of escape from a makeshift marriage (Figs. 2 and 3).

There are numerous occurrences of an ironic take on true and lasting love in *Cœur fidèle*. When Jean is released from prison, he does not immediately go in search of Marie, as the scenario would suggest. In fact, his first stop is for a drink in a bar, where in fumbling in his pocket for a match, Jean inadvertently discards her photograph on the floor for a fellow patron to retrieve once he has left. The intertitle at this moment reads "*Cœur fidèle*...." Next, in a mockery of the melodramatic trope of a relentless pursuit of the beloved, there is a leisurely depiction of Jean's search for employment over the course of several days.

That they meet again at all is entirely an accident. When Jean encounters Marie outside a charity hospital, the presence of her infant prevents him from identifying himself; instead he follows her home. But even in finding Marie trapped in misery and desperation, living in a garret room with Petit-Paul, Jean is unable to act in any but the most token way: he gives her pocket money to purchase medicine for the child.

Figs. 2 & 3: Shifting relationships in Cœur Fidèle

Driven away from Marie's room by the imminent arrival of an intoxicated Petit-Paul, Jean visits another bar, where he has an encounter with the woman of the port, whose mischievous gossip and morally suspect mobility provoke most of the confrontations in the film. She lends a sympathetic ear and hand as the camera cuts in to signify a growing intimacy. And then, superimposed over a close-up of Jean, there is a slow pan from a distorted close-up of the woman of the port to one of Marie, a slippery substitution. This subjective moment in the midst of their conversation seems to indicate the ease with which either woman could occupy the position of the object of desire. Jean relaxes into comfort in the presence of the wrong woman, resting his head on her shoulder as she tenderly kisses his forehead. But then the camera cuts out as he catches himself doing so, a development shown through a series of gestures whose artifice is underscored by the shadow of his hands cast on the wall. This moment is a wry demonstration of the redirection of a surge of accidental sentiment toward the object rationally determined as appropriate.

> At its simplest, the accident of love reduces itself to its gestures. Civilization has infiltrated everything; it has transformed, multiplied, perfected everything, everything except the amorous accident which remained barbarous, natural, sincere![22]

Recoiling from his own faithlessness, Jean reluctantly returns to Marie and, one agonizing step at a time up the stairs to her room, to form.

The words 'for ever' hang over *Cœur fidèle* like a reproach, both in the form of graffiti on the wall of the bar where Marie works, and non-diegetically as in the epilogue (Fig. 4). That they are in English and thus defamiliarized is important; Epstein is deliberately putting space between the words and their significance. This is in emulation of the modern poets he praises for destabilizing stale relationships between words and their denotative meaning while privileging the acrobatic associations that may be engendered when words become sounds, symbols, or intellectual games. Embedded within 'for ever', for instance, is a scathing pun; pronounced in French it becomes 'faux rêvé' [false dream].[23] In *Cœur fidèle*, Jean's dejection about the rewards of a successful reunion is a demonstration of the inherent danger of cleaving too closely to this false ideal.

The heart shape as a sign for love ossified into predetermined conventional forms serves a similar function in the film. Jean and Marie believe that a heart-shaped chalk mark on a wall by the docks functions as intimate communication, but its inherent universal legibility belies this misconception. The woman of the port reads the sign, and, as is her wont, amuses herself by thwarting these machinations toward the morally-appropriate union. She uses the information to incite a murderous rage in Petit-Paul, whose passion, according to the scenario, is "violent, odious, but sincere," thus provoking the violence that ends the film.[24] The

Fig. 4: "For Ever" as Graffiti in Cœur Fidèle

heart shape also appears at the moment in the film when Petit-Paul is coercing Marie to join him at the fair while Jean waits in vain for her on the dock. Jean sees a woman approaching at a distance, and lets himself believe that it is Marie. At this moment there is a close-up of Jean framed by a heart-shaped mask. But as she approaches, it becomes clear that she is just another itinerant woman and not Marie. Jean, inhibited by the form, forgoes the opportunity.

For Epstein, love and aesthetic pleasure are both general sentiments that reside in subconscious memory, periodically erupting through the threshold of consciousness in search of an object. Each is an emotional reflex, and being a reflex is "irrational, unreflective, and irresistible."[25] Indeed, given that for Epstein the subconscious operates according to a kaleidoscopic logic of contiguity and similitude – that is to say, of magic – they are virtually interchangeable.

Epstein makes this claim about the magical structure of the subconscious in a 1922 volume of philosophical speculations, *La Lyrosophie*, a companion piece to *La Poésie d'aujourd'hui*.

> Sentimental knowledge develops through contiguities and similitudes. And if in this development one sees ellipses, gaps, slips of the tongue, digressions, chaos, it is erroneous to name them as such, what would be ellipses, gaps, etc. in the rational continuity....[26]

Whereas the logic of the continuity of reason is a linear one of cause and effect that may be deduced, in the grammar or logic (neither word comfortably applies, although Epstein uses them both) that determines associations of sentiment, causes are created to the measure of effect. This mode of determinism, which to Epstein is one of the laws of memory, has two facets. On the one hand, connections are made between sentiments that come into contact by having been experienced in direct temporal contiguity, enabling substitutions that engender fresh metaphors. The other mode of subconscious association is homeopathic and metonymic; when a magician throws water at the sky expecting rain, it is a futile attempt to externalize this logic. In both cases, the associations made are subjective and entirely subject to chance.

In "Freud ou le Nick-Cartérianisme en psychologie," an essay that purports to refute the very basis of Sigmund Freud's at the time sensational psychoanalytic method, Epstein takes this magical structure of the subconscious as a given.[27] His claim is that Freud's method and that of the magician share the same fallacy: that psychic determinism is identical in form to the logical determinism that governs cause and effect in the external world. Thus in applying deductive reasoning to psychic research and denying the fundamentally elusive nature of subconscious motivations and association, psychoanalysis is therapeutically ineffective and even deleterious. What Freud misses, according to Epstein, is that which is grasped by the narrator critiquing phrenology in Edgar Allan Poe's "The Imp of the Perverse": "Induction, a posteriori, would have brought phrenology to admit, as an innate and primitive principle of human action, a paradoxical something, which we may call perverseness, for want of a more characteristic term."[28] Psychoanalysis is entertaining, however, Epstein admits, which is perhaps why he associates the method with the popular detective characters Nick Carter and Sherlock Holmes.

La Lyrosophie is Epstein's most expansive description of the transformation of subjectivity in modernity. In Epstein's view, the general intellectual fatigue – understood as a biological or chemical phenomenon – that follows from the speed of modern life and its concomitant increase in the speed of thought, contributes to the general development of a more complete mode of apprehension of the world, lyrosophy. In the lyrosophical mode, intellectual fatigue has created lapses in conscious attention, which allows the subconscious to flood consciousness with emotion, and possibly stimulate a revelatory analogy structured according to a magical logic of contiguity and similitude. That Newton being struck on the nose sparked the discovery of universal gravitation is one such revelatory analogy.[29]

Epstein adopts the metaphor of the two faces of a coin to explain how, together, conscious and subconscious knowledge transform distinct two-dimensional views into one coherent three-dimensional aspect.[30] And yes, sentiment – that is to say, love – is for Epstein a form of knowledge, one that provides a truth that is closer to the object than the truth provided by reason. Whereas the rational procedures of science seek truth, and do provide general data that may be shared among observers, scientific truth is:

a function of the future, that is to say, a function of hope, a function of senti-ment. [...] Truth, outside of science, is a sentiment. [...] The state of love, on the contrary, does not seek the truth. It contains it. [...] In general, it does not call the truth, truth, only certitude. Love is sure of itself.[31]

In transforming the concept of truth into that of certitude, Epstein shifts its locus from the object to the subject. One may have conviction in, say, the beauty of a woman, but that beauty is not a property of the woman. It is projected upon her as the general sentiment of love emerges from the undifferentiated soup of sub-conscious memory and overpowers the idea of this particular woman.

Beauty is a thing in itself, that is to say, in us. It can be projected on almost any object or person who, immediately, will become beautiful. Everything depends on the quality, the force of our subconscious....[32]

But that it is projected makes the beauty of the woman no less true.

Epstein incorporates into *Cœur fidèle* the idea that love is a projected subcon-scious sentiment in the sequences in which Jean waits for Marie by the docks. There are long passages in which close-ups of Jean are intercut with superimposi-tions of shots panning past Marie's face and the surface of the water. In 1924, Epstein explained the quasi-Kuleshov effect of this passage to Porte as evocative of both memory and a flood of emotion:

For Jean, the sea evokes the memory of the rendezvous, every evening, on the jetty, with Marie. [...] And the poetry, the sweetness of this vision of sea and sun, drowns the close-up of Mathot in a melancholy [...] that it would not have without that, believe me![33]

Although he does not explicitly associate the sea with the subconscious in this conversation, Epstein's writings during this period are pervaded by such meta-phors as to describe reason as an îlot in *la mer subconscient*.

The idea of love as projection is also a central theme of Epstein's *La Glace à trois faces* (1927). In this film, three very different women each see their own desires and fears embodied by the unnamed leading man, played by René Ferté, whose demeanor oscillates between frivolity and a deadpan dispassionate elegance – bearing a striking resemblance in this respect to Buster Keaton – that accommo-dates such diverse projections. Pearl, a wealthy society woman surrounded by suitors and dripping with jewels, considers him to be "a man of extraordinary strength, calm and tyrannical." To Athalia, the worldly sculptor, he is infantilized, an enervated exotic plaything on a par with her pet monkey. And finally, to the young seamstress Lucie, whose pinpricked fingertips and insecurity about the position of her pinkie while holding a teacup bespeak a difference in class, he is a sophisticate beyond her reach. Each woman imagines herself to be very much in love, but the lover is actually just a mirror who reflects and deflects the women's desire.

The central conceit of this essay is that the kaleidoscope is analogous to Epstein's notion of the subconscious, in that substitutions and associations are motivated according to a magical logic of contiguity and similitude, and that the structural principle of the ensuing patterns may only be intuited through ongoing substitution via the rotational motion of the device. Thus far, the focus largely has been the extent to which *Cœur fidèle* and *La Glace à trois faces* engage the idea that love is an arbitrary projection of subconscious overspill – the product of a fatigued consciousness – onto an object whose attraction is more a product of that which is projected than a property of the object itself. But the idea that the beautiful is more a mirror than a property is crucial to Epstein's take on poetic effect as well.

> Poetry in general appears to me impossible without the intense and particular participation of the subconscious. This enormous speed of thought, this rapid comprehension of metaphorical analogies, this unique perspective of the intellectual plane, this succession of image-details make poetry, because they engage the life of the subconscious and set spinning this top of a hundred mirrors.[34]

Given that both love and aesthetic pleasure are functions of subconscious sentiment, the dynamic that these films represent applies equally to the experience of *photogénie*.

Indeed, Epstein is explicit about the extent to which sentimental conviction is the foundation of his claim that cinematic representation animates what is represented. Consider his explanation of how cinema provides an experience of 'knowledge through love':

> ...on the screen you see what is not there and cannot be there. You see this unreality more specifically, sentimentally, with all the precision of real life. The film shows you a man who betrays. You know perfectly well first that there is no man, then that there is no traitor. But the film addresses itself to your always aroused 'knowledge through love'. It created, by the phantom of a thing, a sentiment, and as this sentiment cannot live without the thing for which it is made living, and as this sentiment also tends above all to conserve its life in it, the fallacious thing will live for you. Or rather a sentiment-thing

will live, and you will believe better than in a traitor: you will believe in a betrayal.[35]

That it is the betrayal rather than that particular traitor that is animated by sentimental conviction is what Epstein means when he says that cinema generalizes.[36] And yet, given that this nexus of sentimental associations underlying the general concept of betrayal is essentially private, as well as contingent upon the unique self created by the subconscious, this particular fallacious thing lives in this way only for you.

These are indeed strange arguments. Itself lyrosophical, La Lyrosophie has a kaleidoscopic rhetorical structure. That is to say, it progresses via a mobile logic of contiguity and similitude. What to Epstein are instantiations of reason and the subconscious, respectively, are treated as if interchangeable. That is to say, *that is to say*. Often, what turns the kaleidoscope is the expression *c'est-à-dire*, employed without full elaboration of reasoning to connect one term to the other. The manifestations of reason are: the sentimental, otherwise described as a pale intellectual reflection of genuine sentiment; the alexandrine in poetry; the scientific method; grammar; a word's denotation; any and all human institutions such as marriage; morality in general; deductive logic; and, by virtue of its sentimentality and logical structure, the melodramatic form. The subconscious, on the other hand, has domain over: sentiment; the aesthetic; the poetic; the sexual drive to perpetuate the species and of which all human endeavor is a sublimation; love and all other emotions; religious feeling; truth; and the ineffable.

As another example of how a kaleidoscopic mode of argument operates, let us consider how Epstein approaches the idea of scientific evidence. Were the evidence upon which all scientific knowledge rests to require an argument to support it, it would no longer be the absolute foundation. Thus it is ineffable; thus evidence too is sentiment; thus it is a product of the subconscious. Anything at all that is ineffable is subconscious; and anything that is subconscious is ineffable. Thus science, despite claims to objectivity and centuries of an increasingly futile effort to suppress and exile sentiment, is lyrosophical.[37]

Epstein first became interested in the question of the relationship of the subconscious to artistic creation and aesthetic response when the works of Remy de Gourmont captured his imagination and enthusiasm in the late 1910s. Like Gourmont, Epstein considered physiology crucial to an understanding of artistic creation. Similarly, they both related the aesthetic to the sexual drive. Epstein quotes Gourmont on this point in La Poésie d'aujourd'hui: "The aesthetic emotion, in its purest, most disinterested form, is thus only a derivation of the genital emotion."[38] In addition, Gourmont's project of the dissociation of ideas that had become reified as immutable truths – words or concepts encrusted with stale emotional associations – was one that Epstein emulated at least until the 1940s. But the most important affinity in this context is Gourmont's conviction that the subconscious is the source of inspiration. Rational consciousness may only collaborate in creative thought and artistic endeavor, as it serves a fundamentally critical, and in Epstein's case, homogenizing, function.

For scientific justification of the notion of the subconscious as the seat of the aesthetic, Epstein relies largely upon evidence provided by the Polish experimental psychologist, Edouard Abramowski, whose findings appeared in French in *Le Subconscient normal* in 1914.[39] In this work, Abramowski seeks to demonstrate experimentally a comprehensive theory of memory. That the subconscious is the domain of sentiment and the aesthetic, both ineffable, is a central tenet. It is Abramowski's view that when fatigued or distracted, what is perceived but not intellectually elaborated into conscious verbal or mental representation is still stored in the subconscious as generic sentiments that function as affective potential. The process of forgetting an intellectually elaborated perception undergoes a reduction to undifferentiated affect and is similarly stored.

This amalgam of the forgotten and the passively perceived, stored in the form of generic sentiments, constitutes the continuity of the self, one's *coenesthésie*. Simultaneously spiritual and physiological, this baseline determines an individual's particular mode of subconscious association, the shape of one's imp of the perverse, as it were. Epstein adopts the term in *La Lyrosophie*, quoting Abramowski's definition of '*individualité cénesthésique*: "the sentiment of ourselves, that conserves its unity and continuity despite all the variations in the conditions of life, health, and thought; it's the profound base of our character and our temperament...."[40] In *Coeur fidèle*, Jean's emotional consistency regardless of circumstance is a reflection of the dominance of his *coenesthésie*; the logic of cause and effect bears no relationship to his emotional response.

Abramowski's research protocol was designed to access the subconscious by separating subconscious memoration and recognition from the processes of memory that involve intellectual elaboration into words or mental images akin to pictures. For instance, each of his experiments included the variable of induced mental distraction and fatigue, usually in the form of the subject's simultaneous absorption in mentally calculating sums. He also utilized alcohol and such gambits as unexpected loud noises to this effect. For his first experiment, concerning recognition, Abramowski designed the image to be perceived by the test subject – the rather valiant Mme. M – to resemble the images in a kaleidoscope, specifically because this resists verbal representation: "They were arabesques of different colors and forms, difficult to retain in words and to classify."[41] What he claims to demonstrate with this exercise supports Epstein's thinking about sentimental certitude. Recognition, and by implication, memory in general, is found to have a dual structure. First, there is an instantaneous surge of certitude from the subconscious that takes the form of a sentiment, in this case, of familiarity. This 'primitive fact' is the essence or 'central kernel' of the recognition and "cannot be described in representative terms" such as words or mental pictures.[42] The surge of certitude is followed by a gradual intellectual elaboration into a conscious memory that is subject to doubt (Fig. 5).[43]

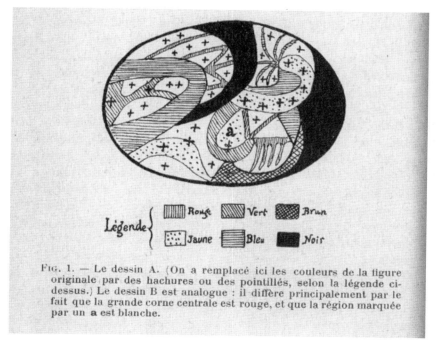

Fig. 1. — Le dessin A. (On a remplacé ici les couleurs de la figure originale par des hachures ou des pointillés, selon la légende ci-dessus.) Le dessin B est analogue : il diffère principalement par le fait que la grande corne centrale est rouge, et que la région marquée par un a est blanche.

Fig. 5: Abramowski's Sentimental and Intellectual Recognition

Another series of experiments concerned the relationship of language to distraction and mental fatigue. In the first, for instance, Abramowski had the subjects read aloud from a series of fifty words flashed in two-second intervals. The subjects then were instructed to write down all of the words that they had retained. The conclusion drawn from these exercises is that a major factor in the recollection of a word, particularly one perceived in a state of distraction, is "the influence of the affective tone of the word, of its symbolic value. The evocation provides the depth, not the surface of the word...."[44] In an exercise designed to induce a dysgnosie [dysgnosia], or a sentiment of étrangeté [the uncanny], Abramowski had a series of young women (and one man) focus all of their concentration on the word 'fly' for what to them was an indeterminate amount of time, but turned out to be approximately five minutes. Several temporarily lost the ability to associate the word with a mental image of a fly, and thus Abramowski concludes that étrangeté is a perception in which the object is separated from its representation as a result of a fatigue-induced inability to concentrate. Clearly, these experiments provided Epstein with what he took to be experimental verification of the central hypothesis of his poetry criticism, that a chronic intellectual fatigue and the attendant hyperactivity of the subconscious was indeed the catalyst for the transformation of language in modern poetry.

The specific experiment that Epstein cites most frequently is the one in which Abramowski establishes that "the aesthetic element is found in the generic sentiments of the forgotten."[45] According to Abramowski's reasoning, this is because the memory of an object is more beautiful than the perception of it. The experiment proceeded as follows: subjects were instructed to learn 'by heart' a series of seven reproductions of prints by prominent pre-modernist artists while subject to variable degrees and kinds of distraction. The subjects produced verbal descriptions of the images immediately and then eight days later. Twenty-five or fifty days later, the subjects compared their memories – at this point presumed to be largely subconscious – to the actual images. Abramowski found that in at least half of the cases, subjects were surprised to discover that they had misremembered the spatial relations of an image, exaggerating the scale of the space, the perspective, and the sky. He attributes this to lacunae in the intellectually elaborated memory image; the excess space corresponds to the details of the image that are presumed to have been forgotten, or otherwise directly absorbed into the subconscious. The other common surprise that emerged when the subjects compared their memories to the reproductions was that, in a majority of cases, subjects found that the image was not as beautiful as their memory of it. François Boucher's *La Cage* (1763) most frequently produced this result – eight out of twelve times. Abramowski attributes this to the unexpected interruptions and irritating electrical sound that distracted subjects from fully intellectualizing their mental image while initially viewing the print. The remaining pictorial details bypassed this process, he claims, and because they were passively received they became associated with the subconscious sentiment of aesthetic pleasure.

Abramowski is particularly interested in paramnesia – the appearance in consciousness of either the forgotten, or perceptions that had never been intellectually elaborated in the first place. He makes the claim, and claims to demonstrate, that art is an instance of paramnesia. "The unique problem and goal [of art, and religion for that matter] is the *rememoration of the forgotten*, the search for complete representations that correspond to these generic sentiments ... under the threshold of consciousness."[46] But given that, for Abramowski, both language and representational images are in the domain of conscious intellectual elaboration, there remains a bedeviling quandary. As Abramowski puts it,

the artist never expresses all that he possesses in memory. There always remains an *irreducible* part that despite all his efforts to translate it into representative expressions, remains in the state of generic sentiment of the forgotten. This part, it is 'beauty' itself.[47]

KATIE KIRTLAND

The artist must somehow transmit this irreducible facet of the memory to her audience by evoking in them a sentiment that is equally real, and equally resistant to representation. Abramowski does pepper his study with critical discussions of poetry, mainly to claim that a succession of poetic images provokes an emotional fusion that is analogous to the emotional tint that one's *coenesthésie* casts upon every lived event.[48] But he leaves the practical solution of the artist's problem to the aesthetes, artfully evading the question of whether or not he himself is a Symbolist.

Epstein articulates the quandary that poetic effect is a function of the evocation of that which cannot be represented by an intellectually elaborated form, in terms similar to, although perhaps more poetic than, Abramowski's:

> Because it is in the moment when the most precious words would be pronounced that words may fail. That in the force of emotion the poet finally comes to have nothing more to say, constitutes poetry itself. The most subtle thoughts inscribe themselves on the illegible inverse of the most common words, and between the lines, as if with this ink called sympathetic [invisible ink], because, without a doubt, only ineffable sympathies can decipher it.[49]

As the means of inscribing thoughts in invisible ink on the inverse of words, Epstein proposes abrupt, disjunctive metaphors akin to Newton's apple. In the aesthetic of the kaleidoscope, the subconscious is projected onto the conscious intellectual plane. Through the ensuing simultaneity and disorder, such "monstrous analogies" – by virtue of their logic of contiguity and similitude – dislodge the word from its conventional significance. Whereas a single word, or an exhausted metaphor, is static and fixed in meaning, the collision of ideas in a fresh metaphor is a form of "comprehension in movement." Epstein envisions a kind of play with words – la *pensée-association* – that operates on a deeper level than their denotative meaning, oscillating between consciousness and subconsciousness: "Sometimes surge words whose signs bizarrely can be reduced to their sonority alone, to an inexplicable coloristic association."[50] The magical logic of the subconscious is the sole guide motivating these associations.

The attempt to formulate a definition of *photogénie* is always a perilous undertaking. Indeed, if an aesthetic response to the screen involves evoking the viewer's projection of subconscious sentiment onto it, *photogénie* is, by definition, resistant to formulation in words. Epstein's remarks on the subject are descriptions, not definitions, of the photogenic. But it is remarkable how closely these scattershot descriptions correspond to what to Epstein are the "stigmata of the subconscious": "Suddenness of its apparition, immediate perfection, sentimental halo, affective aspect, apparent indetermination as to its causes."[51] Abramowski believed himself to have circumvented the process of intellectual elaboration through induced distraction and fatigue, and thus to have discerned the operation of the subconscious. According to Epstein, poets are able to express the inexpressible through monstrous analogies that destabilize language. But how, as a practical matter, did Epstein as a filmmaker during this period encourage the accident of *photogénie*?

That mobility on the screen creates conditions conducive to *photogénie* goes without saying. It is important to note, however, that particular modes of mobility should not become reliable tricks, or a style template. "Like contemporary literature, the film accelerates via unstable metamorphoses. [...] The film borrows [from fashionable clothing] certain charms, and such a faithful image of our infatuations, aged five years, remains suitable only for the lantern of the fairground."[52] To Epstein, the aesthetic effect of cinema is subject to the modernist logic, first and best articulated by Baudelaire, in which novelty and beauty are inextricably combined.

Given the temporality of *photogénie*, that it is an incidental eruption in the midst of what is generally a narrative medium, the circumvention of intellectual elaboration is only possible in fragments. Thus such moments must be housed in a form. They may even be housed in an ossified form, such as the melodrama, of course, but in such a way that acknowledges and disrupts its status as form. This is clearly the compositional strategy of *Cœur fidèle*. *La Glace à trois faces* also disrupts conventional narrative exposition in that each of the three initial episodes is narrated by a different woman, and that in each, the same thing – almost nothing – happens: the character and milieu of the relationship is clearly articulated from the woman's perspective, and then the gentleman caller sends the woman a dismissive note and drives away. There is a general suggestion that the episodes are narrations of the past, but this remains ambiguous, and there are no markers whatsoever to establish temporal relations between the episodes. Indeed, they feel simultaneous. It is only in the final episode – effectively an epilogue – that there is an actual event, the accidental encounter when the bird and the reckless driver disastrously collide.

As a director of silent film actors, Epstein developed a novel strategy that corresponds to the idea that the language of cinema should be exclusively visual. In an interview with Musidora conducted for the Cinémathèque Française in 1946, Gina Manès, who plays Marie in *Cœur fidèle*, recounts that in order to minimize the mouthing of words on the screen, Epstein would direct his actors to condense their lines: "Thus, for example, when one had to say 'Good day, madame, I am pleased to see you,' he told us to say 'day madame pleased see you.'"[53] With similar effect, in editing a sequence depicting a spoken line, Epstein would cut at the moment when the actor began to speak, insert the intertitle, which most likely had been designed as much for its visual properties as for its words, and then cut back to the actor just as the line was completed. "Thus the actor retained his natural expression and this prevented the flapping of useless jaws."[54] The effect of this editing strategy is that interpersonal encounters, whether confrontational or amorous, are structured as a series of close-ups, thus enhancing the emotional intensity and photogenic potential.

Concomitantly, Epstein shaped his filmmaking practice in order to enable chance, subconscious intuition, and improvisation to guide the execution of the film. This involved an attempt to bypass as much as possible the formulation of its visual aspects into words prior to shooting.

> There is a kind of thought through action that precedes conscious thought. One makes a thing and then after thinks that one made it because one was called by the will to achieve it. This could be a perfect psychological illusion and one could very well make things entirely by chance....[55]

That the scenario for *Cœur fidèle* was spare and sparingly followed has already been mentioned. In a 1950 interview, Epstein tells Henri Langlois that he only prepared detailed shooting scripts when compelled by a producer to do so; apparently Alexander Kamenka of Films Albatros was particularly demanding in this regard. But after *La Belle Nivernaise* (1923), these were fictional documents. Instead, Epstein would spend the early morning hours of each day of shooting provisionally planning the day's work: ten to twelve shots.[56] In "Mon Frère Jean," Marie Epstein quotes her brother as he, in 1927, associates this attitude toward the shooting script with the idea of the limitations of language as a representational medium that shapes his poetry criticism:

> The shooting script must never be a shackle. Artistically, it is a mnemonic device. [...] All writing is too rigid, if one holds oneself to the letter, or too feeble, because it never contains enough spirit. One carries one's film secretly in the heart....[57]

That Epstein associates the practice of making a film with the revelation of a secret carried in the heart reiterates the connection between love and artistic creation in his thinking. Each involves the investment to the point of saturation of a form or an object with the particular cast of one's *coenesthésie*, the point of contact between one's subconscious and the world.

> Nothing can explain this continuity between love and the world. Love creates itself in an ineffable and secret manner, in creating the creature. Invisible, it renders itself visible; incomprehensible, it makes itself comprehensible; supernatural, it gives itself a nature.[58]

It is for this reason that in the early 1920s, Epstein claimed that cinema is essentially subjective as well as animistic. Like love, *photogénie* is less an expression than a manifestation of what is essentially inexpressible.

This essay begins by immediately following an epigraph in which, in 1946, Epstein defines a pure cinema as one that would dispense with words with his objection to being pigeonholed as an advocate of Pierre Porte's conception of a pure cinema of visual abstraction. The purity whose relationship to cinema interests Epstein is not a question of plastic deformation; although in the early 1920s he clearly believes that this may contribute to a film's photogenic potential. Rather it is one that inspires sentimental conviction through destabilizing ossified representational forms, effectively bypassing the rational relay between love and the world.

Notes

1. Jean Epstein, "Cinéma Pur?: Une Enquête aupres de l'Homme du Métier," *Forces Françaises*, no. 7 (November 1946), Fonds Jean et Marie Epstein, Bibliothèque du film, Paris, EPSTEIN241-B60 3/3. I hereafter refer to this archive as "Fonds Epstein."
2. Pierre Porte, "Pure Cinema" [1926], trans. Richard Abel, *Abel1*, p. 387.
3. Jean Epstein, "L'Objectif Lui-Même" [1926], *ESC1*, pp. 128-129.
4. My analysis of *Coeur fidèle* (1923) is based on the DVD issued by Pathé Classique in 2007. This version, a reproduction of the print in the Cinémathèque Française film archive, was subject to several cuts by censors and has some editing errors. For a list of the shots excised from the film, see "Renseignements Divers: Cœur fidèle" (transcript), Fonds Epstein, EPSTEIN80-B21 (1/2) 4/12. For a discussion of the editing problems, see Epstein's interview with Henri Langlois: "Jean Epstein: Réunion du 18 Mars 1950" (transcript), Fonds Commission de Recherche Historique, Bibliothèque du Film, Paris. CRH62-B3, pp. 4-5. I hereafter refer to this archive as "Fonds CRH."
5. "Coeur fidèle et l'Opinion de la Press," *Cinéa-Ciné pour tous*, no. 27 (December 15, 1924), p. 27.
6. "Jean Epstein: Interview [1946]" (transcript), Fonds CRH, CRH47-B2, pp. 7-8.
7. Waldemar George, "Accusation," *Les Arts à Paris* (November 1924), Fonds Epstein, EPSTEIN80-B21 1/12 (1/2).
8. Jean Epstein, "Presentation de 'Coeur fidèle'" [1924], *ESC1*, p. 124.
9. Epstein, "L'Objectif lui-même," *ESC1*, pp. 127-128.
10. Jean Epstein, *La Poésie d'aujourd'hui, un nouvel état de l'intelligence* (Paris: Editions de la Sirène, 1921), p. 139.
11. Jean Epstein, "Magnification" [1921], *Abel1*, p. 237.
12. Marie Epstein, "Mon frère Jean" (transcript), Fonds Epstein, EPSTEIN153-B35 4/4 13/14, p. 9.
13. Jean Epstein, "Les films de Jean Epstein vus par lui-même," in *ESC1*, p. 55.
14. "Jean Epstein: Réunion du 18 Mars 1950" (transcript), Fonds CRH, CRH62-B3, p. 6.
15. Pierre Deval, "Agrandissement," *Promenoir*, no. 6 (June 1922), pp. 14-16.
16. Fernand Léger, "La Couleur dans la vie (Fragment d'une étude sur les valeurs plastiques nouvelles)," *Promenoir*, no. 5 (n.d.), pp. 66-67.

17. Fernand Léger, "The Origins of Painting and Its Representational Value" [1913], in Léger, *Functions of Painting*, trans. Alexandra Anderson, ed. Edward F. Fry (New York: Viking Press, 1973), p. 9.
18. Epstein, *La Poésie d'aujourd'hui*, p. 5.
19. Léger, "The Spectacle: Light, Color, Moving Image, Object-Spectacle" [1924], in Léger, *Functions of Painting*, p. 44.
20. Epstein, "Scénario Cœur fidèle" (transcript), Fonds Epstein, EPSTEIN152-B34.
21. "Jean Epstein: Réunion du 18 Mars 1950" (transcript), Fonds CRH, CRH62-B3, p. 30.
22. Jean Epstein, "Amour Indigent (A propos des Don Juanes)," *La Revue Mondiale* CXLX, no. 18 (September 15, 1924), p. 177.
23. My thanks to Christophe Wall-Romana for noticing this pun.
24. Epstein, "Scénario Cœur fidèle" (transcript), Fonds Epstein, EPSTEIN152-B34.
25. Epstein, *La Poésie d'aujourd'hui*, p. 33.
26. Jean Epstein, *La Lyrosophie* (Paris: Editions de La Sirène, 1922), p. 47.
27. Jean Epstein, "Freud ou le Nick-Cartérianisme en psychologie," *L'Esprit nouveau*, no. 16 (May 1922): 1857-1864.
28. Edgar Allan Poe, "The Imp of the Perverse" [1850], in *Complete Stories and Poems of Edgar Allan Poe* (Garden City, NY: Doubleday and Company, Inc, 1966), p. 272.
29. Epstein, *La Poésie d'aujourd'hui*, p. 138.
30. Epstein, *La Lyrosophie*, p. 126.
31. Epstein, *La Lyrosophie*, pp. 42-43.
32. Epstein, *La Lyrosophie*, p. 63.
33. Pierre Porte, "Une Loi du cinéma," *Cinéa-Ciné pour tous*, no. 9 (March 15, 1924), p. 12.
34. Jean Epstein, "Le Phénomène Litteraire," part 4, *L'Esprit nouveau*, no. 13 (December 1921), p. 1433.
35. Epstein, *La Lyrosophie*, pp. 34-35.
36. Jean Epstein, "The Senses I (b)" [1921], *Abel1*, p. 243.
37. Epstein, *La Lyrosophie*, p. 18; infra, 282.
38. Remy de Gourmont, "Le succès et l'idée de beauté," in *Le Chemin de velours*, quoted in Epstein, *La Poésie d'aujourd'hui*, p. 32.
39. For a more in-depth analysis of the relationship of Epstein's early film and poetry criticism to Gourmont and Abramowski, see Stuart Liebman, *Jean Epstein's Early Film Theory, 1920-22* (PhD Dissertation, New York University, 1980).
40. Epstein, *La Lyrosophie*, pp. 56-77. The passage originally appears in Edouard Abramowski, *Le Subconscient normal* (Paris: Librairie Félix Alcan, 1914), p. 137. See also Epstein, *La Poésie d'aujourd'hui*, pp. 82-86, 154-157, 189, 209.
41. Abramowski, *Le Subconscient normal*, p. 8. Incidentally, the viewing device also resembled a kaleidoscope. Mme. M was instructed to look into a tube that had been fitted with a wheel upon which the images were attached. When the designated amount of time for each image had elapsed, the wheel was turned.
42. Abramowski, *Le Subconscient normal*, p. 22.
43. Abramowski, *Le Subconscient normal*, p. 20.
44. Abramowski, *Le Subconscient normal*, p. 71.
45. Abramowski, *Le Subconscient normal*, p. 318. Among other places, Epstein cites the experiment in *La Poésie d'aujourd'hui*, pp. 43-44.

46. Abramowski, *Le Subconscient normal*, p. 235.
47. Abramowski, *Le Subconscient normal*, p. 325.
48. Abramowski, *Le Subconscient normal*, pp. 416-417.
49. Jean Epstein, "Pourquoi j'ai tourné 'Pasteur'" [1923], ESC1, p. 114.
50. Epstein, *La Poésie d'aujourd'hui*, p. 101.
51. Epstein, *La Lyrosophie*, p. 205.
52. Epstein, *La Poésie d'aujourd'hui*, pp. 179-180.
53. "Gina Manès: Interview par Musidora [1946-8]" (transcript), Fonds CRH, CRH46-B2.
54. "Jean Epstein: Interview [1946]" (transcript), Fonds CRH, CRH47-B2, p. 6.
55. "Jean Epstein: Réunion du 18 Mars 1950" (transcript), Fonds CRH, CRH62-B3, p. 2.
56. Ibid., p. 20.
57. Marie Epstein, "Mon frère Jean" (transcript), Fonds Epstein, EPSTEIN153-B35, p. 7.
58. Epstein, "Amour Indigent," p. 177.

Distance is [Im]material:[1] Epstein Versus Etna

Jennifer Wild

> Then through the city, coursing in the lists,
> It travels, forming islands in its midst,
> Seeing that every creature will be fed
> And staining nature its flamboyant red.
> Charles Baudelaire, "The Fountain of Blood" (1857)

> – You didn't know that Etna woke up?
> – I don't know this gentleman and I don't give a damn about his awakening.
> Vincent Gédéon, "Les Opinions de Vincent Gédéon" (1923)

> What we used to call art begins at a distance of two meters from the body.
> Walter Benjamin, "Dream Kitsch" (1927)

In 1923, Jean Epstein traveled to the island of Sicily to film Mount Etna's latest eruption. Stuart Liebman's pioneering research on Epstein has confirmed that the resulting film produced by Pathé Consortium, La Montagne infidèle, is now lost.[2] Yet, the eponymous first chapter of Epstein's book, Le Cinématographe vu de l'Etna (1926), survives not only as one of the most evocative texts about an encounter with the live volcano. It also persists as one of the most powerful early texts on film aesthetics and technological mediation – the epicenter of the modern aesthetic experience according to Epstein.[3]

Throughout the "Etna" chapter, Epstein uses the classic convention of anthropomorphosis not unlike the humorist cited in the epigraph, but toward far more philosophic ends.[4] Etna is described first as a "great actor" whose molten incline later took on "an obstinate, human face."[5] The volcano's fullest human incarnation in the essay is also its most startling. It is followed by a phrase that continues to strike film scholars with its signifying force:

We felt ourselves to be in the presence of someone lying in wait for us. The laughter and the stunning cries of our eight mule-drivers quieted. We marched in the silence of a thought that was shared until I felt it before us like an eleventh, gigantic person. *I don't know if I can communicate the degree to which this, this is cinema, this personage of our preoccupation.*[6]

In this passage, Epstein neither posits a facile comparison of Etna to the cinema nor simply shifts to a cinematographic discourse; nor does he, in my view, describe this experience "as if he were in a film," as the phrase has been otherwise interpreted.[7] Rather, by equating the experience of the volcano's force at a distance with the cinema's signifying force that also occurs at a distance, Epstein begins to transform the classic Romantic paradigm of a solitary, sublime encounter with nature into a treatise on modern aesthetic experience.[8] He provides the initial parameters for what in modernism can be thought of as the technological sublime, and the role that distance – as well as proximity – plays in its experience.

Epstein's thought undeniably shares the intellectual and experiential topos of such (technological) visionaries as William Blake, Georg Simmel, Henri Bergson, and Edgar Allan Poe. There is a particularly striking correspondence between Epstein's and Walter Benjamin's influences insofar as both derive important strains of their thought from Jewish mysticism, modernist literature, and the cross-pollination of yet other disciplines.[9] Benjamin's concept of aura is especially pertinent to Epstein's modern technological sublime. Not only do both conceptualize distance and proximity as essential components of the epistemological and aesthetic transitions inherent in modernity, they conceive of the transitions themselves as primarily perceptual distinctions tied to the history (and historicity) of technology and its engagement with social and aesthetic experience.

While the Benjaminian aura is most frequently summarized as "[a] strange tissue of space and time: the unique apparition of a distance, however near it may be,"[10] Miriam Hansen has shown that the term possesses a far more complex history in Benjamin's thinking as it developed in and around the Munich Kosmiker circle and the writing of vitalist Ludwig Klages, in particular. Benjamin's aura is both "*medium* of perception" and a *method* used to "reimagine" classical and modern experiential structures.[11] However, Hansen suggests that by the time he formulates aura in "The Artwork in the Age of Its Technological Reproducibility," Benjamin had overlaid the concept with the Kantian notion of "beautiful semblance" such that distance and nearness become "spatiotemporal categories that define antithetical perceptual regimes."[12] While Hansen maintains that Benjamin nonetheless continues to invoke the (Goethean) sense of distance and nearness as a "polarity" rather than simply as an oppositional antinomy, she rightly observes that the term's deployment in the artwork essay constitutes a calculated – if necessary – political move of reduction.[13] It was only in this way that Benjamin could, at that moment, detail the conditions for *productive* and collective self-alienation in technological modernity by way of reception and innervation. While Benjamin detailed the power of particular films (by Chaplin, Mickey Mouse films) in this regard, cinematic reception generally would emerge thus as the modern collective experience *par excellence* capable of "detonating" the "otherwise destructive potential" of "distorted, mass-psychotic responses to modernization."[14]

The "Etna" essay is, in essence, a treatise similarly devoted to exploring productive self-alienation, and the role that proximity and distance play in the collective sphere of technological modernity. As the center of Epstein's encounter with the natural world in this essay, however, Etna has been considered more as a trope for his own "interior cinema" – one that frames the travel-narrative of his self-discovery – than as a radical figure in the evolution of his modern aesthetic theory. It follows that critics have heard Epstein's essay and its narrative purely in the Romantic key, and as foregrounding the sublime encounter with the volcanic as Kant did: "Consider [...] volcanoes with all their destructive power. [...] [W]e like to call these objects sublime because they raise the soul's fortitude above its usual middle range and allow us to discover in ourselves an ability to resist which is of a quite different kind...."[15]

In a similar vein, the essay's image of a *tempête* (tempest), a similarly violent yet more ephemeral natural phenomenon, has proven especially productive for scholarly reflection on this essay and Epstein's theory more generally: toward the essay's end, Epstein famously transposes his ascent toward the volcano's dynamic spectacle upon his equally disturbing descent within a mirror-lined, spiral staircase.[16] Indeed, the essay's sudden, tourbillon-like turn down the sloping staircase proves to be a crucial point in the essay whereupon Epstein confronts a deconstructed version of his body, himself. He writes:

> In the morning two days before, as I left the hotel for this trip, the elevator had been stopped since six-thirty between the third and fourth floors [...] To get down, I had to take the grand stairs, still without a handrail, where workers sang insults directed at Mussolini. This immense spiral meant vertigo. The whole shaft was lined with mirrors. I descended surrounded by my many selves, by reflections, by images of my gestures, by cinematographic projections. Each rotation caught me by surprise in a different angle. There are as many different and autonomous positions between a profile and a three-quarter view as there are tears from an eye. Each of these images lasted only an instant, no sooner glimpsed than lost from sight, already another [...] And there were images of images. Third images were born from second images. The algebra and descriptive geometry of gestures loomed [*apparaissaient*] [...] Looking at one and then another, I acquired another awareness of my relief.[17]

For some, this passage reveals the apex of Epstein's theory of film spectatorship and of cinema as an "epistemological machine" – a position that takes Epstein's language to be similar to the passive and "objective" work of the camera.[18] For others, it further anchors Epstein's place within the Romantic tradition[19] that, in the words of literary scholar Frances Ferguson, might be summarized in the following way: "The viewer creates a singular nature by seeing a face in the landscape; the landscape creates the singular viewer as the projection of its perspectival movement."[20]

Early on in La Lyrosophie from 1922, however, Epstein made it clear that his aim as a theorist was not simply to adumbrate the Romantic sensibility for his contemporary moment, but instead to formulate a revisionist stance toward it. In this ranging philosophical work of literary theory, he clearly positioned "science," or what should also be understood as technology, in relation to "sentiment," or what Epstein translates in this context as the Romantic inheritance:

> Romantics we are, that is to say sentimental [sentimentaux]; but we are also so reasonable that we inaugurate romanticism from reason and reason from romanticism, in what I call lyrosophy. Science begins thus a new, and perhaps last, phase of its history, and intelligence [begins] more of a metamorphosis in its life, a crisis, a molting.
>
> For more years to come, or even a dozen, the learned ones won't be able to take seriously this sort of threat and psychological cataclysm that I am anticipating. They will be able to ridicule them as visions [imaginations] and phantasmagoria. But, seriously, who doesn't know what science has always been?[21]

We learn here, and in La Lyrosophie more generally, that Epstein sought a fully modern approach to the categorization and description of the dialectical tensions within both modern literature and the subject's transitional epistemology in the face of technology. Nietzsche's philosophy played a central part in his efforts, although, as Chiara Tognolotti has pointed out, Epstein's sources were rarely direct but instead "vulgar" secondary texts that distilled Nietzsche's metaphorical richness, use of contradiction, and rejection of systematicity that greatly appealed to Epstein's rhetorical and stylistic sense as a writer and thinker.[22] A central distinction from Benjamin in this context, it should be pointed out, is Epstein's declarative interest in spiritualism and in experimental and parapsychological writing by figures such as Edouard Abramowski and, as I will explore in depth, Sir Walter Moore Coleman.[23] Whereas Benjamin resisted using aura for its connection to both theosophy and spiritualism, in La Lyrosophie and in later publications such as Etna, Epstein formulates key aspects of his counter-Romantic approach by liberally drawing from and in some cases re-transcribing the abstract postulates of experimental, spiritualist-infused psychology, alongside those drawn from scientific studies and technological history.[24]

When Epstein wrote "Etna" in 1926, he brought his literary-philosophical and spiritualist thinking to bear on what had become his central preoccupation by this time: the cinema. He also drew explicitly from late eighteenth and twentieth-century technologies to theorize his encounter with Etna's natural spectacle of violence and, more specifically, to move beyond an idealized account of nature that maintained distance as a paradigmatic measure of self-preservation and individuation in an encounter with the sublime. In Epstein's view, technology both mediates the experience of distance and overcomes it; it thereby provides him the tools with which to formulate the modern aesthetic encounter as "a reflexive relation to the modality of vision rather than to its contents," as Rosalind Krauss describes the essential if "fetishized" position of sight in the modernist paradigm.[25] Following Trond Lundemo's observation, Epstein's notion of the sublime is neither Kantian nor Burkean, but is instead "a *technology* that presents new material forms of space and time."[26]

In the opening paragraph of "Etna" we find the first technological metaphor that inaugurates Epstein's new theoretical approach to classic aesthetic problems and that signals his interest in formulating a revision of the classic sublime encounter insofar as it is conveyed by way of, or mediated by, modern technology:

> The fire spread (*se communiquait*) to the red corner of the sky. At a distance of twenty kilometers, the murmur was delivered in instants like a far away triumph, with thousands in applause, an immense ovation. What tragedian, from which theater, has ever known an equal thunderstorm of success, the earth suffering but overcome, cracking open in curtain calls. A dry shiver ran suddenly in the ground where we had placed our feet. *Etna telegraphed the extreme tremors of its disaster.*[27]

First, Epstein reroutes the magnitude of Etna's power within the sounds of an approving audience, and in turn figures the volcano's geographical distance within the dialectical relationship between actor and vociferous collective.[28] In effect, Epstein's perception exceeds the purely visible realm of appearance as audible expression; however, he does not register merely "applause" but also the force of approval it signifies: the distance of the spectacle is overcome, summarized, and "delivered" by the expressive force of its reception. Distance here is conceived less as a separation between observer and object observed than as an actor through whom communication travels. Then, in a telling catachresis, Epstein turns to the late eighteenth-century technology of the telegraph in order to depict the powerful, supersensible communication achieved in its overcoming of distance. Like the wireless telegraph (*télégraphie sans fil*; T.S.F.), whose powers to transmit bypass the visual realm, Etna's force reaches Epstein as the invisible material of vibrating waves. "Do we know what the T.S.F will be in ten years? Without a doubt an eighth art that will be as much an enemy of music as cinema is now to the theater. We do not know much more about what cinema will be in ten years," Epstein mused in the second chapter of *Etna*.[29]

Beyond such speculation, however, Epstein uses the T.S.F at the beginning of "Etna" as a figure for cinematic perception that, first, takes place across distance by way of modern technology; and that, second, is an invisible communication emitted from, yet different than, the object of predilection. As Charles Altieri has summarized Hegel's concept of force, Epstein similarly sought to convey that "our most elemental experience of force is as something whose effects are visible in or on the objects of perception but that cannot be the simple object of our attention, since we cannot refer to the force within the same pictorial model we use to refer to the objects."[30] By substituting the telegraph for a "pictorial" model of the volcano, Epstein denotes the volcano's force as that which is perceived above and beyond its mere visual perception in the landscape. By distinguishing the force of the volcano from the volcano itself, Epstein engages in a dialectical process that clarifies his own perceptive faculties from the content of perception. In so doing, he qualifies not only the transformation of his own consciousness in the act of perception, but also the autonomy and immanence of the natural world that he later likens to cinema's similar "eruption" of sublime force that was, in 1923, rendering a significant challenge to the classically conceived bases of the work of art: "The philosophy of cinema is to be written. Art can't imagine the eruption that threatens its foundations."[31] In this way, Epstein's essay can be understood as a meditation on apperceptive and self-conscious awareness that emerges from an encounter with a force that affects perception, yet that cannot be reduced either to the object of perception alone or the affective state of the perceiver – as is the case of the telegraphic emission.

Yet, because his account signals the overcoming of both physical and psychical distance as the sublime technological encounter, Epstein's use of telegraphic mediation deserves more attention for how it specifically revises the Romantic paradigm. Epitomized by Epstein's receipt of the volcano's telegraphic emission, the distance that formerly maintained a subject's integrity in a sublime experience is here broken down or technologically bridged in modernity. One might say that modern technologies quite naturally and by their design overcome the distance that once threatened to undo the subject; however, the telegraph and cinema also mediate it such that the subject might marvel at the (sublime) psychical and physical overcoming: "In Nancy," Epstein recalls, " an auditorium of three hundred people groaned out loud upon seeing a kernel of wheat germinate on the screen."[32] To invert Benjamin's (late) formulation for aura, this unique apparition of a nearness, however far an object may be to the viewer (we should recall that the screen nonetheless maintains a distance), is an effect of Epstein's technological sublime more broadly. The expression of radicalized self-consciousness – an audience's audibly expressed stupefaction, weeping at the sight of one's self on screen, or at the fragmented sight of one's reflection in the mirrors of a spiral staircase – Epstein insists, is "not a result of mere self-interest [présomption de soi] or of exaggerated coquetry." Rather, "if the first movement before our own cinematographic reproduction is a kind of horror, that is because, as civilized individuals, we lie about nine-tenths of our selves every day. [...] Abruptly this gaze of glass pierces us with the light of its amperes."[33] Hence, Epstein's position corrects the conventionally Romantic stance that delineates the mind as a "lamp" projecting outwards upon the external world such that "we create nine-tenths at least of what appears to exist externally," as Christopher North (John Wilson) put it.[34] The "action at a distance" that structures the Romantic encounter with the sublime's boundlessness (in Kantian terms) is overturned in Epstein's thought: technology mediates and overcomes distance, and, in so doing, claims phenomenological experience as knowledge received and revealed rather than projected from within the subject.[35] In Epsteinian thought, it is within this essential reversal that a thoroughly modern, and productive, self-consciousness manifests as one coefficient of cinema's technological sublimity.

In order to more fully explore the new experiential possibilities Epstein saw in the modern technological sublime of cinema, and the role of proximity and distance therein, the rest of my essay will be devoted to examining other, primarily nineteenth-century writings on Etna. These put Epstein's departure from the classic paradigms of Romanticism into clearer focus, while they additionally demonstrate the role played by the volcano's classical sublimity in the modernist vocation more generally. A renewed focus on the legacy of distance and technology's mediation thereof in the literary and (para)scientific field that surrounded Epstein not only reveals his position in a broader modernist context of writers who similarly attempted to revise the tenets of the Romantic aesthetic encounter. It also animates the continuity between Epstein's aesthetic project concerning cinema and his earlier theoretical, spiritualist, and literary efforts to complicate the tenets of Romanticism such that they could speak to his contemporary, technologically canted moment.

★ ★ ★

There was no dearth of writing on Etna by the time Epstein transformed his experience at the volcano's site into a meditation on the technological sublime and the cinematic image. From ancient Greek odes to essays written during the sixteenth through nineteenth centuries, Sicily and its volcanic phenomena had been the subject of texts from a wide range of disciplines and literary genres. Beginning with Pindar's description of Etna as a "monster,"[36] these accounts often transform the volcano into a telluric figure that, as Noah Herringman has cogently argued regarding eighteenth-century scientific writing, emerges less as an "object of knowledge" than as an "actor and agent."[37] Mediating scientific, natural-philosophic, and historical-aesthetic discourses, Etna was a sublime trope and a trope for the sublime that exposed the lyrical underside of scientific inquiry and development. In many accounts, the experience of Etna importantly positioned both phenomenological and aesthetic observation as an expression of knowledge in and of itself. In the words of nineteenth-century spiritualist and geographer, Élisée Reclus, who in 1866 described seeing the Sicilian volcano, "You feel frightened, as if before a living being, at the sight of this group of hills that murmur and smoke, and whose cones grow incessantly from the debris projected from the interior of the Earth."[38] By way of metaphor and catachresis, the geological discourse in Reclus' passage emerges from a phenomenological encounter that serves as the basis for a positivist account of the phenomenon of volcanic activity and the "coagulation of lava." For Epstein, such an image would become equivalent to an encounter with cinematic movement: "A thousand arms and legs intertwine, fuse, and unravel, overlap, are joined, melt and multiply [...] Everything foams, vibrates, crackles, overflows, breaks out, molts, strips, surges."[39] Although he did not liken his experience directly to the cinema, in Georges Bataille's 1939 account of Etna we find an interesting parallel to movement and its threatening force: "[o]ne could not possibly imagine a place which demonstrated more clearly the fearful instability of things..."[40]

Nineteenth-century texts by Alexandre Dumas (père) and Guy de Maupassant frame an experience of Etna's volcanic activity in positivist as well as aesthetic terms, while their travel narratives detail arduous ascents up Etna's façade as testaments to the mysteriousness of being in the world. In 1920s France, texts by these authors would have been read by travelers preparing for a trip to Sicily: written for a general if literary public, Dumas' and Maupassant's first-person accounts were vivid travel guides whose description of natural sublimity appealed to readers interested in foreign travel and the experiential thrill or fantasy of mastery it provided. While the writing of these authors helps to foreground the extent of Epstein's modernist departure from a nineteenth-century ethos, it is in the modernist writing of Auguste de Villiers de L'Isle-Adam and Poe that Epstein's modernist enterprise finds particular resonance. Considering Epstein's film *Fall of the House of Usher* (1928), Poe's influence on Epstein is no mystery, yet the poet's oeuvre extends much further into Epstein's theoretical project than simply by providing source material for his films and writing. Although, at the end of "Etna," Epstein claims that Villiers "never dreamed of an equal soul-confessing machine" capable of the "analytic power" of the cinema's "gaze of glass,"[41] Villiers' style abstracts a Romantic encounter with Etna such that its force becomes resonant as, precisely, a sublime modernist agency. Insofar as Poe and Villiers both conceive of "experimental transfers" at a distance in both literary and scientific terms, they further corroborate Epstein's fascination in experimental psychological transfers across distances that he first discusses in *La Lyrosophie*, and that I will reorient with respect to the modern technological sublime found in "Etna."

Dumas père's *Le Spéronare* (1842), part of his collection called *Impressions de voyage*, opens the narrative of ascension along Etna's façade by casting the author's own privilege within the terms of Nature: only a small, seasonal window permitted safe voyage to the summit's crater. Dumas' advantageousness provides his voice documentary authority as he goes to great lengths to describe each stage of the voyage, carefully inserting the names of literary figures who preceded him on the journey, as well as historical information regarding Etna's past eruptions that make it, perpetually, "in construction." While the effect of Dumas' contribution survives primarily as an adventure tale, at moments he notes his perceptual and corporeal alienation as a significant part of the experience:

> All of this was terrible, somber, majestic; I saw and perfectly sensed the poetry of this nighttime voyage, although I was so cold that I did not possess the courage to exchange a word with Jadin [his travel companion] to ask him if all these visions weren't the result of the numbness I was feeling, and if I wasn't having a dream. [...] We left the *casa Inglese* [a protective cottage found along the upper route of the ascent]. We began to distinguish the objects: all around us stretched a vast plane of snow in the middle of which [...] arose Etna's cone. Below us, everything was in darkness. [...] It is this cone, eternally mobile, that changes form with each new eruption, damaging the old crater, and reforming itself with a new one.[42]

With each step he takes on the upper crest, his description augments in suspense as the earth becomes more "crumbly," and as the sulfurous fumes multiply and become nearly too much for Dumas to bear.[43] Once at Etna's summit – a position Epstein's text only truly takes in the book's title, *The Cinematograph Seen from Etna* – Dumas finds a source of unrivaled spectacle: Malta "floated on the horizon like fog; around you, all of Sicily, seen from a bird's eye view [...] its fifteen towns, its three hundred villages; its mountains that resemble hills [...] its rivers that appeared as silver threads." It taught him to "forget everything, fatigue, danger, suffering."[44] And in a "radically subjective lyrical expansiveness,"[45] to use Altieri's words, that only the Romantic ethos could provide, the view instantiates in Dumas the power of individualism and presumption as he "admired fully, without restriction, with good faith, with the eyes of a body and the eyes of the soul." "Never had I seen God so close, and consequently so big."[46]

By 1890, fellow Frenchman Maupassant published *La vie errante* in which the details of Etna's treacherousness conclude in a claim toward a general aesthetic theory of art akin to the Symbolists: "A work of art is superior only in the case when it expresses at one and the same time a symbol and the exact reproduction of a reality."[47] Naturalistic though his style may have been, Maupassant's critical stance toward modern technology throughout this text places him well within the reach of Romanticism's own rejection of it. The book begins with the author's declaration of *lassitude* (weariness) – a theme that we might recognize in Epstein's *La Lyrosophie* as the modern "fatigue" of the artist.[48] Unlike Epstein's altogether modern concept of "fatigue" that results from the intensified experiential conditions of modernity, Maupassant's comment follows upon a willful critique of what he understands to be the message of the *Exposition Universelle*: the predominance of "industry and sale" over the purer, more natural impulses that guided knowledge-seekers of times past. In this passage, we should note the likely reference to Edison:

> But does not the genius of the one who, with one grand leap of his mind, jumped from the fall of an apple to the great law that reigns over this whole universe seem born of a more divine germ than that of the sharp American inventor, the marvelous manufacturer of bells, megaphones, and lightning apparatus?
>
> Is not that the secret vice of the modern mind, the sign of its inferiority in its triumph? [...]
>
> At all events, these things which interest us to-day in a practical way do not absorb us as do the ancient forms of thought, for we are far too much the poor, irritable slaves of a dream of delicate beauty that haunts and spoils our lives."[49]

Maupassant decides that "it would be good to see Florence again," whereupon the second chapter, "Night," commences a willful if somewhat naïve travel narrative in which he searches for opportunities to discover ancient forms of knowledge and/or "genius." Passing lithely between documentary account and metaphysical speculation, his narrative modes reveal the author's curiosity in the aesthetic and literary revolutions that were taking place in his era. In a fit of sleeplessness, for example, Maupassant queries Baudelaire and Rimbaud for their heightened perceptual understanding of nature, a discussion that swiftly incorporates the contemporary scientific study of synesthesia as well as a reference to the experimental thinker Hippolyte Taine. In this context, Taine is likely mentioned for his application of scientific positivism to humanistic inquiry, if not for his own *Voyage en Italie*, published the same year as his *Philosophie de l'art en Italie* (1866).[50] It is important to recognize Maupassant's guiding, theoretical emphasis on empiricism, however skeptical it may be: for this writer, empiricism's potentially torturous power derived from the senses nonetheless aids the modern poet's expressive development of form:

> The mind, that blind and hard-working Unknown, can know, understand, discover nothing except through the senses. They are its only providers, its only agents between Universal Nature and itself. It works exclusively on the materials furnished by them, which they, in turn, can gather only in proportion to their own sensitiveness, strength, and acuteness.
>
> The value of thought evidently depends directly upon the value of the organs, and its breadth is limited to their number. [...]

There are five senses, and only five. They reveal to us, by interpreting them, certain properties of surrounding matter, which possesses also a number of other phenomena that we are unable to perceive. [...]

But suppose [man] had been given other organs, powerful and sensitive, gifted with the faculty of transforming into acute perceptions the actions and attributes of all the inexplicable things that surround us – how much more varied would be the extent of our knowledge and emotions.

It is into this impenetrable domain that every artist attempts to enter, by tormenting, violating, and exhausting the mechanism of his thoughts.[51]

In the context of this passage, Maupassant's previous reticence toward technology seems to anticipate what Epstein would claim as the most revelatory aspect of the cinema medium, and that he would eventually extrapolate from his experience before Etna: cinema's ultra-sensory capability to, in Maupassant's words, "transform into acute perceptions the actions and attributes of all the inexplicable things that surround us."

For all of these implicit connections between them, Epstein's qualitative difference from Maupassant (and Dumas) is brought into relief by comparing the moments of geological discovery that appear in each writer's travel-narrative. Like Maupassant, Epstein also apparently traveled from Etna's facade to the former quarry-prisons of the Latomies where the famous geological formation called the "Ear of Denys the Tyrant" (also referred to as the Ear of Dionysius, following Caravaggio) can be found. Maupassant's encounter with the "surprisingly magnified" sounds echoed in the Ear of Dionysius led him to aesthetic conclusions that he transposed upon an image of human form. Immediately following his encounter with the "subterranean hall" of the Latomies, Maupassant entered a museum whereupon he saw her, the Venus [of Syracuse]: "It was not a poetical woman, an idealized woman, nor was it a divine or majestic woman, like the Venus de Milo, but it was a real woman, a woman such as you love, such as you desire, a woman you would fain clasp in your arms."[52] The rhetorical link Maupassant makes between the auditory reproduction in the cave and the statue's replication of human form prepares him for his most explicit claim for nature's "snare of reproduction" as, he reminds us, Schopenhauer referred to it.[53] With the power to both conceal and reveal "the disquieting mystery of life," mimetic representation in Maupassant's terms strikes with a magnitude similar to an encounter with the sublime, although it echoes also within the vein of Symbolist thought whereby the "perceptible and the ideal or spiritual worlds intersected."[54]

On the contrary, Epstein's encounter with auditory reproduction during his visit to the Latomies incisively amputates – disfigures – any remnant of the ideal from his perception: the return of the "real" is painful; it is aggrandized at the expense of Epstein's perceptual integrity; it is a force altogether distinct from its sources; it is, furthermore, self-alienating but productively so. Describing his visit to the Ear of Dionysus, Epstein draws an explicit parallel between Nature, distance, and a newly formed sense of self-awareness. The first line of the quote below places Epstein in the mirror-lined staircase beholding his own fractured reflection:

> Looking at one and then the other, I took in another awareness of my own relief. Parallel glimpses were repeated exactly, were sent back, reinforcing themselves, attaining themselves in an echo with the more superior force than that of acoustic phenomena. Even the smallest gesture became enormous, like at the Latomia of Paradise when words are spoken at the deepest point in the Ear of Denys the Tyrant, thanks to the rock's (roc)[55] *sensitivity, they swell and roar at the top of their lungs.*[56]

Once again doubled within an acoustic phenomenon (recall the "applause" figured in the text's earlier section), this perceptual event occurs across the dialectical distance between what Epstein casts out and what returns magnified and disfigured. Distance here is framed as the conduit for sound as well as echo, but insofar as the return is marked by radical transformation, Epstein's modern, technological perspective refutes the primacy of mimesis as a structuring element of aesthetic experience or representation.

Further, in its ability to obliterate the narcissistic crust that formerly prevented the apprehension of one's own real appearance in the world, the Latomies' depths, and that he likens to the spiral staircase, become a force, an agency, that differentiates between, as Alteiri notes, a "world of pure perception and one in which awareness of the world proves inseparable from the intricacies of self-consciousness."[57] If in Epstein's self-discovery narrative we recognize the traces of a sublime encounter, we must also acknowledge his insistence that cinema possesses an "analytic power" to destroy – disfigure, de-figure – what had previously amounted to "ideal" in both mimetic formations and in the previously dominant aesthetic terms of, for example, Romanticism, to which Maupassant adhered. Epstein concludes this passage with a ranging description of his new self-awareness brought on by the technological animus of perceptual distance:

> This staircase was the eye of another, even more spy-like tyrant. There it was as though I descended through the multifaceted perspective of an insect. Other images by their contrary angles intersected and amputated themselves; diminished, partial, they humiliated me. This is the extraordinary moral effect of such a spectacle. Each perception is a disconcerting surprise that offends. Never had I seen myself so and I looked at myself with terror...Such a lesson of reverse egoism is merciless. An education, an instruction, a religion, had patiently consoled me from being. Everything was to begin again.[58]

While Epstein sought the insight of contemporary art historians such as Henri Focillon in his own work, he departed from any stance that upheld a singular aesthetic view in its entirety. Focillon did just this in 1922 when in Epstein's journal *Promenoir* he declared: "I remain loyal to the principles expressed by Kant so clearly in his *Critique of Judgment*: art is an activity of play (*jeu*), perfectly free and disinterested, and upon which no constraint weighs."[59] Not least because he would have deemed such staunchness outdated, Epstein also sought the insight of authors who were similarly at work to define "The Future of Science" (the title of the last chapter in *La Lyrosophie*) as an agent of aesthetic illumination. Because science and technology indeed weighed heavily upon Epstein, Poe's *Eureka*, a radically analogical scientific theory and poetic treatise on universal oneness, would have provided Epstein with a significantly more powerful source for his thinking on the technological sublime than academic art historians' more conventional writing. Poe's prose poem was first translated into the French language by Charles Baudelaire in 1863, and it is generally cited in relation to Epstein for its opening scene that bypasses an account of any arduous, physical travail upon Etna's façade for an immediate description of an onlooker's view atop the volcano's summit. Poe writes:

> [...] I propose to take such a survey of the Universe that the mind may be able really to receive and to perceive an individual impression.
>
> He who from the top of Ætna casts his eyes leisurely around, is affected chiefly by the extent and diversity of the scene. Only by a rapid whirling on his heel could he hope to comprehend the panorama in the sublimity of its oneness. But as, on the summit of Ætna, no man has thought of whirling on his heel, so no man has ever taken into his brain the full uniqueness of the prospect; and so, again, whatever considerations lie involved in this uniqueness, have as yet no practical existence for mankind.[60]

Uncanny though it may be with respect to Epstein's "Etna,"[61] the filmmaker would have been drawn further into the poem's depths, as it also functioned – as Paul Valéry described it in his introduction to a 1923 illustrated edition of Baudelaire's translation – "an abstract poem, one of the rare modern examples of a total explanation of material and spiritual nature, a cosmogony."[62] As an "aesthetic cosmology," John Irwin argues that "just as Poe makes the ongoing mystery at the heart of his three [Dupin] detective tales the mystery of the self's structure, the puzzle of self-consciousness, so in *Eureka* by presenting the universe as an apotheosized self, he makes this same mysterious structure the central puzzle of the universe...so Poe in *Eureka* links the concept of infinity to the reflexive structure of self-consciousness..."[63]

Epstein would have also, I think, closely followed the concepts of magnitude and distance that Poe used throughout *Eureka* with regard to a number of telluric, astral, atomic, and conceptual forces.[64] In fact, Poe's illustration for one such force, "irradiation," would have been helpful for Epstein's conceptualization of the technological sublime and its characteristics of mediated distance and experimental transfer (Fig. 1).[65] From Poe's illustration of the "degree" of light's outward diffusion (or inward, as "concentralization") from a singular source upon variously distant planes, Epstein would have taken an efficient summary of Eureka's thesis concerning the "continuous outpouring of ray-streams" from the universe, as well as the identical reciprocity of "matter and spirit"[66] and their endless "rejuvenescence" in the universe.[67] Epstein may have also perceived a method by which to think about the components of cinematic reception: representational force, its source, and its recipient. Summarized as it is in Poe's graphic, the shared point between Epstein and Poe is that the reception of force – for example, gravity as the received force upon objects, or the cinema image as the received force of light projected upon a screen – is conceived as the reception of matter, a claim that exacts a "concrete relativity" between a subject's perceptual faculties, her bodily identity, and the visual experience of representation.

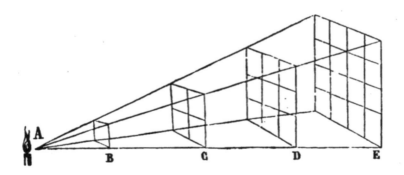

Fig. 1: Poe's original illustration as it appeared in Eurêka

Jacques Aumont similarly interprets the central axis of Poe's metaphysical tale in relation to Epsteinian thought, arguing that for Epstein cinema "becomes a creator of worlds, and of material worlds. Or, if we wish a less metaphorical definition, it becomes an instrument to test hypotheses on the relation of our psyche to the physical laws of the universe. [...] [T]he cinema provides access to these laws."[68] Although cinema was Epstein's particular tool for the measurement and assessment of such laws, he was not as interested as Poe in defining them in scientific terms. Rather, he concentrated on cinema's concrete diffusion of matter through its "gaze of glass" (or through what Poe otherwise called the "hollow

JENNIFER WILD

sphere of glass"): cinema's delivery of variously experiential forces by way of distance or proximity.[69]

For this reason, the dynamic scale of the close-up deserves special attention as the vehicle through which the "atoms" of the image were delivered with particular force in Epsteinian thought. In his legendary essay, "Magnification," Epstein declares in no uncertain terms the link between the proximity of the close-up, the magnitude of its reception, and the sublime geological aspects of this encounter:

> I will never find the way to say how much I love American close-ups. Point blank. A head suddenly appears on screen and drama, now face to face, seems to address me personally and swells with an extraordinary intensity. [...] The orography of the face vacillates. Seismic shocks begin. Capillary wrinkles try to split the fault. A wave carries them away.[70]

According to the OED, "orography" came about during the mid-nineteenth century (1846) as the science of the description of mountains; in contemporary terms, it is the science of geomorphology. Importantly for Epstein, the proximity of the close-up – or the camera's ability to render objects at a closer range despite the screen's stable distance (here, Poe's theory of irradiation bears directly) – is capable of rendering the world's force in terms of a telluric encounter. As in his experience with Etna only a year or so later, here Epstein delineates the overcoming of distance as the sublime encounter provided by – mediated by – the technology of the cinematic close-up. By attributing the force of cinema to the agency of magnification, Epstein asserts that cinema's effects cannot be reduced either to the object of perception alone, or to his stimulated, phenomenological state. We could say that the close-up "telegraphed" cinema's supersensible capacity so to render Nature independent from, yet seated within, the technology that delivers its force across a distance.

Epstein's particular interest in the close-up makes it evident that the technological sublime turns more concisely around cinema's capacity to mediate perception across distance than cinema's function to pictorially represent. As an explicitly modernist predilection, this is also the case for Villiers who, in his 1888 tale, "Etna chez soi" (Etna at Home), chooses never to represent the eponymous volcano but instead constructs his modernist allegory around an experimental transfer in literary perception. Like a snow-capped peak barely visible behind the clouds in the troposphere, Villiers' title summons Etna's image, but then displaces it out of view in the deeply analogical field of its text that performs the violence, explosiveness, and centuries-old threat of destruction for which Etna was known. The last in Villiers' volume of Histoires Insolites (Strange Stories), and published two years after what is perhaps his best known novel, L'Eve future (Tomorrow's Eve, 1886), "Etna chez soi" is a fictional manual for anarchist revolutionaries. It borrows directly from contemporary advancements in engineered explosives (the author cites, among others, the work of Eugène Turpin, and Captain J. M. Lewin of Sweden) in order to effect what Paola Salerni calls an "experimental transfer" of Etna's "explosive" signifying force to the lexical domain and the reader's imagination.[71] This is an operation that Epstein extrapolates and reroutes concerning the explosive, signifying force of cinema insofar as the concept of *photogénie* is itself never named in the "Etna" essay: like steam involuntarily rising from a crater's rocky source, *photogénie* issues forth – unnamed, invisible – from Epstein's catachreses that invoke the volcano's "psychology of organic movement."[72]

The discursive parameters of Villiers' literary experiment possess a conceptual plasticity that, after supplying the "real" know-how to create an initial "eruption" of violence, draws the figure of a volcano's molten flow within the final, orgiastic image of Paris in ruins:

> And suddenly the vociferation of a screaming multitude, the thousands of panicked cries of men and women choking in a vertiginous panic – recalling for example (and with such magnification [*grandissements*]) the horrifying catastrophes at the theaters in Nice, Exeter, and our own Opéra-Comique – suddenly these explosions and all of these cries of carnage, at last, reach the two killers.
>
> The mist seems to have taken on a reddish shade, over there! And, at the same moment, the other five arrows were sent flying. And the surrounding retaliations begin again, mixed with the sounds of crumbling, with the fracas of the powder kegs, in the purple light that burns in the distance. The capital, prevailing in its countless roar over the swaying of carriages and the whistles of parting trains, had become, in a quarter of an hour, nearly equal to Sodom under the fire of the heavens. Sudden mass graves are piling up.[73]

The writer rectifies revolutionary violence ("The future is in explosives" reads the text's epigraph, penned by Prince Kropotkine) by figuring it as natural occurrence within an elaborate prosopopoeia wherein, following Paul de Man, "one begins to perceive a world of potential ghosts and monsters."[74] But by transforming Etna's natural force into this ghostly, textual "monster," Villiers' narrative mode emerges as a distinctly modernist strategy that forcefully subverts any kind of Romantic impulse. Villiers does not simply place an explicitly drawn political or satirical face upon the volcano to incite either symbolic "freedom"or "revolution" as earlier visual uses of the volcano had (Fig. 2).[75] Instead, he subsumes natural, sublime violence within the materialism of anarchist alchemy and action. Thus, he sacrifices the rarified individualism of a Romantic encounter with the natural world in favor of an experience whose power emerges from the collective and material conflagration of politics, science, and aesthetics: it is this fire that is capable of penetrating the appearance and distance that, in the Romantic order, maintained concepts of individuation, and that held Nature at a distinct, self-preserving remove.

Fig. 2: *La Caricature*

But insofar as Villiers substitutes the materiality of anarchist alchemy for the distant ideal of natural sublimity, he also anchors revolutionary change with the scientific exactitude of explosive recipes. The numbers, terms, descriptions, and volumes of each chemical operation become explicit variables of transformation put forthrightly into the hands of the reader so that she too may exact materiality from the penumbra of Romanticism's individualist sublime. Couched as they were within scientific materialism, Villiers' experimental literary transfers may have satisfied Epstein's own desire for scientifically explicit accounts – explanations – of the "revolutionary" forces harbored within nature, art, and the subjective experience when mediated by technology. Such accounts would legitimately and scientifically "inaugurate romanticism from reason and reason from romanticism" – as Epstein wrote in *La Lyrosophie* – as well as bridge the unfathomable distance between phenomenology and scientific reason as technology so efficiently did.

In the writings of "lyrosoph" Walter Moore Coleman, Epstein found an approach that dared to openly combine the materialism of science with the mystery of subjective experience that he sought in his theory of lyrosophy: "Every time in which, in one way or another, the personal coefficient of the observer manifests within a scientific observation, we have the right, nearly always correct, to speak of lyrosophy."[76] Although Epstein quotes an unnamed text by Coleman in La Lyrosophie ("Lyrosophie and personal coefficient once again chez Walter Moore Coleman") that ostensibly explored the phenomenon of the "human aura" as the origin of telekinesis,[77] Epstein devoted a long section to Coleman's experiments a year earlier in Bonjour Cinéma. Permit me to quote at length this passage from the essay "The Extra Sense:"

> One more example. M. Walter Moore Coleman has shown through meticulous observations that at certain moments all the movements (locomotor, respiratory, masticatory, etc.) of a group of the most diverse individuals, including both animals and men, without being synchronized at all, are subject to a given rhythm, a specific frequency which may be either uniform or based on a simple musical ratio. Thus, when one day the lions, tigers, bears, and antelopes in the Zoo at Regent's Park were walking and chewing their food at 88 movements per minute, the soldiers walked around on the lawns at 88 steps per minute, the leopards and the pumas walked at 132, that is, in the ration of 3/2, do-sol, and the children ran at 116, that is, in the ration of 3/4, do-fa. There is, thus, a sort of euphony, an orchestration, a consonance whose causes are obscure. We know how the crowd scenes at the cinema, when there is a genuine mentally active crowd, produce effects that are rhythmic, poetic, and photogenic. The reason for this is that the cinema, in a way better and different from that of our eye, knows how to disengage this cadence and to inscribe this rhythm, both the fundamental and its harmonics. Do you remember how Griffith always had his characters move, even at the risk of having them oscillate on the beat, practically from one foot to the other in many of the scenes in True Heart Susie? It is here that the cinema will one day find its own prosody.[78]

Like the hollow glass tube that for Poe demonstrated the equal diffusion of relational energies across distance, and like the volcano that "telegraphed" the waves of its disaster, Epstein here conceives of cinema as a scientific instrument imbued with similar powers of transmission. It "disengages" unnamed forces from their invisible, mystical, non-scientific realm and transports them to the visible and material plane in a process that demonstrates the layered, vibrating, and quantifiable relay of life's relational energies as artful cadence.[79]

The author of Mental Biology: Experiments in Telergy or the Supersensory Control of Vital Activities at a Distance to which Epstein refers above, Coleman (1863-1923) was an American fellow of the Physical Society who authored a range of works concerning the biological and physical sciences, including textbooks.[80] Coleman's parapsychological research in Telergy attempts to supply a scientific account of the relational parameters between disparate things and their expressive rhythms or force. In short, his aim was in "making subconscious activity amenable to quantitative tests," while "[t]he word telergy ('far-working')," Coleman tells us, "is used by Sir Oliver Lodge and others in the sense of the unconscious control of vital activities at a distance."[81] Coleman finds that telergic force affects the will and mood (hence, indirectly, emotion and thought), and is "reciprocal": it simultaneously affects the most apparent functions of any two subjects such as heartbeat, breathing, blinking, voice, mastication, and locomotion, or "muscular activity in general."

Although Coleman notes that he has never found records of telergy "operating the physiological mechanism through space" and opts thus for the more recognizable agent of "telepathy," it is clear that for Coleman this mysterious force bridging "the reality of distance" holds the key for an altogether new concept of consciousness and its "social origin."[82] As experiments in telegraphic waves attest, Coleman argues, telergic forces exist in an as yet unknown region wherein the communication between entities erupts in a mysterious synchrony that can be parsed out in musical ratios (Fig. 3). In effect, the study of telergic action (found in crowds, "in most assemblies, in companies of soldiers, in flocks of birds, in herds, and even between two or three individuals") is a study of the (im)materiality of distance and the "properties and modes of action of this unnamed force" or agency that bridges it.[83]

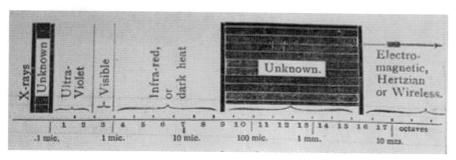

Fig. 3: Coleman, Experiments in Telergy

Clearly, Epstein utilized Coleman's experiments to explain how, in Liebman's words, "the cinema uncovered or at least confirmed the existence of immanent physical laws."[84] But it was more insofar as it also permitted Epstein to radically define his theory of film as also a conceptual operation upon the distance between the poles of science and mysticism, phenomenology and aesthetics, Romanticism and Modernism. On the one hand, "The cinema is true," and on the other, "The cinema is supernatural in its essence."[85] And yet, it is also "psychic." The theoretical expanse between these seemingly disparate elements of Epstein's reasoning in fact orients us to the force of mediation that works in his theory to restructure the Romantic ideal for his modern moment:

To see is to idealize, to abstract and to extract, to read and to choose, to transform. On screen, we see what the camera has already seen: a double transformation, or rather, because it is thus multiplied, a vision squared. A choice within a choice, a reflection of a reflection. Here, beauty is polarized like light; it is the beauty of a second generation, a daughter, but a daughter born before its time from its mother whom we love with our naked eye. It is a slightly monstrous daughter. That is why the cinema is psychic. It presents us with a quintessence, a product twice distilled.[86]

Like the return of a sound distorted by echo, and like the monstrous refraction of Etna's violence subtended beneath Villiers' worldly figuration of destruction, the cinema image here is an experimental transfer providing a return of the real beyond the scope of Epstein's original, subjective encounter with it. To see the cinema image is not simply to "see" the world, he explains. Rather, it is to see it by way of technological mediation across distance, hence by way of a return that frames the modern technological sublime as also a relation to pastness, to history. It is in this sense that Epstein's theory finds its closest *rapprochement* to Benjamin's aura as Hansen explains it: "...by insisting on both the aura's internally retrospective structure and irreversible historicity, [Benjamin] can deploy the concept to catalyze the ensemble of perceptural shifts that define the present – such as the ascendance of multiplicity and repeatability over singularity, nearness over farness, and a haptic engagement with things and space over a contemplative relation to images and time – and posit this ensemble as the signature of technological and social modernity."[87]

As Jacques Rancière has argued, Epstein's aesthetic paradigm demonstrates the specifically modern collision of "fictional with sensible matter," a place where "the sensible and the intelligible remain undistinguished" as similar if not identical "textures."[88] In this way, Rancière continues, cinema "literalizes a secular idea of art in the same stroke that it actualizes the refutation of that idea: it is both the art of the afterwards that emerges from the Romantic de-figuration of stories, and the art that returns the work of defiguration to classical imitation."[89] However, the priority of return in Epstein's theory is contingent upon modern technology's ability to mediate and scientifically materialize both literal and figurative distances inherent in phenomenological or aesthetic encounters.[90] The monsters still lurk and return in Epstein's post-Romantic aesthetic paradigm, delivered again and again in cinema's force that permits the "supersensible beyond" to come into being by way of reception. Just as telergy's mediation implies reciprocity between its subjects, the spectatorial encounter with cinema, Epstein argues, "procures such unexpected encounters with one's self."[91] Indeed, the most horrific, monstrous encounter in the "Etna" essay is found in the "moral effect" of self-consciousness before one's own image mediated, returned by way of cinema's glass gaze that the author extrapolates from his own refracted reflection in the mirror-lined staircase: "I would have run far to escape this spiral movement where I seemed to be thrust toward a hideous center of myself."[92]

Epstein, like Benjamin, presses us to recognize the distinct agency of cinematic reception/perception as one part of the reciprocal coefficient that defines the modern aesthetic experience – as well as the modern technological sublime. As also a collective, rather than solely individualized, receptive possibility, cinema's mediation of distance redirects the phenomenological experience of seeing toward an altogether transformative encounter with, as Altieri succinctly summarizes, "consciousness becoming conscious of itself. Consciousness has to see itself caught up in this logic of appearance and otherness."[93] As an "analytic force,"[94] in Epstein's words, that is reducible neither to the Natural object perceived nor the subject's own perceptual state before it, cinema's transmission across distance demonstrates – again in Altieri's words – the mind's "simultaneous sense of its bondage to appearance *and* its freedom to bring our values and causes within a world that now on one level exists for consciousness, hence as appearance."[95] The cinematic image of a revolver efficiently demonstrated this fact for Epstein: "The desires and the despair that it represented; the mass [*foule*] of combinations to which it was key; all the endings, all the beginnings that it permitted to be imagined, all of this provided it a kind of freedom and moral person. Such a freedom, such a soul, are they more epiphenomenal than our alleged ones?"[96]

The extent to which, for Epstein, this experience is attributable solely to cinema's mediation of distance becomes even more apparent in "Langue d'Or," the third essay in *Etna*. Epstein writes:

> In this darkness that is favorable to the phenomenon of telepathy, that is to say to the most far away understandings [*compréhensions*], to the most secret correspondences of the spirit, the astonishing language was born, of a nature that we didn't expect of it, assimilable by sight and not by sound. It is not read, it is seen, and this 'sight' is very well the most nuanced exercise, the most subtle, the most attentive, the most specialized of all the exercises of the gaze.[97]

Once again Epstein replaces the pictorial model of cinema with a metaphor – telepathy – in order to summarize the particular activity of seeing the cinematic image as a sublimely modern transfer, as well as to exact cinema's particular force from its identity as a modern, "natural" fact. We know that, through the work of Coleman, telepathy was for Epstein linked to the experimental psychological sciences as it was also to the mystical. But a few pages later, he states: "A *telegraph* without words teaches the exact sense of the soul of a people."[98] In this phrase, we are faced with the same figure of mediation he first used to describe the phenomenological encounter with Etna's invisible communication. We are then, in a sense, returned to that place where Epstein could best think about:

the most animated living machine, this zone of quasi absolute death that encircled the first craters by one or two kilometers [...] At two hundred meters the rapids of fire appeared suddenly from a nearly circular crevasse and devoured the slope, forming a river of red like ripe cherries and as big as the Seine in Rouen.[99]

From out of the appearance of this violent, sensuous world, cinema rose up like its sublime underside as though, in Hegel's words, "each is solely through the other, and what each thus is it immediately no longer is, since it is the other."[100] Stripping Epstein of his own analytic powers such that he could only and simply assert, "I don't know if I can communicate the degree to which this, this is cinema, this character of our preoccupation," the volcano prompted Epstein to understand cinematic mediation as a distinctly material force and sublimely modern agency. It assisted Epstein's recognition of a post-Romantic aesthetic experience wherein, by way of the camera's glass gaze that mediated (im)material distances, "Mountains, as well as this Etna, signify."[101]

Notes

1. Arthur Conan Doyle, *Our Second American Adventure* (Boston: Little, Brown, and Company, 1924). This comment, without brackets, appears in the context of Doyle's description of Dr. Littlefield's experiments with animals in Seattle. Thanks go to Ken Eisenstein for supplying me with this reference. I wish to express my sincere gratitude to Miriam Hansen, Karl Schoonover, Sarah Keller, and Jason Paul. Each read and insightfully commented upon early drafts of this essay, and I am grateful for how each in their own way impelled me to track its end. I dedicate this essay to the memory of Miriam Hansen.

2. See Stuart Liebman, *Jean Epstein's Early Film Theory, 1920-1922* (New York University: PhD Dissertation, 1980). The Bibliothèque du film, at the Cinémathèque française, holds an archive related to *La Montagne infidèle*. To my knowledge, at least one anonymous film about Etna's 1923 eruption is conserved in the Gaumont-Pathé Archives: *Eruption de l'Etna en 1923* (DD 119 349).

3. Jean Epstein, *Le Cinématographe vu de l'Etna* (Paris: Les Ecrivains Réunis, 1926). I will hereafter refer to the chapter as "Etna," and the book as *Etna*.

4. Vincent Gédéon, "Les Opinions de Vincent Gédéon," *Le Journal Amusant* No. 217, (Saturday, July 7, 1923), p. 14.

5. All translations, unless otherwise noted, are mine. Epstein, *Etna*, pp. 9, 12; infra, 288, 289.

6. Epstein, *Etna*, p. 12; infra, 289. Emphasis mine. It should be noted that my translation of the key sentence in italics differs from Liebman's initial treatment of it. Liebman first translated it as, "I don't know if I can make myself understood, but the figure with whom we were all preoccupied was the cinema." See Stuart Liebman, "Visitings of Awful Promise: The Cinema Seen from Etna," in *Camera Obscura, Camera Lucida: Es-*

says in Honor of Annette Michelson, eds. Richard Allen and Macolm Turvey (Amsterdam: Amsterdam University Press, 2003), p. 93.

7. Liebman, "Visitings of Awful Promise," p. 93.
8. Much of my understanding of the Romantic sublime comes from Thomas Weiskel, *The Romantic Sublime: Studies in the Structure and Psychology of Transcendence* (Baltimore: Johns Hopkins University Press, 1976). See especially chapter 2, "The Ethos of Alienation: Two Versions of Transcendence." See also John T. Ogden, "The Power of Distance in Wordsworth's Preludes," *PMLA* 88, no. 2 (March 1973): 246-259.
9. For accounts of Benjamin's and Epstein's "cross-illumination," see Rachel Moore, *Savage Theory: Cinema as Modern Magic* (Durham, NC: Duke University Press, 2000) and Christophe Wall-Romana, "Epstein's *Photogénie* as Corporeal Vision: Inner Sensation, Queer Embodiment, and Ethics," in this volume.
10. Walter Benjamin, "The Work of Art in the Age of its Technological Reproducibility" [Second Version, 1936], trans. Edmund Jephcott and Harry Zohn, in Benjamin, *Selected Writings, Volume 3: 1935-1938*, eds. Howard Eiland and Michael W. Jennings (Cambridge, MA: Belknap Press of Harvard University Press, 2002), p. 105.
11. Miriam Hansen, "Benjamin's Aura," *Critical Inquiry* 34 (Winter 2008), p. 342; 375. It is from this essay by Hansen that I best understand Benjamin's various influences to which I refer here.
12. Hansen, "Benjamin's Aura," p. 355.
13. Ibid., pp. 356-357.
14. Ibid., p. 374. See also Miriam Hansen, "Of Mice and Ducks: Benjamin and Adorno on Disney," *South Atlantic Quarterly* 92 (January 1993): 27-61.
15. Immanuel Kant, *Critique of Judgment*, trans. Werner S. Pluhar (Indianapolis: Hackett Publishing Company, 1987), p. 120.
16. Philippe Dubois, "La Tempête et la Matière-Temps, ou le Sublime et le Figural dans l'Oeuvre de Jean Epstein," in *Jean Epstein: cinéaste, poète, philosophe*, ed. Jacques Aumont (Paris: Cinémathèque française, 1998), pp. 267-323.
17. Epstein, *Etna*, p. 16; infra, 291.
18. Mikhail Iampolski, "Epstein: Théorie du Cinéma Comme Topologie," in *Jean Epstein*, ed. Aumont, pp. 110, 114.
19. Liebman, "Visitings of Awful Promise," pp. 91-108. In Liebman's keen comparison to the narrative patterns of Romantic poetry and to the Kantian sublime, he makes reference to Kant's "mathematical sublime," and to Rousseau and Wordsworth. See also Dubois, "La Tempête et la Matière-Temps," p. 276.
20. Frances Ferguson, *Solitude and the Sublime: Romanticism and the Aesthetics of Individuation* (New York: Routledge, 1992), p. 139. Though Ferguson's topic in this chapter is William Gilpin and British travel literature in the eighteenth and early nineteenth centuries, hers is a particularly important account considering Epstein's own travel narrative that sets *Etna* into motion.
21. Epstein, *Lyrosophie*, pp. 216-217.
22. Chiara Tognolotti, "L'alcool, le cinéma et le philosophe. L'influence de Friedrich Nietzsche sur la théorie cinématographique de Jean Epstein à travers les notes du fonds Epstein," *1895*, no. 46 (2005), p. 40. To corroborate her observation, it should be mentioned that at the end of "Etna" Epstein names the French philosopher Jules de

Gaultier who authored *De Kant à Nietzsche* (Paris: Société du Mercure de France, 1900) and *Nietzsche et la réforme philosophique* (Paris: Société du Mercure de France, 1904), among other books on Flaubert and "le bovarysme".

23. My essay can be seen as a companion to Katie Kirtland's essay in the present volume. She recasts with acumen the importance of Edouard Abramowski's experimental psychology to Epstein's concepts.

24. Hansen details Benjamin's distaste in "Benjamin's Aura," p. 357.

25. Rosalind Krauss, "Antivision," *October*, no. 36, special issue, 'Georges Bataille: Writings on Laughter, Sacrifice, Nietzsche, Un-Knowing' (Spring, 1986), p. 147.

26. Emphasis mine. Trond Lundemo, "The Cinematograph Seen from Etna – Recurrent Figures and Stylistic Devices in Epstein's Films and Writings," in *Jean Epstein: intelligensen hos en maskin–The Intelligence of a Machine* (Stockholm: Svenska Filminstitutet, 2001) p. 49. Thanks to Patrik Sjoberg for supplying me with this source.

27. Epstein, *Etna*, p. 9 (my emphasis); infra, 288.

28. On magnitude in Kant's aesthetic category of the sublime, see Jean-François Lyotard, *Lessons on the Analytic of the Sublime*, trans. Elizabeth Rottenberg (Stanford, CA: Stanford University Press, 1994), especially chapter 3.

29. Jean Epstein, "De Quelques Conditions de la Photogénie" [1924], *Etna*, p. 25; infra, 294.

30. Charles Altieri, "The Concept of Force as a Frame for Modernist Art and Literature," *boundary 2* 25, no. 1 (Spring 1998), p. 201.

31. Jean Epstein, *Bonjour Cinema* (Paris: La Sirène, 1921), p. 35.

32. Epstein, *Etna*, p. 11; infra, 289.

33. Ibid., p. 19; infra, 292.

34. Christopher North, cited in M. H. Abrams, *The Mirror and the Lamp: Romantic Theory and the Critical Tradition* (New York: Oxford University Press, 1953), p. 60.

35. Immanuel Kant, "Metaphysical Foundations of Natural Science," trans. James W. Ellington, in Kant, *The Philosophy of Material Nature*, vol. 2 (Indianapolis: Hackett, 1985), pp. 60-61; cited in Berthold Hoeckner, "Schumann and Romantic Distance," *Journal of the American Musicological Society* 50, no. 1 (Spring 1997), p. 59.

36. Pindar, "Pythian Ode I" (lines 15-27), in *Pindar: Olympian Odes, Pythian Odes*, ed. and trans. by William H. Race (Cambridge, MA: Loeb Classical Library, 1997), p. 215.

37. Noah Heringman, "The Style of Natural Catastrophe," *The Huntington Library Quarterly* 66, nos. 1/2 (2003), p. 98.

38. Élisée Reclus, "Le Mont Etna et L'Eruption de 1865," *Revue des Deux Mondes* 58 (July-August 1895), p. 117.

39. Jean Epstein, "Ciné Mystique" [1921], trans. Stuart Liebman, in Liebman, *Jean Epstein's Early Film Theory*, pp. 302-303. See Lundemo, "The Cinematograph Seen from Etna," p. 23.

40. Georges Bataille, "The Ascent of Mount Aetna," trans. Annette Michelson, *October* 36, special issue, "Georges Bataille: Writings on Laughter, Sacrifice, Nietzsche, Un-Knowing" (Spring 1986), p. 103. It should be noted that in this short essay, Bataille mentions that his companion, Laure (Colette Peignot), had written a letter to filmmaker Jean Grémillon in 1937 about their experience ascending Etna.

41. Epstein, *Etna*, p. 19; infra, 292.

42. Alexandre Dumas (père), *Impressions de Voyage: Le Spéronare* (Paris: Walder, 1854), p. 123.

43. Dumas, *Impressions de Voyage*, p. 123.

44. Ibid., pp. 122-123.

45. Altieri, "The Concept of Force," p. 193.

46. Dumas, *Impressions de Voyage*, p. 123.

47. Guy de Maupassant, "The Wandering Life," in *The Complete Works of Guy de Maupassant, Vol. 11: "The Wandering Life" and Short Stories*, trans. Alfred de Sumichrast and Adolphe Cohn (London: The Stratford Press, 1917), p. 76. Though I refer to this translation, I have also consulted the original: Guy de Maupassant, *La vie errante* (Paris: Société d'Éditions Littéraires et Artistiques, n.d.).

48. On Epstein's concept of "fatigue," see Kirtland's essay in this volume.

49. Maupassant, "The Wandering Life," p. 6.

50. See Hippolyte Taine, *Voyage en Italie*, 3 vols. (Brussels: Ed. Complexe, 1990); Hippolyte Taine, *Philosophie de l'art en Italie: leçons professes à L'École des Beaux-arts* (Paris: G. Baillière, 1866). Of equal interest are Taine's more general writings on the philosophy of art: *Philosophie de l'art* (Paris: Hachette, 1909). Taine appears in Epstein's *La Lyrosophie*, p. 159. Epstein mentions Taine's "sad dissertation on the little industry called art" that nevertheless had an "astonishing depth as descriptive science."

51. Maupassant, "The Wandering Life," pp. 15-16.

52. Ibid., p. 76.

53. Ibid., p. 78.

54. Tom Gunning, "Loïe Fuller and the Art of Motion: Body, Light, Electricity and the Origins of Cinema," in *Camera Obscura, Camera Lucida: Essays in Honor of Annette Michelson*, eds. Allen and Turvey, p. 79.

55. Note that *roc* can literally mean rock, but it can also be translated to signify the mythical Persian bird, or the chess piece, rook.

56. Epstein, *Etna*, p. 16; infra, 291.

57. Altieri, "The Concept of Force," p. 200.

58. Epstein, *Etna*, p. 16-17; infra, 291-92.

59. Henri Focillon, *Promenoir* 5 (1922), p. 64. Thanks to Katie Kirtland who graciously shared her copy of this source with me.

60. Edgar Allan Poe, *Eureka: A Prose Poem* (New York: George P. Putnam, 1848), p. 8. Available online at http://www.eapoe.org/works/EDITIONS/eurekac.htm. Accessed 2 December 2011. For a good summary of critical writing about *Eureka* and of the work's contemporary reception, see Barbara Cantalupo, "Eureka: Poe's "Novel Universe," in *A Companion to Poe Studies*, ed. Eric W. Carlson (Greenwood Press, 1996), pp. 323-346.

61. As Susan Welsh has pointed out, Poe's reference to a bird's eye view from Etna's summit is not his invention, but rather that of German explorer Alexander Von Humboldt; Poe in fact dedicated *Eureka* to Humboldt. Poe's recapitulation of Humboldt's scene that is originally found in *Cosmos* (1845) functions to highlight Poe's intuitive and analogical method that strived to "protect the 'impression' of absolute reciprocity from the kinds of limitation and dilution imposed by rules of thought and exposition. [...] Poe proposes a 'survey of the universe' that will enable the mind 'to receive and to perceive an individual impression'" (Susan Welsh, "The Value of Analogical Evidence: Poe's 'Eureka' in the Context of a Scientific Debate," *Modern Language Studies* 21, no. 4

[1991], pp. 10-11). We should recall that Dumas did not "whirl," but instead made the effort of enumerating each thing apparent in the vast landscape as something singularly valuable to his individual consciousness of "oneness."

62. Paul Valéry, "Au Sujet d'Eurêka," in Edgar A. Poe, *Eurêka ou Essai Sur L'Univers Matériel et Spirituel*, trans. Charles Baudelaire, ornements dessinés et gravés sur bois par Alfred Latour (Paris: Editions d'Art Edouard Pelletan, Helleu et Sergent Editeurs, 1923), p. xx. Iampolski notes that Valéry's "Au sujet d'Eurêka" was published in the journal *Variété* in 1924, and that Valéry's text resembles Epstein's method in *La Lyrosophie* – a claim I agree with. However, Valéry's essay originally appeared as the introduction to the limited, illustrated edition (1923) of Charles Baudelaire's translation of *Eureka*. It is highly likely that Epstein would have encountered this edition first, and, as Iampolski suggests, would have been inspired if not quite influenced by Valéry's essay, especially for how he evaluates Poe's power to unify disparate modes of inquiry. Valéry thoughts on the cosmogenic genre are especially pertinent:

Just as tragedy does to history and psychology, the genre of cosmogony touches on religions, and that it confuses in places, and on science, which it necessarily distinguishes by the absence of verifications. It consists of sacred texts, admirable poems, excessively bizarre stories, charged with beauty and ridicule, physio-mathematic research of a depth that is sometimes worthy of an object less insignificant than the universe. (Valéry, "Au Suject d'Eurêka," pp. xx-xxi)

Alfred Latour, a friend of Valéry, illustrated editions of works by André Gide, Raymond Poincaré, and Maurice Maeterlinck. In 1928, his woodcuts were included in an edition of Baudelaire's *Les Fleurs du Mal*.

63. John T. Irwin, "A Platonic Dialogue; *Eureka* as Detective Story; Marked with a Letter; The Tetractys and the Line of Beauty; Letter as Nodal Point; A Shared Structrue; Thematizing the Acts of Reading," in *Edgar Allan Poe*, edited with an introduction by Harold Bloom (New York: Chelsea House, 2006), p. 48.

64. Poe mentions the forces of gravitation, attraction, and repulsion, among others. See Poe, *Eureka*, especially pp. 37-52. Available online at http://www.eapoe.org/works/essays/eureka3.htm. Accessed 2 December 2011.

65. As part of Poe's original text, the graphic appeared in an early edition of Baudelaire's translation of *Eureka* (Paris: Michel Lévy, frères, 1864), reproduced here. It subsequently appeared in the 1923 edition cited above; it was not illustrated by Latour, but maintained its place as a component of the text.

66. As was the assertion of Poe critic, A. D. Van Nostrand (1968), cited in Cantalupo, "Eureka," p. 325.

67. As Kenneth Silverman called it; cited in Cantalupo, "Eureka," p. 326.

68. Jacques Aumont, "Cinégénie, ou la Machine à Re-monter le Temps," in *Jean Epstein*, ed. Aumont, p. 107.

69. Poe also invites the reader to envision a physical agency conducting the diffusion of force. He writes: "For convenience of illustration, let us imagine, in the first place, a hollow sphere of glass, or of anything else, occupying the space throughout which the universal matter is to be thus equally diffused, by means of irradiation, from the absolute, irrelative, unconditional particle, placed in the centre of the sphere" (Poe, *Eureka*,

p. 54; available online at http://www.eapoe.org/works/essays/eureka4.htm. Accessed 2 December 2011).

70. Jean Epstein, "Magnification" [1921], Abel1, p. 235.

71. Paola Salerni, *Anarchie, langue, société: L'Etna chez soi de Villiers de l'Isle Adam* (Paris: Presses Paris Sobonne, 2004), especially pp. 96-126.

72. I take "psychology of organic movement" from I. Madison Bentley, "The Psychology of Organic Movements," in *The American Journal of Psychology* XVII, No. 3 (July 1906): 293-305.

73. Auguste Villiers de l'Isle-Adam, "Etna chez soi," in *Histoires Insolites* (Paris: Librairie Moderne, 1888), p. 309. Thanks to Mireille Dobrzynski for her help translating this passage. Incidentally, a fire engulfed Paris' Opéra-Comique in May, 1887; *The New York Times* reported that a "noisome smell arises from the ruins of the Opéra Comique. [...] The stench shows that there must still be many bodies under the debris" ("The Opéra Comique Disaster," *The New York Times* [30 May 1887]).

74. Paul DeMan, "The Epistemology of Metaphor," *Critical Inquiry* 5, no. 1 (Autumn 1978), p. 21. This essay also appears as the first chapter in DeMan's *Aesthetic Ideology* (Minneapolis: University of Minnesota Press, 1996).

75. This figure is published in Haringman's article. I have obtained it from its original source, *La Caricature*, 3 année, no. 135, vol. 6 (1833), pl. 279, though I am grateful for Haringman's research that first brought this evocative image to my attention.

76. Epstein, *Lyrosophie*, p. 184.

77. Ibid., p. 195.

78. Epstein, *Bonjour Cinema*, pp. 40-41; "The Extra Sense," trans. Stuart Liebman, in Liebman, *Jean Epstein's Early Film Theory*, p. 290.

79. This is similar to Benjamin's concept of innervation; see Miriam Hansen, "Benjamin and Cinema: Not a One-Way Street," *Critical Inquiry* 25, no. 2 (Winter 1999): 306-343. Thanks to Jason Paul for pointing this out.

80. Walter Moore Coleman, *Mental Biology. Second Part. Experiments in Telergy or the Supersensory Control of Vital Activities at a Distance* (London: Woolridge and Co., n.d.). I shall refer to the text as *Telergy* and the concept as telergy. The text's first footnote contextualizes this work: "This series of papers, to be printed later in book form, consists chiefly of sets of experiments. The first paper was on "The Cause of Sleep" (1910). Others will be on "The Heart and the Mind" (fore-, sub-, and self-consciousness), "The Breath and the Spirit (the dynamics of mood and emotion), "Body and Soul" (with experiments on the physiology of the nirvanic state carried out with the aid of Buddhist monks in the Orient)." Ostensibly, Coleman was born in Texas, but spent much of his time as a teacher and researcher in Berlin and London. For a resumé of his activities, see: http://www.tshaonline.org/handbook/online/articles/CC/fco20.html. Many of his other, less experimental publications are available online. Special thanks are due to John Paul Stonard who graciously located, copied, and sent this text to me from the British Library.

81. Coleman, *Mental Biology*, p. 1.

82. Ibid., p. 3.

83. Ibid., p. 2.

84. Liebman, *Jean Epstein's Early Film Theory*, p. 209.

85. Epstein, "Le Sens 1 bis" [1921], pp. 31, 43 (my translation). We would be wise to also recall Epstein's essay "Ciné-Mystique" [1921] that appears in *Bonjour Cinéma*, pp. 111-118.

86. Epstein, "The Extra Sense," *Jean Epstein's Early Film Theory*, p. 289.

87. Hansen, "Benjamin's Aura," p. 354.

88. Jacques Rancière, *Film Fables*, trans. Emiliano Battista (New York: Berg Publishers, 2006), p. 3.

89. Rancière, *Film Fables*, p. 11.

90. Epstein's theory could undoubtedly be explored further within the terms of the uncanny's return via technology. See, for example, Tom Gunning, "Re-Newing Old Technologies: Astonishment, Second Nature, and the Uncanny in Technology from the Previous Turn-of-the-Century," in *Rethinking Media Change: The Aesthetics of Transition*, eds. David Thorburn and Henry Jenkins (Cambridge, MA: MIT Press, 2003), pp. 39-60.

91. Epstein, *Etna*, p. 18; infra, 292.

92. Ibid., p. 16; infra, 291-92.

93. Altieri, "The Concept of Force," p. 205.

94. Epstein, *Etna*, p. 18; infra, 292.

95. Altieri, "The Concept of Force," p. 206.

96. Epstein, *Etna*, p. 13; infra, 290.

97. Epstein, "Langue d'Or" [1922], in *Etna*, p. 36; infra, 297.

98. Ibid., p. 38; infra, 298.

99. Epstein, *Etna*, p. 14; infra, 290.

100. G. W. F Hegel, *Phenomenology of Spirit*, trans. A. V. Miller (New York: Oxford University Press, 1977), p.86.

101. Epstein, *Etna*, p. 13; infra, 289.

"The Supremacy of the Mathematical Poem": Jean Epstein's Conceptions of Rhythm

Laurent Guido

Jean Epstein's ideas about rhythm, expressed in a series of talks, articles, and books from the early 1920s to the late 1940s, cannot be fully understood without being situated within a larger theoretical debate over the aesthetic and social potential of the cinematic medium. Already discussed at the beginning of the 20th century as a key concept in many artistic and scientific fields, the notion of rhythm occupies a central position among the early attempts by French critics and cinéastes to grasp the so-called "specific *langage*" of film. I would like to emphasize a historical-contextual approach, according to which "French film theory" does not amount to a coherent discourse, but instead gathers together a set of conflicting views on similar issues and problems. In the 1920s, rhythm clearly stood out as one of the central conceptions within these theoretical debates over ways to define and to legitimize cinema as an art form.[1] I will start by examining two well-known notions that are closely related to rhythm in Jean Epstein's film aesthetics: movement and *photogénie*. Studying the connections between movement and *photogénie* will foreground the rhythmic properties that early commentators and theorists observed in film. More importantly, these connections will help define Epstein's thoughts about cinematic rhythm, which lay at the intersection between art and science, and refer as much to a recognition of modernity's most revolutionary aspects as to the persistence of traditional philosophical ideas and values.

Movement is a recurring preoccupation among critics and cinéastes writing about the aesthetics of film during the twenties. At the time, critics frequently asserted that cinema epitomized a new kind of mobility, resulting broadly from the major changes brought about in everyday life by the new techniques and practices associated with industrialization. According to many French film critics of the twenties, movement characterized not only concrete and daily existence, but also the aesthetic experience itself. Moreover, the plastic arts were considered primarily a static means of expression, from which cinema should absolutely differ. As the art historian Elie Faure puts it in 1920, only film gives "new plastic impressions" from "a mobile composition, constantly renewed."[2] One year later, in his book *Bonjour Cinema*, Jean Epstein follows Faure in describing film as "all movement, without any obligation to be stable or balanced."[3] Epstein sees stability and balance as the main flaws of painting and sculpture, which he harshly condemns for their superficial attempts to depict movement. The director Marcel L'Herbier takes the same position, maintaining that cinema expresses "a taste for perpetual movement," which explains why it must struggle against the "tendency toward immobility" represented by the plastic arts.[4] L'Herbier's apparent contradiction is echoed in the same year by Leon Moussinac, who blames the static arts for being "breathless" and claims that these "immobile towers" will soon "collapse" thanks to the positive action of cinema.[5] Not only traditional arts such as sculpture, painting, and architecture but also a mechanical medium such as photography are perceived with a hostility that pervades texts from Ricciotto Canudo to Louis Delluc.[6] A similar hostility towards immobility constitutes the starting point for Germaine Dulac's conception of movement, which she unfolds in an important article entitled, "Le film, son esthétique, ses entraves" ("Film, Its Aesthetics, Its Hindrances").[7] If Dulac rejects every means of expression that appears to her as essentially "frozen in its immobility," she acknowledges that film itself is comprised of immobile images whose rapid succession generates what is merely an illusion of animation. She admits that it is "the sensitivity of the photographic images recording a phase of movement [which], by means of their multiplicity, succeeds in building up the whole movement."[8] However, Dulac doesn't seem to be bothered by this artificial dimension of filmic movement, which had been identified and stigmatized previously by Henri Bergson in his book, *Creative Evolution* (1907). On the contrary, Dulac seems to be fascinated by this ability to set immobile elements in motion. Her position anticipates a stand taken by Jean Epstein in such late writings as *Intelligence d'une machine* (1946). In this book, Epstein follows other early film theorists, such as Rudolf Arnheim,[9] who believed movement is not to be found in the immobile images set into motion by the projector, but in the spectator's inner perception of the moving images shown on the screen: "The animation and the merging of these shapes take place not in the film, neither in the camera lens, but in man itself. Discontinuity becomes continuity only after having gone into the spectator."[10] Cinema is thus based on static images, but it goes beyond this elementary stage by making these immutable images move.[11] Hence, when Epstein points out the marvelous ability of film to "turn a discontinuity into a continuity" or, more precisely, to "synthesize discontinuous and immobile elements in a continuous and mobile set," he is responding to Bergson's concern that film embodies a scientific conception of movement and has nothing in common with the real, inner motion that Bergson places at the heart of his philosophical system.[12]

According to French film theorists, cinema seems on the contrary to fit Bergson's ideal process, which is to get closer to the true and infinite "mobile reality" he locates beyond the reach of human language and intelligence. Whereas Bergson himself perceives cinema as an embodiment of the technoscientific inability to apprehend the most important level of reality – that is, the indivisible continuity of a perfect inner duration – many early advocates of film embrace its almost mystical ability to reveal new aspects of the universe. When Germaine Dulac compares cinema to "an eye wide open upon life, more powerful than our own eye and which sees what we don't see," she follows Canudo, who defines film as the "art to express the invisible through the visible,"[13] or Abel Gance, who believes that cinema is able to "translate the invisible world through the visible world."[14] This property of the cinematic medium, this possibility to see the world and its objects with a superhuman keenness is one of the various notions that many critics and theorists have described as *photogénie*. For instance, Louis Delluc, Léon Moussinac, Juan Arroy, and Epstein himself all define *photogénie* as a specific revelation of beauty or moral value in things that are being filmed.[15]

However, there is an additional detail in many of these definitions, which reminds us that *photogénie* cannot really be effective without movement and, furthermore, without timing and rhythm. Among the leading French film theorists, Epstein is one of the most dedicated to this connection between *photogénie* and rhythm. When he specifies in 1924 that the additional "moral value" brought about by the cinematic technique[16] only applies to what he refers to as the "mobile aspects of the world, of things, of souls," he echoes Louis Delluc's earlier urge to "qualify, develop, measure" filmed objects with "rhythm, humanity, outburst," without which *photogénie* would seem "powerless."[17] But Epstein's stand refers above all to his own previous definition of *photogénie* in *Bonjour Cinema* (1921): *Photogénie* is one of the "sensory logarithms of reality," specifically associated with the possibility to expand and multiply "mobility."[18] By alluding to a mathematical term such as "logarithm," Epstein demonstrates his obsessive commitment to the idea of a systematic and rational analysis (and control) of the constantly shifting processes of cinema. Moreover, these processes are not only related to movement, which evolves in time, but also to the spatial configuration of every frame. In this regard, Epstein affirms in 1923 that the "photogenic aspect figures among the time-space variables"; and that "a dimension is photogenic if it moves and changes simultaneously in space and time."[19]

Epstein's statements about the spatiotemporal quality of *photogénie* lead, in my opinion, to one of the essential, if obvious, properties of rhythm: namely, rhythm can refer not only to aspects related to space (for instance the calculation of the rhythmic proportions of volume and space within the frame), but also to time and movement. Thanks to its ability to bridge space and time, the concept of rhythm is very popular in the aesthetic discourses, systems, and methods of the early twentieth century, and especially in early theories of film. As stated by Canudo, cinema synthesizes the "[r]hythms of time" and the "[r]hythms of space."[20] Therefore, cinema links together dimensions traditionally divided in the classical view of fine arts, as theorized since Lessing. Apart from this aesthetic aspect, the notion of rhythm has a more general sense, most often following the all-encompassing definition by Plato, "order within the movement" (Laws 665a). Hence, rhythm turns out to be very useful for understanding all types of movement, be they related to philosophy, science, society, or culture. Hence, scientists use the term on the one hand to describe fundamental, archaic, and traditional movements, from the biological pulses to human gestures related to work or dance, and on the other hand to characterize new types of movements generated by modern life and the machine age, including new modes of transportation and communication. The obsession with rhythm during this period makes it the key principle for understanding how the new movements of modernity shaped themselves according to a very traditional view of universal harmony. As Epstein puts it in his later writings, "cinema brings us back to Pythagoras and Plato's poetry [in the sense that] reality is only the harmony of Ideas and Numbers."[21] He elaborates on this argument the following year, when he affirms that modern science has revealed the "supremacy of the mathematical poem," a privileged way to conceive reality. He also calls this basic principle "the number in motion, the plural and quantized movement."[22] So, if we take into account Epstein's opinion that photogénie explores movement in both space and time, only rhythm seems to be able to control, channel, and organize mobility.[23] As the theorist Paul Ramain – at the time one of the leading proponents of the "musical analogy" (or "musicalist" trend) – reminds us, "Every movement, be it visual or acoustic, creates a more or less symmetrical chain of elements, comprising moments of softness and moments of strength. This is cadence. This is rhythm!"[24]

From movement to rhythm: an outline of film history

Underlying Jean Epstein's definition of photogénie is an aesthetic program that encourages filmmakers to focus on the rhythmic exploration of motion. In fact, rhythm was a primary concern for many French filmmakers of the 1920s. For instance, Germaine Dulac argues that cinema must, first and foremost, be centered on the "knowledge of movement and visual rhythms."[25] Dulac's work is especially important for its delineation of the stages leading from movement to rhythm, as found in "Le film, son esthétique, ses entraves." This article is among her finest contributions to film theory: from a teleological and determinist position (typical of avant-garde criticism between theory and militancy), Dulac gives an outline of film history up to her day, according to the different types of movement that cinema has produced. In this section, I will show how Dulac's account of movement relates to Epstein's own theoretical project, particularly in the ways they link aesthetic discourses with film practice. Many of their views are based upon the critical appraisal of concrete films, which they evaluate according to a progressive and idealistic view of film art. Specifically, both Dulac and Epstein consider cinema's capture of reality as a mere starting point for their artistic endeavor, in which rhythm is destined to play the essential role.

Dulac begins her history of cinematic movement by claiming that early cinema produced only a *mechanical* movement, which is mainly linked with the most trivial aspects of life itself: it is an "ordinary vision of people and animated things, going, coming, agitating, without any other purpose than moving in the frame."[26] Note the choice of the word "ordinary" (*banal*). The same year (1927), Epstein suggests that the contingency created by the camera's capture of reality is basic material in need of a creative step: "This ordinariness studied, explored thoroughly, broken down, multiplied, detailed, applied, will give to the cinematic drama a striking human relief, a hugely amplified power of suggestion."[27] Epstein thus echoes his own, aforementioned definition of *photogénie* as a multiplied and expanded movement: even the radically new dimensions of reality, which are unfolded for the first time by the cinematic device, must be apprehended by human artistry.

In Dulac's opinion, this elementary, mechanical movement is only the "scientific and material basis" of the "capture of movement, taken directly from life itself."[28] She gives the example of an early film, the arrival of a train at a station, which seems to be "the capture of a raw movement, a machine with its rods, its wheels, its speed."[29] Even if Dulac perceives some reality in that type of image (she refers to it as the "*vrai cinématographique*"), she specifies that this obvious impression of truth results more from the "sensation of speed" than from the ontological realism of the moving image, a realism she nevertheless describes as an "exact observation of characters and their gestures."[30] Dulac's reasoning, like many of her fellow avant-garde critics and filmmakers, is deeply rooted in a desire to surpass mechanical movement in order to reach a more elaborate level of artistic creation.

According to Dulac, the early mechanical phase was actually abandoned for the benefit of *narration*.[31] In earlier essays on the connections between film, theater, and literature, she says that narration is another way of structuring movement, a principle capable of building up dynamic structures, such as relationships between tension and resolution.[32] Dulac regrets this turn away from mechanical movement to what she calls a "fictitious narrative" movement, which involves, in her opinion, film's submission to other means of expression and to a series of plots and characters. Yet, she indicates that it is within the framework of narrative film that the first signs of a truly rhythmic cinema became evident. She argues that rhythm made its decisive appearance when film evolved from a series of frames without any reciprocal relations to a succession of shots "which are dependent on each other and follow a psychological logic."[33]

The psychology of characters linked to narrative movement can thus be organized in a more rational and systematic way. Contemporary historical studies have shown that this kind of systematization occurred when editing practices were standardized according to continuity principles honed in the American fiction film. After the First World War, French film critics began writing about the ongoing standardization of narrative cinema; and in 1924, Epstein suggests that American cinema carried out the first concrete experiments involving *photogénie*, a "precocious and unconscious cinematic sense," a "sketch of "space-time *ciné-grammes*"[34] which D. W. Griffith organized in "the classical shape of abrupt, intersecting endings."[35] Epstein notably praises the "measured way in which [Griffith] assembled all these fragments of scenes, according to mathematical proportions between shot lengths...." This calculation "ravished spectators who at that moment discovered a new sensation: visual rhythm."[36] The notion of rhythm therefore lies at the heart of the narrativization process associated with the American feature films discovered in France after the Great War.[37] Chaplin, Fairbanks, Griffith, William Hart, and Thomas Ince are the main figures whose enthusiastic reception among early French critics establishes the advent of a cinematic culture, but whose major influence on French cinéphiles would decline in the mid-twenties.

Even if Dulac is hostile towards narration, she considers this *rhythmic narrative movement* as the epitome of technical progress: thanks to the development of the rhythmical properties of film art, cinema "goes forward to the visual idea [...] From the shots, from the necessary fragmentation, the cadence stood out, from juxtaposition rhythm was born."[38] She implicitly refers to montage when she evokes the "logic" according to which "a point of movement must [always] anticipate another one."[39] In Dulac's mind, the next stage in the history of cinematic movement was already explored by some French filmmakers who were associated with the avant-garde and who occasionally emphasized rhythm over narration in their films.[40] This practice is one of many aspects of the stage that Dulac calls "impressionism." Considered a minor notion at the time, impressionism later became a prevalent expression in film historiography, in spite of being defined in different, sometimes conflicting ways – from Georges Sadoul's *Histoire générale du cinéma* to David Bordwell's thesis on Impressionist cinema. The rhythmic practices to which Dulac refers were most often based upon fast editing practices, comprising typical acceleration patterns. Essays, lectures, and special anthology screenings during the early twenties often featured a familiar set of recurring examples taken from these avant-garde experiments.[41] These examples included the fair sequence from Epstein's *Cœur fidèle* (1923), the car and the lab sequences from *L'Inhumaine* by Marcel L'Herbier (1924), Mosjoukine's wild dance from *Kean* by A. Volkoff (1925), and the circus scenes from *La Galerie des Monstres* by Jaque Catelain (1925). The best example – and the most often mentioned – is without a doubt *La Roue* (1922) by Abel Gance. In her 1927 essay on movement, Dulac, like many other critics of the time, sees La Roue as a "great step forward," appearing as a multiplied, rhythmic version of the early train film which she regarded as an embodiment of mechanical movement. Dulac refers to the "impressionist" trend either as a *symphonic poem of images* when it relates to the expressivity of each image or as a *visual symphony* when she wants to emphasize the structure of time – that is, the rhythm. In both cases, narrative patterns (causality, psychology, etc.) do not play an essential role anymore; instead, Dulac shifts her focus to the temporal expressivity of rhythm, to "the length of images, their opposition, their harmony."[42]

Dulac shows that some sequences from La Roue showcase the formal, geometrical properties of filmed objects and not their meaning or narrative value. In her opinion, the art of motion seems to be "at last rationally understood." Here, Dulac echoes Fernand Léger, who praised the plastic value of La Roue,[43] and Epstein, who perceived in it a major development in the history of montage, a step beyond Griffith's achievements in editing.[44] This idea would be revived in the 1980s by Gilles Deleuze, in his book L'Image mouvement, where he evokes the "French School," which was led by Abel Gance and was characterized by a logic of quality and bravura, a school in which filmmakers concentrated mostly on "the amount of movement and on the metrical relations allowing to define it."[45]

About *inner* and *outer* rhythms

In order to tackle these "metrical relations" more thoroughly, one must take into account an article Leon Moussinac wrote in 1923 in which he raises, more precisely and systematically than any other text from the time, the question of cinematic rhythm. In this article, which would be republished two years later in his landmark contribution to film theory, *Naissance du cinéma*, Moussinac makes a very important distinction between inner rhythm and outer rhythm.[46]

Inner rhythm is the structuring principle of movements within the frame: on the one hand, movements by people and things themselves and, on the other hand, movements generated by the camera. In 1921, Epstein addresses this specific problem, inspired by a passage from a book by the biologist Walter Moore Coleman (*Mental Biology*, notably dealing with "Experiments in Telergy"), who proposes that, at any particular moment, there is a common rhythm synchronizing every single movement coming from a human or animal group, be it a gesture or breathing, and that this common rhythm could be reduced to an elementary musical bar. Epstein suggests that cinema should find inspiration in such relations for the pace of its own gestures, a pacing that he describes as both "rhythmic" and "photogenic." In his opinion, film is able to "catch this cadence, inscribe that fundamental rhythm with its harmonics." This is what Epstein calls cinema's own "prosody."[47]

Regarding this rhythmical apprehension of bodily motion, which is a recurring pursuit in early French psychological and anthropological studies (besides works by Théodule Ribot and Pierre Janet, see the tremendous artistic and cultural impact of Marcel Jousse's thesis on rhythmical gesture in 1925),[48] Epstein makes various statements during the twenties in which he often praises very fast movements taken from traveling cameras placed on horses, cars, trains, and planes. He calls this practice the "extreme" mobilization of cinema, fitting the new rapid conditions of everyday modern life.[49] I have shown elsewhere how Epstein posits this energetic view of modernity through a much-favored metaphor of dance.[50] But, quite early on, he also warns against the excesses of this culture of speed: in fact, rhythm does not relate solely to fast movements, but also to slow ones. Epstein refers for example to the gestures of the actors in his film L'Auberge rouge (1923, from Balzac's novel). There, the idea was to find a filmic equivalent of what Epstein calls the "dreamlike life allure," which corresponds to the peculiar "psychological rhythm" of Balzac's novel.[51]

About outer rhythm, Moussinac's call to create "cinematic bars" (just as there are "musical bars") constitutes a real obsession in the early work of Gance, Dulac, L'Herbier, and Epstein. In order to structure film sequences according to simple and repetitive metrical patterns, they specify in several of their shooting scripts the actual number of images (that is, the number of photograms) that are required for any specific shot.[52] Two fundamental patterns appear when analyzing some of the famous "rhythmic" sequences mentioned above: the systematic alternation of a few similar shots and a gradual increase in speed (or decrease in length for each shot), in order to produce striking climactic effects.[53] The funfair scenes in Cœur fidèle seem to organize on a rhythmic basis the contingency and ordinariness of the mechanical movement I discussed earlier: images of crowds which are channeled and set in motion according to very simple and repetitive pulses; people in seesaws, swing-boats or merry-go-rounds; alternating figures and various subjective point-of-view shots. All these features aim to generate what Epstein himself refers to as a "photogenic dance" in which spectators are supposed to be mobilized as well via direct, primary identification with the camera. In Bonjour Cinéma (1921), he already qualified as "photogenic" the "landscape's dance" taken from a train or car at full speed, and looked forward to a time when he would be able to depict "a dance taken successively in the four cardinal directions. Then, with panoramic shots [...] the theater seen by the dancing couple. An intelligent editing will reconstitute [...] the life of dance, both according to the spectator and the dancer, objective and subjective."[54] In Cœur fidèle, such visual composition is structured through elementary rhythmic successions, which testify to a precise measurement of shot length. Marie (A) and Petit-Paul (B) are treated as true visual motives, which can be arranged in a metrical way. There are, for instance, A-B-A series of shots in which B exactly equals the sum of A + A'; or AB-A-B-AB series in which the addition of the two outer shots

(AB) equals the sum of the two inner shots (A and B). This metric conception is theoretically supported, at least at the beginning, by Epstein. According to him, the "rhythmic" passages of a film must be "composed of frames where one has determined in a very precise manner the length and the proportions between the shots."[55] He underscores the necessity for the shot lengths to remain in an "elementary ratio," in order to strike the eye with more efficiency. For instance, in a fast editing piece, Epstein estimates that "a series of 2-4-8 images creates a rhythm which will surely be ruined by the introduction of a 5- or 7-image series."[56]

At first, Epstein appreciates these "rhythm selections" or "rhythmic fragments," seeing in them the ability to "separate style from anecdote," a necessary experiment for the future development of film art.[57] But, from the mid-1920s onwards, he begins to think that productions such as La Roue suffer from their heterogeneity. In 1926, for instance, he says that La Roue's fast editing sequences look like an "accident in the film."[58] Such rhythmic passages should not appear as self-sufficient, but instead refer to the overall structure of the work in which they are inserted, according to logic and dynamic principles. This flaw is the same aspect of French cinema that the Russian critic, Yuri Tynyanov, would criticize in the "Formalist" book Poetika Kino (Poetics of Cinema) in 1927, calling it the logic of eclecticism: a part of a film follows the rules of "old" editing, devoted only to representing the scene and the fabula, while another part is clearly devoted to "new," avant-garde montage as a perceptible element of construction.[59] Even La Roue's director, Abel Gance, does not defend this hybrid conception of film as a series of potentially detachable pieces. In 1923, he warns that "there would be art if the fragment was a piece inscribed in a mosaic from which it cannot be separated without compromising the perfect harmony of the whole. But it ain't so, the great mosaic does not exist, the fragment is only a mere fragment."[60]

Towards *Photogénie* pure

It is well known that, after the mid-1920s, and most notably in a 1924 lecture about photogénie, Epstein becomes quite skeptical of some avant-garde theories and ideas; he is especially hostile towards fast editing, which, in his view, has turned out to be a mere trend appearing in every documentary or dramatic film, losing any real aesthetic interest.[61] Therefore, "movement symphonies" in the manner of Cœur fidèle seem to him as annoying and ridiculous as "Caligarism," the derisive term used by some French critics of the time to refer to German Expressionism.[62] Consequently, in 1924, Epstein calls for a more complex study of cinematic rhythms, notably in comparison to musical equivalents, but without falling into what he refers to as "easy and deluding analogies."[63]

Unlike literature or theater, music is constantly used as an analogy by many film theorists of the twenties (Canudo, Moussinac, Ramain, Emile Vuillermoz, and, of course, Dulac), who regard it as an emblematic means of expression that can help filmmakers create their own, autonomous language of cinema. At first sight, it seems quite paradoxical for an art to find its own specificity through another art. Nonetheless, music functions here as a model for structuring motion not only through its mastery of rhythm but also through its various techniques, structures, harmonic systems, and melodic developments. If rhythm is an element common to cinema and music, allowing useful comparisons between these two means of expression, other references to so-called absolute relations between musical harmony and visual elements (that is, between certain chords or notes and certain shapes, colors, or frames) seem far less convincing, and are grounded only in the lyrical, metaphorical language that frequently characterizes early film theories. When Dulac affirms in 1925 that cinema should first and foremost try to find out its own "visual symphony made of rhythmic images," she is appealing to Romantic tradition, like most of her fellow filmmakers and critics involved in the musicalist trend.[64] On the one hand, this obsessive allusion to music refers to the philosophical tradition of the early nineteenth century (Hegel, Schelling, Hoffmann, and Schopenhauer), according to which music has a privileged relation to immateriality and the inner movements of the soul. As many French filmmakers grappled with cinema as a means for revealing invisible thought – the stream of consciousness or the inner *durée* as identified by Bergson – they found themselves naturally attracted to this Romantic aesthetic.[65] On the other hand, the idea of "pure music" is an aesthetic conception developed from the mid-nineteenth century onwards by critics such as Eduard Hanslick, who strongly opposed the idea that music should be applied to narrative or scenic performances and praised those aspects of music that fit the requirements of an absolute, autonomous art form. Besides (and mostly thanks to) its influence in the field of plastic arts and poetry, the concept of pure art became a major issue in the French debates about film aesthetics. In the twenties, this issue led to various conflicting views on the role of abstraction in film and its relation to representational features. In order to grasp more clearly Jean Epstein's own position, one should not underestimate the subtleties of this complex set of discourses.

Most critics and filmmakers affiliated with the avant-garde shared a common idea of cinema, which was to restrict narrative elements to a unifying subject or theme (which they most often describe as a kind of "pretext") in favor of a more rhythmical and specifically visual way of structuring movement in film; however, they greatly differ on what they mean by *pure* cinema. For Ramain, Faure, Moussinac, Gance, and a majority of the avant-garde supporters, pure cinema is more the ideal of a stylized narrative, inspired by Wagnerian operas in which essential subjects and ideas were reduced to a dynamic series of musical themes. For others, led for a time by Dulac, the future of film instead lies in a tendency towards abstraction, beyond the hybrid aesthetics she describes as "impressionism."[66] While this position is notably advocated by Henri Chomette[67] and René

Schwob,[68] the most convincing definition of it is given by Louis Chavance in a 1927 essay.[69] Chavance draws a very clear line between *visual symphony* and *pure cinema*. According to him, a visual symphony is essentially based upon abstract movements executed by geometrical shapes, as in the early films by the German filmmakers Walter Ruttmann and Hans Richter. It creates an immediate emotion, needing neither "representation" nor "imagination." Visual symphonies are thus very different from pure cinema, which consists of figurative images and fragments captured from reality which are then integrated into rhythmic developments such as the urban symphonies and the surrealist films near the end of the twenties – for instance, in films produced at that time by the same Ruttmann and Richter.[70]

The opposition that Chavance draws between abstraction and non-figurative realism fits perfectly with the dichotomy Jean Epstein describes in an article titled "Bilan de fin de muet" ("Assessment at the end of silent cinema"), written in 1931. Epstein differentiates the *absolute film* – with its geometrical abstraction, which he strongly rejects – from *photogénie pure* – which embodies a renewed interest in filming nature and great human creations and which Epstein praises (like Jean Tedesco[71]) in a reactionary stance. In Epstein's opinion, the pursuit of *photogénie pure* originates in an impulse to resist the oversimplification implied by absolute films, which are certainly able to capture motion "very close to its principle," but, "as every abstraction, are quickly annoying."[72]

Although on opposite sides, Chavance and Epstein acknowledge the same difference between two aesthetics of cinematic purity. Both agree to reject narration, even as a stylized form based upon visual leitmotifs, but they disagree about abstraction. On the one hand, Chavance calls for displays of non-figurative shapes (the visual symphony, which fits into the absolute film hated by Epstein). On the other hand, Epstein praises a photogenic purity centered upon filming the universe (which fits into pure cinema according to Chavance). However, there is an intermediary position, in which *photogénie pure* does not necessarily imply a refusal of geometrical abstraction. This idea is notably sustained by Dulac, who theorizes abstraction as the main goal of artistic cinema, but observes it mostly in documentary and scientific films dedicated to the tiny, invisible movements of nature (for instance, films using fast-motion to reveal the movements of a plant or wheat germ). This stance – of locating abstraction in nature – is in keeping with an approach chosen by many abstraction theorists such as the futurists Bruno Corra and Arnaldo Ginna, who, in 1910, foresaw the "Art of the Future" as a series of moving harmonic colors based upon the observation of nature.[73] In addition to the ideas developed by the painter Frantisek Kupka in his essay *Creation in the Plastic Arts* (1910-1913),[74] there are also the conceptions, more contemporary to Dulac, that Kandinsky outlined in 1926 in *Point et ligne sur plan* (*Point and Line to Plane*). Looking for a new method of plastic composition inspired by music, Kandinsky insists on finding within nature itself the minimal structural elements that are necessary to create a lexicon of essential geometrical shapes.[75] This is exactly what Dulac sees in the scientific films she considers as foreshadowing pure cinema: they not only contain an expression of rhythm and speed, but also various displays of shapes, lines, curves, light, or shades,[76] all of which she finally refers to as the only "sensitive factors" of film.[77]

Epstein evidently would agree with the premise, according to which any real artistic expression originates in the essential and harmonious *langage* of nature. For example, in 1924, he draws parallels between the cinematographic treatment of movement and the "astonishing life of plants and crystals" and, two years later, between cinema and the eruption of Mount Etna.[78] This type of comparison stems from Epstein's early interest in science (he left impressive notebooks on various topics such as biology, physics, and mathematics).[79] In accordance with the neo-platonic idealism of the era, and a broad renewal of Pythagorean models and ideas, Epstein frequently depicts the universe as a rhythmically regulated geometrical system. In an unpublished note, he evokes

the symmetry which one observes in most aspects of nature: structure of molecule, steadiness of crystal, axis of stem, alternation of leaves, radiance of petals, spirals of seashells, balance of right and left in almost all living beings. Still more amazing is the mystery of symmetries which unite microcosm to macrocosm, which repeat the infinitely small in the infinitely large, and the universe in the atom.[80]

By seeing these "harmonious connections" as potentially related to some "intellectual optical effect," Epstein reveals his constant fascination with the human mind's powers to read, comprehend, and even manipulate the external world. As a new perceptive mode inherited from science, cinema appears as the most effective tool to accomplish such goals. Like many of his fellow avant-garde filmmakers and critics, Epstein in fact perceives the cinematographic device as a prosthetic means able to reveal the universe.[81] Hence, he describes the "strange gaze" of cameras, thanks to which "rivers, forests, snows, factories, railroads, and the sea have unveiled on the screen their intense and personal lives."[82]

There are many examples of these preoccupations in Epstein's work, the most famous one being the sequence from *Le Tempestaire* (1947) in which Father Floch's magical mastering of time is echoed in specific cinematic devices, such as reverse motion. There is also slow motion, which appears to be a crucial aspect in Epstein's rhythmical treatment of temporality. Epstein's use of slow motion by means of a Debrie high-speed camera in *La Chute de la Maison Usher* (*The Fall of the House of Usher*, 1928) has been frequently commented upon, and notably by Epstein himself.[83] In an interview, he justified the recourse to slow motion as a way to enhance the filmic capacity of discovering life's most subtle movements:

There are an infinite number of movements, of expressions, as much among my human actors as among the things that act in my films and in all the details of every landscape that the normal camera is mechanically incapable of comprehending, of seizing, of reproducing. It's not a question of the use I make of this slow motion, of simply or bizarrely decomposing a few subtle plastic aspects of the mobile world.[84]

This rejection of superficial distortion echoes Epstein's condemnation of the avant-garde's unsystematic praise of fast editing or highly fragmented framing. This statement also refers to Epstein's early belief (taken from Walter Moore Coleman, as I discuss above) in a world within which all gestures are in fact perfectly synchronized. Epstein's own theory ultimately owes less to the modernist aesthetics typical of the twenties (based on speed, discontinuity, fragmentation, and so on), which he perceived early on as purposeless and prematurely canonical, than to a persistent reference to the technical and scientific abilities of the cinematic medium. Slow motion epitomizes cinema's technoscientific capabilities, which hold, for Epstein, deep philosophical notions on time and movement. In his article "L'âme au ralenti" ("The Soul of Slow Motion," 1928), he reminds us that "this power of separation which belongs to the mechanical and the optical super-eye makes the relativity of time clearly manifest."[85]

Again, Epstein was not alone in expressing such views. Many French film critics from the twenties echoed similar ideas about cinema's prosthetic abilities, as was notably demonstrated by the enthusiastic reception of the *Cinématographie ultra-rapide* – slow motion – presented publicly on several occasions during the 1920s by the Marey Institute. In spite of the utilitarianism professed by the creators of this device (especially for the Taylorist standardization of factory work), film critics were especially interested in its aesthetic value and its power to reveal the hidden gestures in movement's flow. Emile Vuillermoz estimated that it rendered "the fundamental rhythm of life 'readable,'" and used a choreographic metaphor: "all is dance in the universe. [...] Dance of muscles, dance of the life of vegetation, dance of water and fire, dance of volumes and lines."[86] By identifying an intimate relationship between the tool of cinematography's vision and the rhythmic ordinance of nature, this claim indicates one of the key foundations on which rested many French conceptions of cinema in the early twentieth century. From an obsession with the upbeat tempo of modern life to the unveiling of nature's elemental vibrations, Epstein's various stands on cinematic rhythm originate from this common ground, and evolve from it in order to offer a provocative conception of film's dynamic relation to the world.

Notes

1. This was the topic I researched a few years ago and which eventually led to the pub-
    lication of my book, *L'Age du Rythme: Cinéma, musique et culture du corps dans les théories
    françaises des années 1910-1930* (Lausanne: Payot, 2007). This research was centered
    upon a series of statements which can be found in lectures, articles, magazines, and
    books and which constitute an important part of the vast discursive framework that
    Richard Abel and Nourredine Ghali have referred to as "French film theory" and
    "*avant-garde* theories" respectively. See Abel1; and Noureddine Ghali, *L'avant-garde ciné-
    matographique en France dans les années vingt: Idées, conceptions, théories* (Paris: Paris Expéri-
    mental, 1995).
2. Elie Faure, "La cinéplastique," *La Grande Revue*, no. 104 (11 November 1920); reprinted
    in Faure, *Fonction du cinéma: de la cinéplastique à son destin social* (Paris: Gonthier, 1963), p.
    26.
3. Jean Epstein, "Grossissement," in *Bonjour Cinéma* (Paris: Ed. de la Sirène, 1921); ESC1,
    p. 94.
4. Marcel L'Herbier, "Le cinématographe et l'espace," *L'Art cinématographique*, vol. 4
    (Paris: Félix Alcan, 1927), p. 19.
5. Léon Moussinac, "Cinéma: expression sociale," *L'Art cinématographique*, vol. 4 (Paris:
    Félix Alcan, 1927), pp. 24 and 46.
6. See for instance Louis Delluc, *Photogénie* (Paris: Ed. de Brunoff, 1920). Reprinted in
    Delluc, *Écrits cinématographiques, Tome I: Le Cinéma et les Cinéastes*, ed. Pierre Lherminier
    (Paris: Cinémathèque française/Cahiers du cinéma, 1985), p. 36.
7. Germaine Dulac, "Les esthétiques, les entraves, la cinégraphie intégrale," in *L'Art ciné-
    matographique*, vol. 2 (Paris: Félix Alcan, 1927), pp. 29-50; reprinted in Dulac, *Écrits sur le
    cinéma: 1919-1937*, ed. Prosper Hillairet (Paris: Paris experimental, 1994), pp. 98-105.
    Translated as "Aesthetics, Obstacles, Integral *Cinégraphie*," trans. Stuart Liebman,
    Abel1, pp. 389-397.
8. Germaine Dulac, "L'essence du cinéma. L'idée visuelle," *Les Cahiers du mois*, nos. 17-18
    (1925). Reprinted in Dulac, *Écrits sur le cinéma*, p. 62.
9. See Rudolf Arnheim, "Motion" [1934] in *Film As Art* (Berkeley: University of California
    Press, 1957), p. 181.
10. Jean Epstein, *L'Intelligence d'une machine* (Paris: Ed. Jacques Melot, 1946); ESC1, pp. 261-
    263.
11. This is the reason why film is understood by many early critics as an improvement
    over the plastic arts. Ricciotto Canudo points out this dimension in 1911: "[F]ilm shifts
    the painting from its immutable and eternal space to time, in which it unveils and
    changes." (Ricciotto Canudo, "La naissance d'un sixième art. Essai sur le cinémato-
    graphe," *Les entretiens idéalistes* [25 October 1911]; reprinted in Canudo, *L'Usine aux
    images* [Paris: Séguier-Arte, 1995], p. 33). For Canudo, film thus constitutes a "[p]lastic
    art in movement," an expression which would be used often in the following decade.
    See, for example, Faure, "La cinéplastique," in Faure, *Fonction du cinéma*, pp. 32-33.
12. Epstein, *L'Intelligence d'une machine*, ESC1, 259.

13. Ricciotto Canudo, "Une maison de films latins," *La Revue de l'Epoque*, no. 4, (24 February 1922), in Canudo, *L'Usine aux images*, p. 56.

14. Abel Gance, "Le cinéma, c'est la musique de la lumière," *Cinéa-Ciné pour tous*, no. 3, (12 December 1923), pp. 11-12.

15. See, respectively, Louis Delluc, "Photogénie," *Comoedia Illustré* (July-August 1920); reprinted in Delluc, *Écrits cinématographiques, Tome II, Volume I: Cinéma et cie*, ed. Pierre Lherminier (Paris: Cinémathèque française/Cahiers du cinéma, 1986), pp. 273-274; Léon Moussinac, "Etapes," *Le Crapouillot* (March 1927), p. 17; Juan Arroy, "Danses et danseurs de cinéma," *Cinémagazine*, no. 48 (26 November 1926), p. 427; and Jean Epstein, "De quelques conditions de la photogénie," *Cinéa-Ciné pour tous*, no. 19 (15 August 1924), ESC1, pp. 137-138; infra, 292-96. Epstein defines *photogénie* as "every aspect of things, beings and souls, which elevates its moral quality by cinematic reproduction."

16. Epstein, "De quelques conditions de la photogénie," ESC1, pp. 137-138; infra, 294.

17. Louis Delluc, "La Sultane de l'amour," *Paris-Midi* (11 January 1920); reprinted in Delluc, *Écrits cinématographiques, Tome II, Volume II: Le Cinéma au quotidien*, ed. Pierre Lherminier (Paris: Cinémathèque française/Cahiers du cinéma, 1990), pp. 59-60.

18. Epstein, *Bonjour Cinéma* [1921], ESC1, p. 94.

19. Jean Epstein, unpublished speech [1923], ESC1, p. 120.

20. Canudo, "La naissance d'un sixième Art," in Canudo, *L'Usine aux images*, p. 32.

21. Epstein, *L'Intelligence d'une machine*, ESC1, p. 334.

22. Ibid., p. 334; Jean Epstein, *Le Cinéma du diable* (Paris: Jacques Melot, 1947), ESC1, p. 387.

23. Jean Epstein, *Feuilles libres* (April-May 1922), ESC1, p. 108.

24. Paul Ramain, "Des rythmes visuels aux rythmes cinématographiques," *Ciné*, no. 16 (January 1926), p. 196.

25. Dulac, "Les esthétiques," in Dulac, *Écrits sur le cinéma*, pp.104-105.

26. Ibid., p. 99.

27. Jean Epstein, "Temps et personnage du drame," *Cinégraphie* (15 November 1927), in ESC1, p. 181.

28. Dulac, "Les esthétiques," in Dulac, *Écrits sur le cinéma*, p. 100.

29. Ibid., p. 100. The film to which Dulac refers is not the famous *Vue Lumière* shot at La Ciotat, since Dulac indicates that this train arrives in Vincennes Station, although the two films are clearly similar.

30. Dulac, "Les esthétiques," in Dulac, *Écrits sur le cinéma*, pp. 99-101.

31. Ibid., p. 100.

32. Dulac, "L'essence du cinéma," in Dulac, *Écrits sur le cinéma*, p. 63; Germane Dulac, "Le mouvement créateur d'action,"*Cinémagazine* (19 December 1924), in Dulac, *Écrits sur le cinéma*, p. 47.

33. Dulac, "Les esthétiques," in Dulac, *Écrits sur le cinéma*, p. 101.

34. Epstein, "De quelques conditions de la photogénie," in ESC1, p. 139; infra, 294.

35. Ibid., p. 139; infra, 294.

36. Jean Epstein, "Bilan de fin de muet," *Cinéa-Ciné pour tous* (January-February 1931), ESC1, p. 233.

37. See especially Eileen Bowser, *The Transformation of Cinema, 1907-1915* (New York: Charles Scribner's Sons, 1990).

38. Dulac, "Les esthétiques," in Dulac, *Écrits sur le cinéma*, p. 101.

39. Dulac, "L'essence du cinéma," in Dulac, *Écrits sur le cinéma*, p. 65.

40. This practice is one of many aspects of the stage that Dulac calls "impressionism." Considered a minor notion at the time, impressionism later became a prevalent expression in film historiography, in spite of being defined in different, sometimes conflicting ways, from Georges Sadoul's *Histoire générale du cinéma* to David Bordwell's dissertation on impressionist cinema. See Dulac, "Les esthétiques," in Dulac, *Écrits sur le cinéma*, pp. 101-102; Georges Sadoul, *Histoire générale du cinéma*, vol. 4 (Paris: Denoël, 1975), p. 477; David Bordwell, *French Impressionnist Cinema: Film Culture, Film Theory and Film Style* (PhD Dissertation: University of Iowa, 1974). See also Richard Abel, who defines this same hybrid trend as "narrative avant-garde," in Abel, *French Cinema: The First Wave, 1915-1929* (Princeton: Princeton University Press, 1984), pp. 277-526.

41. See Christophe Gauthier, *La passion du cinéma: Cinéphiles, ciné-clubs et salles spécialisées à Paris de 1920 à 1929* (Paris: Ecole des Chartes/ARFHC, 1999).

42. Dulac, "Les esthétiques," in Dulac, *Écrits sur le cinéma*, pp. 102-103.

43. Fernand Léger, "Le spectacle. Lumière, couleur, image mobile, objet-spectacle," *Bulletin de l'Effort moderne* (1924); reprinted in Léger, *Fonctions de la peinture* (Paris: Gonthier, 1965), p. 140.

44. Jean Epstein, *Le Cinématographe vu de l'Etna* [1926], ESC1, pp. 139, 148-149; infra, 294.

45. Gilles Deleuze, *Cinéma 1. L'image-mouvement* (Paris: Les Editions de Minuit, 1983), pp. 61-62.

46. Léon Moussinac, "Du rythme cinégraphique," *Le Crapouillot* (March 1923); reprinted in Moussinac, *Naissance du cinéma* (Paris: J. Povolovski et Cie, 1925), pp. 75-84.

47. Epstein, *Bonjour Cinéma*, ESC1, p. 92.

48. See Guido, *L'Age du Rythme*, pp. 268-273.

49. Jean Epstein, "Le cinématographe continue," *Cinéa-Ciné pour tous* (November 1930), ESC1, p. 224.

50. See Laurent Guido, "Rhythmic Bodies/Movies: Dance as Attraction in Early Film Culture," in *The Cinema of Attractions Reloaded*, ed. Wanda Strauven (Amsterdam: Amsterdam University Press, 2006), pp. 150-151.

51. Jean Epstein, "Rythme et montage" [1924], ESC1, p. 121.

52. See Guido, *L'Age du Rythme*, pp. 117 and 454n36.

53. See my detailed analysis of a few dance sequences in Laurent Guido, "Le corps et le regard: images rythmiques de la danse dans *La Femme et le pantin*," in *Jacques de Baroncelli*, eds. Bernard Bastide and François de la Brétèque (Paris: AFRHC, 2007), pp. 232-241; and "Entre performance et modèle stylistique: la chorégraphie au cinéma," in *Lo stile cinematografico/Film style*, eds. Enrico Biasin, Giulio Bursi, and Leonardo Quaresima (Udine: Forum, 2007), pp. 499-522.

54. Epstein, *Bonjour cinéma*, ESC1, pp. 94-95.

55. Epstein, "Rythme et montage," ESC1, p. 121.

56. Unpublished speech [1923-1924], ESC1, p. 121.

57. Jean Epstein, "L'Element photogénique au cinéma" [1924], ESC1, p.145; infra, 300.

58. Epstein, "Pour une avant-garde nouvelle," ESC1, p. 148 infra, 303.

59. Yuri Tynjanov, "Des fondements du cinéma" [1927], in *Les formalistes russes et le cinéma. Poétique du film*, ed. François Albera (Paris: Nathan, 1996), p. 87.

60. Abel Gance, "Ma Roue est incomprise du public," *La Revue Hebdomadaire*, no. 25 (23 June 1923); reprinted in Gance, *Un soleil dans chaque image*, ed. Roger Icart (Paris: CNRS/Cinémathèque française, 2002), p. 57.

61. Epstein, "Pour une avant-garde nouvelle," ESC1, pp. 148-150; infra, 302-05.

62. Jean Epstein, "Le regard du verre," *Les Cahiers du mois*, nos. 16-17 (1925), ESC1, p. 125; infra, 309.

63. Epstein, "L'Element photogénique au cinéma," ESC1, p. 146; infra, 300.

64. Dulac, "L'essence du cinéma," in Dulac, *Écrits sur le cinéma*, p. 66.

65. Ibid., p. 66. This is explicitly one of the aspirations of impressionism as defined by Dulac.

66. Dulac, "Les esthétiques," in Dulac, *Écrits sur le cinéma*, p.103.

67. Henri Chomette, "Seconde étape," *Les Cahiers du mois*, nos. 16-17 (1925), pp. 86-88.

68. René Schwob, *Une mélodie silencieuse* (Paris: Bernard Grasset, 1929), pp. 191-192

69. Louis Chavance, "Symphonie visuelle et cinéma pur," *Cinéa-Ciné pour tous*, no. 89 (15 July 1927), p. 13.

70. Chavance, "Symphonie visuelle et cinéma pur," p. 13.

71. *Comœdia*'s inquiry on *cinéma pur*, quoted in Jean Tedesco, "Pur cinéma," *Cinéa-Ciné pour tous*, no. 80 (1 March 1927), pp. 9-11.

72. Epstein, "Bilan de fin de muet, " ESC1, p. 236. See also the way Epstein despises Eggeling's work and an "old avant-garde, only for writers" in Jean Epstein, "L'objectif lui-même," *Cinéa-Ciné pour tous* (15 January 1926), ESC1, p. 127.

73. Giovanni Lista, *Futurisme: Manifestes. Proclamations. Documents* (Lausanne: L'Age d'Homme, 1973), p. 292.

74. Frantisek Kupka, *La création dans les arts plastiques* (Paris: Cercle d'Art, 1989), p. 197.

75. Wassily Kandinsky, *Point et ligne sur plan* [1926] (Paris: Gallimard, 1991), pp. 16-17 and 44.

76. Dulac, "Les esthétiques," in Dulac, *Écrits sur le cinéma*, pp. 103-104. Dulac's description is reminiscent of Elie Faure's discussion of the plasticity of cinematic movement, in which he evokes the eruption of Mt. Vesuvius (see Faure, "La cinéplastique," in Faure, *Fonction du cinéma*, p. 24).

77. Dulac, "Les esthétiques," in Dulac, *Écrits sur le cinéma*, pp. 103-104.

78. Epstein, "De quelques conditions de la photogénie," ESC1, p. 139; infra, 295; and *Le cinématographe vu de l'Etna*, ESC1, pp. 131-134; infra, 289ff.

79. Jean Epstein, *Contre-pensées: Réflexions de Jean Epstein, de M à Z*. Fonds Jean et Marie Epstein, Bibliothèque du film, Paris, EPSTEIN224-B57. See also Epstein's unpublished notebook, "Notes sur des auteurs, des savants, des philosophes signalant leurs conceptions" (EPSTEIN108-B26).

80. Jean Epstein, "Symétrie," in *Contre-pensées: Réflexions de Jean Epstein de M à Z*. Fonds Jean et Marie Epstein, Bibliothèque du film, Paris, EPSTEIN224-B57.

81. See Guido, *L'Age du rythme*, pp. 44-47.

82. Epstein, "Bilan de fin de muet," ESC1, p. 237.

83. See the early study by Charles H. Harpole, "Probes into the Actuality of Fantasy in Jean Epstein's *La Chute de la Maison Usher*," pp. 8-12. Manuscript sent by Harpole to Marie Epstein. Fonds Jean et Marie Epstein Bibliothèque du film, Paris, EPSTEIN122- B29.
84. Quoted in Pierre France, "L'Edgar Poe de Jean Epstein," *Photo-Ciné*, no. 12 (April 1928). This is the version translated and published in the Program notes of the retrospective screening of Epstein's works. Anthology Film Archives, Oct. 1971, p. 5.
85. Jean Epstein, "L'Ame au ralenti," *Paris-Midi-Ciné* (11 May 1928), ESC1, p. 191.
86. Emile Vuillermoz, "Devant l'écran. Mouvements," *L'impartial français* (21 May 1926), p. 2.

The "Microscope of Time": Slow Motion in Jean Epstein's Writings

Ludovic Cortade

Jean Epstein's numerous writings, many of which have not been translated into English, testify to a paradoxical conceptualization of movement. Early on, Epstein was aware that the film medium entails immobility insofar as it relies upon photographic recording. In his 1923 talk, "On Some Conditions of *Photogénie*," Epstein points out that *photogénie* is possible only with the successive mobilization of these photographic images, and that this mobilization alone allows for the revelation of movement: "[T]he mechanism of cinema constructs movement by multiplying successive stoppages of celluloid exposed to a ray of light, thus creating mobility through immobility, decisively demonstrating how correct the false reasoning of Zeno of Elea was."[1] By drawing on Zeno's famous paradox, Epstein acknowledges the role of immobility from a technical perspective: it is the discontinuous succession of motionless frames which eventually conveys the impression of continuity and movement, the basic ontological problem of cinema to which Epstein would return throughout the remainder of his career, as exemplified in *L'Intelligence d'une machine* (1946):

> All film provides us with the obvious demonstration of continuous movement, which is formed at what we could call a deeper level, by immobile discontinuities. Zeno was therefore correct to suggest that the analysis of movement results in a series of still images; his only error was to deny the possibility of this bizarre synthesis which actually reconstitutes movement through the addition of pauses and which the filmmaker creates by virtue of our feeble vision.[2]

From a stylistic perspective, however, the art of cinema clearly relies on movement. Acknowledging the central role that immobility plays in the cinematic apparatus, Epstein nonetheless discards it when it comes to devising a conception of *photogénie*. He states in 1923 that "only the mobile and personal aspects of things, beings and souls may be photogenic."[3] Indeed, Epstein makes the case for the primacy of movement throughout his career as a filmmaker and theorist: in an article published in *Les Temps modernes* in 1950 (three years before his death), he posits that "still life is abominable on screen: it commits a sin against the very nature of cinema, it is a barbarism."[4] While Epstein's severe condemnation of "still life" in cinema recalls the obsession with speed among the avant-garde of the 1920s, Epstein's investigation of movement, in both his films and film theory, was more complex than this outright rejection of stillness suggests.

Though the celebration of movement remains the backbone of Epstein's theory, his writings bear witness to an attempt to bring cinematic movement to the threshold of immobility. Conversely, immobility for Epstein is nothing but a potential movement. In this respect, a distinction should be made between Epstein's condemnation of "still life," which is actual immobility, and his inclination to the cinematic representation of the "inanimate" or "repose" – terms which by contrast designate the potentiality of movement.

Epstein's ambitious theoretical exploration of slow motion entails two stages. In spite of the growing interest in slow motion by numerous directors at the time, the texts written between 1921 and 1928 do not refer to slow motion. However, they constitute an important step in Epstein's theory, introducing a dialectical tension between movement and repose which laid the foundations of his approach to slow motion, as testified by his works in 1928 and thereafter. 1928 was a turning point in Epstein's career, not only because he completed *The Fall of the House of Usher*, a film which is emblematic of the director's use of slow motion, but also because it is from 1928 onwards that Epstein formulates and revises the characteristics he assigns to slow motion. For Epstein, this technique presents a tension between movement and immobility, giving rise to a "tragedy" of duration, and also imbues the image with transparency, revealing the hidden movements of reality which would otherwise remain invisible to the naked eye, thus making slow motion a "microscope of time."

1921-1928: Prelude to slow motion

Between 1921 and 1928, Epstein does not mention slow motion in his writings: the technical methods he advocates during this time include camera movements, close-ups, and editing. Epstein's relative lack of interest in slow motion is surprising given that other French "impressionists" testify to an enthusiasm for this multi-faceted technique.[5] Slow motion was at the time regarded as an all-purpose device whose function could be comical, dramatic, scientific, or "photogenic." The majority of these writers agree that slow motion reveals a state of the soul that escapes the normal speed of filming or captures a movement in nature that otherwise would elude our perception.[6] In 1920, Colette expresses her fascination for slow motion and time-lapse photography in scientific films; she recalls that "a 'slow motion' shot rose from the ground, immobilized itself in the air, then held on a seagull suspended on a breeze. [...] These spectacles are never forgotten and give us the thirst for further knowledge."[7] In 1921, Louis Delluc is equally enthused by this device which reveals unknown aspects of reality: "And what to say of what is added to them by this extraordinary invention of the slow motion technique [ralentisseur]? [...] Men have, in this analysis of images, a grace that we did not suspect of them."[8] In 1924, Germaine Dulac sees in the use of slow motion a device that reveals the soul: "Slow motion intensifies tics, accelerations, it intensifies sounds. A state of the soul described by speed."[9] In the same year, slow motion was used comically in René Clair's Entr'acte, while in 1926, Dimitri Kirsanoff emphasizes the acute perception of reality through slow motion, a hybrid device giving rise to both the transformation and revelation of movement: "Slow motion is stranger because the dimensions of its 'time-movement' are not the same as the dimensions of the 'time-movement' that we know. And because we find strange and mysterious things attractive, a horse's jump in slow motion is more beautiful for us than a natural jump – as it is the opposite of what could have been produced."[10]

While Epstein does not mention slow motion before 1928, his early reflections on time and movement reveal an interesting distinction between the "still life" and the "inanimate," which represent two aesthetic categories of stillness: namely, the still life is an essential entity which is perceived through actual immobility, while the "inanimate," or "repose," comprises the starting point of a potential movement. As early as 1922, Epstein attends to the beauty of the inanimate, making what seems to be a paradoxical statement: he has "uncovered the as yet little-known beauty of inanimate objects, all prodigiously alive."[11] This perception of life in spite of immobility was refined and reinforced in his text of 1926, Le cinématographe Vu de l'Etna, in which he expresses his sensitivity to the secret movements of landscapes and objects: "One of the greatest powers of cinema is its animism. On screen, nature is never inanimate. Objects take on airs."[12] One can detect the far-reaching influence exerted by Bergson on Epstein in these passages. In "La perception du changement," a text in La Pensée et le mouvant, the philosopher argues: "There is indeed change, but in this change, it is not the objects that are changing: change does not require anything in order to occur. There is movement, but there is no invariable, inert object that moves: movement does not imply mobility."[13] Whether we perceive actual or potential movement, the world is always a perpetuum mobile because what we call "immobility" is inscribed in duration. Hence, Epstein's distinction between "still life," which is necessarily detestable, and the beauty of the lively "inanimate" is not as paradoxical as it seems.

To Epstein, still life and cinema are a contradiction in terms because the perception of "motionlessness" turns out to be inscribed in the duration of perception itself: in this sense, actual "immobility" is nothing but a potential movement. It is for this reason that Epstein bans freeze frames from his aesthetic, contrary to figurative strategies common in the 1920s such as the sudden petrification in René Clair's Paris qui dort (1923) or the freeze frames in Dziga Vertov's films. To

Epstein, immobility as such is inconceivable because it does not reflect the complexity of perception which is inscribed in duration. In this sense, the "immobilization" of the moving image is the expression of a death drive, which Serge Daney will later analyze in the case of freeze frames:

> A freeze frame (a return to inanimateness = death drive) implies that there are images beyond which movement does not continue. This can be any one of the 24 images per second of recorded film. Yet at some point, they are no longer just any images: they are, in essence, the end point.[14]

Avoiding the death drive of the freeze frame, Epstein attaches more importance to the subtlety and ambiguous duration that characterizes the perception of the "inanimate" as opposed to "still life." Movement and stillness should not be considered separate entities, for it is the dialectical tension between the two that makes possible the perception of time. Epstein was aware as early as 1922 that "We must recognize that no one is able to experience time, in and of itself, outside of movement and repose."[15] Consequently, if Epstein posits that the inanimate actually gives rise to a virtual movement, conversely, the representation of movement should not reach its climax. This point is crucial, for it paves the way for Epstein's later view that slow motion is the simultaneous synthesis of actual and potential movement.

The dialectic of movement and stillness is developed on the basis of the distinction Epstein makes in *Le cinéma et les lettres modernes* (1921) between an "aesthetic of proximity" and an "aesthetic of suggestion." The "aesthetic of proximity" designates the revelation of movement through the use of film techniques, especially the close-up. In "Magnification" (1921), he posits that "the close-up, the keystone of the cinema, is the maximum expression of this *photogénie* of movement. When static it verges on contradiction."[16] This "aesthetic of proximity" emerges from a theological frame of reference. His approach to cinematic movement consistently links the notion of the film's revelation of the world to the notion of transubstantiation: "It is the miracle of real presence, of evident life."[17] In fact, Epstein's texts, and more specifically the vocabulary he uses, often carry religious connotations. For instance, Epstein's aesthetic of proximity is based on the real presence of movement on the screen, drawing a parallel between the spectator's gaze consuming the image and the worshipper's mouth consuming the host:

> The close-up modifies the drama by the impact of proximity. Pain is within reach. If I stretch out my arm I touch you, and that is intimacy. I can count the eye-lashes of this suffering. I would be able to taste the tears. Never before has a face turned to mine in that way. [...] It's not even true that there is air between us; I consume it. It is in me like a sacrament. Maximum visual acuity."[18]

Epstein's aesthetic of proximity thus echoes the Eucharist and its dogma of the presence of Christ's body in the host. This theological backdrop is all the more relevant to Epstein's conception of slow motion, for it raises the issue of continuity versus discontinuity, which was a staple of the medieval scholastic controversy around the transformation of the host and its inscription in time. Thomas Aquinas poses that time is necessarily continuous; hence the instant of the host's transformation is indivisible because it cannot be simultaneously a piece of bread and the body of Christ.[19] Rather than following this Christian dogma of change and continuity, Epstein's understanding of time is marked by a greater tension between continuity and discontinuity, thus aligning his approach to time with a deviant argument defended in the fourteenth century. Scholastic philosophers such as Landulf Caraccioli, Ugo di Novocastro, and Jean Baconthorpe questioned the dogma of continuity and made a case for the principle of contradiction, allowing for the juxtaposition of continuity and discontinuity, bringing together two contradictory states during the transformation of the host, which is both the body of Christ and a simple piece of bread.[20]

In this respect, Epstein's writings testify to a certain consistency in regard to his interest in the issues related to continuity and discontinuity. Twenty-five years after Le cinéma et les letters modernes, Epstein elaborates on this conception of time in L'Intelligence d'une machine, an ambitious text theorizing cinema in light of the latest scientific debates: drawing on quantum physics and the works of Heisenberg, Planck, Bohr, and de Broglie, Epstein discards the distinction between continuity and discontinuity, just as in the early 1920s he blurs the distinction between mobility and immobility.[21] By recognizing the moment of indeterminacy separating these two stages of movement, Epstein treads the tenuous line separating actuality and virtuality and lays the foundation for his later formulation of slow motion as the simultaneous representation of movement and stillness. Thus, the "aesthetic of proximity," including its religious origin in the celebration of "real presence," is dialectically linked to its negation: the "aesthetic of suggestion." While the former designates actual movement, which is captured by the camera and consumed as a "sacrament" by the spectator's gaze, the latter designates the potentiality of movement, conveyed by the "inanimate." In other words, the revelation of the world through movement is made possible in as much as the actual commencement of movement is deferred, a theoretical stance which lays the foundation for Epstein's conception of slow motion: "On the screen, the essential condition of the gesture is never to be attained. The face does not express like that of a mime, it does better, it suggests. [...] Of an action that begins astutely, the development adds nothing to intelligence. One foresees, one guesses."[22] Epstein demonstrates hostility toward the resolution of tensions brought about by the culmination of movement. In 1921, he gives a description of the ambiguous duration which precedes the opening of the mouth, thus combining the "aesthetic of proximity" and the "real presence" of a face moving in close-up, with the "aesthetic of suggestion": "Instead of a mouth, the mouth, larva of kisses, essence of touch. Everything quivers with bewitchment. I am uneasy. In a new nature, another world. The close-up transfigures man. For ten seconds, my whole mind gravitates around a smile. In silent and stealthy majesty, it also thinks and lives. Expectancy and threat."[23] This explains his fascination with the ambiguity of the frozen duration that precedes the commencement of movement: "Waiting for the moment when 1,000 meters of intrigue converge in a muscular dénouement satisfies me more than the rest of the film."[24]

Epstein places his "aesthetic of suggestion" under the auspices of tragedy, with its tension of opposing movement and stillness, avoiding the resolution of such tension in a dénouement:

> Generally speaking, the cinema does not render stories well. And 'dramatic action' is a mistake here. Drama that acts is already half resolved and on the healing slope to crisis. True tragedy remains in abeyance. [...] Now the suspense is at freezing point. Waiting. One sees nothing as yet, but the tragic crystal which will create the nucleus of the drama has begun to form somewhere.[25]

The tragedy of duration Epstein discusses in this text refers to the power of the film medium to make visible the virtual animation of seemingly lifeless objects and bodies over time. While slow motion is not specifically discussed, Epstein paves the way for his conceptualization of it, bringing together actual immobility and potential movement. He assigns a tragic dimension to duration, for the tenuous line separating actual stillness and potential movement plunges the viewer into a perceptual double-bind: if the perception of stillness over time gives rise to the expectancy of a continuous movement, the actual cinematic representation of a movement is undermined by the discontinuity instilled by Epstein ("I must interrupt"). It can thus be said that he elaborates a fetishism of movement based on a celebration of waiting:

> Even more beautiful than a laugh is the face preparing for it. I must interrupt. I love the mouth which is about to speak and holds back, the gesture which hesitates between right and left, the recoil before the leap, and the moment before landing, the becoming, the hesitation, the taut spring, the prelude, and even more than all these, the piano being tuned before the overture. The photogenic is conjugated in the future and in the imperative. It does not allow for stasis.[26]

If the photogenic does not allow for stasis, it nonetheless relies on repose; while the former designates a type of immobility which does not give rise to any movement ("still life"), the latter designates the "inanimate," in the sense that

Epstein assigns to this word – namely, the propensity of a figure to move. It may be argued that the significance Epstein assigns to the duration that precedes movement is a remnant of a conception of time that sparked the debate around eighteenth-century theories of French neo-classical art.[27] In the Salon of 1763, Denis Diderot shows enthusiasm for the Pygmalion myth, a popular subject of eighteenth-century French sculpture, including Pygmalion aux pieds de sa statue qui s'anime created by Diderot's friend, Étienne-Maurice Falconet. The work represents the instant during which Pygmalion realizes that Galatea, the statue he sculpts, is becoming animate. What is at stake in Diderot's critical judgment of Falconet's work is whether his friend indulged in representing the climax of the action or chose to defer it on the basis of an aesthetic of suggestion. While the first part of the text is full of praise, Diderot eventually concludes by reproaching Falconet for having represented the culminating point of action: the moment where Pygmalion is literally moved, which is to say, the moment in movement. For Diderot, the sculptor's movements of surprise must be "contained and moderate." He advises Falconet to represent not the climax of the surprise experienced by Pygmalion but the instant that precedes it. As much in Diderot as in Epstein, the "inanimate" is not the opposite of movement; it is the prelude to, and therefore a modality of, movement. Indeed, one can argue that the frozen imminence which exacerbates the potentiality of movement and fascinates Epstein from 1921 onward is a remnant of the paradoxical definition of "repose" given by Diderot in his Detached Thoughts on Painting [Pensées detachées sur la peinture] (1775-1781): "Life is in the figure which is in repose. Artists have attached a particular sense to the word 'movement.' Of a figure in repose, they say that it 'has movement,' which is to say that it is inclined to move."[28]

Between 1921 and 1928, Epstein's writings clearly show that he attached great importance to the potentiality of movement rather than its actualization: "repose," "inanimate," and the "suggestion" of movement substitute for "still life" and "stasis," both of which epitomize the death drive of cinema. The texts of this period paved the way for his marked interest in slow motion from 1928 onwards. The year is a turning point not only in his theoretical approach to slow motion, but also in his own practice: though Epstein first attempted to use slow motion in his film of 1923, L'Auberge rouge, a use which is barely detectable, it is in 1928 with The Fall of the House of Usher and thereafter that he refined his views and explicitly discussed the characteristics of slow motion – most importantly, a tragic conception of duration and the revelation of reality through the "microscope of time."

A tragedy of duration

The role of literature in shaping Epstein's views on cinematic time cannot be overestimated. In L'ABC du cinéma, a text completed in 1921 (the same year as Epstein's Bonjour Cinéma and Le cinéma et les lettres modernes), Blaise Cendrars states that "the whole of classicism is conveyed by biceps flexing in slow motion."[29] Cendrars' conception of classicism ought to be discussed in light of Simultaneism, a movement whose ramifications were still palpable in the French avant-garde after World War I. From this perspective, the so-called "classicism" of slow motion does not designate a mere magnification of movement: it is the visual synthesis of the conflict between movement and immobility, conveying a sense of a "simultaneous present."[30] Cendrars' definition of slow motion pertains to the classic tragedy: the ambivalence of slow motion may be regarded as a remnant of the inner conflict experienced by characters who are subject to a set of passionate and duty-bound conflicts resulting in a geometry of double-binds. Likewise, the frozen dialectics of slow motion opposes the temptation of actual movement and the withholding of it. In that sense, slow motion is a tragedy of duration.

The tragic paradigm of slow motion appears in light of further elements pertaining to the literary context under which Epstein made The Fall of the House of Usher, adapted from the eponymous short story by Edgar Allan Poe. Luis Buñuel, who was then Epstein's assistant, recalls that he had met Symbolist playwright, poet, and essayist Maurice Maeterlinck during the making of the film.[31] Maeterlinck, who expressed a strong interest in cinema, was himself strongly influenced by Poe.[32] At the end of the nineteenth century, Maeterlinck forged a conception of drama which was deprived of heroism, staging characters who are sensitive to the unknown and the sublime, and who experience the mere act of living as a tragedy. In "The Tragical in Daily Life," a chapter from The Treasure of the Humble, a collection of mystical essays first published in 1896, Maeterlinck situates the corporeal language of his characters in the wake of the tradition of static actors in Greek tragedies: "I do not know whether it be true that a static theatre is impossible. Indeed, to me it seems to exist already. Most of the tragedies of Aeschylus are tragedies without movement [...] What have we here but life that is almost motionless? [...] It is no longer a violent, exceptional moment of life that passes before our eyes – it is life itself."[33] Stillness lies at the crux of Maeterlinck's works, at the expense of the climax of dramatic action: movement comes to a standstill and excavates the hidden, mystical dimension of life. It should be stressed, however, that stillness is always inscribed in duration and consequently turns into a stream of perceptions – the passage of life.

The dialectics of movement and immobility forged by the Symbolist writer sheds light on Epstein's adaptation of The Fall of the House of Usher, a film that testifies to an extensive use of slow motion which the director himself places under the auspices of tragedy:

> It now seems impossible to me to make a film without a high-speed camera at my disposal. [...] Slow motion really brings a new set of possibilities to dramaturgy. Its ability to dismantle feelings, to enhance drama, to infallibly repre-

sent the sincere movements of the soul is such that it obviously surpasses all the other known tragic modes.[34]

Epstein's conception of slow motion stands in contrast with that of Colette, for instance, in that Epstein's cannot be considered a special effect whose function is to simply ravish the gaze of the viewer. On the contrary, Epstein clearly assigns a dramatic function to slow motion which excavates and magnifies the subtle variations of the state of mind of a given character, without calling attention to the distortion of time it implies. In other words, what is at stake is whether slow motion should be transparent or convey a sense of self-reflexivity. In May 1928, Epstein discarded a conception of slow motion that would spectacularize the marks of enunciation: "At no time in the film will the spectator be able to say to himself: this is slow motion."[35] Indeed, The Fall of the House of Usher distinguishes itself by its use of "subtle slow motion."[36] In 1948, twenty years after making The Fall of the House of Usher, Epstein specifies the transparency of the technique he had been using extensively since 1928:

> This film best captures its tragic and mysterious atmosphere through the systematic use of a subtle slow motion and through the ratio of 1.5:1 or 2:1 that not only allows for a precise reading of gestures and expressions, like through a magnifying glass, but also automatically dramatizes, prolongs, and holds them in suspense as if waiting for something to happen. The actor can usually perform anything: he comes in, sits down, opens a book, flips through the pages; only the camera gives him a profound gravity, burdens him with an inexplicable secret and makes him a fragment of tragedy through the simple reduction of the temporal ratio of this performance.[37]

To Epstein, slow motion is not an artificial entity destined to demonstrate the technical possibilities of the medium or a filmmaker's intention. On the contrary, most important for Epstein is the undetectable and fluctuating line separating the slightest movements of a muscle. It is the organic character of duration that brings together movement and immobility in such a way that the viewer is not able to pinpoint the use of the slow motion device nor to analytically separate the successive stages of a movement. Slow motion is not a special effect: it reveals the world and exposes the spectator to the conflicting forces inherent to it. In "L'âme au ralenti" ("The Soul in Slow Motion," 1928), Epstein analyzes the kinetic uncertainty perceived in duration and which corresponds to a middle ground between movement and immobility. In slow motion, the spectator experiences the impossibility of isolating the precise moment at which pain or its quintessential manifestation, crying, emerges:

I am not aware of anything more absolutely moving than a face delivering itself from expression in slow motion. First a thorough preparation, a slow fever which one does not know whether to compare to a morbid incubation, a progressive maturity or more grossly, to a pregnancy. Finally all of this effort overwhelms, ruptures the rigidity of a muscle. A contagion of movements animates the face. [...] And when the lips separate to finally indicate a cry, we have born witness to the entirety of its long and magnificent dawn.[38]

Slow motion discards any clear-cut distinction between movement and immobility because it organically inscribes the experience of duration in the plasticity of the image.

By focusing on the prelude to actual movement and the kinetic indeterminacy preceding its commencement, Epstein draws on themes he had already developed prior to 1928, especially the notions of the inanimate and repose, which, as I discussed earlier, stand in contrast with the still life. In his 1931 essay, Bilan de fin de muet ("Assessment at the End of Silent Cinema"), Epstein works on the assumption that the use of slow motion is not an alteration of the world but rather the revelation of its ambiguity, precisely because the technique presents us with the spectacle of a frozen dialectic inscribed in duration. The film medium gives rise to a "temporal perspective" whose "simplest effects, slow motion and fast motion, are always striking, penetrating the world with a life as new and as fertile as the extraordinary, surreal life that one finds looking into a microscope."[39] Four years later, in his Photogénie of the Impondérable (1935), Epstein builds on the theme of the revelation of the world through slow motion, emphasizing in the very title of the text the fact that recorded phenomena reveal themselves over time in unpredictable ways. Hence, Epstein mentions the importance of the ongoing fight between conflicting micro-movements which cannot be perceived by the naked eye: "What the mind does not have time to retain, what the eye has neither the time nor the capability to see in an expression – the prenatal pains, the birth, the evolution, the struggle between inter-current feelings (which ultimately determine the outcome) – slow motion displays all of this at will."[40]

The advent of the sound era in French filmmaking did not make Epstein's use of slow motion obsolete, despite the fact that the vast majority of sound films were under the influence of a theatrical approach to speech that seemed incompatible with any visual distortions of movement and time. However, in Mor'Vran (1930), one of Epstein's first sound films, the director remains attached to the visual resources of slow motion he used in both The Fall of the House of Usher and Finis terrae (1929), the first film he made in Brittany. The final shot of Mor'Vran, for instance, is filmed in discreet slow motion, capturing the dramatic explosions of waves along the coast. The impression of prolonged duration is not conveyed by the soundtrack, as the viewer's attention is caught in the uncanny visual sensations created by the waves, which seem to come to a standstill and hover in the air in moments of kinetic indeterminacy. The dramatic function of slow motion in Epstein's films of the early 1930s remains merely visual, thus exemplifying the director's early skepticism towards sound film.

It should be stressed, however, that Epstein's reluctance to use the resources of sound changed over time. In his "Le gros plan du son" ("The Close-Up in Sound"), a text focusing on his film of 1947, Le Tempestaire, Epstein explores the aesthetic and technical aspects of a slow-motion sound, a technique that was eventually made possible thanks to the collaboration of sound engineer Léon Vareille and composer Yves Baudrier. Le Tempestaire features a mysterious old man called "le tempestaire," who has the power to control the movements of waves by blowing on a crystal ball through which he keeps an eye on the tempest. Epstein's experiments seem to signal a resurgence of the myth of "frozen words" [paroles gelées] exemplified by Rabelais.[41] The author of Le Quart Livre devises a fantasy in which words would be encapsulated in the cold but freed – and audible – when brought close to a fire. However, a distinction between the two should be made: while Rabelais envisioned a sonic equivalent of the "freeze frame," Epstein by contrast inscribes sound in time and seeks micro-distortions in order to reveal a soundscape which would otherwise be imperceptible. The difference between the two is that the former links sound to the instant, whereas the latter uses duration to reveal sound in its subtlety: "[Slow motion] enables phenomena to be spread out over the duration; it constitutes a sort of microscope of time."[42] In Le Tempestaire, the movements of the raging sea gradually slow down to the point where the spectator can barely make a distinction between movement and immobility. The ocean seems to come to a standstill: "...in extreme visual slow motion the eye no longer perceives the choppiness of the sea, which now appears as a solid, frozen surface."[43] The subtle distinction between the expiration of movement and the gradual solidification of the waves conveys a tragic experience of duration that plunges the spectator into an instant of kinetic ambiguity. In Le Tempestaire, the use of slow motion is transparent; in this respect, Epstein remains faithful to his conception of slow motion first expressed twenty years before, when making The Fall of the House of Usher. Even when the waves are reversed by the old man, the faith that is placed by the spectator in the revelation of the world through slow motion is not undermined. Roger Odin has demonstrated that the spectator's belief is preserved, despite the fact that this technique tends to foreground the marks of enunciation.[44] For Epstein, the transparency of slow motion lies in the dialectic between movement and stillness, in "the uncertain relationship between that which is animated in the shot, and that which seems to be motionless," as Raymond Bellour puts it.[45] The impossibility of establishing whether the waves will continue their movements, become frozen, or even go backward lies at the crux of Epstein's conception of slow motion.[46] It is the experience of the uncertainty of time and movement that constitutes the spectator's belief in slow motion, a transparent image crystallizing the conflicting forces of the tragedy of duration. In this respect, Epstein's conception of slow motion embraces the definition of *photogénie* he gave at his 1923 conference: "I would describe as photogenic any aspect of things, beings, or souls whose moral character is enhanced by filmic reproduction. And any aspect not enhanced by filmic reproduction is not photogenic, plays no part in the art of cinema."[47]

Conclusion

Epstein assigns three characteristics to slow motion: *photogénie*, the revelation of unknown features of the world; transparency, avoiding any reflexivity the spectator might perceive; and tragedy, based on the inseparability of movement and immobility in the perception of duration.

Epstein's conception of slow motion needs to be compared to the debates in French film criticism of the 1950s. The intersections between Epstein's and André Bazin's writings have long been underestimated, especially because Bazin develops a conception of the potentiality of movement which, to a certain degree, recalls Epstein's work. The author of *What is Cinema?* was familiar with Epstein's films; in 1953, the Cinémathèque française organized an Epstein retrospective at the Cannes Film Festival which Bazin reviewed:

> The only time this year when we have felt the spirit of Cinema was during the Epstein retrospective, not so much because of the snippets of films presented by Henri Langlois, but because of the fervor and reverence conveyed in the speeches of Jean Cocteau, Abel Gance, Charles Spaak, and Jean Dréville. Everyone who was there was there out of love and respect for cinema – it was only about art. In the middle of the Festival, this small ceremony almost took the shape of an initiation ceremony, or a mass in catacombs. We left it feeling revived, as if we had taken communion.[48]

Bazin was struck by the foregrounding of the film medium in François Campaux's documentary *Matisse* (1946), and developed in his review an analysis which paved the way for his essay on Clouzot's documentary: "Un film bergsonien: *Le Mystère Picasso*."[49] It may thus be argued that Bergson is the common denominator between Epstein's and Bazin's theories of duration.

> We all remember this deeply moving moment (in an otherwise mediocre documentary): Matisse's hand fumbling about in slow motion on the canvas. [...] [T]he work of fine art, completed, is timeless; it offers itself to us in a block of timeless space, unlike music, poetry, or novels. Cinema, an intermediate and mixed art, so to speak, restores to us, from space and time, that privileged instant in which creative time will crystallize, for eternity, in patches of color or in masses of stone, and solidify like a cast of bronze in a mold.[50]

Bazin was interested in the resources of slow motion, as long as it preserved the transparency of the film medium over the display of the marks of enunciation. According to Bazin, the function of slow motion does not lie in demonstrating the power of the technique, but rather in capturing and organically revealing the ambiguous stages of the deployment of movement as duration. In that sense, Bazin is not only Bergsonian; he is also is Epsteinian.

Moreover, although the author of "The Myth of Total Cinema" was interested in the evolution of the techniques of the seventh art, he placed the emphasis on the psychology of the viewer. Technological breakthroughs are manifestations of the mental categories of the spectator: in other words, the consistency of the spectator's myths overcomes the avatars of technique. Epstein's texts bear witness to a remarkable consistency in his conception of the tragic duration inherent to the "microscope of time." From 1921 to 1927, Epstein developed his conception of duration without presenting a single occurrence of slow motion in his writings. These texts nonetheless encapsulate his views on slow motion, even before he comprehensively discussed and made extensive use of the device from 1928 onwards. It may thus be argued that Epstein's assessment and practice of slow motion did not originate in the technique itself. Rather, his theory of slow motion draws on a complex frame of references, including the early twentieth century (Maeterlinck) and the avant-garde of the 1920s, particularly Cendrars' Simultaneism. It should also be stressed that Epstein's theoretical foundation can be traced back to the debates gravitating around time and movement long before the invention of cinema, as demonstrated by the similarities between his "aesthetic of real presence" and the Christian dogma of transubstantiation on the one hand, and the "aesthetic of suggestion" and Diderot's preference for repose on the other. Consequently, slow motion in Epstein's writings should be regarded not only as a device rooted in the technological history of cinema, but also as a mental category that invokes a much older dialectical tension between movement and immobility that cuts across centuries and different types of media. Slow motion is impure. From this perspective, Epstein anticipates Bazin.

Notes

1. Jean Epstein, "De quelques conditions de la photogénie" [1924], in *Le Cinématographe vu de l'Etna* (Paris: Les écrivains réunis, 1926), ESC1, p. 138; *Abel1*, p. 315; infra, 293. Unless otherwise stated, all citations from the French are translated by Megan D. Russell, Emily Teising, and Wesley F. Gunter, Ph.D. candidates in the Department of French at New York University. I warmly thank them for their collaboration.
2. Epstein, *L'Intelligence d'une machine* [1946], ESC1, p. 261.
3. Epstein, "De quelques conditions de la photogénie," ESC1, p. 138; *Abel1*, p. 317; infra, 295. Epstein endorsed Blaise Cendrars' views on cinema, who praised the "camera that is no longer immobile, that simultaneously records all the shots, that shakes,

that gets things going" (Blaise Cendrars, *L'ABC du cinéma* [Paris: Les Ecrivains réunis, 1926], cited in Stuart Liebman, *Jean Epstein's Early Film Theory, 1920-1922* [New York University: Ph.D. Dissertation, 1980], p. 99.)

4. Jean Epstein, *Alcool et cinéma*, ESC2, p. 203.

5. Jean Epstein, "Les Films de Jean Epstein vus par lui-même" (unpublished in Epstein's lifetime), ESC1, p. 59.

6. Stuart Liebman has pointed out this paradox: "It is even more surprising that Epstein only implicitly approved of the use of slow motion that excited many early film theorists because later in the 1920s he enthusiastically recommended this technique and used it in *La Chute de la Maison Usher* (1928). In the formative period of his film theory, camera movement, close-up, and editing were the principal strategies he recommended" (Liebman, *Jean Epstein's Early Film Theory*, p. 243).

7. *Colette at the Movies: Criticism and Screenplays*, eds. and trans. Alain and Odette Virmaux (New York: Ungar, 1980), cited in Liebman, *Jean Epstein's Early Film Theory*, p. 95.

8. Louis Delluc, "Cinégraphie," *Le Crapouillot* (February 6, 1921), p. 3.

9. "Conférence de Madame Germaine Dulac. Faite à la Séance des Amis du Cinéma donnée le 7 décembre dans la Salla [sic] du Colisée," *Cinémagazine* 1 (9 December 1924).

10. Dimitri Kirsanoff, "Les Problèmes de la photogénie," *Cinéa-Ciné pour tous* 62 (1 June 1926).

11. Jean Epstein, "Comment j'ai conçu et exécuté le film du *Centenaire de Pasteur*," *L'Illustré* (1922), ESC1, p. 112.

12. Epstein, *Le Cinématographe vu de l'Etna*, ESC1, p. 134; infra, 289.

13. Henri Bergson, "La perception du changement," republished in *La Pensée et le mouvant. Essais et conférences* (Paris: PUF, 1993), pp. 161-162.

14. Serge Daney, *L'Exercice a été profitable, Monsieur* (Paris: P.O.L, 1993), pp. 38-39.

15. Jean Epstein, "T.," *Feuilles libres* (April-May 1922), ESC1, p. 106. For a study of the category of "repose" in cinema, see Ludovic Cortade, *Le Cinéma de l'immobilité: style, politique, réception* (Paris: Publications de la Sorbonne, 2008), chapter 3, pp. 59-79.

16. Jean Epstein, "Grossissement" [1921], ESC1, p. 94; Abel1, p. 236.

17. Jean Epstein, *Le cinéma et les lettres modernes* (Paris: Éditions de la Sirène, 1921), ESC1, p. 66.

18. Epstein, "Grossissement," ESC1, p. 98; Abel1, p. 239.

19. Emile Dumoutet, "La non-réitération des sacrements et le problème du moment précis de la transsubstantiation," *Recherches de science religieuse* (1938), pp. 580-585; See Alain de Libera, "L'instant du changement selon saint Thomas d'Aquin," *Métaphysique, histoire de la philosophie. Recueil d'études offertes à Fernand Bruner* (Neufchâtel: La Baconnière, 1981), pp. 99-109.

20. Simo Knuutila and Anja Inkerti Leatinen, "Change and Contradiction: A Fourteenth-century Controversy," *Synthese* 40 (1979): 189-207.

21. See Epstein, *L'Intelligence d'une machine*, pp. 259-286.

22. Epstein, *Le cinéma et les lettres modernes*, pp. 66-67.

23. Jean Epstein, "Le Sens 1bis," *Cinéa* 12-13 (June/July 1921), ESC1, p. 87; Abel1, p. 243.

24. Epstein, "Grossissement," ESC1, p. 93; Abel1, p. 235.

25. Epstein, "Le Sens 1bis," ESC1, p. 86; Abel1, p. 242.

26. Epstein, "Grossissement," ESC1, p. 94; Abel1, p. 236.

27. In eighteenth-century Europe, Shaftesbury, Lessing, and Diderot took an active part in these debates; see for instance Dominique Chateau, "Narrativité et médium dans la peinture (à propos d'un opuscule de Shaftesbury)," *Littérature*, no. 106 (June 1997): 107-122.

28. Denis Diderot, *Pensées détachées sur la peinture* (Paris: Hermann, 1995), p. 388.

29. Blaise Cendrars, *L'ABC du cinéma*, p. 10. Richard Abel discusses the influence of Cendrars on Epstein in "The Contribution of the French Literary Avant-Garde to Film Theory and Criticism (1907-1924)," *Cinema Journal* 14, no. 3 (Spring 1975): 18-40.

30. Richard Abel, "On the Threshold of French Film Theory and Criticism, 1915-1919," *Cinema Studies* 25, no. 1 (Autumn 1985), p. 26.

31. Luis Buñuel, *My Last Breath*, trans. Abigail Israel. (London: Vintage, 1994), p. 89.

32. Maeterlinck states that "the moving picture presents an art as authentic and as epochal as the Primitive Italian Renaissance" (*The New York Times*, 18 January 1920).

33. Maurice Maeterlinck, *The Treasure of the Humble* [1896], translated by Alfred Sutro. (New York: Dodd, Mead & Company, 1906), pp. 106-108.

34. Jean Epstein, "L'Edgar Poe de Jean Epstein," *Photo-ciné* (April 1928), ESC1, pp. 188-189.

35. Jean Epstein, "L'âme au ralenti," *Paris-Midi* (May 11, 1928), ESC1, p. 191; "The Spirit of Slow Motion," trans. Tom Milne, *Afterimage*, no. 10 (Autumn 1981), p. 34.

36. Jean Epstein, "Dramaturgie dans le temps,"*La Technique cinématographique* [28 November 1948] ESC2, p. 92; infra, 351.

37. Epstein, "Dramaturgie dans le temps," ESC2, p. 92; infra, 351.

38. Epstein, "L'âme au ralenti," ESC1, p. 191; "The Spirit of Slow Motion," p. 34, translation modified.

39. Jean Epstein, "Bilan de fin de muet," *Cinéa-ciné-pour-tous* (January/February 1931), ESC1, p. 230.

40. Jean Epstein, *Photogénie de l'impondérable* (Paris: Éditions Corymbe, 1935), ESC1, p. 253.

41. François Rabelais, *Le Quart Livre*, chapter 56: "Comment entre les parolles gelées Pantagruel trouva des motz de gueule," *Œuvres complètes* (Paris: Gallimard, 1955), pp. 692-694.

42. Epstein, "Le gros plan du son," ESC2, p. 112; infra, 369.

43. Epstein, "Le gros plan du son," ESC2, p. 111; infra, 368.

44. See Roger Odin, *De la fiction* (Bruxelles: De Boeck Université, 2000), particularly the chapter entitled, "De la lecture fictionnalisante à la lecture performative – *Le Tempestaire* de Jean Epstein," pp. 117-118.

45. Raymond Bellour, *L'Entre-Images 2* (Paris: P.O.L., 1999), p. 198.

46. See Philippe Dubois, "La tempête et la matière-temps, ou le sublime et le figural dans l'œuvre de Jean Epstein," in *Jean Epstein: cinéaste, poète, philosophe*, ed. Jacques Aumont (Paris: Cinémathèque française, 1998), pp. 267-323.

47. Epstein, "De quelques conditions de la photogénie," ESC1, p. 137; Abel1, p. 314; infra, 293.

48. André Bazin, "Pour un festival à trois dimensions," *Cahiers du cinéma*, no. 23 (May 1953), p. 10; see also "Le festival de Cannes (suite et fin)," *L'Observateur*, no. 156 (7 May 1953).

49. André Bazin, "Un film bergsonien: *Le Mystère Picasso*," *Cahiers du cinéma*, no. 60 (June 1956).

50. André Bazin, "Le film d'art est-il un documentaire comme les autres?" *Radio Cinéma Télévision*, no. 75 (June 1951).

A Different Nature

Rachel Moore

Il y a toujours un rapport secret entre le voyageur et la terre qu'il paraît choisir pour s'arrêter.

There is always a secret bond between the traveler and the land where he apparently elects to rest.[1]
Jean Epstein

Jean Epstein's writing highlighted cinema as the preeminent modern form, addressing the changing nature of labor and its fatigue, the new relative conception of time and space, and the virtuosity with which the camera machine gave perceptual access to a nerve-wracking world. His films were dramatic vignettes about love, friendship, and loss that engaged in variations of speed, magnifications of objects and bodies, manifold angles, and superimpositions. The films operated in parallel pursuit with his theoretical work to meet perception's evolving demands. These qualities situate Epstein comfortably within the historical avant-garde, and indeed his writings are a continuous point of reference for filmmakers and theorists alike to describe a radically different, modernist cinema throughout much of the history of experimental film. Shattered perception, speed, and movement were key to both his films and his theoretical writing, which emphasized the ways the moving image could make bodily contact with the spectator. The significance of the camera's mechanical nature to accomplish this bodily effect comes through clearly in his evocation of other sorts of moving transport:

The landscape may represent a state of mind. It is above all a state. A state of rest. Even those landscapes most often shown in documentaries of picturesque Brittany or of a trip to Japan are seriously flawed. But "the landscape's dance" is photogenic. Through the window of a train or a ship's porthole, the world acquires a new, specifically cinematic vivacity. A road is a road but the ground which flees under the four beating hearts of an automobile's belly transports me. The Oberland and Semmering tunnels swallow me up, and my head, bursting through the roof, hits against their vaults. Seasickness is decidedly pleasant. I'm on board the plummeting airplane. My knees bend.[2]

Cinema begins with the external world; in this case, a landscape passes through the machine and ends affecting the body. From a moving vehicle, landscape becomes a 'landscape dance' that moves the body. Without such mediation, landscape is merely 'a state.' Perhaps in part to work through this tension between the natural and the technological, Epstein turned to landscape and to Brittany in particular for the latter part of his career. Given his enthusiasm for the modern and the mechanical, along with his disdain for the pictorial, the choice to spend the better part of his last two decades filming at places that were at the time markedly un-modern is striking. Epstein's personal engagement with these places may well remain their secret. But there is clearly more at stake when an eminent modernist with a passionate investment in the potential of cinema spends the better part of two decades filming on four small islands off the coast of Brittany. This paper aims to situate this film work, often relegated to the docile genre of pictorialism, within the context of Epstein's various theoretical concerns. Further still, the work becomes more significant when viewed in its broader social and intellectual context. What follows here looks to the work of ethnography and Critical Theory in order to situate the set of films Epstein made in Brittany – including Finis Terrae (1929), Mor'Vran (1930), L'Or des mers (1932), and Le Tempestaire (1947) – within the larger modernist project, not for the sake of categorization, but rather to try to account for the peculiar relationship between nature and artifice exemplified in two astounding minutes of cinema: the penultimate scene of Epstein's penultimate film, Le Tempestaire, which traverses nature's depths with the height of cinematic artifice, fusing technology with sorcery, the modern with the un-modern. While Bruno Latour may finally be correct that "we have never been modern," the onset of the twentieth century in Europe saw significant changes that brought people in contact with technologies and societies that were new to them.[3]

In France, ethnography and a fascination with cultural difference flourished in the twenties. Whether in the form of the Surrealists' interest in African art objects or the founding of the Institut d'Ethnologie in 1925, "the other," as James Clifford put it, "was a crucial object of modern research."[4] In post-war Germany, Marx had left a gaggle of scholars (who now come under the heading of Critical Theory) scrambling to overcome a trend toward reification through engagement with contemporary labor, art, and the everyday life around them. The interplay between French Surrealism and ethnography yielded the idea that the Other was a serious alternative to the unsteady ground of modern reality whose abstract nature, best articulated by Georg Lukács' landmark essay of 1923, "Reification and the Consciousness of the Proletariat," required new creative methods.[5] In both the French and German cases, reality was no longer straightforward; therefore its representation and, hopefully, transformation, set scholars and artists alike on uncharted paths. Despite his early friendship with Blaise Cendrars, Epstein was not directly connected to either the Surrealists or French ethnography, and he certainly did not read German Marxism. As his writing clearly indicates, however, he was indeed living in the same, newly enigmatic world.

In the context of 1925 Paris, Michel Leiris describes the emergent modernity that was associated with the current influx of Africans and African Americans to which Paris was in thrall:

> The *Revue nègre* enjoys a smash season at the *Theatre des Champs-Elysées*, follow-ing on the heels of W.H. Wellmons's Southern Syncopated Orchestra. Spiri-tuals and *le jazz* sweep the avant-garde bourgeoisie, which haunts Negro bars, sways to new rhythms in search of something primitive, savage...and comple-tely modern. Stylish Paris is transported by the pulsing strum of banjos and by the sensuous Josephine Baker "abandoning herself to the rhythm of the Char-leston."[6]

While the avant-garde bourgeoisie sought "something primitive, savage...and completely modern" according to James Clifford, 1925 also saw Paul Rivet, Lucien Lévy-Bruhl, and Marcel Mauss establish the Institut d'Ethnologie for fieldwork training and the publication of ethnographic scholarship. The antics in the wake of the 1924 Surrealist Manifesto were in full swing, and France was engaged in a minor war with anti-colonial rebels in Morocco. This is the stage Clifford sets to ground the concept of 'Ethnographic Surrealism,' which grows out of a commu-nion between the arts and sciences that share in the project of defamiliarization. For Clifford, this is a significant, if short-lived, historical moment, when every-thing was equally valuable as art and as an object of study, largely through the mechanism of radical contact – that is to say, through maintaining difference by decontextualization, juxtaposition, and collage. At that point in history, "reality was no longer a given, a natural, familiar environment. The self, cut loose from its attachments, must discover meaning where it may – a predicament, evoked at its most nihilistic, that underlies both surrealism and modern ethnography."[7] The look to other cultures, then, was a way of dealing with the modern 'predicament.' Radically different practices and beliefs provided a new lens through which to look at your own society not so much to understand or represent other people, but to open up new creative ground. To look at Epstein's film work on the Breton Islands through the lens of Ethnographic Surrealism is to ask what this contact with difference generated in terms of his artistic and theoretical project.

One of Epstein's essays, written in January of 1926, exemplifies both the influ-ence of engaging with otherness and the valences of modern progress encoun-tered as part of the context for his work. He writes: "But that young black, who used to kneel in worship before the headlights on explorers' cars, is now driving a taxi in Paris and New York. We had best not lag behind this black."[8] Epstein's staged encounter between "this black" and the explorer's headlights, in its his-torical context, enunciates Parisian projections of primitive modernism.[9] In its immediate context, however, he is arguing for a refinement of *photogénie*, away from exploiting the many technical feats only cinema can accomplish and towards their more subtle deployment. Those that desire to hang onto this form of enchantment, he writes, "should buy a kaleidoscope, a plaything for a second childhood."[10] The refinement of *photogénie* brought with it shifts in location and subject matter. The artistic and ethnographic urge towards contact with the radically other emerges first in Epstein's writing as contact with cinema – for it is cinema that is alien and magical – and then as contact with the Breton Islands, distinguished by their isolation and strangeness. Epstein's early invocation of animism and "primitive religions" sets cinematic perception loose to wildly explore all that met his eye, as if his camera were a spirit that could go anywhere, and could imbue things captured on film with magical powers:

> I would even go so far as to say that the cinema is polytheistic and theogonic. Those lives it creates, by summoning objects out of the shadows of indifference into the light of dramatic concern, have little in common with human life. These lives are like the life in charms and amulets, the ominous, tabooed objects of certain primitive religions. If we wish to understand how an animal, a plant or a stone can inspire respect, fear, or horror, those three most sacred sentiments, I think we must watch them on the screen, living their mysterious, silent lives, alien to the human sensibility.[11]

Here Epstein claims that such elemental things as stones acquire the power to elicit emotion, if not religious significance, through the mechanism of the camera. The alien nature of the camera is key to its power to transform objects into things that can inspire sentiment. This contrast of the mechanical with emotion is more than a rhetorical turn; rather it characterizes the basis of Epstein's approach to filmmaking.

Epstein's writing often stages the encounter between the primitive and the technological, between science and poetry, between objective reality and the world the film creates – to put it more generally, between nature and second nature. Second nature is the nature that culture makes, largely through mimetic practices through which we take un-natural things to be natural. The headlights scene is staged at the intersection of nature (a projected primitive authenticity) and second nature (which casts that authenticity in a blinding, mystifying light). From this encounter, the specter of a different nature – Epstein called it a second reality – emerges, one that has the properties of both nature and second nature but blurs the difference between them. Small wonder, then, that he calls the thing that turns, morphs, mimics, and mutates reality the "metal brain."[12]

In its recognition of the difference and confusion caused as film images gained significant ground on reality, Epstein's thought echoes the work of Georg Lukács, who in 1920 formalized the difference between nature and second nature. For

Lukács, the difference between nature and second nature was clear, even if both ultimately depended upon the alienation of the senses. People find themselves isolated from first nature through their own folly: "Estrangement from nature (the first nature), the modern sentimental attitude to nature, is only a projection of man's experience of his self-made environment as a prison instead of as a parental home."[13] First nature does not signify anything, nor does it include feeling. In contrast, second nature, despite its disaffection, even displays a hint of subjective presence: "...second nature is not dumb, sensuous and yet senseless." For Lukács, it is "a complex of senses – meaning – which has become rigid and strange, and which no longer awakens interiority; it is a charnel-house of rotting interiorities." Here, second nature's effect is to flaunt meaning, but a meaning that doesn't resonate in any genuine way with a person.[14] Lukács's definition of second nature posits a world that alienates and yet has power over us; moreover, "this second nature could only be brought to life – if this were possible – by the metaphysical act of re-awakening the souls which, in an early or ideal existence, created or preserved it."[15] Thus second nature is riddled with meaning that has been distorted from its cultural origins beyond human recognition, access, and control.

However inadequate Lukács' metaphysical solution to the problem of reclaiming second nature may now appear, the problem of "reawakening" as set forth in The Theory of the Novel was to animate much of Critical Theory's subsequent work. Adorno, in his address to the Frankfurt chapter of the Kant Society in July of 1932, saw in Lukács' introduction of second nature the division between "a meaningful and a meaningless world"[16] – that is, an immediate world and an alienated world of commodities" that, in Adorno's words, "supplies neither a meaning for the subject in search of a goal nor sensuous immediacy as material for the acting subject."[17] As to first nature, Lukács says, "it can only be defined as the embodiment of well-known yet meaningless necessities and therefore it is ungraspable and unknowable in its actual substance."[18] In Epstein's later work, the Breton Islands can be seen as a foil to second nature, if not exactly a place where first nature was knowable.

In Epstein's early writings, however, second nature emerged with alarming clarity and he greeted it with enthusiasm. He points to the mimetic phenomenon of second nature in relation to first nature within the context of film viewing: "I see what is not and I see this unreal thing exactly."[19] Second nature is so good at taking nature's place that the values attached to the distinction between nature and second nature become difficult to maintain: "Even though it's merely light and shadow whose only material element is the cloth on which it's projected, as a spectator, I do not doubt that they exist."[20] A phantasmagoric situation ensues:

Actors who thought themselves alive here show themselves to be more than dead, less than nothing, negative; while others and objects that are inert seem suddenly to feel and think, to transform themselves, to threaten and to live the life of insects, accelerated twenty metamorphoses at a time. As they exit, the crowds, [...] preserve the memory of a new found land, or a *second reality*, silent, luminous, rapid and shifting. It is a feeling – something far better than an idea – that cinema brings into the world.[21]

As Lukács wrote a year before, second nature has subjective presence; it acts upon us. Epstein's second reality, while formed under the conditions of second nature, is a different nature still, for it appears to bring feeling into the world. The 'feeling' with which the audience is left at the movie theater is both a physical transformation and a memory of direct contact brought on by second reality. People become things, things take on life, and in so doing create a second reality that generates feeling.

Epstein was far from sanguine, however, about this second reality: "Life fragments itself into new individualities. Instead of a mouth, the mouth, larva of kisses, essence of touch. Everything quivers with bewitchment. I am uneasy. In a new nature, another world."[22] This new and other world, accessed by cinematic attention, is the world that has been hidden by naming, by classification, by mere "symbols of reality uniform, proportionate, elective metaphors" – in other words, by the mechanisms of reification.[23] In opposition to this process, the camera reveals the secrets hidden in reality's apparent uniformity. In Epstein's view, you don't know a place until you have filmed it, through close-ups and multi-faceted inspection. Our senses, by contrast, merely present us with symbols of reality that are "uniform, proportionate." These are symbols, in Epstein's words, "not of matter" but of "energy." Epstein continues: "We say 'red,' 'soprano,' 'sweet,' 'cypress' when there are only velocities, movements, vibrations."[24] With a codifying stamp like 'red,' a word masks the disorderly complex of energies at work, but film can capture the forces in the color that our language cannot. Our senses have been impoverished by symbolization, in much the same way we use a word to simplify, order, and thus contain a more raw and dynamic reality. Just as the convention of language turns energy and matter into static dead things, to see according to a conventional perspective deprives things of their formless vitality. To follow Epstein in the process of undoing the shackles of language and liberating our overly trained senses is difficult. It is a matter of seeing "what is," which is always dressed up, shaped not only by language, but also by the conventions of seeing and the hegemony of form.

For Georges Bataille, the difficulty of seeing 'what is' arises because of the authority of form, which requires things to take shape, have form; shape up! The lack of form, by contrast, is always degraded. In Bataille's essay of the same name, "formless" is a term that denigrates where it has no right to do so. It is:

a term that serves to bring things down in the world, generally requiring that each thing have its form. What it designates has no rights in any sense and gets itself squashed everywhere, like a spider or an earthworm. In fact, for academic men to be happy, the universe would have to take shape. All of philosophy has no other goal: it is a matter of giving a frock coat to what is, a mathematical frock coat."[25]

The power of form over a world that simply 'is' for Bataille and the tendency to make uniform what is fragmented for Epstein present formidable obstacles. In his discussion of photogénie, Epstein not only voices the difficulty of defining a concept that refers to things for which there are no words, but also suggests, as does Bataille's advocacy for the formless, that photogénie is elusive, underfoot, and at risk of being trod upon:

> Photogénie is not simply a fashionably devalued word. A new leavening; dividend, divisor and quotient. One runs into a brick wall trying to define it. The face of beauty, it is the taste of things. [...] Elusive, it is often trampled underfoot like the promise of riches with which an undiscovered coal-seam emblazons the earth.[26]

Although photogénie is jeopardized precisely because of its characteristic elusiveness, it derives its strength from its relationship to the camera, which can give us access to "velocities, movements, and vibrations." Although our human senses fail to see what simply is, the camera succeeds precisely because it is not human and therefore not spoiled by intention.

Epstein's writing presents the same temporal and spatial elasticity as cinema, expanding moments of encounter with the world from a close-up outwards, beginning at cellular levels, or condensing a complex scene into one word. As was his claim for photogénie, his writing circumvents conscious cognition and instead grabs you with the tempo of a good film. Epstein records his surroundings in fragments, by shifting angles and focus, by breaking down the environment into close-ups. Gliding along the Seine, for example, his attention is drawn to the lights' glow, to the moths clustered around them, and finally to the ash marks left by the touch of their wings on someone's forehead.[27] The boat, like the camera, turns landscape into a "landscape dance." Epstein's interest in minutiae often makes it difficult to get a concrete purchase on the scene as a whole. From his interest in the moth's ash residue to his curiosity about what lies beneath appearances – that is, "the consistent world of our practical experience" beneath which "hide the surprises of a reality that is very diffuse" – Epstein can be seen as a reader of ruins and fragments.[28] "The consistent world of our practical experience" to which one is habituated – the world of frock coats which has become second nature – hides another reality that is diffuse, formless, and invaluable.

Reducing the world to ruins and fragments was the crucial 'awakening' from the second nature that so preoccupied Lukács, Benjamin, and Adorno. "For radical natural-historical thought," wrote Adorno, "*everything existing* transforms itself into ruins and fragments [...] where signification is discovered, in which nature and history interweave."[29] Seeing things in pieces rather than whole, where their shape or name makes them impervious to history, that is the task of the radical historical materialist. Like the elusive moments of photogénie, these readings of the material world are fleeting, transient, and precious.

Epstein's atomist, materialist understanding of the world, with references from Democritus[30] to Lucretius,[31] renders the world ripe for cinematic inspection, but the camera's transformation of the world is also "an occult business." Like the Epicureans, Epstein turned to the world of matter for the material of enchantment; however, the transformation of matter into cinema was, for Epstein, religious. Cinema was "animistic, polytheistic." Quite simply, Epstein wrote, "the cinema is supernatural."[32] The close-up, for example, has powers of divination, just as the study of an organ's cells can determine the organ's pathology. Indeed, Epstein's medical references blend seamlessly with cinema's supernatural powers: "Possibilities are already appearing for the drama of the microscope, a histophysiology of passions, a classification of the amorous sentiments into those which do and those which do not need Gram's solutions."[33] In histophysiology, the microscopic structure of cells and tissues is related to the entire organ; something can be detected about the heart, for example, by focusing on its smallest component. Someday, wrote Epstein, "Young girls will consult [close-ups] instead of the fortune-teller."[34] The close-up as a fortune-teller for matters of the heart resurfaces later in his film work on the islands, but his point here is that close-ups help us understand the truth of things better. They do this precisely because they do not show things in their entirety, but rather cut them up and expose them. "While we are waiting," he continues, "we have an initial sketch in the close-up. It is nearly overlooked, not because it errs, but because it presents a ready-made style, a minute dramaturgy, flayed and vulnerable."[35] The close-up shows the formless underbelly that is shrouded by the tendency to name and order things. The alien sensibility of the camera offers entrance into a second life, one through which the world's matter becomes the source not only of understanding but also of enchantment.

Epstein's exhaustive explorations of the sensibility the modern world requires to perceive it puts him at the advance front of the modernist project, in both artistic and theoretical terms. In what appears to be a retreat from modernity, however, Epstein turned his camera toward that which he felt to be already authentic, the Breton Islands. His interest in this environment commences with his work on Finis Terrae, filmed on the island of Ouessant beginning in the summer of 1928. He then continued by returning multiple times, eventually making six films on the islands of the archipelago and three in mainland Brittany, the last of these in 1948.

The islands of the Ouessant archipelago were thinly populated, barren, and at that time, free from modern technology.[36] The islands were marginal to the French state and dominated by the church. Houat Island, for example, was known as a theocracy and did not become fully part of the French administrative system until 1891.[37] Even the islands' relationship to the church was not simple, for the rector had a significant financial and bureaucratic hold over the villagers. In 1903, the rector was not only parish curate, but also head of the fishermen's union, city toll collector, post officer, captain of the port, justice of the peace, notary public, letter writer, pharmacist, and doctor, to name but a few. As late as 1973, he was still public letter writer, solicitor, chemist, and owner, on behalf of the church, of the island's self-service shop. Through his ability to extend credit, he had absolute power over the people's finances. He also controlled their access to alcohol as well as to the foyer of the church, which was the only suitable festive meeting place.[38] This control belied the deeper ways in which the demands of fishing life on the islands did not align with Catholic practices and beliefs. For example, a fisherman would not be able to attend mass routinely, and there was a rift between life on land – associated with the church, women, and children – and life at sea, which was exclusively male and was associated with more traditional religious beliefs and customs than those of the Catholic church. Death at sea was such a dominant fact of life that talk inevitably turned to that topic, according to Paul Jorion's 1982 account of his fieldwork from 1974-75. According to Jorion, the beliefs associated with death at sea that lie outside the Catholic Church are various products of the life of these men at sea where religion is a matter between them and the heavens. The fortunes and misfortunes of fishing were attended to by magical as well as religious observation. It is into this complex context that Epstein brings his metal brain.

Ouessant Island is at the very margin of the nation-state, historically and physically. Insofar as the center needed the periphery to authorize the modernist project, the countryside is an important part of the conceptual furniture of the nation-state. Epstein arrived in this region curious about how the technological progress so endemic to the city might find ways to impact the Islands and why the people there nevertheless seemed, in his eyes, to prefer their isolation. While he went there for authentic, raw material, he also noted how modern life was seen through the islanders' eyes. When a merchant, for example, came to demonstrate the wireless, Epstein described the scene with mockery. There was so much static, he wrote, the only thing you could hear clearly was Poland.[39] Although he clearly saw the islands as "terres vierges pour le cinéma," they were not unknown territory.[40] Vincent Guigueno's study, Jean Epstein, cineaste des îles, stresses the point that to see Epstein's first trip there as a "shock" is a serious mistake. He had visited the area, though not this island, as a child; he had read and derided novels and travel journals that painted the people as simpletons, exotics, or primitives; and he had written passionately against the heavy-handed and uncaring behavior of the church. Moreover, the area, though remote, had long been a site for adventurous tourists, artists, and writers in the summer months. The island was virgin territory for his cinematic encounter, but not for Epstein himself.

Epstein wrote of Ouessant: "In this place and people is resumed the mystery of men dedicated to land that is but rock, to a sea which is but foam, to a hard and perilous trade suffering a meager self-sufficiency."[41] Why, Epstein asked, so close to the mainland, do they prefer this risk? Lukács' description of first nature is a possible response: "When the structures made by man for man are really adequate to man, they are his necessary and native home; and he does not know the nostalgia that posits and experiences nature as the object of its own seeking and finding."[42] The islanders operate within nature, whereas Epstein is looking from outside and would be, in Lukács' view, looking at a product of his own objectification. Given the many artifices that ensnare filmmaking, such as make-up, acting, sets, and lighting, along with Epstein's reverence for the material world, the islands seem to have offered him precisely what Lukács had claimed was no longer accessible: "[t]he first nature, nature as a set of laws for pure cognition, nature as the bringer of comfort to pure feeling."[43] Time and again, Epstein writes of the camera's unique perceptual access to the world, through which one could see the minutiae and energies otherwise hidden by the habits and prejudices of human perception. For Epstein, the world of matter already is full of energy and drama, if we would only train the camera upon it. The Island, free of all manner of make-up, sets, and acting, was a place where "existing reality" could make more direct contact with the camera than in urban or staged settings. Writing of filming *Finis Terrae*, he said, "Most films are an invention which the author tries to make seem real. [...] I have tried to achieve dramatic illusion in reverse, as it were, by lending an existing reality to the more general characteristics of fiction."[44] To present the camera with a location generally free from mediation and artifice, flush with natural matter – stones, plants, seas, skies – surely featured in his choice of these locations.

It is difficult to pinpoint what prompted Epstein to go to Ouessant Island to make *Finis Terrae* because he was uncertain about his own motives: "Drawn by what I no longer know," he wrote, "I went to Brittany to seek the authentic elements for this film which became *Finis Terrae*."[45] The film was, in his words, "the reproduction of a brief drama comprising events which really happened, of authentic men and things."[46] But it was specifically the *mixture* of artifice and nature that provided the formula for Epstein's investigation there. The narrative of *Finis Terrae* builds upon this natural setting and its native people. It tells the story of the friendship between two men, Ambroise and Jean-Marie, who languish in the hot sun on a small island to which they have sailed to gather kelp. Insofar as the story was derived from a local newspaper clipping, it is comprised of "events which really happened." As to "authentic men and things," the characters are played by Islanders – men and women in their native setting, acting out that story. The simplicity of the story obscures its subtle and complex psychodramatic elements, in which a series of perceived slights and rebukes escalates to a brief violent moment. Their bottle of wine smashes on the rocks, a sad, brutal occurrence on this island where alcohol was a uniquely valued commodity to which the priest controlled access[47] and where red wine was worth double its price in currency.[48] Worse still, Ambroise has cut his finger, and the wound begins to fester. In the ensuing drama, Ambroise lies in the hot sun, sweating, his pain ignored by Jean-Marie. Lying in a hammock at dusk, Ambroise becomes delirious and falls into a dream-like state. *Phare du Creach*, one of the most powerful lighthouses in the world, appears, although it is otherwise not within his field of vision in the film.

Until this moment, the film had been designed to show the workings of kelp gathering in almost ethnographic detail, occasionally employing slightly slowed motion for the sea and the actors' emotions. The appearance of the lighthouse marks a dramatic change in the film's style, introducing a kind of hallucinogenic encounter. Ambroise's delirium is crosscut with a direct beam from the lighthouse as if refracted in Ambroise's eyeball, although it is not. The cinematic exchange between bodily pain and technological ocular power, between his arm and the lighthouse, repeats. Intercut with his memory of the breaking bottle, the lighthouse and its light create a dizzying spectacle from which he eventually wakes. While the lighthouse is not a camera, it nonetheless evokes *photogénie* and produces its effects insofar as it communicates directly with Ambroise's body. The lighthouse appears once more in the film when the doctor tries to locate the men after an absence of three days. (Although the people announce they are going to the Stiff lighthouse, also on the island, it is clearly *Phare du Creach*.) Although they learn the sea is rough, they nonetheless embark on a rescue mission. Ambroise's life clearly at risk, Jean-Marie puts him in a boat and attempts to row back to the larger island but his efforts are hardly a match for the current. When the fog sets in, the voyage looks impossible. Meanwhile, the doctor has set out with a search party, and the two boats eventually meet in the sea passage, where the doctor drains the wound and Ambroise begins to recover. Returned to the main island, the drama is over, and Ambroise's healing begins.

Although the drama has ended, the film has not. An important, epilogue-like ending reasserts Epstein's investment in examining the tension between technology and nature in the film. The doctor is called away to another patient, and the film ends with his walking away towards an empty landscape, a little drunk due to the thankful offices of Ambroise's mother. Though the film began as the story of a friendship, it ends abruptly with the doctor walking off, with a boy at his side, their backs to the camera. The ending highlights the doctor's role in the drama and his position relative to the community; moreover, it suggests an affinity between Epstein, who trained as a doctor, and the character in the film. When we are introduced to the Dr. Lesser, he is shown playing his gramophone for a group of children, immediately associating him with modern technology and a privileged outsider status. This is precisely Epstein's own status, and in the end – after having brought modern mediation (in the doctor's case, modern medicine; in Epstein's case, the camera) into direct contact with the rugged, hazardous, primitive landscape – he departs. Epstein wrote of this filmmaking experience: "Leaving the Ouessant archipelago, I felt I was taking with me not a film but a fact. And once this fact had been transported to Paris, something of the material and spiritual reality of the island life would henceforth be missing. An occult business."[49] If one understands Epstein the director as the technological doctor, once the story is over, and his work is done, he rightly packs up and leaves, taking this "fact," namely the film, along with him.

While the action of *Finis Terrae* largely takes place on land, shots of the water dominate. Water, with its inherent movement, is by nature photogenic, and Epstein's filming of water is almost trance-like. While this creates a kind of filmic reverie, it also reflects the omnipresence of the sea's danger – whether because it is too calm or too tempestuous for safe travel – in the Islanders' lives. Belle-Île-en-Mer, the much larger island on which *Le Tempestaire* was shot in 1947, shares in the isolation and danger of the Ouessant archipelago. The film's prelude swings wildly back and forth, panning the ocean and sky in the midst of a storm as if attached to a ship's boom gone out of control. The drama opens in stillness, a stillness reminiscent of René Clair's *Paris qui dort* (1925), with fishermen frozen in motion, looking out at the sea, and women caught in the midst of spinning wool and knitting.[50] The film winds into motion, a motion that increases in intensity as the storm gathers its forces.

Structurally, the film crosscuts the drama of nature with a simple human drama, a wife's fear of her husband's death at sea. The constant proximity of death exercised a strong hold on people's daily lives that extended religious practices and beliefs beyond Catholicism. Death at sea could mean a lost body, and with that the threat of chaos for its soul. Jorion writes, "by his presence the priest manages to keep things under control when death seems to be threatening, but the coming of the night...brings non-Christian beliefs concerning the dead back to the mind."[51] While spinning wool at home during the day, a woman is frightened by an ill omen that she believes concerns her husband; by nightfall she is terrified. She inquires about the Tempest Master, whose ability to control storms had saved Islanders from danger long ago. She first stops at the lighthouse to find out what can be done about the storm. The two men there point to the wireless and say that sometimes it can help. She doesn't even glance at the wireless; instead she asks about the Tempest Master, now a reputed drunk.[52] She hurries off in search of him. As she exits the lighthouse, the camera crosscuts between the Tempest Master in his garden with a close-up of the wireless, continuing to pit his magical powers against the wireless. Upon entering the house, the noises of the impending storm are temporarily shut out. After repeated appeals, the Tempest Master unveils his glass ball, and conjures the sea.

With Le Tempestaire, Epstein was both expanding the photogenic properties of cinema to sound, and refining, sobering his optical strategies. In 1926, Epstein had said that the cinema of the kaleidoscope was a thing for children. After filming Le Tempestaire some twenty years later, Epstein noted that within the category of the fantastic, film can do anything: "Trick photography can do everything, change pumpkins into coaches, divide the waters of the sea, make magic carpets fly, compel John the Baptist, once he has been beheaded, to carry his own head to Herod."[53] However, for Epstein, these tricks are amusing but not convincing; all such devices will eventually cease to astound. He dismisses the magic of tricks, which exist merely to deceive, and distinguishes another sort of magic: "On the opposite pole to the fabricated marvels, laboriously worked out and burdened with decrepit futility, there exist, everywhere about us, true mysteries which the motion picture camera discovers by itself, with a prodigious insight."[54] The revelation of true mysteries doesn't require tricks (complicated technical refinements, photo-montage, etc.): "the camera discovers them by itself." Indeed, "the only sorcery the film requires is the basic faculty, of its organic and natural power of making things and events larger or smaller in space or time."[55] Film's basic facility to expand and condense time brings it back to its roots in consciousness, for film, Epstein notes, was able to replicate the feeling of time.[56] He is not interested in the trickery of deception, but in a far more serious sort of magic: "Slowed down eight times, a wave also develops an atmosphere of sympathetic magic."[57] The derision of tricks puts pressure on those moments in these later films when he uses overtly disorienting, or re-orienting cinematographic methods used for a more serious purpose than "contrived miracles." These moments are associated with both technology and the risk of death. In Le Tempestaire, sorcery and technology combine as they did in Finis Terrae, only this time through cinematic as well as narrative devices, to save the husband's life by quieting the impending storm.

The Tempest Master deploys the imitative form of sympathetic magic by blowing at the stormy sea's image in the glass. With this first attempt, as if to put sorcery and science in competition, the scene is rapidly inter-cut with shots of the wireless. The filming of the sky speeds up, accompanied by high musical shrieks; then the alchemy begins as the sound of the slowed-down waves enters the room. Disorienting, almost impossible views made possible by the camera lens, coupled with reflections at the level of mise-en-scène, signal the collapsing of technology and magic. At one point, the close-up of the crystal ball condenses four spatial layers: the Tempest Master holds the ball, and the sea churns within it, while this already- complex image is superimposed onto a seascape outside, as the young woman's face is reflected on the surface of the glass ball. The close-up of the orb shows the sea, which then appears in full screen. Epstein repeats this cut from the shot of the sea in the orb to the full-screen shot of the sea several times, as if to emphasize that the camera has taken over the sorcerer's role. The sorcerer blows onto the glass for the second time, the sea stops and ultimately reverses its motion, followed by a parallel reversal in the sound, until finally the seas relax, tranquil. He blows a third, final time; the glass orb falls to the ground and shatters, and at that moment the husband appears.

While Epstein had left his "tricks" far behind, in this scene he demonstrates the ability to convey a new, cinematic nature. The object under the lens's indifferent scrutiny – the object in close-up – is at once the glass orb and the sea. In Epstein's terms, such a close-up should give us access to something else: "respect, fear or horror." In the context of this island story, the camera's power is even graver, for it faces off with the fact of death at sea and subjugation to nature at its most extreme. The sea is the face of death, both in the individual story and in the way Epstein has built its image in the film, returning to its muscular waves, noisy foam, and swirling currents over and over again, as if death itself were underneath with all its energies colluding to pull in the living. The moment when the crystal ball (in close-up in the Tempest Master's hand) is superimposed onto the sea yields the viscerality that defines *photogénie*. Nature (the sea) and second nature (the lens through which we see it, the glass ball) combine; the sea's movement and its sound slow down, stop, and reverse in a moment of physis. Momentarily, cinema's sorcery is palpable.

Adorno notes that it is not to nature but to second nature that we must attend in order to deal with its deadening effect on modern life. Epstein went to the end of the earth, where the risk of death at sea was an everyday fear, to film nature unadorned. He did so not to redeem nature, but to demonstrate the camera's magical power. No longer merely a mimetic tool that turns nature into second nature, in the film's confrontation with death, Epstein goes beyond the limits of nature versus second nature, which continually keeps us in such a double bind. Critical Theory referred to such an event as 'awakening.' In the case of this film, the conflict between nature and second nature is finally staged as a confrontation with death. It is death, as Benjamin wrote in *The Origins of German Tragic Drama*, that most profoundly distinguishes between the immediate and the mediated world. He writes, "Death digs most deeply the jagged demarcation line between physis and signification."[58] Cinema continually rests atop that line between visceral natural eruptions (physis) and the conferral of meaning (signification). *Photogénie* transports the secrets of the material world – their significance – through sight and sound to the body of the spectator. Its use in this scene not only conjoins the technological with the magical, but also shows the redemptive possibility that cinema can stave off death. Not so much the death of a person, but the stultifying conundrum of modernity's phantasmagoria.

From the point of view of ethnographic surrealism, Epstein's filming on the Breton Islands was an encounter between the camera and the elements of nature in a site free from theatrical trappings, a place of "true mystery." Epstein focused on movement in nature and the minutely slowed-down actions of his non-professional actors; however, in rare bursts of photogenic frenzy, the encounter also affected a head-on collision with other optical and aural technologies, which form stylistic, if not narrative, climaxes within the films. In the case of *Le Tempestaire*, sorcery wins over the wireless, only to have that power purloined by the camera. Recalling Epstein had predicted that "Girls will consult [close-ups] instead of the fortune teller," we can see that he has labored to make his own theory an actuality. However, the cinematic engagement with sorcery here tells us squarely where our faith and skepticism lies, whether or not we think the camera's reversal of motion has a sympathetic effect on the tempestuous ocean. Condensing interior and exterior spatial planes, stopping and reversing time, and lowering the sea's thunder, it is cinema, not sorcery, that emerges victorious. Using film's manipulation of time and space, cinema no longer merely copies physical reality to make an uncanny double (this unreal thing, exactly), but changes fate. Epstein's boldest ethnographic-surrealist move is to usurp the sorcerer's power.

From the point of view of Critical Theory, these films can be seen as experiments with second nature's transformative potential. Adorno wrote, "Whenever 'second nature' appears, when the world of convention approaches, it can be deciphered in that its meaning is shown to be precisely its transience."[59] Second nature reveals its meaning through its ephemerality. Second nature can be remade to be useful, immediate, and human through critique from the inside. The elements of Epstein's scene could not be more raw (water, sky, earth) nor the technology more manifest. By reducing the film down to the elements of nature and technology, and charging them through their friction, Epstein forces open a new, different nature.

Clifford elaborated on a brief historical moment to theorize a Utopian concept, hoping to influence anthropologists to take up a direction lost to the discipline. Adorno and Benjamin understood the chances for "awakening" from second nature as fleeting but not impossible. Epstein's thoughts on *photogénie* too often suggest that it is an ideal that is rarely realized. In 1928, he wrote, "Until now, I have never seen an entire minute of pure *photogénie*. Therefore, one must admit that the photogenic is like a spark that appears in fits and starts."[60] The alchemy these ideas ask us to seek out is ephemeral by nature; at best they refer to momentary transformations. Epstein's cultural encounter on the island allowed him to assert the power of the camera in confronting such an environment; his stark union of nature and second nature produced a moment that transcended those confined categories. Ethnography's radical encounter with cultural difference to produce creativity and Critical Theory's "awakening" are nebulous, fleeting, and difficult to locate. Utopian thinking however, demands that we look.

Notes

1. Jean Epstein, "Approaches to Truth" [1928], trans. Tom Milne, Abel1, p. 423.
2. Jean Epstein, "Magnification" [1921], trans. Stuart Liebman, Abel1, p. 237.
3. Bruno Latour, *We Have Never Been Modern*, trans. Catherine Porter (Cambridge, MA: Harvard University Press, 1993).
4. James Clifford, *The Predicament of Culture: Twentieth-Century Ethnography, Literature, and Art* (Cambridge, MA: Harvard University Press, 1988), p. 120.
5. Georg Lukács, "Reification and the Consciousness of the Proletariat" [1923], in *History and Class Consciousness: Studies in Marxist Dialectics*, trans. Rodney Livingston (Cambridge, MA: MIT Press, 1971), pp. 83-222.
6. Clifford, *The Predicament of Culture*, p. 122. Clifford here cites Michel Leiris and Jacqueline Delange, *African Art*, trans. Michael Ross (New York: Golden Press, 1968), p. 33.
7. Clifford, *The Predicament of Culture*, p. 119.
8. Jean Epstein, "The Lens Itself" [1926], trans. Tom Milne, *Afterimage*, no. 10 (Autumn 1981), p. 17.
9. On primitivism in modernist art, see Robert Goldwater, *Primitivism in Modern Art* (New York: Vintage, 1967); and *"Primitivism" in 20th Century Art: Affinity of the Tribal and the Modern*, 2 vols., ed. William Rubin (New York: Museum of Modern Art, 1984).
10. Epstein, "The Lens Itself," p. 18.
11. Jean Epstein, "On Certain Characteristics of *Photogénie*" [1924], trans. Tom Milne, Abel1, p. 317; infra, 295.
12. Jean Epstein, "The Senses I (b)," [1921], trans. Tom Milne, Abel1, p. 244. For a fuller discussion of the importance of the camera as a "metal brain," see Rachel Moore, *Savage Theory: Cinema as Modern Magic* (Durham, NC: Duke University Press, 2000), esp. pp. 93-95.
13. Lukács, *The Theory of the Novel*, p. 64.
14. This might remind us of Walter Benjamin's comment in "This Space for Rent," an episode in "One-Way Street," in which he writes of advertising and film: "Thereby 'matter-of-factness' is finally dispatched, and in the face of the huge images across the walls of houses, where toothpaste and cosmetics lie handy for giants, sentimentality is restored to health and liberated in American style, just as people whom nothing moves or touches any longer are taught to cry again by films" (Walter Benjamin, "One-Way Street" [1928], trans. Edmund Jephcott, in Walter Benjamin, *Selected Writings, Vol. 1: 1913-1926*, eds. Marcus Bullock and Michael W. Jennings [Cambridge, MA: Belknap Press of Harvard University Press, 1996], p. 476).
15. Georg Lukács, *The Theory of the Novel* [1920], trans. Anna Bostock (Cambridge, MA: MIT Press, 1985), p. 64.
16. Theodor Adorno, "The Idea of Natural-History" [1932], trans. Bob Hullot-Kentor, *Telos*, no. 60 (Summer 1984), p. 117.
17. Adorno, "The Idea of Natural-History," pp. 117-18.
18. Lukács, *The Theory of the Novel*, p. 64. Also quoted in Adorno, "The Idea of Natural-History," p. 118.

19. Jean Epstein, "Cine-Mystique" [1921], trans. Stuart Liebman, *Millennium Film Journal*, nos. 10-11 (1984), p. 192.
20. Epstein, "Cine-Mystique," pp. 192.
21. Epstein, "Cine-Mystique," pp. 192-193.
22. Epstein, "The Senses I (b)," *Abel1*, p. 243.
23. Epstein, "The Senses I (b)," *Abel1*, p. 244.
24. Epstein, "The Senses I (b)," *Abel1*, p. 244.
25. Georges Bataille, *Visions of Excess*, trans. Allan Stoekl (Minneapolis: University of Minnesota Press, 1985), p. 31.
26. Epstein, "The Senses I (b)," *Abel1*, pp. 243-244.
27. Jean Epstein, "Le Cinématographe dans l'Archipel" [1928], *ESC1*, p. 197.
28. Jean Epstein, "The Universe Head Over Heels" [1946] trans. Stuart Liebman, *October*, no. 3 (Spring 1977), p. 22. This text is excerpted from Epstein's book, *L'Intelligence d'une machine* (Paris: J. Melot, 1946). It is also interesting to note that for Adorno, attention to ruins and fragments was crucial to 'awaken' from the false world of second nature. "For radical natural-historical thought," wrote Adorno, "*everything existing* transforms itself into ruins and fragments ... where signification is discovered, in which nature and history interweave" (Adorno, "Idea of Natural History," p. 121). Seeing the pieces rather than the whole (in which the shapes or names of things have made them impervious to scrutiny) was for both Adorno and Walter Benjamin the historical materialist's task.
29. Theodor Adorno, "Idea of Natural-History," trans. Bob Hullot-Kentor, *Telos* 60 (Summer 1984), p. 121.
30. Epstein, "The Universe Head Over Heels," p. 22.
31. Jean Epstein, *Le Livre d'Or du Cinema, 1947-48*, trans. Robert Lamberton, Anthology Film Archives notes, n.d., unpaginated.
32. Epstein, *Le Livre d'Or du Cinema*.
33. Epstein, "Magnification," *Abel1*, p. 238.
34. Ibid., p. 238.
35. Ibid., p. 238.
36. Paul Jorion, "The Priest and the Fishermen: Sundays and Weekdays in a Former 'Theocracy,'" *Man* 17, no. 2 (1982), p. 276.
37. Jorion, "The Priest and the Fishermen," p. 283.
38. Jorion, "The Priest and the Fishermen," pp. 282-284.
39. Vincent Guigueno, *Jean Epstein, cineaste des îles: Ouessant, Sein, Hoëdic, Belle-Île* (Paris: Éd. Jean-Michel Place, 2003), p. 1. While it may have been simply chance that brought clear sounds only from Poland through the wireless that day, it is difficult to ignore the fact that Poland was Epstein's birthplace and childhood home. That this novel piece of modern technology brought the islanders sounds that were incomprehensible, but brought to Epstein voices from his former homeland may have equally been the source of his derision.
40. Jean Epstein, "Les Cinématographe dans l'Archipel" [1929-1930], Fonds Jean et Marie Epstein, Bibliothèque du film, Paris, EPSTEIN96-B24. Cited in Guigueno, *Jean Epstein*, p. 26 n34.
41. Epstein, "Approaches to Truth," *Abel1*, p. 424.

42. Lukács, *The Theory of the Novel*, p. 64.
43. Ibid., p. 64.
44. Epstein, "Approaches to Truth," *Abel1*, p. 423.
45. Ibid., p. 423.
46. Ibid., p. 424.
47. Jorion, "The Priest and the Fishermen," p. 284.
48. Jean Epstein, "Anthology Film Archives Presents," trans. Robert Lamberton, n.d., 9.
49. Epstein, "Approaches to Truth," *Abel1*, p. 424.
50. Jorion's article on fishing life in the archipelago remarks on how much time the men spend staring at the sea and talking amongst themselves, as well as the severe division of the sexes in daily life there.
51. Jorion, "The Priest and the Fishermen," p. 275.
52. Jean Epstein, "The Cinema Continues" [1930], trans. Richard Abel, *Abel2*, pp. 63-68.
53. Jean Epstein, "The Reality of Fairyland" [1947], in Bachmann p. 43.
54. Ibid., p. 43.
55. Ibid., p. 43.
56. Jean Epstein, "Timeless Time" [1946], trans. Stuart Liebman, *October*, no. 3 (Spring 1977), pp. 20-21.
57. Ibid., p. 20.
58. Walter Benjamin, *The Origins of German Tragic Drama* [1924-1925], trans. John Osborne (London: Verso, 1998), p. 166.
59. Adorno, "The Idea of Natural-History," p. 120.
60. Epstein, "Magnification," *Abel1*, p. 236.

Cinema Seen from the Seas: Epstein and the Oceanic

James Schneider

Traveling among the islands of Brittany, filmmakers – myself included – have interrogated the crosscurrents of the cinematic and the oceanic. We have navigated these waters accompanied by the specter of Jean Epstein's own explorations of the region from 1927 to 1948. My investigations of this fluid space have given form to latent proposals found in Epstein's work, which he had begun to elaborate just before his disappearance, among them the theoretical and practical role he accorded to the non-human in the filmmaking process. His cinematic experiment in Brittany began by developing a profound collaboration with the real, initially via the island population with whom he engaged. This evolved into one of Epstein's most striking propositions: that by using cinema to grant perspective to the non-human – to the oceans, the tides, the tempests – humankind gains a vital perspective on itself, a seeming reversal of perception and perspective.

Over several years, I recorded sounds and images on and between the islands of Brittany.[1] Part of this time, I was perched over the Atlantic on the westernmost island of Ouessant, where Epstein shot his last, unfinished film. Once I filtered this material, I placed it in interaction with elements from the vast archives Epstein left behind: interviews, manuscripts, notes scrawled on scraps of paper, newspaper clippings, and images from his films. The connections between these elements have provided clues to understanding the mysterious impulse that drew Epstein to the islands and have revealed the inspiring space his work inhabited when he parted company with cinema. An image of Epstein's oceanic experience/ experiments emerges from three principal sources: materials that document Epstein's making of the maritime films, his theoretical writings on cinema, and the results, half a century later, of my own search – camera and microphone in hand – for the residual traces of his work in Brittany.

Epstein's motives for choosing to work among these rugged islands are evident in the nature of the place itself. Here the cinematograph finds itself operating in a space characterized by potent entities, where an interpenetration of death, fear, and unpredictability are all embodied in and directed by the ocean's flux. When Epstein began filming off the western coast of Brittany in 1927, he found cultures that had remained virtually untouched by industrial society, functioning largely as they had for centuries, poor but self-sufficient, hardened against the elements, and anchored in moral, superstitious, and religious traditions. Coupled with the severe natural environment and treacherous waters, this was and remains today a land of extremes. Amidst this harsh reality, Epstein tested the extent to which the region was receptive to his avant-garde techniques and to his broader aspirations for cinema, on both human and geophysical registers. To reconsider cinema within this oceanic realm today is to reassemble an image of how cinema can mutate and evolve when faced with an abundance of the real.

Epstein did not immediately understand his "impulse toward the exterior," the strange attraction which drew him from a secure position within the Parisian avant-garde toward the unfamiliar edge of France and the European continent.[2] The westernmost tip of Brittany is at the margins of European identity and culture: France but not France, an in-between space and yet a specific location, a metaphorical site for cinema. In 1921, Brittany had already entered Epstein's consciousness, as he observed in *Bonjour Cinema* that the region was indubitably other than the "picturesque" it was popularly known for. By the late 1920s, these insular environments appeared in his films as uncorrupted by industrial or popular culture: "[D]ifficult to access for tourists, this is virgin terrain for cinema."[3] From the outset of Epstein's maritime cycle, the islands function as marginal zones defined by fluctuations between presence and absence, solid and liquid, life and death. The tensions inherent in the place itself provided an ideal laboratory for testing and developing an aesthetic that itself combined avant-garde techniques with realist subjects. Over the next two decades, Epstein confirmed the justness of this impulse to bring his avant-garde cinema to the "extrème occident."

Two films stand as key references to his later maritime period: the dynamic whirlwind of an auto-portrait, *La Glace à trois faces* (1926) and the "deliverance" from his obsession with Edgar Allan Poe's supernatural in *The Fall of the House of Usher* (1927). According to one piece of evidence that lists sites in Brittany that he visited, it was while shooting *Usher* that the region first seduced him. His return trips took him further and further west, until eventually (in 1928) he brought a camera to film a few tests. This marks the beginning of Epstein's conscientious process of allowing himself to be guided by cinema's discoveries. It is following his contact with the landscapes and peoples of the region in his first Breton film, *Finis Terrae* (1928), a lyrical but threadbare narrative featuring kelp gatherers (*goëmonniers*), that he pieces together his own motivations for an unanticipated yet enduring shift to Brittany. He wrote: "After *Usher*, I believed that without the sound film, the color and 3D film, progress toward the creation of a second reality was stopped short. In the meantime, I tried to obtain the dramatic illusion backward, so to speak, by giving an existing reality the more general characteristics of fiction."[4] Epstein initially sensed the islands' harrowing events and mythical narratives as beyond real, defying rational thought and able to offer a much-needed boost to the art. In 1928, he thus inaugurated a phase in his work he called "Approches à la vérité" ("Approaches to truth") which would continue until the end of his life.[5] As Epstein's treatise on his empirical-materialist experiment in Brittany and as a theoretical guide to Finis Terrae, it establishes his revelation that in a realm where human and natural life interact, the fantastic should be unveiled rather than manufactured. These "approaches" were also propositions for ways to expand popular film genres through avant-garde research.

Prior to filming in Brittany, Epstein presented a vision of a technically advanced cinema whereby exterior filming would one day become obsolete. Studios would be able to create all decors synthetically with full control over color and perspective. His initial experiences in Brittany not only radically changed this imagined future, but fomented a rupture (at great professional cost) with the artifice and technical dependence of his Parisian period. Heading west, Epstein abandoned the urban exterior settings, stage sets, and oppressive infrastructure of studio film production in favor of a "second reality." Removing the exoskeleton of industrial production exposed his cinema to previously undocumented elements and landscapes. Epstein's films now would be shaped by the very reality they previously would have framed. In particular, the innate and unwieldy power of the ocean precipitated new ways of conceptualizing and making films.

The move to the outer reaches of Brittany served as a conceptual displacement, removing the filmmaking process from one cultural milieu in order to test it in another. His later maritime films stand as experiments that work through an array of techniques and theories. The results from these "research" films were nearly imperceptibly folded into his subsequent experiments. Again transposed back to Paris and the urban environment, elements of films such as Mor'Vran "lost some of their magic" according to Epstein, but the aspects that weathered this second part of the cycle confirmed their enduring value. Epstein's close-ups, slow motion, acceleration, and special effects innovations – in short, the elements that contribute to photogénie in its technical sense – interacted with the material presence and creative potential of these natural spaces. Epstein's role was as an enabler for the cinematograph, searching for ways the cinematograph could access the unknown and the peripheral. His return trips to Brittany confirmed his belief that the encounter between cinema, the "intelligent machine," and the oceanic expanded human perception and understanding, and disturbed the "very foundations of philosophy." From Epstein's filmic experiments, texts, and interviews, it becomes clear that much of his important later writings, including L'Intelligence d'une machine and Esprit du cinéma, are the result not only of his erudition, curiosity, and genius but also of his empirical work of filmmaking during this period – as his sister, Marie Epstein says, not making "films according to his theories, but rather theories according to his films."[6]

Epstein's experiments in Brittany began on a familiar scale, by filming "indigenous actors," with their oceanic environment operating largely as dramatic support. The initial access to the oceanic was thus through the inhabitants themselves. Just as the surrounding seas determined the overall ambiance of the films and the production schedules, the inhabitants created the essence of their own representation. In other words, the actual "acting," as with other narrative decisions, was only imposed as far as necessary, the non-professional actors "rigorously determining the sense of the work." For Epstein, inhabitants who lived within the environment, with all its volatility and seemingly supernatural occurrences, became when filmed a projection of their experience in this space. The emulsion of the film absorbs and transmits, as Epstein put it, "the action they've already accomplished, of anything else they aren't capable." Having spent their lives on and surrounded by water, these actors possessed an oceanic quality peculiar to the region: "Isn't their character a reflection of it? Have you noticed that they never affirm how much volatility, fluidity there is in them; like the sea, their thoughts are perpetually moving, everything moves within them; in the very way they look, their physical appearance, there is something moving."[7] For Epstein, cinema is seen to invest all filmed subjects with a trace of the oceanic. Likewise, filming these island inhabitants upon whom the ocean has placed "its hidden mark" draws the film towards the fluidity and unfamiliarity embodied by the inhabitants.

Epstein foresaw this use of non-professionals as a technique that would evolve beyond his time, predicting that non-professional actors of every "social class" would some day participate in fiction films. This was part of his overall project of locating the exceptional in, and rendering visible, the forgotten and the voiceless. After *Finis Terrae*, all of his Breton films featured non-professionals, with the exception of *Île Perdue* (1938). This was a keystone of his "Approaches," but was only a part of both a larger dialogue with the islands and a more responsive and adaptable method of production. What is particularly striking is that these films to this day continue to operate as an integral part of the inhabitants' identities, as documents of their cultural trajectories. Over the two decades he intermittently worked in the region, much of his time was spent absorbing the local lore, documenting recent and ancient tales. The scripts he carried to sea were minimal scenarios within which local narratives could develop. A local guide would help to find actors and locations and provide logistical information. Whether François Morin on Ouessant or Christian Lanco on Belle Isle en Mer, the guides were charismatic and well known.

Following the hardships and near-deportation that Epstein experienced during World War II, there is a clear change in the perspective of his maritime films from the 1940s. The role of objects, nature, and the ocean in particular take on far greater importance in these films and indicate yet another departure from his earlier works. However, Epstein's pre-Brittany films foreshadow the centrality of the aquatic in his later films. In *La Belle Nivernaise* (1923), *Cœur Fidèle* (1923), *Double Amour* (1925), and *Le Lion de Mogols* (1924), water becomes an element of psychological import, linked with notions of exile and destiny. The aquatic scenes in these films are also where one finds the more frequent use of double exposures; the liquid element was already inspiring and facilitating experimentation. In a scene from *La Glace à trois faces* (1927), the protagonist rows a small boat as one of the three lovers says to him, "I am but a poor girl." We see him smile at her as if to say, "It doesn't matter," followed by a close-up of her calloused hand. She then smiles a sad smile and dips her hand into the water as the boat glides along. The water takes on the role of an undiscriminating purifying element. Epstein would later humorously criticize films whose only natural settings were the same sort of harmless bodies of water found in the Parisian peripheries. But if these tranquil waters could create such effects, the larger question remains what the power of the ocean would be. Would it be a healing force? A provider? Or a future director of human activity on earth?

While being interviewed on the subject of his final film, *Feux de la mer*, Epstein was asked what attracted him to creating maritime films and working on the islands. He responded that he was motivated by fear. It was fear of the ocean, and more importantly, "fear that demands we do what we fear to do."[8] The ocean and its islands represent for Epstein a "perverse" kind of potential which both recognizes a spectral power beyond our understanding or control and inspires one to feel reinvigorated with the desire to live, to respond to fear with actions designed to remain among the living. In this sense, the ocean's forcefulness, unpredictability, and reign over humankind position it as an ultimate cinematic subject; indeed, it is my opinion that spending long periods of time with the sea should be a required ritual for all aspiring filmmakers. While for some, the train persists as the reigning metaphor for cinema, for Epstein (and I concur) it is the ocean and seafaring vessels. This is also perhaps the case for Andrei Tarkovsky's film *Solaris*, in which another planet's ocean functions as an omnipotent and unknowable entity, evading human understanding and humbling humankind while manifesting its powers in unpredictable and dangerous ways. Oceans decide the rhythms of daily life and who lives or dies, whether heroically or terrifyingly, as in Poe's *Descent into the Maelstrom*. Poe's image of that decisive moment, when the surface of the northern seas opens up, also encapsulates the power Epstein sensed in the oceanic. It is the point when the buoyancy of man's ingenuity surfaces and he resolves not to be drawn into the depths, but it is also the moment that confirms the fragility and resignation of those who go down with the ship.

As much as they take lives, the seas surrounding the islands of Ouessant and Sein in particular are viewed to this day as benefactors in the minds of the inhabitants, as if the seas could simply materialize desired objects. On the islands, I heard the typical tales of the once-bountiful seafood catches but also of barrels of rum and wine washing up on shore, as well as containers of shoes, oranges, cigarettes and (the less practical) hundreds of plastic ducks. And then, of course, there is the increasing amount of trash. The houses themselves were once constructed with pieces of wood that floated ashore; one just had to wait one's turn. Epstein pointed out after his first shoot in the archipelago, "The primary virtue of water is patience."[9] This revelation is as important for the island residents as it is for filmmakers learning to adapt to an alien temporality and spatiality. The ocean's proper cycles are inextricably linked with its majestic and continuous movements, its mysterious conveyor belts, global currents, and the altering weather patterns and microclimates it shapes. It is a fluctuating, breathing entity with neither commencement nor terminus. The cinematograph, uniquely capable of adapting and representing these temporalities, also takes cues from oceanic notions of distance, spacing, and continuity. The waters separating the islands and continents from each other act as interstices between the distant locations of shots or locations cut together. Water dominates the surface of the Earth but generally is considered a *nowhere*, while its currents create the continuity between all the *somewheres*. And as Thales advanced some 2,600 years ago, water is the world's primary unifying force, the world itself a sphere floating on liquid substance.

For the islanders the continent persists as the "other side," and to move there is a small death. The greater death is the other "other side," an unknown that Epstein would treat as a fear comparable to the vastness of the ocean itself. Cinematographically, the seas are a way to consider the passage from life to death. This notion first appears in *The Fall of the House of Usher* (1928), where the coffin is carried across the waters prior to burial. Many years later in 1953, this time without a film camera and in deteriorating health, Epstein had one last wish to travel – to the sea. Plans were made to drive to the coast with his sister, Marie, but the night before their departure he died. After *Usher* yet prior to this final suspended voyage came his maritime films, in which characters teeter constantly on the edge of mortality, held in the squalls of tempestuous seas. As a vessel constantly navigating between the worlds of the living and the dead, the animate and inanimate, cinema is in its element on these islands and at sea. Brittany's islanders have lived for centuries with hundreds of ships sinking in their waters, with sailors regularly lost at sea, anonymous bodies washing ashore. There were also those who joined the merchant marine and simply disappeared. Death's prominent role in the social fabric of the islands is quite particular, especially as it relates to cinema. The ports of the region were, and to a lesser degree still are, a point of departure for the open seas, where death navigates hand-in-hand with life, especially for fishermen. Two years after Epstein had attempted to reach the shores one last time, his guide and closest friend on the islands François Morin, himself suffering from heart troubles, was lost at sea in the waters off the mythical Pern Point at the tip of Ouessant. The Morin family related to me a telling encounter which occurred during one of Epstein's many visits to Ouessant. Epstein asked Morin's sister, Madame Drolec, who also plays the mother of Ambroise in Finis Terrae, how she coped with her husband's death at sea. According to family members, Epstein was surprised to hear her say that it was for the best, that having borne so many children it was a relief, for every time her husband returned from months at sea she wound up with another child. The open discussions regarding death's role continue to serve as therapy on the islands, along with the acknowledgement that it has a purpose and the ocean a place in executing its call. Close-ups of sailors' faces serve in Epstein's films as echoes of mortality, its marks engraved on their visages. The same applies for filming the widows of lost sailors such as Madame Drolec, her real loss transposed to the potential loss of her fictional son in Finis Terrae.

With the knowledge that below the surface of the seas is a graveyard of ships, the ocean's fluid horizon separates the living and the dead. The perspective of death, "a marvelous knower of man," is yet another state of being from which to solicit another approach to the living. During the maritime period this social trait expands both the dramatic and structural aspects of Epstein's filmmaking, as a narrative theme and as another angle from which to enlarge the psychic space of the film. Death acts as an invisible force, always lurking just beyond the visible. Through the instruction of its works executed by the seas, and as one of man's ultimate fears and unknowns, it acts as a final instructive perspective. As Epstein points out, "death makes us his promises by way of the cinematograph."[10] Chance and risk in this tragic oceanic realm can, in principle, draw cinema toward new forms. As a child, Epstein's first experience of cinema coincided with a small earthquake that took place while he was traveling with his family in Croatia. His sister, Marie, recounted her brother's formative experience, adding that for some time after "he no longer wanted to attend a spectacle that provoked such dangerous phenomena, and which he believes can provoke even more dangerous ones."[11] These elements of danger and unpredictability merge with Epstein's profound belief in cinema's power to unveil what lies beyond common understanding, its capacity to alter our relation to both the unknown and the unknowable. Placed in formal and physical precariousness, cinema would also assure itself a continuingly divergent path from the repetition of standardized narrative or documentary forms. With animate and inanimate objects and phenomena spontaneously entering into the filmmaking process, cinema is guaranteed ongoing permutations. The decors, the actors, and the weather remain uncertain until fixed to the emulsion, and even then, as with L'Or des mers, the entire film might have to be re-shot, the rushes having been ruined by humidity. Epstein muses, "This victory of the unpredictable is in no way deplorable. On the contrary, it contributes a fresh element to cinematic art." Epstein held that the human spirit requires this element of the irrational and "external" so that rational thought would not dominate all human activity. In essence, the ocean fulfills this irrational function throughout his maritime films. To this effect, integrating unpredictability into the cinematic process acts as a form of control mechanism while paradoxically marking a loss of control. And the greater the role of the unpredictable, the more that failure and incompleteness becomes a possibility, as Epstein felt of a few of his maritime films such as Mor'Vran. This he accepted as part of the experimental process of advancing the art of cinema.

In 1947, with L'intelligence d'une machine (date places it in the maritime period), Epstein cinematically describes the frontier between land and water and the primordial space in which our ancient ancestors first crawled ashore: "All of man is no longer any more than a being of smooth muscles, swimming in a dense environment, where thick currents still carry and mold this clear descendant of the old marine fauna, of the waters, mothers."[12] This pre-Socratic attraction to the viscous, humid, and primordial finds its aesthetic counterpart in the turquoise waters, foggy coastlines, and strange rock formations of the Breton islands, the ideal space for a mutating cinema to evolve. Corsicans, islanders from a far calmer Mediterranean sea, shiver at Ouessant's nine-foot tidal differential, revealing rocks invisible only a few hours earlier while the inhabitants of Molène speak of strange mountainous forms that appear on the horizon. In such a place where forms blend, objects seem alive, and the eyes play tricks, natural phenomena effortlessly transform into protagonists or antagonists, much like Victor Sjöström's The Wind (1928), in which the wind has a will and a way of its own. In Epstein's films, these phenomena develop on a plane with human beings, creating an atmosphere of suspended potentials. The environment performs much like the unbiased non-professional actors, directly transmitting the authentic "movements" found within it.

Epstein continued to de-center the human to a greater and greater degree over the two decades of his maritime films. Brittany provided unlimited material for fracturing, dislocating, and re-contextualizing human reality. The shift in perspective is apparent in Mor'Vran (1931). An intertitle of this film reads "The sea speaks" as the non-human unwinds itself from the narrative. Sixteen years later, with Le Tempestaire, a second effort at a similar narrative structure, these entities inform and interact with each other, granting one another perspectives as a series of reflections. In this film, described by Epstein as "my first avant-garde film since L'Or des Mers in 1932,"[13] the majority of screen time is completely devoid of human presence; humans are "no more than symbolic figures against a background of earth and sea."[14] The film is a remarkable mise-en-scène of humankind's perilous status on earth. Humans are transformed into immobile objects surrounded by a furious sea. Early in the film they figure as still images, then as the winter storm unfurls on Belle Île en Mer, all they can do is run from shelter to shelter.

Le Tempestaire is Epstein's prototype for his largely unrealized project of cinema's convergence of human and non-human perspectives. For this, sound operates as a key vehicle, yet was unavailable to Epstein during the filming of Mor'Vran. Le Tempestaire, "a poem of the sea told by the wind," was the only opportunity for Epstein to truly experiment with access to perspectives through the "mechanical ear," opening up a whole field of possibilities regarding the expression of these entities by way of their own proper voice quite apart from mankind's perspective. In Le Tempestaire, the sound of the ocean is played in slow motion, backward and forward, with frequencies and textures drawn from the chaos of the winter storm. Epstein predicted cinema would one day make use of a "sound perspectivism," whereby we could not only see objects expressing themselves but enter them audibly. Sound is one of the key aspects of Epstein's largely undeveloped projects for cinema, an aspect which to this day is still arguably underutilized in cinema.

The shift towards an animist approach to filmmaking appeared early on in Epstein's work. Yet, it was after World War II and his decades-long engagement with natural settings and phenomena such as storms, seas, wind, and clouds that human figures were markedly de-centered. He seized on opportunities to multiply perspectives in natural settings as he had previously done in Le Pas de la Mule (1930) or his film about the eruption of Mount Etna, La Montagne infidèle (The Unfaithful Mountain, 1923). The title of the corresponding text, Le Cinématographe vu de l'Etna (The Cinema Seen from Etna, 1926) underscores the relocation of subjectivity from the camera to the mountain, or the non-human subject. Other unrealized films promised greater use of the non-human, such as Au Péril de la mer, for which Epstein argues to potential producers that not only the ambiance but its budget will profit from an abundance of exterior, characterless "ad hoc" shots. Epstein suggests a pantheist-perspectivist cinema could develop alongside the emerging science of quantum physics: "[A]n animism is being reborn. We know now that we are surrounded by inhuman existences."[15] The cinematograph, as a vehicle for appropriating perspectives, is ideally placed to interrogate man's place in the terrestrial narrative, just as Galileo's lens once did or as Doris Lessing also attempts to do by investigating the perspective of extraterrestrials in order to analyze earthlings' destructive behavior from the vantage point of space. By engaging natural, rather than mechanical inhuman perspectives, cinema is capable of inexhaustibly recognizing and analyzing the fictions and realities of civilization. This blending of un-preconceived, "irrational," natural, and outer perspectives contrasts with computer-generated works in which perspectives are either recreated or entirely manufactured. Furthermore, this essay itself could be considered a sketch for a much larger research project on Epstein's late theory and practice as it relates to the "geophilosophy" developed by Deleuze and Guattari in Mille Plateaux.[16]

As the protagonist of Le Tempestaire frets about her fiancé perishing at sea, clouds are accelerated, gestures slowed, temporality fluctuates, and the tempest master Floch blows into his crystal ball, the metaphorical cinema-eye accessing parallel dimensions of existence and knowledge as the storm calms. In the original script, however, Floch collapses and dies from exhaustion after engaging with the movements of time and the natural elements. In this alternate ending, death once again lies just beneath the surface. The figure of the *Tempestaire*, either dead and martyred or alive and active, represents a vestige from an idealized pre-war era, when the preferred "intelligent machine" was not the apparatus of war but rather cinema's advancement of human thought.

Epstein's only two realized post-war films were *Le Tempestaire* and *Feux de la mer*, both shot in Brittany, both using fear of the unknown and the imaginary no man's land separating life and death at the world's end as a pressure zone powering cinema. In the realm of the invisible and unrealized, the fiction film *Bag Noz* remains one of the many post-war projects that he planned for the region.[17] According to the script, which is drawn from local myth and adapted to a World War II setting, the "boat of the night" would make port one last time on the island of Ouessant, en route to the "exterior ocean" as it carried souls to the beyond. Drifting into the land of shadows and fog, the sailors intuitively navigate the fog and deceive the German marines, peering metaphorically into a freeze frame, into mortality, but return to the island to tell the tale. Surviving Epstein to this day, the real and mythological oceanic realms of Brittany remain an inspiration for filmmakers, where cinema can die and be reborn again and again. Yet the residual image of Epstein's oceanic cinema remains perched on these outer edges of reality not as a model but as an infinitely flexible cinematic ideal.

Notes

1. The islands of Ouessant, Sein, Molène, Bannec, Balanec, Belle Ile en Mer, Hoedic, and Houat.
2. Jean Epstein, "Vertu et danger du hasard" [1947], ESC2, p. 86.
3. Jean Epstein, interviewed in *L'Ami du peuple* (November 11, 1929).
4. Jean Epstein, *Le Cinématographe dans l'archipel*, unpublished manuscript [1929-1930]. Fonds Jean et Marie Epstein, Bibliothèque du film, Paris, EPSTEIN96-B24.
5. Jean Epstein, "Les Approches de la vérité," ESC1, p. 191.
6. Marie Epstein, in rushes for filmed interview by Mado LeGall, for the film *Jean Epstein*, Termaji (La Huit Productions, 1995).
7. Jean Epstein, interviewed in *Mer et Outre-mer* (November, 1948).
8. Jean Epstein, "L'ONU confie onze films à onze nations différentes," radio interview, 1950. Institut national de l'audiovisuel.
9. Jean Epstein, "Le Cinématographe dans l'archipel," ESC1, p. 197.
10. Epstein, "Le Cinématographe dans l'archipel," ESC1, p. 199.
11. Marie Epstein, unpublished biography of Jean Epstein.
12. Jean Epstein, *L'Intelligence d'une machine*, p. 58.

13. Jean Epstein, cited in "*Le Tempestaire*, un film 'Oceanique,'" *L'Écran* (November 1947).
14. Epstein, interviewed in *Mer et Outre-mer* (November 1948).
15. Jean Epstein, *Photogénie de l'imponderable*, ESC2, p. 13.
16. See Mark Bonta and John Protevi, *Deleuze and Geophilosophy: A Guide and Glossary* (Edinburgh: Edinburgh University Press, 2004).
17. Jean Epstein, project proposal for *Bag Noz* [circa. 1940]. Fonds Jean et Marie Epstein, Bibliothèque du film, Paris, EPSTEIN34-B14. "Bag Noz" is Breton for "Night Ship."

A Temporal Perspective: Jean Epstein's Writings on Technology and Subjectivity

Trond Lundemo

The essence of technology, Martin Heidegger explains in "The Question Concerning Technology" (1953), is nothing technological. It is a matter of the *Erscheinung* ("coming to presence") of Being of the work of art.[1] The later writings of Jean Epstein also identify a question of technology to be answered in the realm of aesthetics and in processes of subjectivity. Instead of serving the development of a necessarily strained and reductive analogy between Heidegger's concepts and Jean Epstein's writings on cinema – indeed, Heidegger's apparent techno-skepticism and Epstein's celebrations of film technology immediately seem irreconcilable – this relationship may prompt us to ask which is the "question concerning technology" informing Epstein's theory. The "automatic subjectivity" of cinema asks the essential question of technology: whether it acts isomorphically in relation to our consciousness and our perception, and thus serves as a mere tool for our actions and for our thinking, or if it invents an intelligence and a philosophy of its own.[2] Anyone familiar just with the titles of Epstein's books and articles knows his immediate answer to this question: there is a philosophy of the cinematograph and an intelligence of the machine. However, as the essence of technology is nothing technological, the answer is more complex than a complete separation between human and technology. How does this other perception, this differing space-time, relate to "everyday" human perception? How does it produce different ways of thinking and other forms of subjectivity?

I will approach these questions by looking at a central paradox in Epstein's writings: if the technology of cinema automatically sets off other perceptions of time, space, and movement, this difference should apply to all films. That is not the case, however. There is clearly an aesthetics of cinema informing Epstein's writings, where only some films in certain ages of cinema fulfill this potential for transgression of the human boundaries of time and space. The relative lack of analyses of specific films in his writings indicates that Epstein instead describes an un-realized cinema yet to come. The paradox that these transgressive qualities only exist in certain films at certain times while remaining an automatic aspect of the technology is highlighted in Epstein's description of the configuration of the senses in cinema, namely in the relationship between the ocular and the haptic. A third topic of great importance for the development of cinema technology as an essentially *other* perception than that of the human register is the concept of the "temporal perspective." Cinema introduces another modality of time into our everyday regime of space-time, always making the one refer to the other without assimilating the temporality of cinematic technology to our perception. Epstein never defines "a nature of cinematic time," since it is open to an infinity of modulations and variations. While everyday human perception tends to separate space from time, cinema, according to Epstein, is a form that thinks by investing space with time.[3] This irreducible distance between the two regimes of perception of time and space means that cinema technology is not a tool for human intention and action, but forms different patterns of subjectivity and being than those that exist outside cinema. Cinema cannot be assimilated to human perception and is not structurally isomorphic with the mental apparatus.

The powerful canons of film historical periodization have grouped Epstein's films with the "French Impressionists," leading scholars to find in them stylistic figures as illustrations of subjective visions.[4] This persistent view of his films has also prejudiced the reading of his theory into an "Impressionist" agenda shared with other theorist-directors of his time like Louis Delluc, Germaine Dulac, and Abel Gance. While Epstein's early writings sometimes offer space for such projections on the part of the reader, his writings from the mid-thirties on seldom do. One possible reason why, up until today, his more consistent later texts have received less attention than his early writings is that the break not only with the "period" of impressionism but also with the "program" projected onto the movement doesn't fit with the expectations of the material. One element of resistance to the modernist avant-garde offered by Epstein's both early and late writings is exactly the automatic powers of the technology of cinema, making cinema inassimilable to a subjective artistic vision or intention. Moreover, the significant absence of analyses of films as "works" also runs counter to the position of the artwork as the cornerstone of modernist aesthetics.

Automatisms

Another French philosopher of technology and individuation, Gilbert Simondon, criticized Western civilization for having failed to develop a culture of technical objects, in his 1958 dissertation *Du mode d'existance des objets techniques*.[5] Instead, technology has been seen as either a passive tool for human needs or as having a mind of its own, threatening to usurp the human mind. Both of these positions are based on the idea of an isomorphic relationship between mental processes and the way technology works. Epstein's concept of "the intelligence of a machine" does at first glance look like a target for Simondon's criticism of notions of intellectual robots and artificial intelligence. Instead, the two theorists actually hold a similar position towards the question of the relationship between mind and machine. Epstein's "intelligence of the machine" designates an irreducible difference between the machine and the human mind. In a passage called "The Philosophy of the Cinematograph," he claims:

> The cinema is one of these intellectual robots, still partial, that fleshes out representations – that is to say, a thought – through photo-electrical mechanics and a photo-chemical inscription. [...] This result would already be remarkable if the cinematographic thought only did what the calculating machine does, to constitute itself in the servile imitation of human ideation. But we know that the cinematograph, on the contrary, marks its representation of the universe with its own qualities, of an originality that makes this representation not a reflection or a simple copy of conceptions, of an organic mentality-mother, but rather a system that is individualized differently, partly independently, which contains the incitements for a philosophy so far from common opinions, the doxa, that one should perhaps call it an anti-philosophy.[6]

This philosophy is only valid for the screen. The technology of cinema is not just an augmentation of human vision but a different visibility altogether. This function in cinema is "individualized differently," as it projects "an automatic subjectivity" onto spectatorial subjectivity without these two dimensions ever coinciding with each other.

This leads us to a consideration of what is sometimes a paradox, sometimes an ambivalence in Epstein's theory. As Nicole Brenez has pointed out, Epstein's theory of cinema presupposes that the cinematographic technology has these powers to transform at its outset, and that every film necessarily performs these functions.[7] She confronts this with a position, exemplified by quotes from Abel Gance, Robert Bresson, and Jean-Luc Godard, where cinema is called upon to realize its true, still unattained, potential. While both positions are medium specific in that they pose that there is a power in cinema that exists nowhere else, Epstein's stance relies on the automatic powers of the technology, while the latter position depends on the work and artistic agency. Epstein's position in this crucial question is inconsistent, however.

On the one hand, in line with his view of cinema's automatisms, he rarely analyzes single films. In an early text he singles out the Bell & Howell camera as the true artist in cinema, and only after the technology comes the director, photographer, or editor, in the last of whom one often wants to invest the artistic powers of the Seventh art.[8] Epstein's theory of cinema is one at code level, so to speak, one that emphasizes that the techniques of inscription are the true "content" of the medium. This position breaks decisively with the cult of the singular work or of the artist that is so central to the modernist aesthetics within which

Epstein is so often grouped. By consequence, the idea of automatic powers of ideation in technology has important consequences for the role of Epstein's own films in relation to his writings. Nothing in his films would make them more interesting than any other films as examples of these powers of cinema if they were automatically shaped by the technology. True to the principle of automatism, Epstein only occasionally comments upon his films, and unlike many of his contemporary filmmaker-theorists, like Eisenstein and Vertov, never analyzes them at length.

The idea of an automatism of the medium is also what leads him to criticize abstraction, surrealism, futurism, and, more generally, the avant-garde. These movements have not realized the surreal powers internal to the technology, he claims.[9] All kinds of surrealism and abstraction are already present in cinema, and any attempts at stylizing the pro-filmic fail to acknowledge this fact. Epstein intervenes in the art debates by saying that the avant-garde film movements lack a theory of the dispositif of cinema, and for this reason reproduce the same narratives and shapes in cinema as in literature, art, and music.

On the other hand, Epstein repeatedly contradicts this "automatic" paradigm. He develops a normative aesthetics of cinema that goes against his theses on the automatism of the apparatus. Even if he only rarely makes observations on style in films, and less and less so in his later work, he still comments on movements and developments in cinema. Writing in 1930, Epstein claims that just like the old films set up the camera in the "wrong" position, the microphones are directed in primitive ways today.[10] The only moments of phonogénie – Epstein's neologism for sonic effects analogous to the photogénie of the image – recorded so far have been in faulty fragments of actualities. "Bilan du fin de muet" is brimming with these appreciations about good and bad films.[11] In "La naissance d'un mythe," about Charlot, he notes that Chaplin has not developed the dispositif of cinema, but used it in a marginal and personal way, true to a British music-hall tradition.[12] Epstein is also critical of the concept of the 'sound film' in 1929, arguing that, in fact, it only contains a few chansons.[13] And in 1946, he worries that cinema has not cultivated its most important powers and has instead gotten caught up in the representation of fiction.[14]

Nicole Brenez positions Epstein's theory of cinema's automatism in opposition to the idea – shared by Gance, Bresson, and Godard – of a potentiality in cinema that remains unfulfilled; however, this account doesn't take into consideration Epstein's ambivalence about this issue. Epstein's inconsistency becomes apparent in the concept of photogénie, which is at the same time a property of the technology of cinema and yet only realized on rare occasions. In an early text on the concept, which gradually loses its importance in his later writings, only a few films have attained fragmentary flashes of this quality. Discussing some of the works of his contemporaries from the French 'avant-garde' many years later, he states: "Certainly, there are sequences by Delluc that are mysteriously successful:

true cinema made almost entirely without any specifically cinematic means."[15] The idea of a "true cinema" even persists after the abandonment of the concept of *photogénie*, and is opposed to films not realizing this potential, contradicting the thesis of the automatic powers of technology. Epstein made the compilation film *Photogénies* for exhibition in the Vieux-Colombier ciné-club in 1925, after which the shots were disassembled. The selection of shots illustrating this key concept in the film culture of the 1920s seems to demonstrate that "true cinema" only occurs in certain places and particular states.

Epstein finds the reproduction of movement as we see it, in the fixed single-shot cinema, uninteresting.[16] This comment on the early cinema, in which he, like so many of his contemporaries, fails to see all its transforming powers, demonstrates that it is in figures of time constructed through editing, slow motion, and superimposed movements that the potential of cinema may be realized. Epstein's concept of movement does not concern movement in the image (which he terms as static), but moving perspectives, editing, and aberrations of movement. Almost all discussions of what cinema can do in Epstein's writings are made up of examples of movements being halted, accelerated, or reversed. This causes problems for the theory of the philosophy of the "lens itself", the automatic powers of transformation of the camera.[17] Rather, it is the powers of cinema to suspend time, to instigate intervals in the flow of time, which can bring something new to our perception. There are technologically determined automatisms in the reversibility of shooting and projection, but these seem in Epstein's writings only to be uncovered through montage and composition. The automatic powers of technology need excavation by making one movement enter into a relationship with another, and by projecting cinematic time onto spectatorial time. These configurations and juxtapositions are what Epstein addresses as the temporal perspective.[18] When time is no longer an absolute, aprioristic, and irreversible dimension but becomes inextricably linked to space, it becomes open to a multiplicity of perspectives.

This concern with specific temporal and energetic figures in cinema is motivated by Epstein's theory of the technology's automatic powers. However, these powers often remain virtual and are seldom actualized. At the outset of the cinematographic technology there are sets of forms and powers, of which only a few are realized given specific historical and social conditions. This virtual element in Epstein's writings complicates his tendency towards technological determinism, as the existence of the technology is no guarantee for the realization of its powers, and compels Epstein to analyze cinema's specific temporal figures. The result of this complex position is a time-based medium specificity, where cinema is the technology that opens up to a multifaceted temporality. The intervals and spacings of this *heterochronia* require a consistent theoretical and practical work. This is the way cinema invents temporalities and distributes space.

The senses of cinema

By offering a different perception of the world to the human sensory apparatus, cinema re-invents the distribution of space and time. The technological conditions for making cuts and incisions into the streams of time and space form a medium-specific organization of the senses. When space is inextricably invested with time, the entire body participates in observation. Epstein's theory is unambiguously corporeal, as he understands vision as a form of touch, and often evokes the whole sensory register. Henri Langlois observed this:

> For Jean Epstein, everything is a three-dimensional object, and the lens is not an eye, a means to record, but a means to appropriate the reality of things, just like the child is never satisfied with just looking, but touches and feels things at the same time, to obtain the total vision...[19]

However, Langlois' comparison with the child's coordination between vision and touch misses out on the irreducible differences between human perception and cinematic technology. While it is important to note that Epstein's theory doesn't belong to the ocular-centric theories of vision found in many of the so-called "impressionists," neither is it an early instance of the film phenomenology emphasizing the corporeality of vision in cinema.[20] Cinema doesn't just replicate the human forms of apprehending the world, as they vary according to cultural, historical, and physical circumstances; instead, it projects the space and time of a machine onto our everyday sensory apparatus.

If Epstein's film theory doesn't only elaborate on the technology as a different visibility but as another intelligence and new philosophy, it is because it engages the whole of the sensory apparatus as part of a mental process. Epstein's resistance to ocular-centric theories of vision is based in the same view of technology as his rejection of a phenomenological model for cinematic embodiment. Epstein's writings ask which kinds of embodiment are engaged in the technologies of moving images, in which ways they imply processes of individuation, and how these questions depend on a notion of medium specificity in cinema. Epstein's implied question should become ours: How can cinema make us think of embodiment in new ways? Is it possible to invent forms of perception in cinema that neither presuppose a disembodied eye nor are limited to the construction of an environment where the actions of the phenomenological body can be simulated? As in Jonathan Crary's well-known discussion of the embodiment of vision, from Goethe's color theory through optical toys of the nineteenth century and up to cinema, the issue rests with the temporality of the image.[21] Epstein sees cinema as a machine able to defy the irreversibility of time and the second law of thermodynamics, as well as a means of access to the hidden movement and temporality of all objects. Time not only embodies vision, but also invents new configurations of sensory perception.

Jean Epstein's theory of cinema allows us to ask these questions because it understands the sound and moving image as a form of perception and thinking that is radically different from that of our everyday perceptions and our established world view. The haptic refers to a kind of visuality that defies the hierarchies of vision and touch – it doesn't subordinate the eye to touch (the manual), or touch to the eye (the tactile) – by inventing a different regime of visuality. This is Gilles Deleuze's definition of the concept of the haptic in relation to painting, but it has rarely received much attention from writers on the concept.[22] In Epstein's view (even though he never refers to the haptic specifically), this alternative sensorium is instigated by the technology of the moving image and brings with it important consequences for the processes of individuation in cinema. This is also a feature of the various image-types Gilles Deleuze devises in his books on cinema.[23] Deleuze's taxonomical project is certainly absent in Epstein's writings, but there is an important connection between their projects: both understand subjectivity as being formed according to variations in movement and intervals in time.

Malcolm Turvey, in "Jean Epstein's Cinema of Immanence: The Rehabilitation of the Corporeal Eye,"[24] reads Epstein's writings as an alternative both to the ocular-centrism of psychoanalysis and to the "corporeal approach," the two positions traced by Rosalind Krauss in her discussion of avant-garde movements of the first decades of the film century.[25] His outline of Epstein's complication of this dualistic framework of avant-garde theory is a highly valuable contribution to the critique of a dichotomy that marks film theory to this day; the scopic regimes of the apparatus giving way to general phenomenological approaches reconstituting the role of the body in visual perception. According to Turvey, Epstein sees the camera as an instrument to make visible the interior life of human beings that cannot be seen by the naked eye. Furthermore, it also extends beyond humans and explores the interior movements of objects. In Epstein's theoretical writings, sight is capable of relating to the world, to truth, at the same time as it is an embodied eye, a corporeal vision. Turvey's reading of Epstein's theory as an alternative to the "two avant-gardes" is still based on a phenomenological model of vision, however. Turvey draws on Wittgenstein's concept of aspect-dawning, which implies a shifting *recognition* of a visual motive (e.g. the duck-rabbit figure). Turvey expands on this concept in his book *Doubting Vision* in order to show that Epstein makes 'mistakes' in the use of perceptual concepts when describing the powers of cinema to see time and the inner movement of things.[26] Cinema's "revelation" of emotions and family resemblance, which are the examples from Epstein's early writings that Turvey chooses to discuss in relation to aspect-dawning, are properties of Wittgenstein's concept of "seeing-as,"and depend not on technology but on recognition.[27] These properties depend on a familiarity of forms, in which visual technologies transform nothing. In its foundation in the concept of a *recognition* of images, this theory has to sacrifice medium specificity.

Turvey's discussion of Epstein's corporeality takes as its point of departure Rosalind Krauss' considerations of two strands of the avant-garde. However, Turvey does not dwell on Krauss' discussion of the role that empiricism plays in Hermann von Helmholtz's theory of perception.[28] Helmholtz finds, through an investigation of the workings of the stereoscope, that vision is not an anatomical sensation but a mental act. As Jonathan Crary observes, Helmholtz's theory of vision poses the retina as part of the nervous system and, implicitly, as a part of the brain.[29] For Krauss, this is important for understanding the conceptualism of Marcel Duchamp and his investigations of perception, for instance in the *Large Glass*. Helmholtz's position within "The Empirical Theory of Vision" – compare his belief that alternative geometries could be illustrated – is complicated by the need for a theory of "unconscious inference" based on previous experience. This theory cannot account for sensory illusions. The problem is caused by the fact that if illusions didn't have a shape to begin with, they could not be illusions since it is *experience* that makes them have a form. The recognition of forms encounters problems in the question of the recognition of *new* forms. This problem, discussed by Krauss, also causes problems for Turvey, since the recognition aspect of the "dawning" also bears on experience, and would not account for illusions of movement. Even if Epstein sees a "higher truth" in cinema, and refuses to see cinematic forms as illusions, his examples of wheels turning backwards and the estrangement of close-ups cannot be accounted for by experience and recognition, but rather rely on the idea of a different vision at work in the cinematic apparatus.

Epstein's theory of cinema is governed by rules of perceptual processing that differ from those of recognition. Recognition draws on a finite resource of images. Even if this resource could be seen as virtually limitless through our "tertiary memory" – that is, our memory constituted by mediated sounds and pictures of events we have never experienced firsthand – it is still based on coherent sets of sensory data triggering our recognition. In spite of its shifting aspects, the process of recognition depends on shifts between static images, as in the duck-rabbit figure. Recognition halts movement in order to function; it singles out an instant in a flow of time. This is in contrast to the model of vision operating in Jean Epstein's theory, which is based on movement and change. Epstein's writings are concerned with conveying the ephemerality of cinema, as figures written in the sand on the beach, continuously eradicated by the waves of the sea. In one of his last essays, Epstein calls for a "geometry of the instable," at home in quicksand, that will "command a logic, a philosophy, good sense, a religion, an aesthetics, based on instability."[30] In his writings, the impossible arrestment of motion in cinema is highlighted as an element disallowing recognition of forms. The temporal perspective of cinema projects a differing time into our everyday experience of time and movement, to give access to another time and space, and to other configurations of sensorial perception.

Turvey's critique of Epstein's "revelationism" is based on the claim that Epstein confuses space and time as visible categories, which a "better" vision would remedy.[31] This confusion is rather on Turvey's part, since Epstein's argument is that cinema offers a different, and not only "better" or more powerful, multi-sensorial perception that transcends the division between the space and time of human consciousness. Epstein does not claim that the reason why the fourth dimension is invisible outside cinema is because the eye is not powerful enough. The major contribution and the main point of Epstein's writings is the very change of perceptual categories produced by cinema. This is a multi-sensorial, haptic, and extra-phenomenological dimension in Epstein's philosophy, which completely sets aside the question of seeing "more and better."[32]

Turvey locates his evidence in human visual perception and demonstrates that Epstein's claims for the powers of cinematic technology are properties humans cannot possibly see. For this reason, Epstein's theory of the otherness of cinematographic perception and philosophy is never targeted.[33] Rather than taking this feature of Epstein's theory into account and considering it as a property of his argument, Turvey prefers to diagnose it as a flaw in his use of perceptual categories. But the "category mistake" is less on the part of Epstein than on Turvey himself.[34] When considering the same "mistakes" in the work of Béla Balázs, Turvey disregards the huge differences in the two authors' theories of technicity.[35] Indeed, the "revelationist tradition" consists of very different theoretical positions.

Turvey identifies a "corporeal eye" at work in Epstein's theory, but his view leads to a position where the processes of visual embodiment can take place in any medium. This move misses the originality that Epstein's writings offer to an established theory of the avant-garde and seriously undermines Epstein's argument about technical conditions for perception and thinking. What makes Epstein's writings stand out from the phenomenological approach to embodiment and subjectivity is that cinema is a machine that confronts our everyday perceptions and ways of thinking by offering a radically different logic and temporality, thereby implying very different formations and positions of subjectivity. His theory of embodiment is not based on the phenomenological idea of the body or of the subject, but on subjectivity as being formed in the *dispositif* of cinema.

Epstein often describes the processes forming subjectivity in cinema as an alternative to psychoanalysis. Actors do not recognize themselves on the screen. Cinema counters our self-impressions and reveals true identities. This is why cinema produces a split of the subject, as an ongoing process of individuation. Already the simple technique of shooting in reverse motion disturbs our conception of the universe. Cinema allows us to look at things in a different way because it is not governed by the principles of human psychology and consciousness, but instead disturbs our conception of the universe as well as our image of ourselves. Consequently, Epstein argues for a "cine-analysis" instead of the talking cure of psychoanalysis:

> Blown up 20 times, bathed in light, shown naked and confused, man
> finds himself before the cinematic lens cut off from all his lies, confessing, intimate, shameful and maybe true. The psychoanalysts of today teach us that lies are our grace of life, first imagined, then learned, then appropriated. I recommend the beautiful experience of cinematographic psychoanalysis, which is far more precise than the symbolism where etymological cards are drawn in the Freudian school. [...] Every one of the angular interpretations of a gestus [in the film *dispositif*] has a deeper meaning, which is intrinsic since the eye that reveals it is an inhuman eye, without memory, without thought. Most of all, I cannot say, as it was fashionable to do some time ago, that every image of a film should be conceived as seen by one or the other of the characters in the preceding image. This subjectivism is absurd. Why refrain from profiting from one of the most rare qualities of the cinematographic eye, *to be an eye outside of the eye, to escape the tyrannical egocentrism* of our personal vision? Why force the sensible emulsion only to repeat the functions of our retina? Why not seize with force a unique occasion to form a spectacle in relation to another center than the one of our own visual ray? *The lens is itself.*[36]

Epstein's non-representational position makes his theory exceed the stable position of the subject crucial to many phenomenological readings of intention and experience.

A temporal perspective

In Jean Epstein's view of the *dispositif* of cinema, temporal figures that depend on the technology of movement are invented. Cinema instigates diffractions of light and cuts in the streams of time. The visualizations of these processes are to be found in various ways in the many prisms and mirrors in his films (of which *La glace à trois faces* is perhaps the least revealing, because the alternative perspectives on the same person are narratively, if not ocularly, motivated by characters in the story). As all *dispositifs*, cinema regulates the possible enunciations and visibilities of an epoch, which in turn affects a third factor, the production of subjectivities.[37] Foucault's *dispositifs* install spatial confinements. These spatial arrangements of the epoch of big institutions like the prison, the hospital, and the factory are also temporal ones. The factory regulates the distribution of time (e.g., between work-time and leisure), the prison between wasted, useless, and empty time when one is "doing time" and productive time. Epstein understands cinema as a *dispositif* that distributes time in new ways. The visible and the enunciable are subjected to a *temporal perspective* that performs an alternative partition of the sensible that is material in the formation of subjectivity.

The theory of an "innovation of time" in cinema could be understood as a typically avant-garde program. It involves modernist notions of medium specificity, the production of new forms in the work, and the exceeding of the traditional boundaries of the medium. On the other hand, as is revealed by a recurrent criticism of the avant-gardes for ignoring the surrealizing effects of technology and for being based on the principles of creative subjectivity, there is an important part of Epstein's work that is at odds with such theories.[38] It is instructive to look at Epstein's position in the context of the recent debate about modernity in film studies, where David Bordwell, among others, has challenged the idea that modernity implied shifts in processes of attention, memory, and perception itself.[39] The former position claims that perception itself cannot be altered in a short time span. Tom Gunning rightly notes that very few would raise such a radical claim as the occurrence of a fundamental shift in human perception, and that what is debated is a position caricatured by Bordwell and his followers. [40] Epstein's theory of technology offers an interesting element in the debate, as he claims that cinema can present an automated perception that confronts everyday perception. The new forms of perception emerging in modernity do not have to be related to the human sensory apparatus directly, as cinema is an intermediary technology that acts on our perception and creates new configurations of time and space. Epstein's theory thus avoids one of the arguments against the modernity paradigm by radicalizing the claims of the modernity thesis: new forms of perception occur in the *dispositif*, but these are in every way separated from the human architecture of perception. Still, they are subjectivity-forming processes because they project another mode of perception onto human perception.

Epstein's writings on slow motion and decomposition of movement focus on a virtual dimension of the image co-existing with the actual image. When he conceives of his famous film *La chûte de la maison Usher* in terms of "the soul in slow motion" in 1928, this is a cinematographic soul and not a human one.[41] Close-ups and slow motion do not help the spectator to see closer or better, but open up a different world. Superimpositions or decomposed motion are not representations of mental processes like attention, contemplation, or fantasy. It is a different world that can only exist within the technology of cinema, and which always confronts the human psychological world. This irreducible distance between the human psychological apparatus and the technology of cinema is one reason for Epstein's refutation of psychoanalysis,[42] whereas he embraces 'the optical unconscious' of cinema already in his first texts.[43] It is also why Epstein often invokes cinema as a form of hypnosis, which, as discussed with great care by Raymond Bellour, differs from the psychoanalytic paradigm in that it is constituted by a force from the outside, and not by an analysis of a subjective interiority.[44]

The world in fast, slow, or reverse motion is not an image of our world that has been manipulated or tampered with. It is a world of different physical and geometrical dimensions. Whereas our everyday perception is set in a spatial and temporal linearity, cinema offers a temporal perspective. The technology of cinema can invent a deferral of time, undertake selections and contractions of time, and form intervals in time. This is what constitutes temporal innovations in cinema. Cinematic time is reversible, and Epstein argues how cinema can display a refutation of the second law of thermodynamics, that of entropy.[45] Epstein writes of the transforming powers of slow motion in cinema as a technique accessing an elasticity of time, capturing the coagulation and relative viscosity of fluids and the suspension of solidity in things.[46] Slow motion is not a diminution of movement, but rather its intensification. The halted pace of movement approaches the core of movement itself.

In Epstein's writings about the differences between cinematic movement and our everyday perception, there is often a double figure of movement. Every movement enters into a relation with its counterpart, which is also its condition. It is especially the post-World War II books on the movement of sound that opens this line of reflection on time in Epstein's writings. Slow motion of sound, its decomposition and "close-ups," leads Epstein to approach slow motion in relation to a virtual image, sonorous or visual. His interest in "decomposition" of sound is connected to the margins of human perception:

> If this deepening of sounds is pushed far enough, it is lost in the inaudible domain of the infra-deep. There, the vibrations of air are decomposed and slowed down to the extent that the ear is insensitive to this movement that appears still, in other words silent, in the same way as when in exceedingly slow motion, the eye stops perceiving the agitation of the sea, for instance, which appears as a solid, frozen surface.[47]

The absolute intensification of movement of sound invokes the inaudible, and in the image it is linked to stillness. It is evident in this passage that the range of frequency of human perception of sound and the visual can be transgressed through cinematographic inscription. But it is equally clear that it is a relation between movement and stillness, sound and the inaudible, that is formed in cinema. Decomposition of sound is, like that in the image, a means of analysis, but also a spacing between what is heard and its silence, between the moving and the still. The absolute intensification of movement means making it communicate with its absence, opening an interval between the two sides to all sounds and all images. The technology of cinema functions as a production of a virtual time. Every image is invested with a virtual side and every sound is connected to its own silence.

These double-sided sounds and images are far from any representation of our perception or our mental processes, but a center of indetermination between the stimulus and the reaction it sets off. Epstein's writings keep returning to the disruption of any linear cause-and-effect patterns in cinema and how there is a suspension between a received and an executed movement instigated between images. The three stylistic figures shaping Epstein's cinematic work are superimposition, the decomposition of movement, and the reflected image. It should be kept in mind, however, that these figures seldom work in isolation from each other. Images in slow motion are often superimposed by images with decomposed or halted movement. One mode of movement is coupled to its counterpart that is also its condition. The intensification of movement takes place in the face of its own suspension; sound evolves in relation to a domain beyond perceptual thresholds. This transgression and effacement of categories, solid or liquid, sonorous or silent, is cinema's revolutionary invention, according to Epstein, and it rests on a superimposition of movements and temporalities.

This superimposition of different temporalities invests every present moment with its respective hindsight. The property of cinema is to modulate one time in another time, according to Epstein. We are set in front of a *dispositif* producing a complex, multifaceted time, one that confronts our accustomed perception of time as a continuous succession of present points. The elasticity of time, the variable viscosity of matter, is a result of the multiple temporal registers at work in Epstein's writings and in his films. Where there is a fluidity of the perception of space, there is also a *porosity* of time in disintegrated layers.

Epstein's use of superimpositions subscribes to his technique of putting the image in connection with its outside, with silence and stillness. Epstein's critique of the single-shot cinema of the early years is based on the idea that cinema must always be a relation between images.[48] One should point out the historical shortcoming of this argument, since early cinema frequently deployed various forms of superimpositions and established relationships between images through the distributor's provisional editing and programming. However, the statement that the moving image that is not involved in montage is not yet cinema is an important theoretical principle in Epstein's philosophy. In Epstein's films, there is a frequent technique of inserting fleeting superimpositions between images, sometimes hardly identifiable, that relates a moving image to its stilled counterpart. The superimpositions of Madeleine's face when she is painted by Roderick in *La chûte de la maison Usher* is a famous example, as is the sequence of Madeleine's resurrection, in which oscillating shots of interior spaces, timepieces, and the guitar are superimposed onto static images. This technique does not mean that the virtual is actualized in the superimposed still, but rather that the relationship between movement and stillness opens a virtual dimension. Since cinema is not bound by a singular time but consists of a system of coordinates that range over a variety of times, there is a synthesis of multiple temporalities in cinema that keeps their differences and varieties intact. An image is always a relation of temporalities in Epstein's writings and films.

Epstein refers to this spatiotemporal variability as the fourth dimension, which offers another perspective on matter: "The cinematograph is actually the only instrument that records an event according to a system of four reference points. This makes it superior to man, who doesn't appear to be constituted to grasp a continuity of four dimensions by himself."[49] Human perception understands time and space as distinct, linear, and given entities, whereas cinema allows for deferrals and variations in space-time. This relationship of cinema's technological capacity for four-dimensional perception to the human psychology of perception is central to Epstein's concept of *photogénie* in his early writings and to the 'temporal perspective' in his later texts. The following passage describes this relationship and demonstrates that cinema is not a prosthetic medium – that is, a way to see better – but rather an intelligence that shapes and describes the world in its own right, intervening between the world and the human mind:

> Man's physiological inability to master the notion of space-time and to escape this atemporal section of the world, which we call the present and of which we are almost exclusively conscious, is the cause of most "accidents of matter and knowledge," most of which would be avoided if we could directly seize the world as the flow that it is. [...] Such is also the clairvoyance of the cinematograph, which represents the world in its overall, continuous mobility. True to the etymology of its name, it discovers movement where our eye sees nothing but stasis.[50]

Human perception is here described as inadequate and illusory, which is not an uncommon trait in descriptions of cinema technologies. Mary Ann Doane comments on the discourses of the shortcomings of our physiology which give rise to the "afterimage" theory of cinematic movement; and these flaws in perception also give rise to other myths, like that of "subliminal" images in advertising.[51] Malcolm Turvey discusses the "distrust in human vision" in Epstein's theory, privileging the early writings, and finds in *La chûte de la maison Usher* an attempt to put this theory into practice.[52]

In the passage above, one can also see that the movement of the image and sound is entering into a relationship with the fixed, the still, and the silent. This way, an interval between the still and the moving, between sound and silence, is formed in cinema's relationship with our everyday sense perception. It could even be claimed that this relationship is always present in cinema, since it supplements our perception with another perception and thus creates a true image of movement, opens up for thinking a virtual dimension of the sound-image. However, this virtual sound-image cannot be isolated, as it is always related to our perception of the world. It is a presence of the image itself, as it presents itself to us. "By developing the range of our senses and by playing with the temporal perspective, the cinematograph renders perceptible through sight and sound individual beings we thought invisible and inaudible and divulges the reality of certain abstractions."[53] Cinema develops the bandwidth of our senses by giving access to coordinates in time. By making perceptible that which is invisible and inaudible, these properties are no longer virtual. Yet, the imperceptible is always present in cinema as a virtual dimension outside of what is heard and seen.

One should speak in two different senses of a virtual dimension in Epstein's theory of cinema. There is a historically conditioned virtuality that could have been actualized given the right conditions, or that could become actual in the future. This is the cinema for a time to come, as I will shortly return to, that so heavily shapes so many of Epstein's analyses of things moving outside the cinema. On the other hand, there is the virtual that cannot become actual, which always enters into relations with the image without becoming audible or seen.

A cinema to come

It is striking how often Epstein provides examples of the transgressive powers of cinema from outside cinema. As discussed above, this is a major paradox for a medium-specific theorist. It is peculiar that the climbing of Etna, the perception of wheels turning backwards, or the descent through a mirrored staircase should provide the best examples of the radically other perception of cinema. In an often quoted passage from *Le Cinématographe vu de l'Etna* (1926), Epstein describes his descent of a mirrored staircase, comparing it to "the optical facets of an immense insect," as a visual form of psychoanalysis.[54] This description of fragmentation, repetition, and multiplied images is already another perception; but it is only at the end of the passage that he reaches the conclusion that cinema serves this self-estrangement far better than what is described. While cinema itself cannot be described, the written text accounts for an extra-cinematic perception only to point out the principles of perception taken much further by the cinema.

There may be two reasons for this tendency in Epstein's writings to look outside cinema in order to describe its effects. First, Epstein is aware that cinema is "an unattainable text," in the same way as it is described by Raymond Bellour in the 1970s.[55] Any departure from cinema, as in written descriptions and illustrations, halts the movement of the image and subverts the space and time of cinema. If writing belongs in a different set of spatiotemporal coordinates altogether, and every attempt at describing cinematic movement is bound to fail, descriptions of extra-cinematic perceptions may evoke the properties of cinema as well as do close readings of films. This is the reason why Epstein never offers a systematic account of how the perception, intelligence, or philosophy of cinema works, but rather chooses to explain how these things differ from the human registers of experience and consciousness.

The "unattainability" of cinema lies not only in the immobilization and limitations in verbal description, however. There is, secondly, Epstein's ambivalence, discussed above, between cinema as an automaton and his idea that cinema has not yet realized its powers. This position has affinities with Jean-Luc Godard's recurrent discussions of the shortcomings of cinema, especially in his references to Epstein in *Histoire(s) du cinéma*. The subject of Epstein's writings is, to a large degree, a cinema to come. Cinema still 'escapes us' because it is a *dispositif* in which virtual dimensions are yet to be actualized. It is a machine whose intelligence is still not working. It invents a space and time for a mode of thinking that is yet to come. The account of the descent down the staircase in *Le Cinématographe vu de l'Etna* describes an embodiment that only exists virtually in cinema, as a temporality that is still to be invented but which becomes possible thanks to an inhuman perception that penetrates light and image. The haptic is not about how the subject applies its sensorial faculties to cinema, but how cinema forms new regimes of sensation and new modes of subjectivities, in a time to come. It describes a different temporality at hand in the "intelligent machine" of cinema, that always exists as a virtual dimension of the image, always yet to be actualized: "We are no longer concerned here with the existing cinema, but with the one which will perhaps exist in a century or two."[56]

What is Epstein's recurring "question concerning technology"? Like Heidegger's, it is concerned with the "coming to presence" of Being in art. The essence of technology is nothing technological, but rather the processes by which it forms subjectivity. This is an important aspect of Epstein's "paradox": if the automatic powers of cinema precede the aesthetic dimensions of the work (like montage, framing, and composition) technology would inadvertently set off new forms of perception and subjectivity. However, Epstein's examples of the transgressive powers of cinema exploit the "temporal perspective" of the technology through figures of deferral, reversal, and deceleration demonstrates that the transgressive powers of cinema lie with aesthetic choices. There is a utopian dimension in Epstein's philosophy: only with a cinema to come will there be pervasive revolt against the reign of the present, and only then will a variability of time prevail. Towards the end of his life, Epstein observed that popular cinema explored the properties of temporal variability less and less. Perhaps the cinema to come will never be realized and must always remain in the future. Its realization would mean that the virtual would become actual, and that the technology of cinema would coincide with human perception. Epstein's theory of cinema depends on the differences between human perception and mechanical perception. Perhaps this dissimilarity is the true answer to the "question concerning technology" in Epstein's philosophy.

Notes

1. For a good discussion of technics and aesthetics in Heidegger's philosophy, see Sven-Olov Wallenstein, "Towards the Essence of Technology," in *Essays, Lectures* (Stockholm: Axl Books 2007), pp. 305-326.
2. Epstein returns to concepts of an automated subjectivity of technology on various occasions: "The camera [...] could become [...] an eye associated with a robotic imagination and equipped with an automatic subjectivity" (Jean Epstein, "Naissance d'un langage [1947], ESC2, p. 63).
3. Jean Epstein, *L'Intelligence de une machine* [1946], ESC1, pp. 282-286.
4. This is David Bordwell's perspective in *French Impressionist Cinema: Film Culture, Film Theory, and Film Style* (New York: Arno Press, 1980), p. 113. Malcolm Turvey, however, points out how *La Chûte de la maison Usher* (1928) deviates from the techniques of visualizing human perception ascribed to the Impressionist movement. See Malcolm Turvey, *Doubting Vision: Film and the Revelationist Tradition* (New York: Oxford University Press 2008), pp. 26-28.
5. Gilbert Simondon, *Du mode d'existance des objets techniques* (Paris: Aubier 1958).
6. Epstein, *L'Intelligence de une machine*, ESC1, p. 310.
7. Nicole Brenez, "Ultra-moderne. Jean Epstein contre l'avant-garde (Repérage sur les valeurs figuratives," in *Jean Epstein: Cinéaste, poète, philosophe*, ed. Jacques Aumont (Paris: Cinémathèque française, 1998), pp. 205-206; see also the essay by Brenez in this volume.
8. Jean Epstein, *Bonjour Cinéma* [1921], pp. 38-39; ESC1, p. 92.
9. Jean Epstein, "Le délire d'une machine" [1949], ESC 2, p. 119; infra, 372-78.
10. Jean Epstein, "Le cinématographe continue" [1930], ESC1, p. 227.
11. Jean Epstein, "Bilan du fin de muet" [1931], ESC1, pp. 229-237.
12. Jean Epstein, "La naissance d'un mythe" [1934], ESC1, p. 239.
13. Jean Epstein, "De l'adaptation et du film parlant" [1929], ESC1, p. 201.
14. Jean Epstein, "L'Avant-garde pas morte" [1946], ESC1, pp.
15. Jean Epstein, "Naissance d'un langage," ESC2, p. 66.
16. Jean Epstein, "Logique du fluide" [unpublished], ESC2, p. 211; infra, 396.
17. Jean Epstein, "L'objectif lui-même" [1926], ESC1, pp. 128-129.
18. Epstein's complex medium-specific approach could be seen as parallel to that of Etienne-Jules Marey, who took no interest in the synthesis of chronophotography as the reproduction of human perception of movement, but who worked insistently on producing a projector that could synthesize movement as loops, time-lapse synthesis, slow motion, and reverse motion. Marey, *Le mouvement* (Paris: Jacqueline Chambon 1994 [1894]), pp. 309-311.
19. Henri Langlois, "Jean Epstein: L'Oeuvre filmique," ESC1, p. 9.
20. Vivian Sobchack's elaboration of analogies between the history of cinema technology and the growth and development of the sensory faculties of the child is perhaps the most famous instance of this theoretical complex, which is radically at odds with Epstein's theory of cinema. See Vivian Sobchack, *The Address of the Eye: A Phenomenology of Film Experience* (Princeton: Princeton University Press 1992), pp. 248-259.

21. Jonathan Crary, *Techniques of the Observer: On Vision and Modernity in the Nineteenth Century* (Cambridge, MA: MIT Press, 1990).
22. Gilles Deleuze, *Logique de la sensation* (Paris: Editions de la difference, 1981), p. 99.
23. Gilles Deleuze, *Cinéma I. L'image-mouvement* (Paris: Minuit, 1983); and *Cinéma II. L'image-temps* (Paris: Minuit 1985). See also D. N. Rodowick's discussion of subjectivity in Deleuze's image typology in D. N. Rodowick, *Gilles Deleuze's Time-Machine* (Durham, NC: Duke University Press, 1997), pp. 33-37.
24. Malcolm Turvey, "Jean Epstein's Cinema of Immanence: The Rehabilitation of the Corporeal Eye," *October*, no. 83 (Winter 1998), pp. 25-50.
25. Rosalind Krauss, *The Optical Unconscious* (Cambridge, MA: MIT Press, 1993), especially chapter 3.
26. See Turvey, *Doubting Vision*, pp. 61-67.
27. Turvey, *Doubting Vision*, pp. 68-69.
28. Krauss, *The Optical Unconscious*, p. 133f.
29. Jonathan Crary, *Suspensions of Perception: Attention, Spectacle, and Modern Culture* (Cambridge, MA: MIT Press, 1999), p. 153.
30. Epstein, "Logique du fluide," ESC2, p. 215.
31. Turvey, *Doubting Vision*, pp. 53-54.
32. Ibid., p. 15.
33. Ibid., p. 23. Turvey seems to be aware of this crucial point in Epstein's theory in quoting one of its clear expressions, but chooses not to pursue this dimension of the argument.
34. Ibid., p. 14.
35. Ibid., p. 38.
36. Epstein, "L'objectif lui-même," ESC1, p. 128f.
37. Giorgio Agamben, *Qu'est-ce qu'est un dispositif?* (Paris: Payot & Rivages, 2007), pp. 41-42.
38. Jean Epstein, "Le délire d'une machine" [1949], ESC2, pp. 120-127; infra, 372-78.
39. David Bordwell, *On the History of Film Style* (Cambridge, MA: Harvard University Press, 1997), pp. 142-146.
40. Tom Gunning, "Modernity and Cinema: A Culture of Shocks and Flows," in *Cinema and Modernity*, ed. Murray Pomerance (New Brunswick, NJ: Rutgers University Press, 2006), pp. 297-315.
41. Jean Epstein, "L'âme au ralenti" [1928], ESC1, p. 191.
42. Jean Epstein, "Freud ou le nick-cartérianisme en psychologie," *L'Esprit nouveau*, no. 16 (May 1922): 1857-1864; reprinted in *Jean Epstein*, ed. Aumont, pp. 139-46.
43. "Even more beautiful than a laugh is the face preparing for it. I must interrupt. I love the mouth which is about to speak and holds back, the gesture which hesitates between right and left, the recoil before the leap, and the moment before landing, the becoming, the hesitation, the taut spring, the prelude..." (Jean Epstein, "Grossissement" [1921], ESC1, p. 94; translated as "Magnification," trans. Stuart Liebman, in Abel1, pp. 235-241). This description of the close-up – which for Epstein always is a close-up of time as much as in space – resembles the description by Walter Benjamin of the optical unconscious in the Artwork essay. The term is not employed by Epstein, who approaches the analysis of the world through cinema as "ciné-analyse." See Jean

TROND LUNDEMO

Epstein, "Ciné-analyse ou poésie en quantité industrielle" [1949], ESC2, p. 57; infra, 346.

44. Raymond Bellour, Le corps du cinéma: hypnoses, émotions, animalités (Paris: P.O.L., 2009), pp. 96-97.

45. This is one of the few issues where I cannot follow Mary Ann Doane in her excellent discussion of cinematic time. Temporal manipulations in cinema are not only illustrations of deviations from the law of entropy and the irreversibility of time, they also form new configurations of time when projected upon human perception. See Mary Ann Doane, The Emergence of Cinematic Time: Modernity, Contingency, the Archive (Cambridge, MA: Harvard University Press, 2002), pp. 112-122.

46. Epstein, L'Intélligence d'une machine, ESC1, p. 288. See also, Jean Epstein, "Logique de temps variable"[unpublished], ESC2, p. 217; infra, 401.

47. Jean Epstein, "Le gros plan du son" [1947], ESC2, p. 111; infra, 368.

48. Epstein, "Logique du fluide," ESC2, p. 211; infra, 396.

49. Jean Epstein, "Photogénie de l'impondérable" [1935], ESC1, p. 250. Translated as "Photogénie and the Imponderable," trans. Richard Abel, in Abel1, p. 189 (translation modified).

50. Epstein, "Photogénie de l'impondérable" [1935], ESC1, p. 250; Abel1, p. 189 (translation modified).

51. Doane, The Emergence of Cinematic Time, pp. 80-81.

52. Turvey, Doubting Vision, pp. 21-28.

53. Epstein, "Photogénie de l'imponderable" [1935], ESC1, p. 251; Abel1, p. 190 (translation modified).

54. Jean Epstein, "Le Cinématographe vu de l'Etna", ESC1, pp. 135-136; infra, 291.

55. Raymond Bellour, "Le texte introuvable," in Ça cinéma, no. 7-8 (1975). Translated as "The Unattainable Text," trans. Ben Brewster, in The Analysis of Film, ed. Constance Penley (Boomington, IN: Indiana University Press, 2001), pp. 21-27.

56. Epstein, "Le Photogénie de l'impondérable" (1934), ESC1, p. 239. This quote is reproduced out of context in Epstein's collected writings on cinema, but it seems that Epstein is clearly pointing to a philosophy of a cinema to come, since this piece is followed by a couple of the main points from a later version of this same text (published in January 1935, two months after its initial publication). It is this later version that marks the beginning of Epstein's stronger philosophical leanings. See Jean Epstein, Photogénie de l'Impondérable (Paris: Ed. Corymbe, 1935).

Ultra-Modern: Jean Epstein, or Cinema "Serving the Forces of Transgression and Revolt"

Nicole Brenez

Jean Epstein disappeared over half a century ago, in 1953. Yet, few filmmakers are still as alive today. At the time, a radio broadcast announced the following obituary: "Jean Epstein has just died. This name may not mean much to many of those who turn to the screens to provide them with the weekly dose of emotion they need."[1] Since then, oblivion has swallowed up the cinema of small doses, but the aura of Epstein, defender of great ecstasies, has only continued to grow. The process was not achieved without breaks and detours, as the brilliant and erudite historian Jean Mitry, for example, wrote in 1966: "Neglecting content in order to pursue only form, his work is now in the past and has become considerably outdated."[2] For Mitry, only *Cœur fidèle* (1923) would survive. Meanwhile, today's cinephiles and analysts are passionate about Epstein's most avant-garde and experimental films (*Six et demi-onze* [1927], *La Glace à trois faces* [1928], *La Chute de la maison Usher* [1928], *Le Tempestaire* [1948]), as well as the entire Breton period. As a theoretician and three-sided film director (a member of the Parisian avant-garde, a Breton grappling with the real, a man faced with industry demands), Epstein worked and inspired. His thinking intrigued the greatest creators of the period in any given field: philosophy, cinema, and music, from Gilles Deleuze to Philippe Grandieux. In Europe, four signs among others marked the 2000s: first, the publication of a pioneering and richly documented book by Vincent Guigueno, *Jean Epstein, cinéaste des îles*;[3] second, the making of a film essay by experimental director Othello Vilgard (co-founder of the Etna laboratory, thus named as a tribute to Epstein) called *À partir de Jean Epstein*;[4] third, the publication in German of an anthology of texts by Epstein, initiated by Alexander Horwath, the director of the Vienna Filmmuseum in Austria;[5] and fourth, the shooting of *Jean Epstein, Young Oceans of Cinema* (2011) by the American director James June Schneider, dedicated to the Breton portion of Epstein's work.

Paradoxically, Jean Epstein's importance as a stylist, a poet, and a theoretician has grown in spite of the absence of his films: many of his masterpieces never underwent restoration (*Mor'Vran* [1931], *L'Or des mers* [1933], *Les Berceaux* [1934]), many of his films remain invisible, and the fundamental anthology of his writings on cinema published over thirty years ago is out of print and now sells for a small fortune in specialized bookstores. The aesthetic shock is only more deeply felt when discovering masterpieces that ought to be the object of scholarly editions instead of owing their continued circulation to pirated videos shot from the screening of an old and poorly preserved copy. Once reduced to *La Chute de la maison Usher*, Epstein's cinematic work now emerges as a permanent effort toward an increasingly fierce and desperate realism that might answer to the demands of analytic accuracy – on Epstein's own terms, a cinema that is simultaneously photogenic, demonic, and rebellious.

From *Le Cinéma du diable*:

> On the skin of sorcerers, possessed men, heretics, agents of the Inquisition in the old days looked for points or zones of insensitivity, which served to prove that a man belonged to Satan. At the very heart of the cinematograph, we discover a mark whose meaning is much less dubious: the indifference of this instrument toward lingering appearances that remain identical to themselves, and its selective interest for all mobile aspects. This last predilection goes as far as to magnify movement where there was hardly any, and to generate it where it was deemed missing. Yet, the fixed elements of the universe (or those appearing to be so) are the ones that condition the divine myth, while the unstable elements that evolve more quickly and thus threaten the restfulness, the equilibrium and the relative order of the first one are symbolized by the demonic myth. If not blind, the cinematic function is at the very least neutral when considering the permanent characters of things, but it is extremely inclined to highlight any change or evolution. It is therefore eminently favorable to the devil's innovative work. As it was outlining its very first aesthetic differentiation between the spectacles of nature, the cinematograph was choosing between God and Satan, and siding with the latter. Since whatever moves, transforms and comes in replacement of what will have been, proved to be photogenic, *photogénie*, as a fundamental rule, clearly dedicated the new art to the service of the forces of transgression and revolt.[6]

I. Two Sides of a French Critical Tradition

Cinema always already lost

Abel Gance, Robert Bresson, and Jean-Luc Godard dissociate actual cinema from possible cinema. They criticize the limited character of the former and proclaim the unlimited *de jure* nature of the latter.

NICOLE BRENEZ

Abel Gance: "Cinema has only developed a small portion of its possibilities: cinema is, and must absolutely become, something other than what it is, something other than what it is made to be."[7]

Robert Bresson: "I think that the cinematograph is not yet fully realized, there have been attempts, they have been stifled by the theater. It may be that the conditions fit for the cinematograph will be a very long time in coming. The cinematograph is lost from sight, decades may be necessary to find it again."[8]

Jean-Luc Godard (positive version): "And cinema is going to die soon, very young, having failed to give what it could have given, so we must... we must quickly go to the bottom of things."[9]

Jean-Luc Godard (negative version): "So cinema has been useless, it has not achieved anything and there have been no movies."[10]

Cinema forever innate

Conversely, Louis Delluc, Jean Epstein, and Gilles Deleuze defend the principle of cinema as genius, conceived as an immovable set of characteristics and powers that thus irrigate movies, even independently from an artistic project.

Louis Delluc: "I know but one pioneer in cinema.
It is cinema."[11]
Jean Epstein: "Intelligence of a machine."[12]
Gilles Deleuze: "Cinema is always as perfect as it can be."[13]

For Jean Epstein, cinema is in itself "an experimental device that builds – that is, that conceives – an image of the universe."[14] Such a conception determines two attitudes: 1) the exclusion of cinema as envisioned by plastic artists outside the legitimate field of art cinema; 2) the investment of all theoretical energy upon the device's spontaneous and permanent properties, for instance at the expense of the study of films (unlike Louis Delluc) or a reflection on the history of forms (unlike Gilles Deleuze).

Stemming from such a protocol, a line of artists begins to form for whom art consists of looking for purely cinematic forms of expression – that is to say, resulting from cinema's properties regarding one, several, or all cinematic elements (shot, angle, character development, narrativity). This tradition of great formalists takes us from Jean Epstein to Philippe Grandrieux, via Stan Brakhage or F. J. Ossang.

II. The Figurative Stance

But going back to Jean Epstein, why should a central part of cinema be rejected? Is it simply a matter of taste or does refusing it help establish an enlightening perimeter? What does this anti-cinema rejected by cinematography consist of exactly?

Let us first accept a note whose violence is out of place within the sum of Jean Epstein's affirmative and lyrical writings. Epstein develops the idea that cinema is magical because it proves to be capable of getting over certain limits of representation (it goes "above the resemblance of things" and "this efficiency superior to forms is the cinematograph's highest achievement"). He then feels the need to add that these transgressions and this accomplishment have nothing to do with a specific avant-garde cinema.

"It would be an 'absolute' misinterpretation in the reader's mind, if he saw these living images as similar to those of Viking Eggeling, Richter or Man Ray's films, which are only forms, and the lowest at that, nothing but the most animal-like rhythms. Likewise, living words are opposed to the boundless words of Dadaist works. If this remark appears useless, may my fear of being misunderstood be excused."[15]

Despite his vehemence, Jean Epstein's hostility toward the avant-garde is no temporary attitude. At least five other occurrences can attest to it:

1. The cinema of plastic artists is a cinematic pathology.
Epstein, in an interview: "'In your opinion, do films fashioned according to the cubist or expressionist taste represent the quintessence of cinema?' This time, my answer was even more categorical: 'No, it is but an accessory of cinema and almost an ill-state for this accessory.'"[16]

2. The cinema of plastic artists is an infantile degree of cinema.
Epstein recounts a visit from Miklos Bandi, a friend and collaborator of Viking Eggeling. He takes the opportunity to share his feelings about *Symphonie diagonale* and Fernand Léger's films: "If this abstract cinema delights a few, they should buy a kaleidoscope, a toy for the second stage of childhood, upon which a very simple device could impress a regular and forever variable rotation speed. For my part, I believe that the age of kaleidoscope-cinema has passed."[17] And it is not only a rejection of pure abstraction, but also a refusal to challenge the aesthetic principles implemented by the Futurists and the surrealists.

3. The cinema of plastic artists is "garbage."
Epstein begins by attacking the Futurists: "Ah, I fear the futurists, who itch to replace true dramas with fake ones made out of anything and everything: aviation and magma chamber, consecrated hosts and world wars."[18]

4. Sincere but perfectly useless.
Next, Epstein is invited to assess the standing of silent movies, buried as he has been since the generalization of talkies in a "time of confusion," and no doubt

with a certain nostalgia. The report he then gives shows a degree of affability toward abstract and surrealist cinematography:

> Absolute films describe the evolution of more or less complicated geometrical forms; they show a harmoniously mobile descriptive geometry; they capture the essence of cinematic pleasure; they represent movement closest to its prin- ciple; like any abstraction, they quickly create weariness. Surrealist films visua- lize deep thought, the logics of feelings, the dream-like flux that, without cine- matic language, would remain hermetically inexpressible. Such films require from the authors a complete sincerity that is difficult to achieve. The authors already calculate their chances of communicating their feelings through images with a Freudian correlation table; a symbolic language comes to exist, but I believe, as Novalis does, that we cannot understand the hieroglyph.[19]

Epstein tries to rationalize his rejection; and an interesting paradox emerges from his reasoning. Let us remember, for instance, the admirable parking lot sequence in *La Glace à trois faces*: the protagonist's car passes each level of the spiral-shaped building on its way down. Speed increases; the decor becomes blurred and turns into broad bands of white on a dark background; the sequence shot absorbs the fast montage; cinema becomes a pure flash of black and white. Another such visual event could be found in the kinetic treatment of a lighthouse seen from a feverish conscience, or the reduction of sea currents to their shiny glare in *Finis Terrae* (1930), or even in some very blurry shots of the sea in *L'Or des mers* that cancel out the motif to retain only the trace of its movement. *As a cinematographer,* Epstein reintegrates Walter Ruttmann or Hans Richter's plastic vocabulary in the way that, two years later, Eisenstein dialectalizes Malevich's Suprematism in the centrifuge sequence of *The General Line* (1929); for Eisenstein, pictorial avant- garde represents the negative moment of formal invention, the erroneous form that has to be reclaimed, integrated, appropriated, and overcome.[20] "Instead of looking for pure *photogénie* within the mobility of patterns, certain authors found it much more abundant in nature."[21] *As a historian,* Epstein divides, splits, decrees what is incompatible, as if to better separate himself not from what might be closest to him, but rather from the other aesthetic solution, the one that threatens the very foundation of his writing – even though the images sometimes prove to be identical and the preoccupations to be mutual.

5. The cinema of misinterpretation, the unnecessary cinema.

Commenting once again on the cinematic initiatives of Surrealism, Epstein puts an end to his benevolent digression:

> The surrealists were slow to acknowledge that the instrument of derationaliza- tion they dreamed of already existed well within their field of application; and

when they finally took notice of cinema, they used it incorrectly in such a literary, pictorial and artistic way that this experiment was immediately throttled by its esotericism.[22]

Cinema's inherent surrealism, fighting against the "surrationalism" of the social system, condemns in advance the research of the Surrealists and that of their "unfortunate cousins," the Futurists: such initiatives come late and are unnecessary, fruitless, and, at worst, come close to being impostures.[23] Epstein reserves one of his most vicious remarks for Buñuel's epigones: "Trickery made the mistake worse in a few films that pretended to be surrealist."[24]

Thus, Epstein consistently distinguishes between good and bad avant-garde and, symmetrically, does not hesitate to defend the legitimacy of a rear-guard in the form of a future "Cinema Institute" conceived as an "organization that regulates and fixes a multi-faceted art, a ductile language, and an unruly technique": "Cinema also needs a rear-guard whose inglorious mission is to conquer nothing but to cling to the spot and simply die there."[25]

Where does the limit stand between good and bad avant-garde? It is as simple as it is crucial: Jean Epstein's cinema cannot stand without a referent – and it is never closer to its own genius than when it has to elaborate this for itself, for example by exploring the effects of the kinetic sensation produced by modern speeds in La Glace à trois faces, or the effects of dread produced by the existence of photography in Six et demi onze. He must demonstrate the real so as to show an actual break between abstract and Epsteinian cinema, but not between the modernist writing of Six et demi onze (a demonstration of inner turmoil) and the harsh, documentary-like writing of L'Or des mers (a demonstration of material and spiritual poverty). Such an aesthetic imperative simultaneously determines the double rejection of plastic abstraction (Eggeling, Richter, Duchamp no doubt) and the metaphoric drift (Man Ray, Surrealism); it opens the field to which Jean Epstein devotes his energy, in his films and his writing, namely, that of figurative investigation. What are, then, by contrast, the figurative values invented, advocated, and indicated by Epstein's work? Even if the term is not often verified, it seems to us that Epstein offers one of the first, one of the only, overall reflections on cinematic description, including its three main dimensions: experimentation, invention of real presence, and consumption, each opening onto a major proposition in terms of montage.

III. Descriptive Experimentation

On many occasions and in many expressions, Epstein opposes narration to another system of representation that would be more specific to cinematic genius – we can call it a system of description:

NICOLE BRENEZ

There are no stories. There have never been any stories. There are only non-sensical situations; without a beginning, a middle, or an end; with no inside or out; we can look at them from any direction; right becomes left; without limits of past or future, they are the present.[26]

Once Aristotle is buried and the elementary reflexes used in comprehending phenomena are rejected, the work of descriptive experimentation can begin. Like an artistic protocol, this experimentation unfetters one's sight: "We ask to see; because of a mentality of experimentation; out of desire for more accurate poetry; out of analytic habit, because of a need for new errors."[27]

Experimentation thus substitutes to narrative conventionality the power of scientific reasoning, which it transposes into the aesthetic domain and subordinates cinematography to three vocations: claiming the figurative acuity of analysis; accessing a re-cutting of phenomena by means of figurative synthesis; acknowledging its own genius thanks to the choice of a fertile yet well-defined field of research – that of movement.

Analytical decomposition

"Analytical force," "analytical power"[28]: Le Cinématographe vu de l'Etna makes it the "original property of the lens" as well as "the inexhaustible source of the cinematic future." Spontaneously, the cinematic apparatus shatters or dissolves appearances; it grazes, betrays, anatomizes, and unfolds phenomena. To the "orthoscopic definition" of things, cinema opposes the plurality of its "optical interpretations...recognizable and unrecognizable."[29] With description, cinema sides with expolition, namely circumstantial, detailed, and affirmative description; or even with amplification, which is an endless expansiveness of the descriptive element. In practice, it means that the motifs are filmed as serials; one shot is not enough to present them, at least two are always needed, and narrativity adjusts to accommodate many more.

Lability – *photogénie* – theory of movement

Description has two virtues: it is cognitive (it unveils, it reveals); it is hermeneutic, it modifies the very notion of knowledge and generates a new mode of thinking; creating a "descriptive style" is doing "philosophical work."[30] Therefore, the description will be even more complete in that it is responsible for what relates to the infra- or the ultra-natural. That is what the term *photogénie* designates.

In Epstein, the term *photogénie* refers to three main aspects: the principle of non-identity, or the referent's lability, in other words the unstable character of things that always shy away from definition; the motif's moral increase by way of its transposition into an image (or to put it differently: cinema is fetishistic and engenders divinity); and the typological account of movement by cinema, whose key function consists in "representing a movement by another movement."[31] In

"Bilan de fin de muet," for instance, Epstein enumerates the dynamics implemented by cinema to grasp the essential mutability of phenomena: evolution, variation, series of metamorphoses, continuity within change, development, current, link, flow. As regards the literary description of movement, Epstein's inventiveness proves limitless. He must sometimes resort to rare expressions (the "*ruptilité*" of cinematic time[32]) or newly-accepted uses of language, as if it demanded to be altered, deflected, or bent by the fluctuation of phenomena. Hence the unexpected use of the verb "experimenting": "The dunes crawl: minerals flourish and reproduce; animals get bogged down in themselves and get transfixed; plants gesticulate and experiment toward the light; water sticks; clouds break."[33]

Epstein's cinematography establishes the measure of its aptitude: namely, it creates an experimental cosmogony.

Synthetic discovery

Synthetic discovery constitutes the first major event in montage in Epstein's succinct reflection. Sometimes, description uncovers dimensions of the real that do not match any of the standard cuttings within the realm of experience; it exhumes figurative links and detects "Monsters."

On several occasions, Epstein mentions an evening devoted to screening family movies: in the string of films and the vital successivity of individuals, a new form of entity is revealed, which is family ties, the sense of each one belonging to all – it is the Angel, the Dynasty, the Monster: "What an enlightenment for the individual to know the monster whose family member he is, the mother-soul he originates from and into which he enters."[34]

Cinema again asks the question of human community: here again the film dissolves the principle of identity. But, while in the case of natural motives Epstein works on the exchange of substances and properties ("water sticks, clouds break"), this time the entity itself is affected. The individual no longer exists, he is but a porous figure, the "vagueness of the fundamental experience of similarity," an exceptional case within the more essential circulation of analogies that cinema spontaneously reproduces.[35] The automatic elaboration of such figurative synthesis may constitute the most striking effect of descriptive experimentation, which, even though the cinematic world is "famously ghostly," grants access to the real itself: "Quite curiously, it is the ghosts on the screen that are in charge of reminding realism of a thought that, out of over-rationalization, divorced the real."[36]

This means that cinema proves more just, more faithful to the real than the way in which our perceptive physiological apparatus comprehends it. But what happens, then, when cinema no longer works on resemblance – which detaches phenomena from their contours by throwing them into the channels of metamorphosis – but rather on presence, which attaches the motif to itself? Real presence is invented.

NICOLE BRENEZ

IV. "Real Presence"

From Georges Demenÿ to John Cassavetes, from Robert Bresson to Pier Paolo Pasolini, cinema has often considered its aesthetic horizon to be an ideal of mimesis exalted in a claim of presence. Jean Epstein expressed this ideal most beautifully:

> "It is the miracle of real presence,
>   manifest life,
>   open like a beautiful pomegranate,
>   its skin peeled off,
>   easily assimilated,
>   barbaric."[37]

As in Cassavetes, Pialat, or Bresson, real presence obviously does not adopt the shape of appearances; it is always an epiphany. In Epstein, real presence is subject to two conditions: descriptive precision or exactitude, and critical intensity, which presupposes diving into an "inside perspective," one that attends to the phenomenon not in order to show it but to "undo it," deliver it, and strip away "illusion after illusion."[38] Real presence is not a given, it springs up from opposition (the denouement) and must express the dizziness of one's inner self. As such, cinema constitutes a revelation of phenomena. Real presence can then be unveiled in certain privileged locations.

The underground passage

"Like oil potentially exists in the landscape haphazardly probed by the engineer, so does *photogénie* conceal itself there, along with an entirely new rhetoric."[39]

Real presence exhumes the unconscious of the referent and the effect of its transposition into a motif; cinema is a "photo-electric psychoanalysis" (the title of a chapter in *Intelligence d'une machine*). Hence the tears of dread, the terror of actresses who see themselves on the screen for the first time and do not recognize themselves, a primitive experience of *photogénie* to which Epstein often returns.

The reverse side of transparency

"I would that we were capable of reading in the transparency of the image their most secret reverse side. This other side of the little story, and the only one that counts, is called subject."[40]

"Pasteur can be a subject," Epstein concludes. What is the meaning of this unexpected perspective, this reverse side of transparency strangely reminiscent of *inframince*, which Marcel Duchamp developed in the 1930s? Epstein offers a typology quite different from the classic arrangement between visible and invisible, manifest and concealed: a dialectic of transparency and figurativeness (the critical denouement). Things are there, but only cinema can see them for what they are. In other words, it measures itself to their unstable, disorderly, relative, and unintelligible nature.[41] Real presence requires shifting toward the figurative; the phenomenon – a face, a river, a speed – must be recovered from the perspective of its strangeness. And this strangeness does not refer to a mystery, to something dark and shameful (that would be the solution of German Expressionism that Epstein denounces ceaselessly) but to an essential alteration, to the profoundly unidentifiable and impure dimension of things that cinema detects, welcomes, and develops. Strangeness does not stem from an enigmatic lining of the real but from an "excess of obvious facts."[42]

From a narrative point of view, the lightness, the lack of consistency, and the affective irresponsibility of the figure of anonymity, elaborated by the protagonist with faded and whitened features in La Glace à trois faces, testify to the catastrophic nature of the unidentifiable. We can think of it as a deficiency, an unbearable loss, a morbid escape – and Epstein's great pieces indeed are all tales of anxiety. But each shot in the film debates the plastic splendor of alteration – the Breton documentaries, by slowing down descriptive speed, find a way to solidify the ephemeral and only retain from the figurative its monumental beauty. The sea constitutes the motif par excellence in this study on the divergence of the thing from itself. All the wave shots in Epstein's work form the most rigorous figurative investigative undertaking there may be. The investigation does not focus on nuances (as in impressionist pictorial series), but truly on differences (the sea is never confined; it never possesses the same consistency; its status changes from one shot to the next; no sea can gather all these figurative states; each occurrence dismisses the whole). Whether it is an analogy, a transfer, or a leap, real presence may only rise up thanks to an ontological shift.

Prosodic constellation / euphonic montage

With euphonic montage, we are no longer dealing, as was the case with the family monster, with a synthesis of similarities. But similarly, we now have to detect remote agreements and draw another type of figurative link, another connection between different entities. Real presence reveals the deep harmony between what is seemingly unrelated. For instance, Epstein relates one of Walter Moore Coleman's experiences on musical synchrony: let there be a crowd making random movements; suddenly, in one instant, the apparent disorder in the trajectories between soldiers, children, and animals are part of a musical consonance: "This is where cinema will one day find its own prosody."[43] (Let us note that Epstein here brilliantly anticipates a plastic demonstration that Ken Jacobs will enhance with images in Tom Tom the Piper's Son in 1969; also, the discovery of a metric order within chaos constitutes one of the century's scientific revolutions.)

Thus, the Epsteinian description does not submit to the order of appearances: in order to express things, it builds the entity of resemblance through accumulation, the "surreal resemblance" – it is the synthetic discovery; it respects the formal genius of cinematography – it is the difference, the reverse side of transparency; it detects the agreement where there are no links – it is the prosodic constellation. But, conversely, description asphyxiates standard relationships and destroys expected correlations: this is the invention of continuity as negativity, the devouring that is going to restructure not only standard cutting of cinematic matter, but also the links established between the cinematic image and the gaze.

V. World Devoured by Cinema

Epstein refers to the ordinary link between shots by using the sewing model of the basting stitch. In needlework, the basting stitch is a rough, indicative stitch that precariously and imprecisely brings pieces of cloth together while leaving them as fragments.[44] In cinema, the basting stitch refers to a type of agreed-upon link between things; all in all, it precedes the image's own work. Against the basting stitch, Epstein defends the invention of teratological forms of linking or explosion that "unmask the supposed convention of order within creation," that acknowledge the disappearance of the defining principle of identity, and that divide up the world once again.[45]

Extreme hapticality

Epstein's reflection, like his practice, strives to systematically bring back into play cinema's most mysterious link, the one going from the eye to the image.

"Never has a face yet leaned upon mine. At best, it is hot on my heels, and I am the one pursuing it forehead against forehead. It is not even true that there is air between us; I eat it. It is in me like a sacrament. Maximum visual acuity."[46]

Eisenstein had given a lot of thought to the ways in which an image could come out of the screen and pierce through to its spectator, drill through his mind, or run him over; but with Epstein's expression, "I eat it," the image could not be taken any further, it admits to its nature as a fantasy conducive to incorporation, to euphoric introjection.

From the point of view of the motif, the elaboration of such figurative confusions can be found everywhere: *Finis Terrae*, for instance, only reaches its conclusion when two antagonistic boys, one sick, the other exhausted, both at the bottom of a boat "forehead against forehead," end up switching arms. One boy's healthy arm is exchanged for the other's gangrenous limb, or rather, they share the same one, a big white stump that has become the shape of their common story. "It is not even true that there is air between us."

First theory of syncopation

The ultimate link thus becomes perceptive syncopation: "May I look through his eyes [the character's] and see his hand reach out from under me as though it were my own, may intervals of opaque film imitate even the blinking of our eye-lids."[47] If the haptic image injects itself into the body like an immaterial host, under cover of such organic eclipses, the film similarly becomes a body.

With such an invention, Epstein anticipates what will become one of the common traits of cinematic modernity: fades to black internal to the image. We can see how those by Jim Jarmusch, Leos Carax, or Gus Van Sant, like the fades to black in the pool sequence in *Cat People* (Jacques Tourneur, 1942), confuse rather than make out phenomena, creatures, and bodies. But Epstein also anticipates the somatic use of the flicker in Tony Conrad or Paul Sharits, for whom the image's perceptive interruption and plastic flickering are directed not only to the eye but also to the body as a whole; the body has become entirely visible, inside and out, remodeled by the intensity of intermittent light.

Affirmation of an erotica of continuity

In between phenomena, cinema must not express the rationalized, identity-defining passages but the sensitive, tactile, libidinal weaving. Negative devouring becomes natural; the dynamics of continuity are desire: "In fact, whether we go from a man's eye to a woman's belt, it frankly expresses, but only at the junction point, a desire."[48]

Syntax sways from having to describe the phenomena epicenter, the complex of attraction and distancing that acts in between creatures in an underhanded manner. For Epstein, only images are capable of conveying the world's economy because, contrary to strictly verbal and rational thinking, they always turn out to be concrete and metal, always factual, dreamlike, exact and surreal at the same time: *Six et demi onze* highlights the magical properties of photographic recording. A woman finds herself destroyed from a distance by the development of her photographic portraits, while through the same pictures a man discovers his own secrets and his own truth. The images are endowed with "affective valences"; provided that cinema recognizes and goes deeper into such valences, it can reveal this old dream of humanity: "what would have been necessary was to truly exchange, from mind to mind, the images of one's thoughts."[49] In the same way that Freud turned telepathy into a prototype to investigate the various states of the image (from the passing of an image as memory to image as volition, affective prospecting), thought transmission constitutes for Epstein an archaic model of choice used to express the symbolic powers of cinema, "this essential, mental television."[50]

This is why one of Jean Epstein's privileged thinking projects pertains to the treatment of mental images. In *Cœur fidèle*, *La Glace à trois faces* (especially the brilliant episode "Lucy" and its white flashes), *L'Or des mers* and so many others, what carries through Epstein's different periods has to do with the invention of mental images that make it possible, on the one hand, to turn film shots into virtual elements (they represent an anticipation, an anxiety, a non-linear relationship to time, and a non-existing one to action) and, on the other hand, to materialize on screen the spectator's mental movements thanks to a montage linked to desire.

Jean Epstein presents the world as a circulation of analogies; the link between things described in terms of likeness and aversion, telepathy as dream of cinema: is Epstein's meditation regressive? Was it necessary to go back to ante-classical modes of thinking in order to bring cinematography to its achievement? Of course not: such reflections are part of a more expansive perspective, in which all the historical propositions regarding the powers of the image serve the cause of cinema. Since his conception of being is not identity-related, Epstein summons an analogy: it is a lever used to question resemblance, this foundation of figurative cinema that is no longer the phenomenon's autonymic resemblance to itself but a critical wrenching, a vacillation, a transition ("changing all states in transitions"[51]): "Man needs a powerful poetic antidote to sublimate the wastes of his individualism."[52] Epstein's reflection frequently seems already posterior to the end of Foucault's Les Mots et les Choses (1966), written twenty years after Esprit de cinéma. Because his conception of the image is ultra-modern, Epstein absorbs the archaic: the image captures, reveals, devours; it is capable of more mobility than the movement of its motifs;[53] and this mobility includes the action of dissonance, eclipse, and disorganization, all the forms of critical denouement that speak in favor of "the indispensable illogical continuity."[54] Since Jean Epstein's cinema operates in the field of description, it does not distinguish between fiction and documentary, so that between the 1920s and 1930s, between Parisian modernist essays and modern Breton documentaries, there is no aesthetic break: differences in motifs and speeds appear, of course, but also the same intention of finding, for each film, its own form, away from issues of genre or any type of compliance. As such, Epstein's main heir is not so much Carax, who owes him much in terms of visual principles, as Godard. In fact, the latter's hostility toward experimental cinema – which is resolutely absent from Histoire(s) du cinéma, although his work often borrows from it – seems to have been subtler since the discovery of Hollis Frampton's texts.

According to Epstein, it was necessary to deny plastic abstraction in order to better engulf it, and to deploy ultra-figurativeness. In other words, it was necessary, in L'Or des mers, to invent these shots of drawings in the sand that prefigure Cy Twombly. They are like a dream of dancing in which the sole leftovers are the intervals between gestures, quasi-abstract wave shots that provide further allegorical figurativeness, or the moving, heart-wrenching camera gaze of a young woman desperately in love. This camera gaze will have a lasting echo in the history of forms, which it nonetheless never claimed to represent. Epstein can thus rightly claim for himself this power with which he credited cinema as a whole. "Screen love contains what no love had contained until now, its fair share of ultraviolet ray."[55]

VI. Jean Epstein and Guy Debord, Telepathy vs. Hypnosis

In a piece of writing from 1949 that foreshadows Guy Debord's *La Société du specta-cle* written in 1967, Jean Epstein composed an incredibly violent analysis on "the methodical organization of repression" that is the cinematic institution.

Cinema is an "emergency palliative and a strong medicine, administered in doses of one and a half hours of uninterrupted inhibition and hypnosis. [...] A crowd-oriented dramaturgy is necessarily in keeping with an analysis that may not be the most diverse, but of the most similar individual tendencies. And an age of general *planisme*, of typecasting of mentalities, of methodical organization of repression, and consequently of popularization and standardization of mental ills, requires even more critically the same popularization and standardization of the poetic antidote, in order to proportion its effect to that of censorship. [...] The movies with the most profitable reservations in the course of a given year only give a measure of the collective neurosis and introspection during that year."[56]

Guy Debord:

"As necessity finds itself to be a social dream, the dream becomes necessary. The spectacle is the bad dream of a fettered modern society that, in the end, only expresses its desire to sleep. The spectacle is the watchman for that sleep."[57]

If we still doubted the critical and political properties of Epstein's endeavor to visually recast phenomena, watching one of his lesser-known movies would suffice to assuage our misgivings: *Les Bâtisseurs*, produced in 1938 by the Ciné-Liberté group (an offshoot of CGT, the General Confederation of Labor). It prepares the ground for a social policy in construction, for instance by questioning Le Corbusier. In the opening of the film, two workers perched on the scaffolding of a cathedral re-invent the history of religious architecture from the point of view of the workers, the builders, and the people. Like the model figures that show the scale on a map, we can mentally superimpose these little characters onto each one of Jean Epstein's shots and linking shots. He gives them the responsibility of clearing any metaphysics within representation, giving us back "this presence of a body, this mass through which things are thought," as Philippe Grandieux put it so well as he was referring to the author of *L'Or des mers*.[58]

Translated by Mireille Dobrzynski
This essay is a revised version of an earlier essay, "Ultra-moderne. Jean Epstein

contre l'avant-garde," in Jean Epstein. Cinéaste, Poète, Philosophe, ed. Jacques Aumont (Paris: Cinémathèque française, 1998), pp. 205-21.

Notes

1. René Jeanne, Service des Relations culturelles broadcast, RTF, 1953; cited in Pierre Leprohon, Jean Epstein (Paris: Seghers, 1964), p. 155.
2. Jean Mitry, "Jean Epstein," in Dictionnaire du cinéma, eds. Raymond Bellour and Jean-Jacques Brochier (Paris: Éditions universitaires, 1966), p. 255.
3. Vincent Guigueno, Jean Epstein, cinéaste des îles: Ouessant, Sein, Hoëdic, Belle-Île (Paris: Jean-Michel Place, 2003).
4. The essay was shot in Parisian and Breton locations known to the author of L'Or des mers, with the help of his correspondence. One chapter was shown in November 2003 at the Cinémathèque française during the retrospective "Jean Epstein, Quickly," celebrating the fiftieth anniversary of his death.
5. See Jean Epstein. Bonjour Cinéma und andere Schriften zum Kino, eds. Nicole Brenez and Ralph Eue (Vienna: Filmmuseum/SynemaPublikationen, 2008). The present essay constitutes a new version of the foreword to this anthology.
6. Jean Epstein, Le cinéma du diable (Paris: Jacques Melot, 1947), pp. 43-45; ESC1, p. 347.
7. Cited by Pierre Leprohon, "Jean Epstein: L'œuvre écrite," ESC1, p. 13. Leprohon thinks that Gance's proposition "summarizes Jean Epstein's written and cinematic work." We believe he is mistaken.
8. Robert Bresson, quoted in François Weyergans' documentary, Robert Bresson ni vu ni connu (1994).
9. Jean-Luc Godard, Lettre à Freddy Buache, 1982.
10. Jean-Luc Godard and André S. Labarthe, "Le cinéma pour penser l'impensable" (1994), in Limelight florilège, ed. Bruno Chibane (Strasbourg: Ciné-fils, 1997), p. 14.
11. Louis Delluc, "Novateurs, primitifs, primaires" (1923), in Delluc, Écrits cinématographiques, Tome II, Volume I: Cinéma et cie, ed. Pierre Lherminier (Paris: Cinémathèque française/Cahiers du cinéma, 1986), p. 345.
12. Jean Epstein, L'intelligence d'une machine (Paris: Jacques Melot, 1946), ESC1, pp. 257-334.
13. Gilles Deleuze, "Preface to the English Edition," in Cinema 1: The Movement-Image, trans. Hugh Tomlinson and Barbara Habberjam (Minneapolis, University of Minnesota Press, 1986), p. x.
14. Epstein, L'intelligence d'une machine, ESC1, p. 333.
15. Jean Epstein, "La vue chancelle sur les ressemblances..." [1928], ESC1, p. 184.
16. Jean Epstein, "L'essentiel du cinéma" [1923], ESC1, p. 120.
17. Jean Epstein, "L'objectif lui-même" [1926], ESC1, p. 128.
18. Jean Epstein, Le cinématographe vu de l'Etna [1926], ESC1, p. 133; infra, 289.
19. Jean Epstein, "Bilan de fin de muet" [1931], ESC1, p. 236.
20. See S. M. Eisenstein, "La centrifugeuse et le Graal," in La non-indifférente nature, trans. Luda and Jean Schnitzer (Paris: Union générale d'éditions, 1975), pp. 103-140.
21. Epstein, "Bilan de fin de muet," ESC1, p. 236.
22. Jean Epstein, "Le délire d'une machine" [1949], ESC2, p. 119; infra, 372.

23. Jean Epstein, "Finalité du cinéma" [1949], ESC2, p. 49.

24. Jean Epstein, "Le Grand Œuvre de l'avant-garde" [1949], ESC2, p. 72.

25. Jean Epstein, "Naissance d'une académie" [1946], ESC2, p. 75.

26. Jean Epstein, "Le sens 1bis" [1921], ESC1, p. 87.

27. Jean Epstein, "Grossissement" [1921], ESC1, p. 97.

28. Epstein, *Le Cinématographe vu de l'Etna*, ESC1, p. 137; infra, 292, 308.

29. Jean Epstein, "Le Film et le monde" [1951], ESC2, p. 159.

30. Jean Epstein, "Logique du fluide" [unpublished], ESC2, p. 211; infra, 396.

31. Jean Epstein, "Rapidité et fatigue de l'homme spectateur" [1949], ESC2, p. 51; infra, 339.

32. Jean Epstein, "Le Film et le monde" [1951], ESC2, p. 162. "*Ruptile*" is a term from botany: "That which opens by irregular tearing, as enclosed parts swell up [*grossissement*]" (entry from Littré).

33. Epstein, "Le monde fluide de l'écran," ESC2, p. 149; infra, 401.

34. Epstein, "L'Intelligence d'une machine" [1946], in ESC1, p. 245. See also Jean Epstein, *Photogénie de l'impondérable* (1935): "No, no one in this assembly that seemed free, in what he had been, in what he was, or in what he would be. And whether it is through one mouth or another, it was the family that answered me through its one unique voice, with its permanent mode of thinking that would carry on through many past, present and future bodies. When the cinematograph turns a century old, if we now have the means to establish experiences and preserve the reel, it will have been able to capture striking and highly instructive appearances in the family monster" (ESC1, p. 252).

35. Epstein, "Logique du fluide," ESC2, p. 214; infra, 398.

36. Jean Epstein, "Logique de temps variable" [unpublished], ESC2, p. 221.

37. Jean Epstein, *Le Cinéma et les Lettres modernes* [1921], ESC1, p. 66.

38. Jean Epstein, "Fernand Léger" [1923], ESC1, p. 115.

39. Epstein, "Grossissement," ESC1, p. 98.

40. Jean Epstein, "Pourquoi j'ai tourné *Pasteur*" [1923], ESC1, p. 114.

41. Cinema tears its audience "away from the petrifying enchantments of a perfect order, from the dream of an exact measure, from the illusion of total intelligibility" (Epstein, "Logique du fluide," ESC2, p. 211; infra, 396).

42. Jean Epstein, "Cinéma, expression d'existence" [1950], ESC2, p. 138.

43. Epstein, "Le sens 1 bis," ESC1, p. 92.

44. "The link that, indeed, often compensates for the discontinuity of images is just a basting thread, not as much a part of the nature of these images, or that of their model, than of the witnesses' opinions – which may be nothing but prejudice, illusion" (Jean Epstein, "Réalisme de l'image animée" [1950], ESC2, p. 205).

45. Epstein, "Logique de temps variable," ESC2, p. 217; infra, 401.

46. Epstein, "Grossissement," ESC1, p. 98.

47. Ibid., p. 95.

48. Jean Epstein, "Réalisation de détail" [1922], ESC1, p. 105.

49. Epstein, "Finalité du cinéma," ESC2, pp. 34-35.

50. Jean Epstein, "Civilisation de l'image" [1950], ESC2, p. 143. Cf. Sigmund Freud, "Psychanalyse et télépathie" (1921), and "Rêve et télépathie" (1922), in Freud, *Résultats,*

idées, problèmes. Tome II, 1921-1938 (Paris: Presses universitaires de France, 1985), pp. 7-48.

51. Epstein, "Cinéma, expression d'existence," ESC2, p. 137.
52. Epstein, "Finalité du cinéma," ESC2, p. 38.
53. "And some of these images are capable of imitating, and even going beyond the mobility of their models" (Epstein, "Civilisation de l'image,"ESC2, p. 139).
54. Jean Epstein, "Tissu visuel" [1947], ESC2, p. 96; infra, 355.
55. Epstein, "Le sens 1bis," ESC1, p. 91.
56. Jean Epstein, "Ciné-analyse ou poésie en quantité industrielle," ESC2, pp. 56-57; infra, 343-44.
57. Guy Debord, "La Société du spectacle," in *Œuvres cinématographiques complètes: 1952-1978* (Paris: Champ libre, 1978), p. 66.
58. Philippe Grandrieux, "Physique de l'éblouissement. Entretien sur *La Vie Nouvelle*," interview by Nicole Brenez (Paris, 23 October 2002); translated by Adrian Martin as "The Body's Night: An Interview with Philippe Grandrieux," *Rouge* no. 1 (2003). Available online at http://www.rouge.com.au/1/grandrieux.html. Accessed 8 December 2011.

Thoughts on *Photogénie Plastique*

Érik Bullot

It is said that in 1637, the Jesuit Athanasius Kircher asked to be taken into the crater of Mount Vesuvius in order to take a closer look at the volcano about to erupt. In his book of 1665, *Mundus subterraneus*, Kircher presents a comprehensive inventory of the geological knowledge of his age, interweaving considerations of underground water networks, petrifaction, and insect formations, even dedicating a chapter to fireworks. A phantasmagoria enthusiast who was among the first to codify the principle of the magic lantern, Kircher saw a relationship between the sight of the erupting volcano and these proto-cinematic projections of light.

With the rise of the digital film, whether shot on cell phones, distributed on YouTube, or exhibited in art museums or galleries, cinema is currently undergoing a similarly eruptive metamorphosis. The medium seems to exceed its own boundaries; but is this medium still cinema? Has the art of cinema stayed the same through this digital transformation, or has it changed? For me, this question raises the issue of plasticity. Plasticity: the ability to bestow form on a substance, but also contradictorily, the resistance of the substance to this very transformation. Plasticity differs from elasticity, which holds the possibility of reverting to an original form without retaining the imprint of its transformation. Rather, plasticity designates the propensity of a material to undergo permanent deformation, the capacity to change in response to environmental demands as neurons and synapses change their internal parameters in response to their experiences, their memories. Is cinema plastic? Can it transform itself and/or resist deformation?

Contemporary visual art would seem to represent the limits of cinema's transformation and plasticity. As a filmmaker, my own work explores these limits. My films are situated midway between documentary and the installation film. I can shoot a film for a screening or a museum. Do these possibilities mean cinema has become a plastic art?

I will put two questions face to face. Is cinema a plastic art? And if so, what constitutes the plasticity of cinema? It was in the mid-twenties, during the prolific period of silent cinema, that the plasticity of cinema – the form bestowed upon its material basis but also the medium's resistance to its deformation – was most often called into question. This line of inquiry is found in two famous remarks: one from 1922 by the art historian Élie Faure in the aptly-named article "De la cinéplastique,"[1] and the other from 1926 by Jean Epstein in his book *Le Cinématographe vu de l'Etna*.[2]

Faure endeavors to situate cinema within the spectrum of the other arts and, like a prophet, he defines plasticity as cinema's distinctive vocation. Not only is cinema the plastic art *par excellence*, it also comes closest to its "truth" when emphasizing its plasticity. Plasticity, then, is the very essence of cinema. Faure's text ends with a description of Mount Vesuvius. Recounting the spectacle of the erupting volcano, he writes: "I thought I saw in it a formal symbol of this grandiose art whose seed we perceive, and which the future doubtless has in store for us: a great moving construction constantly bringing itself back to life under our eyes from sheer internal force, and which the great variety of human, animal, vegetable and inert forms help build."[3]

Striving to define *photogénie* as cinema's peculiar virtue, Epstein's essay opens onto a superb description of his ascent of the erupting Mount Etna, which offers a metaphor for the animistic power of cinema: "As we climbed on our mules' backs toward the active crater parallel to the lava flow, I thought of you, Canudo, who threw so much of your soul into things. You were the first, I think, to have sensed how the cinema unites all the kingdoms of nature into a single order, one possessing the most majestic vitality."[4]

For these two authors, the attraction of the volcanic eruption represents the ultimate metaphor of cinema's plasticity. Just as lava fuses different states of matter, the cinematic image produces dissimilarity without rupturing its resemblance to its referent. *Photogénie* hinges upon the existence of a gap between resemblance and difference. Epstein says that cinema would be useful for justice because it works like a proof, revealing not truth or falsity but rather producing both truth and skepticism of truth. Epstein was likewise fascinated by the relationship between nature and the cinematic image. Cinema's plasticity is at work within these tensions. Like *photogénie*, plasticity designates the capacity of the cinematic image to achieve a quantum leap, both mimetic and dissimilar. Cinema has the power to constitute an autonomous language of visual signs, akin to gestures and ideographs. This is undoubtedly why the debate about plasticity is so closely tied to the silent cinema, which invented a real alphabet of signs and gestures through the art of editing.

But exactly what is this plastic attribute of cinema? Faure first notes a particular tonal or pictorial quality of cinema that revealed itself to him "in a flash": "The revelation of what cinema can be in the future came to me one day: I kept the memory intact, of the commotion I felt at noticing, in a flash, the magnificence evidenced in the affinity between a piece of black clothing and the gray wall of an inn."[5] The harmony of muted colors is detached from the things themselves.

Plasticity is a quality of abstraction. According to Faure, plastic cinema rids itself of the subject in order to favor the affinities of light amidst masses and volumes. "The sentimental framework must be but the skeleton of the autonomous organism represented by the film. It has to wind its way through time under the plastic drama, as an arabesque circulates through space to arrange a painting."[6] These visual games, subject to continuous variations, define the plasticity of cinema by transforming the film through "a system of values ranging from white to black and constantly combined, moving, changing on the surface and the depth of the screen."[7] This description already reveals what precipitates the comparison between cinema and the volcanic eruption: a tremendous power of modulation. Faure describes the plume of smoke emanating from Vesuvius as a vast, plastic medium: "Inside this cloud, massive volumes of ash were constantly forming and deforming, all contributing to the formation of the great sphere and producing on the surface a forever moving and variable undulation, all the while maintained, as though by means of a central attraction within the mass, which neither shape nor dimensions seem to alter."[8] The expression "forever moving and variable undulation, all the while maintained" conveys precisely the plastic virtue of cinema, its capacity to receive a form while resisting deformation – that is to say, the interplay between abstraction and representation, between plastic mobility and a pattern's rigidity. It is probably the perception of this regulatory principle in cinema – the tension between constant, undulating movement and the stabilization of a structure through which the plastic line winds its way – that prompted Faure to evoke the image of the volcano.

The attraction of an erupting volcano never ceases to fascinate; it offers the image of an interregnum. Let's keep in mind that the different interactions of the various states of volcanic matter (liquid, solid, gaseous) distinguish the eruption's dynamic types: the effusive, in which flows of liquid lava predominate; the extrusive, in which solid elements abound within a generally dense, highly viscous lava; the explosive, which give birth to brutal explosions of pressurized gas and spew ashen clouds into the sky; and finally, the mixed type, with intermediate characteristics. It is this unstable equilibrium of elements, upon which the lava's high or low level of viscosity depends, that models the flow's morphology. Lava comes close to complying with the definition of plasticity; it is given a form according to the different types of eruptive dynamism, all the while resisting deformation thanks to the explosive mode, which releases the over-pressurized matter. It is not surprising that this scene – the constant modulation of matter between the form's continuous effusion and threat of explosion – should have fascinated both Faure and Epstein.

Cinema's plasticity designates its capacity to abstract "in a flash" a distinct motif within the continuum of forms. For Faure, the harmony of black and gray exerts a tension – never resolved – between its autonomous visual power and its role within the diegesis. This tension belongs to plasticity.

Doesn't Faure's description of the gap between the continuous modulation of form and the discontinuous (momentary) flash of the motif precisely match the definition of *photogénie* Epstein provides in *Le Cinématographe vu de l'Etna*? *Photogénie* presupposes an amplification of the cinematic sign. "I will describe as photogenic any aspect of things, beings and souls that increases its moral quality through cinematic reproduction."[9] The photogenic leap characterizes both a gain and a gap between the object and its reproduction. This gap is comparable to Faure's plastic perception of film, which consists of isolating a figure within a continuous framework. But where does this photogenic quality lie? Epstein continually hesitates to ascribe *photogénie* exclusively to objects, techniques, or spectators. Is it intrinsic to movement, a gift within one's gaze, or a process? It at once characterizes a quality of the object (a face can be described as photogenic); the animist power of the medium, capable of revealing this quality; and a virtue of film technique. Thus, *photogénie* belongs to none of these terms in particular, yet conveys the specificity of each – and their respective gaps. It serves as a regulating principle.

Based upon photographic resemblance and upon the difference made possible by the expressive leap, *photogénie* tries to settle on a mobile and contradictory point hinging on both surprise and anticipation. This is undoubtedly why *photogénie* allows for reflection upon the plasticity of cinema: it connects in an improbable configuration the modulation of forms arising from the continuum of photographic reproduction with their deformation, which arises from the medium's expressive power. Epstein writes that "[s]light teeters upon similarities." This game involving modulation and rupture gets to the very heart of the structural principle of cinema caught between the continuous impression of movement and the discontinuous reality of film's photographic nature.

Defined as the gap between the power of metamorphosis and the threat of rupture that regulates its excess, *photogénie* attempts to juxtapose two opposing propositions, yet without offering a solution. How does one anticipate the photogenic revelation? How does one reconcile calculation and surprise? How does one establish a method from shimmering, intermittent, discontinuous qualities? Such is the logical and poetic challenge of *photogénie*. In terms of semantic mobility – action, quality, state – *photogénie* performs magically. It internalizes non-contradiction in the meeting of opposites, ruins the principle of identity, reveals the plurality of time and its reversibility, and evinces cinema's animistic and metamorphic powers. In this respect, one can notice the links between *photogénie* and the magical force that Marcel Mauss describes:

We are therefore entitled to conclude that the notion enclosing that of magic power has existed everywhere. It is that of pure efficiency, which is nonetheless a material substance that can be located, as well as a spiritual one, which acts at a distance and yet through direct connection, if not by contact; mobile

ÉRIK BULLOT

and shifting without any movement, it is impersonal while assuming personal forms, both divisible and continuous.[10]

Photogénie, situated between terms that evoke it but do not contain it, acts like a magic power; it is a variable of time. "Like the philosopher's stone," Epstein writes as a reader well acquainted with the Kabbalah and alchemy, "the cinematograph holds the power of universal transmutations. But this secret is extraordinarily simple: all this magic can be reduced to the capacity to bring about variations in the dimension and orientation of time."[11]

If plasticity designates the power to model time, does cinema have the power to model its own history? Indeed, the perception of cinema's plasticity is linked in Faure's text to the future of the medium. Not only is this perception sudden and dazzling, but it is also accompanied by a feeling of foreboding for the future of the seventh art. Plasticity produces a strange confusion, one which suggests that cinema operates in the future perfect tense. Its plasticity is thought to be in the making. It remains unstable, uncertain. It is the vocation of cinema to be a plastic art, but this vocation has yet to come: it must be established and verified. However, doubts concerning the limits of cinema's plasticity can be found in Faure's text. Specifically, Faure is skeptical of cinema's capacity to become a collective art. Without predicting the introduction of talkies (he writes in 1922), he conceives plastic cinema as a power yet to come that faces growing threats from industry and commerce. Hence the figure of the volcano, with its unpredictable and untimely returns to activity, in which plastic cinema lays dormant; it is a figure that plays on the contrast between the continuous modulation of forms and their explosive fate, the promise of art and the threat of its ossification.

For Epstein, the fate of cinema must obey the imperative injunction expressed by photogénie: "Cinema must strive to gradually and eventually become strictly cinematic, i.e. to use only photogenic elements. Photogénie is the purest expression of cinema."[12] Still, it is a difficult injunction to grant, for it is whimsical and unpredictable. "Until today, I have not yet seen pure photogénie lasting a full minute," Epstein writes.[13] Photogénie possesses the same fleetingness as does the plastic power of cinema revealed to Faure "in a flash." "One must admit," Epstein continues,

> that it [photogénie] is a spark and an exception by fits and starts. I like the mouth about to talk yet still silent, the movement swinging from right to left, the backward step before taking a leap, and the leap before the stumbling block, the fate, the hesitation, the compressed spring, the prelude, and, even better, the piano being tuned before the opening. Photogénie operates in the future and imperative modes. It does not recognize the present state of being.[14]

Epstein likewise perceives a lethal power in the spectacle of the erupting volcano. Evoking Mt. Etna, he writes: "The place where I reflected upon the most beloved living machine [cinema] was this quasi absolute death zone that circled the first craters within a one or two kilometer radius."[15]

By locating a tension between effusion and explosion at the heart of cinema, between the splendor of a revelation and its unstable fate, Faure and Epstein define a discontinuous temporality polarized by this tension: on the one hand, effusive metamorphosis – expressed by the animism of the close-up, the kingdoms of nature elapsing in slow motion, the modulation of forms – and on the other hand, the explosive rupture produced by photogenic splendor. It is a temporality for which the volcano offers a metaphor, both for Faure's notion of plasticity and for Epstein's *photogénie*. This plasticity implies a temporality torn between the creation of modulated forms and their possible disappearance: "[I]f volcanism is the fastest geological phenomenon to guarantee new terrestrial landforms, it is also the only one able to annihilate them almost instantaneously."[16] Unstable and reactive, cinema's plasticity is a promise and a threat, a virtuality that may not be actualized. To this extent, we may consider that cinema is a plastic art without being plastic in itself. Such is its paradox. Its effusive-explosive history is that of a continuous-discontinuous invention, with the unpredictability of a volcano.

What about the history of cinema as a plastic art? For Epstein, the cinematic image evokes preverbal language, akin to the ideogram, by offering visual simultaneity instead of the consecutiveness of articulated language and by developing contradictory and reversible logics devoid of causality: "All the details simultaneously pronounced beyond the words trigger the words at their root, and before the words themselves, toward the feelings that precede them."[17] For Faure, cineplastics is based on a genealogy inspired by dance and pantomime. I will not discuss at this time the theoretical relevance of cinema as an ideograph, but I will point out that it is precisely because cinema does not speak that it is said to be of a plastic quality. Even if Epstein later tried to theorize sound as another plastic element of cinema, *photogénie* remains primarily tied to the visual nature of the cinematic sign. However, this denial of speech is only ostensible, since Epstein supposes that cinema constitutes in itself a universal language: "In this darkness said to be favorable to phenomena of telepathy, that is to say the most distant comprehensions, to the most secretive connections between minds, the surprising language was born, of an unexpected nature, which can be processed by sight but not by sound."[18]

Photogénie is the name given to the plasticity of cinema and, as we have seen, is itself reactive and amorphous, belonging to each of the terms defining it. Doesn't *photogénie* thus specify the tension between the plastic nature of the visual sign, which predates spoken language, and the very possibility of constituting a non-spoken language? Is *photogénie* the name for the impossible coexistence of a language formed without speech and yet miming the power of the spoken word? It is not surprising that Epstein asks these questions in the years immediately preceding the coming of the talkies. Although they triggered a temporary setback for the theory of cineplastics, talkies would only more concretely materialize the tension between speech and the visual sign, a tension that silent films (and their critics) already invoked in the specter of a lost, original, and universal language of which they would be the ghost. The history of cinema as a plastic art will therefore be marked by the struggle to overcome speech, as a stutterer stumbles over language, tripping over the explosive and continuous series of consonants. Charles Van Riper, the famous speech pathologist, defines stuttering as "a disorder in the synchrony of articulatory movements, prompting an impediment in their temporal adjustment during the pronunciation of phonemes."[19] Shouldn't cinema as a plastic art be defined, paradoxically, as a "disorder of synchrony" that not only affects the film itself – subjected to the disparities between its narrative content and formal construct, between sound and image (the technical definition of asynchronous cinema) – but also describes the history of the medium as an instrument of discontinuous temporality, mediating the dissimilarity between stillness and movement? *Photogénie* names this disorder.

The history of cinema confirms this disorder. Cinema as a plastic art falters. Its history is discontinuous, broken, alternating between ruptures and repetitions; it proceeds by leaps and bounds. I will not dwell on this transgressive history, which remains to be written. Instead, I will look more closely at the model of temporality cinema devises, and the ways in which time can invest cinema with a future. As an invention with no future, as Louis Lumière famously put it, what is the fate of cinema today? Can cinema's unstable powers of effusion and deflagration even allow for a future? At a time when the digital evolution of the image shatters the photographic continuum, can we still find a future for the plasticity of cinema? Or have we moved from a plastic art to a "plasmatic" art? I will take up a notion put forth by Sergei Eisenstein about Walt Disney's animated films and his characters' continuous transformations. Struck by the parallel between animism and animation, Eisenstein ponders the variability of forms. How can a form vary continuously? Eisenstein calls this power of metamorphosis "plasmaticity," which he also recognizes in the variations of fire and clouds:

> A faculty I will name 'plasmaticity' since, here, the being reproduced in the drawing, the being of the given form, the being having achieved a certain appearance behaves like the original protoplasm that did not yet have a 'stabilized' form but was capable of adopting one, any one, and, one level at a time, of evolving until it attached itself to any – to all –forms of animal existence.[20]

If plasmaticity does indeed describe a power of metamorphosis close to plasticity, it nevertheless presupposes polymorphism without a point of rupture. The animated characters' bodies, even fragmented, abstracted, animalized, and transmuted, can still return to their initial forms; they are elastic, but not plastic. Then again, placing the fate of plastic cinema in the animated film was one of the prophecies that concludes Faure's "De la cinéplastique." A parallel can probably be drawn today with the digital image. By cutting the umbilical cord between the image and its referent, the animated film and the digital image move somewhat away from the explosive pole of plasticity, thereby giving way to a power endowed with elasticity, much like morphing. If photogénie is defined by a fluid triad of motif, medium, and process and is not based solely on photographic ontology, can it make allowances for its own evolution? Can the plastic model express the plasmatic leap?

We are currently witnessing an unprecedented dissemination of cinema in social space, thanks to computers, digital cameras, and a wide range of distribution and exhibition technologies. These media relentlessly mingle image and inscription. My mobile phone is all at once a camera, a dictation machine, a typewriter, a calculator, a video monitor, and, sometimes, a telephone. The computer combines and confuses all these functions. This interchangeability between the linguistic and the visual influences my own practice. I have made a video with a cell phone, Visible Speech, which intertwines two texts: Diderot's "Lettre sur les aveugles" and a definition of "visible speech" with Alexander Melville Bell's system of phonetic notation which illustrates the physical movements that produce the sounds of language. These texts are read by synthetic voices that serve as "blind voices." My documentary, Speaking in Tongues, encourages linguistic speculation by showing artificial languages from Esperanto to imaginary tongues. It also renders homage to the Russian poet Velimir Khlebnikov who invented the phonetic language Zaum, and to the Canadian artist Michael Snow who performs in a completely improvised language in the film. In a way, Speaking in Tongues is a "silent movie," because language is a plastic material that can be transformed. An old problem now renewed, my films explore the plastic dimension of cinema between word and image. The digital complicates not only the interaction of word and image but also the relationships between abstraction and representation, transformation and stabilization; these are some of the challenges now facing the plasticity of cinema. If, as Jean Epstein reminds us, "death makes its promises to us by way of the cinematograph," should we today mourn plasticity?

Translated by Mireille Dobrzynski. This essay is a revised version of an earlier essay: "Photogénie plastique," in Plasticité, ed. Catherine Malabou (Paris: Ed. Léo Scheer, 2000), pp. 194-207.

Notes

1. Elie Faure, "De la cinéplastique," in *L'arbre d'Éden* (Paris: Crès, 1922); reprinted in Faure, *Fonction du cinéma: de la cinéplastique à son destin social* (Paris: Gonthier, 1964), pp. 16-36.

2. Jean Epstein, *Le Cinématographe vu de l'Etna* (Paris: Les Écrivains réunis, 1926); ESC1, pp. 131-152; infra, 287-310.

3. Faure, "De la cinéplastique," in Faure, *Fonction du cinéma*, p. 34; Abel1, p. 266.

4. Epstein, *Le Cinématographe vu de l'Etna*, ESC1, p. 133; infra, 288.

5. Faure, "De la cinéplastique," in Faure, *Fonction du cinéma* p. 25; Abel1, p. 260.

6. Ibid., p. 32; Abel1, p. 264.

7. Ibid., p. 25; Abel1, p. 260.

8. Ibid., p. 34; Abel1, p. 266.

9. Epstein, *Le Cinématographe vu de l'Etna*, ESC1, p. 137; infra, 293.

10. Marcel Mauss, "Esquisse d'une théorie générale de la magie" [1902-1903]; reprinted in Mauss, *Sociologie et Anthropologie* (Paris: PUF, 1997), pp. 110-111.

11. Jean Epstein, *L'Intelligence d'une machine* [1946], ESC1, p. 323.

12. Epstein, *Le Cinématographe vu de l'Etna*, ESC1, p. 138; infra, 293.

13. Jean Epstein, "Grossissement" [1921], ESC1, p. 94.

14. Ibid., p. 94.

15. Epstein, *Le Cinématographe vu de l'Etna*, ESC1, p. 134; infra, 290.

16. *Géologie 1*, Encyclopédie de la Pléiade, dir. J. Goguel (Paris: Gallimard, 1972), p. 555.

17. Epstein, *Le Cinématographe vu de l'Etna*, ESC1, p. 143; infra, 298.

18. Ibid., p. 142; infra, 297.

19. Cited in Anne van Hout and Françoise Estienne-Dejong, *Les Bégaiements: histoire, psychologie, évaluation, variétés, traitements* (Paris: Masson, 1996), p. 112.

20. S. M. Eisenstein, *Walt Disney* (Strasbourg: Circé, 1991), p. 28.

Fig. 1: Jean and Marie Epstein, 1905 (Zopott, Poland). Courtesy Cinémathèque française Iconothèque

Fig. 2: Jean Epstein, date unknown

Fig. 3: Jean Epstein during the filming of Le Tempestaire on Belle Isle sur Mer, 1947. Courtesy Mado Le Gall, Private Collection

Fig. 4: A bar fight develops in Coeur Fidèle (Jean Epstein, 1923) © la Cinémathèque française

Fig. 5: Ivan Mosjoukine as Prince Roundghito-Sing in Le Lion des Mogols (Jean Epstein, 1924) © la Cinémathèque française

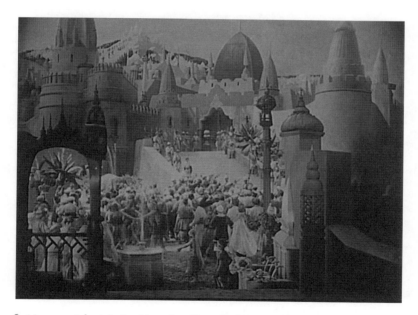

Fig. 6: Monumental set in Le Lion des Mogols (Jean Epstein, 1924) © la Cinémathèque française

Fig. 7: Behind the scene in Le Double amour (Jean Epstein, 1925) © la Cinémathèque française

Fig. 8: Les Aventures de Robert Macaire (Jean Epstein, 1925) © la Cinémathèque française

Fig. 9: La Glace à trois faces (Jean Epstein, 1927) © la Cinémathèque française

Fig. 10: La Chute de la maison Usher (Jean Epstein, 1928) © la Cinémathèque française

Fig. 11: Finis Terrae (Jean Epstein, 1929) *Courtesy of Agnès Berthola and the Musée Gaumont*

Fig. 12: Life at sea, Mor'Vran (Jean Epstein, 1930) © *la Cinémathèque française*

Fig. 13: In quicksand in L'Or des mers (Jean Epstein, 1932) © la Cinémathèque française

Fig. 14: A symphony of superimpositions in L'Or des mers (Jean Epstein, 1932) © la Cinémathèque française

Fig. 15: Le Tempestaire (Jean Epstein, 1947) © la Cinémathèque française

Translations

Introduction: Epstein's Writings

Epstein's film criticism is among the most wide-ranging and poetic writing about cinema; it also constitutes an essential foundation to the history of French film criticism that mainstream Anglophone film studies customarily assigns to André Bazin. Almost as soon as Epstein's writings about literature and then cinema were published, they were held to be among the most insightful and provocative in the new criticism – nowadays we would say 'theory' – of the 1920s. Contributing articles to the plethora of newly emerging literary and journalistic venues for the cinema such as Cinéa-Ciné-pour-tous and Photo-Ciné in France, Epstein also manages several successful entries internationally, for example with articles appearing in Broom (Rome) and Zenit (Zagreb). There was a wide dissemination of Epstein's films and criticism, seen for example in Pudovkin's mistaken impression that The Fall of the House of Usher was shot entirely in slow motion[1] to a fairly substantial knowledge of Epstein among the Czech avant-garde of the 1920s and 30s, some of whom knew of La Lyrosophie.[2] Given this international exposure, it is all the more surprising that Epstein did not immediately rise to the stature his work deserved in cinema studies as it developed as a discipline.

Epstein's critical writing covers a wide range of interests and approaches to cinema. It plays a significant role in developing a language for discussing the potential of film as an art, for example. Moreover, it arrives as an early entry in the debate about cinema's relation to realism. First, Epstein examines the importance of the relationship of the spectator to the world depicted on screen; a bit later, after his first encounters with filming in Brittany at the end of the 1920s, he also develops an understanding of how actors (or inhabitants of the places where he filmed) function cinematically, as part of the landscapes they occupy. In this, his work connects to later iterations of the realism debate, for example through Italian Neo-Realism. While several aspects of Epstein's notion of cinematic realism are examined in exciting and productive ways within the critical essays of this volume – Rachel Moore on the Brittany films and Ludovic Cortade on "the basic ontological problem" taken up in Epstein's work, for two very different examples – many more of the implications of Epstein's notions of realism remain to be explored.

As suggested in the introduction to this volume, the earliest formulations of Epstein's theories about the cinema develop in relation to literary concerns, particularly cinema's affinities with poetry's temporal and image-making capacities. Simultaneously, Epstein begins to develop several related concerns, including elaborating the concept of *photogénie*, which marks the early exuberance of his thinking about the expressive potential of cinema. This aligns him with later thinkers like Roland Barthes, whose notion of the *punctum* seems particularly indebted to Epstein's thinking about *photogénie*,[3] or Gilles Deleuze, whose time-image, for instance, bears important relationships with the kind of affect made possible for Epstein in the cinematic domain.[4]

Sections of later texts in Epstein's oeuvre, including *L'intelligence d'une machine* and *Cinéma du diable*, attest to a crisis in Epstein's thought, perhaps precipitated by the Nazis' rise to power, World War II, the Holocaust and the use of atomic bombs, and culminating in the impossibility for Epstein to make films for several years. All of these issues suggest a tension between Epstein's Franco-Polish ethnicity (French father, Polish mother) and shared Catholic-Jewish heritage, a tension that manifests itself in the global crises of the age, a crisis between humans and machines in *L'intelligence d'une machine*, and between Good and Evil in *Cinéma du diable*. While we may note that through his faith in the cinematograph's transgressive, transformative power, Epstein, on the side of cinema, also tends to side with the devil, we also marvel at how his negotiation of Manichean cultural values in these writings involves a remarkably complex set of strategies, none of which leads him to tidy conclusions or validates strictly dualistic thinking.

Epstein's thinking touches on enduring concerns for cinema studies and provides a tool for intervention in current debates about the nature of cinema. His earlier work anticipates the interdisciplinary, cross-medial approaches to thinking about cinema's place within the arts, culture, and history. His later work makes new media seem if not exactly old, then certainly something with significant antecedents. Epstein is persistently and insistently contemporary because of his "ultra-modern" understanding of the ways cinema participates in the crisis humanity feels when confronted with the machine (see Nicole Brenez's essay in this collection).

As we see it, Epstein's developing theory of cinema is thus important for a number of reasons, among which is its modernist intervention. As Christophe Wall-Romana notes, that intervention is less dystopian than we might imagine when we see how often he refers to conditions of modern fatigue. In fact:

...in marked contrast to Freud who tends to define the modern condition as a series of endings, destructions and lacks (spiritual hunger, isolation, alienation, etc.), Epstein treats it instead as the experience of a new kind of excess – a nervous condition which he paradoxically encapsulates in "la fatigue." This is one of Epstein's more radical redefinitions: rather than being caused by energetic depletion, for him modern fatigue proceeds from an inchoate potential and desire for expression which leads to a state of restless stimulation. Fatigue is an un-actualized potential.[5]

Moreover, in its most salutary manifestations, Epstein claims that cinema serves an important function within the social conditions from which modernism derives, providing an outlet for the otherwise underestimated, underchallenged spectator. A similar optimism about cinema marks the full range of Epstein's writings.

The comprehensive representation of Epstein's writing collected here allows us to remark upon several of these tendencies and important themes in his work, and to reconsider some that have been understood less well than they might be. For instance, a rich history surrounds the development of Epstein's most enduring and possibly most misunderstood concept: *photogénie*.[6] According to Epstein, *photogénie* concerns the special quality that photography confers upon that which is photographed. Laid out in the greatest detail in writings that date from the early 1920s, Epstein outlines the way in which the camera confers "personality," "life," or "soul" upon the things it addresses. He insists upon the cinema as a vehicle to express this vitality:

> [...] The cinema must seek to become, gradually and in the end uniquely, cinematic; to employ, in other words, only photogenic elements. *Photogénie* is the purest expression of cinema.
> What aspects of the world are photogenic, then, these aspects to which the cinema must limit itself? [...] A moment ago I described as photogenic any aspect whose moral character is enhanced by filmic reproduction. I now specify: only mobile aspects of the world, of things and souls, may see their moral value increased by filmic reproduction. [...] To things and beings in their most frigid semblance, the cinema thus grants the greatest gift unto death: life. And it confers this life in its highest guise: personality.[7]

For Epstein, the personality of things becoming visible depends upon the mastery of the camera by the most creative, engaged practitioners of the cinematic medium (e.g., Abel Gance, D.W. Griffith, Marcel L'Herbier); mastery of the medium consists of both what is shown (selection) and how it is shown. *Photogénie* describes the transformative process through which cinema brings out the soul of objects in motion through the devices of photography and in time.

Notwithstanding the importance of this concept to cinema studies, even a partial story of *photogénie* has not yet been told in the Anglophone world. The reception of *photogénie* has often been monolithic. This owes a lot to those critics who dismiss Epstein's theories as inconsistent or unsystematic and contradictory. American critics have often lumped all the French film critics of the 1920s together under a term – Impressionists – which, while perhaps appropriate to some, does not really apply to Epstein in either its descriptive or prescriptive sense. That is, Epstein is not merely interested in using technical effects to reveal the subjective interiority of his characters in hopes of achieving a Romantic rhetoric on film. Nor may his work be characterized by the sense of "impressionistic" as it is used pejoratively to describe a theory devised off the cuff and with little underlying substance to support it. The concept of *photogénie* is far more complex than this: it involves a tripartite psycho-physiological relationship among apparatus, object, and spectator; it at once evokes mystical or "revelationist" connotations as well as decidedly modernist ones (that involve, among other things, the limits and expansions of perception, cognition, and affect).[8]

Another connection that has not yet been fully explored is the relationship of Epstein's sense of realism to the very influential publication of André Bazin's essay on "The Ontology of the Photographic Image."[9] Epstein never explicitly attempts to lay out an ontology of photographic or moving images, but his writings nevertheless show a persistent engagement with the nature, meaning, and essence of the image. His writings are concerned with the cinema's relationship to the world and return again and again to interrogate the photographic basis of cinema (and, contrary to Bazin, usually to point out its limitations) and the effect that cinema's ontology has on the presentation and perception of time. Putting these works side by side, it seems that Bazin comes off as rather more of a classicist, with Epstein more attuned to the transgressive impulse, as we see especially in his insistence on reality as a constantly mobile, transformative premise.

Undoubtedly, Epstein's contributions to theorizing these issues are many and deserve greater scrutiny, which we hope this collection will inspire. To support this hope with practical assistance, we have provided a selection from each of Epstein's major books – most of them translated into English for the first time.[10] In addition to significant excerpts from every period and major publication of Epstein's written oeuvre, we include the complete text of *The Cinema Seen from Etna* (*Le Cinématographe vu de l'Etna*), the book that perhaps most persuasively and entertainingly combines serious theoretical arguments, incisive criticism, poetic prose, dogmatic views, and unrestrained cinephilia.

All of Epstein's books include excerpts that were themselves first published – often in slightly or significantly different forms – as articles in journals or given as lectures. We note this provenance of his collections because it is important to remember that Epstein was not writing weighty tomes of film theory outside of a lived film practice and immersion in his contemporary cinematic and artistic milieu. His theorizations were conceived as responses to issues in which he was fully immersed as an artist and citizen of the modern world. Introducing each translated work is a brief note that situates the text within Epstein's oeuvre, cinema history, or the development of similar concerns elsewhere, providing the reader with contexts in order to access better the full range of Epstein's evolving thoughts about the condition, practice, and potential of the cinema.

A word on the translations

As we have edited this selection of translations of Epstein's work, we have tapped the talents of several translators, many of them contributors to the critical essay section of this book, and all of them engaged for one reason or another with Epstein's thinking. Naturally, each one approaches Epstein's complex, playful, syntactically-difficult, inspiring, and sometimes maddening prose with a slightly different strategy; as the remarkable Lydia Davis commented, after having intimately consulted a dozen previous translations of *Madame Bovary* in preparation for her own translation of Flaubert's novel: "The great variety among the translations depends, of course, on two factors: how each translator handles expressive English and how liberally or narrowly each defines the task of the translator."[11] The translations here emphasize different aspects of Epstein's work by cleaving more or less closely to the lines by which Epstein's thought – full of digressions (often several within one sentence) and extended or abandoned metaphors – unfolds in the original language. Just as Davis later noted that "Perhaps Flaubert was mistaken when he believed that the success of the book would depend entirely on its style – since various of his translators over the years have composed deeply affecting versions that do not reproduce it," we sincerely hope that the assortment of styles within the translations we have assembled here advances their intended effects and provides ample inspiration for further work on his oeuvre.[12]

Notes

1. V. I. Pudovkin, *Film Technique and Film Acting*, ed. and trans. Ivor Montagu (New York: Grove Press, 1960), pp. 179-180.
2. See *Cinema All the Time: An Anthology of Czech Film Theory and Criticism, 1908-1939*, eds. Jaroslav Andel and Petr Szczepanik, trans. Kevin B. Johnson (Praha: National Film Archive, 2008), especially two texts by Karel Teige, "Photo Cinema Film" (pp. 124-144) and "The Aesthetics of Film and *Cinégraphie*" (pp. 145-154).
3. A more detailed discussion of *photogénie* follows. Barthes' *punctum* intersects with *photogénie* in its inexplicability, its unpredictability, and the intertwining of camera, object, and spectator, as well as in its instantaneous and transient powers of transmission: "However lightning-like it may be, the *punctum* has, more or less potentially, a power of expansion" (Roland Barthes, *Camera Lucida*, trans. Richard Howard [New York: Hill and Wang, 1980], p. 45).
4. See Gilles Deleuze, *Cinema 2:The Time Image*, trans. Hugh Tomlinson and Robert Galeta (Minneapolis: University of Minnesota Press, 1989).

5. Christophe Wall-Romana, *Cinepoetry: Unmaking and Remaking the Poem in the Age of Cinema* (PhD Dissertation: University of California-Berkeley, 2005), pp. 180-181.

6. For a thorough discussion of the history of the concept of *photogénie* see Katie Kirtland, "What Was *Photogénie?*", in her forthcoming dissertation, *The Depth of the Image: Animation and Revelation in Jean Epstein's Theory of Cinema* (University of Chicago).

7. Epstein, "On Certain Characteristics of *Photogénie*," *Abel1*, pp. 315, 317; infra, 293, 294.

8. On the "revelationist" tradition, see Malcolm Turvey, *Doubting Vision: Film and the Revelationist Tradition* (New York: Oxford University Press, 2008).

9. André Bazin, "The Ontology of the Photographic Image," in *What Is Cinema? Vol. 1*, trans. Hugh Gray (Berkeley: University of California Press, 2004), pp. 9-16.

10. The only other book of enormous significance to a sense of Epstein's work is his *Ganymède, essai sur l'éthique homosexuelle masculine*, which Christophe Wall-Romana addresses in his essay in this collection. It may be found in the archive of Epstein's materials at the Bibliothèque du film, Paris (Fonds Jean et Marie Epstein, EP227-B59).

11. Lydia Davis, "Introduction," in Gustav Flaubert, *Madame Bovary*. (New York: Viking, 2010), p. xxiii.

12. Ibid., p. xxiv.

270   JEAN EPSTEIN

La Poésie d'aujourd'hui, un nouvel état d'intelligence

Introduction

Epstein wrote his first book, La Poésie d'Aujourd'hui, in the summer of 1920, and it was published just after he arrived in Paris in 1921. Focusing mainly on aesthetic and literary concerns (it was well received as a statement on modern poetry), it also sketches out several of the issues Epstein would develop over the course of his writings, including intellectual attention and fatigue; the role of reverie, affect, synesthesia and coenaesthesia in comprehending one's relationship to the visible world; and how literature and cinema mobilize these concepts. He turns explicitly to the cinema in a late chapter, excerpted here, to demonstrate affinities between poetic strategies and cinematic ones.
– Sarah Keller

★ ★ ★

Cinema and Modern Literature [1921]

Translated by Audrey Brunetaux and Sarah Keller

[Jean Epstein, "Le cinéma et les lettres modernes," La Poésie d'aujourd'hui, un nouvel état d'intelligence (Paris: Éditions de la Sirène, 1921), pp. 169-180.]

Cinema saturates modern literature. And inversely, this mysterious art is imbued with a great amount of literature. It is true that, to date, the cine-literary collaboration has mostly produced filmic adaptations such as Le Crime de Sylvestre Bonnard [director unknown, 1919] and Au Travail [Henri Pouctal, 1919], films which would be impossible to criticize too harshly and which have led astray this emerging, still-hesitant mode of expression that nonetheless stands as the most subtle one we have ever known, the most attuned to the moment.

If viewing a second-rate film made by some mindless director who only knows about literature from the French Academy and its cohorts makes us think of modern literature in spite of him, or rather without his being aware of it, that's because there exists a natural interplay between this new form of literature and cinema that functions on several levels.

First of all:

Modern literature and cinema are equally enemies of theater. Any attempt to reconcile them is pointless. Like two different religions, two aesthetics cannot live side by side without coming into conflict. Under attack from both modern literature and cinema, theater, if not already at the point of death, will progressively grow weaker. It is a foregone conclusion. When even a good stage actor has to struggle just to exist with the excess verbiage of a forty-line monologue in verse so regular as to ring false, how can theater hope to compete with the screen, where every fibril of movement is visible and where I'm delighted to see a man who does not need to act because, simply human, most beautiful animal on earth, he walks, runs, comes to a halt, and sometimes turns his face to the voracious audience.

Cinema and the new approach to literature need to support each other by superimposing their aesthetics.

a) Aesthetic of Proximity

The succession of details with which modern authors have replaced narrative development and the first close-ups generally attributed to Griffith are part of this aesthetic of proximity.

> Between the spectacle and the spectator, no barrier.
> One doesn't look at life, one penetrates it.
> This penetration allows every intimacy.
> A face is seen under a magnifying glass, exhibiting itself; it flaunts its fervent geography.
> Electric waterfalls cascade into the fault lines of this relief, and collect under the 3000 degrees of the arc lamps.
> This is the miracle of real presence,
>> life made manifest,
>> opened like a beautiful pomegranate
>> and stripped of its covering,
>> easily absorbed,
>> barbaric.
> A theater of flesh.
> No vibration escapes me.
> A shift in shots upsets my equilibrium.
> Projected onto the screen, I land on the line between the lips.

What a valley of tears, and how silent!

The lips become agitated and begin to quaver. They tremble, part, slip away, and flee:

Splendid warning for a mouth set to open.

Compared to the drama of muscles moving in close-up, how paltry a theatrical performance made of words!

b) Aesthetic of Suggestion

One no longer tells; one shows. This allows the pleasure of discovery and creation. More personally and without restrictions, the image comes together.

On the screen, the essential quality of a gesture is that it does not come to an end. The face doesn't mimic expressions, but, better, it suggests. When laughter is interrupted, we imagine it from our glimpse of its advent. And in Hayakawa's palm, just barely beginning to open, upon such a broad path of gestures, our thoughts find their bearings.

Why?

Developing an action that begins so skillfully adds nothing to it. We can anticipate; we can already foresee the rest.

For anyone who knows their arithmetic, the givens of a problem suffice.

How tedious to read all the way through a simple solution which we could have discovered more quickly on our own.

And above all, there is the unfilled space of a gesture that the mind, which is quicker, plucks from its cradle and then races ahead of.

c) Aesthetic of succession

In calling them "movies," the British have understood that remaining faithful to what comprises life lies in the representation of its incessant movement. A rush of details constitutes a poem; and the editing of a film gradually intertwines and combines shots. The centrifugal process comes later, and from the base we extract the general impression. Cinema and literature, everything moves. The rapid angular succession approaches the perfect circle of impossible simultaneous action. The physiological utopia of seeing things "together" is replaced by an approximation: seeing them quickly.

d) Aesthetic of Mental Quickness

It is at least possible that the speed with which we think might increase over the course of a lifetime or over successive generations. No two people think at the same speed. Thus the slowness that bothers us in Italian films, where gestures drag out across the screen like slugs, testifies to Italians' slowness of thought. The time spent figuring things out is longer for the Italian brain than for the French. That which mysteriously interests and deceives the Italian spectator, we, the French, catch onto in a matter of seconds.

For this and many other reasons, there will never be an international cinema for the elite.

Fast-paced films lead us to think quickly. It's a kind of training, if you will.

In the aftermath of some Douglas Fairbanks films, I may have experienced some stiffness, but never boredom.

This speed of thought, which the cinema records and measures, and which in part explains the aesthetic of suggestion and succession, can also be found in literature. In just a few seconds we have to decipher ten metaphors, and if we fail, comprehension founders. Not everyone can keep up; slower minds are as delayed in literature as they are in cinema, and they end up getting on the nerves of their neighbor with their string of constant questions.

When reading Rimbaud's *Illuminations* aloud, there is on average one image per second.

They come at the same pace in Blaise Cendrars' *Nineteen Elastic Poems*, at certain points a bit slower.

Elsewhere, in Marinetti (in Italian), you hardly come upon even one image every five seconds.

This is the same difference that exists in films.

e) Aesthetic of sensuality

In literature: "no sentimentality!" – not visibly.

In cinema, sentimentality is impossible.

Impossible because of extreme close-ups and of photographic precision.

What is the point of having platonic flowers when the audience is looking at a face illuminated by forty arc lamps?

Americans, who have understood certain aspects of cinema relatively well, have not always understood this one.

f) Aesthetic of metaphors

The poem: a cavalcade of metaphors that rear up.

Mr. Abel Gance was the first to create visual metaphors. If you make allowances for their being distorted by slowness and disguised by symbolism, this was a major discovery.

The principle of the visual metaphor is adaptable in dreams and normal life; on the screen, it is a fixed given.

On screen, a crowd. A car pushes its way slowly through. Ovation. Hats off. White splashes of hands and handkerchiefs dance above heads. An indisputable analogy recalls these lines by Apollinaire:

"When human hands were all in leaf"[1]

and these others:

"The sky was filled with lakes of light.

And human hands flew up like milk-white birds."[2]

I immediately imagine a superimposition that emerges from the fade-in, then jumps into focus and stops abruptly:

dead leaves falling down and swirling, then a flock of birds.

But:

QUICKLY (2 meters)

WITHOUT SYMBOLISM

(the birds should be neither doves nor crows, but simply birds)

Within five years we will write cinematographic poems: 150 meters of film with a string of 100 images that minds will follow.

g) Momentary aesthetic

Not many literary critics have failed to claim that a beautiful poetic image must be eternal. This is silly. First of all, "eternal" does not mean anything. Let us say: long-lasting. But an image cannot last long. Scientifically speaking, reflected beauty wears thin: the image becomes cliché when it ages. Racine, in his time, had to offer his audience numerous and quite stunning images. What remains of them today? Platitudes. Whereas the success of a performance once depended on the text, now it is the performance that saves the text. How can a work of literature withstand such a reversal? All that is left of Racine's work is its rhythm, half of what it used to be. An image can emerge from a cliché, provided that it has been forgotten first. Let's forget about Racine. Let's not talk about him for three hundred years. A new audience will rediscover him and, sincere at last, will take pleasure in his works.

The written word always ages, but more or less rapidly. Today's written word will age very quickly. This is not intended as a criticism. I know that some people gauge the value of works of art by the duration of their success. They return their verdict: "This will be a classic," or "This will soon fade from memory." They speak of posterity, of centuries, of millennia, and of eternity as mentioned above. They despise passing trends. They no more know how to measure their pleasure than the faded games of generations gone by.

All the same, we should be spared this sentimental blackmail. My great-grandfather might have loved Lamartine and worn pants with foot straps. Filial affection doesn't oblige me to take up foot straps, but am I supposed to love Jocelyn? Masterpieces aren't read much anymore, and when they are – oh, tombs! What a dance on your gravestones! A page from a classic isn't always a complete page: it is too general. Certain works are so closely bound to a certain period that once that time has gone by, there is nothing left but an empty husk. But for fellow travelers, what a mirror they provide! Same thing in the classroom: that which the pedant enjoys in Corneille, Corneille justifiably held in contempt. I would not wish upon my worst enemy to produce a classic and therefore the future makings of a bunch of hogwash.

Literary movements hasten their own replacement. Those that are closely tied to human sentiments observe that, in ten years, both humans and their sentiments change. Its very exactitude quickly turns literature into impenetrable brush. Symbolism has already begun to degenerate into foolishness, but it did offer genuine pleasures. One style doesn't suffice for a whole generation. In the last twenty years the path of beauty has reached a new turning point. The quickness with which we think has increased; fatigue rushes in. That things one wrongly calls Cubism only last for months, not years, shouldn't be held against them. People who came of age fifty years ago sometimes run out of breath trying to keep up. Most of them criticize. It is the old quarrel of the ancients and moderns, which the moderns have always won.

Like contemporary literature, film hastens volatile metamorphoses. From autumn to spring, aesthetics change. One speaks of eternal canons of beauty whereas any two successive catalogues from Bon Marché give the lie to such nonsense. Nothing appeals to our sensuality with as keen a sense of the times and as fine an ability to adapt as fashion. From here, film adopts some of the same magnetic charms, and it is such a faithful image of our childlike infatuations that five years later, it is only suitable for the fairground lantern.

Notes

1. Guillaume Apollinaire, "L'émigrant de Landor Road/The Emigrant from Landor Road," in *Alcools*, trans. Donald Revell (Hanover, CT: Wesleyan University Press, 1995), p. 103.
2. Apollinaire, "L'émigrant de Landor Road/The Emigrant from Landor Road," p. 101.

Bonjour Cinéma

Introduction

Bonjour Cinéma, published in October 1921, features at its center a set of essays Epstein had published in film journals earlier in the same year and then revised for this collection. The first of these articles, "Grossissement," appeared in Epstein's own arts journal Promenoir in the February/March issue; "Le Cinéma Mystique" (renamed here "Ciné Mystique") and "Le Sens 1 bis" appeared in Louis Delluc's magazine Cinéa in the spring and summer of that year. Surrounding this core of essays is every manner of textual, poetic, and graphic play: in addition to several poems and pithy statements about the cinema, the slim volume includes pages whose designs derive from the world of movie fandom (posters, programs, fan magazines, music sheets, etc.) and several drawings both by Claude Dalbanne and Epstein himself. Bonjour Cinéma simultaneously sketches out several of the issues that were deeply important to the development of Epstein's theory of film – photogénie among them – and pays homage to popular moviegoing through an exuberant, infectiously enthusiastic approach to cinema.
– Sarah Keller

★ ★ ★

Continuous Screenings [1921]

Translated by Sarah Keller

[Jean Epstein, "Séances continuelles," Bonjour Cinéma (Paris: Éditions de la Sirène, 1921), pp. 13-15.]

Continuous Screenings

In close-up
pale sunshine

this face reigns
The enamel mouth stretches out
like a lazy awakening
then turns laughter upside down
up to the edge of the eyes
Without good-byes the waltz retreats
I am taking you, cinema,
and your china wheels
which I feel when I embrace
your trembling enduring
skin, so close,
spread out in the arc-light glare
How beautiful this lantern is
which repeats its dramatic light –
I have seen your 1 2 3 step
moving away on the lawns
and your silent laughter
which rushes toward me
full in the face
The gallop of flight
escaping into the cab –
hooves trample,
the auditorium, tango air,
Pursuit in the saddle
driving over the hill
In the dust, the heroine
reloads her gun
Next to a man
I walked through the snow
everything against his back
an eye on his coat
He was running along with great strides
without turning his head
he feared it was getting cold
every moment he pressed forward
my supernatural cinema
The tracks of documentary
come in through my mouth –
the lopsided hill
slips away and lies down
this seasickness is excellent
in the ocean liner cabins

with tracks for the blowtorch
I congest the earth
In my deck chair
I resign myself to shipwreck
Blocked at every right turn
Tunnel to starboard
Under the belly of a blimp
I slide in by plane
the nose, the propeller in air

I have been to the Belle Hélène theatre
I was well-shaved –
Cinema I am taking you

La Lyrosophie

Introduction

Epstein's La Lyrosophie (1922) is a companion piece to his La Poésie d'aujourd'hui, un nouvel état d'intelligence (1921). Although La Lyrosophie only skirts the question of the cinema, its philosophical speculations serve as the armature upon which he constructs his film theory. In La Lyrosophie, Epstein claims that the general intellectual fatigue that follows from the speed and telescoping of space in modern life, and a concomitant increase in the speed of thought, contributes to a mode of subjectivity he calls lyrosophie. In the lyrosophical mode, the enervation of the control of reason over the subconscious elicits the projection of subconscious sentiment onto the conscious intellectual plane. As aesthetic pleasure is a function of – and analogous to – the stimulation of subconscious emotional associations, themselves ineffable, what is elaborated is a theory of poetic language in which the sign, independent of the reader's wholly subjective projection of beauty upon it, is aesthetically inexpressive. But in poetry, in which fresh, disjunctive metaphors reign, and in play, in which words also function as autonomous sounds, thus destabilizing language itself, the aesthetic becomes a genuine possibility. Epstein conceives of the aesthetic effect of cinematic representation in terms analogous to that produced and experienced in the lyrosophical mode: it is a function of the investment of objects with an intensified sense of life via their position in an atemporal nexus of the viewer's subconscious emotional associations.
– Katie Kirtland

★ ★ ★

Excerpts from *La Lyrosophie* [1922]

Translated by Christophe Wall-Romana

[Jean Epstein, La Lyrosophie, 4th ed. (Paris: Éditions de La Sirène, 1922), pp. 16-20, 31-35, 45-46, 74-77, and 181-182.]

The Scientific Order Opposed to Feeling

[...]

All the sciences thus endeavor to constitute for themselves a proper domain from which feeling and its logic are banned. The more exact the science, the stricter the banishment. The reasons for this rigorous exclusion are easily understandable. Any science, any logic, any knowledge rests in the last analysis on the evidence [*évidence*].[1] Any proof at its crucial point appeals to the evidence. General geometry rests on Euclid's postulate, which is evidence incarnate. Evidence, it stands to reason and almost by definition, is indemonstrable. To demonstrate it would mean to state an argument more evident yet, which would consequently be singularly obvious [*évident*]; and this would therefore destroy evidence. Hence evidence is indispensable and ineffable. *Hence evidence is a feeling.* And it is a pure feeling, a feeling that is its own species, such as those we take hold of in dream-life, for example. All of traditional logic thus has for its unique and indispensable linchpin what it most despises: an affirmative feeling. This feeling of evidence: sciences are neither able to, nor do they want to, exclude it; yet, drawing their life from its pure integrity, they must necessarily ensure its complete isolation. The same way one refines sulfur, sciences refine their postulates of evidence. However, we know how rare pure, generic feelings are, that they take place only in special intellectual or almost a-intellectual states, that they more than easily combine with each other, and that from these combinations there result the mixed and rough feelings – hatred, pride, lust – that animate us. It is therefore incumbent upon the sciences, so as to mine this pure ore, this invaluable radium of the feeling of evidence, that they should cultivate it in a zone from which all other feelings are absent. Hence order is foremost the sacrifice of passion. This non-feeling and pure intellectual state, self-conscious to the utmost degree, is quite rarefied. While all sciences aspire to it, few truly reach it, and many remain midway in intermediary states – half-feeling, half-reason. And around this part of the island that has laboriously emerged, this island of pure reason, there lies truly an immensity of feeling, graspable and thought-dependent at its surface; and lower, subconscious and unsayable; and lower still, unconscious, unknown, but fecund. From the depths of this confusion, where everything and nothing can be imagined – nothing, as before the world was created – there gushes to the summit the most systematized of pure intellectual states, retaining like a geyser the heat-feeling of its depths: the feeling of evidence. But only this feeling, single and pure. Because if evidence is corrupted, it becomes analogy. Then at a lower depth, analogy becomes metaphor. At this point, science enters a lyrical state. Science is dead. Lyrosophy is born.

Particulars of Love

[...]

Let's take cinema as [an] example. Like mathematics and like the knowledge that comes from love, cinema is essentially subjective.[2] The same way the mathematician demonstrates on paper properties that are not intrinsic to the paper, on screen you see what is not and cannot be on the screen. Moreover, you see this unreality specifically and feelingly, with all the particularities of real life. A movie shows you a man who betrays. You know full well first of all that there is no such man, and secondly that there is no such betrayal. Yet the movie addressed the ever-wakeful knowledge that comes to you from love. It created, through the ghost of a thing, a feeling; and since this feeling cannot live without the thing for which it was made, and since this feeling too obeys the law of preservation, the false thing will come alive for you. Or rather there will come to life a thing-feeling, and you will believe in more than a traitor – you will believe in a betrayal. You now need this very betrayal, since you have the feeling of it – and such a particular feeling that no other betrayal than this imaginary one will satisfy it.

Experimental Science and the Experience of Feeling

Science is experimental. Feeling is experience [*expérience*] itself.[3] Nothing in the knowledge that comes from love can be acquired other than through personal trial. Such knowledge is therefore closer to the thing and to the object than scientific knowledge, which, as we know, is often indirect, even bookish. Science recognizes a certain faith: even if the experiment fails, you still believe that hydrogen can combine with chlorine. That's because the conclusion is here outside of the experience, and the conclusion is general, while the experience is particular, and in order to reach a conclusion you can very well replace one try by another. For love, the experience, just like the conclusion, are in the realm of the individual. Experience is its own conclusion. Nothing is truly general. There are as many conclusions as experiences, and if the experience fails, there is no conclusion. Hence while science demonstrates, feeling is itself the essence of the demonstration, that is to say, the pure affirmative. And if it does not succeed in being this complete affirmation, it is but an absurdity, a nullity. Science progresses; feeling is immediately everything or nothing.

The knowledge of feeling is a passion. Lyricism takes sides with everything, and nothing of what it knows leaves it indifferent, for as soon as there is knowledge in a lyrical state, instantly this knowledge is perfect – that is, it becomes love, passion, possession, and self-forgetting.

Science looks for causes through the study of effects. Lyricism creates causes in proportion to effect, that is, it invents them.

The Rule of The Kabbalah Is Such That It Espouses Passion Rather than Opposing It

The mystical principle is that intelligence, or more precisely spirit, or more precisely yet, the soul, penetrates things. Representation thereby becomes a phenomenon. To a fact there answers within man an indelible philosophy with which this fact fuses. The word, the exterior sign of representation and the interior sign of the thing, is identical with the representation and the thing. Thus there are no longer representations of things, but thing-representations. To designate means to create. Because the universe is the verb, the verb is the universe. Abstraction is a general matter. Reality and its metaphysics have the same value for the soul, because the soul takes hold of the fact and interprets it; interpretation is a second fact, inseparable from the former, its Siamese twin.

In short, the Kabbalist never considers the world as exterior, located outside of himself, but considers it always after he has absorbed it within himself. Everything to him is introspection. He does not differentiate between two categories of phenomena: objective and subjective. All are located for him on a unified plane of consideration, a subjective plane – that is to say, that of feeling. And in this unified plane, this network of feelings, the most varied equivalences, associations, equalities, and correspondences take place. The suppleness of the logic of feeling allows these to occur while rational logic brutally forbade them to reason. Through the operation of the soul, the object passes into the state of feeling and, having become feeling, henceforth lives like one, that is, by associating itself. If, as the Kabbalist writes, "Twelve letters – *he, vav, zain, chet, tet, jod, lamed, nun, samek, ayin, zade, kaf* – he has founded, he has traced, engraved, combined, weighed, and permuted, and he has made with them the twelve constellations, the twelve months of the year, the twelve directors of the soul," it is, in terms of pure logic, even less than an absurdity: an incomprehensible and null nonsense.[4] But in the logic of feeling, such associations between the letters of an alphabet and constellations or months of the year are perfectly normal and, in terms of feelings, justifiable by contiguity or similitude (but the similitude of feeling). Hence a child who sees, while learning her alphabet, as is common, the image of an angel next to the letter A, might her entire life conserve a feeling of equivalence between the letter A and the representation of an angel, a feeling repressed by reason, half-forgotten within the subconscious, but capable at any moment, if the circumstances arise, to emerge within consciousness.[5]

The Lyrosophical Misunderstanding

The lyrosophy of language thus leads to bestowing a double meaning or rather a double series of meanings to each verbal expression.[6] One of these series contains reasonable, logical, and stable meanings whose individual variations are rather limited. The other series is formed by affective meanings coming in the wake of logical meanings. These affective meanings are infinitely more complex, more precise – and precise otherwise – and more changing. With them, the word is plainly much richer and more broadly expressive; it says more things and, by way of feeling, says them poetically. At the same time, it is exposed to being fuzzy and favoring misunderstandings. It is more intelligent since it offers the possibility of having more things be understood, but it runs the risk of not succeeding in communicating the one thing it most intends, among the things it can say.

It behooves us to propose here an apology of misunderstanding. To misunderstand means to become aware of a meaning until then virtual within the sentence, which, once corrected, still possesses both meanings. To misunderstand certainly means first to miss understanding, but also to understand something else, hence more, since this other thing is in excess of the meaning strictly intended.

Notes

1. Epstein plays on the concept of *évidence/l'évident* throughout this section. Although translated as "evidence" or "evident" in all but one case (noted in the text), we should read in every use of this word both the sense of proof and of the obvious. See note 3 below.

2. In the preceding section, Epstein describes both mathematics and the knowledge of love as subjective but precise states of being; they negotiate subjectivity and objectivity at once. For example, in the field of mathematics, Epstein writes: "...other marks of subjectivism: these figures that have no value other than the subjective. It is subjectively that the line is straight, the circle round, and the angle right; objectively it doesn't matter what the line, circle, and angle are." *La Lyrosophie*, p. 32.

3. See note 1, above. Epstein here may be speaking equally of human experience and scientific experiment, as well as possibly a combination of the evidence of the senses and the (apparent) rules obvious in the world's natural order (editors' note).

4. This citation is from the *Sefer Yetzirah* [Short version], 5:2. The "directors of the soul" are parts of the human body.

5. Later in the text, Epstein draws an explicit analogy between Kabbalah and cinema: "The cinema names things visually: as spectator I do not doubt for a second that they exist, and I link this whole drama and so much love to a few signs made of light and shadow. Never, even in the Kabbalah, was designation so thoroughly the same as creation. And, after this creation, I conserve the feeling of a second singular reality, *sui generis* and cinematographic." *La Lyrosophie*, p. 93.

6. Epstein provides a discussion on the "lyrosophy of language" in the chapter preceding this one:

    If lyrosophy appears in contemporary thought, we can anticipate that it likewise appears in language. Similarly, the fact is that if today the modification of language is the most lyrosophical thing we've seen for a hundred years, nevertheless, because there has always been language, it has always lived lyrosophically. Just as Kabbalah is the intensification of a mysticism which for many a long age already contained its rudiments, the germ of lyrosophy, this other kabbalah, which is going to blossom tomorrow, already exists.

Each word in its adult form possesses two sides: it is intelligible on one hand and moving on the other. These two qualities generally depend on each other and are therefore, in this way, contradictory. Furthermore, they are variable, because if the emotion conferred by a word increases, its intelligibility decreases and vice versa. *La Lyrosophie*, pp. 167-168.

Le Cinématographe vu de l'Etna

Introduction

Le Cinématographe vu de l'Etna was Jean Epstein's fourth published book and the second he devoted exclusively to cinema. Many, but not all, of the articles and lectures on cinema he had published or delivered since 1922 are included, sometimes in augmented or revised form, but none of his other contemporary writings on literature and the visual arts. Circumstantial evidence suggests that it was composed and delivered to the printer before the end of 1925 since it fails to include two short but interesting texts, "L'Opera de l'oeil" and "L'Objectif lui-même," both published in the first weeks of January 1926. The seven short essays extend some of the principal theoretical points first enunciated in Bonjour Cinema: film as a universal language; the transformative powers of the camera apparatus that made it as central to the creation of film art as the men who set up the framing and turned the crank. It is perhaps equally notable for its literary flair. The loosely organized, meandering meditations on the diverse theoretical topics he treats are replete with metaphorical turns of phrases and cultural references that are at once suggestive and elusive, illuminating and frustrating. These strategies were and would remain a distinctive feature of Epstein's reflections on the art to which he devoted his life.

– Stuart Liebman

* * *

The Cinema Seen from Etna[1]

Translated by Stuart Liebman[2]

[Jean Epstein, Le Cinématographe vu de l'Etna (Paris: Les Écrivains Réunis, 1926).]

Sicily! The night had a thousand eyes. All sorts of smells shrieked at once. An unfurled coil of wire brought our car, swathed in moonlight as if surrounded by mosquito netting, to a halt. It was hot. Impatient, the drivers broke off singing the most beautiful love song, striking the car with a monkey wrench and insulting Christ and his mother with a blind faith in their efficacy. In front of us: Etna, the great actor who bursts onto the stage two or three times each century, whose tragic extravagances I had arrived to film. An entire side of the mountain was a blazing spectacle. The conflagration reached up to the reddened corners of the sky. From a distance of twenty kilometers, the rumbling at times seemed to be a triumphal reception heard from afar, as if a thousand hands were applauding in an immense ovation. What tragedian in what theater ever knew such a thunderous success? The earth, suffering but held in thrall, exploded during the curtain calls. A harsh shudder suddenly ran beneath the ground where we stood. Etna's tremors telegraphed the vast scale of its calamity. After that, a great silence descended in which one could once again hear the drivers' songs.

The roads at the foot of Etna had been closed as a precaution. At every crossroad, the black shirts demanded our travel authorization. But these soldiers for the most part did not know how to read, and the multi-colored brochure which had covered my tube of aspirin had a greater effect on them than the Prefect of Catania's authentic signature.

At Linguaglossa, the mule-drivers waited for us in front of the flowing lava, black and shot through with purple like a beautiful carpet. The wall of embers advanced by caving in again and again. Under its impact, the houses, badly protected by their holy images, exploded, making a sound like nuts cracking. Huge trees only touched at the bottom of their trunks by the fire instantaneously burst into flames, from their roots to their tops, and burned like so many roaring torches. The day dawned. The mules, uneasy, tensed their nostrils and flattened their ears. Some of the men, feeling helpless, wandered around.

Glorious volcano! I have never seen expressions comparable to yours. The conflagration had covered everything with the same colorless color, grey, dull, dead. In front of one's very eyes, every leaf on every tree passed through all the colors of autumn until, cracked, twisted and scorched, they fell into the fiery blasts. And each naked, blackened tree held itself upright for but an instant during this scorching winter. There were no more birds, no insects at all. Like the roadway of a bridge when a very heavy truck rolls across it, the earth, lined with thin crevices, was continually traversed by tremors. The lava collapsed with the noise of a million plates breaking at once. Pockets of gas burst, hissing as softly as snakes. The inferno's smell, an odor without scent, filled with tingling, acrid sensations, poisoned our lungs to their very depths. Under the sky, pallid and parched, death truly reigned. The battalions of soldiers, bureaucrats, engineers, and geologists contemplated this distinguished natural actor, who rekindled in these democrats an idea of absolute power and divine authority.

As we climbed on our mules' backs parallel to the lava flow toward the active crater, I thought of you, Canudo,[3] who threw so much of your soul into things. You were the first, I think, to have sensed how cinema unites all the kingdoms of nature into a single order, one possessing the most majestic vitality. It inscribes a bit of the divine in everything. In front of me, at Nancy, a room with three hundred people moaned when they saw a grain of wheat germinate on screen. Suddenly, the true visage of life and death, of a terrifying love, appeared, provoking these religious outcries. What churches, if we only knew how to construct them, could accommodate a spectacle like this, where life itself is revealed. To discover unexpectedly, as if for the first time, everything from a divine perspective, with its symbolic profile and vaster sense of analogy, suffused with an aura of personal identity – that is the great joy of cinema. No doubt, there were games in antiquity and "mysteries" during the Middle Ages that produced this much piety and amusement at the same time. In water, crystals as beautiful as Venus grow, born as she was, replete with the most elusive symmetries, correspondences, and charms. A heavenly game, thus do worlds fall – wherefrom? – into a space of light. It is the same for thoughts and words. All life is covered with ordained signs. In order to grow and unite, rocks make beautifully steady gestures as if they were meeting beloved memories. Under the sea, angel fish and those voluptuous organs, the secretive jellyfish, dance. Insects appear as large as battleships, as cruel as the intellect, and devour each other. Ah, I fear the futurists who are itching to replace true dramas by false ones made with whatever is at hand: aviation and central heating, consecrated hosts and the world war. I fear they will only write some third-rate acting scenes for the crystals and jellyfish of cinema. Why does one even need to imagine? The wooden shoes of our mules pawed the site of a veritable tragedy. The earth had an obstinate, human face. We felt ourselves to be in the presence of someone lying in wait for us. The laughter and dazzling shouts of our eight muleteers were all there were. We marched along silently, so sharing a single thought that I felt it in front of us like an eleventh gigantic person. I don't know if I can make myself understood about this, but the figure with whom we were all preoccupied was the cinema. And what a character it is! It was as if we had come into the presence of an old and powerful man who rushed around, myopic and rather hard of hearing. You waited for a response, but you understood him less than he understood you, undoubtedly because your languages are different and your thoughts unfamiliar to each other. I once had a friend, a quite Europeanized Chinese man. One morning we were studying flowers in the botanical garden; suddenly, my comrade got angry for no reason at all. I was never able to penetrate the insurmountable anger and sorrow with which he surrounded himself much like the Great Wall does his country. Thus, quite often the extreme points of human sensibilities are inaccessible to us, and sometimes an entire soul, full of power and cunning, is forbidden to us. As if in front of one of these [souls], I stood before Etna.

One of the greatest powers of cinema is its animism. On screen, nature is never inanimate. Objects take on airs. Trees gesticulate. Mountains, just like Etna, convey meanings. Every prop becomes a character. The sets are cut to pieces and each fragment assumes a distinctive expression. An astonishing pantheism is reborn in the world and fills it until it bursts. The grass in the meadow is a smiling, feminine genie. Anemones full of rhythm and personality evolve with the majesty of planets. A hand is separated from a man, lives on its own, suffers and rejoices alone. And the finger is separated from the hand. An entire life suddenly is condensed and finds its most pointed expression in this fingernail which mechanically torments a thunder-charged fountain pen. There was a time not so long ago when hardly a single American drama was without a scene in which a revolver was slowly pulled out of a half-open drawer. I loved that revolver. It seemed the symbol of a thousand possibilities. All the desires and desperation that it represented, the multitude of combinations to which it was a key. It allowed us to imagine all sorts of endings, all kinds of beginnings; and all of these endowed this revolver with a kind of freedom and moral character. Is such freedom, such a soul, more epiphenomenal than the one we claim to be our own?

When the whole man finally appears, he is seen for the first time ever with an inhuman eye. The place for me to think about this most beloved living machine was this almost absolutely dead zone extending one or two kilometers around the first craters. The most careful surgeons prepare their operating rooms less antiseptically. I slept on the ashes which were warm and moving like the skin of a large animal. Two hundred meters away, fiery rapids surged from an almost circular crevice and rushed down the slope to form a river as red as ripe cherries and as large as the Seine at Rouen. The vapor covered the sky with a porcelain whiteness. Little gusts of fetid, angry wind raised eddies of ash which fluttered just above the ground, strange seagulls living at the edge of the gigantic conflagration. The mule-drivers held the noses of the mules that wanted to flee and could not be tied up anywhere. Just like a child who plays too close to a fire and who, it is said, will have an accident, Guichard,[4] my cameraman, shot a lap-dissolve whose value no one, I think, will fully appreciate. A tall man suddenly appeared through the fumes, jumping with incredible temerity from rock to rock along the crater's edge, like some bizarre guardian angel of a place certainly more propitious than any other to magical transformations. He approached with long strides. He was old and dry, with ashes powdering every hair in his goatee; the whites of his eyes were very red, his outfit singed here and there, and he had about him the general air of a sorcerer. I was not so sure that he was not a real devil, but he claimed to be a Swedish geologist. While speaking to me he made gestures with a metal thermometer as long as an umbrella. This man had been living very calmly for a week solely in the immediate company of this volcano. A few steps away, he camped under a tent where he could see equally clearly by day or night and through which the shaking ground stirred a constant current of air. His pockets were filled with chunks of lava and papers. Taking out his watch, he noted down the exact time of our encounter. He cupped his hands to form a megaphone, and his mouth practically at my ear, he shouted some words which I barely made out: "Today everything looks as if it will remain calm. But yesterday, an Italian journalist descended half insane." I already knew this; as we ascended we had met his guides as they were coming down, badly shaken and eager to talk. Where we were, the noise was that of a hundred express trains scorching past a metal viaduct. After a few minutes, the roaring became like silence, propitious to the imagination. And all about us lay ashes.

Two days before, as I left the hotel for this trip, the elevator was stuck between the third and fourth floors from six-thirty in the morning on. The night clerk, already a prisoner in the cabin for three hours, shook his wretched body, softly groaning into the carpet. In order to descend, I had to take the large staircase, still lacking a banister, where workers were chanting insults at Mussolini. This immense spiral of stairs portended vertigo. The entire shaft was lined with mirrors. I descended surrounded by images of myself, by reflections, by images of my gestures, by cinematic projections. At every turn I was caught from another angle. There are as many different and independent positions between a profile and a three-quarter view as there are tears in an eye. Each of these images lived but an instant, no sooner caught sight of than lost from view, already something else. Only my memory could hold on to one of their infinite number, and by doing so, missed two out of every three. Tertiary images were born from secondary images. An algebra and descriptive geometry of gestures came to light. Certain movements were divided over and over; others were multiplied. I tilted my head and to my right I saw only the square root of a gesture, but to the left, this gesture was raised to the eighth power. Looking at one, then the other, I acquired a different conception of my three-dimensionality. Parallel perceptions were in perfect accord with each other, reverberated against each other, re-enforced each other and then were extinguished, like an echo, but with a speed far greater than acoustical ones. Tiny gestures became very large, just as when words spoken as softly as possible into the ear of Dionysius the Tyrant at the Paradise of the Latomies, swell into a booming shout, thanks to the conductive nature of the rock.[5] This staircase was the eye of another sort of tyrant, an even greater spy. I descended as if moving across the optical facets of an immense insect. The opposing angles of other images cut across and amputated each other; reductive and fragmentary, they humiliated me. For the moral effect of such a spectacle is what is so extraordinary. Every glance brings a baffling surprise that insults you. I had never been seen this way before and I regarded myself with horror. I understood those dogs that bark and the apes that fly into a rage in front of a mirror. I thought myself to be one way, and perceiving myself to be something else shattered all the vain notions I had acquired. Each of these mirrors presented me with a perverse view of myself, an inaccurate image of the hopes I had. These spectating mirrors forced me to see myself with their indifference, their truth. I seemed to be in a huge retina lacking a conscience, with no moral sense, and seven stories high. I saw myself stripped of my sustaining illusions, surprised, laid bare, uprooted unfeelingly and presented truthfully, exactly for what I was. I would have run a long way to escape this spiraling movement in which I seemed thrust down toward a terrifying center of myself. Such a lesson in egotism in reverse is pitiless. An education, an entire course of instruction, a religion had patiently consoled me to be as I was. Everything had to be begun anew.

Even more than this kind of play with tilted mirrors, cinema produces similarly unexpected encounters with oneself. The uneasiness experienced in front of one's own filmed image emerges suddenly and is widely shared. By now the story of the little American millionaires who cried after seeing themselves on screen for the first time has become a commonplace anecdote. And those who do not cry are troubled. One should not understand such an effect as merely the result of presumptuousness or exaggerated coquettishness. For the mission of cinema does not seem to have been precisely understood. The camera lens is an eye which Apollinaire would have called surreal (without any relationship to today's surrealism), an eye endowed with inhuman analytic properties. It is an eye without prejudices, without morals, exempt from influences. It sees features in faces and human movements that we, burdened with sympathies and antipathies, habits and thoughts, no longer know how to see. For anyone who even briefly considers this statement, every comparison between theater and cinema becomes impossible. The very essence of these two modes of expression is different. Thus, the other original property of the cinematic lens is its analytic power. Cinematic art ought to depend on it. Alas!

If the first response to our own cinematic reproduction in front of us is a sort of horror, it is because every day we civilized individuals lie (no need to cite the theories of Jules de Gaultier or Freud) about nine-tenths of who we are.[6] We lie without knowing it any more. Suddenly this mirror's gaze pierces us with its amperes of light. The inextinguishable source of the cinematic future lies in its analytic power. Villiers hardly dreamed of a comparable machine to confess souls.[7] And I see very clearly new inquisitions drawing overwhelming evidence from films in which a suspect is captured, flayed, and meticulously betrayed in an unbiased way by this very subtle mirror's gaze.[8]

★ ★ ★

On Certain Characteristics of *Photogénie*[9]

Translated by Tom Milne

The cinema seems to me like two Siamese twins joined together at the stomach, in other words by the baser necessities of life, but sundered at the heart or by the higher necessities of emotion. The first of these brothers is the art of cinema, the second is the film industry. A surgeon is called for, capable of separating these two fraternal foes without killing them, or a psychologist able to resolve the incompatibilities between these two hearts.

I shall venture to speak to you only of the art of cinema. The art of cinema has been called 'photogénie' by Louis Delluc.[10] The word is apt, and should be preserved. What is 'photogénie'? I would describe as photogenic any aspect of things, beings, or souls whose moral character is enhanced by filmic reproduction. And any aspect not enhanced by filmic reproduction is not photogenic, plays no part in the art of cinema.

For every art builds its forbidden city, its own exclusive domain, autonomous, specific, and hostile to anything that does not belong. Astonishing to relate, literature must first and foremost be literary; the theater, theatrical; painting, pictorial; and cinema, cinematic. Painting today is freeing itself from many of its representational and narrative concerns. Historical and anecdotal canvases, pictures that narrate rather than paint, are rarely seen nowadays outside the furnishing departments of the big stores — where, I must confess, they sell very well. But what one might call the high art of painting seeks to be no more than painting, in other words color taking on life. And any literature worthy of the name turns its back on those twists and turns of plot that lead to the detective's discovery of the lost treasure. Literature seeks only to be literary, which is seen as a justification for taking it to task by people alarmed at the idea that it might resemble neither a charade nor a game of cards and be put to better use than killing time, which there is no point in killing since it returns, hanging equally heavy, with each new dawn.

Similarly, cinema should avoid dealings, which can only be unfortunate, with historical, educational, novelistic, moral or immoral, geographical or documentary subjects. The cinema must seek to become, gradually and in the end uniquely, cinematic; to employ, in other words, only photogenic elements. Photogénie is the purest expression of cinema.

What aspects of the world, then, are photogenic, these aspects to which cinema must limit itself? I fear the only response I have to offer to so important a question is a premature one. We must not forget that where the theater trails some tens of centuries of existence behind it, cinema is a mere twenty-five years old. It is a new enigma. Is it an art or something less than that? A pictorial language, like the hieroglyphs of ancient Egypt, whose secrets we have scarcely penetrated yet, about which we do not know all that we do not know? Or an unexpected extension to our sense of sight, a sort of telepathy of the eye? Or a challenge to the logic of the universe, since the mechanism of cinema constructs movement by multiplying successive stoppages of celluloid exposed to a ray of light, thus creating mobility through immobility, decisively demonstrating how correct the false reasoning of Zeno of Elea was?[11]

Do we know what radio will be like in ten years' time? An eighth art, no doubt, as much at odds with music as cinema currently is with the theater. We are just as much in the dark as to what cinema will be like in ten years' time.

At present, we have discovered the cinematic property of things, a new and exciting sort of potential: *photogénie*. We are beginning to recognize certain circumstances in which this *photogénie* appears. I suggest a preliminary specification in determining these photogenic aspects. A moment ago I described as photogenic any aspect whose moral character is enhanced by filmic reproduction. I now specify: only mobile aspects of the world, of things and souls, may see their moral value increased by filmic reproduction.

This mobility should be understood only in the widest sense, implying all directions perceptible to the mind. By general agreement it is said that the dimensions deriving from our sense of direction are three in number: the three spatial dimensions. I have never really understood why the notion of a fourth dimension has been enveloped in such mystery. It very obviously exists; it is time. The mind travels in time, just as it does in space. But whereas in space we imagine three directions at right angles to each other, in time we can conceive only one: the past-future vector. We can conceive a space-time system in which the past-future direction also passes through the point of intersection of the three acknowledged spatial directions, at the precise moment when it is between past and future: the present, a point in time, an instant without duration, as points in geometrical space are without dimension. Photogenic mobility is mobility in this space-time system, a mobility in both space and time. We can therefore say that the photogenic aspect of an object is a consequence of its variations in space-time.

This definition, an important one, is not simply a mental intuition. A number of films have already offered concrete examples. First, certain American films, demonstrating an unconscious and highly precocious feeling for cinema, sketched the spatio-temporal cinegrams in rough outline. Later Griffith, that giant of primitive cinema, gave classical expression to these jostling, intersecting denouements that describe arabesques virtually simultaneously in space and time. More consciously and more lucidly, Gance – today our master, one and all – then composed his astonishing vision of trains swept along on the rails of the drama. We must be clear why these racing wheels in *La Roue* comprise the most classic sentences yet written in the language of cinema. It is because in these images the most clearly defined role is played by variations, if not simultaneous at least approximately so, in the spatio-temporal dimensions.

For in the end it all comes down to a question of perspective, a question of design. Perspective in drawing is a three-dimensional perspective, and when a pupil executes a drawing which takes no account of the third dimension, the effect of depth or relief in objects, it is said that he has done a bad drawing, that he cannot draw. To the elements of perspective employed in drawing, the cinema adds a new perspective in time. In addition to relief in space, the cinema offers relief in time. Astonishing abridgements in this temporal perspective are permitted by the cinema – notably in those amazing glimpses into the life of plants and crystals – but these have never yet been used to dramatic purpose. If, as I said earlier, a draftsman who ignores the third spatial dimension in its perspective is a bad draftsman, I must now add that anyone who makes films without playing with temporal perspective is a poor director.[12]

Moreover cinema is a language, and like all languages it is animistic; in other words, it attributes a semblance of life to the objects it defines. The more primitive a language, the more marked this animistic tendency. There is no need to stress the extent to which the language of cinema remains primitive in its terms and ideas; so it is hardly surprising that it should endow even the most inanimate objects it is called upon to depict with such intense life. The almost godlike importance assumed in close-ups by parts of the human body, or by the most lifeless elements in nature, has often been noted. Through the cinema, a revolver in a drawer, a broken bottle on the ground, an eye isolated by an iris are elevated to the status of characters in the drama. Being dramatic, they seem alive, as though involved in the evolution of an emotion.

I would even go so far as to say that the cinema is polytheistic and theogonic. Those lives it creates, by summoning objects out of the shadows of indifference into the light of dramatic concern, have little in common with human life. These lives are like the life in charms and amulets, the ominous, tabooed objects of certain primitive religions. If we wish to understand how an animal, a plant, or a stone can inspire respect, fear, and horror, those three most sacred sentiments, I think we must watch them on the screen, living their mysterious, silent lives, alien to human sensibility.

The cinema thus grants to the most frozen appearances of things and beings the greatest gift in the face of death: life. And it confers this life in its highest guise: personality.

Personality goes beyond intelligence. Personality is the spirit visible in things and people, their heredity made evident, their past become unforgettable, their future already present. Every aspect of the world upon which the cinema confers life is elevated only if it possesses a personality of its own. This is the second specification which we can now add to the rules of photogénie. I therefore suggest that we say: only the mobile and personal aspects of things, beings, and souls may be photogenic, that is, may acquire a higher moral value through filmic reproduction.

An eye in close-up is no longer the eye, it is AN eye: in other words, the mimetic decor in which the gaze suddenly appears as a character... I was greatly interested by a competition recently organized by one of the film magazines. The point was to identify some forty more or less famous screen actors whose portraits reproduced in the magazine had been cropped to leave only their eyes. So what one had to do was to recognize the personality in each of forty gazes. Here we have a curious unconscious attempt to get spectators into the habit of studying and recognizing the distinctive personality to be seen in the eye alone.

And a close-up of a revolver is no longer a revolver, it is the revolver-character, in other words the impulse towards – or remorse for – crime, failure, suicide. It is as dark as the temptations of the night, bright as the gleam of gold lusted after, taciturn as passion, squat, brutal, heavy, cold, wary, menacing. It has a temperament, habits, memories, a will, a soul.

Mechanically speaking, the lens alone can sometimes succeed in this way in revealing the inner nature of things. This is how, by chance in the first instance, the *photogénie* of character was discovered. But with the proper, by which I mean a personal, sensitivity, one can direct the lens towards increasingly valuable discoveries. This is the role of the author of a film, commonly called a film director. Of course a landscape filmed by one of the forty or four hundred directors devoid of personality whom God sent to plague the cinema as He once sent the locusts into Egypt looks exactly like this same landscape filmed by any other of these film-making locusts. But this landscape or this fragment of drama STAGED BY someone like Gance will look nothing like what would be seen through the eyes and heart of a Griffith or a L'Herbier. This is how the personalities of certain men, the soul, and, finally, poetry erupted into the cinema.

I remember still *La Roue.* As Sisif died, we all saw his unhappy soul leave him and slip away over the snows, a shadow borne away in angels' flight.

Now we are approaching the promised land, a place of great wonders. Here, matter is molded and set into relief by personality; all nature, all things appear as a man has dreamed them; the world is created as you think it is; pleasant if you think it so, harsh if you believe it to be. Time hurries on or retreats, or stops and waits for you. A new reality is revealed, a reality for a special occasion, which is untrue to everyday reality just as everyday reality is untrue to the heightened awareness of poetry. The face of the world may seem changed since we, the fifteen hundred million who inhabit it, can see through eyes equally intoxicated by alcohol, love, joy, and woe, through lenses of all sorts of madness: hate and tenderness; since we can see the clear thread of thoughts and dreams, what might or should have been, what was, what never was or could have been, the secret forms of feelings, the startling face of love and beauty – in a word, the soul. "So poetry is thus true, and is as real as the eye itself."

Here poetry, which one might have thought mere verbal artifice, a figure of style, a play of antithesis and metaphor – in short, something next to nothing – achieves a dazzling incarnation. "So poetry is thus true, and is as real as the eye itself."

The cinema is poetry's most powerful medium, the medium most capable of realizing the unreal, the 'surreal,' as Apollinaire would have said.

This is why some of us have entrusted to it our highest hopes.

★ ★ ★

Langue d'Or[13]

Translated by Mireille Dobrzynski and Stuart Liebman

Almost as much as they hate one another, human beings love one another. And they dream of a prodigious universal tongue that would facilitate their monetary and emotional exchanges. But if the tenacious will to understand each other which led to the development of Esperanto was not checked by the vertigo that stopped Babel's expansion as the tower tapered off in the clouds, that desire was nonetheless in vain. A methodical framework alone is not enough to build the quivering architecture of speech. Patient in their work, facile in their ability to imitate, and logical in their efforts at synthesis, scholars [of Esperanto] succeeded in coining words: leaves without trunks or roots. They also developed a grammar, but without having to incorporate thousands of generations of a hundred thousand living hearts. Artificial and lacking in inspiration, their lingo ended up being forgotten, after having amused a few sufficiently uneducated anarchists; one cannot even say that it died, since, strictly speaking, it was never born.

But, springing forth from the dense mass of things, a spark was struck from the tragic friction between peoples; the universal tongue, reigning over the six thousand idioms of the world, was meant to be. It came into being. So many ears pricked up to record its first syllable. And the first syllable emerged without breaking the silence, so that many who were listening too hard still haven't been able to hear it, although it has been speaking for about ten years. In the darkness said to be favorable to telepathic phenomena – that is, to the comprehension of the most remote things and the most secret correspondence between minds – the surprising language was born; its nature was unexpected, easily assimilated through the eye but not through the ear. It isn't read, it is seen, and this act of "seeing" is truly the most nuanced exercise, the most subtle, the most exacting, and the most specialized of all visual exercises. The cinema, both popular and high-brow, familiar and spectacular: a universal language. Its undeniable share of requisite vulgarity produces deep roots that sustain its life. A modern machine of frightening complexity. A golden language, much more expensive than was silence in a time long ago when speech was silvery. Each celluloid word consumes dollars, marks, francs. And it cannot be pronounced except upon the say-so of bankers, pregnant with capital, after signing contracts in which hundreds of thousands are pledged, exchanged, won, promised, lost, divided, and multiplied. Each word must pay for insurance and customs duty, be amortized and rake in a lot. For this word to be pronounced properly – that is to say, to be pronounced in a way that pays, amortizes, rakes it in – some curt, tough, buttoned-up men in black who represent gold, who think gold, who give, protect and recover gold, have decreed and applied a cinematic canon more meticulous and more authoritarian than the classical rule of the three unities.[14] Something upheld to a greater extent than this rule, probably.

And I can only clumsily express just how difficult this language is. It is agony, like a nightmare in which one fights against sleep, finally to pronounce a syllable in a faltering, liberating breath. The world is made up of four simple elements; film is composed of all the others acting for or against each other, accumulating straightforwardly in sums, and collapsing into pyramids of secondary elements. The human face, so soulful, attacked by electricity. Light, a shower of fire, cooks and reheats the face, corrodes and ripens it, gives it luster, coats and paints it in the colors of passion. The face cracks, is peeled apart, splits in half all the way to the bottom, suffers and laughs, then rises like a revered sun. The touch of amperes inscribes thoughts on the forehead. The arc-light bears the shadow of memories into the eye that it frames, pins to the star's gaze a strength of will, and blows, like God, onto the clay of mouths so that even the saddest feelings about love might appear as a smile. But if the arc-light should blink, farewell to profound perspectives of feeling! May the actor, yielding to the storm of clarity, cease to forget himself and thus reclaim the soul being torn from him. The lens is quarrelsome. Do not think for a moment that it is taking photographs. It displays what is hidden, hides what is displayed, first wants something, doesn't want it the very next moment, composes and recomposes, then resolves its very personal vision despite all the blinkers in ways contrary to any expectations. And, male that it is, it impregnates the film, until that moment said to be virginal, even more unpredictably than human beings are born. Film is also reticent. One evening, we all had to turn our backs on it so it would stop its cruel whims. Our gazes disturbed it: who knew?

And from so many fevers and burns, from so many sweating hands and hearts, from work that wears one down like love itself, what is left? A film image, a reflection of what we wanted, filtered a hundredfold, weakened, faded, wounded a hundred times by the one hundred adverse realities it had to overcome, almost dying, born after at least five months of effort for a life lasting but sixty-five minutes, then, dream that it is, forgotten.

Because it is so complex, this language is also incredibly subtle. All the details pronounced – expressed without recourse to words – simultaneously trigger the words that lie at their roots as well as the feelings that precede them. Then the screen turns on its silent loudspeaker sky. The atmosphere of Swedish films, cold as reformed religion, is unloaded on foreign hearts at the speed of light. Hayakawa's gaze, as heavy as an oath, crushes us white men, who do not know what honor in the East is, or a love without kisses, a fire under ashes, or a fifteen-year betrothal. A wordless telegraphy teaches us the precise meaning of peoples' souls. All around the earth are roads upon roads along which we love and kill each other; seas and still more seas, on whose shores people sit, their chins on their fists, waiting; and cities forty stories high where men fall asleep on their phone every night and die one day, finally happy, having had no time to notice it. There is an album of the world's hearts, in sarcophagi made of gelatin.

And this is even more beautiful: in the same way that pleasure and pain in living things only express the instinct of self-preservation, the film's financial necessities similarly determine its moral qualities (I dare not speak of artistic qualities; it is obvious that cinema is already more than an art). In order to satisfy its need for capital, films tend to extend beyond the borders of the country that produced them. This is not necessary; it could be cut. It is a vital necessity. Cinema will either be a global form of writing, or it will be nothing more than a kind of theater made worse by photography. For a long time now, the first American images have flown above our heads with the lassos of the Wild West. Then we got to know Ince and his rustic dramas. Today we like Griffith – a brutal Jew and restrained Protestant – who is the very incarnation of passion. They know little about the five or six films we could show them. Thus far, Gance, your *J'accuse* alone fell from so far high up and down into American hearts that they became heavier.

★ ★ ★

The Photogenic Element[15]

Translated by Tom Milne

The cinema is at that happy period when new forms of expression for thoughts and human emotions meet with misfortune. If I said that the young arts, the young sciences, the young philosophies waxed strong on easy successes, you would not believe me. Their successes were always difficult, blended with the measure of failure that tempers character. I mean that cinema is in its apostolic period, an era corresponding in the history of religions to their militant days. And if I call them happy, very happy, these difficult times cinema is going through, it is because they alone, through their very difficulty, permit the explosion of great enthusiasms. Above all, they alone conjure the will and the talents that are the most valuable, the *individual* aspect of these enthusiasms. These pioneering individuals are missionaries sent by the Cause to prepare its triumphs and convert the barbarians.

Tonight my thoughts cannot but turn to memories of two of these missionaries for the cinema: Canudo and Delluc. And there must certainly be some of us who will admit to having been converted to the cinema by one or the other, or possibly both, and to owing them heartfelt thanks.

Canudo was the missionary of poetry in the cinema; Delluc, the missionary of *photogénie*.

As early as 1911, Canudo published an essay on cinema so farseeing that one cannot reread it today without being astonished. In 1911, when cinema for years to come was to be, in both theory and practice, no more than a holiday diversion for schoolboys, a darkish place of assignation, or a somewhat somnambulistic scientific trick, Canudo had understood that cinema could and should be a marvelous instrument for lyricism. And although this new lyricism really only existed then as a prophecy, he immediately foresaw its limits and possibilities, its determinate and indeterminate qualities.

The concept of painting was born on the day when color sprang as an abstraction into the minds of our very remote ancestors. Similarly, the concept of sculpture or architecture was born the moment the notion of volume emerged in the human mind. In 1919, Delluc formulated and wrote of this word which for a time seemed magical, and to this day retains its mystery. With the notion of *photogénie*, the concept of cinema as an art was born. For how can one better define the undefinable *photogénie* than by saying: *photogénie* is to cinema what color is to painting and volume to sculpture – the specific element of that art.

If Canudo quickly scanned the reaches of cinema's horizons, Delluc discovered this *photogénie* which is a sort of refractive moral index to this new perspective.

It was Canudo, in those sessions at the Salon d'Automne, who first thought of publicly presenting selected extracts from films, of building up an anthology of cinema. This notion of a cinematic anthology was extremely valuable because, through these fragments of film, it drew attention to cinematic style: it isolated style from narrative. This attempt to analyze cinema's resources should be pursued even more rigorously: by taking not extracts from various films, but images in the strict sense. And not images from various films, but images in a quality of style, a photogenic quality. Those programs at the Salon are in fact still very much in the flow of evolution and refinement today. It is this classification of cinema's resources that I propose should be undertaken more in the spirit of a grammarian or a rhetorician.

An army commander should, I presume, know exactly what armaments he has at his disposal, the range and caliber of the guns with which he is to fight. A writer should know the value of the word combinations he will employ in writing. And to understand this art of writing, he learns grammar and rhetoric, both consciously and unconsciously. But we filmmakers, who should have a detailed knowledge of all the elements of cinematic expression, find any such grammar or rhetoric totally lacking. My aim is to attempt to establish the premises for a cinematic grammar.

We must not, however, yield to facile and misleading analogies. It would be convenient to say: a long shot is like a substantive phrase, and the close-up stressing a detail in the overall view is comparable to an adjective which underlines some quality in the substantive. This would be easy but erroneous, because a detail shot is often more important, more substantive than the long shot, which exists only in relation to the detail. And where repetition, for example, is often used as a means to reinforce expressiveness in writing, repetition of the same images in a film weakens their effect.

The grammar of cinema is a grammar uniquely its own.

Unattended, without words, an air of conviction alights from the screen on eighteen hundred pairs of eyes. Words slither like wet cakes of soap around what we try to say. This evening a friend, trying to put everything too precisely into words, suddenly shrugged twice and said no more. I believed him, as others might have been persuaded verbally, on the strength of this wearied silence. And when a scientist takes pains to use words with precision, I no longer believe. I know his words respond to definitions not within him or me, but outside and between us, in some lecturer's diplomatic, imagined nowhere. There are, too, at least twelve words for each thing, and at least twelve things for each word; strictly speaking, therefore, no word is the word for a thing, and no thing is the thing for a word. On the line of communication by speech we are interrupted by an unexpected static of feelings. Everything remains to be said and we give up, exhausted. Then the screen lights up its silent loudspeaker sky. How convincing is this language dispensed by a square, sputtering eye. The screen captures a theft of automobiles. Above these heads, between the arc lamp and screen, Babylon passes, intangible as smoke, reconstructed in flashes of light.

All details that are expressed without recourse to words simultaneously trigger the words that lie at their roots as well as the feelings that precede them. Just as the mathematician indubitably demonstrates on paper properties that are not there, so a thousand eyewitnesses in front of a cinema screen would swear on their lives to what cannot be there. The film shows a man who betrays; nevertheless there is no man and no betrayer. But the ghost of something creates an emotion which nevertheless cannot come to life unless the thing be for which it was created. So an emotion-thing is born. You believe in more than a betrayer, you believe in a betrayal. Now you need this betrayal; because you feel it, and feel it so precisely that no other betrayal but this imaginary one will satisfy you.

In this unreality, validated by emotion, authenticity is absurd and universal. If conventions seem so very out of place here, it is not that they are insufficiently plausible; on the contrary. These limitations – obstacles so stimulating to the theater – cannot be permitted by a form of imagination that casts them all aside from the outset. Whereas in grammar the part – not without effrontery – replaces the whole, here the whole is substituted for by the part which is better equipped to excite emotions. "In those times, it was..." says the storyteller; here, instead of having been, things are, and the time is always today, a continual today in which yesterday collides with tomorrow at a speed of 3,600 seconds per hour, bringing past and future into the present.

Already this is more than an art. So it is no longer an art just when the herd of critics, journalists, artists, actors, orchestra leaders, and pyro-engravers, all regularly twenty-five years behind the times, finally admit that among the arts, cinema is one. Is it already a language? In the absence of words, it has the chance to discover a profound precision. But will cinema ever secure seekers of its stable, unimpeachable, universally perceptible elements?

★ ★ ★

For a New Avant-Garde[16]

Translated by Stuart Liebman

I just want to say this: you have to love it and hate it at the same time – and love it as much as you hate it. This fact alone proves that the cinema is an art with a very well-defined personality of its own. The difficulty lies above all in the choice of what is right to hate about it. And if this choice is difficult, it is because it must be revised at extremely short intervals.

Indeed, the best friends of an art always end up becoming infatuated with their ideas. And because art as it evolves goes beyond its rules at every moment, these best friends of yesterday become the worst enemies of tomorrow, fanatics devoted to shopworn methods. This continual overturning of friendships is characteristic of the slow evolution of all the arts.

Thus it is that today at last – at last, but a little too late – some methods of cinematic expression, still considered strange and suspect a year ago, have become à la mode. Being fashionable has always signaled the end of a style.

Among these methods we can chiefly include the suppression of intertitles, rapid editing, the importance accorded to sets and to their expressionist style.

The first films without intertitles were made almost simultaneously in America and in Germany. In America it was in a film by Charles Ray, La Petite Baignade [The Old Swimmin' Hole, 1921], distributed and titled here, though only after considerable delay. Retreating from its novelty, the distributors were careful to add about fifteen intertitles to the film. In Germany, it was Le Rail [Scherben or Shattered, 1921] by Lupu Pick. I haven't come here to justify the so-called "American" title – incorrectly named, for it is, alas, often French too – that beforehand first explains to the spectator what he is about to see in the next image, then afterwards tells him a second time in case he either wouldn't see or understand. Certainly, the suppression of the title has had its value as a new method, not entirely in and for itself, but as a useful one among others. And Lupu Pick, who must be considered the master of the film without titles, last season presented us with a kind of cinematic perfection, that is, Sylvester [New Year's Eve, 1923], perhaps the most filmic film ever seen, whose shadows conveyed the extremes of human passion on film for the first time. And the theory that is the basis for the film without titles is obviously logical: cinema is made to narrate with images and not with words.

Except that one should never go to the limits of theories; their furthermost extent is always their weak point where they give way. For one can't deny that watching a film absolutely free of intertitles is, for psychological reasons, depressing; the subtitle is above all a place for the eye to rest, a punctuation point for the mind. A title often avoids a long visual explanation, one that is necessary but also annoying or trite. And if you had to limit yourself to films without titles, how many otherwise beautiful scenarios would become unrealizable. Finally, there are various kinds of information that I still believe are more discreet to provide in a text than through an image; if you must indicate that an action takes place in the evening, maybe it would be better simply to write it than to show a clock face with the hands stopped at nine o'clock.

Obviously, in a good film an intertitle is only a kind of accident. But on the other hand, advertising a film by stating that it has no intertitles, isn't that like praising the poems of Mallarmé because they don't have punctuation marks?

Rapid editing exists in an embryonic state in the gigantic work of Griffith. To Gance goes the honor of having so perfected this method that he deserves to be considered its inspired inventor. *La Roue* is still the formidable cinematic monument in whose shadow all French cinematic art lives and breathes. Here and there, attempts are being made to escape from its hold and its style; it is still difficult. And if I insist on this point, it is so that what I am going to say in a moment cannot in any way be construed as a criticism of *La Roue*. It contains, moreover, elements far more noble, more pure, and more moral than the discovery of the rapid editing technique, which seems to me nothing more than an accident in the film. But if in *La Roue* this is a very fortunate accident, how disagreeable it becomes in so many other films. Today, rapid editing is abused even in documentaries; every drama has a scene, if not two or three, made up of little fragments. 1925, I predict to you, will inundate us with films that will precisely correspond to this most superficial aspect of our cinematic ideal in 1923. 1924 has already begun, and in a month four films using breakneck editing have already been shown. It's too late; it's no longer interesting; it's a little ridiculous. Wouldn't our contemporary novelist be ridiculous if he wrote his work in the Symbolist style of Francis Poictevin[17] where, invariably, he uses the word "remembrance" [*resouvenance*] for "memory" [*souvenir*] and "disheartenment" [*déséspérance*] for "despair" [*déséspoir*]?

If you must say about a film that it has beautiful sets, I think it would be better not to speak about it at all; the film is bad. *The Cabinet of Dr. Caligari* is the best example of the misuse of sets in cinema. *Caligari* represents a serious cinematic malady: the hypertrophy of a subordinate feature, the great importance still accorded to what is an "accident" at the expense of the essential. I do not want to talk primarily about *Caligari*'s shoddy, "ready-made for thirty francs" expressionism, but about the principle of a film that is hardly anything more than photographs of a group of sets. Everything in *Caligari* is a set: first, the décor itself; next, the character who is as painted and tricked up as the set; finally, the light, which is also painted – an unpardonable sacrilege in cinema – with shadows and half-tones illusionistically laid out in advance. The film is thus nothing more than a still life, all its living elements having been killed by strokes of the brush. Along with a thousand other things, cinema has borrowed sets from the theater. Little by little, if it is independently viable, cinema will pay back its debts and this debt as well. No more than it revived the theater, the work of painters will not succeed in reviving cinema. Painting is one thing, cinema something else entirely. If the "Théâtre d'Art" declared at its birth: "The word creates the décor as well as everything else…," the "Cinéma d'Art" now being born declares: "The gesture creates the décor as well as everything else." In cinema, stylized sets ought not and cannot be. In the fragments of those few films that are almost true cinema, the sets are anatomical, and the drama played in this intimate physical arena is superlatively ideal. In close-up, the eyelid with the lashes that you can count is a set remodeled by emotion at every instant. Beneath the lid appears the gaze which is the character of the drama and which is even more than a character: it is a person. With its imperceptible movements whose religious secret no emotional microscopy has yet been able to reveal, the circle of the iris transcribes a soul. Between the tuft of the chin and the arc of the eyebrows an entire tragedy is won, then lost, is won anew and lost once more. Lips still pressed together, a smile trembles toward off-screen space, within those wings that are the heart. When the mouth finally opens, joy itself takes flight.

If I criticize three techniques especially misused by modern cinema, methods that now enjoy a belated vogue, it is because these methods are purely material, purely mechanical. The mechanical period of cinema is over. Cinema must henceforth be called the photography of delusions of the heart.

I remember my first meeting with Blaise Cendrars.[18] It was in Nice, where Cendrars was then assisting Gance in the production of *La Roue*. We were speaking about cinema and Cendrars told me: "*Photogénie* is a word…very pretentious, a bit silly; but it's a great mystery." Gradually, much later, I understood how great a mystery *photogénie* is.

Each of us, I assume, may possess some object which he holds onto for personal reasons: for some it's a book; for some, perhaps a very banal and somewhat ugly trinket; for someone else, perhaps, a piece of furniture with no value. We do not look at them as they really are. To tell the truth, we are incapable of seeing them as objects. What we see in them, through them, are the memories and emotions, the plans or regrets that we have attached to these things for a more or less lengthy period of time, sometimes forever. Now, this is the cinematographic mystery: an object such as this, with its personal character, that is to say, an object situated in a dramatic action that is equally photographic in character, reveals anew its moral character, its human and living expression when reproduced cinematographically.

I imagine a banker receiving bad news at home from the stock exchange. He is about to telephone. The call is delayed. Close-up of the telephone. If the shot of the telephone is shown clearly, if it is well-written, you no longer see a mere telephone. You read: ruin, failure, misery, prison, suicide. And in other circumstances, this same telephone will say: sickness, doctor, help, death, solitude, grief. And at yet another time this same telephone will cry gaily: joy, love, freedom.[19] All this may seem extremely simple; they may be regarded as childish symbols. I confess that it seems very mysterious to me that one can in this way charge the simple reflection of inert objects with an intensified sense of life, that one can animate it with its own vital import. Moreover, I confess that it seems much more important to me to concern ourselves with this phenomenon of cinematic telepathy than to cultivate two or three almost purely mechanical methods too exclusively.

M. Jean Choux, the film critic of the newspaper *La Suisse*, has written apropos of *Coeur fidèle* the lines that I reproduce below and they do not apply solely to this film.

"How close-ups deify. Oh, these faces of men and women displayed so harshly on screen, solid as enamel and more powerfully sculptural than the Michelangelo-esque creatures on the ceiling of the Sistine Chapel! To see a thousand immobile heads whose gazes are aimed at and monopolized and haunted by a single enormous face on the screen toward which they all converge. What an excruciating conversation. An idol and the crowd. Just like the cults in India. But here the idol is alive and this idol is a man. An extraordinary meaning is emitted from these close-ups. In them, the soul is extracted in the same way one isolates radium. The horror of living, its horror and mystery, is proclaimed. This pitiable Marie, this Jean, and this Petit-Paul, have they no other purpose than to be this Marie, this Jean, and this Petit-Paul? It's not possible! There must be something more."

Certainly there is something more.

Cinema is its herald.

★ ★ ★

Amour de Charlot

Translated by Jennifer Wild[20]

All critics, today, from all journals all over the world marvel at Charlot. He deserves perhaps a bit more than that.

In England – August 1914 – I saw one of his first films. Laughing entirely too loudly, I endured my neighbors' discourteous remarks. In those days I would have been stupefied that some might find a sad genius in Charlot. One critic from

L'Opinion – I have completely forgotten his by-line – had not yet recognized the Bergsonian essence of this comic. Stockpiles of cream pies smacked laughter right on his face. No sooner had twenty-eight shots of a revolver at point-blank range created a sense of malaise than a dive with both feet over the piano dissipated it. In those days Charlot was often drunk and always unrefined. He wasn't very honest, or courageous, or truly agile. He was a fiery man, deceitful, and sensuous. Just as in the Gospels of Childhood, playmates dropped dead as punishment for a practical joke. A drunken hiccup disrupted romantic meditations. With love in his heart, a bum no sooner lifted the skirt than mallet blows on the head settled into a series of fainting spells. There were quite a few dead men and a broken whiskey bottle. There was neither pity nor heroism. Drownings and betrayals, wicked deals where everyone was fooled, failed schemes, the right of the strongest, owners of overly strapping ladies, kisses that Charlot landed as knock-out blows. Ordeals, too.

This ordeal was entirely ridiculous. Everything backfired. We roared. It wasn't even sad, since it was well done. And Charlot was so crudely common that he didn't even garner admiration. Women, as I recall, loathed him. I loved him like a vice. It was a beautiful time.

Charlot has become resigned. He is less unhappy and much sadder. Since he hardly drinks, he is not able to forget the grief he has endured. Without alcohol, he is at the mercy of the worst affairs of the heart. Almost honest, devoted and unhappy, he now uses the mallet and the brick to pave his way to a love life, and these crude instruments poorly serve a passion that is almost speculative. But he has learned how to raise his eyes so sorrowfully that the hearts of beautiful girls capsize like small, over-loaded boats. The women catch him by surprise and vice versa. Then he is naïve and even dopey, each time a bit more so. Having frequented only disreputable bars and shady pastry shops for six years, his seductiveness is now that of a virgin. He can't even be accused of inspired love. Everything happens by chance. But if it's about goofing off or eyeballing something, he immediately regains his powers, becomes transparent and invisible, splits himself in two, displays tails when the coin shows heads, smiles and passes out. The chase goes haywire in the stairway. Three wrong directions converge under a table, leaving a total of three individuals blacked out. Except him, everyone takes the wrong door, picks the wrong pocket or opponent. Policemen run into each on the stairway landing. Saved by a ruse, Charlot's face indulges a sumptuous melancholy that is the luxury of safety conquered. The respite after battles leads to heartache. A distracted and desolate solemnity falls like the night. Iris. End.

Your people, o fair king, are not made up of critics who admire you. O doleful prince of a celluloid tale, we are three hundred million who love your heart swimming in the throes of passion.

★ ★ ★

Amour de Sessue

Translated by Mireille Dobrzynski and Stuart Liebman

> *"The will generates minds of a kind with which reasonable minds have nothing in common."*
> – Paracelsus

As foreigners, it would be a sacrilege if we could understand this notion of honor swathed in silk. In decent films in which kisses are implied, what do we understand? And what do we understand of you, dancer, waiting in the teahouse for five years, faithful to the postcard sent by your fiancé, a servant in Frisco, who is saving unheard of sums? The sweetness of honorable words and genuine manners, both thoroughly out of place in New York. Young girls kneel to read, vertically and from right to left, the great misfortunes that ocean liners import from across the Pacific. There, life is pitched in white contempt, and sometimes one is lucky enough to hold a boxer prisoner by just his little finger. And there, too, is the even paler laughter of American women who would never marry a man of color. As a student, it is about learning medicine without forgetting the ancestral gods and, just because it is termed a suicide, not losing the strength to perform hara-kiri after lighting the candles and carefully laying out the mat. So faithful is he to such a conception, stabbing himself if he fails, can we understand the nature of his vengeance?

This is beyond us, and yet so *cornélien*, if *cornélien* were not so closely associated with the *baccalauréat*.[21] Hayakawa, the Japanese actor long associated with *Forfaiture* [*The Cheat*, Cecil B. DeMille, 1915], alone lives according to what he ought to be. This excessive probity surprises us, kind and fun-loving daredevils that we are. His pride in the purity and pedigree of his style aims at a poetry that, without him, we are no longer capable of.

If comparisons are to be made with such a face, other actors, with the possible exception of Nazimova, do not fight with equal weapons. They begin from nothing, he from a repose that is already at the point of revealing everything. So much so that if he speaks, his words simply contribute to the breakdown of an immobility that is in itself expressive. Tragic, and like the symmetry of snow crystals, this eloquent stillness by nature yields to the thawing of an emotion that then becomes surprise, excess, relief from expectations: spring in the midst of ice. He hasn't performed yet and he has already dispensed with grand gestures. With this spontaneous expression, a blank check for unlimited amounts of sadness, he appears among extras who are suddenly swept away by his violent, forlorn silhouette. And he cannot shoot some pool or walk across a bedroom without our being deeply moved. What is strictly necessary and sufficient in a determined expression is reflected in his natural dramatic performance, which takes on a surprising perspective – indirectly and by chance – if not to say two things at once (or at least to speak vaguely).

He calls the young girl, and before leaving he gives her the god who has died for love as a keepsake. He extends his hand, halfway between the two of them; and he pulls it back, having torn through the distance between them with his twisted fingers. One leaves something. One takes something away. He closes a door. In the garden – even though the lawn lies between us – he listens to a voice with all his might, but not to any of the words. For him, when it stops, everything will be over. Then the close-up flares to challenge us; an eyebrow is raised, but it is still a part of the episode, the anecdote, and the game. A prodigious sense of persuasiveness comes over the room in question. Over and above a dramatic screenplay, the screen violently conveys a colossal horde of burning desires and continual worries, of spiritual things, that *photogénie* graces with holiness and poetic personality.

Neither comprehensible nor reasonable, it is sympathy itself.

Notes

1. The editors wish to give special thanks to Stuart Liebman for his careful reading of this translation and for writing the notes, with the exception of notes 9, 13-15, and 19-20, which were provided by Sarah Keller.
2. Material added at the end of the essay has been taken from the version of the last part of the Etna essay that was originally published as "Le Regard du verre," in *Les Cahiers du mois*, nos. 16/17 (1925): 9-12. These additions will be placed in footnotes.
3. Ricciotto Canudo (1879–1923) was an Italian poet and film theoretician active in France from the early 1900s. His manifesto, *The Birth of the Sixth Art*, published in 1911, argued that cinema was a synthetic "Seventh Art," "a superb conciliation of the Rhythms of Space (the Plastic Arts) and the Rhythms of Time (Music and Poetry)." In Paris, he established an avant-garde magazine *La Gazette de sept arts* in 1920, and one of the first independent film clubs, CASA (Club des amis du septième art) in 1921. *L'usine aux images*, a collection of his essays, was published posthumously in Paris and Geneva in 1927.
4. Paul Guichard served as Epstein's cameraman for his Etna documentary, *La Montagne infidèle*, as well as for several of his other films including *Coeur fidèle* (1923) and *La belle Nivernaise* (1924). He also filmed Germaine Dulac's shorts *L'Invitation au voyage* (1927) and *The Seashell and the Clergyman* (1928).
5. Epstein is referring to a famous quarry site near the Sicilian city of Syracuse where the rock formations, named after a legendary tyrannical ruler, amplify whispered sounds.
6. Jules de Gaultier (born 1858; died 1942) was a French philosopher and essayist, known especially for his theory of "bovarysme" (the name taken from Flaubert's novel), by which he meant the continual need of humans to invent themselves, to lie to themselves.

   On page 11 of "Le Regard du verre," Epstein introduced this paragraph in a slightly different way: "The lenses of the cinematographic eye possess two major original properties on which all cinematic art should depend. The first of these qualities is its analytic or psychoanalytic force (without any need to bring in Freud or Jules de Gaultier)."

7.   Jean-Marie-Mathias-Philippe-Auguste, comte de Villiers de l'Isle-Adam (1838–1889) was a French Symbolist writer and close friend of the poet Stéphane Mallarmé. He was perhaps best known for his novel L'Eve future (1886).

8.   On page 12 of "Le Regard du verre," Epstein concludes this part of the essay as follows: "But I do not wish to say that one ought to work in cinema by following certain theories, neither these nor any others. The symphonies of movement that have lately become à la mode, are now very irritating. Caligarism only offers photographs neither better nor worse than those in the Salon des Artistes Français. Pretentious styles appear as soon as inventiveness ceases, in cubism as much as in 'rapid' montage, or in the sort of cinematic subjectivism that has become ridiculous because of its use of superimpositions. One can only write if you yourself feel and think. I would like to board each of my films the way a traveler does who arrives at the next to last minute with six trunks still to register, a ticket to buy and a seat to locate. He leaves, but does he know where he is going? God's grace is the sole timetable without slip-ups. He arrives in the country of surprises. It is the land that has been promised to us."

9.   This chapter first appeared in translation by Tom Milne as "On Certain Characteristics of Photogénie," Afterimage, no. 10 (Autumn 1981): 20-23; it was reprinted in Abel1, pp. 314-318, and appears here with minor changes by Stuart Liebman.

10. Louis Delluc (1890-1924) was one of the first film critics in France to publish a daily column, as well as collections of his essays on the cinema. By 1920, he turned to scriptwriting and directing. Epstein served as his assistant on the film Le Tonnerre (1921).

11. The pre-Socratic Greek philosopher Zeno (490-430 B.C.) was famous for creating paradoxes about, among other things, motion, distance, and time.

12. Epstein uses the term cinégraphiste, a synonym for a film director, but one very aware of the graphic dimension of cinema, which was often used in French critical discourse during the late 1910s and 1920s. He thereby establishes a parallel between a cinema artist and the "draftsman" (dessinateur) in the first part of the sentence.

13. Literally this title is translated as "Golden Language," which Epstein takes up in the essay; it also echoes Langue d'oc (a dialect associated with southern France) and its counterpart of Langue d'oïl (the dialect from which modern French is derived), sounding out Epstein's interest in the localizable facets of a global/universal language.

14. The so-called "law of three unities," – it regulates a play's action, place, and time – was first sketched by Aristotle in his Poetics, and ultimately received its most restrictive, "neo-classical" form in seventeenth-century France in the works of Molière and Racine. The concepts held that a play should have one main action, with no or few subplots; it should be staged in a single physical space and not represent more than one place. Finally, the action should occur over no more than 24 hours. Epstein's own cinematic practice, as well as that of many of his contemporaries, radically contested this "law."

15. This chapter first appeared in translation by Tom Milne as "The Photogenic Element," *Afterimage*, no. 10 (Autumn 1981): 23-27, and is reprinted here with minor corrections by Stuart Liebman.

16. This chapter first appeared in translation by Stuart Liebman as "For a New Avant-Garde," in *The Avant-Garde Film: A Reader of Theory and Criticism*, ed. P. Adams Sitney (New York: New York University Press, 1978),pp. 26-30; it was reprinted in *Abel1*, pp. 349-353, and appears here with minor corrections by Liebman.

17. Francis Poictevin (1854-1904) was a minor French Symbolist writer and notorious dandy who served as the model for the character Des Esseintes in Joris-Karl Huysman's famous novel. *À rebours* (1884), translated into English either as *Against the Grain* or *Against Nature*. http://fr.wikipedia.org/wiki/Joris-Karl_Huysmans.

18. The Swiss francophone poet and novelist Blaise Cendrars (1887-1961), Epstein's early mentor, helped him publish his first books on French poetry (*La Poésie d'aujourd'hui*, 1921) and the cinema (*Bonjour cinema*, 1921) with the avant-garde Parisian house Éditions de la Sirène. Cendrars also wrote several early essays on film in the late 1910s and early 1920s that were eventually published in his *L'ABC du cinema* (Paris: Les Écrivains Réunis 1926).

19. Epstein is here outlining an intuition of what Lev Kuleshov and Vsevolod Pudovkin demonstrated in their "Mosjoukine Experiment."

20. Special thanks are due to Anne Magnan-Park for her insightful assistance.

21. The French adjective *cornélien* refers to a situation in which love and duty conflict. The term derives from the French dramatist, Pierre Corneille (1606-1684), whose works famously stage dilemmas that force characters to choose between passion and honor, and then to suffer the tragic and inevitable consequences of their choice. Epstein disparages the term's superficial popularity among the French *baccaulauréat* exams.

L'intelligence d'une machine

Introduction

L'intelligence d'une machine was published in January 1946, after more than a ten-year hiatus due to the war, when Epstein had to go in hiding. While the topic reflected in the title of the book had been a constant preoccupation throughout Epstein's previous writings, this text pursues in depth topics that will remain central to all his later publications. He here approaches cinema as a philosophy of time and space more consistently than before, and methodically construes arguments in the field of physics, mechanics, and thermodynamics. The concept of photogénie loses much of the importance it had in earlier writings, and references to film examples are almost absent. Instead, he searches in cinema for an intelligence and a philosophy of time other than those based on our brute sense impression. Because this discourse is far away from that of most "Impressionist" and avant-garde theory, his later writings have often been overlooked in France as well as abroad, where few of the post-war publications have been translated until now.
– Trond Lundemo

Excerpts from *L'Intélligence d'une machine* [1946]

Translated by Trond Lundemo

[Jean Epstein, *L'Intelligence d'une machine* (Paris: Éditions Jacques Melot, 1946). Selections reprinted in ESC1: pp. 310-16.]

The Philosophy of the Cinematograph

Cinema is one of these intellectual robots, still partial, that fleshes out representations – that is to say, a thought – through photo-electrical mechanics and a photo-chemical inscription. One can here recognize the primordial frameworks of reason, the three Kantian categories of space, duration, and causality. This result would already be remarkable if cinematographic thought only did what the calculating machine does, to constitute itself in the servile imitation of human ideation. But we know that the cinematograph, on the contrary, marks its representation of the universe with its own qualities, with an originality that makes this representation not a reflection or a simple copy with conceptions, of an organic mentality-mother, but rather a system that is individualized differently, partly independently, which contains the incitements for a philosophy so far from common opinions, the doxa, that one should perhaps call it an anti-philosophy.

★ ★ ★

Quantity, Mother of Quality

Indivisibility of space-time
The fundamental difference between the human intellectual mechanism and the cinematographic mechanism of apprehension and expression is, in the first case, that notions of space and time can exist separately, and that the human mechanism even demands an effort to conceive of their perpetual union. And in the second case, every representation of space is automatically given with its dimension in time. This means that space is inconceivable outside of its movement in time. Consequently, man can keep the image of a posture or the memory of an utterance present in the mind for several seconds or longer if his attention doesn't get tired, as if its duration didn't exist. The cinematograph, however, cannot furnish the same image or sound without a temporal rhythm, usually adjusted to twenty-two or twenty-three images per second. In human comprehension, there is space and there is time, out of which a synthesis of space-time is hard to construct. In the cinematographic comprehension, there is only space-time.

Absolute relativism
We know that cinematographic time is essentially variable, while temporal rhythm as normally perceived by man is, by contrast, constant: yet another difference between the intellect of the living being and that of the mechanical being, which remarkably reinforces the former. Against static space and invariable time – usually considered independent from each other and, as such, forming the two primordial, classical categories of human understanding – is opposed space-time, which is always mobile and changing, the unique frame within which the cinematograph inscribes its representations.

The variation of cinematographic time and the interdependence that connects it with its space bring forth continuous transformations correlative to all the shapes located in this four-dimensional continuum. This most general relativity is conveyed by the rupture and confusion of all the seemingly fundamental and solid classifications of the extra-cinematographic universe. According to the various momentary forms taken by the space-time dimensions, discontinuity may become continuous or continuity discontinuous, stillness produces movement and movement stillness, matter may acquire a mind or lose one, the static may be animated or the living frozen, chance may be determined or what is certain may lose its causes, ends may become origins, and evident truths may be immediately perceived as absurdities.

These changes in primordial qualities depend on variations of the duration and size of the observed objects in relation to their point of reference, which is the one closest to the observing subject – the human scale. Quality is a consequence of measurement, of numbers. Quality results from quantity. Quantity and quality become correlative and interchangeable notions, which must be able to merge with each other in a quantitative-qualitative continuity, co-variable with the continuity of space-time. Accordingly, the philosophy of the cinematograph only sees one principle in Aristotle's second and third attributes.

[...]

Man, the only measure of quantity in the universe

If, at the root of things, every differentiation only has a quantitative signification, only some idea of the size of phenomena remains as the foundation of their distinction, classification, and knowledge. An object, being, or event is positioned in its qualitative realm of space, time, and logic according to its dimensions. Actually, space is straight or curved, matter is continuous or discontinuous, the mechanical is determined or given to chance, laws are causal or probabilistic, dependent upon whether one studies [these things] on a scale that is medium, infinitely small, or infinitely large.

However, this immensity, or happy medium, or smallness of things – these are all always evaluated with reference to man. It is the scale of man and the dimensions immediately useful to him that decides the measurement, according to which one values every size, number, and quantity. It is only the distance applied to a phenomenon, departing from human dimensions, that makes it small or big, and which determines the spatial, temporal, and logical areas where it takes place. Consequently, the complete relativity of every aspect of nature has only one point of departure, only one point of reference, only one judge: man, or rather, the height, weight, and shape of man, the length of his extremities, the orientation of his vision and hearing.

All our systems of knowledge, all our science and all our philosophy, all our convictions and doubts, all our eternal truths and ignorance are exactly adjusted to this average height of one hundred and seventy centimeters at which we carry our foreheads above the ground. One may doubt that the disposition of Cleopatra's nose has changed the face of the earth, since love is not always oriented towards beauty. But surely other theodicies and cosmogonies, a different mathematics and logic could function with a human race reduced to the size of bacteria or inflated to the size of the Himalayas.

All constructions of thought only admit as their final criterion the human dimension, of which we feel the episodic and precarious character. This shows the scandalous vanity of our pretensions and the impotence of our need to hold on to a stable ground outside of us, to a small scrap of absolute certainty, to a hint of the presence of stable existence. All the efforts of the intelligence to escape the relative are as embarrassingly futile and absurd as the attempt of someone who is drowning in quicksand to pull himself up by his hair. Man is the only measurement of the universe, but this measurement is itself measured by what it purports to measure: it is the relative of relativity, an absolute variable.

Relativity of Logic

The incredible reversibility of time
The reversibility of time is a possibility confirmed by cinema's representation of the universe and constitutes a major difference in relation to the properties of our usual universe. This reversibility appears so rarely and is so completely foreign to all our exterior experiences that it seems incredible to our mental faculties. It seems a pure game of the machine, an artificial and comical appearance without any real significance compared with the invariable order of succession observed everywhere else. Still, whether one likes it or not, temporal reversibility takes place in cinematic representation with a regularity that makes it a principle of this system, as certain as any principle may be. We have difficulties in understanding that the principles of identity and rigorous causality cease to be applicable in the world of atoms. Still, we listen to the arguments of physicists, no matter how subtle their theories are. By contrast, even if the cinematograph visually proves to us, with a much stronger evidentiary force, the ambivalence of the order in which phenomena happen on the world of the screen, and even if this world is closer and better known to us than the world of atoms, we hesitate to devote the slightest attention to the reversibility of filmed actions. The cinematic world – one says with contempt – is only a fictional world.

Legitimacy of fiction
However, fictional doesn't mean false or nonexistent. Nobody could deny the practical usefulness of the work of the imagination. "Everything one invents is true," Flaubert affirmed. Even if everything one invents weren't true, it would become so. Today, most psychologists and psychiatrists, be they supporters or adversaries of Freud, recognize that the imaginary world *par excellence* – the dream – holds a superior psychological truth compared to objectified and ostensibly realistic extroverted and rationalized thought. When freed of most of the logical and

moral limitations of outer life, the personality of the dreamer can actually manifest itself more freely and reveal its intimate nature in dream-images.

The cinematograph, machine of dreams
The procedures employed by the discourse of the dream, allowing for a profound sincerity, have their analogies in cinematographic style.

One very common kind of synecdoche, where the part stands for the whole, works this way. A detail, in itself minimal and banal, is magnified and repeated, and becomes the center and the driving force of a whole scene as it is dreamt or seen on the screen. This could be, for example, a key, a knotted ribbon [nœud de ruban], or a telephone, which the dream or the screen shapes into a close-up, and which is charged with immense emotional force as well as all the dramatic signification attributed to this object when it was noticed for the first time in waking life or at the beginning of the film.

Further, and consequently, in the language of dreams as in the language of cinema, these image-words undergo a transposition of meaning, a symbolization. It is no longer a matter of key, ribbon, or telephone. The key could more correctly be translated as, "Do I dare to commit this indiscretion required for my rest?"; the ribbon as, "She loved me so!"; the telephone as, "By now he must be out of danger." But the real truth is that these signs are scribbles [grimoires] summing up a whole universe of impressions, lived, living, and to be lived, that no verbal expression could convey in their entirety.

Finally, the action of the dream, like that of the film, unrolls each at its own pace, cut up and reconnected again ad libitum, where the simultaneous can be drawn out to succession, and the successive can be compressed and happen at the same time, to the extent that the difference from exterior time may go all the way to inversion.

The prejudice against the dream of a machine
The magnification and allegorization of details, the growth and transformation of the signification value of these symbols, the particularity of time: all these analogies between the language of dreams and the language of the cinematograph should lead us to believe that the two are constitutionally predisposed to express highly faithful psychological truths with a deep exactitude in the figuration of mental life.

But, on the contrary, this is perhaps what causes or strengthens the general skepticism one can see towards the philosophical disposition of cinematographic images. The completely introverted dream life, in spite of it being infinitely richer in emotions and sincerity, is seen as dangerous, damned, and inferior to mental waking life, which after all is only a quite banal, extroverted schematization of the former.

Le Cinéma du diable

Introduction

Epstein discusses film in light of great technical discoveries that have been questioning political institutions, scientific and religious dogmas since the Middle Ages. Celebrating the rebellious spirit which lies at the crux of the printing press, the astronomical lens, and medical dissection, Epstein provocatively states, "Evil should be considered a benefactor to humankind." In the wake of these breakthroughs, the cinematographer sets the base of a libertarian philosophy inspired by evil, for the optical device magnifies movement in its slightest variations and reveals photogénie. Cinema exerts a subversion of literature, reason, and logic alike by exposing the viewer to a new universal language. Influenced by the latest developments in quantum physics, Epstein devises a conception of cinema that expresses the relativity of space and time through the use of editing, close-ups, slow motion, and time lapse. The last section of the text develops a contrary stance: despite its "evil" nature, cinema should also be regarded as a cathartic experience for the masses. According to Epstein, the cinematic spectacularization of violence and subversion is necessary because it neutralizes the viewer's negative impulses and therefore reinforces the stability of the social body. Le Cinéma du diable thus poses a challenging paradox: while the film medium is intrinsically and historically subversive, it should also be used as a conservative device that aims at social control.[1]

– Ludovic Cortade

* * *

Indictment

Translated by Franck Le Gac

[Jean Epstein, "Accusation," Le Cinéma du diable (Paris: Éditions Jacques Melot, 1947), pp. 11-20.]

Up to the years 1910 to 1915, going to the cinema constituted a somewhat shameful, almost debasing act, and no person of quality ventured into it until pretexts had been found and excuses made. Since then, the spectacle of cinema has undoubtedly earned a few titles in nobility or snobbishness. Meanwhile, to this day, the arrival of a fairground cinema stirs trouble and disapproval among honorable people in some counties. There are even some small towns whose scarce and struggling theaters remain disreputable places where the local reputable citizenry would not be seen without embarrassment.

In truth, in this mid-twentieth century, few people even among believers dare speak the Devil's name, so deft has the trickster been at exploiting the blunders of both his enemies and followers in order to shroud himself in a thick veil of ridicule – not unlike the way hands have to dabble in ink to get to the cuttlebone. Yet how many moralists, even non-believers, loudly claim that cinema is a school of stupefaction, vice, and crime! In Christian terms, what does that amount to, if not the idea that the phantasmagorias of the screen are inspired by the devil to defile humankind?

Should it come as a surprise, in fact, that the Devil is taken as the instigator of the moving image, since he has so often been held responsible for other achievements of human ingenuity? Diabolical, the invention of the telescope which, as he foresaw, caused Roger Bacon to be thrown in jail for twenty years; which exposed the old Galileo to the severity of the ecclesiastical court and to imprisonment; and which terrified the cautious Copernicus to his deathbed. Diabolical, the invention of printing, whose pernicious use religious authorities and their secular counterparts rushed to control immediately – for long centuries and counting. Diabolical, the study of the human body and medicine, condemned by St. Ambrose; anatomy and dissection, banned and punished with excommunication by Boniface VIII. Diabolical, da Vinci's secret plans and his dreams for a machine that would rise up in the air. Tricks of the demon, automatons, be they the work of a saint, shattered to pieces by another saint; the first steamboat, which Papin could not spare from the terrified wrath of a fanaticized people; the first automobile, Cugnot's *fardier*, a steam car which met with a similar fate; the first hot-air balloons, which pious countrymen tore to shreds with their pitchforks; the first railroads, which illustrious scientists accused of spreading plague and madness; and finally – to put a stop to an enumeration that may go on forever – the cinematograph.

In this medieval mindset, which has not completely disappeared, the Devil appears as the great inventor, the master of discovery, the prince of science, the toolmaker of civilization, the master of ceremonies for what is called progress. Thus, since the most widespread opinion holds the development of culture as a notable benefit, the Devil should mainly be considered as a benefactor of humankind. However, faith has not yet gotten over the divorce that separated it from science, which remains suspect in the judgment of many believers and is often cursed as the impious work of the rebellious spirit.

JEAN EPSTEIN

In primitive society, priest and scientist at first were one. Then, as religion froze its doctrine into dogmas allowing for little variation, science evolved by formulating propositions farther and farther apart from the traditions of theodicy. The disagreement came to tear the spirit into two enemy parts. Through force or persuasion, through the authority of revelation or the subtlety of reasoning, humans long tried to re-form the original unity of their knowledge, both supernatural and natural, either by seeking to subject science to religion, or by trying to reconcile the two harmoniously. That was in vain. Faith repudiated science; science excluded faith. And who, over the course of centuries, enticed a number of orthodox magicians onto a heretical path, turning them into black sorcerers with obscure alchemists for students, the forerunners of lucid scientists? Who if not God's enemy, Satan?

More specifically, the Devil found himself accused of continuously renewing human instruments. In fact, tools have exerted a decisive influence on the evolution of thought that saw cosmogony rise up against theology. As a general rule, each time humans create an instrument after their own idea, the instrument in turn and in its own way reshapes the mentality of its creator.

If, with the help of the Devil, humans invented the telescope, the telescope invented the images of the sky, which compelled Copernicus, Galileo, Kepler, Newton, Laplace, and so many others to think in a certain way rather than another: after these images and not after others. Without a telescope to animate and direct their intelligence, these discoverers could not have discovered anything, nor could they have produced any of their grand theories; and most likely, we would still imagine the earth as immobile, set in an inextricable entanglement of stars revolving around it. In equal measure, the optical mechanism of lenses and the intuitive and deductive organism of humans have played a role in establishing the Copernican system, the laws of Kepler, and a whole magnificent movement of thought that resulted in the current Einsteinian relativism, beyond which it will probably keep expanding.

This scientific and philosophical movement – one of the most important in the history of culture – has mostly been fueled and guided by constantly new appearances collected by telescopes in the peripheral, astronomical universe since the fifteenth century. This effort aims to explore the realm of the infinitely great, and has given rise to a vast metaphysics which should be called a metaphysics of the telescope, for telescopic and macroscopic instruments of this kind play the role of primordial operators in it. Indeed, the existence and use of an instrument is at the root of the immense, immeasurable difference between stages in the general philosophical, religious, and psychological development of a contemporary of Ptolemy and a contemporary of Einstein (a difference that exists from a certain point of view, which encompasses a very wide range of the mind).

A second, large body of scientific and philosophical doctrines originated in another type of instrument – the microscope. Without the microscope, for instance, there would probably not have been any microbes or microbial theories: no pasteurization or glory for Pasteur. There again, lenses provide – that is, they produce – images, select them in order to make them visible within the invisible, separate them from what will remain unknowable, suddenly raise them from non-appearance and non-being to the rank of perceptible realities. And this first selection, on which the whole ulterior development of thought depends, is the product of the instrument alone, according to the arbitrary law of its particular similarities and receptivity. A given magnification and a given coloring make a given form appear, a form out of which a new conception will emerge. If observers did not have this magnification or this coloring at their disposal, the form they derive from formlessness would never be promoted into existence, nor would its theory. And another magnification and another coloring would present a different appearance, leading to a different medicine, to other cures perhaps. The instrument, which in time may more or less be controlled, at its inception involves a completely random empiricism that directs thought according to the data it does or does not provide.

Stemming from the examination of the microcosm, an ideological current developed later but at a phenomenal pace, yielding today's quantum physics and wave mechanics – both systems which will manifest their force of expansion for a long time to come. This movement of thought receives its impetus and its primary orientation from perpetually renewed appearances, which have been for scarcely a hundred years collected by microscopes, ultramicroscopes, electronic hyper-microscopes, spectroscopes, etc., from the so-called central universe: cellular and nuclear, molecular and atomic. In this instance, the goal is to discover the infinitesimal, and multiple biological and ultraphysical speculations have come out of this in-depth exploration. They constitute the group of what should be referred to as the philosophies of the magnifier, since this type of instrument is their main operator.

There is a hierarchy in the world of machines. Not all of them are key instruments such as those of enlarging or magnifying optics, whose influence stimulated and transformed the life of ideas as a whole. But there are no tools, as humble as they might be, whose use has not more or less marked our mentality and our customs in the long term. Undoubtedly, the cinematographic instrument itself reshapes the mind that designed it. The question in this case, rather, is whether the reaction of the creation to the creator has a quality and magnitude that justify a suspicion of participation in the diabolical work perpetually opposed to traditional permanence.

In this instance, it is not only about the superficial mischief denounced in accusations of immorality against such-and-such film restricted to audiences sixteen and older, which has nothing specifically cinematographic to it. The genuine trial of the moving image introduces problems of a more general scope. Does the cinematograph belong in this category of machines, of operators that, like the telescope and the microscope, discovered vast original horizons in the universe, of which we would know nothing without these mechanisms? Is it able to bring within the range of our perceptions domains so far unexplored? Are these new representations bound to become the source of an intellectual current so deep and wide-ranging that it could alter the whole climate in which thought moves, that it could deserve the title of philosophy of the cinematograph? Finally, if the screen truly announces its advent, is this philosophy part of the anti-dogmatic, revolutionary, and libertarian – diabolical, in a word – lineage already comprising the philosophies of the telescope and the magnifying glass?

The answers to these questions are not self-evident, as the cinematograph is only fifty years of age and has wasted three quarters of this half-century, in a sense, providing public entertainment, believing it was just an art of spectacle, duplicating the novel and the theater, becoming an industry and a commerce, neglecting the development or even the plain acknowledgment of all its other, less lucrative powers. This gilded make-up and the moving eloquence of the "seventh art" were not able, however, to completely conceal a few signs that let us know that the ghosts of the screen may have something else to impart to us than their fables of laughs and tears: a new conception of the universe and new mysteries in the soul. The reprobation of professional virtue-mongers with their petty scandals conveys an immense, deep-rooted anxiety in the style of the common morality – yet one whose signification can no longer find its full expression. Still, a few of these upholders of the present order know that their tremor of fear and indignation does not only owe to a richly sensual image. Their fear comes from farther away and encompasses more: it can sense the monster of novelty, of creation, pregnant with all the fast-transforming heresy of a continuous evolution.

Let us open the proceedings. The cinematograph pleads guilty.

★ ★ ★

To a Second Reality, a Second Reason

Translated by Sarah Keller

[Jean Epstein, "A seconde réalité, second raison," *Le cinéma du diable* (Paris: Éditions Jacques Melot, 1947), pp. 219-233]

That the senses deceive is the most clichéd platitude. It implies that reason – which one also calls common sense – can in unreliable data discover and correct errors committed by five or ten other deficient senses. If the lesson we have been taught by the cinema had to be boiled down to one sentence, it would be this: in its own way, reason deceives us as much as the senses. Our conclusion, itself powerfully logical: how can reason, which works with the results of a deceived sensibility's experience, yield anything other than a quintessence of misconceptions?

Behaving like a complex, sensorial super-organ, the cinematograph provides new images of the world, which reason suspects at first of falseness, even more than it would with organic and natural data. Nevertheless, though working with information received secondhand, as a sub-part of the brain, reason likes to present itself as some manner of super-reason, with the authority to overturn the judgments arrived at by simple reason on the grounds that, because they are ill-informed, they are therefore incorrect.

Thus, in the most general way, thanks to the *photogénie* of movement, the cinematograph shows us that form is only one unsettled state of a fundamentally mobile condition, and that movement, being universal and variably variable, makes every form inconstant, inconsistent, fluid. Solids suddenly find their supremacy threatened; they are but one particular genre of appearances within systems of ordinary experience on a human scale, which are either in constant motion or only slightly and uniformly varying. Fluidity – the reality of the cinematographic experience – is also the reality of a scientific outlook, which sees in every substance a gaseous structure.

Another important difference between the notions of first reason and second reason is due to the extreme manner in which the cinema mobilizes spatial relations, which is another aspect of the *photogénie* of movement. On the screen, the part can be equal to or greater than the whole. This seemingly absurd correlation, inadmissible to common sense, must nonetheless be admitted as valid, not only in the cinematographic domain, but also in the realm of the greatest mathematical generality, that of set theory.

A third, critical difference between the reality that is directly perceptible and the reality of the screen, and between the two corresponding kinds of reasoning, again stems from the *photogénie* of movement when it functions in a temporal perspective. As is its custom, the screen presents events in a rhythm of successions more or less rapid than that of normal observation. The ability to discern either the acceleration or slowing of one world in relation to another presupposes a constant speed of movement, common to both, which allows us to establish a comparison. Indeed, this constant does exist: the speed of light. Moreover, this speed – because we don't know any greater velocity and because it guarantees practically instant transmission of every signal – universally serves to mark the present as the starting point for every series, the zero coordinate of time. When an electric discharge occurs in a stormy atmosphere, we know it first by lightning, then by thunder, because the light travels through space faster than sound. It is this quantitative difference in the speed of travel that separates the lightning from the thunder, creating a separation, an interval, a relief, a perspective which we call time, which we believe to be time. If every message that reached us construed the spatial distance in exactly the same way, we wouldn't be able to identify a notion of time as distinct from space. Between the sight and the sound of a soccer ball bouncing beside us, we note no passage of time. Between the sight and sound of the same ball falling a few hundred meters from us, we already observe a slight lapse in time. This can only be the result of what is different in the two experiences. And yet what has changed is simply a spatial distance.

It's not that, from this perspective, time doesn't exist; rather, it's the allegorization of a certain way of negotiating distance, of a certain action in space, which we estimate by comparing it with the displacement of light. And if the cinematograph manages to create new temporalities, it is precisely because it knows, through acceleration and slow-motion, how to modify the relationship usually observed between the natural movement of people and things and the standard displacement of rays of light. Here, too, time amounts to being only the space consumed, through a quantitative difference with the consumption of space by light. However, in this case, there isn't a virgin space, a place of nothingness where no thing resides, nothing happens. The expanse exists only insofar as it has been traveled; it is space that has been acted upon, traveled through, negotiated; it exists only if it is also time.

In both reality and in classical models, space and time constitute two separate frameworks, where things coexist or occur in series following an unchanging order. Here, phenomena can be localized and assessed with certainty, through means of a system of fixed sizes linked to an absolute standard. This absolute determinism, this *fixisme*, stems from the fact that here, space and time, which constantly remain as they are, condition a continuity or a discontinuity always equal to itself in all its points, in all its moments. When there is movement in this homogenous domain, it can only be uniform movement or uniformly accelerated or slowed down. As a result of the limited degree of these variations and the slowness with which they occur, this movement grants forms a relative permanence and gives the field in which they exist an apparent symmetry. There derives from all of this an ideology whose multiple branches, while they may contradict each other on a host of points, are all in agreement as to being, in general terms, philosophies of solidity and permanence.

For example, in matters of religion, there is but an immutable God, which is the ultimate conceit, but a conceit to which everything relates and from which everything receives its prize of being unvarying for all eternity. Mathematics, at this stage, is the science of finite numbers only, wherein the Greeks endeavored to exclude any suspicion of the infinite with a trepidation that still resurfaces among many of our contemporaries when confronted with anything that doesn't calculate precisely. Euclidian geometry isn't conceivable anywhere other than in a solid world, in the experiential framework within which it was born. If our habitat were not on terra firma, but were liquid or gaseous, if a Euclid of fish or bird intelligence had composed works of aquametry or aerometry, we wouldn't have such rigorous notions about sea swells or the symmetry of the winds. All physics taught in the schools – even when it deals with liquids or gases, to say nothing of radiation – takes the law of solids both as its point of departure and its culmination. Moreover, the very concept of laws implies permanence and rigidity. All science is but a search for this permanence, for an invariable law of relations bridging the changes in things, and that remains immutable at the very heart of that which isn't stable.

In cinematographic representation, space and time indissolubly unite to make a space-time framework in which things coexist or succeed each other in an order and at a pace that can be variable to the point of reversibility. There, in order to define phenomena, there are only systems of shifting relationships that cannot be linked to any fixed value. This nearly total mobility, this general relativity, defines a domain that does not always remain as it has been. Continuity on screen is heterogeneous, because the movement that reigns there is not only variable but variable in an unpredictable fashion, variable with inconstancy, variable to the point of being able to reach relatively enormous accelerations and decelerations that can profoundly alter the nature of first reality. In such a domain of movement, the form is not retained; symmetry disappears. Two instantaneous, successive shapes of the same object cease to be super-imposable. From this is born an ideology that cannot be based on the experience of a world of solids: it is rather a philosophy of the fluid, where nothing and no one are what they are, but become, rather, whatever they become. In this sense, one could say that the cinematographic universe is Sartrean, but its existentialism isn't limited to psychology and morality; it is also and foremost physical, geometrical, mathematical, and logical.

In a universe where everything moves and changes, one risks losing all sense of rule, apart from those laws defining this mobility and change. This may explain why one already sees some slack in the defining relations of ultra-physics and ultra-mechanics, which have become more flexible. In the infinitely small, as in the cinematographic universe, the invariable has been eclipsed, which may point to its uselessness and portend its disappearance. The scholar, the philosopher, and the cineaste all wonder with deep worry what the power of the mind will be in worlds where permanent structures that seem necessary to any kind of knowledge are loosening, dissolving, and fading away. Probably, like a last haven of limited security, there will remain the law above all laws, the law of large numbers: probability. Except that this is not a true invariable, but a substitute, or expedient, presented in the form of a limit that is more or less problematic in terms of variance. It is not a law that characterizes an order; instead it is an indication of the failings of the absence of laws, which reveals the deficiencies that prevent us from perfecting disorder.

It isn't surprising that people are anxious as they realize the importance of change in their own experience and thought. Again, so long as the new reality seemed destined to remain a rarity, one limited to laboratories where it was produced at great cost and effort, its revolutionary influence seemed interesting only to a small number of the most learned speculators, whose theories could hardly have an appreciable impact on practical life, on common sense. But all of a sudden there is Hiroshima, Nagasaki, the Bikini islands, with the splitting of atoms suddenly emerging in human customs and morals, bringing far more than the power of a weapon of war – the proof that all we have imagined of the strange organization of the infinitely small is not an utterly wild dream. And then there is Freudian therapy affirming, through the criterion of usefulness, the existence of a deep soul in which the eccentricities of behavior are no longer imaginary, either. And finally there is the cinema, which, playfully it sometimes seems, publicly translates the universe through forms even more confused, more preposterous than all those that scholars managed secretly to guess. Atom-splitting, psychoanalysis, cinema – this grouping, though disparate in appearance, combines three methods of accessing a second reality where rational logic may well not suffice.

It is necessary, however, to point out that this irrationalism now appearing on the cultural horizon is in fact excessively rational and, in a sense, even more rational than the Cartesian method of blind and exclusive faith in the infallible rightness of rational judgment. It is reason itself, in fact, that warns us of its own disadvantages. It is the critique effected by the second reason that reveals the gaps and abuses of the first reason. If a certain public acutely feels the development of irrationalism in the contemporary mentality as a danger, we must also recognize that the despotic expansion of logic that has characterized thought in the preceding centuries has also been fraught with peril.

Though necessary at first, it is misguided to try to rationalize everything, to analyze everything and reduce everything to an abstraction; to attempt everywhere to separate the thing from its attribute, the form from movement, the object from its number; to coerce the mind into valuing only that part of itself formulated according to the classical rules of spoken and written expression. Vocabulary, grammar, and syntax are the machinery with which we translate ideas, which are above all images. But this machinery cannot function without betraying the thought-image: without misrepresenting it; without either impoverishing it or weighing it down; without simplifying it or overloading it, alienating its original sense and sincerity. The more a sentence is a sentence, the more beautifully formed it is, the more it risks being a thick accumulation of lies. From Racine to Valéry, the great art of the writer is the game that has become increasingly difficult in which, according to the rules, he requires the reader to guess the emotions the text hides while claiming to express them. That in the end, nine out of ten readers may not understand anything, or understand whatever comes to their minds, is the ultimate achievement of this style. The author's thought and the psychology of his characters are just word games.

Thus language transformed that wild and shadowy habitat for feeling that is poetry into a French garden, drawn geometrically, fallaciously clear, and then led it to degenerate into a fallaciously obscure labyrinth just as much as a perfectly ordered masterpiece, and definitively purged of all sincere emotion. In scientific and philosophical domains, where the sentimental trend develops with less force, rational thinking has made out even better. Words have proliferated like a cancer, spreading a Taoist nominalism, casting a veritable magic through which it is enough to name a thing to bring it into being. The first concrete reality is nothing more than a memory of a distant starting point for so many systems that reason derives from itself, and, having never met its own image, it takes this reflection as if it were a certified copy.

All of this is too specious for it to last indefinitely. Over the last few dozen years, there have emerged islands of another, scandalous reality – a reality that refuses to conform precisely to a rational framework. There, logical thought finds itself disoriented and at times impotent. The game of induction and deduction misfires, fails. To understand the innovation in the structure of things, we need innovation in the nature and organization of our thought processes as well. In returning to the concrete – but to a second form of concreteness – we develop and restore to favor an ancient mode of thinking through images and analogies, through visual representations and metaphor, which had fallen nearly into obsolescence. This analogical and metaphoric order pervades the more narrowly rational order, adding to it but not necessarily destroying it, much as a knight on a chessboard, with its indirect, bounding progress, makes its way rectilinearly through other pieces that advance in straight lines, and joins with them to complete an overall strategic position.

The majority of the islands of the new reality are difficult to access. Only shrewd physicists and audacious psychiatrists manage to get to them – and only by breaking in. Only cinema invites the general public in. To even moderately attentive viewers, the screen shows at least a hint of the fluid and metalogical universe, of a mobility with four variables, of a becoming that conforms to no standards, of a reality that is just an inconstant association among numerous movements. And even the inattentive spectator receives from film a mental orientation that encourages him to think outside of rational, grammatical, and syntactic rigor, estranged from and on the margin of words, beyond and before them, to think according to the sentimental and magical mystique of images.

If this mystique is dangerous because it draws on what is deepest and most human in mankind, because it stirs the best and the worst of the soul's secret powers – well then, the cinematograph is dangerous and it's high time people began reacting. Already, the book – that ultimate synthesizer of classical language – let itself get contaminated: it is now ashamed of an overwritten, overly correct text, as if this were equivalent to lying. Already, the newspapers present their accounts rendered like "films" of this or that, composed in a telegraphic style, in which, moreover, as many words as possible are replaced by pictures. Already, walls abound with posters meant to be understood by passers-by who don't have to stop or slow down, and which employ all methods of the moving image: close-ups, superimpositions, parts bigger than the whole, etc. In frequenting the cinemas, the public have unlearned to read and think as they read or write; it grows accustomed to looking and thinking as simply as it sees. Among producers of films, the word "visualizing" became fashionable for some years. In fact, there is no better way to characterize film than by saying it visualizes thought. Thus, after the craftsman and the scholar, one sees the spectator appearing, a new sub-variety of reasoning being. The knowledge acquired through slow, abstract, rigorous reasoning has been pervaded by knowledge gained directly through feelings, one that is immediate, practical, and supple – a kind of poetry that we acquire above all through what we see. Paradoxically, the return to the concrete is also a return to the mystical, to the mystique of a beauty, a goodness, a truth that is no longer immutable but perpetually moving, always relative, and infinitely transformable. The old battle between the Ancients and Moderns ceases to be undecided. The new man of the street, the new average French person, has taken the side of mutability over fixed forms, of becoming over permanence. And, certainly, the cinema has played a role in this. If this is a work of the Devil, well then, cinema is diabolical, and it's already too late to declare holy war against it, for that war has already been lost.

Note

1. For a detailed examination of *Le Cinéma du diable*, see my article, "*Cinéma du diable*: Jean Epstein and the Ambiguities of Subversion," SubStance 34, no. 3 (2005): 3-16.

Later Works

Introduction to *Esprit de cinéma* and *Alcool et cinéma*

These last two books of Jean Epstein were published posthumously in 1955 and 1975 respectively. *Esprit* reprises a number of articles Epstein published in journals in the years 1946-49 (with one short text from 1935), and *Alcool* may be considered in part a variant of *Esprit*, since half of it recapitulates sections of that book almost verbatim. Taken together, these works represent a last summation of Epstein's thoughts about cinema. They echo central themes and ideas found in two of his other synoptic efforts, *L'Intelligence d'une machine* (1946) and *Le Cinéma du diable* (1947), notably the insistence that cinema as a mechanical apparatus discloses our universe anew. *Photogénie*, close-ups, reverse and slow motion, and a loosening of cause and effect, display a different face of nature which paradoxically accords both with certain discoveries of modern physics and aspects of pre-Socratic, pagan, and materialist thought.

The fundamental dualism of Epstein may be seen in the parallel oppositions of 'intelligence' and 'evil,' and 'spirit' and 'alcohol'. On the one hand, we find an Apollonian tendency to understand cinema as an idea, a development in the realm of the mind and science, while on the other hand, cinema directly and challengingly reconnects modern viewers to a Dionysian embodiment, to art and poetry. Since Epstein rarely cites Nietzsche, we might do better to point to Charles Baudelaire's duality of *le moderne*, which combines a deeply material belonging to the present moment with a much more ethereal relationship with the past and the eternal. While Baudelaire is cited scarcely more than Nietzsche, Epstein's reverence for Poe together with his apology of evil, alcohol, and corporeal experience are unmistakably Baudelairean.

But *Esprit* and *Alcool* also contrast with *L'Intelligence d'une machine* and *Le Cinéma du diable*, the latter two centrally concerned with time and temporality and written in a taut lyrical-philosophical style. Both compilations of articles published in mainstream journals, *Esprit* and *Alcool* display a register akin to cultural chronicle – indeed close to our current cultural studies – more so than philosophical critique. As for content, they focus on four main aspects, two of which are new to Ep-

stein's thought. The old foci are cinema as an alternative to – yet also a form of – language; and cinema as 'surreal' in a way that contrasts with Surrealism. In both cases Epstein deepens previous reflections started in the 1920s. The main new conspicuous interest is sound, as attested by the development of the notion of *phonogénie* as a sonic parallel to *photogénie*, and illustrated in the beautiful *Le Tempestaire* (1947). Second, more than the rest of his oeuvre, these two books look backwards as much as forward, probing the history of silent film and cinema at large, and mulling over moviemaking as a specific craft, with specific techniques worth addressing as such. This makes them possibly the most approachable of his theoretical works from the viewpoint of contemporary film studies, even though they display less of the incisive, tonic, and poetic verve of his best books such as *Bonjour Cinéma* (1921) and *Le Cinéma du diable*.
– Christophe Wall-Romana

Esprit de cinéma

"The Logic of Images"

Translated by Thao Nguyen

[Jean Epstein, "La Logique des images," *Esprit de cinéma* (Genève: Éditions Jeheber, 1955), pp. 37-41.]

Every novice screenwriter knows that no film character can simply put his umbrella somewhere in the middle of a scene without such a gesture leading to consequences that need to appear in the film's conclusion. This captious finalism flourishes with utmost wealth in the most faux, the most arbitrary genres: those of melodrama and detective stories. But, truth be told, no author who seeks a certain amount of success dares stray too far away from this rational order and dares give in to sentimental illogicality, which more closely characterizes the behavior of real beings. So, at first view, it seems to us that filmed narration docilely obeys all rules of formal logic.

These rules, however, have been conceived to assemble words according to grammars that constitute as many little codes of an abridged and common reason that are available to all: speaking and writing correctly means reasoning soundly, in the classical sense. Yet, even though cinema is now talking, film also and primarily uses images. And one can ponder if verbal logic truly applies to image groupings – if it is legitimate to extend, as we often try to do, the value of syntactic principles and rhetorical techniques, be they oratory or literary, to visual discourse. A fairly sure answer should arise from the comparison between the laws of grammar that direct the order of sentences, and the rules of editing, in which filmed sequences appear. Without a doubt, cinematographic language has not found its Vaugelas or its Littré,[1] but it already possesses well-established customs, whose broad lines have been inventoried. And, already, an important difference appears between word and image constructions.

From one idiom to another, grammar varies more or less; thus does logic as well, and sometimes in a very subtle manner. Until now, philosopher after philosopher has tried, in vain, to draw, through those differences, a grammatical diagram shared by all languages in order to paint a minimal portrait of a humanly universal logic. On the other hand, at this time, editing and montage techniques only offer completely negligible national variations; thus, such techniques pretty much embody the very architectural constant of the human spirit that grammarians fail to isolate. We do not know how Eskimos, for example, would conceive the cinematographic treatment of a subject, but we know that they easily understand films of any origin that depict a simple life. However, it remains to be seen if such a general form of visual language can be considered logical.

Admittedly, a scenario usually appears as a kind of great syllogism, conforming to the scholastic rule: *Omne praedicatum est in subjecto*. That is to say that, the drama having been set, one no longer needs to innovate but rather needs simply to inventory drama's elements and characters in order to see the inevitable denouement which was already and completely present in the primary data. The crime bears the trace of a left-handed, poor-sighted culprit who wears espadrilles. Now, Paul is left-handed, poor-sighted, and he wears espadrilles. Therefore, Paul will be hanged. Such dramaturgic logic, completely similar to the grammatical one, is incapable of inventing, of creating something new, something true, something real. It only knows how to abstract, in the form of a hypothesis, the attributes of the subject and to isolate, in order to make it more apparent, a conclusion that existed beforehand – as is – involved in the knowledge of the starting point. If this analytical process has followed certain principles that we shall study later, its result gives the impression of being something true and real, whereas it is only correct in relation to a rule of the game, like a checkmate that is brought about correctly, but to which we cannot lend any character of truth or reality.

However, visual language proves resistant to abstraction, and with difficulty separates qualities from their object. The image remains a symbol that is close to concrete reality, infinitely richer in knowable content than the word that constitutes an already very refined diagram. Moreover, the cinematographic image lives quickly. It modifies its content, it changes meaning every second, whereas the content and the meaning of the word vary slowly, sometimes from one year to another, sometimes from one century to another. The animated image, which would require a lot of time to be broken down into its elements in fact because of its richness, eludes, through its instability, the kind of analysis that has ample time to dwell on the permanence of the word. So, because of the very nature of its elements that only capture, when it comes to forms, those related to movement, cinema does not lend itself well to the analytical, deductive, syllogistic type of exposition and understanding, and film tends to reject any stationary logic, of the grammatical type, that we seek to force upon it.

In movement, which is the essence of cinematographic representation, fundamental principles of formal logic are mobilized, relaxed, wrecked, reduced to a very relative validity. In the screen world, where things never remain what they are, how would the principle of identity keep its rigor? The principle of identity presupposes a homogeneous space-time continuum, in which figures remain superimposable onto themselves. In a space-time that is variable at will, as conceived by the cinematographic tool, each object continually becomes an endless number of *aspects-objects* that oftentimes cannot be compared. When all forms liquefy in a perpetual mobility, the principle of identity becomes as unsuitable to them as it is to ocean waves.

As a result, a corollary principle, the law of the excluded middle, crumbles as well. Either – as we think outside of the screen – Pierre and Paul are not the same height, or Pierre is shorter or taller than Paul. But, on screen, Pierre can sometimes be shorter, sometimes taller than Paul, and it is not impossible that both are the same height. The non-contradiction ceases to be a valid criterion of truth. Zeno's arrow, which is immobile in flight, does not surprise us anymore.[2] Any being combines movement and stillness, solidity and fluidity, languor and precipitation, tininess and immensity according to time-space conventions, where the lens arbitrarily places that being. Had the neurotic Pascal seen a few films, he would have had to find a new support to his anguish other than the size differences between mite and man – a difference that cinema can cancel or reverse at will, like the most banal optical illusion.

Two other fundamental notions of logic – those of non-ubiquity and of simultaneity – crumble into a strange confusion when we try to transpose them onto the world revealed to us by the screen. According to our usual idea of a four-dimensional continuum, it seems obvious to us that an individual cannot be at two different locations at the same time, nor can this individual, should he move, be at the same location at two different moments. But, in the discontinuous and fragmentary cinematographic concept of a time-space made up of autonomous cells, each holding its own references, the terms "the same place" and "the same moment" often lose all meaning from one cell to another. Let us consider the race between the hare and the turtle, filmed in double exposure, at two different speeds: one for the hare, the other for the turtle. Where and when can we possibly say that the hare and the turtle are either at the same location, or at the same moment? At the end of the race, in the heterogeneous time-space created by cinema, the fable's moral could find itself turned upside down. This also shows that moral sense is a sense of logic.

Finally, we believe that two events that uniformly follow each other are linked, one to the other, by a mysterious quality of causality. However, in a reverse film, we may see time and time again the explosion come after the smoke, but we refuse to accept that smoke caused the explosion. Rather, we seek and we find – because one always ends up finding or inventing what one seeks – a complicated series of direct causes that explain and correct a relation screaming of contrary causality. However, a doubt can linger in our mind: is normal causality (which constitutes one of the items – not least among them – of our daily, logical act of faith, and that physicists already repudiate to replace it with statistical laws) another *trompe l'œil*, just like the absurd causality of the film recorded in reverse?

Thus, cinema shows us that classical logic, no matter how great its usefulness, is not an absolutely universal tool completely valid in all knowledge domains. In the discontinuity and heterogeneity of cinematographic time-spaces, logic itself takes on a discontinuous and heterogeneous aspect; it cannot always be extended, such as it is, from one spatial-temporal cell to any other one. We are led to think that several logics may exist, which in the end are parochial. Such plurality is already well known to scientists, various sciences being in the process of devising specific analysis and deduction methods in relation to certain orders of phenomena. Microphysicists do not reason quite in the same fashion as do physicians or geologists. It is therefore natural that cinematographic phenomena, those events that unfold on screen, fit into a special logic of which we can only catch a glimpse. What already appears at the conclusion of the acquired knowledge, thanks to the popularizing power of cinema, is the notion, most certainly important, of the relativity of logic.

* * *

Rapidity and Fatigue of the *Homo Spectatoris*

Translated by Franck Le Gac

[Jean Epstein, "Rapidité et Fatigue de l'Homme Spectateur," *Esprit de cinéma* (Genève: Éditions Jeheber, 1955), pp. 59-68.]

It is readily admitted, following Quinton, that the relation between the successive capacities of intelligence and the products of this faculty at every moment of history form a specific constant in terms of effort and yield; that nowadays a mathematician using tensor analysis experiences neither more nor less difficulty than did a disciple of Pythagoras using the table of the first numbers. Yet it is not so much in the occupations of intellectuals as in the conditions in which any man, including the most average, must live and accomplish his daily work that the difference appears between cerebral tasks from one period to another.

Today the general acceleration of life, through the speeds of means of manufacture and communication; the monitoring of the economy, made necessary by the increasing population of the earth; the more and more meticulous measure of production as well as consumption; the increasingly precise bounding of any activity, in space and time; the efforts towards a more and more accurate adjustment of all gains and all expenses to standards of rational value; all these factors and many other corollaries force the clerk, the factory worker, the housewife, the stallholder, and even those who stroll around into constant attention: at the office, in front of the machine tool, at the market, at the family home, and in the street.

This tension has made the reduction of working hours and the institution of paid vacations necessary. However, while the working day is eight hours long rather than ten or fourteen, this does not imply that we work less today than before, but that we work faster and, as a consequence, that we get tired sooner. Even outside their professional occupations, from the moment they get up to the moment they go to sleep, industrialized and commercialized humans enjoy little leisure time, which has become a sin punishable by at least a fine. A lapse in concentration appears as a damning vice, subject to a whole array of penalties: limitation periods and surcharges, loss of earnings and loss of living, premeditated eliminations and automatic accidents. The law of civilized selection has it that those incapable of a life always on the watch waste away and die. Accordingly, besides the *acute* intellectual fatigue of every evening, which sleep dispels, a muted chronic weariness has settled in, which the relative rest of the five-day week or the summer break can alleviate but only provisionally.

Intellectual fatigue – as psycho-physiology teaches us – acts upon the subordinating center which lies at the base of the brain and regulates the oscillations of mental life between states of wakefulness and states of sleep. In wakefulness, this center maintains the cerebral cortex in a state of effective communication with sense organs, in a state of peripheral receptivity and extroverted activity whose associative channels correspond to thought in its logical organization. The longer and the more intensely nerve cells work this way, the more they charge up with toxins. The subordinating center responds to this poisoning by more or less suspending the relations between the outside environment and the cortex, freeing the latter from ceaseless stimulation by the senses and the rational habits these messages have established. At all the stages of sleep and wakefulness, thought becomes more or less illogical, as can be observed in the dreams and reveries featuring other, irrational types of sequences strongly marked by affective paralogics. Indeed, the inhibition of an extroverted and reasoning cortical activity is accompanied by an increase in the influence of other zones at the base of the brain, considered the centers of affective life.

In general, the cerebral cortex and base may react as stimulants, just as they may mutually inhibit each other, in a rhythm of always unstable equilibriums and alternating predominancies under the control of a – probably complex – center that regulates the state of wakefulness or the state of sleep. This center functions as a center of poetry when it introduces intermediate states between the full exertion and the total eclipse of logical intelligence. And intellectual fatigue, in its moderate degree, in its chronic form, evidently opens the door to half-dreaming and calls for the transformation of reasoning-thought into poem-thought.

Seen from this fundamental psycho-sociological angle, rational activity and irrational activity appear as the inseparable, contradictory, and complementary constituents of a dialectic – to speak Hegelian – which is the life of the mind itself. The excess of one of these mental activities necessarily leads to an exhaustion and intoxication that allow and invite the other to a more vigorous and manifest development. Cast in this light, which is also the light of medicine and hygiene, one can see that organizing a too-strictly rationalized life would amount to creating states of affective need or romantic crises, sooner or later.

Because as a language-spectacle it appeals more to emotions than to reason, because it is the creator of the most prefabricated, digestible, massive, intense, popular poetry, cinema remedies so well some of the ills of rationalist civilization, in which it thus becomes an essential provision. Intellectual fatigue has created, on the scale of the whole of humankind caught up in progress, a need for facile, crude poetry and a receptivity to it which are only increasing. This need and this receptivity have hung on to cinema as to a mainstay, a soft, heroic drug, a staple food.

Thanks to speech, writing, and printing, which propagated the reasoning method, the *Craftsman* had become the *Scientist*. Yet following the law of evolution of animal species, which die away through an excess complexity in the makeup of some of their organs, this human variety, characterized by a highly logical behavior, feels today that it is tangled up in the profusion of its own reason, overwhelmed with this system as with huge boughs, and whose upward spiritual movement does not make it any less bulky, heavy, or awkward.

The excellence of his reason – probably – raised man above animals. However – and though the reasons for this are not known – there are limits to every good, beyond which it becomes a wrong. These limits in their development were reached, for instance, with the shell of lamellibranchia in the Secondary Era, the carapace of the radiated tortoise, the tusks of mastodons, the giraffe's neck, the genitalia of copepods and, from a functional standpoint, the higher brain of man.

At a certain level of hypertrophy, rational thought tends to become paralyzed and disintegrate as an effect of organic fatigue: this effect is both direct, exerted by this thought upon itself, and indirect, a result of the obligation to think rationally ever more, so as to be able to live life as it has been conceived and organized materially by reason. A vicious circle if there is one, where intelligence strains itself in the creation of machines and regulations, which themselves create intellectual fatigue. In this, one could see something like an ingenious process for the obscure will of the species which, aware of the danger of rationalization, would have fitted it with an automatic braking system.

It thus happens today that man no longer has the taste – nor the time, in fact – to read for the sake of reading. While he has to ingest his daily newspaper in haste, he only scans the page, which lends itself quite well to this, half of which involves headlines and titles designed to be read at a glance. Often, illustrations make the knowledge of the little text that remains optional or even are a substitute for the article itself. Photographs, diagrams, posters make it possible to learn an enormous amount of required knowledge without exacting the effort of attention and logical thinking needed for a somewhat coherent reading. Journalists, publicists, and many men of letters now know that they need to have consideration for the intellectual fatigue of their contemporaries, who can no longer be diligent readers; who no longer find themselves in a state to do anything but to watch, and to watch quickly at that, while passing, running, driving, eating, traveling, and thinking about something else to boot.

Indeed, the movement and the haste, the cramming and the cumulation characteristic of modern life add to cerebral fatigue and, just as directly, to the repercussions of this fatigue: laziness when it comes to reading, aversion to reasoning more still while reading. Little by little, the learned man and logician, but weary of being so, develop the attributes of a new mental variety which could be named *Homo spectatoris.*

As it happens, this spectator, a spectator always in movement, discovers cinema – a universal spectacle, a spectacle always in movement. The film brings with it the means to say and learn everything through images that just need to be watched and, to a degree, heard. The most cursory survey – and one may wonder at the fact that a more comprehensive investigation has not yet been carried out – already shows that the audience is much more inclined to be spectators than listeners. The majority of theater patrons hear or understand well often only a slight part of the dialogue. The rest goes unheeded or is misinterpreted, which still does not prevent the film from producing the effect intended by the author, thanks to its visible content.

If this spectacle suits so perfectly the new spectatorial mentality, it is first of all because intelligence, the effort of the higher brain – which, precisely, wants to rest – is little called upon in the comprehension of its visual symbolism, while the sentimental and irrational activity of the base of the brain, of the lower brain, by contrast seeks to be put to work. Yet this is also because the images on the screen essentially constitute a spectacle of mobility, and the pace of such mobility, which reflects the exterior pace of life nowadays, accords with the momentum in which souls live, carried and hurried along as they evidently are by the same movement of events around them. The *photogénie* of movement, the fundamental law of the whole cinematographic aesthetic and dramaturgy, thus reveals a deep signification.

The increasing frequency in human activity constitutes one of the most striking exterior characteristics of our time, on which it puts its imprint in a manner both very visible and very intimate. Acceleration – which may well be a general law of life for immense periods of time and which, from one century to another, is in fact perceptible in history – has now become palpable in terms of personal experience, as everyone can already attest in the course of one's own existence. Our contemporaries need only compare their memories, from decade to decade since their childhood, to acknowledge that man acts and is acted upon faster and faster, and therefore more, from the outside.

The ever higher speed which mechanization imparts to all movements, all relations, all realizations, allows and leads to an increase in the number of all these acts, each of which is a set of movements. The rush of activity thus keeps multiplying, and there is one secret for this acceleration of acceleration, for this exponentially increasing speed which drives civilization – possibly to the brink of disaster. For it is difficult to imagine how the organism could indefinitely resist and adapt to the ceaseless hardening, the tension pushed to the extreme, the jam-packing of a life passing in a flash whose fractions of a second will come to be counted, and which in the end will be examined and will have to be lived like a record-setting raid of efficiency.

This exterior acceleration of work is evidently not without equivalent in mentalities. These high school students, who after class may be heard engaging in passionate discussions on the performances of the latest jet plane hitting the sound barrier, certainly share a new, vivid faith quite opposed to the tradition of the Eleatics.[3] For young generations, speed – the aristocratic symbol of movement – has become an elegance, a snobbery, an abstract good, an ideal. At last, the old pretensions of philosophies of permanence, in which man proclaimed his mastery over a universe frozen in a reassuring solidity, meet with the consciousness, the pride, the glory of another conquest: that of the mobile world, understood in its turn, forced into its most dangerous uncertainties.

In the interest the public has started to show so keenly for all forms of movement, and especially for improvements in movement, one may see the evidence of a capital reorientation of the mind, which is beginning to look less for aspects of the greatest constancy than for those of the greatest mobility. Among other reasons for the current vogue for sports, there is the concurrence between these games, bringing into play and making a spectacle of movements as they do, and the new intellectual and sentimental – and in the end, aesthetic – trend to have appreciation for everything. And the dithyrambs published on a locomotive making the Paris-Bordeaux trip a few minutes shorter or on a swimmer gaining a few seconds over his rival over the distance of a pool no longer appear ridiculous when they are thought of as the signs, coming from an unknowing writer, of a revolution which does not leave any knowledge unreached in the soul.

This new intuition of mobility, this new sense of the world in movement, however, also begs to be expressed in a less abstract aesthetic than that of philosophy and mathematics, and in forms of art less fleeting than that of a scrum in rugby or a skier's jump. Engravers were probably already faced with the issue of representing movement during the Neolithic Age, and the progress of sculptors in ancient Egypt and Greece may be measured by their increasing skill at figuring torsos and limbs that are not as stiff, faces not as numb, clothes not as straight. All such statuary aimed at providing, by way of solution, portraits as exact as was possible, fractions as small as could be captured, and a movement that to this end had to be broken down into a series of punctual freezes. This was a method, a calculation in infinitesimal or differential art, which was reused in painting and countless minor graphic instruments, and which was generally and exclusively practiced until the beginning of this century. Of this system instant photography represents a state of perfection, at least when it comes to the fineness and the comprehensiveness of the analysis.

Yet the real problem, that of reproducing a movement in the integrality of its nature, in the continuity of its evolution, remained unsolved and appeared insoluble. Was it not absurd, indeed, to seek to interpret a mobility through an immobility, a fluidity through a solidness, a becoming through a permanence, a white through a black? Certainly, some thought of animating statues, and the strong appeal, the mix of curiosity and anxiety, past and present, exercised by automatons, homunculi, robots, artificial Adams and Eves – whose fabrication is attributed to great alchemists, great saints, great philosophers and scientists – may be partly explained by the fact that man can imagine the efforts behind them, wishes for and fears the success of a perfect art which he had come to think of as forbidding. However, the attempts that were not only imagination and dupery produced only results which, poor as they might have been, already required a daunting mechanical complication.

At the same time that the use of railroads, bicycles, autos, the telegraph, the telephone, the plane, the radio, and all the instruments designed to beat and beat again speed records became widespread, the problem of the representation of movement, which seemed like a closed matter, came back to the forefront of preoccupations in plastic arts and literature. Literature did the best it could to pick up the pace, shortening its narratives, adopting the telegraphic, spoken style, multiplying contractions, summaries, ellipses, forcing writing into a shorthand that could keep up with the fastest thought.

Sculpture, which could not really model fluids, invented the blur, which at least produced a certain impression of inconsistency. Hands, breasts, masks were seen half emerging from a wave of heavy foam of which they seemed to be made, but for a moment only, ready to disappear again in this swell of marble.

In painting, Cubism and its imitations proposed a projective figuration of the object, on several planes and from several different angles. This complex perspective, the assumed result of shifts in the pictorial point of view, was to give rise to an impression of movement in the spectator's mind, who was also invited to travel in imagination.

Draftsmen began to copy, as symbols of such movement, the flaws of snapshots, at the extreme limit of the power of photography to intercept the appearance of an almost immobile particle within mobility. Thanks to dotted or shaky lines, this resulted in images of stretched autos, fitted with streaks of hatching and with wheels flattened in ellipses.

All these expedients suffered from the same fault, which seemed without remedy: the impossibility of figuring a movement through another movement, as long as no mobile media existed, a media with fluidity, in which the movement of a form could still be imprinted, and which could keep this form of movement intact so as to repeat it indefinitely; the impossibility of integrating all the fragmentary and seemingly immobile appearances of a mobility in the continuity of their evolution, reconstructed by some system, some calculation of integral art.

This is the impossibility cinema has solved, precisely by adding a series of instantaneous and discontinuous photographic infinitesimals into their integral and continuous sequence, which is movement. In this light, the cinematographic camera is first and foremost an integrating, calculating machine. In any case, this machine enabled the most difficult expression, pursued for ages and demanded all at once and urgently by a civilization to which Romanticism and the tyranny of speed had just revealed the paramount value of movement.

The representation of movement made possible by cinema was at first understood in a quite superficial manner and employed in overabundance in this simplicity. The first scenarios never seemed to feature enough accidents, encounters, battles, chases. The art of movement was at first of stereotypical imagery, whose production does in fact continue to this day: there is always a need, in order to satisfy a certain public, for films that respond to a very macroscopic and naively romanced conception of things to come.

However, the camera – learning that, while recording the movements of others, it could also move – approached characters and made close-ups. What was then discovered, in the expressions of a face filling the whole screen, was the world of a much finer mobility. This was still a physical mobility, but it translated in minute detail the mobility of a soul. The close-up thus was a step of enormous scope for the cinema, inaugurating the microscopy of exterior movement and extending the power of figuration of the new language to the realm of interior movements, spiritual movements. Thanks to the close-up, films were no longer limited to the storytelling of obstacle courses and gained the ability to depict a psychological evolution as well.

Slow motion later pushed the microscopy of outer movement to a prodigious degree of sophistication, which begged to be used to the end of a no less penetrating analysis of thought and feeling. Speeded-up motion has created a telescopy or a tachyscopy of movement.[4] And both slowed-down and speeded-up motion have thus caused a new world to emerge suddenly, next to the three already known, more or less – the human scale, the infinitesimal, the infinitely great – a fourth universe that in fact encompasses the three others: that of the infinitely mobile, infinitely slow, or infinitely fast and, in a psychological sense, of the infinitely human.

Cinema thus accords with a civilization that is becoming conscious – and painfully so – of the acceleration of life, not only because it brings the representation of movement in a form that may be used in art as in science, but also because it constitutes, through its images, music, and noises, a language whose understanding may be extremely swift, much swifter than that of spoken or read language. This high speed of absorption by the mind cinematographic discourse owes to its irrationality. Such speed suits civilized mindsets because it rests them from their overworked reason.

★ ★ ★

Ciné-analysis, or Poetry in an Industrial Quantity

Translated by Sarah Keller

[Jean Epstein, "Ciné-analyse, ou poésie en quantité industrielle," *Esprit de cinéma* (Genève: Éditions Jeheber, 1955), pp. 69-76.]

Our scientistic civilization tends to create an order of humanity perfectly suited to the technical and social uses it is to serve. The result is normalized, typified and extroverted to the extreme – and might well be called superhuman, since here the superego, civic and professional, must peremptorily control the individualist fantasy of the ego. The superego, itself as unified and aligned as possible with group averages, allows the formation of homogeneous groups, within which behavior and productivity are certainly predictable. Probably the conjunction of food shortages, economic restrictions, and policing – generally totalitarian mindsets – promote this psycho-technical and psycho-political human *autoplanisme*[5] by contributing in a hundred ways toward diminishing the original spirit of the individual. However, this temperament is not yet so submissive that it does not suffer and complain about the excessive repression imposed on it by the methodical censoring of thoughts, actions, and accomplishments that are useless or even detrimental to communal activities. The permanent controversy, the incessant transactions – the dialectic, if you will, between the rationality demanded by the environment and the irrationality of feelings that animate individual beings – thus seem to have reached the instability and the intensity of a crisis.

In poetry, people have always found the first relief for troubles resulting from external forces that rebuff their true tendencies, poetry being understood in its general[6] sense of sublimation. Thus for example, the Stakhanovist ideal[6] is above all a poetry of forced labor: a transfiguration of the mortifying pressure to struggle until a fixed norm has been reached, into the glorious liberty of voluntarily exhausting oneself beyond that norm; a transference that allows the realization of transcendence within deprivation, with an eye toward the social good. In addition to such methods of heroic poetry in action, other means – traditional and benign, which one includes under the heading of art – remain in use.

Literature, theater, painting, music, sculpture, etc. can probably still bring readers, spectators, listeners into a state of sublimation through resonance with the poetic state expressed by the creator. But, when it comes to interesting a large audience, these diversions often exert too narrow and too particular a liberating effect. In contemporary French letters, there is not a writer who may be called a great popular poet, and it's not that anyone lacks inspiration: it's that literature has ceased being able to serve as a medium for poetry, given to the mass audience, massively riddled with prohibitions, which has to be compelled to self-analyze. For the man of the street – incapable of counting the thousands of orders he is given forbidding him to do and destroy, love and hate, feed himself and expend his energy, cry and wear himself out as he pleases – it is of course necessary, in order even slightly to overcome so many suppressed desires, to have an outlet and a sublimating agent endowed with efficiency proportional to the task: an intense, simple producer and transmitter of poetry in a mass quantity.

It is the cinematographic spectacle – the inventors of which predicted neither its utility nor its success – which rather quickly and as if spontaneously revealed itself capable of making a huge, quasi-global public forcefully participate in moving fictions, where it could consume the excess and wreckage of a prohibited affectivity.

The active power of the cinematographic automaton can be explained first of all in that the discourse of this machine is made principally through animated images, which, by their visual and mobile character, resemble mental images enough that they can imitate those images in their modes of physical structuring, association, and transition. Naturally, the style proper to cinema has defined itself in its use of magnification and isolation of objects in shifting, incommensurable dimensions; in its indefinite or lightning or infinitely sluggish durations; in the impressions of ubiquity it produces; in its symbolism of identity transpositions and emotional transference; in its sequences made by linking up elements after their actual order. All of this in the manner of this old and profound visual thought that dreams and certain daydreams bring forth. Thus the film is found to be particularly apt at both enriching and setting directly into motion the memory and visual imagination of spectators, without having to pass through the operations of crystallization and dissolution of a verbal intermediary.

And yet, all the elements of this visual thought, rooted in the subconscious, are prodigiously rich in affective values, governed by and also governing them. The film proceeds therefore especially by working with emotional evidence and, at that very moment, receives the irresistible power of conviction from it. Because visual thought is fundamentally instinctive, sentimental, and moving, it is well suited to a poetic use and, in the majority of mentalities, indispensably so. Therefore, more than any other means of expression, film seems constitutionally designed to serve as a vehicle for poetry.

Moreover, cinematographic poetry is always administered in circumstances that facilitate contagion. The cinema's darkness, forced immobilization, and exclusion of all other shocks to the sensibilities except that which derive from the film put the spectator in a state of rupture from exterior contingencies and suspension from superficial activities, which is the condition of all reverie. Usually, the creator, the reader, the spectator, or the person listening to poetry have to isolate themselves with effort from their company and forget their routine; and often they are unable to reach that state easily, since a strong facility for suppression is rather rare. However, cinema's spectator, for whom nearly every distraction is eliminated and whose attention is directed toward a sole center – the screen – finds that hypnosis and poetry are generated at the same time.

And it is not irrelevant that this hypnosis is collective. First of all, because the communion of a little crowd feeling the same way provides a sense of its own reality and legitimacy and creates, among individuals, an amplifying current of sympathy. Further, because the use of poetry assumes a social role that can be understood as at least a partial rehabilitation, for a recognition of the right to an existence at least ideal in these tendencies that the self perceives as most its own, as the most original and all the more precious as they are unhappy: sentenced to relegation, devoid of real gratification.

Plato, who exiled poets from his Republic, would *a fortiori* have forbidden cinema as a high-performance poetry machine. But wouldn't the constraint that deprives the most private passions of imaginary satisfaction be more dangerous for the public order, incompatible as those passions are with state norms expressed under check by the superego? Wouldn't such a constraint make the consciences of citizens guilty, anguished by their ignorance of and contempt for themselves in spite of themselves, neurotic through their private disaccord and, in the end, cause them to rise up against the oppression of an overbearing patriotism?

At the cinema, as elsewhere, there can be no productivity without modifying the quality. Since the poetic function of cinema is useful to the masses, film must treat affective themes of sufficient generality to respond to the needs for sublimation in the greatest number of spectators. According to this rule, the choice of a scenario can be among only a few highly banal types with little variation in their dramatic evolution. Originality happens only to be wanted or acceptable in a secondary position, to disguise the obligatory monotony in the content. Books and theater allow the adoption of much more particularized, diverse subjects, as they seek to satisfy a more limited public. But on screen, every exceptional psychology (for example, the genius or the simple-minded) and all heroes not personifying a very widespread ideal (for example, the simple peasant or the paragon of virtue) are usually doomed to failure. The rule for commercial success, while much maligned, is in fact a poetic law, which is to say a psychoanalytic law: for with its millions of souls, the public can truly subscribe to a dramatic fiction only insofar as this fiction responds to agencies sufficiently and commonly present in all of those souls.

This need to adapt cinematographic poetry to the most common agencies prohibits film authors from expressing things profoundly and meticulously in their works; in becoming too particular, the works would prove unprofitable. Hence the impossibility for the spectators to calm their frustrated appetites with delicacy, while precisely discovering themselves through perfect alternative satisfactions. It needs to be confessed: the sincerity that carries the film and which drives it is most often heavy and narrow. These one hundred percent magnificent lovers' kisses, this machine-gunning of bloody and bloodthirsty gangsters, these shifting fortunes – passions, wretchedness, and glory happening to deified typists, to mechanics transformed into billionaires, to athletes revived ten times over; all the most popular themes on the screen are only meager sustenance for tricking that great hunger of a sedentary and civilized people, patiently laborious, tormented by old desires – always vibrant, always thwarted and dismissed – for violent action, for resplendent tragedy, for personal triumph, for impossible love. This is an emergency treatment or drastic remedy for prohibitions: uninterrupted inhibition and hypnosis, as they say, administered in one hour and a half doses. And, leaving their weekly treatment [séance de cure], spectators remain dazed, exhausted, for believing so hard they actually battled, suffered, loved, and vanquished, relieved as when piercing an abscess, as when fever drops after frenzy.

Thus, that which cinematographic poetry must neglect in the finesse of its effects it compensates for in its general efficacy; that which cine-analysis cannot achieve in particulars, it exchanges for the intensity of liberating action. To a dramaturgy destined for the crowd, an analysis – not of the greatest diversity but with the strongest similarities among individual tendencies – necessarily corresponds. And an epoch given to general *planisme* – with its typifying of mentalities, methodical organization of repression, and by consequence popularization and standardization of psychical maladies exacts even more imperiously the popularization and standardization of the poetic antidote as well, to adjust its effect to that of censorship. As limited as the degree of individual characterization reached by cine-analysis should thus be, it represents on the level of greatest common factors the average term of the greatest collective efficiency; and this term surely finds itself defined by the best commercial success.

This does not at all mean that this psychological limit and the commercial index of it are immutable, that it is not necessary to work to move them in the direction of an increasingly more advanced judgment, an increasingly profound curative effect. The most profitable film bookings in the course of the year only provide the measure of neurosis and collective introspection over the course of that year. That this measure constantly changes can well be seen through the effect of puerility that one feels in seeing old film strips, or the disappointment in production companies that imagined they would find the same enormous profits by revisiting two or three times the same subject that succeeded for them the first time.

In certain aspects, the evolution of cinematographic dramaturgy and poetry develops slowly and continuously; in other cases, it proceeds through sudden transformations. But the technical and artistic transformations of profitable films follow a path already paved by either knowingly or unwittingly daring trials; it is a path already marked out by an avant-garde whose works alarm the public in proportion to how much they announce the unknown that will become knowable, the captive that will escape from the unconscious. There are commercial failures that are the pilots for commercial success because they lead by accident or experimentally show the way to develop the cine-analysis from one optimal profit to another.

The cinematographic spectacle first blossomed on the poetic level of serial novels, light-hearted songs, postcards. And the immediate decline, nearly the extinction, of the popular melodrama at the theater confirms the superior force and efficacy with which cinema finds itself capable of stimulating, satisfying, diverting, and using the need for emotion in the greater public. Cinema limited theatrical dramaturgy, even as it encouraged it to propose a finer, more profound, more idiosyncratic psychology on the stage.

But today, the need for cine-analysis and the perfecting of it, developing conjointly, allow films to represent less common, less schematic conflicts. The clientele of the cinema is extended, by way of also interesting minds more prone to introspection – minds to which, until now, dramatic and literary dialogue merely provided explication and a decline in bothersome mental appeals.

And, to keep its proper utility, on which its existence depends, the theater must tend more and more to represent of life that which the cinema finds itself economically impeded in providing, even though technically it is perfectly capable: the subliming idealization. Theater must cultivate a psychology, either of the exceptional case or of an altogether normal, individual case, but analyzed with a meticulousness that in the end reveals the anomaly in every genuine particular. It is in this orientation toward the singular that the current proliferation of little theaters responds, planned for small audiences with singular tastes; these venues present plays that are simply clinical studies of singular neuroses.

This is in no way a negative criticism. The social role and the individual effect of the cinematic as well as theatrical spectacles are like an amusing psychoanalytic lesson and cure where spectators have to become familiar with the natural mechanism of certain troubles of the soul so they will not be frightened by them or suffer from them as from shameful, monstrous diseases; where the mind must be purged of an excess of sentimentality – available for actual use or impossible to use in actuality – through the consummation of this superabundance in a fantasy of passion. Cinema and theater, each in its own way, lead people to know themselves better, in a setting free from mental anxiety. Though they are often called rivals, theater and cinema can nonetheless be considered as equals in their common zeal to invite the spectator to return to the self. If the power, breadth and increasing depth of cinema's action constrains the theater to evolve ever more towards singularity and finesse, there is – in these two processes, one of which pushes the other – a general movement of the mind by which a man endlessly tends to approach, seize, and disarm the dreadful sphinx, which he ceaselessly becomes for himself.

★ ★ ★

Dramaturgy in Space

Translated by Audrey Brunetaux

[Jean Epstein, "Dramaturgie dans l'espace," *Esprit de cinéma* (Genève: Éditions Jeheber, 1955), pp. 120-124.]

Recently, a producer observed that the bigger, the more complicated, the more beautiful, the more expensive the decors on the set are, the less often we show them on screen. It is true that long shots have become rare, maybe even rarer than close-ups. The editing condenses the action in close-shots that only unveil what is necessary for our understanding of the characters and objects and what helps our comprehension of the film. Far from being just a temporary trend, this economy shows a tendency characteristic of cinematographic dramaturgy.

Silent film had already showed this tendency, applying it even more, multiplying extreme close-ups through which facial expressions could replace words and subtitles. Then, the emergence of feature-length sound films marked a decline in this approach at first due to the difficulty and the danger of moving the imperfect soundproof cabins closer to the microphone, cabins where the camera remained locked for a while. However, as the leopard cannot change its spots, soon enough the movement of an approaching camera resumed, without constantly necessitating the use of close-ups, a technique that had taken over as a result of the easy use of dialogue. Finally, after its failure with the first great expansion of color and depth in cinema, the evolution of close-ups, maybe, will soon repeat itself when the audience grows weary of vast shots in polychromatic stereoscopy that will cease to surprise.

On the one hand, it is evident that a film moves us even more when the images are closer to us; on the other hand, the ability to bring and move the spectacle closer to the audience, in space as well as in time, so as to situate the action at the best possible distance and in the best possible duration to obtain the dramatic effect, is an essential quality of the cinematographic instrument. As a result, a cinematographic dramaturgy is one of proximity and more specifically of variable proximity, in opposition to the theater, which can represent an event only at a fixed distance, at a constant pace. Thus, we can say that theater only admits a planar dramaturgy while cinema allows a spatial dramaturgy.

This spatial diversity in the on-screen spectacle significantly determines its psychological nature. A camera lens and a microphone that can approach a face to the point where it captures the smallest movement, the slightest murmur, can and thus must describe tragedies of a great intimacy and of a detailed human truth. For instance, a text by Giraudoux that sounds prestigious when performed by characters standing on stage and heard from a three to five-meter distance – a distance for which the text was written – becomes extravagant when it is recited in a close-up and listened to within a one-meter proximity. This does not mean that cinematographic dramaturgy pretends to exclude all artifice, but it requires a certain capacity for falsehood that is more internalized and natural than externalized and decorative. On screen, as lies are subject to the spectators-listeners' scrutiny due to their proximity, they are themselves forced to become true. There is something of an appetite for documentary in this psychological realism that governs the whole aesthetic of the filmed drama – an aesthetic that represents an immense and endless subject whose logical preface must specify the way, characteristic of cinema, to situate a dramatic action in the spatial frame.

In general, the current technique of the *mise-en-scène* only gives us a discontinuous, fragmentary, and disparate view of a place and décor – closer here, farther there; in terms of perspective, sometimes normal, sometimes plunging, sometimes even tilting the verticals. We can see the surroundings of an action not with our unique pair of eyes, but with a multitude of eyes equipped with all sorts of magnifying lenses and eye glasses that we would sometimes hold at knee-level or at the tip of our fingers, sometimes way above or beside our head. This view would definitely be more intricate than that of the compound eyes found in insects.

However, we are used to mentally re-working the data obtained through our normal vision range, to correcting what we call our innumerable optical illusions so as to build a notion of a sound, straight, homogeneous space where we can orient ourselves following Euclidean rules. Transposing this habit, as different fields materialize on the screen, we automatically and unconsciously try to regroup them into a coherent whole within our classical space, thus solving the puzzle that the filmmaker brought to us out of a legitimate concern for concentrating our attention on a "detoured" drama."

But if, on the one hand, it is necessary for the film director to sacrifice the description of the décor for the narrative of the action, on the other hand it is necessary for the audience to locate quite precisely the elements of this action, risking otherwise neither to understand it, nor to be convinced or moved by it. Our brain works in such a way that the localization of an object is essential to our acceptance of its existence. A thing found nowhere would, of course, not exist, and an event is all the more real, believable, and able to capture our interest if we know where it takes place. Thus, we notice a contradiction between the movement of increasing approximation in cinematographic dramaturgy and the general law of credulity in dramatic fiction.

When the fragmentation of shots makes the localization of an event very difficult, the search for it becomes conscious and disturbing, disrupts the attention, and tends to break the spell of even the most touching film. For instance, in some film from the past season, a few scenes represented limit cases where the difficulty of precisely situating the dramatic effect reached a degree capable of countering the emotion born from the narrative. When a German patrol visited the place where an escaped prisoner was hiding, the spectator's anguish remained uncertain while he was unable to find his way through the décor – a small space yet filmed in discontinuous bits – which wasn't enough for understanding where the hideout was. Throughout the scenes in a prison cell, one felt equally disturbed due to the lack of localization because the décor, though easy to imagine, was never made explicit through the images. Finally, during a long shot in which people condemned to death were rescued thanks to the Royal Air Force bombings, the discomfort came back like slight dizziness due to a loss of spatial orientation, because it wasn't easy for the spectator to piece together all the partial shots of the prison and its whereabouts according to a logic of space following the logic of the dramatic order of events.

But these remarks are not only and necessarily critiques. Among many other lessons, the one surpassing all others is that cinema offers a notion of space more flexible and more diverse than that of the old Euclidean space. Most of the time, films make their philosophical propaganda in such a discreet, patient, and disguised way that the public assimilates it without ever noticing it. Only sometimes a few innovators go against this caution, more or less overdose, and provoke a reaction that forces us to ask questions and to face the fact that we are little by little modifying our way of thinking. In a very large sense, what makes a film shocking is often what makes it worthwhile. The scandal and doubt arising from an image can remind us that cinema leads us to the difficult loosening of our brain's imperious demand to anchor every single reality in a simple space that is rigorously equal everywhere.

In this space, as we knew it before the filmmaker and as we have insisted on representing it since the Renaissance, horizontals form lines of convergence, whereas verticals remain parallel. This is not really a Euclidean space anymore but a hybrid space, half curved and half straight, horizontally curved and vertically straight, where indeed the absurd dream of parallelism hides. In space such as it appears on screen, vertical lines converge as much as horizontal lines, as one would know by looking at a full shot of a cathedral. The cinematographic space thus appears like a fully curved space where any strict parallelism is impossible. On the one hand, we see our usually semi-straight space as a homogeneous continuum. On the other hand, we see the elliptical space represented on screen as discontinuous and heterogeneous. Each different shot constitutes a cell of space that has its own system of references and its own standard for size. From one cell to the other, faces are neither superimposable nor similar. Each shot has its own geometry that works only in this very context. Similarly, Euclidean geometry, also relative, works only in the context of a direct and short-range visual experience.

We could spend more time on these remarks from which ensues, first, the following conclusion: cinema shows the general relativity of notions of space. Space has no absolute reality whatsoever; it is only a more or less precise, more or less facile point of reference, depending as much on the conditions in which vision operates, either through the eye or through a camera lens, as on the skills and habits of the brain that uses it. Searching for the superiority or inferiority of authenticity between classic Euclidean space and elliptical cinematographic space does not make any more sense than wondering whether or not, on a piece of paper, a grid in millimeters is more or less correct than a grid in centimeters. The important thing to know is that all conceivable structures of space are imaginary.

★ ★ ★

Dramaturgy in Time

Translated by Audrey Brunetaux

[Jean Epstein, "Dramaturgie dans le temps," *Esprit de cinéma* (Genève: Éditions Jeheber, 1955), pp. 125-129.]

We automatically tend to consider space and time as two distinct categories, as our teachers (even the most eminent ones) have taught us. Our mental representation of a cubic meter is thus perfectly separated from our notion of a second because it seems to us that we could indefinitely keep in mind the image, for example, of a meter's worth of wood. However, in the cinematographic representation, montage necessarily assigns a certain duration of two or three seconds, in other words a temporal dimension, to this image. Film cannot represent spatial dimensions devoid of temporality. Our mind dissects phenomena according to the Kantian analysis of space and time. The world that we see on screen shows us volumes-durations in a perpetual synthesis of space and time. Cinema presents to us space-time as something obvious.

Somehow, we ended up connecting all the various times of our different experiences – psychological, physiological, historical, cosmic, etc. – to solar and astronomical time, which appear constant. Before the invention of the cinematographic time-lapse, slow motion, and reverse motion, we were unable to conceive what the face of our universe becomes through the modification of its temporal rhythm. But as it plays out, cinema creates these seemingly unimaginable worlds where time speeds are twenty times slower or fifty thousand times faster than those of our clocks. In a documentary about dance or the life of crystalline or botanical species, the screen shows us a partial world endowed with its own particular time that is not only different from ours but also variable with respect to itself: evenly or variably accelerated or slowed down. Between the events of one of these worlds and the events of our reality, we realize that looking for any simultaneity is illusory. In this way, through a visual experience and through obvious facts, the film introduces us to the comprehension of an extremely general relativity.

Here, this relativity presents itself not in the form of a difficult mathematical expression but of an often embellishing, always interesting and instructive metamorphosis of all forms of movement. The rider, the horse, the dancer receive an admirable amount of grace from slow motion. Through fast motion, minerals become alive, plants start to move, clouds explode and blossom in the sky like fireworks. These are the effects we get when enriching the image with a sort of temporal dimension, effects both deeply aesthetic and of an important philosophical meaning.

This discovery of temporal perspective corresponds with the comparison that is suddenly possible to make between several speeds in the sequence of an event, which the cinema creates and sets against the standard of human time in the same way an architect puts a figurine in the model of a monument to evaluate its proportions. Because we only know things through their differences. In a monochromatic world where everything is red, there would not be any color, any red. In a system maintained at a constant temperature, there would not be any detectable and measurable temperature. In a world with a unique speed, time would disappear. If we have a notion of time, yet a confused one, it is because, on the one hand, the elements of our world move at different speeds and, on the other hand, the relationship between these speeds and the main movements of light and earth remains constant. But cinema succeeds in altering this constant which seemed to be an intangible operator of the creation; cinema divides and multiplies a rhythm that was thought to be unique and inoperable; below and beyond the only value that we viewed in absolute terms, cinema shows a time scale technically limited by photographic and mechanical conditions, yet already large enough to add new possibilities of existence, maybe in the most original and the most exclusively cinematographic ways, to the film's aesthetic and dramaturgy.

By its ability to move through space, the cinematographic spectacle already contrasts, in a way, with the theatrical spectacle, which is forced always to situate the action at the same distance from the audience. By its power to describe events in various temporal rhythms, cinema is ready to surpass theater in another way. One will probably object that for a long time, since the *mystery plays* performed in the Middle Ages, the notion of time in drama has differed from historical time; that classical tragedies already condensed twenty-four hours of real time in three or four hours of spectacular time; that today a man's life can be summed up in three acts of forty minutes each. However, this is not actually an acceleration but a discontinuity, of interruptions in time. These chosen portions of time that each act represents always go on at a roughly steady pace. The implied, purely fictitious acceleration happens only during intermission. Regarding slow motion, drama can only give a sense of it in a very boring way. On stage, we can never see what beings and things become within a faster or slower time than our own. The theatrical dramaturgy that can only use a spatial distance functions with only one time speed. Only cinema can quite freely make use of a multiplicity of perspectives with four dimensions in space and time.

Is cinema taking advantage of this talent? That is another question. Through the most common life experience and through the use of a hundred graphic means of expression we have been accustomed to understanding the most diverse and the boldest representations according to the three spatial dimensions. Also, a great mobility in the camera now represents an inherent characteristic of the technique. However, due to its mono-rhythm, time has remained both a blurry and a rigid notion whose transformations are foreign to us. Here, cinema that imitates theater and other domains as well has made particular use of implicit time-lapses, through a subtitle or an answer informing the audience about the twenty years that surreptitiously elapsed between two sequences. Filmmakers have rarely made the effort to designate a temporal gap with a shot in which a landscape in bloom would be covered with snow little by little, in which a garden would, in a few seconds, come back to life after its winter death.

Already in 1910, cameramen probably knew to turn faster to better show and to slow down the exploit of a stuntman on screen, or to hold back on the crank to intensify a chase and show the comic in it. With very few exceptions, this is how, so far, the dramatic use of time variations has been limited, even though its amazing aesthetic and psychological value has been demonstrated by quite a few documentaries. In *The Great Dictator*, Chaplin used slow motion, time-lapse, and even reverse motion to add a graceful and eerie touch to the scene of the globe dance at the end of which he climbs, with an unreal agility, if not the walls, at least the window drapes. In this scene, the technique used to insist on the character's madness obviously has a dramatic implication. The only criticism we can make about it is that this technique was used sporadically, clearly breaking with the rhythm of the entire film. If one were to pick one instance of a continuous use of dramatic slow motion, *The Fall of the House of Usher* – and I apologize for this – is the only one that comes to mind. This film best captures its tragic and mysterious atmosphere through the systematic use of a subtle slow motion and through the ratio of 1.5:1 or 2:1 that not only allows for a precise reading of gestures and expressions, like through a magnifying glass, but also automatically dramatizes, prolongs, and holds them in suspense as if waiting for something to happen. The actor can usually perform anything: he comes in, sits down, opens a book, flips through the pages; only the camera gives him a profound gravity, burdens him with an inexplicable secret and makes him a fragment of tragedy through the simple reduction of the temporal ratio of this performance.

One will object that with shots of dialogues, actors cannot move away from the normal rhythm. Indeed! When handling a Moviola, everybody could see that subtle slow motion dramatizes the voice even more powerfully than it does the image. One can use this effect, if not with a direct recording, at least through the re-recordings.

Besides, our reluctance to use the power of cinema to create something beautiful, strange, and dramatic through the variation of the temporal rhythm is not at all triggered by insurmountable technical difficulties. The real reason for this disinterest is a lack of experience, a laziness, an inadequacy of our mind that is a lot less flexible than the cinematographic instrument in conceiving modalities of time different from those we are used to and constrained to live in. In this case, the powers of a machine surpass those of any organism and appear superhuman. This instance is far from being unique in light of, among others, eye glasses, microscopes, sensors, gauges, electron exhibitors that offer us figures of space that we were obviously unable to imagine with our vision as it is. But since Galileo, scientists have been trying to relax, diversify, and enrich our idea of space by bringing into use an infinite number of visual schemas for five centuries. But cinema, at just fifty years old, is the first system that attempts to make us see time differences not transposed into values of space but represented in values of time itself. This is without any doubt the most important aspect in the originality of this mechanism for animated images. But more years will be needed before we get accustomed to use it more commonly, so that our brain can learn how to use time as easily as space. Humankind will owe to cinema this acquisition that will transform our cultural knowlegde.

★ ★ ★

Visual Fabric

Translated by Franck Le Gac

[Jean Epstein, "Tissu visuel," *Esprit de cinéma* (Genève: Éditions Jeheber, 1955), pp. 130-136.]

Any novel, any poem, any work of art in fact, and any film is fundamentally just organized dreaming. Still, film remains – hence its power – the most similar to the original dream, whose mostly visual form it retains. Vision by vision, the shooting script describes, according to the directing technique, a guided reverie during which the author, in some way, mentally projects to himself the film to come – a reverie as precise, a description as meticulous as the sketch in geometry that we also call projective, out of which the engineer foresees the machine to be built.

Like any reverie, the filmed reverie follows a logical course, a perfunctory one in fact, which evokes the order of spoken and written language – that is, the general rational schema of the mind. To depict and group together events based on their order of coexistence or succession, the shooting script is divided into punctuated sequences, each of which corresponds to a chapter, or a paragraph, or a stanza. In turn, sequences are subdivided into shots which have the richness of sentences or clauses, for each bears the expressive value of twenty, fifty, or a hundred words, taken in their complex and particular sense that results from their combination in the group. The spectator grasps this complex signification of the image immediately – without having the need or the time to dissociate and then readjust its elements – and much more through intuition and emotion than logical analysis and deduction.

If it so often happens that a very simple audience perfectly understands every shot of a film while being incapable of following the thread of the narrative, it is precisely because almost no reasoning is needed to read an image taken in isolation, whereas some, even just a little, is necessary to be aware of the connections existing between different views. This is especially the case when these connections belong to a higher logic than that of mere apposition, as happens every time they assume, from one shot to the next, a relation – direct or indirect – of cause, of purpose, of circumstance, whereas in cinema no conjunctions-guides exist that could indicate with precision the relation at stake. Admittedly, there are means of conjunction for the screen – dissolves and wipes in a thousand forms – yet each of them may be subject to almost all imaginable significations of coordination and subordination, to choose among which only the context can settle. Indeed, how could these links even have become specialized since, just as an image accumulates the value of masses of words, an adverbial shot generally conveys a multiple meaning: of time and place, addition and exclusion, consequence and manner, etc. The wealth of terms in visual language is the result both of the extraordinary concrete precision of this mode of expression and the difficulty it meets in abstracting general signs capable of ordering themselves without polyvalence, without vagueness, unequivocally, following a somewhat subtle logic.

It is therefore important, first of all, to rigorously limit the image (as it always tends to say everything and too much at the same time, both that which is useful and that which is useless) so that it shows only what is necessary and sufficient in eliciting the wished-for emotion and so that it allows understanding of the dramatic development. Second, the same strict economy (which will become clarity) is needed between the shots in order to establish syntactical connections as univocal as possible. It is thus through a measure, not of impossible abstraction but of filtration of the meaning of each image (stripping it of its superfluity), and also through a rule for organizing things according to rudimentary logic, that one can fight against the great congenital flaw of visual language: its confusion due to an excess of data and to overdetermination, leading to a multiplicity of dubious and uncertain interpretations, as in dreams.

Truth be told, up to this point the organization of shooting scripts has only had to conform to a kind of prelogic or superlogic, much more simple and general than grammatical logic; to a set of universal algorithms more related to logistics, to Leibniz's "combinatorial art," which checks the reasonable legitimacy of any succession of ideas against an elementary calculation.

The rule according to which the image should only present dramatically or poetically significant elements brings with it a first spatial determination of the shots (distance and angle of the views). Aesthetics alone, photogénie, can only in exceptional cases justify the presentation of a character or an object in unusual perspectives or dimensions. Even more in cinema than in literature, the style that may be called 'normal' is an impersonal, objective style showing the world in its most frequent appearance, at eye level, within the limits of sharpness bounded in a healthy range: an average vision in which any extraordinary glimpses shed their differences, and which least fatigues the mind by sparing it the deciphering of old resemblances hidden under strange distortions. Few spectators accept being forced out of this idleness to see an image which most will simply deem bizarre if they do not sense at least a vague, practical usefulness in it.

As it happens, however, this usefulness can and must appear, and even become a necessity, when for instance the lens gives a cut-out of the phalanx of a finger leaving an incriminating print in an extreme close-up, or, at ground level, the arrival of a locomotive wheel on a rail whose bolts have been removed. The tendency to show only what must be shown, and to show it in the best possible way, constitutes an indisputable justification, and makes possible – even draws images towards – the greatest variety. An additional license, no less determined though more dispensable, may be granted in the case of a concern for accuracy – in itself a subjective notion – when a world is figured on the screen, not as it is seen by an anonymous, neutral optical system, by a standard eye, but as it appears to the look defined in personal terms, either that of the author or that of one protagonist or another. In the eyes of a moving traveler, landscapes are mobile; in those of a drunkard, houses lean; in those of the loser, the victor becomes a gigantic Hercules.

All these justifications for the differentiation of images are themselves justified by the fear that an arbitrary action, not by the prince, but by the director, may suddenly become a reminder of the existence and the activity of the camera, interposed between spectators and reality, and that it may disrupt the decisive magical operation of the *make believe*,[7] of being deluded into believing. Yet the impersonal style, through its monotony and the fixity of its anchorage point, may just as well betray the lie about the instruments used. To the judgment of a public accustomed to a more flexible technique, a long sequence of ordinary images or the intrusion of an impersonal shot in a dialogue alternately seen from the points of view of the two participants will signal the presence of a cameraman as strongly as could the most daring interpretation.

Subject on the surface and in its broad articulations to a certain logical formalism, the living substance of the film still appears as a dreamlike and poetic fabric whose intimate cohesion is not really of a reasonable nature. A hybrid being, cinema is a game for grown-ups analogous, in its core principle, to children's games: it transfigures aspects of reality and uses them, poeticized and dramatized, to stimulate and wear out a superfluous sentimental dynamism. Literature and theater are equally useful games but, because they play out more in the logical domain of speech, they can set reverie in motion less directly – a reverie that is the natural outlet for unspent passions. Film, by contrast, when it proceeds through images, sounds, and musical noises rather than dialogues, speaks almost immediately, thanks to its own illogicality, to the illogicality of affective life – to arouse and absorb its activity.

This illogicality of cinema surfaces in analogical connections, which must double logical relations between sequences as much as possible. A shooting script always seeks to match the final image of a sequence and the initial image of the following one (or, if not images, then sounds, or another image and sound). It does so through any kind of resemblance or opposition in image or sound, through contiguity from the memory, through symbolization, through any chance association of feelings. Indeed, in the rigidity of a purely logical transition, the reverie of the spectator (put by the film in a state close to hypnosis) may be derailed and broken if the bend is not protected by a guardrail suited to dreaming, by a dream-guard.

Thus there exists a paralogical continuity, a visual or visual-sound image, which demands to be followed, and not only in the passage between two sequences, but also within each of them. Such unity – the only one, to tell the truth, a film cannot dispense with – is both a matter of meaning and feeling. In order for the spell within which the spectator lives another existence to persist, unbroken, the look should be allowed to move from one image to another smoothly, without even being aware of the cut. It is a question of harmony between the dimensions, angles, directions, and speeds of juxtaposed movements. And any shared form – a memory of the shot in the reverse shot, even just the smoke of a cigarette – acts as a bridge on which the eye glides from one shot to another without feeling disoriented. When it turns out to be impossible, the hyphen is given to the ear in the form of overlapping sounds. Here as in dreaming, a hiatus in the fabric of representations constitutes a prodrome, the threat of waking.

The other aspect of this indispensable illogical continuity, connecting all the shots in a series to one another, is that it is sentimental. This emotional connection dominates all others and, if need be, can replace them. So well does it constitute the cement par excellence of any dramatic assembly of views that it makes a sequence of shots appear perfectly ordered and homogeneous, even when they would be a non sequitur had they not exactly communicated the same quality of emotion to spectators and maintained it in them. Accordingly, images (sparrows pecking at crumbs on the ledge of a window, an embroidery frame, hands spreading jam on a slice of bread, a dusty piano with the fall board closed, etc.; or women gossiping at the washing place, a door being double-locked, children catching and tormenting a cat, a mailwoman examining a letter with a suspicious look, an empty pew at church, etc.) cease to seem disparate, as their sentimental concordance is grasped (a deceased woman being missed or the hostility of a village towards one of its inhabitants). There again, the film is built according to the architectural principle of the dream, whose representations have value and come together less because of their literal than their figurative sense, as the latter finds itself attached to a given affective climate.

This sentimental idealization of the image is not a general abstraction but a symbolization peculiar to each case, each scenario. This symbolization makes it possible to push the photographic interpretation of common aspects of reality much farther than the logical rule alone would allow, defining the shot as the necessary and sufficient figure, formed by a given eye in a given physical position and operating state. However, a distortion of appearances may also be done away with altogether. Even photographed in the most banal way, an object may receive from the context an entirely singular meaning: slice of bread and jam = grandmother. Any allegorization will in general be accepted all the more readily when it appears more as a spontaneous, unexpected product of the existence of some preceding images. And it would be quite difficult to use without falseness or ridicule older, all-purpose emblems (heart for love, anchor for hope, skull for death, etc.) incompatible with the realism of the cinematographic image.

The wide-ranging analogy that surfaces between the arrangements of a film's shooting script and the organization of a dream or a reverie may expose the language of the screen to accusations of extreme deception and lying. Rather, this analogy shows the scope of cinematographic realism, which is extroverted and introverted at once and which, better than any other, can provide convincing descriptions of both worlds, exterior and interior. For there also exists a psychic reality, more surely even than a physical one. It is out of faithfulness to mental realism – perhaps the more real of the two – that film so widely dares to transpose the significations of forms, to substitute people for things and vice versa, to use the part for the whole, making the whole less than its fraction, to make the object palpable and active, to represent any fragment of the universe in a deeply melodramatic light.

Certainly, spectators – who for so long have been trained to make the illogicality of their most intimate life subservient, and even to stifle it, to the benefit of the logic needed for their exterior relations – sometimes find themselves surprised as they feel the screen taking them back to their oldest, most natural, and most powerful ways of being moved and of thinking. As engaging, as easy as the path opened by cinema might be, through which the mind currently experiences the probably salutary need to extricate itself from an excess of rational habits, the director should still be careful in striking a balance between archaic elements and romantic renovation. Still, this renewal of the soul, reoriented for a time towards its primitive functions, certainly constitutes the essential goal of cinematographic art, and a shooting script shows an understanding of this end insofar as it straightforwardly uses the linking and interpretation of images according to what is called the logic of sensibility.

★ ★ ★

Pure Cinema and Sound Film

Translated by Franck Le Gac

[Jean Epstein, "Le cinéma pur et le film sonore," Esprit de cinéma (Genève: Éditions Jeheber, 1955), pp. 137-141.]

People often believe that pure cinema is now just something for cinematheques, a relic of the silent era. And yet, in fact, there never did and never will exist any but one problem (more or less apparent, more or less close to its solution) in cinema: the expression of any thing, from the outer world as well as from the inner world, in cinematographic terms, that is, in terms of movement. Which is exactly the object of pure cinema.

In the silent era, cinema could only represent the visual aspect of movement. The stake was then to express everything, the objective and the subjective, as much as possible through the image alone. Subtitles thus became the main enemy that had to be excluded from films because they were not a view, strictly speaking, and because they introduced words, the elements of another mode of expression, of another language, set to the much lower speed of another system of thought than thought through visual representations. In a few seconds of presence on the screen, a moving image shows as though simultaneously a hundred qualities of a thing and the action of this thing, as well as the cause, the goal, the result, the circumstances of this action. To describe this almost instantaneous spectacle, speech – which has to make analytical choices between substantives, verbs, adjectives, and has to assemble them logically into subjects, direct, indirect, defining objects, or adverbial phrases; into main, coordinated, parenthetical, relative clauses – uses at least a few minutes, that is, at least sixty times as much time. Even then, this verbal description always proves to be marred by mistakes and gaps, inaccuracies and aloofness. An image, even with few events, kindles a much richer and quicker mental life than a cluster of words might fuel in the same amount of time. Hence this impression of slowness, which surprised us in the first sound films around 1928.

Verbal thought is slow because it consists of a complicated symbolic system formed of abstract elements, which have to be matched to the data of perceptible reality through an analysis, grouped according to grammatical logic, and on that basis deciphered by the listener or the reader. Not only do these logical operations of abstraction, analysis, and construction take time to be performed, they also interpose, between a spectacle and the emotion this spectacle may arouse, a network of transmission that runs through reason, where criticism may find a place to exert itself and act as a resistance decreasing the intensity of the stream. Everyone knows that the sight of an accident on the street may be deeply moving, even when the account in the newspaper would not have caused the bat of an eyelid. The image corresponds, therefore, to a type of thought both faster and more moving than the thought corresponding to words.

The affinity between image and feeling is an affinity of rhythm. These few seconds during which an image remains on the screen, which are not enough for the reasonable language of words to capture, are more than enough for the spectator to be moved by it, to gain a complete and effective sentimental knowledge of it. Indeed, in the domain of feelings, variations take place at a much faster pace than how quickly the transformations of reasoned thought are formed. And a spectator's emotionalism finds itself capable of immediately using dramatic hints provided by the film as it unfolds, before these may be intercepted by the brake-filter of reason. Hence the prodigious power of conviction issuing from the screen.

These are, very basically, the justifications for pure cinema within the category of silent cinema. And certainly, if like cinema one could design a visual language for universal individual use, if everyone carried in their pockets, instead of a pen, a small device that could record and project immediately all the images of thought, humankind would have at its disposal a means of mutual understanding so miraculously precise and fast, subtle and comprehensive, that next to it speech and writing would appear as barbaric relics.

However, the image suddenly found itself capable of making itself heard as well. The sound of film was at first used mostly musically, which only improved on the established usage of accompanying every projection with an orchestra or a piano player. In fact, the music of the image, like the image itself, is addressed almost exclusively at the feeling of the listener-spectator, and the union of these two agents of expression, which are minimally rational, constitutes a balanced, synchronous couple in action. This balance and this synchronism found themselves destroyed when film became "100% talkie" in the enthusiasm the cinema felt when suddenly cured of its silence. This resulted in a strange and ill-assorted vehicle of thought, one of whose wheels – speech – spun some sixty times slower than the other, image. These two rhythms evidently had to harmonize with each other as much as possible eventually, with one subordinated more or less to the other. The heavy spiritual legacy of classical rationalism, the old influence of spoken and written culture, the ease and the benefits which the imitation of the novel and the theater brought to directors prevailed over the little-apparent practical usefulness, the inexperience and lack of organization of the young visual language, suspect of being suitable only for very subtle poetry, akin to dreaming, this enemy number one of our extroverted civilization. Allowing for exceptions, the image was reduced to the role of mouthpiece, connective tissue, responsible only for ensuring the connection between words.

After 1930, pure cinema thus seemed bound to disappear completely. Words came aplenty to spare the illustrators of film any effort of invention. As to this profound and fleeting unspeakable quality, which the image had sometimes succeeded in capturing, it was crushed by the slow, heavy, and rigid system of speech, which sent it back into limbo, a state it was well used to. Within its views, as in the rhythm according to which these views related to one another, film had lost some of its fundamental originality, its primordial quality, its ability to create or follow a very swift movement of thought.

Certainly, speech could not be excluded from film, nor should it be. But someone had to curb this laziness in which one no longer sought to express oneself faster and more finely than through words and beyond them; in which one subscribed to the pretension of saying everything and being the only one able to do so. For some years now cinema has heeded the call for this reform, producing fewer films that are perpetual, falsely brilliant dialogues in order to also put out works in which speech is gradually reduced to the place it occupies in real life. Unquestionably important, this place is still limited, very limited even: that of moderate subtitling in an old silent film.

With a few directors, a trend towards a return to the outright supremacy of the image may even be observed. However, one can no longer support this image being silent or continuously accompanied by the flow of music: the artifice and deception of these are shocking. Films with very little dialogue thus rely more on atmospheres based on noises to fill their silences. Still clumsily or tentatively used, this resource deserves to be fully exploited, as it belongs in the essentially cinematographic domain, like the image. Just as a view, a noise is addressed at the imagination with a speed and directness that neither require nor allow setting critical reason into motion. If critical reason comes into play, it is only after the fact, and generally too late. Having already resonated in memory and aroused an emotion, it is also based on an already formed representation. Images and noises act synchronously and reach their mental representation simultaneously, whereas speech – when it is not treated only as intonation, which in practice happens more often than is thought – is still going through the mechanism of logical deciphering; without the play of this mechanism, it cannot represent anything nor move anyone.

In its great role as the discoverer of mobility, the cinematographic instrument is as capable of revealing sound movements as visual movements. If we tend to show more interest in the latter, it is because, on the one hand, the cinematograph is still better equipped to describe them in detail at this point; and on the other hand, because sight generally prevails over all other human senses. Yet the domain of pure cinema embraces both the image and the soundtrack, which share the same stumbling block: the word, written or uttered, because it is in itself a form of thought which, if not completely solidified, is very viscous, at the very least.

★ ★ ★

Seeing and Hearing Thought

Translated by Franck Le Gac

[Jean Epstein, "Voir et entendre penser," *Esprit de cinéma* (Genève: Éditions Jeheber, 1955), pp. 142-145.]

For some twenty years, production has been dominated by a misunderstanding whereby a film is held to be a means, not to express thought, but to reproduce speech. This mistake derives from another one, still to this day spread by college regents, many of whom claim that there is no thought without words. A share of our thoughts does indeed result in interior monologues which, in moments of confusion, we may go as far as to mutter. Still, beneath this verbal thought, which is all the more coherent logically because it is closer to consciousness and its oral or graphic realization, there exists a more intimate, less conscious, but extremely active mental life in which images play a very important part. The moving memories of a friend, of a day of vacation, of a loss are thus first and foremost a gallery of *tableaux vivants*, portraits and landscapes, preserved by memory, touched up by oblivion. Only later do words attach to these visual elements, whose affective climate they very imperfectly manage to render. Thought in images is therefore not reserved for dreaming, reverie, or delirium; it is part of the ordinary life of the soul, during the day and at night, and in such a continuous manner that some attention is required to glimpse it and identify it as the foundation of verbal thought.

When silent cinema sought to refine the psychology of the characters in its fictions, it initially used and abused subtitles, then resorted to close-ups, and at last discovered that it was quite naturally capable of representing, through the images of the screen, the images of this profound thought that underpins words. The first flashbacks,[8] or views representing memories, which appeared in a few American films, were characterized by a soft focus which, like italics, indicated that these shots did not belong to the same level of objectivity as the rest of the sequence. At the opera, for instance, Faust sees Marguerite through tulle. In *La Roue*, Gance, in an analogous search for an inner truth, showed shapes gradually growing darker and then disappearing in the sight of a man becoming blind. With some directors, harmonizing the shooting technique with the state of mind of the character supposedly seeing what the audience saw became a permanent concern. The process was quite legitimate, so legitimate in fact that it became commonplace.

However, the real problem – that of putting on the screen, in their authentic illogicality, associations of thought through visual images – had until then been barely touched upon. Suddenly, under the influence of Surrealism, a few authors were able to direct four or five films in which they claimed to describe a purely mental spectacle and drama. Images no longer had to tell what a hero did or said, but what he thought, everything he thought, respecting the apparent disorder of this psychic activity. Yet the public, saturated with verbal logic, demanded that a drama or a comedy be built in every detail as a succession of theorems, and that the arrest of the assassin or the engagement of the fiancés be deducible point by point, with the rigor of a demonstration. And the screenings of the last Surrealist film were stopped by order of the police headquarters on the pretence of obscenity. In truth, the issue was to put an end to an offence, not so much to morals as to one of its old parents, dating back to Aristotle: formal logic. Shortly before the triumph of the talkie, verbal rationalism thus already scored a first victory and, already, put a ban on the romanticism of purely visual discourse.

For long our ancestors, who invented speaking, remained in awe at the power of the word. It was enough to utter: "Do!" "Give!" "Carry!" for a thing to be done, given, carried. It was magic, undoubtedly. When, around the age of thirty, film found itself cured of its silence, it also started believing in the bewitchment of words and their power to create everything: the setting and the fact and the soul of characters. Why labor so much trying to express a few snatches of visual thought when verbal thought seemed to flow on its own in a dialogue or mono- logue? And why linger over the uncertain search for a new optical language when the old verbal languages presented the moving image with their safest commod- ities?

However, we think aloud quite rarely if our thoughts are not meant to be com- municated immediately to some interlocutor. And the typical monologue, that of the actor taking the stage alone or speaking in an aside, constitutes a shocking artifice, even in theatrical conventions. Cinematographic dramaturgy, which is not without conventions but still follows psychological reality more closely, soon reckoned that on the screen that kind of monologue amounted to a comic scan- dal.

Other films featured a more interior form of monologue, closer to truth. Here, it is a doctor doing a morning round in his neighborhood, with commonplace remarks coming to mind: "For God's sake, why did I tie a knot in my handkerch- ief? Another kid who doesn't find life to his taste... in a way, I would tend to agree with him... Ah, there I am, I had to remember little Colter's birthday... That's it... buy him a little present... a toy..." Yet these thoughts, if the attitude and the ex- pression of the doctor match them, are not uttered through his mouth. The audi- ence can hear them whispered by the very muted voice of the walker, by a voice barely spoken and which may give the illusion of a voiced-only thought. Else- where, the same technique makes the entreaties of a woman heard very softly; her whole face is praying, but her lips are not moving. This is certainly an artifice, but the artifice of a plausible effect. And should not the scene from *Jean de la Lune*, in which the rumble of a train turns into a rhythm, be taken as the origin of this system, as the ear deciphers a few words ceaselessly on the traveler's mind?[9]

This old example from *Jean de la Lune* shows perhaps the best and the most delicate use of the technique. For here the danger is of wanting to have verbal thought say too much, and on the model of spoken discourse. Though more logi- cal than thought in images, thought organized in words remains even further removed from the order of oral language than oral language is removed from the perfect geometrical rectitude of the written sentence. Always hedging about its goals; directly linked to the fancy of its genitor, visual thought; time and again modified, diverted, enriched by the interferences of its outsides and of coenaes- thesia,[10] the interior verb follows a much more convoluted, intermittent, disparate progression than, for instance, the thoughts of the doctor mentioned previously might lead one to believe. In *Le Jour se lève*, the monologue of the murderer com- bines snippets related to his crime which he mechanically scans in an old news- paper.[11] Though uttered in a hushed voice, the monologue represents more truth- fully a real arrangement of words coming to mind.

Between the logical order of the speech composed in order to be given or read and the pre-logical relation of a spontaneous series of images, there is an infinity of intermediate forms of thought that are more or less verbalized and rationalized at the same time that they are more or less visualized and sentimentalized. Thought really exists only in this mixed state of images and words, reasoning and emotion. In its chimerical ambition of translating everything through images, silent film had the excuse of not being able to speak, of not being equipped with the instrument necessary in the expression of the spirit of geometry. However, sound film would be unforgivable if it lost its way claiming to convert all the life of the soul into words – if it forgot that it has retained the means to express, through the image, the spirit of subtlety.

★ ★ ★

The Counterpoint of Sound

Translated by Franck Le Gac

[Jean Epstein, "Le contrepoint du son," *Esprit de cinéma* (Genève: Éditions Jeheber, 1955), pp. 146-149.]

In current shooting scripts, one may note that the right-hand column, used for the notation of sound, often features a much more developed text than the left side of the page, reserved for the description of the image. This may lead some to believe that the arrangement of all the sound elements of a film is usually pre-established with the greatest care and in the greatest detail.

In fact, however, of the three means to produce sound – noise, music, speech – the last one almost single-handedly fills the provisions of the shooting script by its importance. In this flow of dialogue, one rarely comes across even a scant indication of the sound of a door being closed or a car starting, or a vague suggestion of some musical accompaniment. And the asset value of speech, as it appeared in cinema some twenty years ago and as it still rules today in many films, undercuts all the other values of image and sound, forcing its own approach on them – an approach which even in the most skillfully disorderly texts remains set by grammatical logic. It may thus have looked as though the talkie had made any construction by the shooting script irrelevant, other than giving places for cuts based on lines of dialogue and sentences. If, nevertheless, it is admitted that there should sometimes be alterations to the regularity of these syntactic caesuras, these are oddities which, according to this system, should be left to a later occurrence of chance, that of editing.

Still, this double use, synchronous and equivalent, of image and speech necessarily produces an impression of dullness, boredom, emptiness in the minds of the spectators-auditors who are neither so distracted nor so narrow-minded that they need simultaneously to see what they hear and hear what they see in order to understand it. For the eye and the ear not to result in a vicious pleonasm when they contribute to putting a datum together, the work assigned to every sense should be quite different. In his memoirs, Casanova considers as an instance of the most serious stupidity the fact of a lover saying "I love you" to the woman loved. Yet this is a mistake nine films out of ten make in nine shots out of ten.

No more understandable would be a piano player continuously hitting exactly the same notes with both hands, one or two octaves apart. The play of image and sound, of sight and hearing, may and should also achieve a sort of two-part counterpoint, in the harmony of more complex significations, which evidently constitute the true art of a language involving two registers of expression. It is useless for a man shown arriving to say "I'm coming." But if, while hearing him say that he is arriving, the same character is shown putting some effort into not coming, or coming only with specific intentions – restricting or amplifying or changing the meaning of the words "I'm coming" – then the audience is puzzled, busy trying to understand, forced, as in real life, to combine and reconcile inconsistent meanings into a worthy lesson. A certain degree of contradiction between image and speech, of falsehood between the eye and the ear, thus seems necessary for a shooting script to offer the opportunity for an intellectual exercise captivating enough, and for an illusion of reality convincing and moving enough. The rule does not only hold true for the public, in fact: all actors know that the sincerity of a character, the pleonasm of synonymous words and gestures, make parts difficult, flat, unrewarding, whereas the deception within a character whose action, face, and voice find themselves perpetually diverging makes for "golden parts."

On the screen, a door shown closing without the noise of this shutting seems like negligence, an error. On the other hand, if the noise faithfully accompanies the image, the effect, too simple and unnecessary, is found to look naive, silly almost. An acceptable solution consists in providing the noise alone over another image, for instance that of the dialogue continuing after the departure of one of the participants. Like speech, noise thus must often be dissociated from the visual aspect of the phenomenon it depends on, when it does not add any particular signification to it. In the end, aesthetic judgments, though they are often believed to be disinterested, are actually always founded on a criterion of usefulness.

This is also why this door noise, which stupidly doubles the image, can become prodigiously interesting and eloquent if an inflection is given to it that adds to dramatic tension. This dramatization of a sound may be simply obtained through the conspicuous place where it is located in the action, or through an acoustic interpretation, a distortion of the sound itself. Either technique amounts to endowing the element of sound with a given character of unreality or, to put it better, of a superior reality, mental and poetic: of surreality. A trend has thus been manifested – for little time and still feebly, in fact – towards personalizing the representation of sound, making it capable of subjective fidelity, of psychological truth, in a manner analogous to that (much more successful) which forced the image to be, if necessary, a thought image.

Films are beginning to appear in which one discovers the murmur of an idea, the whisper of memories-words, the strange reach of sentences one could swear were heard but which were never uttered. The voice of cinema strives with difficulty, slowly, to become a human voice altogether, whose resonance would not only depend on the setting but on the soul as well, where cathedral-like echoes and crypt-like muted sounds also exist. Much more important, and imminent: all beings, all objects will be able to speak. It is the task of scriptwriters to goad sound technicians into capturing the voice – which exists – of a passing cloud, a rejoicing house, grass growing.

Certainly, this inarticulate language of things is, most of the time, but a neutral or irritating noise for our ears, composite and confusing, sometimes barely perceptible. Like our sight, our hearing enjoys only a limited power of separation. The indentations of the soundtrack sing too many cries at once, entangled, compressed, squeezed against one another in an undecipherable hubbub. The eye too can read, but in a superficial and uncertain way, a quick expression on a distant face, transformed by countless movements of muscles and the skin, commanded by a complex emotion. This sum of small gestures needs to appear magnified according to dimensions of space and time, in close-up and semi-slow motion, for its complete signification and deep harmony to be discoverable. However, this technique of analysis seemed so far exclusively reserved for visual elements, and no shooting script provided for sound close-ups in slow motion.

In its spatial dimension alone, as a mere increase in volume set by the potentiometer, the close-up of sound had admittedly existed for ages. But if the plastic form always plays an essential part in visual aspects, in auditory appearances it is their kinetic state, their measures of movement and duration which mainly characterize the phenomenon – whose other, geometric figure, wave-like or spindle-like, generally remains hidden. This explains why musicians have been able to spread the myth of a music existing outside of space, in time alone. This is also why the most interesting enlargement of sound is not obtained by artificially getting closer to the sound source, but by stretching, slowing down vibrations spread over a longer duration. This is why, at last, the sound – which only involves, by way of stillness, the invisible balance of stationary waves – has to lend itself to cinematographic interpretation, which everywhere opts for mobility, better even than the image, where the essential movement is much more caught up in the rigidity of a largely solid world.

★ ★ ★

The Close-up of Sound

Translated by Franck Le Gac

[Jean Epstein, "Le Gros plan du son," *Esprit de cinéma* (Genève: Éditions Jeheber, 1955), pp. 150-160.]

The real fate of cinema is not to make us laugh or cry over the same old tales, which an eminent theater critic once calculated as numbering at most three dozen types. The essential generosity of the cinematographic instrument – like that of all noble instruments, which transform and multiply the power of our senses – consists in enriching and renewing our conception of the universe, making its ways of being accessible to us, that looking and listening cannot directly perceive.

And it is not only that the lens makes us familiar with faraway countries we will never set foot on; that it turns us into witnesses, across time and through walls, of events and lives we would otherwise know as only a date and a name; that it introduces us into the very thought, the way of feeling and understanding of illustrious figures and admired heroes, whose presence and confidence seemed to us like wishes that could never come true. It is also and above all that the screen shows us things, magnified and detailed, in perspectives, relations, movements unknown until then, which force our attention, contradict our patterns of thought, and compel us to revise most of our judgments.

For instance, slow and accelerated motion in particular reveal to us a world suddenly deprived of one of its most evident material qualities: solidity. It becomes a thoroughly fluid world, where the permanence of forms has vanished into a space that no longer knows any symmetry and a time that has ceased to be uniform. This being the case, all the great laws of reason, even the principles of identity and non-contradiction, all of our physics and philosophy appear as local, fortuitous arrangements, relating to a given state of movement – itself quite random, and stabilized around us only in exceptional cases.

In the domain of sound, there has been very little attempt to seek out the innovative interpretations of which film recording is capable. The huge majority of technicians do not concern themselves at all with what the instrument they handle may reveal as uncommon, or never heard before, in the noises it is exposed to. Or, when they do concern themselves with it, they react in horror, with the view of removing like quitch grass any strange novelty, any mysterious disobedience towards which the machine may have found itself pushed by its own nature.

How many directors, when they need a horse's gallop, will ask themselves: let us listen to how cinema translates this sound? And the same who go to this trouble often exclaim afterwards: This is not it at all! Then they will fabricate or buy ready-made a mock gallop, produced by knocking walnut shell halves or suction pads on an ironing board. The general trend thus consists, not in probing the microphone on its personal talent for expressing the music of nature and increasing this whole part of our knowledge that comes from hearing but, on the contrary, to force the mechanical ear and voice to rehash all the old timbres we already know by heart. These efforts in the wrong direction and their imperfect achievements prove, at any rate, that sound cinema is in itself organized also for something else than these parroting exercises; that besides this imitative vocabulary imposed by sound-effects engineers, it involves spontaneous, new, wild accents which will sooner or later entail a transformation of the art of film.

Besides their dramatic and poetic usefulness, will the new sound forms, which cinema would keenly put within range of our hearing, have the power to alter our representation of the universe, down to our most deeply rooted intuitions – as much as did the new visible aspects born on the screen? Probably not. The intelligence of our species is more visual than auditory. In our individual and social life, in the whole development of our civilization, sight has played the part of a conductive sense whose data are the most numerous, the most precise, the most memorable, the easiest to rethink. Even speech, as long as we have not read or seen the words, does not appear to us as something we can get a firm grasp on, and in fact, at least three-quarters of our vocabulary translates mostly retinal impressions. Except in a small minority of particularly gifted individuals, hearing only represents the second outer sense. From the moment an auditory impression calls for a somewhat finer expression, even musicographers find themselves at a loss for adequate words, go on borrowing epithets and metaphors from the language of the eye, or even that of touch, of muscular sense, with the result that writings of this kind present a typical confusion.

The thing is, the ordinary data we receive from hearing are themselves confused, unstable, fleeting, and do not lend themselves to logical examination, definition, or ordered signification. While it is often ineffable, a mere noise may still directly cause a psycho-physiological shock which puts the subject in a state of instantaneous, intense, thoughtless emotion. Sight thus appears, not at all as a sense necessarily and exclusively devoted to intelligence, but as the sense whose information is also subject to the operations of reason, whereas hearing picks up messages that for the most part trigger purely sentimental reflexes. Even in a speech listened to, and as rational as the text might be, what the listeners show themselves most sensitive to, what touches them most vividly and convinces them the most swiftly, is not the intelligible meaning of words but the timbre of the orator, the quality of the sound of the voice. The tone makes the tune, as the proverb goes.

If, therefore, the extension by means of cinema of what is already known of the realm of sound, the harvest of not-yet-heard noises do not seem on first examination to be set to provide great opportunities for ideological renewal, we may on the other hand expect to find important resources there to renew the moving power of films, to bring variety and development to the dramaturgy of the screen.

And on reflection, we have to reckon that this enriched sensibility cannot but eventually entail a certain general evolution of the mind as well.

Since the techniques of slow and accelerated motion best emphasize the originality of the cinematographic vision by creating, through film, forms and movements indiscernible to the naked eye, it was only natural to try and apply the same processes to sound recording in the hope of also putting into play, at once and as much as possible, the interpretive and revelatory power of the machine in the domain of hearing. If accelerated and slow motion bring so much novelty into visible appearances, it is precisely because they reproduce things in a system of relations where, for the first time in the entire history of techniques of representation, the fourth dimension – time – plays the role of a variable, one not any less important than that of the three dimensions of space, and where duration may be figured with the same freedom of interpretation, magnification, or compression as spatial distances. From this perspective, no longer does any form exist seperate from movement; no longer are there any objects to speak of, only events. Similarly, varying measurements of time – of the speed at which sound phenomena succeed one another – bring qualities to these phenomena that we would never know about without the modification in the frequency of vibrations.

Whether one decided to begin with acceleration or deceleration, to which a greater number of natural sounds lend themselves, the instrument had at any rate to be modified in its most sacred principle: synchronism at constant intervals. Even though the problem amounted in fact and very simply to ensuring that during a re-recording the track already printed at normal speed and the track to be printed could run at different speeds – one being the double, triple, or quadruple of the other – from the outset the eminently traditionalist tribe of technicians deemed the endeavor, if not impossible, at least adventurous, complicated, and carrying enormous costs. However, engineer Léon Vareille carried it out perfectly by having a joiner calibrate a block of pulleys, at a total cost of seven hundred francs. Rather than using the roundabout means of re-recording, which is advantageous only economically, one might just as well make direct sound recordings at variable speed, devoting a little resourcefulness, time, and expense to transform a device and synchronize it with a low-speed camera.

If, before it was achieved, the slowing down of sound met with the skepticism of some cameramen, afterwards it was strangely denied outright by a physicist specializing in sensitometry. The scientist, who had just been listening to slowed-down sounds for half an hour, declared right out of the blue that he would not believe his ears; that a priori, before and against any experience, the slowing down of sound already constituted an absurdity, excluded in advance from any condition of possibility. The argumentation started from the cliché according to which music in particular and sound in general consisted in phenomena of pure duration. Surprising deductions followed from this, demonstrating that noises were neither shrinkable nor extensible, as God had made them once and for all.

Accordingly, the deceleration of sound could involve neither deceleration nor sound, but perhaps something else, and what exactly no one really knew.

That music is a phenomenon of pure duration (and any noise, any speech act, any organized series of sound waves are also kinds of music) is an axiom very much in favor with musicians, at the same time that it is an obvious untruth. First of all, because space and time are our two indispensable and inseparable means of thinking whatever may be thought, and without whose cooperation there may be no knowledge of anything. For instance, can we imagine as physically possible a music to whose vibrations no elastic volume of medium would be available – that is, no space to form and propagate?[12] Frequency is not the only way to characterize the shock of sound; there are also amplitude and wavelength, which are spatial measures. Do a score, an orchestration not take into account different sound planes, that is to say, various spatial distances, real or fictitious, at which this or that type of timbre should be located? The interdependency of space and time, their unity, their spiritual consubstantiality have become commonplaces to such a degree that no one should have to argue for them any longer. Let us note, however, that cinematographic deceleration provides yet another striking material experience of it, since the increase in the temporal dimension of a wave necessarily comes as the result of the proportional increase in the spatial inscription of the phenomenon on film. A double or triple expansion in duration is absolutely linked to a double or triple extension of the length of film. Here, time and space are covariant factors.

It is by acting upon the factor of space – and more specifically on one of the elements of this spatial factor, length – that cinema as an instrument causes a corresponding modification in the temporal value of the wave. Thus whenever duration doubles, the frequency of the vibration is obviously divided by two, which is to say that the produced sound has gone an octave lower. By lengthening film footage and time again, a new decrease in frequency is obtained, and with it a new shift towards lower sounds. And so on. One of the effects of deceleration thus lies in sounds becoming lower and, when this is pushed far enough, in their getting lost in the inaudible domain of infrasonic vibrations. There, the vibrations of air are so slowed down and spaced out that the ear will remain insensitive to a movement that sounds to it like immobility, that is, like silence, just as in a visual slow motion taken to the limit the eye stops perceiving the roughness of the sea, for instance, which appears as a solid, frozen surface.

In any case, the transposition of natural noises in (at least) the four perfectly audible lower octaves already makes it possible for a musician to compose a rich and varied sound score for a film. Instead of having at his disposal just two or three sea noises, for example, all roughly in the same tone, the composer will be able to play on a keyboard of twelve or twenty-four or thirty-six or forty-eight different tonalities (with transposition at fractions of an octave), whose combination at the premixing stage will also allow him to diversify the resource infinitely.

It thus becomes possible to create chords and dissonances, melodies and symphonies of noises, which are a new, specifically cinematographic music.

On the one hand, the eye and the ear are insensitive to a very slow movement; they prove incapable of perceiving a difference between the two successive positions of a mobile being when, from one to the other, the spatial distance is very small relative to the time used to cover it. On the other hand, sight and hearing also turn out to be insensitive to a very fast movement; they are powerless when it comes to distinguishing two positions of a mobile being separated by a minimal time interval with relation to the path traveled. For example, the pendulum of a metronome with a short period of swing will not appear moving back and forth around the position of equilibrium. Instead, a hazy grayness occupying the whole space of oscillation will appear. And from a busy street at rush hour, nothing will be made out of human voices, the shuffle of the crowd, the exhaust of engines: only a muted hum will be heard. Too many different tones succeed one another too quickly for listeners to register them one by one and to recognize them; to these listeners, they form an indivisible and undecipherable mixture.

If, however, through a slowed-down recording or re-recording, the frequency at which these vibrations of the air follow one another is reduced, and if the intervals of time between the nodes of wave trains are thereby increased, many of these tones will cease to appear as overlapping one another, as superimposed in our perception, and will become distinctly audible and knowable, just as, through the slow motion of the image, some positions of the swing of the metronome will be made clearly visible and definable. Deceleration therefore increases the naturally limited power of separation available to the organs of vision and audition; it makes the spreading of phenomena in duration possible; it constitutes a sort of microscope of time.

A second effect of deceleration thus enables the ear to analyze auditory impressions more finely. Yet this analytical effect finds itself modified by the first effect: lower sounds. While deceleration may break up a complex sonority into its component parts, it cannot do so without at the same time distorting them, transposing them into a lower tessitura in which they may not always be recognized as what they represent or would represent to regular hearing. A general constraint of the experiment is thus that it alters its object to some degree. This alteration – whose usefulness will appear in other respects – may be remedied only by isolating the elements obtained and by bringing them back to their original cadence through a speeded-up re-recording.

Yet for the poetic or dramatic film, the most interesting result of analysis through deceleration is precisely the creation of sounds whose unusual character may renew and reinforce a moving atmosphere. The great natural sounds – wind, sea, thunderstorm, rock fall, blazing fire – precisely comprise tangled wave packets emitted by very different sources and complex compressions of infinitely particular and numerous tones. These symphonies, which happen too close together in time, represent the perfect material for a work of deceleration by cinema. If, in an artificial noise (skis sliding on snow, for instance), deceleration can detect but the means of the trick (a brush against a silky fabric), in a natural sound (the wind, for example), an analysis reveals not only a gripping transposition of identifiable elements (the rustle of branches, the modulations of telegraphic wires and posts, the song of an air stream in a chimney, shutters banging, etc.), but also many other mysterious timbres which do not even have a name in language. Introduced in a world of unknown tones where the markers of the already heard are rare, hearing leads to an experience of dizziness as well as anxiety, which parallel the astonishment, originating in the look, of images of the world photographed with infrared. These noises as well as these landscapes, until then unknown to man, appear fraught with insecurity, charged with who knows what expectation, what threat.

Such arbitrary dramatic expression – dramatic in itself – which all sounds assume even when their origin remains recognizable, constitutes the third remarkable effect of the deceleration of sound. Indeed, deceleration also performs such dramatization on the image, where the simplest gestures gain added significance, seem to be more thought through, loaded with intentions, hidden meanings, secrets. The dramatizing effect of the deceleration of sound also proceeds from a surprise on the part of listeners, whose attention finds itself awakened and held by something strange. Then and mainly, the lowering of tones triggers a psycho-physiological reaction, according to which we interpret low sounds as messengers of sadness or, at least, as news of importance, to such an extent that the word that conveys the lowness of a musical note and the seriousness of an event is the same (*gravité*).

Thus dramatized, noises become all the better able to constitute a moving sound score, and they may also give a voice to parts played by inhuman or superhuman characters which film dramaturgy has more and more frequently participate in an action. The mere noise of a door being closed, recorded in real life, may already, if suitably placed at the editing stage, assume more dramatic importance than the most clever line of dialogue. Yet this same noise, made lower, extended, dramatized, interpreted by a more or less accented deceleration, will produce a much more striking impression on the audience, one much more precisely geared towards the desired effect.

The transformation of instrumental music and dialogue through deceleration is also of great interest, but their use is more sensitive. Musical instruments and the human voice adjust their vibrations in the perfect proportion needed for understanding their harmonies, the excessive distortion of which would risk destroying their charm and intelligibility. On speech, the dramatizing effect of deceleration is particularly clear, but when it is pushed a little, the space between vibrations also translates as quaver. Slowed-down voices are also old voices, mournful, agonizing, sorrowful; slowed-down cries reach phenomenal intensities in the expression of suffering or dread.

Accelerated sound is no more difficult to obtain than decelerated sound, but its application appears more limited. The effects of acceleration are analogous to those of slowed motion, but in reverse: increase in the frequency of vibrations and consequently higher tonalities, transposition of sounds in the higher octaves. Pushed far enough, acceleration has in principle the consequence of making all the tones vanish in an inaudibly high pitch, in the domain of ultrasounds. Instead of a dramatization of noises, one notes their cheerfulness; they tend to produce an impression of arbitrary comicality, to trigger a reflex of hilarity, which burlesque comedies may advantageously use.

Still, the most intriguing result of acceleration as well as deceleration is without a doubt the creation of original tones. Deceleration produces these by lowering and analyzing vibrations which are too high-pitched, too quick, too close to one another, whereas acceleration obtains them through the elevation and compression of waves which are too slow or too spread out. If deceleration draws periodic movements from the silence of the highest pitches to introduce them into audible reality, acceleration also takes rhythms of air from mute infrasonic vibrations, also turning them into sound entities. We need speeded-up motion to see that a dune crawls, that a crystal reproduces, that a vegetal stem raises its tip in a spiral, that everything moves. We need speeded-up sound to discover that every thing has a living voice, to hear stones and trees speak their true language, the mountain thunder its avalanche, rust eating into iron, ruins complaining of their decrepitude.

Let us note that these important analogies between the accelerations and decelerations of image and sound conceal a deep difference. With the image, neither slow nor accelerated motion modifies the velocity of propagation and the frequency of light waves; they come into play only to change the rhythm by which fixed and complex sets of visible forms succeed one another – sets where the organization of elementary optical phenomena remains constant. With sound, slowing down and speeding up do not change the velocity of propagation of waves either, but they do modify its frequency; they make each audible form vary, directly treating the acoustic phenomenon itself as a variable. By contrast, visual slow and accelerated motion exert their action through indirect means, lengthening or shortening only the intervals between images, between the clusters of countless vibrations which for their part remain unaffected. What is changed is the succession of these clusters; it is a (variable) frequency of (invariable) frequencies. One thus understands what the learned sensitometer did not: that the most extreme acceleration and deceleration, which make any noise disappear into ultrasounds or infrasonic vibrations, may not cause an image to disappear in ultraviolet or infrared, since these processes are capable of distorting individual sound waves, but not individual light waves. Slowed-down sound, which in effect slows down the frequency of the sonic vibration, deserves its name, though it does not slow down the propagation of sound waves. The inaccuracy would be to speak of slowed-down light rather than slowed-down images, since slowing down has no bearing on light vibrations themselves.

★ ★ ★

The Delirium of a Machine

Translated by Christophe Wall-Romana

[Jean Epstein, "Le Délire d'une machine," in *Esprit de cinéma* (Paris: Éditions Jeheber, 1955), pp. 168-179.]

Remarkable is the coincidence in time between the first great flowering of cinema, still silent, and the movement of ideas that was labeled the Surrealist Revolution. What representations could, better than animated images, assemble that language emancipated from the logical rigor of grammatical construction – a language nonetheless universally comprehensible, which Apollinaire had prided himself on forging? What figures of the universe could teach more persuasively than the figures on screen, the ubiquitous life, the perpetual fluidity, the fundamental incommensurability, the absolute singularity, the minute irrationality, the "uninterrupted becoming of any object" which Breton endeavored to reveal from beneath the rational stabilization and simplification of appearances?

However, the Surrealists were slow to recognize that the instrument of de-rationalization of which they dreamt was fully at the disposal of their practice; and, when they finally noticed cinema, they used it against its grain in such a literary and pictorial – in such an artistic – way that their attempts were instantly choked by esotericism.

The fact is that on its own account and without anyone paying great notice, the cinematographic machine was undertaking, in a wholly original way, to renovate and reinvigorate the delirium of interpretation, freeing it from the syllogistic yoke, so as to teach or remind people to use their poetic faculty.[13] Since no philosophy, no science, no discourse, no judgment, no understanding, no narrative, no memory, no sensation exists that is not essentially paranoid; since interpretation is the universal mode of knowledge; since paranoia typifies the function of the mind and the senses, the true genius that cinema makes manifest is its own authentic capacity for surrealization, in a system of unconscious and automatic interpretation inherent to the apparatus itself.

Indeed, cinema provides the wholly automatic recording of a thought – as inhuman and as unconscious as can be supposed – through images whose profoundly unusual, uncanny, and surrealist character begs to be recognized. Only the cinematographic machine by its very action is able to disclose and publish this marvelousness [*merveilleux-là*].

[...]

What, indeed, are the wonders that cinema manufactures by itself out of objects that have long ceased to surprise us?

These wonders may be, first of all, microscopic aspects. Most likely, when we talk to someone, we notice their eyes, but rarely do we devote to them a prolonged and acute attention, rarely do we feel moved, and more rarely yet do we try to consider and understand them as such rather than as integrated within the whole signification of the face. However, an eye that occupies the entire screen suddenly reveals itself to be a monster: a wet and shiny beast with its own movements like those of any animal; which, with its shadowy mouth, projects a force unlike any other form of life; which unveils itself and hides itself, in between two tremulous valves, planted with a long and graceful vegetation of curved darts whose venom we cannot fathom. Or else, the retina – is it a captive planet, a star of living crystal, streaked with blood and oiled with luminous secretions, holding at the center of its brightness, set in the mosaic of the iris, a pole of dark fascination, a crater of never-extinguished night, so heavy with questions and answers, and yet so thoroughly enclosed in its translucent but insuperable envelope? A soul is in there which, from within, moves and lights up this lamp, haunts this well, a few millimeters under the cornea, at a distance no one can measure or cross.

What an adventure is such an encounter with the eye of whomever, surrealized by a close-up! The very mystery of body and soul, the very plot of thought and matter, the very knot of the plurality and unity of the self, the very quid pro quo of the real and the unreal, the very play of subjectivity and objectivity are sprawled on the screen to be touched, palpated, traversed, searched, dissected by the gaze – perfectly inextricable and insoluble. In lieu of strangeness, this is – close to the naked eye – the true grand illusion, the true everlasting lure which, already, puzzles children who break their first watch whose tick-tock they had yearned to hold in their hand.

Every close-up or scaling-down of any interest, every slightly exceptional shot angle, every moving image recorded when the camera is in motion, insofar as it brings us unusual – that is, strange – aspects of things and beings, forces us to pause before such appearances and judge them; placing us again in front of the perpetual mystery of the universe which we realize, in the end, has never been elucidated, as we only became weary of it and forgot it, because of its very perpetuity, because of what we see of it everyday.

The dilation, contraction, and inversion of the course of phenomena in the vectorial dimension of time – of which only cinema allows a visual figuration in temporal terms – provide aspects of the world that are more original and more rare, more unusual and surrealized, and remind us more intensely of the forgotten miracle of the universe, by revealing some of its forms until then unsuspected.

And it is remarkable to notice to what extent the mind is sensitive to such a novelty. It would seem, for instance, rather trivial to see billiard balls roll and hit each other in various directions. However, when the screen shows a billiard shot filmed in reverse, even if the cue hitting the ball is not shown, most movie-viewers, even if they know next to nothing of this game, will note, through minute details, a vicious uncanniness in the motion of the balls or experience a vague discomfort, an intimidation, an anxiety, whose source they cannot locate.

Consciously perceived or not, discrete or overt, such an opportunity that reverse, slow, or accelerated motion images offer to human anxiety essentially devolves from their irrationality. A film showing examples of mineral biology, vegetal intelligence, mechanical nonsense, mixed states of matter, or logical principles made relative presents the apparatus and order of reason as a system of local and temporary conventions in which everything cannot always exactly fit. In front of crystals whose wounds heal or replicate methodically, in front of plants moving their limbs through conditioned reflexes, in front of persons whose awkwardly cerebral gestures fall back on instinctive grace, in front of the acceleration of gravity that has now become the slowing down of lightness, in front of the liquefaction of the universe into unidentifiable and incommensurable forms and movements, today's movie viewers are thrown back into the awful perplexity which, twenty centuries ago, caused Pythagoricians to shiver in front of the incalculability of the square root of two.

All such irrational aspects have the effect, on the one hand, of shaking the credence of reason which they eschew or belie, and, on the other hand, of awakening a plentiful kinship of analogical concepts having the same uncanny character and more or less dormant within the unconscious. Thus, the experience of the cinema fulfills the Surrealist wish to call upon the fecundity of intuitive thought that may be called genius-like since it provides intelligence with fresh data to be logically assimilated and since it points to the insufficiencies, excesses, and errors of the deductive method, at the same time as it points to the qualifications and correctives that hold up to it.

However, the surrealism of cinematographic images may not result only from their concrete character, in isolated shots or in those of the simplest documentaries as lightly dramatic as can be. Whether a form is utterly banal or quite odd, it can either acquire a powerful strangeness or considerably increase its surprising effect if the context gives it, in and of itself and indeed often in an unforeseen way, a special transcendental interpretation, a symbolic signification that is broader or suggests a transfer of feelings.

Everyone knows how easily – too easily – a revolver, a stack of old letters, an empty bottle, or a calendar acquire in a movie the status of symbols, even allegories, and how they can act on the mind, having become surrealist objects, catalysts of wide affective complexes, materializations of the mind partly unexpressed and partly inexpressible. This ease conveys the natural tendency of the language of animated images to surrealize emotionally all appearances. This is because the signs of this language are those of visual thought, always emoted and emoting, always interwoven with subconscious correspondences; a thought in itself naturally surrealist and surrealizing.

[...]

The raw and unusual surrealism that reverse, slow, and accelerated motions produce is also reinforced by dramatic signification. And we note that such interpretations added to images are almost always comical for reverse and accelerated motion, and tragic for slow motion.

Seen in accelerated or reverse motion, gestures become unexpected for the spectator, either because there is not enough time to anticipate them, or because no correct anticipation is possible for illogical consequences. In either case, here a gesture appears to be or is more or less absurd. Now, an absurdity initially provokes laughter, the vulgar form of surprise.

To the contrary, the conclusion of a gesture in slow motion is long awaited by the spectator who, meanwhile, reflects more than is usual on the motivations and consequences of this gesture, bringing to it a vast field of dramatic hypotheses. To obtain such an effect of psychological deepening of a protagonist's movements, a slight slow motion suffices, which is not perceivable in itself but only through the small paranoia of interpretation that this slackness occasions.

An actor lifts up his head from the book he was reading and gazes towards the lens, that is to say, towards an out-of-frame door through which someone is to enter. In normal-speed footage, as soon as the man's gaze leaves the book, the spectator sees the next shot: the door opening with the second protagonist entering. There is no time for doubt or wondering; everything is plain, immediate, logical, clear and ordinary. But in slow motion the lifting of the reader's gaze lasts a few seconds, during which the spectator does not know and wonders who will enter, the same way that the reader on the screen wonders himself: friend or foe, bearer of good or bad news, unimportant or unknown person? An expectation is thereby created – an enigma, a mystery, a dramatic suspension.

Such dramatic surrealizing of acting through carefully measured slow motion can and should be used as a regular device in filmmaking, especially in poetic or fantasy films, but also in the many films that now rely on non-professional actors who tend naturally to move too quickly and do not know how to slow down, how to decompose their pantomime so as to render it more legible or, when they try, do so awkwardly and compromise its veracity.

As in the case of images, there exists a surrealism of cinematographic sounds, but it is only now being discovered and few dare use it. The calls of conscience, the injunctions of duty, the obsessive criticisms of remorse, the refrains that hum in memory, the secret din of dreams, the tumults of nightmares – the soundtrack is timidly trying to let them be heard.

Yet in this domain, too, early research in the heyday of sound cinema took the wrong path and, until very recently, aimed almost exclusively at perfecting the reproduction of falsified sounds, of the most servile imitations of the most banal aural data, of a whole simulated and gaudy hurly-burly. No one bothered to learn how the microphone, the film strip, the loudspeaker could in themselves, by virtue of their nature and mode of working, interpret the true sound of true wind, the true gallop of a horse. And, whenever by chance such an experiment was made, viewers were naively upset that the aural result did not conform to the most ordinary data of hearing. For, what sound engineers, directors, producers, and viewers all wanted was to hear again for the thousandth time the wind and the gallop exactly the way they had heard it a thousand times with their naked ear. It did not matter to them that bellows and whistles, flutes and combs wrapped in tissue paper, walnut shells and suction cups and spoons were needed to fabricate a false wind or a false horse gallop, so long as they seemed truer than the real thing to the standards of the human ear!

Such heresy – similar to wanting to stop telescopes from getting closer and magnifying glasses from making bigger – has not yet ended: still, it is countered by the direct tendency that seeks to know and publish the original sonic representation that the cinematographic apparatus might compose with natural sounds. The aim, for the sound as for the image, is to leave maximum freedom for, and to stimulate and highlight, the authentically singular surrealizing and automatic function of cinema. The aim is to seek occasions for such recordings which amateurs of flat sound hold in contempt, and to cultivate supposedly counterfeit sounds as cinema's personal creation: deformation through resonance or variation of distance, echoes, ambient interferences, distortions and atonalities, murmurs and shouts yet unheard of that resemble nothing else, and acoustic forms whose existence can only be revealed by the microphone.

True, in general, in the current state of technics, the results of sound recording remain far less reliable, less finely perceptible, than those of optical recording. Moreover, the public remains indifferent and as if deaf to the language of noises and only lends its trained and attentive ear to receive speech, to the point of being dissatisfied with blends of music and voice, needing to hear distinctly every word of a song. Finally, the audible universe, since it is less abundant in its diversity of attributes than the visible universe, offers poorer prospects for development and a poorer foothold for an interpretive apparatus.

In view of the relative poverty of the audible elements of representation, the realization of sonic slow motion with its forceful surrealization analogous to visual slow motion, takes on a considerable importance. By lengthening the duration of a noise, the action of slow motion consists in increasing the discriminating powers of hearing. It thereby acquires a capacity for analyzing more finely a sonic set, to distinguish in it otherwise imperceptible components, and to discover timbres until then truly unheard of. Hence, through micro-audition, cinematographic interpretation invents sounds, true sounds, as true and surrealized as images of a nebula, a protozoa, or a bone structure invented by telescopy, microscopy, and radioscopy. Within a tempestuous sea, which to the human ear is merely monotone and confused roaring, rerecording in slow motion reveals a polyphony of such strange and new noises that most of them have no name yet in any language. Every second, the sea creates another cry.

Moreover, this kind of sonic close-up lowers the tonality of sound by slowing down its vibrating frequency. Lengthened to twice its original duration, every sound lowers by an octave. The same noise can then be rerecorded at several octaves or fractions of octaves lower, or else a more or less accelerated replay can displace the sonority towards a higher pitch. Thus, out of real ambient sound, sufficiently interpreted sonic elements can be constituted to compose a sequence of consonances or dissonances, a score, a symphonic or cacophonic music of noises truer than in nature.

The Futurists, poor cousins of the Surrealists, had been the first to guess that the sound domain too could produce the marvelous and the unusual. They ventured out a few experiments of noise music that proved inexpressive because they relied on no instrument – not even a phonograph – capable of powerfully interpreting noises, defamiliarizing them to make them surprising and uncanny. Yet cinema represents a means of surrealizing sound much more broadly and deeply than can the phonograph or the radio which, itself, depends on recordings. Cinema opens the way to the sonic materializations of the fantastic directly extracted from reality.

Slowing, accelerating, or reversing sound is no longer technically utopian nor even difficult. Even speech and music can be processed this way, either in moderation or to the point of complete denaturalization. By lowering voices, slow motion bestows on them the timbre of another personality that we cannot ascertain to be entirely human, with a pained, anxious, and tragic intonation. This dramatization of sound is also perceptible in the most common noises that acquire an extremely moving signification. For example, the trivial creaking of a door replayed in more or less pronounced slow motion becomes an inhuman groan, the mysterious moaning of things, the singular warning of one knows not what disorder, what suffering of matter. Acceleration, on the other hand, by sharpening sonorities infantilizes and feminizes them, interpreting them towards the comical.

The surrealization of sounds through slow or accelerated motion hence moves the auditor in the same manner as the analogous surrealization of images does the spectator. To the psychological explanation of this phenomenon that we have proposed must be added the fact that, through the generalization of our everyday visual and aural experience, we accord to bass tones [sons graves] – as the figurative meaning of the word "grave" indicates – a sentimental prejudice of force and sadness as easily as we tend to overestimate slow gestures as laden with importance and suffering. To perfect the expressivity of protagonists in a movie, slow and accelerated sound, as with images, allow for innumerable effects: discrete and barely perceptible; taken to the extreme of quavering, Punch-and-Judy exaggeration; monstrous rumblings, or that of a trill; a torrent of words ejected as in a spasm, melted in a single piercing cry.

Through such a power of spontaneous interpretation, such a faculty of automatically creating unusual appearances, cinema acts like a paranoid robot coming to the aid of weak, paranoid persons insufficiently able to note or compose strange aspects that can trigger their genius of delirium. But the strong poets too, avid of surreality, whose subconscious manifests its life at the slightest impulsion, will find in the delirium of the machine the stimulant allowing them to dream more intensely and diversely. Whether with minds so deeply and docilely rationalized that they can no longer act on their own, or with minds so rebellious against the dominant rationalization that they seek constantly and everywhere the means to escape it – everyone needs the original poetry that cinema offers.

This brand new marvelousness [merveilleux], it is indeed the cinematographic machine that produces it through its very working. Man only triggers it, at times unaware of its poetic value which may or may not appear on the screen, at other times as a result of a more or less empirical and random forecasting derived by analogy from past surprises. A marvelousness that is automatic because produced through a minimum of human critical intervention. A marvelousness that can be said to be true, real, and objective because it is obtained mechanically out of these sole and selfsame natural and concrete elements that constitute for us the acme of the real, objective, and veridical world; also because this marvelousness is a sensible datum a movie can reproduce a thousand times before a thousand witnesses, always identical to itself.

In cinematographic poetry, the function that in other species of the poetic devolves more from the human subconscious, is in part pre-accomplished by a machine. It combines unexpected interpretations, delivers resemblances foreign to and stronger than logical relations, and creates visual metaphors having the forcible status of objects and engines for daydreaming. The originality, diversity, and the kind of freedom of these representations would not allow us to consider them as other than the acts of a sort of soul, were we not so thoroughly subjected to the egocentric prejudice according to which we cannot understand thoughts other than consciously – and consciousness other than living in an organism – and above all a human one. Yet, truly, do we actually know more about the consciousness of a crystal, an orchid, an ant, a city, a labor union, or a nation than of a machine or factory of the slightest complexity? Objectively, we are wont to suppose a consciousness just as soon as we observe a sensibility that organizes selective choices. Practically, man now knows that he contains within himself a huge part of unconscious psyche. Consciousness is a pure symptom, like a migraine, which may appear when one thinks a lot, but without which we can think notwithstanding, and perhaps just as well. It would be absurd to speak of a camera's headache, but it is plain that this device experiences cold and heat because then it does not work well.

As unforeseeable as its poetic effects may be and as irrational as its propositions may seem, the delirium of cinematographic images is, nonetheless, the end result of a mechanical work and structure that have their own laws, that is to say, their own reason. All the fantasy of the aspects created by the camera results from the application of a system for disorganizing commensurability in both space and time. A principle of anarchy, to be sure, but whose realization is logically announced, inscribed, developed, perfected, through the planning, construction, conduct, and oversight of a mechanical being, rationally organized in itself. Is it but a fortuitous oddity that an apparatus of such highly rational structure should generate, as the product of its working, remarkably irrational products? That it should make manifest a kind of thought that escapes and contradicts reason? It would seem not. It would seem that, in all domains and all cases, in the inorganic as in the organic realm, in matter as in the mind, and in matter as it appears to the mind, the absolutely general rule of rational complication is to tend towards the irrational, the indeterminate, the ungraspable aspects of personality and soul – towards the illusion of freedom. Always, it is with its own plenty that reason ends up strangling itself.

Notes

1. Claude Favre de Vaugelas was an important seventeenth century French grammarian. Émile Littré was author of the massive *Dictionnaire de la langue française*, completed in 1873.
2. See Zeno's paradox of motion of the arrow in flight:
    If everything when it occupies an equal space is at rest, and if that which is in locomotion is always occupying such a space at any moment, the flying arrow is therefore motionless. (Aristotle, *Physics*)
    As Epstein and others (e.g., Henri Bergson) have shown, this paradox has important implications for theories of movement and duration. Epstein makes frequent reference to Zeno as well as the Eleatics, with whom Zeno is associated, throughout *Esprit de cinéma* and his later works.
3. The Eleatics were a group of pre-Socratic philosophers who held the view that although the senses cannot recognize the essential unity of being, such a unity exists: only appearances change. Zeno, whose paradoxes Epstein mentions earlier in the text, is part of this group.
4. A tachyon is a hypothetical particle that travels faster than the speed of light. German physicist Arnold Sommerfeld first introduced the concept in 1926.
5. *Planisme*, often described as a proto-fascist program, developed first in Belgium and exerted an influence in France during the inter-war years; it was a social democratic economic ideology intended to contend with the depression-era economy. An *auto-*

planisme suggests that, living in a regime characterized by the diffusion of ideologies, the citizens monitor themselves and one another without feeling that their freedoms have been curtailed.

6. Alexi Stakhanov was something like a poster child for socialist labor in Soviet Russia in the 1930s: a highly proficient coal miner, he represented the ideal of worker productivity and was held up as a model for the socialist economic system embraced in the USSR at the time. It was reported that Stakhanov repeatedly mined in excess of the expected daily quota, including at one point sixteen times that quota. *Stakhanovism* more generally upholds such ideals of efficiency and hard work effected by laborers.

7. In English in the original French text.

8. The author uses the English term "backshot" in the French text.

9. *Jean de la Lune*: directed by Jean Choux in 1931, it received a good deal of press about its sound sequences. See Philippe Soupault's "*Jean de la Lune* or Cinema on the Wrong Track," Abel2, pp. 75-77.

10. Coenaesthesia is the sense of conscious existence.

11. *Le Jour se lève*: directed by Marcel Carné in 1939, often cited as a classic of French "poetic realism."

12. Epstein refers to volume being the space that serves as a medium for the sound to propagate, so that if that volume were fixed and invariable, music would become unthinkable.

13. "Délire d'interprétation," is a symptom of paranoia that artists such as Salvador Dalí transformed into an artistic method. See Paul Sérieux and Joseph Capgras, *Les Folies raisonnantes: le délire d'interprétation* (Paris: Félix Alcan, 1909).

Late Articles

The Slow Motion of Sound

Translated by Franck Le Gac

[Jean Epstein, "Le Ralenti du son," *Livre d'or du cinéma français* (Paris: Agence d'information cinégraphique, 1948).]

In the fascination that comes down from a close-up and weighs on a thousand faces tense with the same rapture, on a thousand souls magnetized by the same emotion; in the wonderment that ties the look to the slow motion of a runner soaring at every stride or to the accelerated motion of a sprout swelling up into an oak tree; in images which the eye cannot form as large, as close, as lasting, or as fleeting: there the essence of the cinematographic mystery, the secret of the hypnotizing machine are revealed – a new knowledge, a new love, a new possession of the world through the eyes.

Until the very last few years and almost until the very last few months, the soundtrack, assigned to the old forms of speech and music, would reveal nothing to us of the acoustic world but what the ear had itself been used to hearing for as long as one could remember. Drowned in this overabundant triteness, the forerunner – the hum of the wheels on the train that took Jean de la Lune away – did not have any successors for a long time.[1] These days, however, several foreign films attest to research that moves us towards improvements in sound recording – just as image recording improved over fifty years – in the direction of a genuine psychological and dramatic high fidelity, of a deeper and more accurate realism than that of an *omnibus* hearing, taken to be totally reliable. Already, it is no longer about hearing just speech, but thought and dreams as well. Already, the microphone has passed the threshold of the lips and slipped into the inner world of man, on the lookout for the voices of consciousness, the old repeated melodies of memory, the screams of nightmares and the words no one ever uttered. Already, echo chambers convey not just the space of a set, but distances in the soul.

In this refinement of sound cinema, it obviously seemed necessary to experiment with what could be added by the process of deceleration, which keeps enriching the visual reign with so many aspects not yet seen. I raised the issue from a technical standpoint with a sound engineer, M. Léon Vareille, who became interested in it and solved it simply and elegantly, as the mathematicians say. Throughout *Le Tempestaire*, I was thus able to use wind and sea noises re-recorded at variable speeds, up to four times as slow.

The effect of this slowed-down sound, of acoustic vibrations stretched in time, is twofold. On the one hand, lowering the frequency of vibrations results in lower tonalities, going down one octave each time sound is slowed down a unit. The same noise may thus be recorded in several different tessituras. This allows, through editing and mixing, the creation of a genuine, purely sonorous score. Yves Baudrier, who composed this score with great intelligence, also had the talent to thread just an extremely simple instrumental melodic line through this natural music, which allows the sound experience to keep its own importance and does not skew the audience's judgment of it.

The other effect of the slowing down of sound is an analytical effect with complex sounds. Like the eye, the ear has only a very limited power of separation.

The eye has to resort to a closer position and to spatial magnification with a telescope to realize that a fence, which seemed like a continuous surface, is in fact made of posts fixed at intervals. The eye has to use deceleration, that is, a magnification in time, to see that the jab of a boxer, which looked like a simple, rectilinear movement, is in actuality a combination of multiple muscular movements, with infinite variations. Likewise, the ear needs a magnifying glass for sound in time – that is, slowed-down sound – to find out for instance that in a finer reality the monotonous and confusing howling of a storm is made up of a host of very different sounds never heard before: an apocalypse of screams, cooing, rumble, cheeping, detonations, tones and accents, most of which do not even have a name. One may just as well take a more modest example, the noise of a door opening or closing. Slowed down, this humble, ordinary noise reveals its complicated nature, its individual characters, its possibilities for dramatic, comic, poetic, musical signification.

Certainly, most of the time, this inarticulate language of things is merely a neutral or irritating noise to our ears, sometimes barely perceptible. The standard grooves of the soundtrack declaim too many discourses in too little time – entangling, compressing, squeezing them against one another in an undecipherable hubbub. In detailing and separating noises, creating a sort of close-up of sound, sonic deceleration may make it possible for all beings, all objects to speak. The mistranslation of Latin scholars, who had Lucretius say that things cry, will thus become an audible truth. We can already see, we will soon hear the grass grow.

★ ★ ★

The Fluid World of the Screen

Translated by Sarah Keller

[Jean Epstein, "Le monde fluide de l'écran," Les Temps modernes, no. 56 (June 1950). Reprinted in ESC2, pp. 145-158.]

When some filmmakers contrived to push or drag the camera on its wheels – to raise it up or lower it, to tilt, carry, swing, or turn it around – most of these experimenters thought only of seeking out a more artistic, amusing, and ornate descriptive style; they did not dream that they had started to embark upon habituating themselves, of habituating the film and the public, on how best to nullify movement, how to choose it and outline it, how to develop a new awareness of it. In this, the fondness of cinema for mobile aspects of the universe quickly came to transmute nearly all the stable forms into the unstable. The animated image – as animated as the lens, objects, or light make it so – demonstrated throughout its diversity, transition, and inconstancy.

In fact the camera accomplishes all of its movements, hidden or apparent, on behalf of the human eye. This eye sometimes becomes like a multifaceted fixed eye; sometimes like a multiplicity of eyes, each of which possesses a unique perspective; sometimes like a mobile snail eye, an eye mounted on an extendable and retractable stem. It is an eye that can collect data, which happens not always at a more or less fixed distance, a more or less important distance, but also at the nearest point of visibility, almost in contact with the object, and able to maintain this contact if the object moves. The variety and mobility thus granted to the spectator's perspective come to multiply the variety and mobility proper to cinematographic objects. The result is a world on screen where the spectator's attention is called for more frequently and more deeply in terms of a sense of diversity and change than in the real world.

Howsoever mobile and mobilistic the lived and living world has become, cinematographic expression surpasses it with its own universe whose fleetingness it must check, whose metamorphoses it must limit, and whose virulence it must filter, so as not to go against the conventions by which a large part of the public wants to continue to see, hear, imagine, understand. The most original perceptions in films can only be introduced progressively, and can only be accepted in meager doses. Of these instants of surprise, spectators however also experience the appeal, at least vaguely, like a brush with a danger that then becomes domesticated, of making it through a vertigo that is soon mastered. But a number of purely cinematographic expressions remain unused, not even tried – forbidden because they are charged with scandalous surprises.

Mobilization and Decentralization of Space

Here we have a table, which the lens – jumping, sliding, flying – approaches, moves away from, magnifies, shrinks, spreads out, tilts, stoops, raises, broadens, elongates, makes lighter, makes darker, reforms, and retransforms each time that the object presents itself in the shot and through the flow of shots. Without taking into account here other evolutions that the specimen of a table could undergo in recommending itself for a dramatic role, and without wanting to consider more than the variety of accidental aspects that this piece of furniture accrues on the screen, one already often comes to question whether it is a single table, to doubt that one actually knows it, to feel unable to define it, and to wonder whether it isn't actually two or three different tables.

This uncertainty surprises us, since in our experience and usual conception of space, most notable forms seem to be considered equal to themselves. In this space, designed mainly for the use of solids, a single order can always moderate all measures that a spectator brings back in the end to himself, considered the unique center and consistent standard. Space thus employed permanently presents everywhere the same virtues; it is homogeneous and egocentric. Identity is rigorously demonstrable and finds itself with credence to serve as the great principle of all logical development.

In the universe taken up on screen, it is otherwise. The size and the position of the spectator no longer absolutely rate as the benchmark of evaluation and bearings, because this observer finds himself incapable of relating, directly and exactly to this center and to this standard, the situation and dimension of objects that cinematographic reproduction has taken for its models. Indeed, between the human eye and the real object interposes the result of another visual act: preliminary vision through a device whose situation, in relation with the object, is not sufficiently defined in a way to allow constituting a precise comparative system through this intermediary. For that matter, each new position of the apparatus, each shot, raises another ordination of space, always imperfectly determined, often complicated by an arbitrary evolution, due to the movement – poorly understood itself! – of the lens during recording.

If one considers this cinematographic space, varied and variable, in the discontinuous multiplicity of its fixed frames or in the continuity of one of its mobile frames, one sees that the majority of forms do not remain equal to themselves, neither in their transposition from one cell to another in discontinuity, nor in the course of their passage from one moment to another in a constantly evolving perspective. Exterior to objects and invisible, the movement of the observatory apparatus is translated into the figures of objects, where it becomes visible as proper mobility, animating each form and allowing it to change itself. These inconstant figures, non-superimposable, are objects in the filmed world: secondary objects to a second reality. But this is truly all the perceptible reality from the spectator's standpoint. Such objects indicate a non-homogenous, non-symmetrical space where common egocentrism, in its human proportion, finds itself disrupted. Among these ghosts, as evasive in their reciprocal relationships as in their individual structure (as though viscous), no identity can be entirely established.

Diversification of time

The mobility that we read in the world of the screen does not arise only from the mobilization of spatial dimensions and directions, but also from a particular variability in the temporal dimension. In the real world, we are able to modify the speed and thereby the duration of only certain kinds of movement in a limited zone of influence and in restrained proportions; and we feel ourselves incapable of altering any part of the cadences of an immense majority of phenomena which we perceive outside of and within ourselves. Among these cadences that appear to us to be very stable, if not immutable, we have located several time scales of which the ones most commodious in measuring the speed and duration of our own actions are at a premium. In the secondary reality of the screen, the organization of speeds and durations is much more tractable; we can vary movement of the near totality of phenomena produced, and this variation can be in certain cases much more pronounced than the one we may chance to impose upon model phenomena. This proliferation of rhythms is not without confusion when it comes to the comparisons of previously understood speeds and temporal rules previously elaborated, but it also brings with it a host of previously unknown appearances.

Thus in the telescopic and microscopic equipment that distinguish objects that are very far away or spatially very tiny and that spark the blossoming of knowledge, cinema adds the means of discerning, in the very slow or very rapid, that which is temporally separate or too close together for our vision, by tightening it or widening it for our sight. Thanks to acceleration (that is to say tightening), in a year's worth of changes, contracted into three minutes of projection, the observer may form a collective view, grasp a consequence, a harmony, a rule that otherwise would not be discovered. Thanks to slow motion (that is to say widening), whereby sixty seconds of projection stretch out, break down and analyze one second of real movement, the spectator can name and enumerate phenomenal content that otherwise would not be manifested. This tachyonscopy and this bradyscopy, which are just starting to be used methodically, allow an enormous enrichment of visual experience, and the auditory experience would benefit from a similar extension if one were to decide to use the acceleration and deceleration of sound as well, as cinematographic technique easily allows it.[2]

But the popularization of such images and sounds runs into an obstacle in light of public opinion. Indeed, if spectators who are more or less used to changes in latitude, longitude, and altitude will permit, without balking too much, great spatial flexibility in cinematic representations, then they show themselves to be much more suspicious about the generous suppleness afforded by the film world to its durations, of which the natural world offers few examples. Only on the screen can one observe a stone fall from the same height that in natural time would take a second, consuming in this enlargement of temporal nature ten or a hundred seconds. In the earthbound construction of space-time, such information seems contradictory inwardly, contradictory outwardly: misleading, ridiculous, dreadful, unbelievable. This confusion contrasts with the serene confidence we bring – without seeing any injury to reality – to the image of a flea magnified spatially ten or a hundred times.

However, everyone has experienced this confusion in front of images that mix up the categories of stationary and mobile, constant and inconstant, sluggish and lively, according to the three states of matter, the three rules of nature, the three categories of animated beings. The dunes crawl away; minerals blossom and reproduce; animals get caught in lime and become petrified; plants move and strain toward the sun; water gets stuck; clouds break. In addition, film can change a real movement by reversing it, thereby giving it an even more troubling and totally abnormal aspect, to which even the least experienced audience is acutely sensitive. It seems, for example, that there shouldn't be much difference in which direction billiard balls roll and collide. However, when the screen shows a stage in the game filmed in reverse (even if the break isn't shown), most spectators (even if they were never really interested in the game) notice in the tiniest details a repugnant strangeness in the movement of the balls, or vaguely perceive a malaise, an intimidation, which they cannot explain.

Also the change of temporal perspective may be achieved (albeit in a more perfunctory way) through simple editing effects, the principle being the same as that of accelerated projection, but where the constriction of time, rather than being evenly distributed across all passages from one image to another, is reserved irregularly for certain joints between groups of images regularly filmed and printed otherwise. One finds examples of this process in most films and even in amateur cinema, which allows families to collect moving portraits of their members, filmed at reunions, a place where they are also gladly projected. So it appears to be that little Paul, playing with hoops, doesn't have a lot in common with baby Paul, who sucks on his bottle; and that Paul, on his first bike, is again another boy, who would have been renamed Jack or Peter in order to distinguish him from the others; that this Paul or Jack or Peter, as bachelor, soldier, fiancé, have not truly been Paul, nor Jack, nor Peter; that they were also distinct individuals, whom the so-called Paul (who now is welcoming the birth of his first daughter) does not resemble any more than he resembles one or the other of his second cousins. What characterizes the Paul appearing on the birth certificate? Does he even exist in this constant changeability?

Doubtless, with the aid of memory, the human look can also constitute a series of the transformations undergone by a person, but it cannot do so with such meticulous accuracy, concrete evidence, and shocking continuity as film. Without a doubt, we know a thousand ways – commonplace, legal, scientific – by which, year after year, a man self-identifies, but then all of a sudden this statement of the obvious becomes a prodigious, barely comprehensible certainty: a barely altered revelation of a meaning.

Through accelerated projection, slow-motion, reverse direction, through the discontinuities and interpolations possible through editing, cinema delineates a world where durations do not necessarily reproduce the durations of the real world – neither in terms of natural size nor in connection with the constant transformation of that size. In such a sequence of a film, characters' movements occupy and define an ensemble of durations, with time roughly identifiable as the same as that which the spectator recognizes himself to occupy and define in his own movements. In another sequence, dancers move by consuming three or four times more time than that which is needed normally to complete the same gestures in real life. The prevailing time on screen is manifestly no more homogeneous than the space configured on screen. Time here is varied and variable, and, when united with a varied and variable space, it reveals a continuity whose four dimensions, in continual evolution, represent, in our usual system of reference, a sort of caricature by liquefaction. Let us here introduce a standard indifferent to size, and it will itself be reshaped from image to image, deprived of its form and endowed with a hundred forms, incapable of retaining its own measure and providing exact comparisons.

Logic of the melting point
Of dense and extraordinary phenomena, one often hears: that's like cinema! The public associates the screen with a world of overabundant chance encounters and almost unlimited possibilities, where a decapitated person can walk about while single-handedly carrying his head (which continues to hurl invectives). Basic paralogisms contribute to this big dramatic fantasy as well as to their own appearance as a group. They result from the stubborn resistance of filmed objects to the geometrical and mechanical rules viable in reality. In a space-time different from that which fashions the general use of solids that are constricted in their movements, a different logic is also constructed.

The most decisive of the symptoms that mark the resistance of the filmed world to a purely rational construction is the difficulty the spectator experiences in defining the permanent characteristics of an object or a person on screen. The film shows so many particularities and changes among which the spectator must so quickly find his bearings, that he has little choice but to content himself with approximate matches, of summarily hazarded recognitions. The careful application of the principle of identity is a scholarly privilege, and the person who participates mentally in a filmed action can afford it even less than someone busy with his daily occupations. Logically, cinematographic space-time seems first of all like a field with a very virtual and conjectural frame for identity, where identification depends squarely on analogies, through a sequence of temporary hypotheses always subject to re-doing, like the creation of an always-relative truth menaced by incompletion and that involves a degree of incertitude greater than that of observations in the real world.

By the associative paths of logic itself, this play in the application of the principle of identity spreads to corollary principles and deductions. When neither Peter's nor Paul's height can be measured – each of them being arbitrarily shown in close or long shot, emphasized or not by the *mise-en-scène* – one hesitates to determine which of the two is taller. Symptomatic in this regard are the questions that numerous fans pose to editors at magazines about the nature and build of famous actors. These, on screen, appear in a haze of incommensurability, in which all comparisons lose their edge and founder. Contradiction or non-contradiction of a vague identity can only be vague itself, and the effect of an excluded third term can no longer take place, or takes place only within an approximate probability.

Again logically, the slackening of the principle of non-contradiction is passed on to its derivative: the rule of non-ubiquity and non-simultaneity. The three-step test of what's possible can no longer function except in a loose manner. Thus, the spectators allow – under the same, existing scheme of a visible and audible reality – for actions that immediately answer one another, even as they occur from all ends of the earth; for events that come together, having abolished years and centuries; for characters that cross space and time more quickly than light (a young man opens the door to exit his student room in Paris and, crossing the threshold, an acclaimed old man enters a conference room in Edinburgh). These liberties with respect to the logical convention that regulates the occurrence, the duration, and the circulation of directly seen and heard phenomena constitute another convention that gives phenomena on screen a dispersed and amassed presence, an advanced and delayed existence, a leaping and stumbling course. And this extension of the possible fills consciousness in a more confused manner, but more densely as well.

In a field of concurrent events, notably overstretched and cluttered, successions find a place to occur with an ambiguity that can compromise their rational validity. A spectator enters the cinema at the moment when on screen there are images of an automobile, then a train at a dead run chugging along quickly in the same direction; then again the auto, then the train, etc., in one of these chase effects that, dealt with in speedy and rough simultaneous succession, used to be the dramatic climax of many films. But the chase after whom, by whom? The spectator who hasn't seen the beginning of the sequence can attribute its outcome either to images of the locomotive, or of the automobile, etc., with the unaccountable virtue that attaches to seniority when it comes to explaining or even inventing the younger images. For some seconds or minutes, the automobile drivers in the film are sometimes the chased, sometimes the chasers; as characters they are sometimes logically ambivalent or contradictory, sometimes null and void, waiting to assume a sufficient motive for being and acting, depending on whether or not precedence is granted or denied to them in the end.

In one direction of an edited sequence, we see a man training in a stadium, then the same man, stretched out on a chaise lounge in a clinic, and we understand that the practice of sport has caused burnout or an accident. Reversing the order of the images, we figure: the illness is the cause for taking up a regenerative sport. In these two cases, we allow that the facts follow on the screen in the direction of a progressive discovery of the future, which is also the resulting direction for the majority of real circumstances. Elsewhere, the film proposes to show us actions in a reverse order: that of an exploration of the past, starting from the most recent actions and going back to the most ancient facts. Thus, one sees a man at the penal colony, then tried, then arrested after his crime, then jealous of his rival, then in love with the sought-after woman, etc. More or less, the mind of the spectator is thereby shared between two awarenesses of time going in opposite directions: the time lived and the time seen and heard in the film. And, if only intermittently, the spectator must disassociate the meaning of the effect or the cause of observed facts from the order in which they appear. In the seen-heard time of film, the effects of lived time remain effects, only they are foreseen; and the causes remain causes, only delayed. To this day, the greater public gets lost in this sort of representation which, however, is often symbolized schematically – read, thought, but which had until now rarely been achieved in a sufficiently concrete way to be able to trouble consciousness with two competing presences, equal in power but ordered differently. Another public appreciates these mixings-up of one temporal perspective with another, through particularly cinematographic effects.

When we arrive at the inversion, no longer by the interpolation of a few groupings of images in the editing stage, but by reversing the order of succession of all the images between the shooting and the screening, the effects of reality come to occupy the position of causes in a very tight series, whose turnabout clashes even more strongly with the routines of logic. The spectator may well know that he can turn to a finalist explanation by assigning the decisive power to phenomena that have appeared last; he may well have understood that smoke will compel fire, seen that the smoke precedes an explosion on the screen; still, he can't quite give up the scientific interpretation that smoke is caused by combustion. All the same, he ends up allowing that there are two possible determinations for this smoke and fire: by the causes of momentum from behind and by the necessities of traction from the front. When a reversed film shows the rubble of a house fly away and regroup in the form of the exploded building, as absurd as this spectacle looks, it only parodies another logical mode, according to which Cuvier rediscovered lost species by starting with their fossil remains,[3] or according to which detectives in novels reconstitute the crime by starting with clues.

After this moment of confusion, the spectator rediscovers his habitual, logical construction by carefully separating the learned meaning that involves the cause or result of each image's content from the purely ordinal value of these images as their sequence unwinds on film. Since this value does not directly arise from real world successions, reassuring logic advises that we not attribute actual and direct determining authority to it. And the spectator finds himself cured of his slight vertigo.

It remains, however, that the film tends – and would tend all the more if one left it alone – to popularize this incertitude in which we are in relation to the chicken and the egg, in which we don't know which is the effect or origin of the other, nor even if there is an origin or an effect. It is evidently not in calling upon a gymnastics of dissociation of causal relationships and the relationships of precedence that the film makes the givens of the problem as simple and clear as verbal logic frequently presents them to us. In cinematographic representation, causality no longer appears so inherent – neither within nature nor in the order of things. To both of these, instead, cinematographic representation appears to bring meaning: sometimes more, sometimes less, sometimes in one way, sometimes in another, and sometimes without success. Unobtrusively, discretely, films habituate the public to thinking of the universe as looser, watched over from farther away and more distractedly, more inviting to statistical neutrality.

Second reality, but overqualified

In its uncoordinated and non-egalitarian position, in its unsynchronized temporality, in its approximation of logic, it seems that film must produce mixed and vague imitations of reality, themselves mixed and vague, and therefore only meagerly convincing. However, the ultimate decline of the popular theater, the fact that the middle-brow theater and music halls are losing ground, coinciding with the tenfold proliferation of cinemas, show that the public takes the film for the vehicle of fiction whose dramatic and poetic yield is the best: that the public finds in cinema substitute realities most capable of moving and distracting it from lived reality. And it's this way even though the screen offers no real, direct presence, while on stage, real beings are acting.

The paradoxical realism of the cinematographic spectacle comes first from the fact that there, the word does not constitute the exclusive, nor even the most predominant, means of expression. Images bring a mass of information that directly strikes the eyesight (the most active of the cultural senses) without being obliged to pass information via the long, slow, complex path of neurons that encrypt the concrete into the abstract, and disencrypt from the abstract back into the concrete: the logical symbolism of words and their more or less literary assemblage. At the theater, a walk-on part must recount a fire, a hero give a monologue of his past behavior, a heroine declare her trouble in an aside. On screen, the spectator observes for himself the fire, the behaviors, and, upon a face fifteen times enlarged, the least emotion. In fact, at the cinema, word play is well heard and appreciated for its surplus performative value, not for giving information or using persuasion. As for the dramatic sense of words, it comes a bit too late; it only confirms comprehension already established by ocular testimony. This observation with the naked eye, this proof via evidence, has the decisive force of conviction in all trials and also in this debate where the spectator is at the same time witness and judge – where, if there is disagreement between image and word, the document seen is trusted over the commentary, the facial expression over the speech of a character.

If, at the cinema, the word has only the secondary role of making visual information explicit, still the film generally gives this explanation more abundantly than the occasions of real life do. As the theater, very visually limited, is altogether talky; as the cinema, extremely visual, speaks less than the theater; as life, moderately visible, speaks even less than the cinema – of these, it's the cinema that, all in all, usually supplies the representation of the world signified concurrently by the greatest number of means, visuals as well as spokens: the most richly descriptive representation, the most accomplished, and also the most feasible for the public.

Owing to its very abundance and diversity, the visual information provided by cinema probably cobbles together its reality out of rather diffuse and confused beings, of thick and cloudy things that recall the monstrous plates printed over several times instead of one, in which moreover the confusion is always astir with improvements. But the imprecision of such forms does not derive from what little one knows about them; it derives from what we know too well about them. It is true that an object that holds a durationless position or a time of appearance without height or width more or less escapes logical conception, but a phenomenon that presents numerous and different space-time references – not reduced (or not reducible) to a unique group of measurements in four dimensions – also resists its installation in the system of classical knowledge. This therefore comes about only at a certain degree – as with a distinct focus – of determination, beneath and beyond which there is all that exists without having yet been (or without the ability to be) rationalized, on the grounds of being either unqualified or overqualified. It is because moving images find themselves overqualified by the multiplicity of their visible (and, secondarily, audible) interpretations of brute reality that these images do not admit logical structure without dislocating it in proportion to their overload of concrete associations. It is because this overload establishes a luxurious world of differences on screen that the film produces a stronger impression of reality, in proportion to its refusal to allow rational typifying as schemas of perfect resemblance.

Re-education by the absurd

To the degree that people are obliged to have an existence more and more full of reasoning, they feel all the more the need to grant moments of relative repose to their cerebral machinery of rational coordination. And this relaxation of cortical control is more likely to allow thought to give in to sentimental and instinctive influences. A thought of dulled reasoning, a thought of awakened passion, of poetry, then arises. Supporting this effect of chronic intellectual fatigue, the sustained influence of alcohol over civilized man fosters the occurrence of mental activities of a dreamlike character, where the visual abounds and where the possibilities of association flourish. To the bouts of sleepiness of the civilized, film responds with prefabricated mental images, a digest of ready-made dreams.

Numbed but not removed, rational control finds itself alerted, however, as soon as the screen telegraphs some remarkable exception to the routine of verbally exorcised, logically domesticated phenomena: a gigantic eye that takes after an oyster and the moon; a flower that goes back into its bud. Quickly, the insult must be washed away by laughter, nullified for its absurdity. Because, when directors and camera or sound operators do not keep watch carefully enough, despite all of their precautions, cinema by itself snags a lot of discrete or striking nonsense in a reality unseen and unheard, and brings it to a visible and audible reality, just as from the marine depths the nets of oceanographers pull a flock of monsters whose forms at first look fantastical. The more deeply one fishes, the more miraculous the catch is. The more the cinematographic instrument succeeds in liberating itself from the egocentricism of the directly human point of view, to move away from the CGS zone[4] of the human scale, the more it can encounter and reveal figures not yet hewn into classes and subclasses, provisionally without name (or definitively un-nameable), stupid and marvelous.

The mobilism of judgment in the cinema, the *photogénie* of movement (without forgetting acoustic movement) lead to these eruptions of absurdity that come out of reality's limbo, through the weakened logic of the world on screen. Without a doubt, the majority of this strangeness is destined to be more or less quickly domesticated by the rational, as have been the wonders revealed by microscopes and telescopes. However, thanks to its exceptional ability to disrupt the anthropomorphic standardization of space and time, cinema can choose aspects that are inaccessible to any other experience and are particularly difficult to standardize according to the fixed standards of common experience. Sometimes the effort to standardize succeeds above all to weaken the rules of the inflexible world.

Whatever the scenario, each meter of each film teaches first, implicitly, esoterically, this experience of a renewed and still savage reality: a reality from beneath and beyond the right view and the proper time; in fact, past the center which is anywhere and past an inertia now deprived of a system, from before names and before the law of words. The development of educational film confirms that this constitutes a very powerful means of culture. But this cinematic culture is not above contradicting classical culture. The invention of the printing press brought nothing profoundly revolutionary with respect to the mentality of its time. Whatever its subject, every reading is first a grammatical exercise in reasoning, and the book has only greatly assisted the spread of a way of thinking and knowing, verbally and logically, which had already been ascendant for thousands of years and whose triumph was perfectly assured. The invention of cinema introduces a more dramatic character because it contains a threat against a rationalism that has become totalitarian. Rationalism has known and still knows many dissidences, probably, but here it meets a weapon for irrational propaganda with a very powerful capacity for the popularization of thought and knowledge.

In reading "Peter took the knife from Paul," a child only learns a rather empty compartmentalization, from which he does not receive the means to imagine anything. All the knives in the world look enough alike to be Paul's knife, and millions of boys could equally be called by any first name. But, if it's the screen that announces a schoolboy taking a knife from a classmate, then it is a knife-with-a-horn-handle-and-a-nicked-blade-etc. which differs from all other knives; and one child is a fair-haired-kid-with-freckles-and-a-falsetto-voice-etc. and the other a swarthy-kid-with-a-turned-up-nose-and-a-Marseilles-accent-etc.: two boys whose names we'll never know, but each of whom is a completely unique being, and cannot possibly be confused with the other. The book above all teaches abstract categories; the film above all concrete individual beings. At the cinema, children, teens, and adults continually learn and relearn geography, history, professional skills, morals, physics, sociology, etc. – starting or not starting over – not backwards, through syllogisms and theorems in which typography presents the final result of a long and laborious transposition of the facts, but in a natural way, through the facts themselves, presented in a rather unlearned state and thus offered to an illiterate knowledge more rapid, richer, and often more practical than abstract knowledge. Many of these facts are taken in only with trouble and at the risk of a loss in the boxes and lines of their elaboration as scientific facts, and shall end as flawed syllogisms and precarious theorems – all the more flawed and precarious as a fact on screen may have been purged less of its strong, concrete burden of particularity, distilled less carefully into an entity. Reality can become rational only once it has taken, in relation to itself, a certain distance in the mind. The film disrupts this perspective by bringing (or bringing back), all of a sudden, from the farthest to the closest plane of attention, a reality raw enough to have retained its original taste of absurdity. Thus, in the abrupt comparison that can be made between images of a rockslide and the algebraic expression of Newton's laws, there reemerges with strength the particular arbitrariness of the law and the general arbitrariness and absolute absurdity that there is a law. On the strength of etymologies, reminiscences, figurative meanings, and works of art, the amorous crowds embark each day for Cythera. On screen, Cythera is a dry rock. Of course, the action of the book demands the reaction of the film.

Notes

1. Infra, p. 380 n9.
2. Tachyon: see infra, p. 379 n4.
3. Georges Cuvier, French naturalist and zoologist, and author of *Le Règne Animal* (1817).
4. The CGS system is a system of physical measures with the centimeter, the gram, and the second (CGS) as its basic units.

Alcool et cinéma

Logic of Fluidity

Translated by Thao Nguyen

[Jean Epstein, "Logique du fluide," *Alcool et cinéma* (unpublished in Epstein's lifetime), in ESC2, pp. 210-215.]

Spoken language, verbal thought, and their logic have been formed by and for man's relationship with his fellow human beings and his surroundings in order to rule the outside world, and also under the rule and after the model of this world as we perceive it through our naked senses. Depending on circumstances, either immobile or changing figures could predominate among aspects of this physical world, but the human mind gave precedence, a special attention, to diversified forms that with more or less speed appear constant or rigid, as if they were signs and means of safety, markers of exploration and study. Up to this day, we are left, from such esteem for permanence, with an atavistic habit. We always particularly enjoy the most resistant constructions, the hardest materials, unchangeable measurements, obstinate characters, immutable divinities and ideals. We despise fragility, softness, and fickleness. Not only is it our empirical practice and our science, but it is also our religion, our philosophy, and our morals that have been first conceived according to the primacy of solid elements.

Without doubt, Heraclitus reacted against this with his doctrine of universal conflict and universal movement, but, against this Ionian school, Parmenides and Zeno of Elea championed the cult of what always remains equal to itself, the faith in a permanent identity, foundation of the entire rational system.[1] This Eleaticism so profoundly influenced thought that twenty centuries went by before Heraclitus' conceptions could find credibility with a rather wide audience – before Bruno, Hegel, Schopenhauer, Bergson, Engels, et al. succeed in rehabilitating becomingness, change, and flux as essential aspects of being. These new philosophies of mobility found matching and supporting theory in certain sciences that we are beginning to interpret any material, any energy, any life, as a result of the incessant moving of atoms, of a perpetual molecular agitation, of an absolutely general evolution.

But this philosophy as well as this science, neither of which had much visibility and were reserved to a limited audience, could only have an indirect and practically insignificant influence on the masses' mentality. Even when the discovery of faster means of locomotion started bringing celebrity and prestige to speed by drawing attention to all kinds of moving objects and by offering newly moving landscapes to the eye, all this aggrandizement of the mobile experience was relegated to a corner of memory, like a set of information, admittedly precious but exceptional, definitely worth being kept as curiosities, but incapable of rivalry with old and strong static notions.

The customs of cinematographic spectacle, even sooner than with the memorabilia of travel or vertigo, at last earned it the power to popularize a more mobile representation of the world. Perhaps cinema too became static – not to dare make the faintest adjustment of the lens, to struggle to conform to the still powerful principles of Eleaticism and its aesthetic corollary of immobility. However, in a club, some started talking about the photogenic quality of movement and some directors came up with the idea of pushing or pulling the camera on casters, of raising it, of lowering it, of tipping it, of carrying it, of swinging it, of making it turn in a circle. These militants of the cinematographic avant-garde thought that, in doing so, they were creating a new (specifically cinematographic) descriptive style, but they did not realize that they were launching, at the same time and more profoundly, a philosophical enterprise; little did they know that the appearances that their lenses captured, in a way that the eye cannot see well enough or at all, would surprise and little by little prepare countless spectators. This audience, finally, would find itself forced, unbeknownst to it, to fundamentally reform its way of feeling, of imagining, of understanding; it was forced to rip its model of reality from the petrifying spells of the perfect order, from the dream of the exact measure, from the illusion of complete intelligibility.

Saying that the cinematograph is essentially meant to record and reproduce movement is a truism; a truism that we held for a while – even if we do not hold it still – as literally insignificant from an industrial, commercial, or even artistic standpoint. But the gaze of the lens, in and of itself, obeying its organic law, perceives and shows us the mobile aspects of the world, emphasizes them, favors them with a predilection that transmutes even stable elements into unstable ones, solids into fluids. Thus, in the world seen on screen, the spectator, whether he likes it or not, whether he understands it or not, sees his attention drawn, against his classical habits of mind, toward change, malleability, and the fluidity of forms. Even completely still shots that follow each other in the same scene with the same characters and the same décor are shots that were taken from different angles (here lies an elementary rule of cinematographic continuity), which means that these images are the result of camera movements and that they demonstrate the results of such movements.

[...] The animated image, when it is as animated as much as its nature compels it to be, thus shows that everything is diversity and evolution and that no state exists because there is no equation, apart from the state and equation of movements, which is to say rhythm.

For the needs of our outside activity, the relative constancy of human scale, taken as a central marker in relation to forms in the surrounding world that are remarkable for their ample fixity or rigidity, has enabled us to establish a system of reciprocal localization for getting at objects, a system of orientation and assessment of our own movements and of those observed outside of us. This system constitutes our usual configuration of space, whose ideally precise, perfectly rationalized aspect is given by Euclidean geometry.

This entire empirical configuration and its geometric theory rest on the fact that forms seem to remain the same when we transport them from one place to another because they are solid. If the said figures, whatever their motions be, conserve at all times and everywhere their geometric properties, it is – we think – because the imagined space possesses too, at all times and everywhere, the same qualities; in other words it is homogeneous. In this spatial homogeneity, we can slide a figure onto another one without distortion, and that they exactly coincide is proof of their perfect similitude. Identity is thus rigorously demonstrable and is licensed to serve as the great principle to the entire logical development. Without any distortion, we can rotate a figure around an axis or a point in order to superimpose it to another figure, as a proof of a somewhat particular kind of identity: symmetry. We thus say that space – at least space related to solids – is not only homogeneous, but also symmetrical.

Truth be told, that which is likely to show similitude, identity, and symmetry are the bodies put into play that through their performance create a notion of space and which, by their rigidity, characterize that which in turn describes the idea of space as being a certain aspect of this play. But the human mind, just as it personified and materialized space, personifies and materializes the qualities ascribed to this phantasm. Let us remember that homogeneity and symmetry are allegories.

In the world depicted on screen, things are different: the size and position of the spectator do not absolutely hold as a benchmark and a place to get one's bearings, because – as has already been stated – the observer finds himself incapable of bringing the location and dimension of objects as they appear on the cinematographic image intact to this center and benchmark. The situation of the camera is neither sufficiently definable nor sufficiently fixed to base a comparative system common to all of a film's shots on it. So, not only does the configuration of cinematographic space elude the rigorous egocentrism of the Euclidean configuration, not only does it refuse to accept an exclusively human proportionality, but it also accepts no unique center of perspective, no unique standard, whatever it might be.

In fact, with every change of camera position, with every shot, the spectator is offered a new kind of space, which is always partially indeterminate. We are thus dealing with a composite space, of a multiple of spaces, and each space could perhaps be expressed in Euclidean terms, but the grouping suggests the conception of another continuum with very different characteristics. And considering this new space as a simple juxtaposition of ill-assorted Euclidean cells would not be enough to remove its special properties. It would be as erroneous as confusing differential elements with the result of their integration. Indeed, if the shot was taken in motion, we obtain on screen an integration of cinematic space, summoning all the fragments of this space that evolve from image to image into a visual impression of continuity. And this integration does not obey the Euclidian law.

Whether we think about the cinematographic space according to its discontinuity, from cell to cell, or according to its continuous evolution, the visual data – which is, here, the sole information – indicates that most forms do not remain equal to themselves, neither in their transposition from one frame of discontinuity to another, nor during their passage from one moment of continuity to another. Two figures of one and the same object, taken in two different fixed shots or at two different moments of a moving shot, hardly ever conserve their geometric properties, can hardly ever be perfectly superimposed. The relationship between physical sizes has changed; their dimensions behave like variables. The exterior movement of the camera has, in some way, spread to the object, which it has endowed with an interior movement expressed through transformations.

Since configurative relations do not remain everywhere nor at all times the same, the cinematographic space does not appear as a homogeneous space. Neither does it necessarily accept symmetry. It does not possess homogeneity nor symmetry because it represents a space in motion or, to express it better, a space no longer generated (as is Euclidean space) by well-determined positions of the stable shapes of solids, but generated by badly-defined movements of apparitions that are also mobile in their shapes and that behave like fluids.

No geometrician, no physicist can match exactly two clouds, two ocean waves. In the fluidity of the world shown on screen, it is also difficult to establish a perfect identity; there, the principle of identity maintains only a value of approximation – a value that is both more uncertain and larger than the role the principle plays in the representation of the world, which we understand to be reliable. This vagueness of the fundamental experience of similarity and this fuzziness of the primordial axiom of reasoning drag into themselves the entire apparatus of classical logic, as we have seen. What is there to say but that this entire, old rational system relies on the conception of Euclidean space and only works within a certain geometry's limits of validity? When the experience of space changes, geometry changes too, and we need to reason, to philosophize, to moralize, to think differently, according to this other geometry.

Sure, one will say, but Euclidean space is the truest geometry, and the only natural one. Well, what is true is that imagining a Euclidean space satisfies the most frequent needs of our ordinary activity, just like our conception of the meter – which is neither an absolute nor a natural truth – solves many practical problems. What is also true is that, as cinema shows, if we lived on a less firm Earth with fewer fixed markers, or if we were organized to better perceive the mobility of this so-called firm Earth and these so-called fixed markers, we would have to think about a non-Euclidean space.

Within the same package – a room setting – fifteen different shots, fixed and mobile, show us fifteen different spaces, some Euclidean and some non-Euclidean, each being two- or three-dimensional, ordered in relation to different axis systems, accepting different scales. Does this prove that the room really contains fifteen kinds of spaces, just like it could contain thirty-six or a hundred kinds? And which one of these spaces is truer than others? Or does the real space add up to fifteen times three, or one hundred times two, dimensions?

Such diversity of shots instead tends to prove that there is no more a uniquely true space than there is a uniquely accurate perspective: it proves that there are as many spaces and perspectives as we can conceive and that all spaces, as well as all perspectives, belong to the realm of optical illusions. As far as space in general is concerned, only one possibility exists: that of situating, in an infinite number of ways, phenomena considered to coexist; that of thinking, in innumerable ways, about events considered simultaneous. Perhaps we could more easily purge the spatial conception of reality by reappropriating the Cartesian term of *extension* that, after falling into desuetude, distanced itself a bit from the baggage with which it was loaded by the seventeenth- and eighteenth-century usage and for which it was reformed and replaced by the (at first purely) idealistic Kantian designation.

If there is a truth, it lies in the absence of the truth of space and in the lack of specific form of *extension*, where each new aspect of the contents creates the structure for a new phantom container. Thus, through its spatial polymorphism and through the mobility of its *extension*, cinematographic representation is, after all, truer than the classical conception of an immovable geometric frame, unique and universal, underlying all localizations. Slowly, carefully, insinuatingly, cinema effects a great change in mentalities, even those not accustomed to abstraction, by freeing them of fixity fetishism. This fetishism that worshipped five polyhedra as doubly sacred, because they were remarkably solid, remarkably regular, and that saw (and still sees) in nature the work of genius geometricians and architects: that's Euclidian geometricians and architects.

It is said that Euclid used to trace his figures in the sand of Alexandrian beaches, and that he was not concerned that the wind could skew his theorems.

However, a world that is intrinsically animated, like an image on a screen, needs a kind of geometry that remains valid on quicksand. And this geometry of the unstable governs a logic, a philosophy, a common sense, a religion, an aesthetics based on instability.

★ ★ ★

Logic of Variable Time

Translated by Thao Nguyen

[Jean Epstein, "Logique de temps variable," *Alcool et cinéma* (unpublished in Epstein's lifetime), in ESC2, pp. 216-221.]

Furthermore, we need to ask if the theory of space, proposed and demanded by cinematographic representation, can still accept a geometry or a kinematics, since the movement that reigns in this space is so different from geometric and mechanical displacement.

Cinema is one of those very rare instruments that is not only capable but forced to represent a succession by a succession, a duration by a duration. On screen, any phenomenon finds itself inevitably set not only with a length, a width, and a height, but also with a fourth dimension, that of time, which geometry completely neglects in its translations, rotations, and projections, all of which are always supposed to be instantaneous. The animated image can never constitute a purely spatial representation, but, necessarily, a time-space representation to which a geometry of four dimensions (three of space and one of duration) must correspond: a time geometry. The animated image reproduces and demonstrates through evidence the truly inviolable unity of space-time, which, through our habit of Euclidean analysis, seemed like a relativist mystery to us, if not a relativist myth.

Since any movement is a succession, according to the Eleatics themselves, and since any succession can only occur in time, it goes without saying that nothing in an essentially mobile world can exist without occupying a place both in time and in space. The Euclidean trick had succeeded in having us forget this notion, full of elementary realism, or to find it very subtle. Here again, cinema, refusing to confirm an abusive analysis, leads to an understanding, whatever its unknowable or non-existent absolute truth or absolute falseness may be, that better embraces the generality of the phenomenon.

There is more. The dimension of time that we believed was subjected absolutely to the constant rhythm of our standard clocks, the duration of phenomena whose more or less speedy succession we found impossible to see, are shown to us in a varying state by the screen, just like it shows variable spatial data. Without doubt, measured in general at twenty-three images per second, projections adjust, in theory, the passage of time in the cinematographic field to the passage of time in the earthly field, where the recording was made at the same rate. But all we need on screen is to show an old tape, recorded at a slightly slower rhythm, to discover a world living more rapidly, a hurried world so bustling as to be comical. Besides, even in films produced and reproduced at today's normal speed, spectacular time is, in fact, hardly ever in tune with historical time. Whether it be a shot, a scene where characters engage in successive actions while avoiding any pause detrimental to the spectator's interest, or an entire montage that elides days, seasons, or centuries as it pleases, cinematographic transposition almost always accelerates the course of events.

Theatrical time is variable as well, but in a much more moderate way and in a much clumsier fashion. Alone, cinema can represent, through a real, sensible continuity, a course through the universe – not only accelerated but also slowed down at will, in a duration compressible and extensible in relation to our own consumption of time. Alone, cinema can show us a life that is twenty times slower or fifty thousand times faster, in which we discover minerals crawling, crystals blossoming, the elasticity and solidity of water, the viscosity of continents, the gesticulation of plants, the rigidity of clouds flying across the sky like arrows, or the petrifaction of man himself, becoming his own statue.

These remarkable aspects make the fundamental principles of our classifications – which distinguish the immobile from the mobile, the inconstant from the constant, the being from the becoming, the inert from the living, the three states of matter, the three kingdoms of nature, the three categories of living organisms – look precarious. To merge these categories, to unmask the convention of a supposed order in creation, we only need to vary duration sufficiently, to rally the temporal dimension, to add a temporal movement to spatial movement. Making the effects of a superior mobility visible for the first time, combining spatial and temporal changes, is the very special power of the cinematographic tool, whereas, until cinema, all movements that we were accustomed to see took place at a unique and constant speed. Placed in this mobility, which is in a way raised to the second power, all forms are affected and made pliable, remelted or rehardened or reliquefied, proving that they are nothing more than forms of movement. Such a result becomes especially obvious when we vary the speed of shots during the same recording.

One may object that it is an artificial result. But is there an experiment or even an advanced observation that does not employ a device and that does not more or less disrupt natural phenomenon while at the same time communicating new appearances? And yet, we do not consider those to be false.

Today, astronomers tell us that if the Moon does not turn faster around the Earth, it is the Earth that, probably, slows down its movement; that our solar time is unstable. Biologists and psychologists affirm, on the other hand, that organic time flows more slowly in a young being than it does in an older being. But, these small or unclear variations that are difficult to see or are elusive for our senses still remain unknown to most people, who cannot even fathom the possibility of time differentiations because they have not experienced them visually, because they never had the opportunity to compare the diversity of aspects that a phenomenon undergoes during two or several unequal durations. The imagination of the cinematographic instrument alone makes possible this comparison of visible effects of plurality, mobility, relativity, of the frame where successions are ordered and measured.

In cinema's favor, we need to add that the almost microscopic technique of slow-motion and the almost telescopic technique of time-lapse cinematography help us abandon our simplistic faith in a quasi-material existence of a unique and rigid time, merged with earthly or sidereal time. Like space, time has no other reality except from one perspective through which we no longer see approximately simultaneous phenomena creating spatial perspective but distinct events that appear successive. Depending on the duration given to these events and to their intervals, temporal perspective accepts all shortcuts, all elongations. All forms of this perspective can be equally exact, commensurately, but none of them is absolutely true. Asking if terrestrial time is truer or less true than biological time makes barely any more sense than asking if the pink sky at sunset is truer or less true than noon's azure. Declaring that aspects of a scene of germination shown on screen in slow motion are more false than the appearances of the same germination seen in the calendar time, amounts to declaring that a stamp, seen through a magnifying glass, becomes a fake stamp.

Perhaps if the magnificent resources – not only documentary but also dramatic – of slow motion and time-lapse were not used in such a regrettably exceptional manner in films aimed at the general public, spectators would more quickly allay their suspicion about the most original representation that cinema may have shown us to date: the representation of a scaled-up or down universe *ad libitum* in its time dimension.

However, even spectacular films use, more or less discretely and unknowingly, the cinematographic ability to modify duration. If not every shot, then almost each sequence possesses its own rhythm. Images do not represent the same time that reigns in all the shot cells of different spaces. If not every cell, at least several cell groups are presented like as many particularities not only of space, but also of time. As soon as the camera has moved or moves, spatial perspective changes, and as we carefully observe it, rarely does time perspective not also undergo some kind of modification.

We do not always see a temporal variation accompanying each spatial variation, because the camera movements can only occur within restricted limits of time or speed. And temporal variation remains unnoticeable. On the other hand, the latitude of ratios of acceleration or slowing down proves sufficient to show that cinematographic time consumes space, directly due to its speed, if we examine it within its own time-space system, and inversely, if we inscribe it in terrestrial space, in the length of recorded tape. Thus, there exist relations of equivalence between temporal and spatial values. Astronomers, who routinely compute distances in years, are accustomed to this commutativity where time becomes space and vice versa, where time is absorbed by space and space by time, where time-space no longer exists. Cinema affords us an experience which, though it hardly explains the mystery of this unity, summarizes the mystery in this trajectory that needs to be three times shorter and in this film tape that needs to be three times longer, to produce a time that is three times slower.

Time is no more uniform on screen than space is homogeneous, and the projection of any film offers a series of time-spaces that, at first, differ from one another in a discontinuous fashion, but each of them can also continuously vary within its own limits. Cinematographic time-space is thus an irregular complex, made of numerous, juxtaposed little continuities, but the jump between those continuities from one set of references to another rarely occurs without a hiatus. It is a functionally discontinuous group that, through this character, essentially contrasts with the deep-rooted conception that space and time must absolutely be continuous, by virtue of their function which defines their sole nature.

Yet, physicists' works have recently conveyed a new orientation to scientific philosophy, which now accepts the notion of a non-homogeneous time-space, of granular or cellular structure – that is to say, a discontinuous orientation. In the eyes of classical philosophy, there is the abstraction of everyday experience; in the eyes of common sense, these are the atavistic remains and origins of an old philosophy, and such heterogeneous division of time-space can only seem to be an absurd chimera since it does not correspond to any current observation, to any practical use. However, cinema suddenly brings images that enable us to see what things can look like in an irregular and fragmented time-space, one that does not claim to represent faithfully relativists' and microphysicists' time-spaces, but one that makes this type of spatial-temporal frame conceivable. Not only can we now fathom such a frame, but we are forced to reckon that it is endowed with a more subtle realism, that it adapts in a more precise manner to movements of all exterior and interior life.

Perhaps the public is not generally aware of the radical transformation that cinema proposes for the two fundamental instruments – the idea of space and the idea of time – that allow all the other ideas to be thought up. Cinema teaches in a manner that is never really dogmatic and that, here, remains especially implicit. Film only provides another visual experience of nature; the spectator simply needs to collect suggestions from this experience, just like he does by directly viewing the world, from which it took him a long time to sort out and construct a mechanism. But, through repeated suggestions of this second vision, it is quite improbable that the human mind will not end up – unconsciously at first – softening and complicating its diagram of the universe, by synthesizing time-space and by analyzing it as multiple time-spaces with differentiated values – variable and relative ones.

Thus, underneath the level of great logical axioms, the influence of animated images reaches the most deeply-rooted, rational categorizations, which it intends to patiently and almost treacherously repair. [...]

Note

1. See infra, p. 379, n2-3.

Afterword: Reclaiming Jean Epstein

Richard Abel

Do we sense a "historical turn" or return to Jean Epstein as both a major theorist and filmmaker? The April 2008 symposium organized by the Department of Cinema and Media Studies at the University of Chicago certainly awakened that expectation – first, by inviting half a dozen scholars from North America and Europe to present new research on Epstein's theoretical writing and several of his films and, second, by screening a relatively unseen 35mm print of *Finis terrae* (1929), which coincided closely with Pathé's unexpected DVD release of *Coeur fidèle* (1923). This collection of newly translated texts and critical essays should mark a further advance in the "turn" to reclaim Jean Epstein for film theory and film history. My own modest contribution aims to offer a series of notes on *Coeur fidèle* and *Finis terrae*, prompted by the unique opportunity to re-see both films – nearly thirty years after Marie Epstein allowed me to view them at the Cinémathèque française – and by the astute remarks of several scholars during the Chicago symposium.

Coeur fidèle

Coeur fidèle opens with an unusual series of eight shots that I described long ago as follows:

1. High-angle close-up of a table surface as a hand clears it of a plate and a cigarette and then wipes it with a rag.
2. Extreme close-up of Marie's face (45° angle).
3. Medium close-up of a hand picking up a glass and bottle while another hand wipes the edge of the table.
4. Close-up of Marie's face (straight on).
5. Medium close-up of wine being poured from a bottle into a glass, beside which a hand rests on the table.
6. Close-up of Marie's face looking down.
7. Medium shot of Marie pouring wine for a man seated at the table; she corks the bottle, and he lights a cigarette; he begins talking to her.
8. Long shot of the bistro interior: Marie and the man are at the table in the right background, behind a couple at another table, while the edge of the bar is in the left foreground. The bistro owner pushes Marie toward the man at

the table and then exits (foreground left); his wife enters (foreground left) and shakes her head at Marie, who comes over to the bar with a paper in her hand.[1]

There are a number of refinements that could be made in this shot description: for instance, the rough surface of the table in shots 1, 3, and 5 is suggestive of the interior space eventually revealed in shots 7 and 8; the hands in the same shots extend from frame left and seem to belong to the same person. The sequence of shots reverses the recently standardized pattern of American continuity editing, which would begin with an establishing shot defining the diegetic space and then cut in to closer shots. The disorienting reverse order has the effect of calling attention to the close-ups of Marie's face and her assumed hands moving among the objects on the bistro table's surface – and accentuates their potential importance.

This brief opening sequence makes an instructive contrast to one of Lev Kuleshov's re-editing experiments created just a few years prior to Epstein's film for the newly formed Moscow Film Committee in the Soviet Union. Those experiments, which he described as "making new subjects from old films," made Kuleshov acutely aware of how one could organize disparate shots, even from different sources, into a meaningful, rhythmic sequence.[2] The relationship of shot to shot could be more significant than an actor's performance, for instance, and engender associations or emotions beyond those evoked by a single shot. Most germane here is the montage experiment often cited as the "Kuleshov effect," in which a long-take close-up of Ivan Mosjoukine's expressionless face was intercut with various shots from other films: "a steaming bowl of soup, a woman in a coffin, a child playing with a toy bear."[3] Projecting the "new subject" for spectators, Kuleshov discovered that the same shot of Mosjoukine seemed to convey a different emotional effect, depending on its relation to one shot versus another.[4] Although similar textually, Epstein's "experiment" in the opening of Coeur fidèle produces an equally startling but different effect. Rather than emphasize a conjunction of shots in which each image seems to transform the sense of the same actor's expressionless face, his sequence creates an unexpected disjunction in which the three-shot series of Marie's face seems disconnected from the alternating three-shot series of hands moving about the rough table surface. Rather than being bound together through the intercutting, the two series seem almost separate, and Marie's face remains unchanged in its lack of expression. It is as if her character already exists in a space or world distinct from that eventually revealed as the bistro milieu.

Most striking in this opening sequence, however, is the immobility of Marie's face in close-up, which contrasts sharply with the movement of her hands in the alternating medium close-ups.[5] The relatively quick alternation of stasis and movement (the close-ups of her face each last no more than a second) is somewhat reminiscent of another famous sequence in a much later film, Hitchcock's *The Birds* (1963) where medium close-ups of Melanie's stilled face (looking down left foreground, down straight on, down right foreground, and then right) are intercut with point-of-view shots of a flaming trail of gasoline that races from right to left in shorter and shorter shots, ending in a long shot of a car exploding – after which, again in medium close-up, she reacts in shock. In the Hitchcock film, the accelerating combined rhythm of the rushing flame and the cutting intensify the suspense, but the differing "frozen" images of Melanie create a paradoxical sense of knowledge and helplessness: as if in a trance, she realizes what is about to happen yet is powerless to act – much like the film's spectator. The puzzling, if more regular, alternation of stasis and movement in Epstein's film has a very different effect of discontinuity. Marie's gaze seems disassociated from either the objects on the table or her active hands; she is looking yet not looking, her gaze "frozen" into an unchanging blank stare (wherever directed) that accentuates not only her separateness from her environs but also her alienation and the suggestion of a possible "desire for something else."

The print of *Coeur fidèle* that I viewed at the *Cinémathèque française* years ago, first in a small screening room and then on Marie Epstein's hand-cranked moviola, left me even more puzzled about the film's ending.[6] Although the re-mastered print recently made available on DVD resolves some of that puzzlement, Katie Kirtland's essay (in this volume) offers an ingenious analysis of the epilogue that impels me to reframe my own reading of the film's ending. Especially striking is her deft tracing of the numerous "layers of cliché" that undermine the conventional melodrama narrative and ultimately accumulate into a deeply "ironic take" on the *for ever* of lasting love. Let me first accentuate that "ironic take" by noting the structural rhyme between one moment in the *fête foraine* sequence concluding the film's first half – often cited for the intoxicating complexity of its rapid montage – and another similar moment in the epilogue. The first presents a sharp contrast between Marie and her brutal lover Paul (in medium close-ups and close-ups), swiftly circling above the fairground crowds in an amusement ride airplane: while Paul grins with delight, Marie's face remains expressionless, even sullen, and her look closely parallels that of the film's opening, evoking her unending sense of entrapment. The other recapitulates this moment, with Marie and Jean seated together (in medium close-ups and close-ups) in the same circling airplane: now, however, it is Marie who smiles and snuggles close to Jean, while he assumes the mask of immobility, the "frozen" lack of expression, that once defined her. The ironic "role reversal" of this recapitulation strongly suggests that, for reasons that Kirtland has outlined, it is Jean now who feels disengaged, entrapped.

In the midst of this structural rhyme, however, there is an enigmatic insert shot whose potential significance can be traced back to the confrontation that climaxes in Paul's death just prior to the epilogue. This is a high-angle full shot of the crippled woman (played by Marie Epstein) who is cradling Marie and Paul's infant at the bottom of her apartment building's rough wooden stairs. The shot is linked to Jean's look, as if the image were emerging from within, and the crippled woman's equally expressionless face seems to mirror his. The puzzling relationship among these three characters is set in a series of moves marking the film's climactic sequence. The first has Jean very slowly edging Marie toward the door of her apartment and away from her infant's cradle, an action that gains emphasis through a short montage of images, linked by dissolves, in which the cradle seems about to disappear into a distant darkness. The second occurs after the crippled woman shoots Paul, as his body slumps down and comes to rest leaning against the infant's cradle. That this image of Paul and the infant concludes the sequence and is followed immediately by the epilogue creates an inextricable bond between the two, excluding Marie, and that exclusion is recapitulated in the later enigmatic insert. The image of the crippled woman and the infant, as if seen or imagined by Jean, deepens the uncertainty marking the film's resolution. Is it guilt for killing Paul that Jean now shares with the crippled woman (anticipating Hitchcock once more), or does the existence of the infant uncannily conjure up, like a return of the repressed, an involuntary memory of Paul that will continue to haunt these two characters, as well as the spectator. The startling ambiguity of this nexus of images opens up a *mise-en-abyme* in Jean and Marie's romantic relationship.

Finis terrae

During the Chicago symposium, Ludovic Cortade's essay on Epstein's theoretical writings (in this volume) provoked considerable discussion about his late 1920s conception of slow motion and its effect on the screened experience of a film, whether 1) evoking a sense of transparency or non-transparency or 2) accentuating a sense of movement or immobility. Rather than extend the theoretical trajectory of that discussion, let me tease out some implications of how the frequent, consistent use of slow motion seems to function in several sequences in Finis terrae, which I still consider one of his very best films.[7] Before leaving Paris for the most western reaches of Brittany, in the early summer of 1928, Epstein published a short piece, "Fragments of Sky," in which he sought to set himself apart from those critics and filmmakers promoting one form or another of pure cinema as well as those flaunting "avant-garde" techniques for their own sake. Assuming that the film image is "a sign, complex and precise," characteristically he invokes a palimpsest of analogies to advocate something close to the ideal of transparency that would later become central to André Bazin. With language: "To allow time to admire the sign is to distract the spectator from the meaning of the text and turn his interest to its typography." With painting: "Pleasure in plasticity is a means, never an end." And with spirituality: "Images have only to channel their semi-spontaneous charge just as cathedral spires conduct thought into the heavens."[8] Yet the film he shot off the coast of Brittany, edited as *Finis terrae* in Paris and first screened at a specialized cinema, L'Oeil de Paris, in May 1929, is hardly devoid of "avant-garde" techniques, and especially slow motion.

In late 1928, while apparently still editing the film, Epstein published another essay, "Approaches to Truth," in which he explained that he went to Brittany to discover a kind of "authenticity," a "quality of sincerity," among the men gathering kelp on the isolated islands of Bannec and Balenec.[9] Only on his second trip did he believe he succeeded, and, in an unusual admission, he sought to justify his extensive use of slow motion, especially in recording the islanders he chose as actors and specifically the two boys playing Ambroise and Jean-Marie. "Sincerity in expression and natural gestures . . .[are] too fast, too illegible at normal speeds of shooting and projection: only filming at 30 or 40 frames per second can do away with the basically untruthful quality in an actor's performance."[10] Even if Epstein believed he had captured a sense of authenticity in the production process, how would the edited film create a similar sense in projection? What would keep spectators, especially cinéphiles, from being distracted and taking more pleasure in the film's "plasticity"?[11] An answer may lie in the opening scene, in the "staging" of the incident that generates the film's narrative. As Ambroise, in a rush, hands a last bottle of wine to Jean-Marie, it slips out of their grasp and breaks on the rocks; the shattered bottle provokes an argument but also cuts Ambroise's thumb – and the festering wound will force Jean-Marie to set out, with his delirious friend, in a small sailboat for the mainland. This scene is composed almost entirely of close shots (faces, hands, running feet, a bottle, glass fragments, rocks, and sand), some accentuated by fast tracks and dollies but all of relatively short length and marked by slightly slowed motion. Although the subsequent shots lengthen and movement within the frame decreases, the slow motion continues until it becomes almost imperceptible, even "natural." That imperceptibility gives the images an unusual degree of "transparency" that eventually allows a subtle sense of the uncanny to emerge.

Initially, the world of *Finis terrae* is confined to the island of Bannec, where Ambroise's condition worsens and Jean-Marie's animosity grows (he also believes Ambroise has stolen his knife). Not only are the boys' actions and interactions presented in slight slow motion, so are the sea waves that break on rock outcroppings and wash up on a sandy beach, as is the men's work of gathering the kelp into piles for burning. A simple moment of synecdoche, also accentuated by slow motion, first suggests that the sea is more than a source of subsistence and may threaten the men: an empty wooden bowl (once containing their cooked potatoes) gradually is caught in the incoming tide, tilted, overturned, and submerged. As the film shifts near midpoint to the coastal village of Ouessant on the mainland, a lighthouse keeper notices a lack of activity on Bannec and the two boys' mothers persuade the local doctor, Lesenin, and several fishermen to venture out in a rowboat to find out what could be wrong. A lengthy, suspenseful sequence of alternation, marked consistently by slow motion, first climaxes when the two boats meet miraculously in a dense fog, while the two mothers keep watch on the high rocks above a narrow harbor cove. And it climaxes a second time when, after the mothers' long night vigil huddled together under a single shawl, the overcrowded rowboat finally emerges out of the fog and maneuvers through a turbulent sea to reach the harbor dock in safety. Here, slow motion remains so imperceptible – except perhaps when one mother drops a handkerchief and huge waves repeatedly crash against the rocks – that its apparent transparency accentuates the uncanny alignment of these alternating spaces and underscores the bond that, despite distance and difference, links the boys, their rescuers, and their mothers in a community of *caritas*.

This imagined community in *Finis terrae* deserves a final observation. If the sea, as a force of nature, separates men and women and even threatens their existence, it also acts as a mysterious agent of deliverance. In this fable of near death and "resurrection," it is striking that, despite the presence of a village church and the tolling bell that gathers people together, the human agents of that deliverance are secular rather than religious.[12] Two lighthouse keepers, separately, notice that something is wrong on Bannec, but it is the doctor who plays a crucial mediating role, returning the boys to their mothers and saving Ambroise from blood poisoning. Lesenin is a strangely "modern" figure who not only uses proven medical practices to minister to this marginal community but also acts as a benevolent "father" to the village children.[13] The mothers' gratitude is conveyed near the end in a long shot of the doctor sleeping at a kitchen table with several women in quiet attendance, the glowing interior framed by a darkened doorway. How apt too is the film's final low-angle long shot in which a young boy leads the doctor over a grassy hill (to attend to a sick old man), silhouetted against an immense white sky. It is tempting to imagine Lesenin as a fictional surrogate for the filmmaker himself. Both may be outsiders in this pre-modern world, on screen and off, yet they work in respectful collaboration with the villagers and, in Epstein's case, with the kelp gatherers as well. If Lesenin's function is to serve as a "healer" who cares for the sick and wounded, Epstein's is more like that of an ethnographer quite aware that he and his camera are hardly neutral observers but rather provocative participants in the islanders and villagers' confrontation with modernity. One of his aims in editing and screening the film in Paris, as Rachel Moore suggests (in another essay included in this volume), may have been to reverse this confrontation and force Parisians to encounter "the material and spiritual reality" of an "other" culture (however collaboratively captured) within the very borders of France.[14] Yet the point of the encounter was to provoke an understanding – one that recurs repeatedly in his writings – not so much of the "other" but rather of oneself.[15] What the encounter – the "healing" experience of filmmaking in Brittany – may have meant personally for Epstein remains one of several gaps in our knowledge about this incredibly poetic French filmmaker.

★ ★ ★

This timely collection of critical essays and newly translated texts aims to initiate what we all hope will become an ongoing project to reclaim Jean Epstein for both film history and film theory. At stake is the recovery and resituating of his writings as the most original, erudite, and poetic of French theoretical texts in the 1920s, the most sophisticated prior to that of André Bazin, whose own writings owe an often unacknowledged debt to his precursor. Also at stake is the recovery of an early model for what it means to work as both a film theorist and filmmaker: not only do Epstein's theoretical writings and films illuminate one another, the films themselves often do intense theoretical work, extending and complicating his thinking through the continuity and discontinuity of streams of images. This project now depends on a joint effort between scholars and archivists to make more of Epstein's films available on DVD, struck from high quality positive prints, most of them deposited by Marie Epstein at the Cinémathèque française – from *La Belle Nivernaise* (1924), *Six et demi onze* (1927), and *La Glace à trois faces* (1927) to *Mor–Vran* (1930), *L'Or des mers* (1933), and *Les Batisseurs* (1938). And, of course, the marvelous *Finis terrae!*

Notes

1. Richard Abel, *French Cinema: The First Wave, 1915-1929* (Princeton: Princeton University Press, 1984), p. 361.
2. Lev Kuleshov, "In Maloi Gnezdnikovsky Lane" [1967], in *Kuleshov on Film: Writings of Lev Kuleshov*, ed. and trans. Ronald Levaco (Berkeley: University of California Press, 1974), p. 199.
3. This description of shots comes from Vsevolod Pudovkin, *Film Technique and Film Acting* [1929], trans. Ivor Montagu (London: Vision, 1954), p. 140. Kuleshov himself describes them slightly differently in "In Maloi Gnezdnikovsky Lane," p. 200.
4. Ronald Levaco, "Introduction," in *Kuleshov on Film*, ed. Levaco, pp. 7-8.
5. Just two years before, in one of his first essays, Epstein disdained "motionless close-ups"; yet, as if looking ahead to the opening of *Coeur fidèle*, he also lovingly described one such instance of immobility (a face in close up) as an incipient prelude to action, to the "maximum expression of *photogénie*." See "Grossissement," in *Bonjour Cinéma* (Paris: Éditions de la sirène, 1921), pp. 93-108; translated by Stuart Liebman as "Magnification," *Abel1*, pp. 235-240.
6. See Abel, *French Cinema*, pp. 365-366.
7. I was surprised to discover that the analysis of *Finis terrae* I wrote nearly thirty years ago still seems largely persuasive. See Abel, *French Cinema*, pp. 500-507.

8. Jean Epstein, "Les images de ciel," *Cinéa-Ciné-pour-tous*, no. 107 (15 April 1928), translated by Richard Abel as "Fragments of Sky," *Abel1*, pp. 421-422.

9. Jean Epstein, "Les approches de la vérité," *Photo-Ciné* (15 November-15 December 1928), translated by Tom Milne as "Approaches to Truth," *Abel1*, pp. 422-425.

10. Epstein, "Approaches to Truth," p. 423.

11. My own viewing notes on *Finis terrae* from research at the Cinémathèque française are suggestive. The rough notes taken at a screening sometimes include instances of slow motion, but the detailed notes taken during a moviola viewing make no mention of them.

12. In her essay in this volume, Rachel Moore offers an important context for the film's focus on the secular rather than the religious: Ouessant was described as a theocracy until the late nineteenth century and only became part of France in 1891.

13. It is worth recalling that, in the midst of WW I, Epstein initially began to study medicine in Lyon, and his first film was a feature-length fictional documentary, *Pasteur* (1922).

14. Epstein, "Approaches to Truth," p. 424.

15. See, for instance, the amazing, self-reflexive description of his descent into a volcano, in Jean Epstein, *Le Cinématographe vu de l'Etna* (Paris: Les écrivains réunis, 1926), pp. 9-19; infra, 287-92.

Filmography

Silent films

Pasteur (1922). Made on the occasion of the centennial of Pasteur's birth. Directed by Jean Epstein. General supervision by Jean Benoit-Levy. Script by Edouard Epardaud. Camera by Edmond Floury. Interiors shot at Nadal studios, at Joinville-le-Pont, Exteriors on location at Arbois, Dole, Strasbourg, Alias, Pouilly-lo-Fort, at the Pasteur Institutes of Paris and Lille, at the Auguste Lumiere laboratories at Lyons, at the public schools (Écoles Normales Superieurs) in Paris and the Alsace region. Produced by L'Edition Française Cinématographique, Distributed by Pathé-Consortium-Cinéma. First shown at the Gaumont-Palace, Paris, in April 1923. Length: app. 1200 meters.

Les Vendanges (1922). (The Wine Harvest). Documentary of the Narbonne Region. Camera: Edmond Floury, Produced by Édition Française Cinématographique.

L'Auberge rouge (1923). (The Red Inn). Adapted from the tale by Honoré de Balzac. Adapted and directed by Jean Epstein. Artistic Supervision: Louis Nalpas. Interiors shot at Quenn Studio Pathe, sets by Studio des Vignerons at Vincennes; Exteriors at the castle of Vincennes. Camera: Raoul Aubourdier, assisted by Roger Hubert and Robert Lefebvre. Produced and distributed by Pathé-Consortium-Cinéma. Length: app. 1800 meters.

Cœur fidèle (1923). (The Faithful Heart). Written and directed by Jean Epstein. Camera by Paul Guichard, Leon Donnot. Interior shots at the Pathé Studio in Vincennes. Exteriors in Marseilles (the old port of Monosquo). Produced and distributed by Pathé-Consortium-Cinéma. Length: app. 2000 meters.

La Montagne infidèle (1923). (The Faithless Mountain). Lost. Documentary on the eruption of Mount Etna in June 1923. Directed by Jean Epstein. Camera: Paul Guichard. Produced and distributed by Pathé-Consortium-Cinéma. Length: app. 600 meters.

La Belle Nivernaise (1923). (The Beauty from Nivernais). From the short novel by Alphonse Daudet. Adapted and directed by Jean Epstein. Camera: Paul Guichard, assisted by Leon Donnot. Edited by Jean Epstein, assisted by R. Allinat. Interiors shot at the Pathé Studio of the Vignerons at Vincennes. Exteriors on the Seine between Paris and Rouen, and at Vincennes. Produced and distributed by Pathé-Consortium-Cinéma. Length: app. 1800 meters.

La Goutte de sang (1924). (A Drop of Blood). From the story by J. Mary. Partial direction by Jean Epstein. Camera: Paul Guichard, Leon Donnot. Interiors at the Pathé Studio in Vincennes, exteriors at Gorges de l'Herault, Nice. As a result of Epstein's difficulties with the Société des Cinéromans, it was completed under the direction of Maurice Mariaud. Most of the scenes taken by Epstein were not used in the final version.

Le Lion des mogols. (1924). (*The Lion of the Moguls*). Scenario by Ivan Mosjoukine. Directed and edited by Jean Epstein. Camera: Joseph-Louis Mundwiller, Fedor Bourjoukine, Nicolas Roudakoff. Sets by Lachakoff. Costumes designed by B. Bilinsky. Interiors shot at the Albatros studios in Montreuil and at Menchen d'Epinay. Exteriors in Algeria and the port of Marseilles. Produced by Albatros Films. Distributed by Armor Films. Length: app. 2000 meters.

L'Affiche (1924). (*The Poster*). Scenario by Marie Epstein. Directed by Jean Epstein. Camera: Maurice Desfassiaux. Sets by B. Bilinsky. Interiors shot at Albatros Studio in Montreuil. Exteriors at Bougival and in Paris. Produced by Albatros Films. Distributed by Armor Films. Length: app. 2000 meters.

Photogénies (1925). Film edited from stock-footage at the request of the Théâtre de Vieux Colombier. Improvised rapidly with the use of out-takes and newsreel material. This film was later destroyed.

Le Double amour (1925). (*Double Love*). Scenario by Marie Epstein. Directed by Jean Epstein. Camera by Maurice Desfassiaux, assisted by Nicolas Roudakoff. Sets designed by Pierre Kefer. Interiors shot at the Studio Albatros in Montreuil. Exteriors at Nice and on the French Riviera. Produced by Albatros Films. Distributed by Armor Films. Length app. 2000 meters.

Les Aventures de Robert Macaire (1925). (*The Adventures of Robert Macaire*). Five episodes. Scenario by Charles Vayre from L'AUBERGE DES ADRETS (Play by Benjamin Antier, 1832). Directed by Jean Epstein. Camera: Paul Guichard, assisted by Jehan Fouquet, Nicolas Roudakoff. Sets designed by J. Mercier. Interiors shot at Albatros studios in Montreuil. Exteriors at Dauphine, Grenoble, Vizille castle. Produced by Albatros Films. Distributed by Armor Films. Original length: 4500 meters. Short version: 3000 meters.

Mauprat (1926). From the novel by George Sand. Directed by Jean Epstein. Assistant director: Luis Buñuel. Camera: Albert Duverger. Sets designed by Pierre Kefer. Constumes by the Souplet company. Wigs by the Chanteau company. Interiors at the Menchen Studio in Epinay. Exteriors at the valley of the Creuze. Produced by Jean Epstein Films. Distributed by Selections Maurice Roubier. Length: app. 2000 meters.

Au Pays de George Sand (1926). (*In the Country of George Sand*). Documentary on the castle of Nohan. Camera: Porinal. Produced by Jean Epstein Films.

Six et demi, onze (1927). (*Six and a Half, Eleven*) Scenario by Marie Epstein. Directed by Jean Epstein. Camera by Georges Perinal. Sets designed by Pierre Kefer. Interiors at the Studio Nouilly (Roudes) and at the Théâtre des Champs Elysées. Exteriors in Paris, Fontainebleau, Antibes, and the Alps. Produced by Jean Epstein Films. Distributed by Companie Universelle Cinématographique. Length: app. 2000 meters.

La Glace à trois faces (1927). (*The Three-Sided Mirror*). From the short novel by Paul Morand. Directed by Jean Epstein. Camera: Eiwinger. Sets designed by Pierre Kefer. Interiors at the Roudes studio in Neuilly. Exteriors in Paris, L'Isle-Adam. Produced by Jean Epstein Films. Distributed by Studio des Ursulines. Length: app. 900 meters.

La Chute de la Maison Usher (1928). (*The Fall of the House of Usher*). After Edgar Allan Poe. Adapted from Poe's "Fall of the House of Usher" and "The Oval Portrait." Directed by Jean Epstein. Assistant: Luis Buñuel. Camera: Georges Lucas, assisted by Jean Lucas. Sets designed by Pierre Kefer. Interiors at Studio Menchen at Epinay. Exteriors at Magny-en-Vexin, at swamps of Sologne, and on the Breton coast. Assistant set designer: Ferdinand Ochse. Produced by Jean Epstein Films. Distributed by Exclusivités Seyta. Length: app. 1500 meters.

Finis Terrae (1929). Directed by Jean Epstein. Camera: Joseph Barth and Joseph Kottula, assisted by Louis Neo and Raymond Tulle. Produced by Société Générale des Films. Distributed by Mappemonde-Films. Length: app. 2400 meters.

Sa Tête (1929). (*His Head*). Scenario by Jean Epstein. Directed by Jean Epstein. Camera: Albert Bres, assisted by Fred Alric. Assistant director: Marcel Cohen. Interiors at Studio Roudes in Neuilly. Exteriors in the region of Seine-et-Oise. Produced by Gaston Roudes. Distributed by Exclusivites Seyta. Talking version with narration by Bernard Zimmer. Length: app. 900 meters.

Le Pas de la mule (1930). (*The Mule's Pace*). Documentary. Directed by Jean Epstein. Camera: A. Bres. Production: Vieux Colombier.

Sound films

Mor'Vran (1930). (*The Sea of Ravens*). Directed by Jean Epstein. Acted by the fishermen of the Île de Sein, near Brest. Camera: Alfred Guichard, Albert Bros and Marcel Rebière. Assistant cameraman: Henri Chauffier. Natural sets and exteriors photographed on the Île-de-Sein and in the bay of Finistère. Music by A. Tansman and Alexis Archangelsky. Post-synchronized with original Breton music. Produced and distributed by Compagnic Universelle Cinématoqraphique. Length: app. 900 meters.

Notre-Dame de Paris. Documentary. Directed by Jean Epstein. Camera: Emile Monnoit. Produced and distributed by Synchro-Ciné. Post-synchronized. Length: app. 300 meters.

La Chanson des peupliers (1931). (*The Song of the Poplars*). A filmed song. Directed by Jean Epstein. Camera: Christian Matras. Produced and distributed by Synchro-Ciné. Post-synchronized. Length: app. 300 meters.

Le Cor (1931) (*The Horn*). Based on a poem by Alfred de Vigny. Directed by Jean Epstein. Camera: Christian Matras. Produced and distributed by Synchro-Ciné. Post-synchronized.

L'Or des mers (1932). (*Gold from the Sea*). Directed by Jean Epstein. Produced as silent. "Acted" by the inhabitant-fishermen of the Island Hoedick. Camera: Christian Matras. Assistant cameramen: Albert Bres and Joseph Braun. Music by Devaux and Kross-Hertman. Natural sets and exteriors on the islands of Houat and Hoëdick. Produced and distributed by Synchro-Ciné. Length: app. 2000 meters.

Les berceaux (1932). (*The Cradles*). A filmed song. Directed by Jean Epstein. Camera: Joseph Barth. Exteriors shot at Saint-Malo and Cancale. Produced and distributed by Synchro-Ciné. Post-synchronized. Length: app. 300 meters.

La Villanelle des rubans (1932). (*The Villanelle of Ribbons*). A filmed song. Directed by Jean Epstein. Camera: Joseph Barth. Produced and distributed by Synchro-Ciné. Post-synchronized. Length: app. 300 meters.

Le Vieux chaland (1932). (*The Old Barge*). A filmed song. Directed by Jean Epstein. Camera: Joseph Barth. Produced and distributed by Synchro-Ciné. Post-synchronized. Length: app. 300 meters.

L'Homme à Hispano (1932). (*The Man with the "Hispanic" Car*). From the novel by Pierre Frondaie. Written and directed by Jean Epstein. Camera: Armand Thirard and Joseph Barth, assisted by Phillipe Agostini and Arthur. Assistant directors: Louis Delapree and Robert de Knyff. Music by Jean Weiner, conducted by Roger Desormiere. Second recording by Courmes and Gernolle. Sets designed by Lauer & Co. Edited by Marthe Bassi. Interiors at the Braunberger-Richebe Studio in Billancourt. Exteriors at Cannes, in the Provence, at Biarritz, and in the Basque country. Produced by Vandal and Delac. Distributed by Films P. J. de Venloo. Length: app. 2000 meters.

La Châtelaine du liban (1933). (The Lady of the Lebanese Manor). From the novel by Pierre Benoit. Written and directed by Jean Epstein. Dialogue by Pierre Benoit. Camera: Armand Thirard, Joseph Barth, and Christian Matras. Assistant directors: Ary Sadoul and Pierre Duval. Sets designed by Aguettand and Bouxin. Music by Alexander Tansman. Sound recording by Bauge. Interiors at Studio Pathé-Francoeur. Exteriors in Beyrouth (Lebanon), Palmyra (Syria), and at Avignon. Produced by Vandal and Delac. Distributed by Films P. J. de Venloo. Length: app. 2400 meters.

Chanson d'Ar-Mor (1934). (Song of Ar-Mor). After Jean des Cognets. Adapted and directed by Jean Epstein. Ballad-type documentary, spoken in Breton language. Camera: Jean Lucas, assisted by Georges Lucas and Raymond Raynal. Assistant director: Pierre Duval. Music by Jacques Larmanjat, conducted by Roger Desormiere. Choirs and dances arranged by Emile Cueff, assisted by Suscinio. Sound recording by Behrens. Edited by Marthe Poncin. Breton Dialogue by Fanch Gourvil. Natural settings and exteriors in Brittany. Produced by Ouest-Eclair at Rennes. Distributed by Pathé. Length: app. 1200 meters.

La vie d'un grand journal (1934). (The Life of the Great Newspaper). Documentary. Directed by Jean Epstein. Camera: Jean and Georges Lucas. Produced by Ouest-Eclair.

Marius et Olive à Paris (1935). (Marius and Olive in Paris). Scenario by Pages. Directed by Jean Epstein. Assistant director: Pierre Duval. Camera: Joseph Barth and Philippe Agostini. Music by Jean Wiener. Interiors at Studio Photosonor. Exteriors in Marseilles. Produced by Cinemonde. Due to disputes, Epstein withdrew his name from the title credits.

Cœur de gueux (Cuore di vagabondo) (1936). (Heart of the Vagabonds). Scenario by G. B. Seyta, after A. Machard. Adapted and directed by Jean Epstein. Dialogue and Lyrics by Camille Francois. Camera: Mario Albertelli, Tielzi, assisted by Angarelli. Assistant director: Pierre Duval. Music by Jean Lenoir and J. Dallin. Assistant for the Italian version: Giacomo Forzano. Sets by Lucca. Director of production: G. B. Seyta. Interiors at the Forzano Studio and the Studio Tirrenia in Marina di Pisa. Exteriors in the environments of Pisa, Florence, and Livorna. Produced by Seyta and Forzano Films. Distributed by Compagnie Universelle Cinematographique. Length: app. 2400 meters.

La Bretagne (1936). (Brittany). Documentary for the exposition of Art and Techniques. Directed by Jean Epstein. Narration by Leandre Valliat. Camera: Georges Lucas, assisted by Robert Ruth. Music by Henri Casadessues. Songs performed by Yvon Le Mar'Hadour. Dances arranged by Emile Cueff. Sound recording by Behrens. Produced by Jean Benoit-Levy and Grands Reseaux Francais. Distributed by Atlantic Films. Length: app. 1200 meters.

La Bourgogne (1936). (Burgundy). Documentary for the exposition of Art and Techniques. Directed by Jean Epstein. Narration by Leandre Valliat. Camera: Georges Lucas, assisted by Robert Ruth. Assistant director: Pierre Duval. Music by Henri Casadessus. Sound recording by Behrens. Production and distribution: Grands Reseaux Francais and Atlantic Films. Length: app. 900 meters.

Vive la vie (1937). (*Long Live Life!*). Scenario by Marie Epstein and Jean Benoit-Levy. Directed by Jean Epstein. Documentary produced for the French Youth Hostel Association. Assistant director: Pierre Duval. Music by Jean Wiener. Sound recording by Behrens. Interiors at the Billancourt studio. Natural settings and exteriors at the youth hostels of Aix en Provence, Aubagne, Apt, and in the valley of Loups. Produced by Jean Benoit-Levy. Distributed by the ministry of Public Entertainment. Length: app. 1200 meters.

La Femme du bout du monde (1937). (*The Woman from the End of the World*). From the novel by Alain Serdac. Adapted and directed by Jean Epstein. Camera: Enzo Riccioni and Paul Cotteret. Assistant director: Pierre Duval. Director of Production: Jean Rossi. Music by Jean Wiener. Sound recording by Behrens. Sets designed by Roger Berteux at Courbevoie studio. Interiors at Studio Francois Premier. Exteriors on the island of Ouessant. This film was released under the occupation without giving credit to Epstein. Length: app. 2400 meters.

Les Bâtisseurs (1938). (*The Builders*). Documentary. Scenario by Jeander. Directed by Jean Epstein. Camera: Georges Lucas and Robert Ruth. Assistant director: Pierre Duval. Sets: Roger Berteaux. Music by Hoeree and Honegger. Sound recording by Behrens, assisted by Maxime Bachellerie. Interiors at La Garenne Studio. Exteriors at Paris, Chartres, St.-Cloud, etc. Produced by the National Federation of Construction. Distributed by Ciné-Liberte and the Maison des Techniques. Length: app. 900 meters.

La Relève (1938). (*The Relief*). Documentary. Camera: Georges Lucas, Robert Ruth. Produced by Ciné-Liberte.

Eau-Vive (1938). (*Spring Water*). Documentary. Written and directed by Jean Epstein. Camera: Georges Lucas and Pierre Bachelet. Assistant directors: Pierre Duval and Jacques Brochard. Interiors at the La Garenne studios. Exteriors at Rochefort en Yveline. Produced by Jean Benoit-Levy. Distributed privately. Length: app. 1200 meters.

Artères de France (1939). (*Arteries of France*). Documentary produced for the French section of the International Exposition in New York. Scenario by Henri Champly. Directed by Jean Epstein, in collaboration with Rene Lucot. Camera: Georges and Jean Lucas. Assistant director: Pierre Duval. Cooperative production of Les Artisans D'Art du Cinéma. Distributed by Robert de Nesles. Music by Heni Casadessus. Sound recording by Behrens. Length: app. 600 meters.

Le Tempestaire (1947). (*The Storm Master*). Directed by Jean Epstein. Camera: A.S. Militon, assisted by Schneider. Score by Yves Baudrier. Sound recording by Leon Vareille and Frankiel, assisted by Dumont. Director of production: Nino Constantini. Produced by Filmagazine. Distributed in the USA by Martin Lewis. Length: app. 600 meters.

Les Feux de la mer (1948). (*The Fires of the Sea*). Directed by Jean Epstein. Camera: Pierre Bachelet, assisted by Andre Bernard. Assistant directors: Pierre Duval and Jacques Duchateau. Musical score by Yves Baudrier. Sound recording by Leon Vareille. Produced by Films Etienne Lallier for the United Nations. Distributed by the UN. Length: app. 600 meters.

Select Bibliography

Books by Epstein (including chapters previously translated into English)

La Poésie d'aujourd'hui: un nouvel état d'intelligence. Paris: Éditions de la Sirène, 1921.

Bonjour Cinéma. Paris: Éditions de la Sirène, 1921.

> "Grossissement," in *Bonjour Cinéma*, pp. 93-108. Translated by Stuart Liebman as "Magnification," *October*, no. 3 (Spring 1977): 9-15; reprinted with minor corrections in Liebman, *Jean Epstein's Early Film Theory*, 1920-1922 (1980), pp. 293-301; reprinted, with changes, in *Abel1*, pp. 235-240.

> "Le Sens I bis," in *Bonjour Cinéma*, pp. 27-44. Translated by Stuart Liebman as "The Extra Sense," in *Jean Epstein's Early Film Theory*, 1920-1922 (1980); translated by Tom Milne as "The Senses 1 (b)," *Afterimage*, no. 10 (Autumn 1981): 9-16; Milne's translation reprinted in *Abel1*, pp. 241-246.

> "Ciné-mystique," in *Bonjour Cinéma*, pp. 111-117. Translated by Stuart Liebman as "Cine-mystique," in *Jean Epstein's Early Film Theory*, 1920-1922 (1980), pp. 302-305; reprinted in *Millennium Film Journal*, nos. 10-11 (1984): 191-193.

La Lyrosophie. Paris: Éditions de la Sirène, 1922.

Le Cinématographe vu de l'Etna. Paris: Les Écrivains réunis, 1926.

> "De quelques conditions de la *photogénie*," *Cinéa-Ciné-pour-tous*, no. 19 (15 August 1924): 6-8. Translated by Tom Milne as "On Certain Characteristics of *Photogénie*," *Afterimage*, no. 10 (Autumn 1981): 20-23; reprinted in *Abel1*, pp. 314-318.

> "L'Elément photogénique," *Cinéa-Ciné-pour-tous*, no. 12 (1 May 1924): 6-7. Translated by Tom Milne as "The Photogenic Element," *Afterimage*, no. 10 (Autumn 1981): 23-27.

> "Pour une avant-garde nouvelle," Translated by Stuart Liebman as "For a New Avant-Garde," in *The Avant-Garde Film: A Reader of Theory and Criticism*, ed. P. Adams Sitney (New York: New York University Press, 1978), pp. 26-30; reprinted in *Abel1*, pp. 349-353.

L'Or des mers. Paris: Librairie Valois, 1932.

Les Recteurs et la Sirène. Paris: Fernand Aubier, Éditions Montaigne, 1934.

Photogénie de l'impondérable. Paris: Éditions Corymbe, 1935. Excerpts translated by Richard Abel as "Photogénie and the Imponderable," *Abel2*, pp. 188-192.

L'Intelligence d'une machine. Paris: Éditions Jacques Melot, 1946. Excerpts translated by Stuart Liebman as "Timeless Time" and "The Universe Head over Heals," *October*, no. 3 (Spring 1977): 16-25.

Le Cinéma du diable. Paris: Éditions Jacques Melot, 1947.

Esprit de cinéma. Paris: Éditions Jeheber, 1955.
Alcool et cinéma. Unpublished in Epstein's lifetime.

Essays and Reviews by Epstein

"Grossissement," *Promenoir*, no. 1 (February 1921).

[Untitled], *Promenoir*, no. 3 (May 1921).

"Leçons de choses," *Promenoir*, no. 3 (May 1921).

"Le Cinéma mystique," *Cinéa* (10 June 1921): 12.

"Le Sens I bis," *Cinéa* (22 July 1921): 13-14.

"Le Phénomène littéraire," Parts 1-4, *L'Esprit nouveau*, no. 8 (August 1921): 856-860.

"Le Phénomène littéraire," *L'Esprit nouveau*, no. 9 (September 1921): 965-969.

"Amour de Charlot," *Cinéa* (14 October 1921).

"Le Phénomène littéraire," *L'Esprit nouveau*, no. 10 (October 1921): 1088-1092.

"Cinéma," *Zénith* (October 1921).

"Le Phénomène littéraire," Parts 5-6, *L'Esprit nouveau*, nos. 11-12 (November 1921): 1215-1222.

"Le Phénomène littéraire," *L'Esprit nouveau*, no. 13 (December 1921): 1431-1443.

"Douglas Fairbanks," *Cinéa* (16 December 1921).

"Litanies de toutes les photogénies," *Cinéa*, no. 35 (6 January 1922): 14.

"Les Livres de Science: *Role des Colloides chez les Être Vivants par August Lumiere*," *L'Esprit nouveau*, no. 14 (January 1922): 1659.

"Review of El Dorado," *L'Esprit nouveau*, no. 14 (January 1922): 1669-1970.

"Amour de Sessue," *Cinéa*, no. 37 (20 January 1922): 14.

"Amour de Sessue," *Cinéa*, no. 11 (February 1922): 3.

"Nous Kabbalistes," *L'Esprit nouveau*, no. 15 (February 1922): 1709-1713.

Review of Alfred Jarry, *Ubu Roi*; Charles Chassé, *Les Sources d'Ubu Roi*; André Suarès, *Poète tragique*; Jean Paulhan, *Jacob Cow, le pirate*, *L'Esprit nouveau*, no. 15 (February 1922): 1746-1748.

"Critique de l'amour," *Le Vie des lettres et des arts* (February 1922): 12-15.

"La Lyrosophie," *Les Feuilles Libres* (February-March 1922): 33-41.

"Eloquence d'yeux," *Le Crapouillot* (16 March 1922).

"Réalisation de Détails," *Cinéa*, no. 45 (17 March 1922): 12.

"The New Conditions of Literary Phenomena," *Broom* 2, no. 1 (April 1922): 3-10.

"t.," *Les Feuilles Libres* (April-May 1922): 105-111.

"Freud ou le Nick-Cartérianisme en Psychologie," *L'Esprit nouveau*, no. 16 (May 1922): 1857-1864.

"Les Livres" [Reviews of Carl Sternheim, *Libussa*; Paul Neuhuys, *Poètes d'aujourd'hui. L'Orientation actuelle de la conscience lyrique*; and Elie Ehrenbourg, *Et quand meme elle tourne*], *L'Esprit nouveau*, no. 16 (May 1922): 1923-1925.

"Journaux et revues," *L'Esprit nouveau*, no. 16 (May 1922): 1955.

"Le Bel Agonisant," *Zénith* (19 May 1922).

"Le Bel Agonisant," *Promenoir*, no. 6 (June 1922).

"La Lyrosophie," *L'homme Libre* (June 1922).

"A Necessary and Sufficient Literature," trans. B. Gorham Munson, Broom 2, no. 4 (July 1922): 309-316.

"Lampes sur le rail: Quelques mots sur la poésie d'Ivan Goll," Le Disque Vert (July 1922): 69-70.

"Rimbaud," L'Esprit nouveau, no. 17 (Summer 1922).

"Variable: Ame," L'Esprit nouveau, no. 17 (Summer 1922).

"Les Livres" [Reviews of M. Perochon, Poésies; Franz Hellens, Bass-Bassina-Boulou; De Massot, De Mallarmé à 391; Paul Morand, Ouvert la nuit; Jean Paulhan, Le Pont Traversé; Paul Laffittee, Grand Malaise; Jean Cocteau, Vocabulaire], L'Esprit nouveau, no. 17 (Summer 1922).

"Amour indigent: A propos des Don Juanes," La Revue mondiale (15 September 1922): 176-180.

"Langue d'Or," La Revue mondiale (December 1922).

"La Roue," Comoedia (12 December 1922).

"A l'Affut de Pasteur," L'Europe nouvelle (30 December 1922).

"Pourquoi j'ai tourné Pasteur," Gazette des Sept Arts, no. 2 (25 January 1923): 11.

"Abel," La Revue mondiale (March 1923).

"Le Décor au cinéma," La Revue mondiale (March 1923).

"Fernand Léger," Les Feuilles Libres (March-April 1923): 26-31.

"L'Elément photogénique," Cinéa-Ciné pour tous (1 May 1924).

"De quelques conditions de photogénie," Cinéa-Ciné pour tous (15 August 1924).

"Rhythme et montage" [1924], ESC1, p. 121. Translated by Tom Milne as "Rhythm and Montage," Afterimage, no. 10 (Autumn 1981): 16-17.

"Pour une avant garde nouvelle," Cinéa-Ciné pour tous (15 January 1925).

"Poème," La Flandre Littéraire (15 March-15 April 1925): 104.

"Jean Epstein dit," La Flandre Littéraire (15 March-15 April 1925).

"Le Regard du verre," Les Cahiers du mois, nos. 16-17 (October 1925): 9-12.

"Le Cinématographe vu de l'Etna," Comoedia (4 December 1925).

"Opera de l'Oeil," Comoedia (1 January 1926).

"L'Objectif lui-même," Cinéa-Ciné pour tous (15 January 1926). Translated by Tom Milne as "The Lens Itself," Afterimage, no. 10 (Autumn 1981): 17-20.

"Amour de Charlot," Comoedia (16 April 1926).

"Film und Kino," Reichsfilmblatt (25 September 1926).

"Les Grands Docteurs," Photo-Ciné (15 March 1927).

"Hommage à Canudo," Comoedia (2 September 1927).

"Abel Gance," Photo-Ciné (September-October 1927). Translated by Tom Milne as "Abel Gance," Afterimage, no. 10 (Autumn 1981): 27-30.

"Six et demi onze (un Kodak)," Cinégraphie (15 October 1927): 33-35.

"Temps et personnages du drame," Cinégraphie (15 November 1927).

"Art d'événement," Comoedia (18 November 1927). Translated by Tom Milne as "Art of Incidence," Afterimage, no. 10 (Autumn 1981): 30-32; reprinted in Abel1, pp. 412-414.

"Tiempo y personajes del drama," La Gaceta Literaria, no. 24 (15 December 1927): 4.

"Salles et films d'avant garde," Comoedia (31 January 1928).

"La Vie chancelle sur des ressemblances," Photo-Ciné (February-March 1928).

"Des mondes tombent dans un espace de Lumière," Photo-Ciné (February-March 1928).

"Quelques notes sur Edgar Poe et les images douées de vie," *La Critique cinématographique* (17 March 1928).

"Les Images du ciel." *Cinéa-Ciné pour tous*, no. 107 (15 April 1928): 11-12. Translated by Richard Abel as "Fragments of Sky," *Abel1*, pp. 421-422.

"Quelques notes sur Edgar Poe et les images douées de vie," *Photo-Ciné* (April 1928). Translated by Tom Milne as "Some Notes on Poe and Images Endowed with Life," *Afterimage*, no. 10 (Autumn 1981): 32-34.

"Psychanalyse et cinéma," *La Critique cinématographique* (28 April 1928).

"Le Ralenti," *Cinéa Ciné pour tous* no. 108 (1 May 1928): 10.

"L'Ame au ralenti," *Paris-Midi* (11 May 1928). Translated by Tom Milne as "The Spirit of Slow Motion," *Afterimage*, no. 10 (1981): 34-35.

"Opinion sur le cinématographe," *Le Rouge et le noir* (July 1928): 18-30.

"Algunas ideas de Jean Epstein," *La Gaceta Literaria* no. 43 (1 October 1928): 2.

"Les Approches de la verité," *Photo-ciné* (15 November-15 December 1928). Translated by Tom Milne as "Approaches to Truth," *Afterimage*, no. 10 (1981): 35-36; reprinted in *Abel1*, pp. 422-425.

"Nos Lions," *L'Ami du people* (11 January 1929).

"La Mort et le cinématographe," *Cinéa-ciné pour tous* (1 February 1929): 7-9.

"Londres parlant," *Cinéa-ciné pour tous* (15 December 1929): 7-8

"L'île," *Cinéa-ciné pour tous* (July 1930): 33-37.

"L'île (suite en fin)," *Cinéa-ciné pour tous* (August-September 1930): 33-37.

"Le Cinématographe continue..." *Cinéa-ciné pour tous* (November 1930): 5-7. Translated by Richard Abel as "The Cinema Continues," *Abel1*, pp. 63-68.

"Bilan de fin de muet," *Cinéa-ciné pour tous* (January-February 1931).

"Un système graphique en trois dimensions: le cinéma," *Revue des arts et métiers graphiques* no. 23 (15 May 1931): 239-46.

"Misère d'Hoedick," *Vu* (30 March 1932).

"Natur Film," *Neue Zurcher Zeitung* (1933).

"Films de nature," *Cinéa-ciné pour vous* (April-May 1933).

"Photogénie de l'impondérable," *Corymbe* (November-December 1934).

"Intelligence d'une machine," *Interciné* (August-September 1935).

"Naissance d'un mythe," *Corymbe* (January-February 1936).

"Avant-garde pas morte," *Spectateur* (9 July 1946).

"Le Plus Grand Commun Langage," *Ecran français* (17 July 1946).

"Culture cinématographique," *Technique cinématographique* (19 September 1946).

"Charlot débiteur," *Spectateur* (24 September 1946).

"Cinéma pur et film sonore," *Technique cinématographique* (3 October 1946).

"Dramaturgie de l'espace," *Technique cinématographique* (17 October 1946).

"Voir et entendre penser," *Technique cinématographique* (31 October 1946).

"Cinéma du diable," *Le Magasin du spectacle* (6 November 1946).

"Dramaturgie dans le temps," *Technique cinématographique* (28 November 1946).

"Perséides," *Spectateur* (3 December 1946).

"Naissance d'une académie," *Technique cinématographique* (26 December 1946).

"Le Cinéma et les au-delà de Descartes," *La Porte ouverte*, no. 3 (1946).

"Féerie réelle," *Spectateur* (21 January 1947).

"Logique des images," *Technique cinématographique* (23 January 1947).
"Deux Grands Maîtres à filmer," *Technique cinématographique* (20 February 1947).
"Vertu et danger du hasard," *Technique cinématographique* (6 March 1947).
"Le Sens du cinéma," *Technique cinématographique* (20 March 1947).
"Groupement de jeunes," *Technique cinématographique* (3 April 1947).
"L'Age du cinéma," *Technique cinématographique* (1 May 1947).
"Du sujet et de son traitement," *Technique cinématographique* (15 May 1947).
"Découpage – Construction visuelle," *Technique cinématographique* (29 May 1947).
"Découpage – Construction sonore," *Technique cinématographique* (12 June 1947).
"Le Professeur Joliot-Curie et le cinéma," *Technique cinématographique* (26 June 1947).
"Découverte du cinéma," *Opéra* (20 August 1947).
"Découpage – Construction idéologique," *Technique cinématographique* (4 September 1947).
"De la belle technique ou un art plus humain," *Le Figaro littéraire* (6 September 1947).
"Humanité du cinéma pur," *Technique cinématographique* (25 December 1947).
"Le Ralenti du son," *Livre d'or du cinéma français* (1947-1948).
"Les Faux Dieux," *L'Age nouveau*, no. 25 (1948).
"L'Ecole cinématographique française," *L'Age nouveau*, no. 30 (1948).
"Le Grand Epoque du cinéma muet," *L'Age nouveau*, no. 30 (1948).
"Naissance d'un style," *L'Age nouveau*, no. 30 (1948).
"Avant-garde = technique," *Néo-Art* (September 1948).
"Finalité du cinéma," *Mercure de France* (1 February 1949).
"Grand Oeuvre de l'avant-garde," *Ciné-club* (March 1949).
"Pourquoi nos films vieillissent-ils si vite?" *Le Figaro littéraire* (5 May 1949).
"Ciné Analyse ou Poésie en quantité industrielle," *Psyché* (July 1949).
"Culture cinématographique," *Technique cinématographique* (19 September 1949).
"Delire d'une machine," *L'Age nouveau*, no. 42 (October 1949).
"Rapidité et fatigue de l'homme-spectateur," *Mercure de France* (1 November 1949).
"Le Monde fluide de l'écran," *Les Temps modernes* (6 June 1950).
"Cinéma, expression d'existence," *Mercure de France* (1 September 1950).
"Le Film et le monde," *Les Temps modernes* (March 1951).
"Voeux cinématographiques," *Le Figaro* (1 January 1951).

Secondary Works

Abel, Richard. *French Cinema: The First Wave, 1915-1929*. Princeton: Princeton University Press, 1984.
—. *French Film Theory and Criticism: A History/Anthology, 1907-1939. Vol. 1: 1907-1929*. Princeton: Princeton University Press, 1988.
—. *French Film Theory and Criticism: A History/Anthology, 1907-1939. Vol. 2: 1929-1939*. Princeton: Princeton University Press, 1988.
Aumont, Jacques, ed. *Jean Epstein: Cinéaste, poète, philosophe*. Paris: Cinémathèque Française, 1998.
Bordwell, David. *French Impressionist Cinema: Film Culture, Film Theory and Film Style*. PhD Dissertation: University of Iowa, 1974; republished by Arno Press (New York), 1980.

Brenez, Nicole, and Ralph Eue, eds. *Jean Epstein: Bonjour Cinéma und andere Schriften zum Kino*. Wien: Österreichisches Filmmuseum/SynemaPublikationen, 2008.

Cortade, Ludovic. "*Cinéma du diable*: Jean Epstein and the Ambiguities of Subversion," *SubStance* 34, no. 3 (2005): 3-16.

Fieschi, Jean-André. "Jean Epstein." Trans. Tom Milne. In *Cinema: A Critical Dictionary*. Vol. 1. Ed. Richard Roud. New York: Viking Press, 1980. 328-334.

Gauthier, Christophe. *La passion du cinéma: Cinéphiles, ciné-clubs et salles spécialisées à Paris de 1920 à 1929*. Paris: Ecole des Chartes/ARFHC, 1999.

Ghali, Nourredine. *L'Avant-garde cinématographique en France dans les années vingt, idées, conceptions, theories*. Paris: Paris expérimental, 1995.

Guigueno, Vincent. *Jean Epstein, Cinéaste des îles*. Paris: Jean Michel Place, 2003

Hillairet, Prosper. *Coeur Fidèle de Jean Epstein*. Crisnée: Éditions Yellow Now, 2008.

Kirtland, Katie. *The Depth of the Image: Animation and Revelation in Jean Epstein's Theory of Cinema*. PhD Dissertation: University of Chicago, forthcoming.

Leprohon, Pierre. *Jean Epstein*. Paris: Éditions Seghers, 1964.

Liebman, Stuart. "Espacio, Velocidad, Revelacion y Tiempo. Las Primas Teorias de Jean Epstein," *Archivos de la Filmoteca* [special issue on Jean Epstein, eds. Daniel Pitarch and Angel Quintana] (June 2008):

—. *Jean Epstein's Early Film Theory, 1920-1922*. PhD Dissertation: New York University, 1980; republished by University Microfilms International (Ann Arbor, MI), 1981.

—. "Visitings of Awful Promise: The Cinema Seen from Etna," in *Camera Obscura, Camera Lucida: Essays in Honor of Annette Michelson*, eds. Richard Allen and Macolm Turvey. Amsterdam: Amsterdam University Press, 2003. 91-108.

Lundemo, Trond. *Jean Epstein: intelligensen hos en maskin–The Intelligence of a Machine*. Stockholm: Svenska Filminstitutet, 2001.

Mitry, Jean. "Jean Epstein." In *Dictionnaire du cinéma*, eds. Raymond Bellour and Jean-Jacques Brochier Paris: Éditions universitaires, 1966.

Moore, Rachel. *Savage Theory: Cinema as Modern Magic*. Durham, NC: Duke University Press, 2000.

Paci, Viva. "The Attraction of the Intelligent Eye: Obsessions with the Vision Machine in Early Film Theories," in *The Cinema of Attractions Reloaded*, ed. Wanda Strauven. Amsterdam: Amsterdam University Press, 2006. 121-137

Pasquali, Valentina, ed. *L'essenza del cinema: scritti sulla settima arte*. Torino: Fondazione scuola nazionale di cinema, 2002.

Tognolotti, Chiara. "L'alcool, le cinéma et le philosophe. L'influence de Friedrich Nietzsche sur la théorie cinématographique de Jean Epstein à travers les notes du fonds Epstein," *1895*, no. 46 (2005): pp. 37-53.

—. "Jean Epstein's "Intellectual Factory": An Analysis of the Fonds Epstein, 1946-1953," in *Dall'inizio, alla fine. Teorie del cinema in prospettiva/In the Very Beginning, at the Very End: Film Theories in Perspective*, eds. Francesco Casetti, Jane Gaines, and Valentina Re. Udine: Forum, 2009. pp. 515-524

Turvey, Malcolm. *Doubting Vision: Film and the Revelationist Tradition*. New York: Oxford University Press, 2008.

—. "Epstein, Bergson and Vision." In *European Film Theory*, ed. Temenuga Trifonova. New York: Routledge, 2008. pp. 93-108.

—. "Jean Epstein's Cinema of Immanence: The Rehabilitation of the Corporeal Eye." *October*, no. 83. (Winter 1998): 25-50.

Vichi, Laura. *Jean Epstein*. Milano: Il Castoro, 2003.

Wall-Romana, Christophe. *Jean Epstein*. Manchester: Manchester University Press, forthcoming 2012.

—. "Jean Epstein, Filmic Lyricism, and the Affects of Modernity." In *French Cinépoetry: Unmaking and Remaking the Poem in the Age of Cinema*. PhD Dissertation, University of California at Berkeley, 2005. 176-216.

Willemen, Paul. "Photogénie and Epstein." In *Looks and Frictions: Essays in Cultural Studies and Film Theory*. London: British Film Institute, 1994. 124-133.

Notes on Contributors

Richard Abel is Robert Altman Collegiate Professor of Film Studies in Screen Arts & Cultures at the University of Michigan. Most recently he published *Americanizing the Movies and 'Movie-Mad' Audiences, 1910-1914* (California, 2006), co-edited *Early Cinema and the "National"* (John Libbey, 2008), and edited a paperback version of the *Encyclopedia of Early Cinema* (Routledge, 2010). His current project is *Menus for Movie Land: Newspapers and the Emergence of American Film Culture, 1913-1916*.

Nicole Brenez is Professor at the University of Paris-3, Sorbonne Nouvelle. She is the author of *De la Figure en général et du Corps en particulier. L'invention figurative au cinéma* (De Boeck Université, 1998); *Abel Ferrara* (Illinois, 2007); *Abel Ferrara. Le Mal mais sans fleurs* (Cahiers du Cinéma, 2008); and editor of *Poétique de la couleur* (Auditorium du Louvre, 1998); *Jeune, dure et pure. Une histoire du cinéma d'avant-garde et expérimental en France* (Cinémathèque française/Mazzotta, 2001); *Jean-Luc Godard: Documents* (Centre Georges Pompidou, 2006); *Jean Epstein. Bonjour Cinéma und andere Schriften zum Kino* (Filmmuseum/Synema Publikationen, 2008); and *Le cinéma critique* (Publications de la Sorbonne, 2009). She is also Curator of avant-garde film at the Cinémathèque française and a recipient of Anthology Film Archives' Film Preservation Award.

Audrey Brunetaux is an Assistant Professor of French Studies at Colby College. Her research focuses on 20th-century French literature with an emphasis on French Holocaust narratives, cinema, and the visual arts. She explores the representations of Holocaust memory and trauma in Holocaust films, memoirs, and graphic novels.

Érik Bullot is a filmmaker. His work has been screened at the Centre Pompidou (Paris), the Jeu de Paume (Paris), La Enana Marrón (Madrid), the Biennial of Moving Images (Geneva), the CCCB (Barcelona), and elsewhere. His most recent writings include *Sayat Nova* (Yellow Now, 2007), an essay about Parajanov's film; and *Renversements 1. Notes sur le cinéma* (Paris Expérimental, 2009). He is currently director of the postgraduate program in Document and Contemporary Art at the École européenne supérieure de l'image in Poitiers, and teaches film at the École nationale supérieure d'art in Bourges (France). He was visiting professor at the State University of New York at Buffalo, 2009-2011.

Ludovic Cortade is Assistant Professor in the Department of French at New York University. He is the author of *Antonin Artaud – La Virtualité incarnée* (CNRS/L'Harmattan, 2000); *Le cinéma de l'immobilité: style, politique, réception* (Publications de la Sorbonne, 2008); and recent articles on André Bazin, François Truffaut, and Jean-Luc Godard; as well as co-editor of a special issue of *Contemporary French Civilization* celebrating the fiftieth anniversary of the French New Wave (2008). He specializes in French cinema and film theory.

Mireille Dobrzynski holds a PhD in French literature and cinema from the University of Chicago. Her dissertation focuses on a reading of Eric Rohmer's films in light of French classicism. Her interests also include literary and media-related translation.

Laurent Guido is Professor in the Department of Film History and Aesthetics at the University of Lausanne, Switzerland. He researches film historiography and the relations between cinema, music, and dance. His most recent books and edited volumes include *L'Age du Rythme* (Payot, 2007); *Aux sources du burlesque* (AFRHC/Giornate del Cinema muto, 2010); *Fixe/Animé* (L'Age d'Homme, 2010); and *Rythmer/Rhythmize* (a special issue of *Intermédialités*). He is currently working on a book about dance in early cinema.

Tom Gunning is Professor of Art History and Cinema and Media Studies at the University of Chicago. He is the author of *D.W. Griffith and the Origins of American Narrative Film* (1991) and *The Films of Fritz Lang: Allegories of Vision and Modernity* (2000), and he has written on a wide range of subjects related to cinema and photography in numerous journals, including *American Film*, *Camera Obscura*, *Cinema Journal*, *Discourse*, *Film Quarterly*, and *Wide Angle*.

Sarah Keller is Assistant Professor of English and Cinema Studies at Colby College. Her writing focuses on silent and experimental cinema, as well as on intersections between cinema and poetry. Her current project addresses the relationship between Maya Deren's finished and unfinished work.

Katie Kirtland is a doctoral candidate in the Department of Art History at the University of Chicago. She is currently completing a dissertation entitled, "The Depth of the Image: Animation and Revelation in Jean Epstein's Theory of Cinema."

Franck Le Gac is a Paris-based independent translator specializing in academic and scholarly texts on film and the visual arts, mass media, and architecture. He holds a PhD in film studies from the University of Iowa, and teaches film at the Centre Parisien d'Études Critiques and the University of Paris-3, Sorbonne Nouvelle. His research includes the theoretical implications of citation in fiction film and the figurative uses of tennis in cultural and social critique.

Stuart Liebman is Professor Emeritus of Film and Media Studies at Queens College and the Graduate Center of the City University of New York. He received his PhD at New York University in 1980 for a dissertation on the scope and sources of Epstein's early film theory. He subsequently wrote extensively on and translated many essays about early French and post-war German cinema. He has also edited volumes on Jean Renoir's films and politics in the 1930s and Alexander Kluge's cinema. He co-edited the issue of October (No. 72) entitled "Berlin 1945: War and Rape" that won the Association of American Publishers Award for the Best Single Issue of a Scholarly Magazine in 1995, and edited the anthology, Claude Lanzmann's Shoah: Key Essays (Oxford, 2007). In 2006, he was named an "Academy Film Scholar" by the Academy of Motion Picture Arts and Sciences. He is currently working on a study of the first ten years of cinema representing the Holocaust.

Trond Lundemo is Associate Professor in the Department of Cinema Studies at Stockholm University. He has been a visiting professor and visiting scholar at the Seijo University of Tokyo on a number of occasions. He is co-directing the Stockholm University Graduate School of Aesthetics and is co-editor of the book series, Film Theory in Media History for Amsterdam University Press. He is also affiliated with the research project "Time, Memory and Representation" at Södertörns University College, Sweden, and "The Archive in Motion" research project at Oslo University. His research and publications engage in questions of technology, aesthetics, and intermediality as well as the theory of the archive.

Rachel Moore teaches in the Media and Communications Department at Goldsmiths, University of London. She received a John Simon Guggenheim Fellowship for her current project, "In the Film Archive of Natural-History," which investigates the use of old movies and footage in current artistic practice. She is the author of (nostalgia) (Afterall/MIT Press, 2006); and Savage Theory: Cinema as Modern Magic (Duke, 2000), as well as articles on Patrick Keiller, James Benning, and Kenneth Anger. She is a member of the Leverhulme Spaces of Media Project, investigating the use of screens in the urban spaces of Cairo, London, and Shanghai.

Thao Nguyen currently teaches at Grand Valley State University. His research focuses on the literature of the seventeenth-century and theater across the ages. His interests include theater history, theatricality, the relation between literature and the visual arts, and cinema.

Jason Paul was formerly a PhD student in the Department of Cinema and Media Studies at the University of Chicago, and is currently pursuing a degree in archival studies at the University of Wisconsin-Milwaukee. He is also researching the history of camera movement and preparing a collection of essays entitled *Archiving Cinema*.

James Schneider is a filmmaker, video performer, and writer. He studied at the Rhode Island School of Design, and holds graduate degrees in philosophy and aesthetics from the University of Paris-8, Vincennes in St. Denis. In 2011, he completed the documentary *Jean Epstein, Young Oceans of Cinema*.

Christophe Wall-Romana is Associate Professor in the Department of French and Italian at the University of Minnesota, where he is also affiliated with the new Graduate Major in Moving Image Studies. His research has focused on the textual intersections of French poetry and cinema, especially around the post-WWI narrative avant-garde in France. Secondary interests include contemporary poetry, philosophy, and the translation of American poetry into French. He has two books forthcoming: *Cinepoetry: Imaginary Cinemas in French Poetry, 1890-2008* (Fordham, 2012), and the first monograph in English on *Jean Epstein* (Manchester, 2012). His next project will examine the role of cinematic affect in philosophical and literary innovations in the 20th century.

Jennifer Wild is Assistant Professor of Cinema and Media Studies at the University of Chicago, where she is also affiliated with the Department of Romance Languages and Literatures. Her essays have appeared in *1895*, *Frameworks*, *CinémAction*, and *Early Popular Visual Culture*. In 2007, she was assistant curator of the exhibition "Picasso, Braque and Early Film in Cubism" for PaceWildenstein. She is currently completing a manuscript entitled *The Film Stripped Bare: Parisian Modernism in the Age of Cinema, 1900-1926*.

Index of Names

Index of Films and Major Writings by Jean Epstein

*Numbers in bold indicate translations available in this volume.

Index of Films